An Illustrated Dictionary of Little-Known Words from Literary Classics

Mary Ellen Snodgrass

ABC-CLIO

Santa Barbara, California
Denver, Colorado
Oxford, England

Library of Congress Cataloging-in-Publication Data

Snodgrass, Mary Ellen.
An illustrated dictionary of little-known words from literary classics / Mary Ellen Snodgrass.
p. cm.
Includes bibliographical references and indexes.
1. English language—Glossaries, vocabularies, etc. 2. English language—Terms and phrases. 3. Vocabulary. I. Title
PE1689.S675 1995 95—44276
423'.1—dc20

ISBN 0-87436-809-X (alk. paper)

02 01 00 99 98 97 96 95 10 9 8 7 6 5 4 3 2 1

ABC-CLIO, Inc.
130 Cremona Drive, P.O. Box 1911
Santa Barbara, California 93116-1911

This book is printed on acid-free paper ♾.

Manufactured in the United States of America

Is an alewife a barmaid or a fish? In *Johnny Tremain*, alewives are found in a tavern, salted. And what is a cheval-glass doing in Dr. Jekyll's laboratory? Does it have anything to do with horses? While the meaning of some unfamiliar words can be deduced from context or derivation, others are misleading or have evolved into new meanings.

In *Moby-Dick,* nautical terms are pivotal, while *Flowers for Algernon* hinges on psychological jargon. **An Illustrated Dictionary of Little-Known Words from Literary Classics** is a compendium of these terms and others encountered in Western classics as well as multicultural literature and other works outside the traditional canon. School curricula and reading lists from the American Library Association and the National Council of Teachers of English were used to help choose the works covered, a selection that includes the books likely to be leisure or required reading for today's students.

Words such as carcinoma, cenotaph, Grumman, Molotov flower basket, strafe, and tomographic scan—all found and perhaps stumbled over in John Hersey's *Hiroshima*—are defined and their historical background or derivation given. Entries include:

- Architecture: apse, campanile, grotto, peristyle, plinth
- Dance: czardas, gavotte, juba, moochie, taxi tips
- Insults: dandy, momzer, ofay, peckerwood, tosspot
- Supernatural: arch-fiend, cabbala, fakir, gematriya, geomancer
- Weights and measures: dram, fee sheet, intercalary month, stone, verst

Entries are alphabetized and cross-referenced to allow the reader to return quickly to the classic at hand, although some of the eye-catching and befuddling words may inspire browsing. This profusely illustrated dictionary will enhance the literary adventures of teachers, students, writers, literati, and literary neophytes alike.

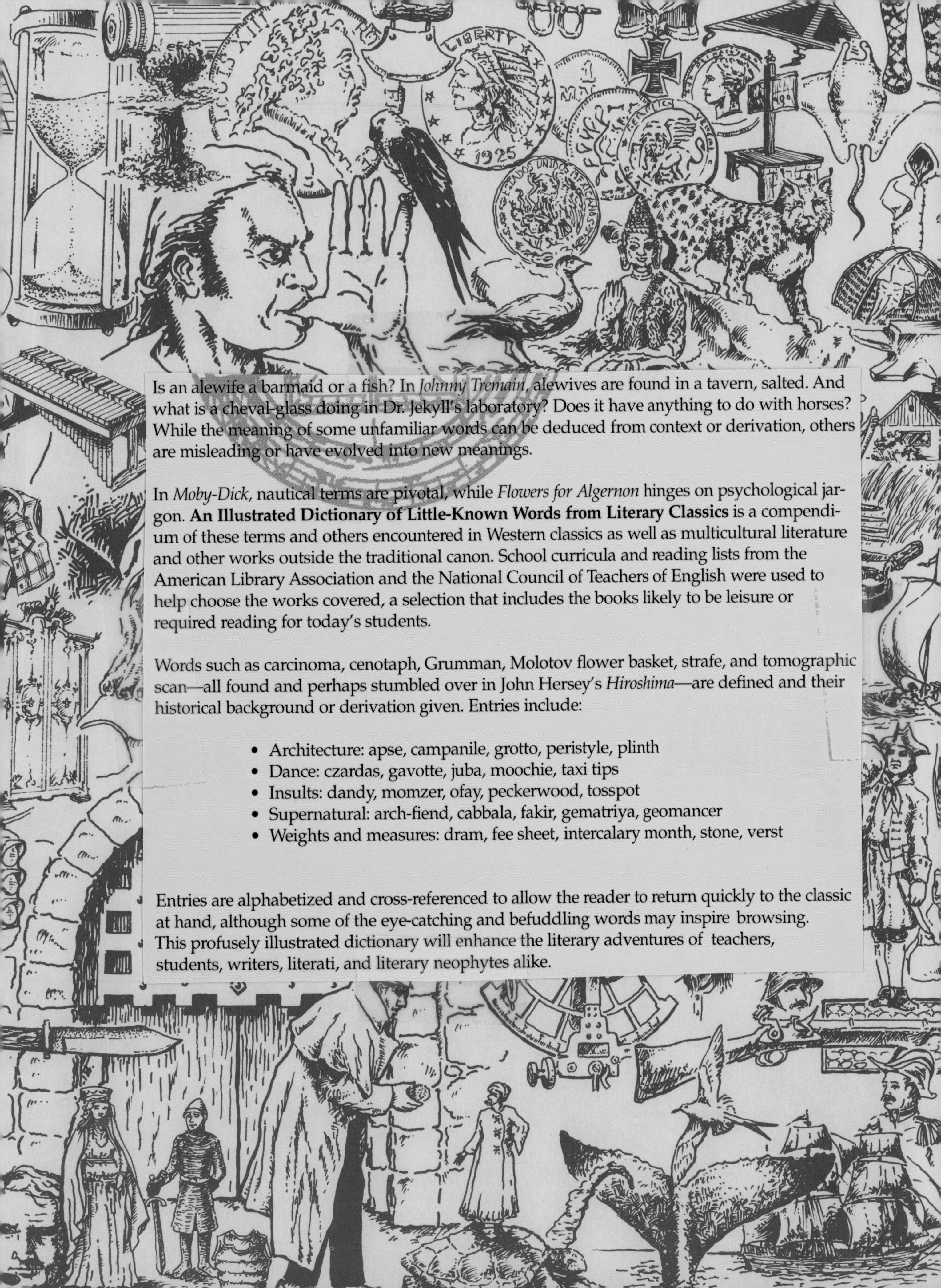

Is an alewife a barmaid or a fish? In *Johnny Tremain*, alewives are found in a tavern, salted. And what is a cheval-glass doing in Dr. Jekyll's laboratory? Does it have anything to do with horses? While the meaning of some unfamiliar words can be deduced from context or derivation, others are misleading or have evolved into new meanings.

In *Moby-Dick*, nautical terms are pivotal, while *Flowers for Algernon* hinges on psychological jargon. **An Illustrated Dictionary of Little-Known Words from Literary Classics** is a compendium of these terms and others encountered in Western classics as well as multicultural literature and other works outside the traditional canon. School curricula and reading lists from the American Library Association and the National Council of Teachers of English were used to help choose the works covered, a selection that includes the books likely to be leisure or required reading for today's students.

Words such as carcinoma, cenotaph, Grumman, Molotov flower basket, strafe, and tomographic scan—all found and perhaps stumbled over in John Hersey's *Hiroshima*—are defined and their historical background or derivation given. Entries include:

- Architecture: apse, campanile, grotto, peristyle, plinth
- Dance: czardas, gavotte, juba, moochie, taxi tips
- Insults: dandy, momzer, ofay, peckerwood, tosspot
- Supernatural: arch-fiend, cabbala, fakir, gematriya, geomancer
- Weights and measures: dram, fee sheet, intercalary month, stone, verst

Entries are alphabetized and cross-referenced to allow the reader to return quickly to the classic at hand, although some of the eye-catching and befuddling words may inspire browsing. This profusely illustrated dictionary will enhance the literary adventures of teachers, students, writers, literati, and literary neophytes alike.

An Illustrated Dictionary of Little-Known Words from Literary Classics

Contents

Preface, vi

A Reader's Guide, xi

Acknowledgments, xiii

Little-Known Words from Literary Classics 1

Bibliography, 317

References, 323

Index by Author and Title, 327

Subject Index, 337

Preface

The best of times—and the worst—for the bibliophile is the literary passage containing a crucial ingredient or metaphor bearing an intrusive unknown—the insidious X factor that intercedes between a hasty read and a full grasp of events, characters, settings, and themes. The flow of a soul-penetrating line from Herman Melville's *Moby-Dick, Typee,* or *Benito Cereno* can slow to a limping plod from the average landlubber's unfamiliarity with a staggering list of nautical terms—binnacle, cuddy, forecastle, hawse-hole, Try-Works, holystone, oakum, flukes, and foretop. A promising segment from Charles Dickens's *A Christmas Carol, Great Expectations,* or *David Copperfield* can befuddle with the Victoriana of clothing, table settings, lodging, and travel—for example, postboy, hackney chariot, liver wing, settle, greatcoat, roasting jack, mangle, épergne, and rush-light. A surprisingly ponderous list of terms from Mark Twain deters understanding of his jaunty text, leaving the reader abuzz with queries about phrenology, yawl, melodeum, towhead, doodlebug, jackboots, temperance revival, taw, and serape. Authors assume that readers will always understand a bit of trivia or an arcane reference to trephining or gallipots, vision quests or nosegays. These writers fail to predict that future generations will falter over the simplest synonym for food, drink, shoe, coat, hat, or bag. The resulting muddle exasperates the discriminating reader and stymies the tentative beginner whose dearth of word skills leaves agape the resulting chasms in meaning.

From my own experiences as reader, teacher, newspaper columnist, textbook writer, and reference book researcher, I know the exasperation of trying to locate the definitive explanation for terms that lie beyond my field of recognition, especially words relating to ships and the sea, foreign currency, obsolete medical treatments, building materials, or warfare and weaponry. In books about ancient times, the Middle Ages, and the Renaissance, editors often provide chapter notes, footnotes, pictures, diagrams, maps, and glossaries. However, for more current titles—*All Quiet on the Western Front, I Know Why the Caged Bird Sings, A Farewell to Arms,* "The Metamorphosis," *The Great Gatsby, The Autobiography of Malcolm X, Never Cry Wolf, Waiting for Godot, A Doll's House,* and *Flowers for Algernon*—there looms a nebulous gray area. Sometimes the word that teases most has a number of simple meanings, but serves a specialized purpose:

- taper—a thin, quick-burning candle
- impress—force a sailor into the navy
- texas—upper deck of a steamboat
- the dragon—Ku Klux Klan
- flip—spiced drink
- stir—solitary prison cell
- junk—trading vessel

These terms offer no handholds except context and a rough guess at similar terms depicted in art, movies, television, general reference, or other books and databases.

The regular use of detailed terminology underscores the importance of history, fashion, and custom to literature, much of which is written by discerning observers, researchers, and historians in a class with Thomas Hardy, Ruth Prawer Jhabvala, John Hersey, Edith Hamilton, Esther Forbes, Daniel Keyes, Jean Craighead George, J. R. R. Tolkien, Maya Angelou, Black Elk, Amy Tan, and George Orwell. Questions such as these puzzle or perplex:

- Why does Charlie Gordon, protagonist of Daniel Keyes's *Flowers for Algernon*, concern himself with the psychosurgery and T-maze performance of a white mouse? Why does he suddenly discover the purpose of his libido, id, and ego?
- In Avi's *The True Confessions of Charlotte Doyle*, why do the ratlines terrify the title character? What does a signature on a round robin indicate to a suspicious captain?

•What does trouble with tappets, clutch plates, an ammeter, and babbitts indicate to the Joad family in John Steinbeck's *The Grapes of Wrath?* How does apoplexy fell Grandpa so quickly? How do exaggerations on placards lead the family to doom?

•Why does Arthur Miller depart from scenes and acts in *Death of a Salesman* and conclude with a requiem? What does the grace period offer the Loman family? Why is Willy so pleased with flashbacks of his son simonizing his car with a scrap of chamois?

•Why does Thomas Hardy begin and end *The Mayor of Casterbridge* with doleful images of Michael Henchard, a laborer bearing wimble and cradle as emblems of his trade? How does the seed drill separate the era of Mayor Henchard from that of Mayor Farfrae? How does a skimmity-ride end all hopes of happiness for Lucetta?

•What type of symbol is the ideograph mentioned in Maxine Hong Kingston's *Woman Warrior?* Is it the same as a rune or seal character? Is it a hieroglyph or part of an alphabet?

These examples and hosts of others spool out like thread through a labyrinth, leaving the reader wondering how a breech-loader can save lives by speeding the soldier's task of charging a muzzle-loading weapon in Esther Forbes's *Johnny Tremain;* why Aldous Huxley exposes his futuristic characters in *Brave New World* to a kiva, peyote, mescal, and a ritual Snake Dance; why Susan B. Anthony compares the disenfranchised female citizen to a serf; and why a riding light lures a condemned man toward an unnamed compassionate double in Joseph Conrad's "The Secret Sharer."

The focus of this book extends beyond trivial quibbles over farthingales and hoop skirts, the purpose of a cuirass or a gorget, the shape of a gateleg table in *1984,* or the therapeutic value of Tom Sawyer's sitz baths. Its purpose resides in the reader's need to picture and absorb as much of the essence as possible to see, hear, feel, taste, smell, and touch the action, to hold and possess it, to absorb every nuance. In short, knowing the terms positions the reader in the action as a willing participant. In pivotal scenes, details can elucidate character reaction and assist the reader in appraising personal traits and tendencies, for example, the limits of female education demonstrated by Mattie Silver's ability to play a potpourri from *Carmen* in Edith Wharton's *Ethan Frome* and Elizabeth-Jane's skill at netting in *The Mayor of Casterbridge.* An example known to most readers of Shakespeare's tragedies is Mark Antony's reading of the will in *Julius Caesar.* What is the real value of the 75 drachmas left to "every several man"? Is the dollar value worth the murder of Rome's strongest leaders and ten years of civil war? Did Caesar actually believe that his will would be carried out? The same need for a knowledge of market value applies to the worth of Reichsmarks in Anne Frank's *Diary of a Young Girl,* which highlights the limited buying power of families and the importance of the black market in supplying food, medicines, and necessities during World War II, as well as to the inheritance left by Winnie's father during the same period in Amy Tan's *The Kitchen God's Wife.* On the comic side, why do characters in Jane Austen's *Pride and Prejudice* rate social status by contrasting modes of transportation? Is there grist for gossip mills in a stately arrival by brougham, barouche, or crested coach as opposed to a mundane trip by dog-cart, fly, or rockaway, as mentioned in Kate Chopin's *The Awakening* and Herman Melville's "Bartleby the Scrivener"? What do the comfort, style, and size of each conveyance say about the traveler's purpose and ability to pay? And more important, does the reader need to make these minute discriminations? From devout book fans I hear a thunderous Yes!

A comprehensive reference work that purports to supply information about vocabulary from significant literature bears the implicit burden of explaining what constitutes "significant." Certainly the canon of long-loved and long-lived touchstones from English and American works deserves primary consideration. Because well-educated people leave high school with a knowledge of certain must-reads, inclusion of venerable classics guarantees vocabulary selected from sources such as these: Arthur Miller's *Death of a Salesman* and *The Crucible;* Charlotte Brontë's *Jane Eyre;* Dickens's *Great Expectations, Tale of Two Cities,* and *A Christmas Carol;* F. Scott Fitzgerald's *The Great Gatsby;* Herman Melville's "Bartleby the Scrivener" and *Moby Dick;* Jane Austen's *Pride and Prejudice;* John Steinbeck's *The Red Pony, Grapes of Wrath,* and *The Pearl;* Jonathan Swift's *Gulliver's Travels* and "A Modest Proposal"; Joseph Conrad's *The Heart of Darkness* and "The Secret Sharer"; Mark Twain's *The Adventures of Tom Sawyer* and *The Adventures of Huckleberry Finn;* Nathaniel Hawthorne's *Scarlet Letter* and *The House of the Seven Gables;* Tennessee Williams's *A Streetcar Named Desire* and *The Glass Menagerie;* Thomas Hardy's *Tess of the D'Urbervilles, Far from the Madding Crowd,* and *The Mayor of Casterbridge;* Thornton Wilder's *Our Town* and *The Bridge of San Luis Rey;* and William Shakespeare's *Hamlet, A Midsummer Night's Dream, The Tempest, Julius Caesar, Romeo and Juliet,* and *Macbeth.* The list must also include the great dystopian works—George Orwell's *1984*, Aldous Huxley's *Brave New World*, H. G. Wells's *The Time Machine,* William Golding's *Lord of the Flies,* and Ayn Rand's *Anthem,* for example.

But the list cannot stop there. An added impetus for the writing of this book is the growth of the multicultural reading list, which presents a mix of peoples, cultures, rituals, customs, religions, and beliefs that carry us into distant realms. This murky territory often blends universals of daily life—food, family, activity, work, rest—with the demands of Native American worship, fundamentalism, Catholicism, Judaism, Islam, and Buddhism as well as folklore, superstition, and the occult. To comprehend the importance of the *curandera* in Rudolfo Anaya's *Bless Me, Ultima* requires some background information about the aims of sorcery and herbal healing. Likewise, an understanding of young Elie Wiesel's studies in cabbala underscores his deep emotional response to the Holocaust, which devastated his homeland and family, leaving him doubtful that fasting for Yom Kippur was worth the danger of moving one day closer to starvation. In addition to these examples, scenes from *Julie of the Wolves, So Far from the Bamboo Grove,* "An Astrologer's Day," *Farewell to Manzanar,* Confucius's "Analects," *I Heard the Owl Call My Name, Born Free, Zlata's Diary, Fallen Angels, Siddhartha, Like Water for Chocolate,* "Miss Youghal's Sais," *The Island of the Blue Dolphins,* and *The Joy Luck Club* take most readers of English onto unfamiliar ground where the knowledge of fen, pice, ulu, tombola, umiak, bo, claymore, cormorant, candlefish, banyan, jampani, and spirit money is rudimentary at best.

As a prod to the reader's compassion and appreciation of the humanities, multiculturalism has done more than demand a more thorough dictionary and development of a multinational vocabulary encompassing terms such as jutka, samisen, punkah, sarod, posole, hamatsa, wonton, abbé, Hajj, *llanero, vaquero, parrain,* and *patrón*. Readings from nontraditional authors force the audience to work harder at picturing behavior and actions. A broadened spectrum of classic literature awakens mental taste buds to fuller savor, one guaranteed to satisfy the palate while stimulating the mind to spice up the bland traditional diet restricted to the Anglo-American experience. As I perused lists of works that have always appeared on reading lists I grasped the importance of blending voices, of appending to works of Victor Hugo, Charlotte Brontë, Nathaniel Hawthorne, Homer, Charles Dickens, and Mark Twain the intricate lore of N. Scott Momaday and Zora Neale Hurston, the zany wit of Charles Portis, the grandeur of Gabriel García Márquez, the philosophical pronouncements of Margaret Atwood, and the indomitable female spirit depicted by Jeanne Wakatsuki Houston and James Houston and by Nobel prizewinner Toni Morrison.

A broadened definition of the canon would also include scriptural titles, notably Confucius's *Analects* and the Bible books of Ruth and Luke. Another serious omission from more traditionally defined lists is the varied, rich experiences of young adult fiction and adventure titles, such as Avi's*The True Confessions of Charlotte Doyle,* Charles Portis's *True Grit,* Conrad Richter's *The Light in the Forest,* Esther Forbes's *Johnny Tremain,* Hal Borland's *When the Legends Die,* Irene Hunt's *Across Five Aprils,* Jules Verne's *Around the World in Eighty Days,* Ray Bradbury's *R Is for Rocket,* Richard Adams's *Watership Down,* and Sir Arthur Conan Doyle's *The Adventures of Sherlock Holmes.*

As I probed curricula and cross-checked required reading lists against shelf lists from the American Library Association, the National Council of Teachers of English, and various book catalogs and anthologies, I pondered longest over the most-loved classics that exist in translation, among them Albert Camus's *The Stranger,* Alexandre Dumas's *The Count of Monte Cristo,* Anne Frank's *The Diary of a Young Girl,* Auguste Flaubert's *Madame Bovary,* Franz Kafka's "The Metamorphosis," *Gilgamesh,* Homer's *Iliad* and *Odyssey,* and Victor Hugo's *Les Misérables.* These, along with such works as Isak Dinesen's stories, Rudolfo Anaya's *Bless Me, Ultima,* Isabel Allende's *The House of the Spirits,* and Edmond Rostand's *Cyrano de Bergerac*, require the careful choice of words that recur in all translations and provide precise vignettes, for example, the making of jet in *Les Misérables;* makeshift sleeping arrangements on an opklap bed in the annexe, the setting of *The Diary of a Young Girl;* and the religious title of the Abbé Faria, mentor to Edmond Dantès in *The Count of Monte Cristo.* To this sizable accounting I added the reading market's growing interest in personal and historical narrative, whether essay, diary, historical commentary, investigative reporting, biography or autobiography, as exemplified by Benjamin Franklin's *Poor Richard's Almanac,* Dr. Martin Luther King's "Letter from a Birmingham Jail," Elie Wiesel's *Night,* Farley Mowat's *Never Cry Wolf,* Henry David Thoreau's *Walden,* Thomas Keneally's *Schindler's List,* Yoko Kawashima Watkins's *So Far from the Bamboo Grove,* and Zlata Filipovich's *Zlata's Diary.*

Speeches by Abraham Lincoln and Susan B. Anthony and a single entry from "The Star-Spangled Banner" cried out for inclusion. To these masterworks I felt impelled to add the historical overviews in Upton Sinclair's *The Jungle*, Scott O'Dell's *The Island of the Blue Dolphin,* and Alexander Solzhenitsyn's *One Day in the Life of Ivan Denisovich*, plus prizewinning stories of Najib Mahfouz, Rabindranath Tagore, R. R. Narayan, Doris Lessing, and Jorge Luis Borges. Frustrated at this point with the impossibility of all-inclusiveness, I listed as often as possible the words that permeate all writing—the lore of the sailing vessel, garments and conveyances, containers and tools, organizations, ritual, and medical treatment. With the inclusion of nearly 800 drawings, the work sprang to life, a source of explanation and encouragement for the armchair traveler enboldened to depart the narrows of a smaller world and reach beyond. Enjoy!

A Reader's Guide

I have simplified the use of this dictionary with numerous aids to the reader, who is more interested in getting back to the story than in searching through cross references for that one small detail, whether **Rose of Sharon, sow belly, Five-Year Plan, skrimshandering, fenian movement**, or **intercalary month.** The entries, spelled as they were in the main source, are alphabetized. Many of these terms appear unusual by modern standards of spelling, capitalization, and punctuation:

paterollers
po' white trash
snap-brim hat
jalousie-blinds
duck-weed
sou'wester
slop-seller
rush-light

A frequent use of hyphens harks back to a nineteenth-century spelling rule that required a hyphen when one noun combined with another but served as a modifier: **duck-weed, jalousie-blinds, slop-seller.** Some unusual terms derive from product names (**meccano set; sen-sen; quonset hut**). Those from foreign languages that have not yet been assimilated into English appear in italics, e.g., ***abrazo, ignis fatuus, llanero, tempura, bonne, a cappella.***

Some of the entries are common to a variety of works. Alongside the entry appear alternate spellings and versions of the word:

griffon/griffin/gryphon
loadstone/lodestone
bandy legs/banty legs
Vestal or vestal virgins
matins/matin
swingel/swingle
nawab/nabob/nob
ruble/rouble
skein/skean/skeane
tie wig/tye wig

Other entries contain synonyms unrelated in spelling:

hoe cake/johnny cake
pop-the-whip/crack-the-whip
ignis fatuus/will-o'-the-wisp
ride on a rail/run out on a rail

Cross-referencing leads readers to the variant found in a particular literary work:

genie *See* djinn
bas mitzvah *See* bar mitzvah
plaster *See* poultice
night bucket *See* slop jar
thurible *See* censer

Obvious pronunciation goes unmarked, as with **Rose of Sharon**, **A.M.E. Church**, **rune**, **O.S.S.**, and **swab.** Where pronunciation proves difficult, the entry follows the H-based system of phonetic spelling, which requires no diacritical marks over vowels. The system follows this simple twelve-part model:

a **as in masque [mask]**
ih **as in mitt [miht]**
ah **as in mop [mahp]**
oh **as in mole [mohl]**
aw **as in maul [mawl]**
oo **as in mousse [moos]**
ay **as in maze [mayz]**
ow **as in mouse [mows]**
ee **as in meal [meel]**
uh **as in much [muhch]**
eh **as in met [meht]**
y **as in mine [myn]**

Note that a few foreign terms retain certain diacritical markings: **épergne, øre, façade, tête-à-tête**.

Each syllable receiving a major stress appears in italic with a stress mark to the right:

adobe (uh. *doh'* bee)
merino (muh . *ree'* noh)
quadrille (kwah . *drihl'*)
jaeger (*yay'* guhr)
chinoiserie (sheen . *wahz'* ree)
thuggee (*tuhg'* gee)

A syllable receiving minor stress appears in italic without an accent mark:

esplanade (*es* . pluh . *nahd'*)
convolutions (*kahn* . voh . *loo'* shuhnz)

Where more than one pronunciation applies, the first phonetic spelling in parentheses represents the more common usage: **fakir** (fuh . *keer'* or *fay'* kuhr).

After the pronunciation appears the formation of alternate, unusual, or questionable plurals:

shaman *pl.* **shamans**
seraph *pl.* **seraphim**
shako *pl.* **shakos** or **shakoes**

If the plural follows conventional English spelling (**effigy/effigies, ululation/ululations**), no plural is listed. In more complex entries, appended advice on spelling provides additional guidance in correct usage:

bilboes usu. pl., rarely **bilbo**
momzer or **momser** or **mamzer** *pl.* **momzerim**

The text or text plus illustration gives a succinct idea of the meaning of the word as it has been used in literature and summarizes the word's etymology where that information will prove useful. For example:

junta (*hoon'* tuh) a self-appointed governing body, council, administrative board, or commission; a military coterie or usurper who seizes control of a country by *coup d'état*, then rules autocratically. Derived from the Latin for *yoke*, the term entered English in the early seventeenth century.

The entry concludes with the title and author of the source and states the situation or usage of each term. For the entry on *junta:*

In *The Crucible*, playwright Arthur Miller notes that the unified group that arrived on the *Mayflower* had been supplanted by splinter groups ruled by a narrow fundamentalist junta.

Thus the reader can pinpoint the location of the term and its use in context for more thorough understanding. An index by author and titles provides a master list of entries from each work.

This book offers other ways of homing in on word meaning. A spectacular array of drawings details the use of tools, depicts obscure plants and animals, and illustrates building terms, architectural details, behavior, or domestic items, for example, **stair rod, amphora, tippet, wimble,** or **biting the thumb.** A majority of entries give general dates or periods when the term appears to have evolved, for example, "before the twelfth century" or "during the Middle Ages." Some are more precise: "in the mid-1800s" or "during the Civil War era." A few, such as **odori,** list exact times (1603). Another small group, including **selah** and **mooche**, leave a limited trail for the word student to follow.

A second index groups entries by subject. The bibliography names the literary classics referenced in this book, and a list of references directs the reader to the sources consulted in its preparation.

Acknowledgments

Dr. W. F. Atwater
U.S. Army Ordnance Museum
Aberdeen, Maryland

Michael Bauman
Temple Beth-Shalom
Hickory, North Carolina

Lynne Bolick
Reference Librarian
Catawba County Library
Newton, North Carolina

Gary Carey
author and editor
Lincoln, Nebraska

Catawba County Department of Social Services
Conover, North Carolina

Michael Coffey
Reference Librarian
Catawba County Library
Newton, North Carolina

Janey Deal, Archivist
Elbert Ivey Memorial Library
Hickory, North Carolina

Jonathan Frock
taxidermist
Arden, North Carolina

Rita Hofrichter
Holocaust Documentation Center
Miami, Florida

Carlotta Holman, Secretary
St. Aloysius Catholic Church
Hickory, North Carolina

Reference Department
Holocaust Museum
Washington, D. C.

Laura Kelleher
reference librarian
Elbert Ivey Memorial Library
Hickory, North Carolina

Reference Department
Lincoln Public Library
Lincoln, Nebraska

Burl McCuiston
reference librarian
Lenoir-Rhyne College
Hickory, North Carolina

Dr. Lotsee Patterson
Department of Library Science
University of Oklahoma
Norman, Oklahoma

U.S. Army Center of Military History
Washington, D. C.

Wanda Rozzelle
Reference Librarian
Catawba County Library
Newton, North Carolina

Mark Schumacher
Reference Librarian
University of North Carolina–Greensboro
Greensboro, North Carolina

Mohamed Bashir Sani
Information Attache
Nigerian Embassy
Washington, D.C.

Juanita Setzer
Reference Library
Elbert Ivey Memorial Library
Hickory, North Carolina

To my secretary, Andrea Pittman, a bushel of thanks for transforming chaos into order. Thanks also to the artists who illustrated the book: Jon Norby, Brice Adams, Chad Bontrager, Stuart Compton, Elizabeth Cornwell, Toinette Feist, Susan Fry, Wes Geiger, Jene Horan, Nicole Horn, Melanie Keys, James Kovac, Heidi Leech, Diana Lyon, Paul Reinhardt, Stephen T. Rose, Anna Schmidt, Walter J. Strength, Valerie Thrall, Paul Trani, and Scott Widing.

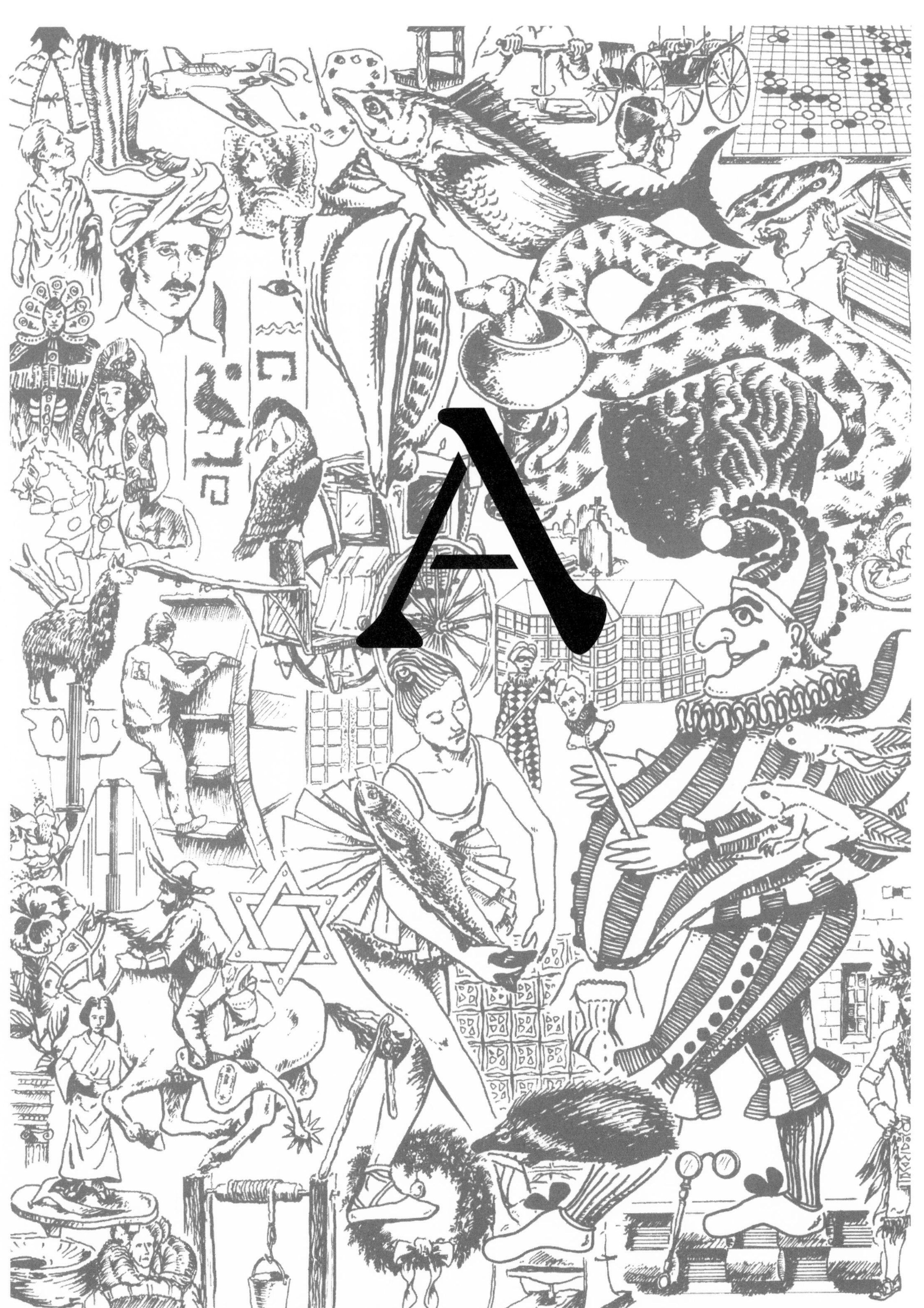
A

abacus (*a'* buh . kuhs) an early form of calculator composed of a rectangular board or frame holding parallel wires, grooves, or dowels fitted with movable beads to serve as memory devices for counting, computing, or teaching arithmetic in early Russia, India, China, Greece, and Rome, where it was reintroduced by Pope Sylvester II about A.D. 1000. Derived from the Greek for *slab,* the word entered English in the fourteenth century. Each column of counters equals a range of values, for instance, ones, tens, hundreds, thousands, and so on. In her autobiography, *I Know Why the Caged Bird Sings,* Maya Angelou refers to seeing Chinese children in San Francisco operating an abacus.

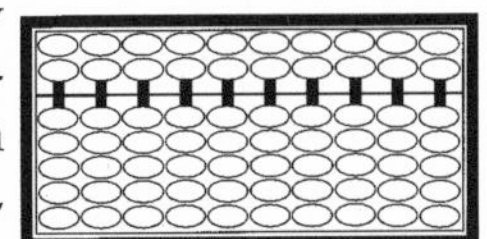

abalone (ab . uh . *loh'* nee) a tasty shellfish, or gastropod, similar to a scallop and highly prized by Indians of the West Coast, who pry them from rocks at low tide. The meat can be dried and stored for winter use; the shiny shells are a common craft material. In early times, California Indians used abalone shells as trade items to be carved into coins, ornaments, buttons, knife hilts, beads, labrets, and fishhooks. The term derives from the Rumsen, a Native American language of California. The carved Kwakiutl mask in Margaret Craven's *I Heard the Owl Call My Name* is made from the pearly white abalone shell.

abbé (*ab'* bay) title conferred on a French chaplain, teacher, cleric, priest, or other official wearing an ecclesiastical costume. This sixteenth-century term derives from the Aramaic word *abba,* meaning *father.* The Abbé Faria, a frail prisoner, serves as a pivotal mentor, educator, and spiritual counselor to Edmond Dantés, the central character in Alexandre Dumas's *The Count of Monte Cristo.*

abbot (*ab'* buht) superintendent of the monks or holy men who occupy a monastery or other religious institution. In the Middle Ages, the abbot served as religious governor and oversaw the monastery's charitable service or scholarly pursuits, such as feeding the poor, visiting shut-ins and elderly people, and translating or copying valuable texts. Dating to the twelfth century, the term appears in Thomas Hardy's *Tess of the D'Urbervilles,* naming the person buried in the stone coffin where Angel Clare places Tess.

ablution (uh . *bloo'* shuhn) ritual washing of the hands or cleansing of the body, often in sanctified springwater, seawater, wine, urine, or blood contained in a ceremonial basin. It is a sixteenth-century term derived from the Latin for *wash.* Alex Haley's *The Autobiography of Malcolm X* describes the Muslim ablution, which begins with right hand and left hand, then proceeds to the teeth, mouth, and nostrils, and concludes with the entire body.

AB master mariner or **able-bodied seaman** a standard designation for sailors capable of commanding vessels at sea or on inland waterways. Among their skills are the crucial jobs of rigging, reefing, and steering a vessel in all weathers; observing safety regulations and courtesies to other vessels; attending to lights and sails; and splicing and "knowing the ropes" or knots—even in the dark during gale weather. Beyond the AB classification are the skilled laborers such as cook, ship's surgeon, navigator, engineer, telegrapher, radar or sonar operator, communications chief, purser, and electrician. Reduced to hobbling and superintending the galley, Long John Silver, once an AB master mariner in Robert Louis Stevenson's *Treasure Island,* remains mentally alert and capable of coercing others to do his bidding. *See also* gale.

abolitionist (a . boh . *lih'* shuhn . ihst) an activist who denounced human bondage by taking part in the antislavery movement that formalized operations in the United States around 1820 and flourished openly from 1833 to 1865, when emancipation was declared. Frederick Douglass took a leading role in producing antislavery tracts, organizing workers, and delivering speeches; Harriet Beecher Stowe wrote the definitive abolitionist novel, *Uncle Tom's Cabin* (1852). In Mark Twain's *The Adventures of Huckleberry Finn,* the central character would rather be called a "low-down abolitionist" than allow his friend Jim, a runaway slave, to be recaptured and sold. *See also* tract; underground railroad.

abrazo (uh . *brahs'* oh) the Spanish term for a ritual hug or embrace between people of the same sex or opposite sexes—particularly welcoming a guest, ending a quarrel, concluding a competition, giving thanks, or preceding a separation or departure between friends, neighbors, or family members. As head of the household, Antonio's father performs the *abrazo* as a ceremonial expression of friendship in Rudolfo Anaya's *Bless Me, Ultima.*

absolution (*ab* . soh . *loo'* shuhn) the formal or sacramental forgiveness of or release from the burden of sin and accompanying guilt. The act usually occurs as a result of private confession to a priest, from acts of contrition, or through penance, which is attained via prayer or ecclesiastical mandate. In the Catholic faith, absolution can be obtained for the dead through prayers asking God to intercede for the departed. The term entered English in the fourteenth century. In his anguish over the execution of his son, Kumalo in Alan Paton's *Cry, the Beloved Country* prays for absolution. *See also* contrition, act of; limbo; penance.

Acadia *See* Cajun.

a cappella (ah kuh . *pehl'* luh) an Italian musical term meaning *in chapel style,* referring to songs performed by congregations, liturgists, choirs, cantors, or soloists without musical accompaniment. In Judith Guest's *Ordinary People,* Conrad raises his self-esteem through his participation in the *a cappella* choir, which he considers a prestigious role in school affairs.

ack-ack fire imitative slang dating to the mid-1920s that denotes anti-aircraft fire from powerful guns of a servomechanism or electronic defense system trained on the sky, which was illuminated at night or in bad weather with searchlights that pinpointed positions of bombers. The advent of missiles has resulted in a more sophisticated antimissile system requiring heat sensors and other chemical and computerized devices to explode incoming shells in the air. Mentioned by Anne Frank in a March 1943 entry in *The Diary of a Young Girl,* ack-ack fire outside the family's hiding place is so loud she can't concentrate. *See also* anti-aircraft.

acolyte (*a'* koh . lyt) the altar attendant or assistant to a priest, minister, or rector. The term, derived from the Greek for *follower* and dating to the fourteenth century, refers to the lay person who performs duties such as cleaning and storing ecclesiastical robes, polishing altar brass, or turning pages during the priest's reading of scripture. In *Gilgamesh,* a ceremonial entourage in the underworld includes priests and acolytes.

acropolis (uh . *krah'* poh . lihs) derived from the Greek for *high point of the city,* a seventeenth-century English term referring to a city's fortified highest elevation, fortress, or safe zone. In particular, as described in Edith Hamilton's *Mythology,* the Acropolis—the citadel, treasury, and municipal and religious center of ancient Athens—is a focal point of fifth-century B.C. Greek architecture and a monument to the goddess Athena, the city's patron.

act of contrition *See* contrition, act of.

acupuncturist (*ak'* yoo . *puhnk* . choor . ihst) a therapist who treats illness with traditional Oriental methods—by inserting, twirling, heating, or charging with electric current thin metal needles or skewers at precise points on the body to stimulate or lessen the flow of energy called *ch'i* or to balance natural elements that govern the life force. Begun with a medical arsenal of bone, wood, bamboo, or stone points, acupuncture, which was described in the *Nei Ching* or *Yellow Emperor's Classic of Internal Medicine* (ca. 2550 B.C.), stimulated or lessened the flow of energy, or *ch'i,* to balance a pattern of natural elements that govern the life force and to countermand dysfunction in organs or systems. Later equipment made of copper, brass, steel, gold, or silver was easier to sterilize and connected better with endorphins, the body's natural painkillers. In John Hersey's *Hiroshima,* victims of the atomic blast turn to acupuncture to tone muscles and improve health, cure disease, strengthen organs weakened by radiation poison, lessen chronic pain, or anesthetize a patient for surgery.

Adam's apple an eighteenth-century colloquial term for the projecting thyroid cartilage in the front of the larynx, an organ that is more prominent in males. The term is a reference from the Hebrew lore in Genesis in which Eve offers her mate an unidentified fruit at the insistence of Satan, who takes the form of a persuasive serpent. *Adam's apple* reflects the legend by suggesting that Adam ate an apple and forfeited Adam and Eve's tenure in the Garden of Eden. To illustrate Billy's delight in a box of pups, Wilson Rawls in *Where the Red Fern Grows* describes the temporary paralysis of Billy's Adam's apple.

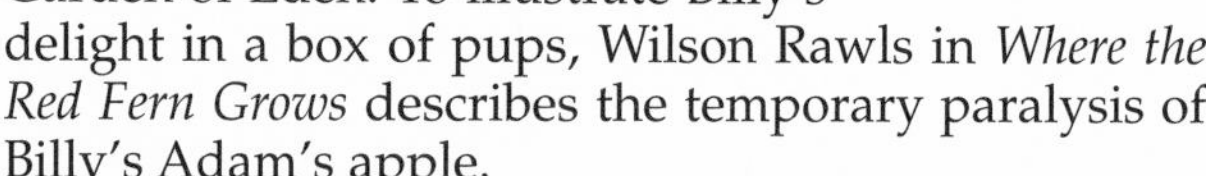

addenda (uh . *dehn'* duh) *sing.* **addendum** a supplement, appendix, or postscript to a letter; codicil to a will or legal document; an additional commentary, tables, or systematized facts positioned at the end of a scholarly treatise for handy reference. The addendum on the condolence note from Meyer Wolfsheim to Nick Carraway in F. Scott Fitzgerald's *The Great Gatsby* helps to distance Wolfsheim from the messy matter of a funeral for a suicide. Wolfsheim contends that he did not know Gatsby's family and prefers to remember his old friend when he was still alive.

adder a brightly patterned snake named for the Latin for *water snake.* Common to Asia and Europe, this triangular-headed, poisonous viper is frequently mentioned in literature, for example, the trained snake that crawls through the vent and commits the murder in

Sir Arthur Conan Doyle's "The Adventure of the Speckled Band," as well as serpents mentioned in William Shakespeare's *Macbeth* and Ray Bradbury's *Fahrenheit 451.*

adobe (uh . *doh'* bee) red-brown brick that is formed of clay, ash, straw, grass, and gravel by hand or in molds and baked or cured in the sun. Homes and other structures made of adobe are cemented with plaster, which has to be reapplied after seasonal rains. A common building material easily obtained in the American Southwest, Mexico, and Latin America—for the churches in William Barrett's *Lilies of the Field* and Rudolfo Anaya's *Bless Me, Ultima*—adobe is cheap, fireproof, and weatherproof. Builders and homeowners prefer it for its durability and traditional subdued glow, which blends well with other earth tones.

adze or **adz** (adz) a twelfth-century Anglo-Saxon term denoting a Stone Age hand tool made with a short or long handle at a right angle to a narrow, arched blade of shell, bone, metal, or obsidian honed on the outer edge. Like an ax, pick, mattock, or hatchet but less precise than a plane, the adze is swung downward to slice, trim, or shape a wood surface. As Calypso helps Odysseus prepare for his journey to Ithaca in Homer's *Odyssey,* the multitalented sailor displays skill with the adze, which he uses to shape a keel.

aegis (*ee'* jihs) Zeus's shield or breastplate, a shaggy torso guard covered with a serpentine design and fringed with gold tassels. The term derives from the Greek for *goatskin.* Described in Edith Hamilton's *Mythology,* this ceremonial armor, which sported the head of Medusa, the snake-haired gorgon, protected Zeus's daughter Athena, goddess of war. Currently, the term denotes divine protection, sponsorship, or the type of controlling, stultifying patronage the title character spurns in Edmond Rostand's *Cyrano de Bergerac.*

African M. E. Church or **A.M.E.** the African Methodist Episcopal Church, a widespread black Protestant denomination founded by Richard Allen in New York City in 1801. In Harper Lee's *To Kill a Mockingbird,* Cal, governess for the Finch family, undergoes hard looks from members for escorting two white children, Scout and Jem, to an austere A.M.E. church for a Sunday service.

after braces the ropes or wires toward the rear, or aft, of a ship that attach a block to the yardarm to adjust a sail horizontally along the beam. The term is taken from the French *bras* for *arm.* In a surprise show of authority, the unnamed captain in Joseph Conrad's "The Secret Sharer" orders his crew to the after braces to trim the sails before breakfast.

after-deck or **poop deck** a ship's deck, platform, or flooring located from the rear, or aft, toward the middle, or ship's waist, the scene of much activity, where the crew attends to changes in the weather and resetting of sails. The term derives from the Dutch for *covering.* In Robert Louis Stevenson's *Treasure Island,* hero Jim Hawkins carefully surveys the after-deck for mutineers before creeping aboard the *Hispaniola.*

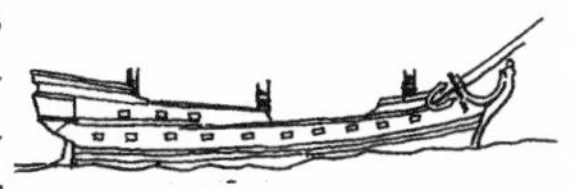

after-image a neurological phenomenon occurring after an unwavering or lengthy gaze. Because of the intensity of the visual illusion, it remains in the mind after the eyes are closed or after the image has moved out of the field of vision. The persistent shape, like a photographic negative, may reverse the colors of figure and background. After an intense jungle experience, Simon's mind retains the after-image of the focal symbol, a fly-blown sow's head on a stick, in William Golding's *Lord of the Flies.*

agate (*ag'* iht) a semiprecious gemstone also called chalcedony or onyx, which is related to quartz and formed in lava eruptions into parallel bands of silica. The stone, which is quarried around the globe, varies in opacity and color, from white to tan, rust, brown, and black, depending on the circumstances of its formation. Agate marbles are called "aggies," a prized possession in Mark Twain's *Adventures of Tom Sawyer.* In Marjorie Kinnan Rawlings's *The Yearling,* Jody inspects a bag of agates that Oliver brings his girlfriend. *See also* taw.

aggie *See* agate.

agoraphobia (*a* . guh . ruh . *foh'* bee . yuh) an irrational or overstated terror of open places or crowds and a strong preference bordering on mania for a reclusive, singular lifestyle within a familiar, confined locale. This psychological malady takes its name from *agora,* the Greek term for *marketplace,* an open-air city gathering spot and commercial center. The aunt in Maxine Hong Kingston's *Woman Warrior* develops agoraphobia after her family curses her.

ague (*ay'* gyoo) any acute illness accompanied by trembling, sweating, disorientation, malaise, chills, and fever, especially malaria or swamp fever. Derived from the Latin for *sharp,* this general medical term entered English in the fourteenth century. In Robert Louis Stevenson's *Treasure Island,* Dr. Trelawny correctly predicts that the pirates will soon come down with ague because they are camped on marshy ground.

airedale (*ayr'* dayl) a tall, long-limbed terrier weighing around 50 pounds bearing a distinctively crisp, wiry coat of patterned black and tan. The name, dating to the late nineteenth century, reflects the area around England's Aire River in Yorkshire. The airedale is bred to hunt and to carry battlefield messages; it adapts well to being a family pet, as described in James Herriot's *All Creatures Great and Small.* In F. Scott Fitzgerald's *The Great Gatsby,* the dog-seller lies to Myrtle that the pup Tom Buchanan buys for her is an airedale.

airie or **airy** *See* eyrie.

alarum (uh . *lah'* ruhm) an archaic or poetic spelling of *alarm,* traditionally used in stage directions to indicate movement, surprise, crowd noises, a disturbing happening or turn of events, riot, war, attack, or a call to arms or battle stations. William Shakespeare uses alarum to indicate offstage fighting during the civil war that follows the murder of the title character in *Julius Caesar* and in the scene in which the title character duels with Macduff in *Macbeth.*

albacore (*al'* buh . kohr) a large, long-finned bluefish tuna common to the warm waters of the West Indies and the Pacific Ocean. A member of the mackerel family, the tasty, white-fleshed fish takes its name from the Arabic word for *precocious.* In Ernest Hemingway's *The Old Man and the Sea,* Santiago follows schools of bonito and albacore far from land and eats raw strips to keep up his strength while he battles his great catch.

Albert chain a watch chain with a crossbar, crest, or emblem at the end. The Albert chain was worn during the nineteenth century to anchor the loose chain end in a vest pocket or to extend it from the lapel buttonhole to the breast pocket, in which the watch was kept handy and safe. The chain takes its name from Queen Victoria's husband, Prince Albert, whose clothing and architectural tastes predominated in the mid- to late nineteenth century. In Sir Arthur Conan Doyle's "The Red-Headed League," Sherlock Holmes sizes up a man who wears an ostentatious ornament dangling from the end of his Albert chain.

albumen or **albumin** (al . *byoo'* mihn) a water-soluble, protein-rich substance separated from blood and used in sugar refining, fertilizer, and cement; in the creation and testing of serum and artificial hormones; and in printing to produce a sheen on paper. Derived from the Latin for *white,* the term entered English in the late sixteenth century. In Upton Sinclair's *The Jungle,* albumen is one of the many byproducts workers extract from the blood of slaughtered animals.

alchemist (*al'* kuh . mihst) from ancient times into the Renaissance throughout Europe and Asia, a chemist, metallurgist, laboratory piddler, or other pseudoscientist who employed astrology, sorcery, incantations, or ritual magic in a vain attempt to produce gold from lesser metals or to discover a universal cure-all or the secret of eternal life. In an interview with his first college teacher in Mary Shelley's *Frankenstein,* Victor boldly names the forbidden works of alchemists he has studied.

alcove (*al'* kohv) a vaulted or arched recess, nook, or inset in a room, exterior wall, or hedge; a curtained or screened niche for sleeping, storage, or the display of art or religious objects. Derived from the Arabic word for *vault,* this architectural term dates to the seventeenth century. In George Orwell's *1984,* a shielded alcove is an essential factor in Winston Smith's ability to hide his secret diary from the screen that monitors his room.

alee (uh . *lee'*) on the sheltered side, shielded from the wind; leeward, the opposite of aweather or windward. A common adverb in sea jargon, the word entered English in the fourteenth century. It plays a significant role in Joseph Conrad's "The Secret Sharer," in which a captain helps a condemned man escape pursuers by slipping alee over the side of the ship into calm waters and swimming to an island where his crime is unknown.

alewife (*ayl'* wyf) *pl.* **alewives** a prolific saw-bellied member of the herring family common to the Atlantic waters off New England. The alewife, a popular, inexpensive food fish reaching 8 to 10 inches in length, swims upriver to spawn in freshwater. In Esther Forbes's *Johnny Tremain,* the title character buys a mundane tavern meal of bread and salted alewives.

alfalfa (al . *fal'* fuh) a nutritious cloverlike forage crop and perennial member of the pea family. Alfalfa, which grows about 30 inches high and produces a cluster of purple, lilac, white, or yellow blooms, originated in Babylon and is commonly grown for fodder worldwide. In John Steinbeck's *Of Mice and Men,* Lenny and George anticipate buying a 10-acre farm and growing alfalfa to feed their rabbits.

Allah (*ah'* luh or ah . *lah'*) the Arabic name for God, or the supreme being in the Islamic or Muslim faith. According to the Koran, Islam's holy book, Allah, the creator, ruler, and judge of humankind, is the author of or inspiration for Muslim scripture, which was recorded by Mohammed, Allah's prophet. In Alex Haley's *The Autobiography of Malcolm X,* the desire to obey Allah influences Malcolm to give up street crime, organize worship centers, and preach to Black Muslims.

Allahu-Akbar (ah . *lah'* hoo . *ahk'* bahr) the ritual invocation at Muslim prayer services, meaning "Allah is the greatest." *See also* As-Salaikum-Salaam.

alligator pepper common name for the offe (oh' fay), an inch-long brown fruit of a shrub native to western Africa. When ground or shredded and blended with kola nut, the torrid seeds form a spicy paste for cooking. Ibo tribesmen who confer during the opening scenes of Chinua Achebe's *Things Fall Apart* share a traditional snack of kola nut and alligator pepper, symbolic of courtesy, congeniality, and welcome. *See also* kola nut.

alluvial fan (uh . *loo'* vee . uhl) the triangular sediment bed or aggregate of boulders, earth, silt, gravel, sand, mud, and debris deposited by a swift current when it pours from a gorge and enters a slower stream or floodplain. On her return to the Japanese internment camp where her family spent World War II, Jeanne Wakatsuki Houston and James D. Houston, authors of *Farewell to Manzanar,* describe the alluvial fan on the barren site in California's windswept Mojave Desert.

almanac (*ahl'* muh . nak) a day-to-day table or annual compendium of data that derives its name from the Arabic for *calendar*. Dating to ancient Egypt, almanacs feature tips on farming; weather; tidal, migratory, and astrological forecasts; animal and herbal lore; holidays; adages; cures; household hints; and humor. The most famous American almanac is Benjamin Franklin's *Poor Richard's Almanack* (1732–1757), which warns "Haste makes waste."

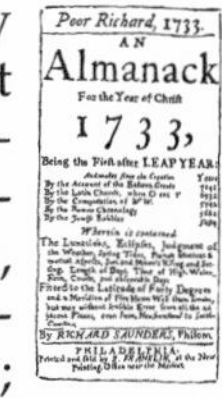

almshouse a poorhouse, charitable distribution center, sheltered workshop, or receiving home founded by altruistic individuals, foundations, or institutions to aid invalids, the aged, infirm, mentally or physically handicapped, or destitute; a workhouse. In Edith Wharton's *Ethan Frome,* Zeena snipes at her husband with a snide remark about Frome's residing in the almshouse. *See also* workhouse.

alpaca (al . *pak'* uh) a woolly member of the camel-like llama family of the Andes Mountains of Peru. The term derives from the Quechua word for *reddish-brown*. Alpaca shearings yield a thin, elastic, silky fiber used in warm, lightweight, high-quality knitted goods such as caps, sweaters, socks, capes, and baby blankets. The speaker in Joseph Conrad's *The Heart of Darkness* recognizes a European gentleman by his fine clothing, including an alpaca jacket that is completely out of place in Congo heat.

alpenstock (*al'* pihn . *stahk*) an awkward staff or hand tool composed of a 6-foot shaft ending in an iron pick. The alpenstock was formerly used by mountain climbers as they reached forward to secure a grip on icy slopes or to dig out a toehold. This tool has been replaced by the ice ax, a shorter, lighter, more flexible tool. Jenny, a honeymooner in Isak Dinesen's "The Pearls," wields an alpenstock as she hikes the mountain slopes of Norway.

amanuensis (uh . *man* . yoo . *ehn'* sihs) *See* scrivener.

Amazon (*am'* uh . zahn) a member of a mythic race of female warriors, native to Asia Minor south of the Black Sea, who allowed no men to live among them except for brief visits from breeders to sire their children; also a female guard at a gate, harem, or palace entrance. In recent times, the term refers to any athletic, competitive, or aggressive woman. According to Edith Hamilton's *Mythology,* the Amazons, led by Queen Penthesilea, were renowned archers who took part in the Trojan War.

amber a yellow, translucent fossilized resin that in prehistory dropped from pines and other trees, encasing gas bubbles, insects, and plants. When mined and shaped, amber is cut and polished to make brooches, ornamental boxes, buttons, buckles, rosaries, and pipe stems or added to lacquer or varnish to enhance sheen. In Thomas Hardy's *The Mayor of Casterbridge,* a description of the remains the Romans buried in English cemeteries, particularly silver coins and amber jewelry, proves the historical presence of an ancient occupation force.

ambrosia (am . *broh'* zhyuh) according to Edith Hamilton's *Mythology,* ambrosia is a fragrant salve, delicious food of the gods, and elixir of life—a fact implied by the Greek derivation from *immortal.* Mortals who ate ambrosia became divine and lived forever. In Harper Lee's *To Kill a Mockingbird,* which is set in the American South during the 1930s, ambrosia is a traditional Christmas dessert blended from coconut, orange sections, and brandy.

A.M.E. *See* African M. E. Church.

amen corner an American colloquialism designating a section of a congregation where fervent worshippers can address God; echo words sung by soloists or the choir; shout for joy; and utter praise, pleas to the Almighty, or comments on the minister's sermon. In Alice Walker's *The Color Purple,* Harpo feels free to flirt with a girl during church services because her father, attentively participating from the amen corner, doesn't observe the irreverence of his daughter's beau.

ammeter (*am'* mee . tuhr) or **calibrated galvanometer** an instrument attached to a dashboard gauge registering the conversion of a direct electrical charge being drawn from a battery for use by a vehicle's engine. The ammeter, invented by Hans Oersted in 1820, measures in amperes or microamperes the direct current that passes through a coil and creates a magnetic field that activates a pointer and scale of numbers. In John Steinbeck's *Grapes of Wrath,* Al Joad, who drives the decrepit family truck over desert roads from Oklahoma to California, keeps a worried eye on the ammeter for signs of electrical problems.

ammonia the common name for NH_3, a colorless, poisonous alkaline gas causing a noxious smell. The Greeks named ammonia for the god Ammon, whose priests extracted the gas from animal hooves and horns. Ammonia was first synthesized by German chemist Fritz Haber in 1909. Its production required temperatures higher than 1000 degrees Fahrenheit. In John Steinbeck's *The Pearl,* the doctor administers to Coyotito some drops of ammonia, which appear to cause abdominal spasms. The doctor gives the baby a white powder to stop the pain; then claims to have cured him of the effects of a scorpion bite.

amphitheatre (*am'* fuh . *thee.* uh . tuhr) a sloped floor containing semicircular tiers or a gallery overlooking a central space, stage, or focal point. Before the cesarean birth of the baby in the concluding scenes of Ernest Hemingway's *A Farewell to Arms,* Catherine is wheeled into an operating room that includes an amphitheatre with seating to accommodate observers or medical students.

amphora (*am'* for . uh) *pl.* **amphorae** a tall, oval footed vase, funeral urn, or storage container tapering to a slender neck flanked by two large handles to facilitate the pouring of wine, vinegar, cider, oil, olives, or grain. Picturing the palace in Ithaca, Homer's *Odyssey* describes the king's locked storeroom, which is stocked with weapons, clothes chests, and stoppered amphorae sealed with wax.

amulet (*am'* yoo . liht) a protective charm, such as a sacred stone, scarab, saint's likeness, rabbit's foot, zodiac sign, or animal tooth, that is applied to a dwelling or boat or is carried or worn to bring luck or fend off accident, illness, witchcraft, sorcery, or other evil. The term, of inexact origin, appears to date to the comic theater of ancient Rome. During the journey to Mexico's capital city, Kino, the central figure in John Steinbeck's *The Pearl,* wears an amulet on a string around his neck.

anarchy (*an'* ahr . kee) a state of riot, rebellion, disorder, social chaos, lawlessness, defiance of authority, or lack of governmental regulation. A Greek term, *anarchy* derives from words meaning *lack of an archon or controller.* In John Knowles's *A Separate Peace,* the winter carnival dissolves into frolicsome anarchy as the boys ignore, violate, or improvise sporting rules; wrestle in the snow; and enjoy freedom from teachers and school administrators.

anemic (uh . *nee'* mihk) insipid, forceless; lacking in nutrients; thin, tottery, weak, pale, faint, queasy, or sickly from insufficient iron in the diet and from the bloodstream's loss of hemoglobin, which carries oxygen throughout the body. From the Greek for *bloodless,* the term sums up a variety of physical symptoms, such as a condition of malaise or weakness that accompanies AIDS, dysentery, or leukemia. Esperanza, the youthful narrator of Sandra Cisneros's *The House on Mango Street,* demonstrates her need of a bagged lunch by holding up a limp, anemic wrist.

aneurysm (*an'* yoo . rizm) a blood-filled sac or dilation bulging outward from a malformed, diseased, clotted, or damaged artery. An aneurysm has the potential to weaken or erode until it bursts and precipitates a life-threatening hemorrhage that can kill in minutes. The term dates to the fifteenth century and derives from the Greek for *spread side.* Jing-Mei Woo's mother, a character in Amy Tan's *The Joy Luck Club,* dies unexpectedly from a cerebral, or brain, aneurysm.

angiogram (*an'* jee . oh . *gram*) a cardiovascular study of the circulatory system and heart function conducted by x-raying the flow of a harmless dye that is injected into the blood vessels. Gary Paulsen's *Winterdance* describes his annoyance with heart disease and its treadmill tests and angiograms, all of which point to an end of the author's dogsledding activities.

anise (a . *nees'*) a plant of the carrot family yielding aromatic seeds used as flavoring for rum punch or for nonalcoholic drinks. The term derives from the Greek for *unequal.* Anise was first mentioned among fourteenth-century English herbal cures. Resembling licorice in flavor, anise is easily detected, as denoted in the pungent fragrance of the wine shop in Charles Dickens's *A Tale of Two Cities.*

annealing furnace a small chamber stoked with wood, charcoal, or gas and supplied with a bellows or source of oxygen to fan the flame to high temperatures to melt, toughen, strengthen, or temper a solid such as silver or steel for shaping. The chief purpose of an annealing furnace is the extraction of impurities and reduction of brittleness, for example, during the tempering of glass for telescopes, mirrors, baking dishes, thermal insulators, acoustical soundproofers, fireproof materials, and silencers and mufflers. In Esther Forbes's *Johnny Tremain,* Dove, the jealous second apprentice, conspires to ruin Johnny, who sends him out for charcoal to stoke the annealing furnace. *See also* crucible.

annexe or **annex** (*an'* nehks) an addition, expansion, or enlargement attached to an existing building. According to Anne Frank's *The Diary of a Young Girl,* the Frank family and four other survivors owe their lives to the cramped two-story, five-room annexe, which forms makeshift quarters within an old spice warehouse in Amsterdam, Holland, to conceal the Jewish inhabitants from the German SS. *See also* holocaust; Nazi; SS.

anorak (*an'* ohr . ak) *See* parka.

antechamber a foyer, entranceway, anteroom, or waiting area leading to a larger room, office, or apartment. Dating to the seventeenth century, this hybrid word derives from Latin for *in front* and French for *chamber.* To conceal his confession from Cosette, his foster daughter, Jean Valjean, the protagonist of Victor Hugo's *Les Misérables,* waits in the antechamber to unburden himself in private to Marius, Cosette's husband.

antelope drive an effective hunting method in which hunters join to yell or wave branches at frightened antelope to drive them down a chosen path and into a corral or blind canyon for slaughter. As described by N. Scott Momaday in *The Way to Rainy Mountain,* the antelope drive of 1848–1849 required the whole tribe to force antelope into a circle to be clubbed to death for food.

antelope medicine the invocation of a supernatural power or force that endows a group with a successful hunt. Making medicine might call for enacting former hunts, collecting sacred objects such as eagle feathers, painting the body or a horse with powerful signs, chanting prayers or incantations, or sprinkling colored sand in symbolic patterns. According to N. Scott Momaday's *The Way to Rainy Mountain,* making antelope medicine precedes the drive near Bent's Fort, Colorado.

anti-aircraft a gun; protective artillery; heat-sensitive, radar- or computer-controlled missile or rocket system; or ground-to-air battery that wards off bombardment by enemy planes or missiles. In Erich Maria Remarque's *All Quiet on the Western Front,* which is set during World War I, soldiers identify the sound made by individual artillery and anti-aircraft weapons. *See also* ack-ack fire.

anti-Christ as foretold in the Bible in John's epistle, the unnamed false prophet, wicked deceiver, or adversary of Christ, who represents goodness and salvation. The Christian Church anticipates that the anti-Christ will oppress Christ's followers and challenge Him for control of human souls during the apocalypse, a cataclysmic war between good and evil in earth's final days. In the concluding scenes of Arthur Miller's *The Crucible,* Deputy Governor Danforth implies that John Proctor is the anti-Christ.

antimacassar (*an'* tih . muh . *kas* . suhr) a crocheted, lace-edged, or tatted doily placed on the back of a chair or sofa to protect the cloth cushions from Madagascar or "Macassar" oil, a greasy hair tonic popular in the nineteenth century that left a stain on upholstery, hatbands, pillows, and shirt collars. In Charles Dickens's *David Copperfield,* Macassar oil is also applied to mustaches to make them silky, lustrous, and manageable.

antinomian (*an* . tee . *noh'* mee . uhn) a theological belief that Christian law, founded on God's grace and the intervention of the Holy Spirit, does not require followers to obey earthly law in matters of social, legal, moral, and sexual behavior. The title character of Thomas Hardy's *Tess of the D'Urbervilles* overhears a spirited antinomian sermon delivered by Alec d'Urberville, her seducer.

anti-Semitism an open hostility toward or persecution of Jews, the prime motivating force in Thomas Keneally's *Schindler's List,* Esther Hautzig's *The Endless Steppe,* Elie Wiesel's *Night,* Anne Frank's *The Diary of a Young Girl,* and Corrie ten Boom's *The Hiding Place.* During interviews and debates, the title character of Alex Haley's *The Autobiography of Malcolm X* is compelled to answer accusations of insubordination to Black Muslim authority, misogyny, and anti-Semitism. *See also* holocaust; Nazi; SS.

antistrophe (an . *tihs'* . truh . fee) in Greek drama, the second of a triad of speeches—strophe, antistrophe, epode—recited by the chorus as commentary on the action. Derived from the Greek for *twisted against,* the term indicates a type of rebuttal to the strophe. During the first ode in Sophocles' *Antigone,* the chorus dances from right to left as it chants the antistrophe, a graphic commentary on Polyneices' savage attack on Thebes. *See also* epode; strophe.

anvil (*an'* v'l) an oblong cast-iron or steel block with a smooth top, square heel, and projecting horn used by a smith as a multipurpose place to shape hot metal. Entering English in the eleventh century, the word derives from Old High German meaning *to beat on.* In his instructions to Cosette on the secrets of making jet, Jean Valjean, hero of Victor Hugo's *Les Misérables,* notes the manufacturer's need for a small anvil.

apex (*ay'* pehks) a vertex, narrowing, or meeting point of two lines or sides creating an acute angle in a plane or multiple points in a three-dimensional view. The Latin term for a *tip, pointed end, acme,* or *summit,* the term entered the English language in the seventeenth century and figures prominently in geometry, graphing, surveying, design, construction, and architecture. In William Golding's *Lord of the Flies,* at the assembly ground in the triangular arrangement of fallen trees, Ralph takes the symbolic leader's place at the apex and faces the island with his back to the lagoon.

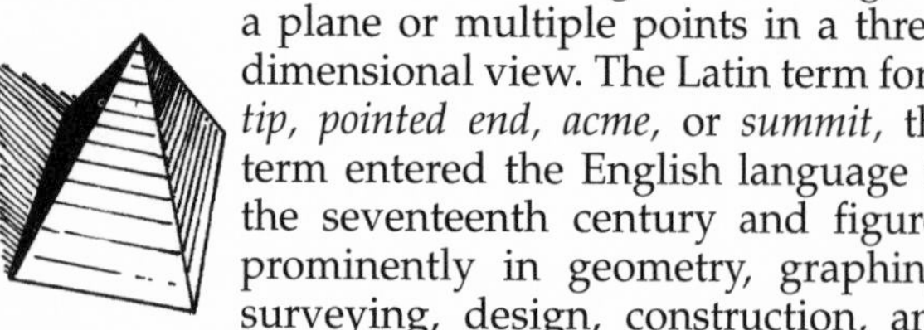

apikorsim (*a'* pee . *kohr* . sihm) a theological term derived from the Greek *Epicurean* and applied to pleasure-loving, luxurious Hellenized Jews; also, irreligious freethinkers, dissidents, or heretics who prefer secularism and noncompliance with church law to obedience and orthodoxy. In Chaim Potok's *The Chosen,* Danny Saunders sees himself as a member of the apikorsim, the educated or atheistic Jews who flout or deny Jewish tradition.

apoplexy (*a'* puh . *plek* . see) commonly known as stroke, a blockage or rupture of a cranial artery marked by temporary or permanent numbness, shock, paralysis, loss of speech, coma, disorientation, or crippling. A currently out-of-date term that was in common use from the fifteenth to the seventeenth centuries, *apoplexy* derives from the Greek for *strike.* In George Eliot's *Silas Marner,* gout and apoplexy were common diseases among the privileged, who ate heartily from rich foods. *See also* gout.

apothecary (uh . *pah'* thuh . *ka* . ree) an archaic term for an herbalist, druggist, or chemist. Following the plague, during which many doctors died, apothecaries served as community medical practitioners. Derived from the Greek for *storekeeper,* the term implies the importance of herbs and pharmaceutical compounds to the work of early pharmacists. In William Shakespeare's *Romeo and Juliet,* Romeo persuades an underpaid Mantuan apothecary to sell him poison.

apotheosis (uh . *pah* . thee . *oh'* sihs) an idealization, glorification, exaltation, epitome, height of realization, or quintessence. From the Greek for *of God,* the term implies elevation to the divine. In "The Bear," William Faulkner labels the bear an apotheosis of the American wild before the arrival of human despoilers.

appliqué (ap . plih . *kay'*) a nineteenth-century French term for a common form of needlework that ornaments by stitching or fastening a decorative piece of fabric, such as a crest, logo, or initial, onto the surface of another fabric, finished table linen, banner, athletic uniform or cap, altar cloth, or ceremonial garment; to overlay or patch. Corrine emulates Olinka men, who appliqué animal figures on quilts in Alice Walker's *The Color Purple.*

apprentice (uh . *prehn'* tihs) a student, novice, or beginner who works without pay, receiving room and board while learning from a master practitioner a certain profession or skill, such as ironwork, blacksmithy, or pharmacy. A sworn and binding indenture, the formal contract to a 7-year period of study, usually from age 14 to 21, often provided tools and uniforms and forbade gambling, strong drink, and late hours. While training in the carpentry trade, the speaker in *Narrative of the Life of Frederick Douglass* reports a fierce battle with four white apprentices. *See also* indentures; journeyman.

apron a leather or waterproof canvas shield in an open carriage that protects passengers and parcels from splashes and blasts of cold air. Derived from the Latin for *table napkin,* the word dates to the fifteenth century and figures heavily in the design of vehicles in the eighteenth and nineteenth centuries as well as the first horseless carriages of the twentieth century. In *Great Expectations,* Charles Dickens writes of Bentley Drummle's awkward leap over the apron of his carriage.

apse a semicircular or polygonal area behind the altar and protruding from the choir end of a traditional cross-shaped church or cathedral. A seventeenth-century architectural term, the word derives from the Greek for *fasten* and refers to a sacred and often domed and highly decorated area. Gene Forrester contemplates the wives and children of staff members, who sit in the apse end of the church in John Knowles's *A Separate Peace.*

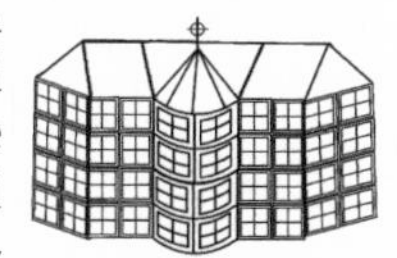

aqua vitae (*ak'* wuh *vee'* ty) brandy or other strong alcoholic drink. Derived from the Latin for *water of life,* the term entered English in the fifteenth century and names a liquid stimulant often used as first aid or as a tonic for anemic, faint, or sickly people. After she finds Juliet's cold, immobile body, the nurse in William Shakespeare's *Romeo and Juliet* calls for *aqua vitae* to revive the girl. *See also* anemic.

aquiline (*a'* kwih . lyn) **face** refers to a long, narrow, almost bridgeless nose prominently shaped like the convex curve of an eagle's beak. The term derives from the Latin *aquila* or *eagle.* In George Orwell's *1984,* Winston Smith recalls the bold, aquiline features of his wife, Katherine, an ominous detail that emphasizes his unpleasant memories of marriage and sex.

arabesque (*a* . ruh . *behsk'*) a graceful seventeenth-century dance pose balancing the performer on one leg while the other leg extends straight out behind the torso parallel to the floor; the opposite arm extends forward and slightly elevated above shoulder level. In the autobiographical *I Know Why the Caged Bird Sings,* Maya Angelou, who was once a tall, ungainly teenager, studies the grace of ballet demonstrated by an arabesque performed by her teacher.

arc-and-compass symbols of work or skilled labor that denote the scope of the Freemasons, a men's secret society originating in 1717, and usually represented by a rectangular layout of a draftsman's right angle overlaying a compass. In Sir Arthur Conan Doyle's "The Red-Headed League," Sherlock Holmes recognizes the arc-and-compass breastpin as an unofficial symbol of membership in the Freemasons.

arch-fiend one of many names for the demon Satan, the fallen angel Lucifer, or the "light-bringer" who became the chief adversary of Christ and the repository of all evil and perversion of good. Entering English in the mid-seventeenth century, the hybrid term derives from the Greek for *primary* and the Sanskrit for *enemy.* In Arthur Miller's *The Crucible,* the author refers to Satan as "arch-fiend," "Lucifer," and "the Old Boy."

archipelago (*ar* . kuh . *pehl'*. uh . goh) a cluster of islands or an expanse of sea- or freshwater strewn with islands. A sixteenth-century term derived from the Greek for *primary sea,* it originally referred to the Aegean Sea before becoming a generic term for all seawaters. In Joseph Conrad's "The Secret Sharer," the neophyte captain anticipates leaving the Gulf of Siam, sailing northeast, and navigating the Malay Archipelago between the Indian and Pacific oceans.

arc-lamp a high-intensity spotlight using the energy produced from an electrical current arcing through vapor between two incandescent electrodes, as with the carbon- or mercury-arc lamp. The term derives from the Latin for *curve.* Invented by electrochemist Sir Humphry Davy in 1808, the device was a powerful source of light in theaters, microscopes, and lighthouses. In Ray Bradbury's *Fahrenheit 451,* the police use arc-lamps to illuminate the path of the escaping Guy Montag, who flees the city after incinerating Captain Beatty with a flamethrower.

argosy (*ar'* guh . see) one of the largest and heaviest of Mediterranean merchant ships. This sixteenth-century term derives from *Arragosa,* a corrupted form of the port of Ragusa, Sicily. In William Shakespeare's *The Taming of the Shrew,*

Tranio, posing as Lucentio, brags that his father owns three argosies.

Ark of the Covenant a portable gold-painted, acacia-wood box measuring 3 feet 9 inches by 2 feet 3 inches by 2 feet 3 inches. It contained the Torah, the laws of Moses, which were originally inscribed on stone tablets. Except for times when the Hebrews carried the ark before the army into battle or during migration, it remained behind a curtain in a sacred niche, the holiest place in the Tabernacle at Jerusalem, which is also referred to as the ark. In Chaim Potok's *The Chosen,* Danny recalls the layout of the synagogue, with the Ark near the Eternal Light. *See also* Torah.

Armageddon (*ar* . muh . *gehd'* d'n) in Christian tradition, the Day of Judgment, when Satan's and God's forces will engage in the last great battle between good and evil, as described in Revelation 16:16. The term, which entered English in the sixteenth century, appears to be a Greek translation of *Mount Megiddo,* a biblical site northwest of the Dead Sea where Deborah's Israelite forces overcame their enemies. In *Black Boy,* the autobiography of Richard Wright, preachers at the Seventh Day Adventist Church concentrate on such fearful images as Armageddon and the Second Coming. *See also* Seventh Day Adventist.

armoire (arm . *wahr'*) an oversized storage cabinet, chifforobe, or wardrobe opened from the center with hinged double doors that feature ornate detailing and hardware and painted scenes or gilt oriental patterns called chinoiserie. Entering English in the sixteenth century, the word, from the Latin for *arms* or *tools,* reflects its original use; later, it served in place of a closet. To the consternation of the head nurse in Ernest Hemingway's *A Farewell to Arms,* Lt. Frederick Henry hides liquor and wine bottles in the armoire in his hospital room and suffers jaundice, for which he could be court-martialed on grounds of malingering. *See also* chinoiserie.

army an independent unit within a nation's land armed forces, comprising two corps and approximately 225,000 troops, commanded by a general; also used to refer to the land armed forces as a whole. In Isabel Allende's *The House of the Spirits,* the term is used in an ironic sense: Senator Trueba opens a bottle of champagne to celebrate the army's overthrow of the leftist government at the same time that the army's torture team incarcerates and torments his son Jaime to death. *See also* battalion; brigade; company; corps; division; platoon; squadron.

arnica (*ahr'* nih . kuh) a mountain herb of the thistle family with fuzzy leaves and bright orangy-yellow daisy-shaped flowers, common to Europe and North America. Arnica heads and leaves are blended in salves and ointments to lessen the pain, discoloration, and swelling of bruises. In Willa Cather's *My Antonia,* Grandma applies a healing poultice and rubs arnica over a bruised chest and shoulders. *See also* herbal medicine; poultice.

arras (*ar'* ruhs) a heavy and often ornate tapestry, curtain, drape, or screen hung over windows, archways, niches, alcoves, and other wall openings to stop drafts and conceal privies or unsightly stone walls. Probably named for a French town in Artois, the word gained common usage in the fifteenth century. Polonius hides behind an arras in Queen Gertrude's boudoir to snoop on a private conversation and meets his fate at the end of the prince's sword in William Shakespeare's *Hamlet. See also* alcove; tapestry.

arroyo (uh . *roy'* oh) a dry creek bed or overflow channel that remains a waterless gully during dry weather or can be used as a ready-made irrigation system when flooded artificially by a diverted stream. As demonstrated by the speaker in N. Scott Momaday's *The Way to Rainy Mountain,* an arroyo can serve as a roadway or passage for a rider, although the dry channels can become dangerous during a flash flood.

art deco (*deh'* koh) a simplistic geometric style, both in architecture and furnishings, formed of clean lines and bold bas-relief, often constructed from shiny plastic, chrome, concrete, or glass. After its brash break with traditional materials and classic lines, art deco dominated architecture, household design, and fashion of the 1920s. In Amy Tan's *The Kitchen God's Wife,* Pearl's art deco bedroom suite, a relic of her teens, is so out of date it appears to have cycled back into style. *See also* bas-relief.

Aryan (*ayr'* ee . uhn or *ayr'* yuhn) a native Caucasian of Gentile or non-Jewish descent, such as a Saxon. Aryans are typically identified as tall, slender, blue-eyed, fair-skinned blondes, or Nordics, whom Tom Buchanan extols as racially superior in F. Scott Fitzgerald's *The Great Gatsby.* In *Schindler's List,*

Thomas Keneally illustrates the value of an Aryan genealogy during Hitler's regime. *See also* holocaust; Nazi; Saxon.

asafoetida or **asafetida** (*as* . uh . *feh'* tuh . duh) a bitter dun-colored herb of the carrot family. The juice from the roots or stem can be dried into gum for potions or teas to soothe a stomachache, colic, or throat spasms; to ease asthma attacks; or to rid the intestines of parasites. The Persian term, which entered English in the fourteenth century, is the source of the word *fetid,* which characterizes the plant's rank smell. In *To Kill a Mockingbird,* Harper Lee mentions the garlicky reek of asafoetida in a scene in which the white lawyer's children attend a black church.

As-Salaikum-Salaam (*ahs* . suh . *ly'* koom . suh . *lahm'*) a ritual Arabic call, invocation, or formal greeting, "Peace be unto you." The liturgical reply in Islamic worship services is "Wa-Alaikum-Salaam" or "and to you be peace." Described in Alex Haley's *The Autobiography of Malcolm X,* traditional greetings of "As-Salaikum-Salaam" follow the morning ablutions and gathering of family members for prayers. *See also* ablution; Allahu-Akbar.

assegai or **assagai** (*ah'* sih . gy) a metal-tipped spear or javelin made of lightweight wood of the assegai tree, a member of the dogwood family. Common to southern Africa, *assegai* is an Arabic or Berber word that entered English during European exploration of Africa in the early seventeenth century. In Joseph Conrad's *The Heart of Darkness,* the manager of an upriver waystation collects assegais and other native trophies. In Lorraine Hansberry's *A Raisin in the Sun,* the African suitor of Beneatha, a main character, is called Mr. Assagai.

assizes (uh . *syz'* ihz)**, court of** a legal hearing, session of a circuit court, or inquest into civil or criminal matters. Entering English in the fourteenth century, the term derives from the Latin term *to sit together.* During the 11-month court of assizes held in Albert Camus's *The Stranger,* three judges determine that Meursault is guilty of murder, a capital offense.

astrolabe (*as'* troh . layb) one of the world's oldest measuring, timekeeping, or navigational instruments, which the Greeks invented in the third century, Arabs perfected, and pilots or helmsmen worldwide used from the fifteenth to the eighteenth century until it was replaced by the sextant. The astrolabe determined the altitude or position of the sun or stars. Consisting of round wooden or brass discs—the first a map of the sun and the most visible stars and the second detailing the times and places when the patterns occur—the handheld device was lifted by a ring while the viewer sited along a rotating bar to calculate an exact location according to the placement of heavenly bodies on the horizon. The astrolabe is a symbol of nautical expertise in Gabriel García Márquez's "The Handsomest Drowned Man in the World." *See also* sextant.

asylum state shelter or protection of a foreign national from detainment or arrest on the basis of political or diplomatic immunity from oppressive governments. A Greek word derived from *no right of seizure,* the term entered English in the sixteenth century and often applied to fleeing criminals or deserters from the army hiding on church property. Yoko Kawashima Watkins's autobiographical *So Far from the Bamboo Grove* describes Korean authorities questioning her mother, a refugee and the wife of a Japanese ambassador, about her need for political asylum during Korea's brutal ousting of the Japanese during World War II.

atoll (*a'* tohl) an oval or ring-shaped coral reef enclosing a lagoon. The word, taken from a Maldivian term, entered English in 1625. Charles Darwin's studies of atoll formation in the Pacific Ocean indicate that an atoll is the result of an eroded volcanic island that collapsed in the center, leaving a barrier reef at the edges. The crew's yarns about castaways marooned on Pacific atolls intrigue the title character in Avi's *The True Confessions of Charlotte Doyle.*

atom-bomb mushroom the result of fission or a chain reaction from the multiple destruction of atoms in a plutonium or uranium core by detonation of an outer shell of less powerful explosives. The updraft from this massive release of energy bursts into a mushroom-shaped effusion of energy emitting light rays, radioactive particles, condensed droplets, and exploding gas. First predicted from the work of Enrico Fermi, the finished explosive was the combined effort of numerous physicists. Atomic power came to fruition through Franklin Roosevelt's Manhattan Project, which was begun in 1942 and resulted in a test of the bomb on July 16, 1945, at Alamogordo, New Mexico, releasing a charge equal to 20,000 tons of TNT. In Ray Bradbury's *Fahrenheit 451,* Granger helps Guy Montag put into perspective the relatively painless destruction of his wife, Mildred, from an atom-bomb mushroom that destroys the city of Los Angeles.

atomizer (*a'* tuh . *my* . zuhr) a propellant that fragments liquid into tiny drops or mist as a means of spreading moisture, fragrance, medicine, or disinfectant. A forerunner of the pressurized spray can, the atomizer requires the manual squeeze of a bulb or the press of a plunger. In Tennessee Williams's *A Streetcar Named Desire,* Blanche DuBois uses her atomizer as a playful weapon against the potentially dangerous Stanley Kowalski, her brother-in-law, who later rapes her.

auger (*aw'* guhr) a primitive T-shaped mining or carpentry tool used to bore holes in wood, earth, ice, or veins of coal. Unlike the brace and bit, the auger consists of a handle at right angles to a centered shaft with a bit, grooved in a spiral or helix, on the end. The word, evolving from the Old English for *spear,* entered English in the eleventh century. In the *Odyssey,* Homer describes Odysseus's skill with an auger and saw to build a new boat to take him away from Calypso's island and home to Ithaca.

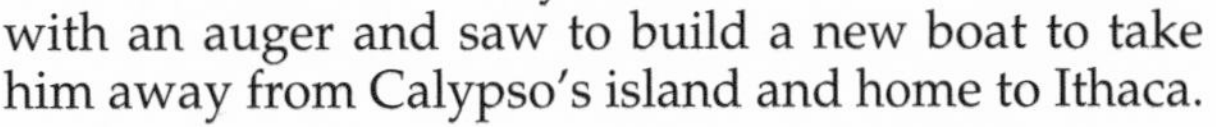

augury (*aw'* gyuh . ree) a divination or prediction of the future based on the study of an omen from nature, such as the flight patterns of birds or the rise or dispersion of smoke. Augurs, or priests, observed and recorded direction, time, weather, and other auspices, or signs, to determine the gods' will or human fate. In Sophocles' *Antigone,* the seer Teiresias practices augury by cooking the fat of a sacrificial bird and by examining the gall bladder and learning that King Creon has brought evil on his subjects. A similar scene in William Shakespeare's *Julius Caesar* indicates through Cassius's reinterpretation of Calpurnia's dream that an unfavorable augury can be twisted to favor or disfavor a venture.

au jus (oh *zhoo'*) a French culinary phrase meaning accompanied by natural drippings, grease, or juices obtained from roasting. *Au jus* can be flavored and used to baste slices of meat or pour over vegetables or bread as a sauce or gravy. Daddy Bailey, master chef and father of Maya Angelou in *I Know Why the Caged Bird Sings,* teaches his daughter to appreciate prime rib *au jus.*

aura (*aw'* ruh) an invisible spirit, breeze, atmosphere, fragrance, sensation, or presence surrounding a person. A mystical emanation, luminosity, or electrical field, often represented in art as a halo or nimbus around the figure of a saint or divinity. Angel Clare, a major character in Thomas Hardy's *Tess of the D'Urbervilles,* feels an aura pass over his flesh when he is in Tess's presence.

aurora borealis (uh . *roh'* ruh boh . ree . *al'* ihs) the northern lights, literally, the Latin for *northern dawn,* a midnight phenomenon viewed by dogsledders in Jack London's *The Call of the Wild* and Gary Paulsen's *Dogsong.* The luminous streams of light that radiate from the horizon in the Southern Hemisphere echo a similar electrical display called the aurora australis. Both bursts of light result from charged particles following the path of solar wind around the earth's poles and produce bands or curtains of colored light. *See also* stratosphere.

automaton (aw . *tah'* muh . tahn) *pl.* **automatons** or **automata** a self-propelled servant, wind-up toy, clockwork, or other programmed device set to perform a predetermined task. Karel Capek's play *R. U. R.* was the first to apply the term "robot" to an automaton, a docile being having no volition, sensation, or intelligence. The concept dates to Greek myths about automatons invented by Daedalus for King Minos, and it recurs in literature in the science fiction of Ray Bradbury, Arthur C. Clarke, and Robert Heinlein.

awl a primitive hand tool made from a sharply honed metal point and wooden or bone handle used for marking, pricking, boring, or piercing leather, canvas, or wood. The awl, which resembles an ice pick or marlinspike, can be threaded for stitching or repairing hard or inflexible surfaces, for example, sails, saddles, boots, or tents. *Julius Caesar,* William Shakespeare's tragedy, opens with a cobbler's pun on all-awl, a necessary tool of the shoemaking trade. *See also* marlinspike.

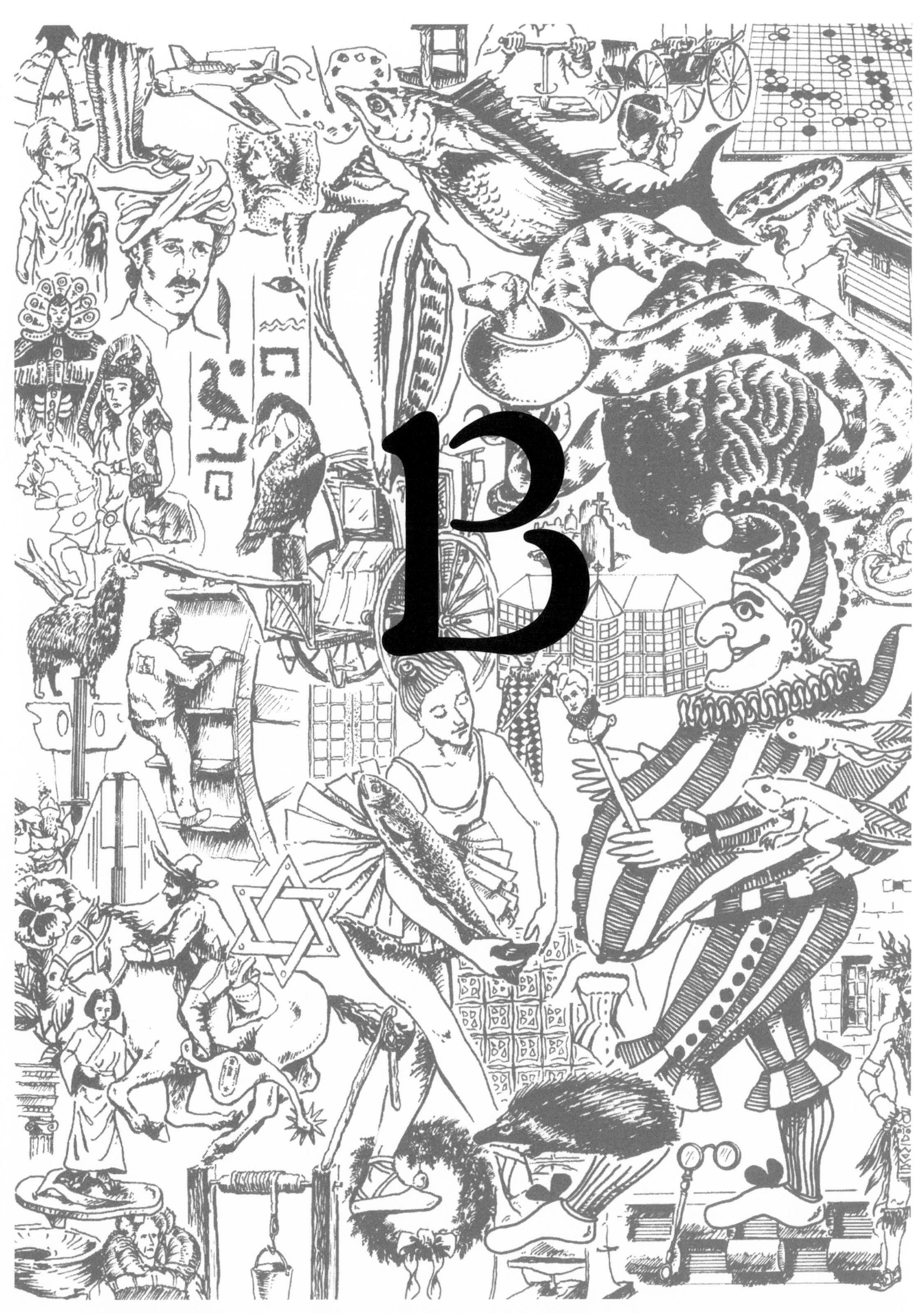
B

babbitt (*bab'* biht) a soft antimony-, copper-, or tin-based antifriction lining that reduces wear when moving parts activate bearings. The babbitt is named for inventor Isaac Babbitt (1799–1862). The term entered the language in the twentieth century as the standard term for antifriction alloys, which decreased the number of breakdowns in car and railway engines, pumps, and mining equipment. While examining a malfunctioning truck on the family's way from Oklahoma to California, Tom Joad, in John Steinbeck's *The Grapes of Wrath,* locates a broken babbitt.

Bacchic rite (*bak'* kihk) a wild, frenzied ritual in honor of Dionysus or Bacchus, the god of wine and fertility, who led his ecstatic train of mostly female followers across the ancient world, from Greece into Asia Minor and back. In their revelry, followers committed unspeakable acts, including sexual orgies, suckling of serpents, and cannibalism of children. In Sophocles' *Antigone,* the chorus reflects on the Bacchic rites, which offended more sedate worshippers and family members. *See also* Maenad.

backgammon (*bak'* gam . m'n) a board game for two—possibly the oldest in the world, dating to 3000 B.C. Players sit at a rectangular board that is separated into two halves by a bar and roll dice to determine how far to advance their 15 counters. The object of the game is to cover a path of 24 pinnacles, to reach the far side of the course, and to remove all the counters by avoiding the opponent's interference. In Jane Austen's *Pride and Prejudice,* Mr. Collins and Mr. Bennet withdraw from the women to play a private game of backgammon.

backstay a strengthening or stabilizing rope connected from a mast to the stern of a ship. At a pivotal point in Herman Melville's *Billy Budd,* the title character answers a summons to the narrow platform screened by devices with suggestive names—deadeyes, backstays, and shrouds—to hear a secret whispered by an unidentified man. *See also* deadeye; shroud.

bailiff (*bay'* lihf) or **bailey** a varied occupation over time, including sheriff's deputy, steward, overseer, or manager of a bailiwick, an area of legal jurisdiction that was a minor portion of a sheriff's territory. The term refers to a rent-collector, custodian or property agent, peace officer, or executor of writs or arrest warrants. In Thomas Hardy's *Tess of the D'Urbervilles,* Mrs. D'Urberville determines Tess's worthiness based on advice from the bailiff.

baldric (*bawl'* drihk) a leather belt or bandolier attached directly to a sword belt and worn from one hip, over the chest, across the opposite shoulder, and down the back to support a weapon, musical instrument, wineskin, canteen, or other burden. The Middle English term entered English in the fourteenth century. The baldric frequently bore a family crest, initial, or insignia indicating allegiance. In Sir Walter Scott's *Ivanhoe,* a yeoman appears wearing a bright baldric across his shoulder to support a horn.

ballad sheet more commonly known as a broadside, a sheet printed on one side only with news, items of commercial interest, and seasonal verse as well as songs or ballads, often composed by a jokester to poke fun at or satirize a public figure, rogue, or object of scandal. In the opening scene of Thomas Hardy's *The Mayor of Casterbridge,* an unnamed man studies a ballad sheet much as a person today would read a newspaper or handbill.

ball and chain a leg manacle, usually attached to one ankle and trailing a length of chain with an iron ball on the end to prevent a convict or prisoner from fleeing. A husband sometimes jokingly refers to a demanding or shrewish wife as the "ball and chain." Used by the speaker in Sandra Cisneros's *The House on Mango Street,* the term implies the restrictions of matrimony in a patriarchal Hispanic neighborhood where men value their macho status.

ballast (*bal'* luhst) the gravel, iron, lead shot, sand, stone, or water used to maintain buoyancy or control or to stabilize the hold in an empty cargo vessel or a hot-air balloon. In Charles Dickens's *Great Expectations,* a busy ballast-lighter, which resembles a barge or skow, gives a bustling commercial atmosphere to the river. In Theodore Taylor's *The Cay,* incoming ballast water is fresh and can be used for drinking.

balm a fragrant herb, such as lemon, mint, or balsamic resin used as scent in laundry rinse water, for washing hair and hands, or for flavoring foods or drinks. Derived from *balsam,* the term, which entered English in the thirteenth century, is a generic category for all soothing salves, ointments, teas, or herbal fixatives such as myrrh applied to the dead to preserve the skin. In Amy Tan's *Joy Luck Club,* Chinese women discuss the making of balm or salve by crushing certain insects with herbs and applying to swollen or burned skin.

balsa (*bal'* suh) a buoyant commercial craft, raft, or fishing boat formed of tule rushes or shaped over a light balsa or corkwood frame and used to ferry bundles and a few passengers across narrow waterways and small lakes. The absorbent balsa wood, taken from a native South American tree, waterlogs easily, but can be dried for continued use and waterproofed with paraffin or tar. Thor Heyerdahl's *Kon-Tiki* describes the sailor's attempt to link Incan balsas with Egyptian boats that might have brought settlers from Africa to South America. *See also* rush.

balustrade a protective barrier, screen, or hand railing topping a wall, parapet, terrace, balcony, gallery, or series of supportive banisters; a coping. In Charles Dickens's *A Tale of Two Cities,* the symbolic balustrade at the home of a doomed aristocrat, which separates him from commoners, is combined with stone urns and decorative carvings of flowers, faces, a gorgon, and lions—a blend of the sublime and menacing elements of his elite life. *See also* gorgon.

bandbox a sturdy cardboard or light wood cylinder with lid used for storage of hats, collars or "bands" and matching cuffs, removable frills, gloves, hairpieces, falls, trains, and ruffs. As fashion additives grew more ornate, expensive, and fragile, people who journeyed over difficult terrain packed their garments and wigs on frames, wrapped them in tissue, and stowed them in bandboxes to protect them from crushing, dust, soot, or moisture. George Eliot's *Silas Marner* describes partygoers arriving at Squire Cass's New Year's party with their fashion accessories packed in bandboxes suspended from their saddles. *See also* ruff.

bandy legs or **banty legs** legs bent or curving outward at the knees, frequently as a result of long stretches of horseback riding; bowlegged. The term, which entered English in the late seventeenth century, may derive from comparison of bowed legs to a *bandy,* a curved hockey stick. In a rare departure from farm drudgery, Mr. Shimerda and his daughter Antonia, the title character in Willa Cather's *My Antonia,* visit Peter, a bandy-legged Russian.

bannock (*ban'* nuhk) a thick circular pancake or loaf made from unleavened, coarsely ground wheat flour, oatmeal, pease, or barley and baked on a hot stone or iron griddle. Derived from the Cornish or Gaelic word for *drop,* the term entered English in the eleventh century. In J. R. R. Tolkien's *The Hobbit,* Bilbo Baggins sings an impromptu song extolling the hospitality of elves, makers of bannocks.

banyan or **banian** (*ban'* yuhn) an Indian ficus or fig tree that produces garnet red figs; the tree, a sacred member of the mulberry family, sends out auxiliary trunks from air roots until it creates an expansive thicket with a high canopy of leaves and vertical columns of trunks that create a natural portico. The tree is named for a Tamil term for *trader* because of the commerce conducted in its shade. The banyan is the spot where the title character chooses to meditate on humanity in Hermann Hesse's *Siddhartha.*

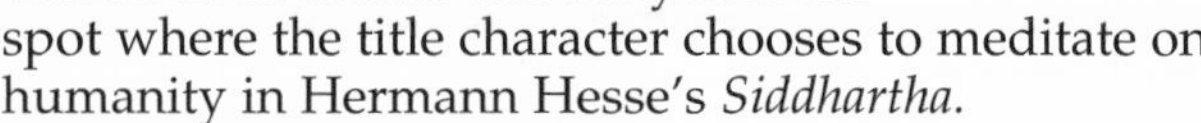

barb a sharply angled metal curl or snell jutting from a weapon, tool, fishing harpoon, leister, or fishhook, which impales the catch more firmly on the point. Derived from the Latin word for *beard,* the term entered English in the fourteenth century. Jack Merridew, the hunter in William Golding's *Lord of the Flies,* intends to increase the killing power of his javelin by adding a barb. *See also* toggle point.

barley a high-starch cereal grain related to grass that produces a distinctive head consisting of eleven rows of kernels. Dating to the twelfth century, the term denotes a useful agricultural crop. Its nutty-flavored grains and bran are used in unleavened flour, porridge, animal feed, malt liquor, beer, and whiskey; its stalks produce soft, fragrant bedding and silage for livestock. In a temporary job after their flight from Weed, California, George and Lenny help a hired crew harvest barley in John Steinbeck's *Of Mice and Men.*

barlow knife a large jackknife or pocket knife with a single, thick folding blade. Named for its inventor, Russell Barlow, an eighteenth-century cutlery maker, the barlow knife is an adaptable tool for cutting, whittling, slicing, or gouging and can be used as a weapon. In Mark Twain's *The Adventures of Huckleberry Finn,* the title character ignores a corpse and collects oddments from a floating house, including clothing and a new barlow knife; much later, Jim reveals that the corpse was Pap Finn.

bar mitzvah (*mihtz'* vuh) a Jewish coming-of-age ritual that originated in the thirteenth century and consisted of a blessing, a short speech by the initiate, and a celebratory meal. A Hebrew phrase meaning "son of the law," bar mitzvah recognizes a thirteen-year-old boy's readiness for manhood and accountability for his sins. The female equivalent is the bas mitzvah, or "daughter of the law." Amid traditional merriment, Danny's brother celebrates his bar mitzvah in Chaim Potok's *The Chosen.*

baron a low-ranking noble or lord of the kingdom who has received a hereditary land grant from the crown; a member of the peerage, which moves upward from baron to viscount, earl, marquess, duke, and king. Originating in the thirteenth century, the title derives from a German term for freeman and confers on the receiver the honorific prefix "my lord" or "your lordship" and on his wife, "my lady" or "your ladyship." In Victor Hugo's *Les Misérables,* Marius's grandfather sneers that his rebellious grandson must accept the responsibility that accompanies the rank of baron. *See also* title.

baronet (*bar'* uh. neht) a rank below baron that royalty sells to a commoner. Less noble than a baron, a baronet is addressed like a knight as "sir." Instituted in the seventeenth century, the hereditary title could be bought, thus adding over £1,000 per grantee to the royal treasury. Sir Henry Baskerville, an honorable English baronet, reports unusual happenings at Baskerville Hall to Sherlock Holmes in Sir Arthur Conan Doyle's *The Hound of the Baskervilles. See also* baron; title.

baroque (buh . *rohk'*) an ornate, exuberant style that infused and invigorated instrumental and vocal music during the first half of the eighteenth century. The extravagance of baroque works focuses on embellishments and complex, interlocking, and often contrasting patterns, for example, those of Georg Friedrich Handel's *Messiah.* Jeanine confuses Conrad by asking him about baroque music in Judith Guest's *Ordinary People.*

barouche (buh . *roosh'*) a showy carriage with two small wheels in front and two larger ones behind, a raised box for the driver at the front, and a shelf to accommodate luggage and a footman at the rear. The coach itself seated four to six with the two or three at the front facing the other passengers at the rear. A folding leather and canvas top could be hoisted over the back seat. In Frederick Douglass's autobiography, *Narrative of the Life of Frederick Douglass,* he comments on the sumptuous carriage collection of Colonel Lloyd, including dearborns, coaches, gigs, and barouches.

barracoon (*bar* . uh . *koon'*) a cage, pen, corral, compound, or enclosed huts built as temporary quarters for slaves, convicts, runaways, or political prisoners awaiting transfer, punishment, or sale. The Spanish term, which is akin to *barracks,* entered English in the 1850s. In Paula Fox's *Slave Dancer,* the slave trader is irate because African chiefs set fire to the barracoon.

barracuda (*bar* . ruh . *koo'* duh) a thin-bodied, predatory tropical fish from two to five feet in length. The barracuda is notorious for its pointed head, deep jaw, needle-sharp teeth, and aggressive attacks on other fish and humans. In Ernest Hemingway's *The Old Man and the Sea,* the speaker builds to an ignoble conclusion by picturing dead barracudas on the beach alongside beer cans.

barricade (*bar'* ruh . kayd) a hastily constructed obstruction, barrier, or fortification to halt attack, rioting, or infiltration by an enemy; a rampart. The term, which entered English in the mid-seventeenth century, derives from the French word for *barrel.* In Victor Hugo's *Les Misérables,* rebel forces heap barrels, carts, sawhorses, scrap wood, boulders, and fence posts as a temporary barricade against musket volleys or a charge by French soldiers.

barrow (*ba'* roh) a cairn, raised gravesite, or stone burial chamber; rounded and heaped over with earth; and found in Alaska, the Aleutian Islands, the Yukon, and throughout the British Isles and Scandinavia. Barrows dating from the Stone Age are designed for multiple interments; those of the Bronze Age accommodate a single chieftain and his weapons, jewelry, and other personal effects. The anonymous epic *Beowulf* describes a lofty stone barrow in hill country in which a secret treasure lies hidden. A mound of stones or earth used as a landmark, territorial limit, or waymarker, is also mentioned in Inuit or Athapascan lore as well as in the books of Farley Mowat, Sir Arthur Conan Doyle, and Thomas Hardy.

barton the land, barnyard, threshing floor, or farm set aside for a private owner rather than leased to a tenant. Deriving from an Anglo-Saxon word for *barley town* or *barley enclosure,* the term dates to the Middle Ages. While he walks, Angel Clare feels sunlight reflected from barton walls in Thomas Hardy's *Tess of the D'Urbervilles. See also* barley.

bas mitzvah (*bahs'* mihtz . vuh) the female equivalent of a bar mitzvah. *See* bar mitzvah.

bas-relief (*bah'* rih . *leef*) a slightly raised pattern, edging, braid, or figure that is carved, sculpted, or molded into an artwork, coin, or wall design to give a raised or three-dimensional impression; low relief. In Edith Hamilton's *Mythology,* carved animals on Mesopotamian bas-reliefs are named among the relics of prehistoric times.

bastion (*bas'* chuhn) a defensible crag or natural position; a bulwark, rampart, or projection of a fortification offering a wide-angled view of an enemy's approach.

Entering English in the sixteenth century, the term derives from earlier words for *build* and *fort*. On the island setting of William Golding's *Lord of the Flies,* a single pink crag, like a symbolic pastel playhouse, stands atop the land and becomes a bastion for Jack Merridew's hunters.

bath-house a wheeled closet that was pulled from the shore into the water, where the bather can enjoy a private place to change clothes, sunbathe, and take a concealed dip in the ocean. Invented in the mid-eighteenth century, the device remained in use in the Victorian Era. Edna Pontellier, the main character in Kate Chopin's "The Awakening," keeps a rug and pillows in the double bath-house she shares with Madame Ratignolle.

battalion (buh . *ta'* lyuhn) a large segment or tactical unit of artillery, foot soldiers, or tanks in a brigade or regiment and roughly a tenth of a division. The battalion, currently 500–1,000 soldiers, is composed of several infantry companies. In Homer's *Odyssey,* Athena, the Greek goddess of war, is capable of combatting whole battalions. *See also* army; division.

battery a gun emplacement, coordinated fire power, or line of defense composed of cannon and heavy artillery intended to guard or retain from enemy encroachment an area such as a harbor, seawall, ship, parapet or rampart, or field encampment. Henry Fleming, the protagonist of Stephen Crane's *The Red Badge of Courage,* turns his attention to a battery of musket fire. *See also* parapet; rampart.

battledoor or **battledore** a flat, lightweight wooden, bamboo, or cork paddle or framed racket with a center woven of catgut or cord. The battledoor is used to bat a ball or shuttlecock in a game similar to badminton or lacrosse. The game piece, popular in the Orient around the first century B.C. and named in the fifteenth century from the French word for *hit,* enables a player to volley a projectile to keep it aloft. In Emily Brontë's *Wuthering Heights,* Ellen searches a cupboard for toys, finding hoops, shuttlecocks, and battledoors. *See also* shuttlecock.

bawd the female go-between, brothel-keeper, madam, or procurer who brings together two distant or timid lovers or who solicits clients for a prostitute or brothel. In William Shakespeare's *Romeo and Juliet,* Romeo's friend Mercutio cries "bawd" at Juliet's nurse, who arranges for the young lovers to share a private time together and who makes arrangements for Friar Laurence to perform their marriage ceremony.

bayonet (*bay'* uh . *neht*) a detachable two-edged dagger or blade that can be used in hand-to-hand combat or clipped onto the muzzle of a rifle for making lethal jabs at the soft tissue of an advancing enemy infantry, a task once performed by pikemen or billmen. First used in 1640 as a short stabbing knife plugged into the end of a musket, the bayonet takes its name from Bayonne, France, home of inventor Maréchal de Puységur. The keeper of the customhouse recalls the use of bayonets against the Chippewa in Nathaniel Hawthorne's *The Scarlet Letter. See also* bill; musket; pike.

bayou (*by'* yoo) a sluggish, marshy creek or watercourse that flows into a lake or river and is best navigated by poling or paddling a canoe, flat-bottomed skiff, or lighter vessel. The term, dating to the mid-seventeenth century, derives from the French spelling of a Choctaw word and typifies a culture or lifestyle of hunters, trappers, and fishers who live in isolated cabins on stilts. In William Faulkner's "The Bear," the main character, an untried boy, hunts bayous and surrounding land for the bear—an aged, but wily quarry. *See also* skiff.

bazaar (buh . *zahr'*) an Oriental marketplace or district shaded with awnings and lined with stalls, barrows, and shops selling a variety of fresh foods, sweets, clothing, housewares, and jewelry. Derived from the Persian term meaning *commercial center,* the early seventeenth-century word often names or characterizes the center of towns and villages in Morocco, India, Pakistan, Malaysia, China, or Tibet. Saunders refers to rumors going around the bazaars about Hugh Conway, protagonist of James Hilton's *Lost Horizon.*

beadle (*bee'* d'l) in colonial times, a uniformed town crier or church sergeant-at-arms bearing a staff as emblem of office, who delivered messages to parishioners, seated worshippers, separated men from women and whites from blacks, and kept order in church by punishing rowdies and undisciplined children and by punching sleepers who snored. In Nathaniel Hawthorne's *The Scarlet Letter,* the beadle oversees a civil matter—the public humiliation of Hester Prynne and her infant before the town pillory.

beaver the chin guard or lower visor on a helmet, which was raised when not in use and pierced with air holes so that it could be lowered, yet not inhibit breathing. Derived from an Old French term for *saliva,* the beaver dates to the eleventh century. In William Shakespeare's *Hamlet,* witnesses to Hamlet's father's ghost recall that he appeared in full armor with his beaver up so that courtiers and guards easily recognized his face.

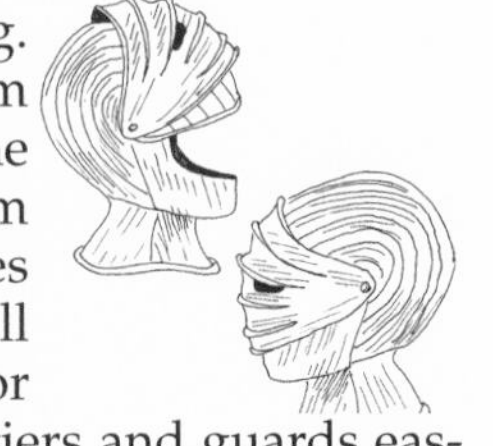

beaver hat a sturdy napped bonnet or top hat formed from beaver pelts, which was common during the seventeenth century. The modish beaver hat became such a status symbol that European traders undermined the beaver population in the New World, where trappers and Indian traders prospered on brisk trade. As a result of the dearth of pelts, eighteenth-century hat makers had to simulate beaver with rabbit fur or matte felt wool. In *Silas Marner,* George Eliot indicates the popularity of Squire Cass's New Year's party by the appearance of beaver bonnets on female guests.

bedlam (*behd'* l'm) chaos or inadequate control, a slang reference to an infamous London madhouse or asylum for the mentally ill and to the uproar and lunatic ravings of mad beggars whom ward doctors granted street privileges, including opportunities to eat in local cafes. The term, which Scrooge lightheartedly mentions in Charles Dickens's *A Christmas Carol,* is a corruption, or elision, of *Bethlehem,* taken from the Hospital of Saint Mary of Bethlehem. The institution, originated in a priory founded in 1247, has treated the insane since 1402.

bed-ticking *See* tick.

begging bowl a shallow dish the size of an outstretched palm, which Buddhist monks proffer in both hands to passersby as a receptacle for food or donated coins, which buy the givers favor with the gods in the afterlife. In Hermann Hesse's *Siddhartha,* itinerant holy men carry their begging bowls, the only possessions allowed by their mendicant order.

beldam or **beldame** (*behl'* duhm) a medieval euphemism for an old woman, hag, virago, or crone who is usually pictured as gnarled, stooped, humpbacked, scraggly haired, and repulsive or menacing. Derived from the French *belle dame* or *beautiful lady,* the word entered English during the early Renaissance and appears in William Shakespeare's *Macbeth* as a synonym for *witch.*

belfry (*behl'* frih) a steeple, cradle, tower, or housing for a bell atop a church or other edifice; also a campanile or separate bell shed, enclosure, or chamber, often accommodating a full scale of church bells, which are played by trained and rehearsed ringers who enter at the ground level and activate the bells with ropes or pulleys. This fifteenth-century term derives from Middle French for *siege tower,* a portable assault weapon. Winston Smth and Julia, his lover, arrange to meet secretly in a bomb-scarred belfry in George Orwell's *1984.*

belle a popular, charming, or attractive girl or lady; a beauty of unquestioned rank or prominence. The Southern usage of "belle" often implies cynicism or mockery, as of a pretentious, self-absorbed, or conceited clotheshorse or flirt. The belle in Mark Twain's *The Adventures of Tom Sawyer* enters church ahead of a line of young heartbreakers, who follow her down the aisle like bridesmaids.

bell-pull a cord, tassel, band, or slender embroidered hanging that attaches to a bell or buzzer in another part of the building. Use of the bell-pull makes no discernible noise upstairs, but summons a servant from the scullery or waiting room. In Sir Arthur Conan Doyle's "The Adventures of the Speckled Band," the bell-pull, which is fake, becomes one of the clues to murder by snakebite.

beret (buh . *ray'*) a Basque worker's flat, disk-shaped cap with a snug-fitting, gathered edge; a biretta, tam, or tam-o'-shanter, as featured in a poem by Robert Burns. Originally a circle of wool, linen, felt, velvet, or leather drawn up by a string passed in and out around the edge, post-medieval models sported slender brims, braided bands, feathers, and appliqués or the characteristic stem at the center. In *Zlata's Diary,* a chronicle of the first years of the Bosnian War, Zlata Filipovich notes that United Nations forces wear either blue helmets or blue berets, which resemble the American green berets. *See also* appliqué.

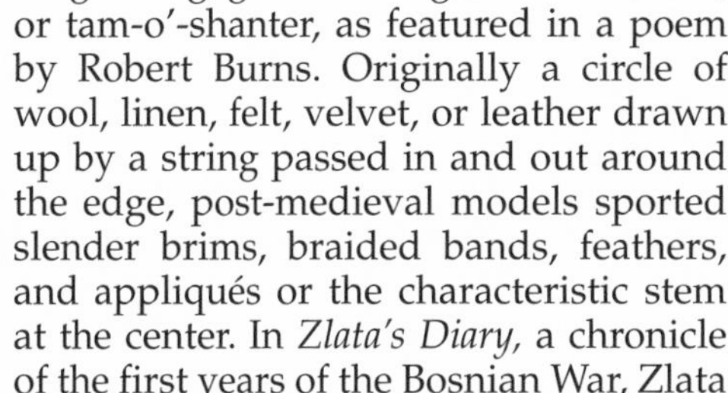

Berkshire boar an English breed of short-legged, straight-backed pig common to the world market and raised in England, Canada, and the United States primarily for tasty, low-fat pork and bacon. The Berkshire boar reaches breeding age at six months; in England, it is slaughtered for fresh pork before it reaches 100 pounds. The markings are obvious—a black body with white on feet, legs, face, and tail. In contrast to Old Major, the beneficent revered patriarch swine of George Orwell's *Animal Farm,* Napoleon, a Berkshire boar, is tight-lipped and menacing.

besom (*bee'* zuhm) a rough round broom or scrub brush consisting of a scraggly bundle of twigs or stubble fastened around a central limb or stick. From an Old English term originating in the eleventh century, the besom was a homely, but necessary home tool that wives often applied to the backs of recalcitrant husbands. In "The Custom House," the introduction to Nathaniel Hawthorne's *The Scarlet Letter,* the author characterizes political reform as a besom, an implacable force crudely ridding the area of a former regime.

Bessemer (*behs'* sih . muhr) **furnace** an early steel-purifying device that forced heated gas through melted pig iron to oxidize and remove silicon, carbon, and other impurities. Invented by English metallurgist and industrialist Sir Henry Bessemer in 1855, the refinement enabled steelmakers to improve the quality of smelted metal and simplify the shaping of rails that required no hammering. In Upton Sinclair's *The Jungle,* the immigrant Jurgis is cowed by the huge flames, clatter, and terrifying heat emerging from a Bessemer furnace.

biddy chicken a newly hatched chicken; a female chicken of any age. In southern idiom, the term implies something of little worth or significance. In Truman Capote's "A Christmas Memory," Buddy and his elderly friend exhibit at their freak show a malformed biddy chicken as well as stereopticon pictures to earn money for fruitcake ingredients. *See also* stereopticon.

bier (beer) a stand, support, or wooden framework with handles on which a slab or coffin is propped while mourners view a corpse; a moveable barrow used to transport a corpse to burial; also, a catafalque, an aboveground sepulchre or tomb, or a coffin and its display stand taken as a unit. In William Shakespeare's *Romeo and Juliet,* Romeo is surprised to find Juliet lying uncovered on a bier in the family vault.

biffin (*bihf'* fihn) a dialect term denoting a round, beef-red cooking apple, often roasted, flattened into a cake, and served with cream and sugar as a dessert. While under the influence of the Ghost of Christmas Present in Charles Dickens's *A Christmas Carol,* Ebenezer Scrooge observes in a shop window a plump, juicy Norfolk biffin filled with succulent treats.

bight (byt) a wide, recessed bay, protected indentation, or rounded bend, gulf, or hollow on a curved beach or coastline. A common term in literature about the sea, the word is prominent in books about the triangular Atlantic slave trade, which took slave ships from the Caribbean to England and into the rounded western shoreline of West Africa to the Bight of Benin. This area is featured in Paula Fox's *Slave Dancer,* in which black traders kept prisoners in barracoons until slavers could select prime specimens to sell at American slave markets. *See also* barracoon.

bilboes (*bihl'* bohz) *usu. pl.,* rarely **bilbo** shackles or manacles composed of a metal bar with loops slid into place and locked at the end. Designed in the sixteenth century and used to immobilize the wrists and/or ankles of one or more prisoners, bilboes were crude forerunners of modern handcuffs, which allow more freedom of movement and cause less hindrance to blood flow. Described in William Shakespeare's *Hamlet* by the title character as similar to the sleepless nights he suffers since learning of his father's murder, bilboes imply immobility and control of a prisoner or mutineer on a ship.

bile a common metaphor for ill temper or crotchety moods, owing to an overbalance of bile in the bloodstream. According to medieval anatomy, the body contained four humors—blood, phlegm, and yellow or black bile. The theory predicted that too much bile, a secretion of the liver, disposed the sufferer to anger, grumpiness, and argumentative behavior. Fuchs, a character in Willa Cather's *My Antonia,* predicts that a snowstorm will take the bile, or irascibility, out of the bulls.

bilge (bihlj) the collected wastewater, oil, and rubbish pooled in the lowest part of a ship. As a slang term, *bilge* refers to foul gossip, nonsense, or illogic. The minister in Margaret Craven's *I Heard the Owl Call My Name* must keep the bilge pumped out of the small boat that takes him up the west coast of British Columbia. In Mark Twain's *The Adventures of Huckleberry Finn,* the speaker makes a joke of the Duke of Bridgewater, whom his fellow conman calls "Bilgewater."

bill a poleax or battle-ax consisting of a six-to-seven foot wooden shaft with a sharpened ax, hook, or blade on the end; a forerunner of the bayonet. In addition to being a watchman, the bill carrier, or billman, sometimes was a ritual figure in the coterie, or security guard, of royalty, for example, the Swiss Guards who stand ceremonial watch at the Vatican. In William Shakespeare's *Romeo and Juliet,* the authorities call for clubs, bills, and partisans, or spears, to end a gang war.

billet troops' destination, assigned quarters, post, or lodgings, whether in tents, barracks, private residences, or public buildings. Derived from the Latin for *bulla,* meaning document, the term also applies to the letter or official orders assigning a soldier or refugee to a post or requiring a civilian to supply board for the bearer. Infantryman Paul Baumer, a naive protagonist at the beginning of Erich Maria Remarque's *All Quiet on the Western Front,* strolls at leisure behind the billets and reads his mail.

bindle a bundle or bedroll packed with food and clothing and carried by a hobo on a stick over the shoulder. By extension, the term, which derives from the Old English verb *bind*, is also a pejorative referring to the carrier of a bindle, who is known as a bindlestiff, usually a rover, scamp, or jobless, homeless person. John Steinbeck names personal items in a bindle in *Of Mice and Men*, one of a series of novels about rootless people known collectively as "Steinbeck's losers."

binnacle (*bihn'* uh . k'l) the casing around a ship's compass, which stood near the helm of a small sailboat or on the bridge of a large vessel for ready access by the steersman. Derived from the Latin *to dwell in*, the word indicates the significance of this instrument, which was never moved and gave pilot and captain immediate reference to direction. In Joseph Conrad's "The Secret Sharer," the protagonist makes a symbolic gesture after rescuing a swimmer—he removes the lamp from the lighted binnacle and examines the swimmer's face, an act suggesting his personal and professional shift of direction.

biopsy (*by'* ahp . see) a surgical removal of cells, fluid, or tissue for medical or scientific study. Derived from the Greek *bio* and *opsis* for "observing life," the term, which entered English in the late nineteenth century, names an intense procedure that scrutinizes or analyzes a representative sample drawn from a subject's body to discover the presence, cause, extent, and type of disease or abnormality. John Hersey describes the biopsy of suspicious organs at the Red Cross Hospital in *Hiroshima*, a journalistic study of the victims who suffered post-radiation anomalies, including cancer and atrophied organs, as a result of the dropping of an atomic bomb on August 6, 1945.

birdshot the smallest gauges or weights of shot, ranging from four to nine, which are round lead projectiles loaded into a shell and discharged from shotguns to kill birds, ducks, and small animals, particularly rabbits and squirrels. The splatter effect can also serve as a deterrent to intruders and housebreakers. In Ken Kesey's *One Flew Over the Cuckoo's Nest*, one ward orderly's weapon of choice against psychotic patients is a sock filled with birdshot.

bit in slave times, a metal disciplinary or restraining device resembling the bit of horse harness, which is placed over a slave's tongue and fastened around the head to silence, imprison, punish, degrade, or humiliate. Paul D, central male figure in Toni Morrison's *Beloved*, is unable to protect Sethe from attackers because he was "tasting iron" from the bit.

bit and bit-roller the part of a saddle animal's bridle or head harness that passes horizontally over the tongue; a rotating or spiraled mouthpiece used as a curb or control. Made of ivory or metal, the bit is the major point of communication between rider and steed. In John Steinbeck's *The Pearl*, the horse shakes his head, clicking the bit and bit-roller between his teeth and causing the trackers to be wary of Kino, their prey.

bite one's thumb to make an insulting or obscene gesture by placing the thumb in the mouth and waggling the fingers to harass, incite, belittle, or indicate contempt or disrespect. Warring gangs of young men loyal to either the Capulets or the Montagues in William Shakespeare's *Romeo and Juliet* antagonize their opponents by making the gesture called biting one's thumb.

bitt one of a pair of sturdy uprights or posts used to secure lines, coiled cables, or an anchor rope on board ship. Derived from the Old Norse for *beam*, the word has been a standard nautical term since the sixteenth century. The old man, Santiago, protagonist in Ernest Hemingway's *The Old Man and the Sea*, imagines that he is the bitt that the great marlin tows out to sea. In Joseph Conrad's "The Secret Sharer," Leggatt is rammed against the forebitts when he throttles his tormentor.

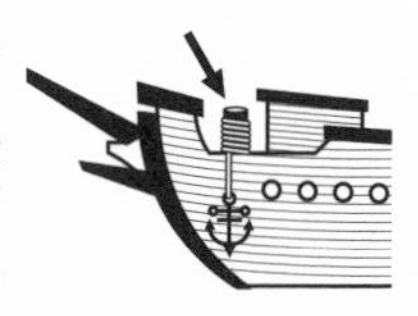

bitter herbs acrid, pungent shrubs, vines, or plants such as artemisia, dogbane, dock, cress, or belladonna. The roots, stems, leaves, flowers, or fruits of these aromatic plants are blended with an alcohol base such as gin or rum into a tonic to stimulate the liver, stomach, and digestive tract to invigorate the body, improve absorption of nutrients, and flush out impurities. Consequently, bitter herbs are key ingredients in herbal tonics and palliatives for indigestion. In Emily Brontë's *Wuthering Heights*, Isabella extracts medicinal juices from Mrs. Dean's bitter herbs.

bittermelon a seedy green member of the squash family that resembles a honeydew melon. Common to Chinese cuisine, bittermelon is dried and served as a vegetable, usually accompanying beef dishes. To Winnie and the other runaway wives in Amy Tan's *The Kitchen God's Wife*, the melon slices they share represent the bitter life of the feudal wife.

bittern a small brown European wading bird with striped or mottled feathers and shorter legs than its relative, the heron. The bittern commonly hunts alone on marshlands, where it feeds on frogs, insects, and crayfish. For its raucous, undulating mating cry, the bittern is nicknamed the thunderpump or stake driver, and possibly derives from the Latin *taurus* for its bull-like roar. In Sir Arthur Conan Doyle's *The Hound of the Baskervilles,* Stapleton attempts to explain away a cry on the moors as the piercing call of the bittern.

bivouac *(bih'* voo . wahk) a night or surveillance patrol camped in the open on improvised bedding. Derived from the Swiss term for *additional watch,* a bivouac is also a night camp, settlement, or temporary quarters offering little shelter and spartan amenities. In Richard Adams's *Watership Down,* the fleeing rabbits avoid a place too infested with foxes to offer a safe bivouac.

Black Belt an African-American settlement or ghetto; an unintegrated strip or development in a city or county that is densely populated by black residents and/or merchants. Parts of the American South are referred to collectively as the Black Belt. Bigger Thomas, protagonist in Richard Wright's *Native Son,* notes that one white man owns most of the rental property in Chicago's Black Belt.

Black Friars priests of the Dominican order who wear black robes and hoods. The mendicant order, founded by Dominic Guzman of Spain and dedicated to preaching, dates to 1215. In Herman Melville's *Benito Cereno,* the reference to Black Friars in the opening paragraphs foreshadows the title character's withdrawal from black people to a monastery shortly before his death.

blackguard *(blag'* uhrd) a scoundrel, vagrant, or rascal whose manners and intentions are inappropriate or suspect and whose language is too foul for polite company. Applied in the sixteenth century to underlings or the lowest servants, the word evolved into a pejorative synonym for an unprincipled, villainous, or outcast person. Henry Higgins, the language teacher referred to in the title of George Bernard Shaw's *Pygmalion,* labels Eliza's father a blackguard before he sees the man.

blacklisted boycotted, banned, penalized, or singled out for censure, suspicion, or exclusion from membership or employment. A seventeenth-century term, the word refers to a black-bordered list of people in disfavor or subject to disbarment. In Upton Sinclair's *The Jungle,* managers blacklist workers who make trouble for the employers by reporting substandard sanitation, hazardous working conditions, or violations of local workplace regulations.

blackout an extinguishment or concealment of all forms of light to hide residences, targets, or strategic positions from an enemy or to avoid an air raid; a precautionary plunge into darkness over a period of bombardment, often nightly. In Anne Frank's *The Diary of a Young Girl,* the families concealed in the annex carefully obscure their hiding place with heavy blackout drapes. *See also* annexe.

black-pudding a rich, juicy pork sausage composed of fat and blood, seasoned with brandy, onion, and spices, and stuffed into a length of intestine or synthetic casing; a French *boudin,* or blood sausage, that is boiled in water or stock, grilled, baked, or fried. Haie, a soldier in Erich Maria Remarque's *All Quiet on the Western Front,* characterizes the sweetness of revenge as "black-pudding."

blanc mange or **blancmange** (bluh . *mahnzh'*) a smooth, sweet white pudding made of cornstarch, milk, and almond or rum flavoring; any opaque gelatinous or starchy molded dessert. Derived from the French *white* and *to eat,* the term dates to the beginnings of the English language. In the "Prologue to the Canterbury Tales," Geoffrey Chaucer's cook is best known as a "blancmanger."

blind man's bluff or **blindman's buff** a game for young children, dating to the seventeenth century, in which the person who is "it" is blindfolded and forced to catch and name a fleeing participant. If the guess is correct, the pursuer passes the blindfold to the quarry, who becomes "it." The game takes its original name from *buffet* because players tease and shove the pursuer. Scout watches Jem play spirited games of blind man's bluff in Harper Lee's *To Kill a Mockingbird.*

blinkers a rectangular pair of leather flaps, blinders, or screens attached to the head harness or bridle of a dray horse, mule, or burro to inhibit side vision or to conceal from the animal a fire, reflection, or another animal that might cause it to bolt or rear. The rebellious livestock of George Orwell's *Animal Farm* reject such degrading harness as blinkers and nosebags.

Blitzkrieg *(blihtz'* kreeg) aggressive assault methods that gain rapid military victory by mounting a surprise mass offensive to catch the enemy unprepared and overwhelm them by land, sea, and air.

Derived from the German for *lightning war,* the term names an intense form of fighting favored by Julius Caesar, who surprised his adversaries by the agility and fierceness of his strike force, which coordinated veteran infantry, artillery, and cavalry into a tightly compacted two-prong formation. In a novel set against the backdrop of World War II, students in John Knowles's *A Separate Peace* adapt blitzkrieg into blitzball.

block and tackle a hoist composed of ropes, lines, or cables wrapped around blocks or pulleys to ease heavy objects forward, up, or down. Dating to 8000 B.C. and refined by Archimedes, the Greek mathematician, the concept of block and tackle is essential to the building of elevators, escalators, and conveyor belts. In Ernest Hemingway's *The Old Man and the Sea,* workers lift dead sharks by block and tackle to the factory ceiling before cleaning, dissecting, and selling the meat.

blockhouse a reinforced square observation tower or fortification equipped with a projecting upper story and loopholes for sharpshooters. Made of thick timbers or concrete walls in more recent times, the blockhouse was the first line of defense in European outposts of colonial Canada and North America during the seventeenth century and served as the model for radiation shields in desert atomic bomb test sites. In Robert Louis Stevenson's *Treasure Island,* the mutineers gain control of the island's only blockhouse.

blood horse a registered horse of recognized value, beauty, quality breeding stock, and speed; a thoroughbred of impeccable ancestry suitable for breeding or demanding a high price. In Charles Dickens's *A Christmas Carol,* Bob Cratchit serves as son Tim's blood horse by hoisting the boy to his shoulders for the walk home from church.

Bluebeard a husband who murders multiple wives and conceals his crimes from the authorities. Derived from Charles Perrault's late seventeenth-century horror tale of *Barbe-bleue,* the husband who forbids his bride to open a locked room where he stores the remains of previous wives, the term currently applies to men who marry and abandon or discard numerous wives. In Maya Angelou's autobiographical *I Know Why the Caged Bird Sings,* she doubts the efficacy of Mama's flashlight against Rippers and Bluebeards. *See also* Rippers.

bluejacket a nineteenth-century slang term referring to a U.S. or English sailor; an enlisted man who wore a short blue double-breasted jacket trimmed in gold braid and gold buttons. In Herman Melville's *Billy Budd,* the lusty crew of loyal British soldiers form a mass of bluejackets, each indistinguishable from the other.

bluetick hound a valuable hunting hound or coon dog distinguished by a black or tricolor coat heavily marked with white or tan. During treatment for psychosis, Chief Bromden, paranoid narrator of Ken Kesey's *One Flew Over the Cuckoo's Nest,* imagines that he hears a bluetick hound baying because he has lost the scent of his quarry.

bluff bank a steep, flattened vertical headland that obscures the view inland from a riverbank or ocean shore; a towering cliff, crag, palisade, or promontory. In Mark Twain's *The Adventures of Huckleberry Finn,* the title character and his companion Jim use bluff banks as landmarks as they guide their raft on the Mississippi River. *See also* mesa; palisade.

blunderbuss a short-barreled, large-bore pistol with a flared muzzle that accommodates an indiscriminate scattering of shot with one discharge. The term, derived from the Dutch for *thunder gun,* refers to common muzzle-loading firearms of the mid-seventeenth century. In Charles Dickens's *A Tale of Two Cities,* blunderbusses in revolutionary Paris fire "shot and ball," a broad-ranged method of crowd control that sprays rioters with fragments of shot and metal chain.

boater an informal flat-topped hat made of woven straw and worn by men and women during the last quarter of the nineteenth century for sporting events and outings. This broad-brimmed hat, popularized by rowers, was woven of natural-colored straw and decorated around the crown with a ribbon or braid. Nettie, sister of the protagonist in Alice Walker's *The Color Purple,* dresses fashionably in a gored skirt, suit jacket, high-topped shoes, and straw boater.

boatswain (*boh'* suhn) the naval officer assigned to posting duty rosters and summoning crew members to their tasks; the petty officer or warrant officer in charge of deck, hull, equipment, and rigging. The term, which entered English in the fourteenth century, derives from the Anglo-Saxon for *boat mate.* In the opening scene of William Shakespeare's *The Tempest,* the boatswain sings out orders to sailors caught in a dangerous storm.

bob nineteenth-century English slang for a shilling, one-twentieth of a pound, a common coin. In Charles Dickens's *David Copperfield,* Steerforth tosses Miss Mowcher two half-crowns, which equals 5 shillings or "five bob." *See also* shilling.

bobby *See* Bow Street men.

bobbysoxer a young girl in white anklet socks rolled or folded into a characteristic cuff. During the mid-1940s, the term applied to all faddish female teenagers. In the autobiographical *Farewell to Manzanar,* coauthor Jeanne Wakatsuki Houston describes herself as a Japanese-American girl trying to be the typically spirited bobbysoxer.

bobcat a short-tailed North American lynx distinguished by a mottled reddish-brown pelt and weighing around 25 pounds; a fierce wildcat known for its piercing scream and for leaping from rocks or tree limbs onto its startled prey, usually rats, rabbits, and squirrels. In Wilson Rawls's *Where the Red Fern Grows,* Billy faces a fearful mountain bobcat, which disembowels Old Dan, the male of Billy's prized pair of hunting dogs.

bobwhite a common southern and southwestern U.S. term for quail; a plump brown game bird about 10 inches long with abundant white markings. The slang name imitates the mating call of the bird, which can be heard in the flats and hill country at evening. Will Tweedy's dog T. R. flushes two bobwhite in Olive Ann Burns's *Cold Sassy Tree.*

bodega (boh . *day'* guh) a wine cellar or small convenience or specialty store selling wine and Hispanic foods, usually in a Spanish-speaking neighborhood. The term, like the French *boutique,* derives from the Latin *apotheca* and dates to the mid-nineteenth century. In Ernest Hemingway's *The Old Man and the Sea,* Manolin brings Santiago tins of hot coffee from the village bodega.

bodkin a slender-tipped stiletto. Later, the word referred to a blunt needle of steel, bone, or ivory; an ornamental hairpin or small awl used to punch holes in leather or cloth or to thread colored twine, tape, or ribbon through a hem. Also, a printer's tool for removing type from a tray. In William Shakespeare's *Hamlet,* the title character envisions a "bare bodkin," referring to an earlier usage of an unsheathed dagger—possible weapons by which the prince can kill Claudius to avenge King Hamlet's murder. *See also* awl.

boll weevil (bohl *wee'* v'l) a gray, long-nosed insect. An agricultural pest that lays its eggs in a cotton boll; the resulting larvae destroy plant fiber. The weevil emigrated north from Mexico and spread into Texas, Louisiana, and Mississippi, precipitating a mass collapse of the South's cotton industry from 1892 to the 1920s. In Paula Fox's *Slave Dancer,* the ship captain nicknames Jessie Bollier "boll weevil."

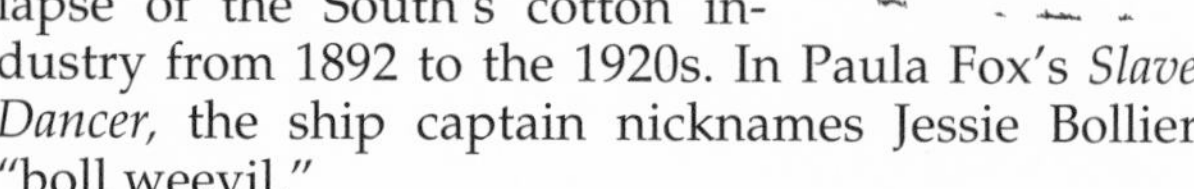

bolster a long, narrow, thickly stuffed pad or upholstered cushion that supports the head and shoulders at the upper end of a bed, cot, chaise longue, or sofa. Derived from the Anglo-Saxon for *bag,* the word, which entered English in the eleventh century, can refer to a luxurious, highly decorative item or a simple roll of fabric used to cushion the head. Petruchio, the antagonist in William Shakespeare's *The Taming of the Shrew,* throws pillow and bolster into chaos to demonstrate his wife Kate's faulty bed making.

boma (*boh'* muh) a temporary pen, picket fence, or enclosure made of brush or sharpened posts, providing privacy or a defensive barrier against intruders or predatory animals. The Swahili term, common to East Africa, denotes a necessary adjunct to a campsite in the wild. Elsa, the domesticated lioness set free in adulthood in Joy Adamson's *Born Free,* searches the boma for her human family.

bond a legal document or certificate requiring a borrower (usually a public utility or government) to repay a loan with stipulated interest. In Alexandre Dumas's *The Count of Monte Cristo,* the villain Danglars falls to financial ruin from unwise investment in Spanish bonds. Nick Carraway, the central intelligence agent in F. Scott Fitzgerald's *The Great Gatsby,* moves to New York to become a "bond man" or bond-seller.

bond-servant *See* indentures.

bones a pair of tapered bone or ivory strips used as a percussion instrument by minstrels and stage performers; clackers or spoons held between the fingers and tapped together or against the thigh or palm of the opposite hand. Bottom, the comic ass-headed actor in William Shakespeare's *Midsummer Night's Dream,* calls for music of the bones and tongs to entertain his lady Titania.

bonito (buh . *nee'* toh) a striped, large-mouthed tuna or tunny of the mackerel family, which is native to the warm waters of the Caribbean, Black, and Mediterranean seas and the Atlantic and Pacific oceans. In Ernest Hemingway's *The Old Man and the Sea,* Santiago follows schools of bonito and albacore, on which larger fish feed.

bonne (bahn) the French term for a nursemaid or governess; an *au pair* girl or hired immigrant who serves as the family babysitter. Sophie, a French-speaking character in Charlotte Brontë's *Jane Eyre,* works for Edward Rochester as the *bonne* of Adèle Varens, his ward and a student of the title character.

boom a wooden bar that stabilizes or extends the bottom of a sail; a spar that alters the angle of a sail. Derived from the Dutch for *beam,* "the booms" names the part of the deck where unused spars are stored. The title character in Herman Melville's *Billy Budd* is resting among the booms when he is summoned by a mutineer to a secret conference.

bootjack a metal stand in a doorway consisting of a 9- to 12-inch blade for scraping mud from the sole of the shoe and a V-shaped end ornament into which the wearer fits the heel of the boot and tugs the foot free. Outside the taproom in Thomas Hardy's *The Mayor of Casterbridge* stands the bootjack, an image suggesting the mundane, servile role that Henchard adopts after Donald Farfrae is elected mayor.

bootlegging producing, transporting, smuggling, distributing, or dealing in illicit liquor, often referred to as moonshine, that lacks the appropriate tax stamp; trafficking in any pirated item, for example, computer software, videotapes, or recorded music. The seventeenth-century term may have derived from smugglers' use of wide-topped boots to conceal such banned or dutied items as were surreptitiously slipped into England. While living in Memphis, as reported in the autobiographical *Black Boy,* Richard Wright takes part in a phony bootlegging deal and realizes that he has been set up as the dupe, or patsy, of con artists. *See also* jackboots.

bos'n *See* boatswain.

bosque (bahsk) a thicket or grove. Derived from the Spanish for *woods* or *forest,* the word is also spelled *bosquet* or *bosket,* a mass planting of hedge in a park or as an ornamental edging for a driveway or berm. To head off vengeful armed men, Antonio forces his way through thick bosque to reach the riverbank and rescue his friend in Rudolfo Anaya's *Bless Me, Ultima.*

bo tree a tall ficus tree native to southern Asia distinguished by pendulous, tapered, heart-shaped leaves; the original plant from which the pipul, or peepul, tree of Ceylon sprouted. A shortened form of the Sinhalese *bodhi,* the term means *enlightenment* or *inspiration.* The bo, which is a sacred fig tree to Hindus and Buddhists, shelters Gotama while he contemplates philosophy in Hermann Hesse's *Siddhartha.*

bots a parasitic gut worm found in horses, sheep, goats, deer, and human beings that results from infestation of the hide or the inhalation or swallowing of the botfly or gadfly larva or maggot, which attacks the nose, mouth, liver, stomach, and intestines and causes dizziness and a staggering gait. James Herriot, in the autobiographical *All Things Bright and Beautiful,* describes home remedies for bots, parasites, and other ailments in livestock. *See also* gad-fly.

bottoms rich, agriculturally valuable delta land along a creek or river; effluvial mud of low country, which is often flooded and used for growing rice or indigo. The title character in Mark Twain's *The Adventures of Huckleberry Finn* searches the bottoms for a wild pig to kill so that he can create a contrived murder scenario to explain his disappearance from Pap Finn's cabin.

bouclé (boo . *klay'*) a fabric woven of an irregular ply of yarn containing a relaxed, knotted, or looped thread, which gives the finished piece a softened texture. Derived from the French for *buckle* or *curl,* the concept was popularized in the late nineteenth century both in weaving and knitted goods. In Tennessee Williams's *A Streetcar Named Desire,* Blanche DuBois asks her sister Stella to check her bouclé garment for wrinkles.

bound feet a traditional form of female mutilation that extended over China's history into the nineteenth century. Parents wrapped a daughter's feet to halt the growth of the arch so that the girl had to step carefully with an exaggerated, mincing step, thus creating an impression of birdlike delicacy and helplessness. As described in Pearl S. Buck's *The Good Earth,* bound feet restricted upper-class ladies to limited movements; conversely, slaves' feet were left unbound so that they could perform heavy chores.

bourgeois type a script style, typeface, or font used in journalistic printing and named from the French for *middle class.* In Sir Arthur Conan Doyle's *The Hound of the Baskervilles,* Sherlock Holmes's keen eye spots the leaded, or wide-spaced, bourgeois type that was the trademark of the London *Times.*

bowie knife a thick steel-bladed fighting, hunting, and utility knife with a curved sharpened tip, stout grip, and one honed edge. Around 15 inches long, the bowie knife gained popularity with American pioneers in the mid-nineteenth century and took its name from its inventor, Texas hero Colonel Jim Bowie, who was killed defending the Alamo. One of Injun Joe's co-conspirators in Mark Twain's *The Adventures of Tom Sawyer* uses a bowie knife to dig a hole in which to hide a cache of coins.

bowler *See* derby.

bowse or **bouse** (bowz) to haul or pull by block and tackle; to hustle or expedite work by vigorous participation or loud calls directing laborers in a concerted effort, for example, in lifting a piano upstairs or lowering a mast into its cradle. An overseer yells for slaves to bowse forward a load in Frederick Douglass's autobiography *Narrative of the Life of Frederick Douglass. See also* block and tackle.

bowsprit (*boh'* spriht) the projecting beam, bow pole, or stabilizing spar on a ship's front timber to which the forestays anchor the front sails. On full-rigged vessels, the bowsprit may sport its own sail, the spritsail (*spriht'* s'l). To Charlotte, heroine of Avi's *The True Confessions of Charlotte Doyle,* the bowsprit on the *Seahawk* resembles a unicorn's horn. *See also* unicorn.

Bow Street men a romanticized investigative force; the forerunner of the English Bobbies, who policed England after 1829. A replacement for the antiquated post-feudal system of constables and justices of the peace, the runners were instituted in the mid-eighteenth century. They earned a questionable reputation for boasting, hiring informers, fencing stolen goods, and claiming more glory, expense remuneration, and reward money than they deserved. In Charles Dickens's *Oliver Twist,* the familiar red-vested Bow Street men investigate the attack on Mrs. Joe, Pip's sister.

box a partially walled booth in a church, restaurant, or coffeehouse or an enclosed balcony chamber offering semiprivate seating for wealthy or aristocratic theater-goers who are willing to pay extra, as described in Sir Arthur Conan Doyle's *The Adventures of Sherlock Holmes.* In Charles Dickens's *David Copperfield,* the box also names the exposed position beside the driver at the front of a stagecoach roof. *See also* stagecoach.

brace and bit a rudimentary D-shaped handle fitted with a set of sharpened points of graduated sizes. When the shaft is turned or cranked with two hands, one at the top and one in the middle, the brace rotates the bit into wood or stone to form a hole the diameter of the bit. As Homer describes in the *Odyssey,* Odysseus's men wielded a spear like a brace and bit to gouge out the eye of the Cyclops Polyphemus and escaped captivity in the giant's cave.

braces suspenders or galluses. *See also* galluses.

bracken an untended expanse of heath, moor, wood, or field overrun with wild fern fronds, heather, rushes, or rough marsh growth. Dating to the fourteenth century, the term derives from the Danish or Swedish for *fern.* In J. R. R. Tolkien's *The Hobbit,* Bilbo and Gandolf wade through bracken that is higher than a hobbit. *See also* rush.

braille a system of clustered raised dots used by sight-impaired readers and writers as a touch alphabet. Adapted in 1853 by Louis Braille from a military system of silent signals, or night communication, the alphabet is widely accepted in schools for the blind and can be easily typed or hand-coded. In Sandra Cisneros's *The House on Mango Street,* Ruthie runs her hand over a text as though she is reading braille.

brain fissure creases, clefts, or concave folds in the cerebrum, or brain, which separate the organ into a series of regular convolutions. In Daniel Keyes's *Flowers for Algernon,* Charlie Gordon reports that dissection of the mouse's brain reveals deepening brain fissures and a smoothing of convolutions—both forewarnings of changes about to occur in Charlie's brain.

brain spoon a slender spadelike instrument used to perforate and/or take a sample of brain tissue on the inner side of the nasal cavity, where no bony structure prohibits insertion. In *Never Cry Wolf,* researcher Farley Mowat reports using scalpels, shears, and brain spoons to examine tissue from small birds and animals of the tundra for signs of disease.

brake *See* bracken.

brand a torch, charred or smoldering stick, or rushes twisted into the shape of a torch; a firebrand or rush-light carried from room to room and used to light fireplaces, chandeliers, sconces, or braziers. In Edith Hamilton's *Mythology,* the three Fates hurl a log into the fire and warn Althea that her son will live until the brand burns into ash. *See also* rush-light.

brazier (*bray'* zhuhr) a portable metal crater, pan, or bowl on a framework, stand, tripod, or legs. The brazier was suitable for holding charcoal or hot coals used in ancient Greece and Rome for cooking, lighting and heating a room, driving away insects, or burning out contagion, dampness, or a musty smell. In Homer's *Odyssey,* Circe's hospitable staff set before Odysseus a blazing brazier, wine, and a feast. *See also* tripod.

breach to break the sea's surface or leap through water into the air and fall back with a loud splash; to make a deliberate display of presence or mastery. From the Anglo-Saxon for *break,* the term dates to the early medieval era. The white whale in Herman Melville's *Moby-Dick* leaps from the depths of the sea and explodes in a spectacular breach of the surface as a warning and enticement to his implacable pursuer, Captain Ahab.

breastplate an oval or rectangular piece of armor similar to a bulletproof vest or umpire's chestguard.

When the ancient Greeks dressed for battle, their typical breastplate fit over the chest or torso and fastened at each shoulder with leather straps, metal hinges, or chain links to free the arms for fighting. The Romans updated the concept with flexible chain mail or link armor around 300 B.C. In Edith Hamilton's *Mythology,* the god Zeus's breastplate is decorated with the likeness of the snake-haired gorgon Medusa. *See also* aegis.

breastwork a temporary chest-high parapet, barricade, or emergency fortification; a makeshift barrier or defense thrown or heaped up in the field from dirt clods, limbs, wagons, furniture, or caissons to protect infantry or artillery during a sudden attack. Henry Fleming, a raw recruit and protagonist in Stephen Crane's *The Red Badge of Courage,* observes men lying in wait behind a breastwork. *See also* barricade; parapet.

breechclout (*breech'* klowt) or **breechcloth** a folded piece of cloth or animal skin that passes between the legs and over a belt to form a garment for males, particularly when mounted on a horse; a loincloth or simple garment for laborers or galley slaves. In some Native American tribes, decorative fringe or stitching adorns the loose ends or edges. Tom Black Bull, protagonist of Hal Borland's *When the Legends Die,* abandons the rodeo circuit and returns to the breechclout and simple life he once loved. *See also* clout Indian.

breech-loader a shotgun, flintlock, or other type of rifle that is loaded near the trigger at the rear of the barrel rather than through the muzzle. Designed in the mid-eighteenth century by English soldier Patrick Ferguson, the first breech-loaders opened at a screw plug for charging. In 1819, New Englander John Hall improved on the system, creating a hinged chamber for quick loading. The unnamed boy in William Faulkner's "The Bear" receives a new breech-loader for Christmas and caries it most of his hunting career to stalk the mythic bear that lives in the Mississippi bayou.

breviary (*breh'* vya . ree) a worship handbook containing the service for the day or a summary or abridgement of the hymns, responses, recitations, and prayers for the seven canonical hours, beginning with matins, or morning service, and concluding with vespers and compline, which ends the day. In Alexandre Dumas's *The Count of Monte Cristo,* the Abbé Faria treasures Count Spada's antique breviary, from which falls the treasure map that leads Edmond Dantes to a massive cask of jewels and coins in a cave at the shore of Monte Cristo.

brickbat a fragment of brick or masonry used as a makeshift projectile; also, a verbal invective, slur, or insult hurled at an adversary. Richard Wright, protagonist of *Black Boy,* gathers a handful of brickbats to hurl at two aggressors.

brig *See* brigantine.

brigade army unit below the division level, consisting of about 5,000 troops in four battalions and commanded by a colonel. While marching with his brigade, Henry in Stephen Crane's *The Red Badge of Courage* experiences the oneness of the group, who seem to grin in unison at the nearness of a battle. *See also* army; battalion.

brigadier a general who commands a large military force consisting of infantry, armored vehicles, support troops, and headquarters; the British use of brigadier equals the American rank of colonel. In Stephen Crane's *The Red Badge of Courage,* infantrymen are proud that the brigadier bragged on their previous show of courage against the enemy. *See also* army; battalion.

brigantine (*brih'* guhn . teen) a light, economical two-masted ship with square rigging and square topsails; a brig. Derived from the Italian for *skirmishing ship,* the term dates to the early sixteenth century when a brigantine was the ship of choice for spies, privateers, slavers, blockade runners, and pirates who employed oars and sails for maneuverability and rapid flight. Mentioned in Jules Verne's *Around the World in Eighty Days* and central to Avi's *The True Confessions of Charlotte Doyle,* the brigantine had a singular weakness—it was top-heavy and easily capsized.

brindle a blending of colors, especially on the hide of a domesticated animal. Brindle streaks, speckles, and spots of tan, brown, black, and white against a gray or taupe background compose a distinctive pelt. The word derives from the Old Norse term for *burned.* In William Shakespeare's *Macbeth,* the cat is described as "brinded," another form of "brindle" suggesting a sprinkling of evil. In Stephen Crane's *The Red Badge of Courage,* the cow that Henry Fleming sees is a brindle.

brioche (bree . *ohsh'*) a crusty glazed bread, bun, roll, or pastry created from linking or stacking balls of lightly sweetened yeast dough in a mold. The ornate loaf incorporates a rich batter of eggs, butter, flour, and leavening and flavorings such as cheese or fruit. Brioche derives from the German term for *break.* The bread, which originated in eighteenth-century Paris, is separated by hand into servings. In Act II of Edmond Rostand's *Cyrano de Bergerac,* Cyrano and his companions enjoy the fragrance and flavor of mounds of brioches and other pastries.

broadside a forerunner of the modern newspaper; a broadsheet. The broadside was printed on one side of the page and featured news, announcements, moral harangues, miracles and phenomena, and advertisements. In sixteenth-century England, broadsides were distributed by hand and often contained humorous doggerel and satiric ballads about topical heroes and villains. The title character in Esther Forbes's *Johnny Tremain* enjoys the fragrant ink and stack of broadsides and notices after landing a job at a patriot's print shop.

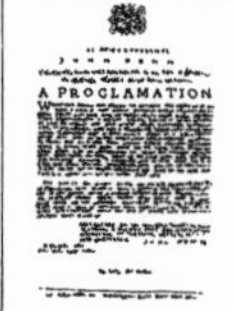

brogan (*broh'* gan) or **brogue** a heavy, coarse, high-topped, low-heeled work shoe. Formed of untanned leather pierced with holes to accommodate a lace, the shoes were common to poor Irish farmworkers. Mentioned in Penny and Ma Baxter's list of necessities in Marjorie Kinnan Rawlings's *The Yearling* is a pair of brogans for Jody.

bromo a popular sedative composed of potassium bromide or sodium bromide, each beneficial as a depressant for headaches or nervousness, an effect discovered by Charles Locock in 1857 and applied to the treatment of epilepsy. Blanche DuBois, protagonist of Tennessee Williams's *A Streetcar Named Desire,* needs a bromo to help her account for the expenditure of family money, which Stanley Kowalski claims as a marital right under Louisiana's Napoleonic code.

bronc *See* mustang.

brontosaurus a semiaquatic plant-eating lizard of the Jurassic Period marked by a huge body, stocky legs, slender neck and tail, and disproportionately small head, which grazed on tender treetop leaves. Its name is neo-Latin for *thunder lizard,* an approximation of the impact of this 85-ton, 82-foot-long beast on the territory it inhabited and of the sound made by lashes of its whiplike tail. The Time Traveller, unnamed protagonist of H. G. Wells's *The Time Machine,* identifies an abandoned building as a museum after he locates the skeleton of a brontosaurus.

brougham (*broo'* uhm or broom) an elegant, discreet lightweight carriage seating up to three passengers, drawn by a single horse, and guided by a driver who sat on a box seat in front of the coach. Named for Lord Brougham, England's lord chancellor, this mid-nineteenth-century conveyance evolved into the Clarence, a sturdier four-wheeled model later used as a taxi, and into a motor-driven coupé of similarly limited capacity. In George Bernard Shaw's *Pygmalion,* a brougham is specified as the wedding transportation for Eliza and Henry Higgins's mother.

brown holland a smooth, tough, unbleached linen or cotton fabric used to make sturdy clothing for work or travel. Named for its country of origin, glazed and sized brown holland was a common, cheap nineteenth-century fabric used for book covers, window and lamp shades, scrim, and furniture and carriage upholstery. The clownish character who beckons to the speaker of Joseph Conrad's *The Heart of Darkness* wears brown holland patched with cloth pieces of various colors and shapes. *See also* scrim.

brucine (broo . *seen'*) a bitter alkaloid potion of the strychnine family derived from nux vomica seeds; a powerful emetic, heart stimulant, or tonic prescribed in small doses to expel intestinal parasites or to boost appetite and a sense of well-being. In Alexandre Dumas's *The Count of Monte Cristo,* the attending physician wishes to conceal the fact that Madame de Saint-Méran died of a dose of brucine originally prescribed for Monsieur Moirtier.

bruja (*broo'* hah) *pl.* ***brujas*** Spanish word for a sorceress, witch, conjurer, or hag suspected of consorting with Satan during midnight dances that accompany the Black Mass. The antidote to the *bruja*'s power is the sign of the cross or the quick action of a *curandera,* a benevolent herbalist. In Rudolfo Anaya's *Bless Me, Ultima,* Gabriel's father believes that Ultima is a *curandera,* a knowledgeable herb doctor who can lift curses and exorcise evil spells that *brujas* cast on people, such as afflicting them with disease or turning them into owls or coyotes. *See also curandera.*

B-29 the lethal high-altitude Boeing bomber employed by American forces during the 1940s. A four-engine, propeller-driven craft around 100 feet long and achieving speeds up to 325 miles per hour. One of these Air Force long-range trans-Pacific workhorses, the *Enola Gay,* carried the atomic bomb that devastated Hiroshima, Japan, on the morning of August 6, 1945; a second bomb run created similar havoc on Nagasaki. The Japanese people described in John Hersey's *Hiroshima* employ spotters to watch for B-29s, the planes most feared during World War II.

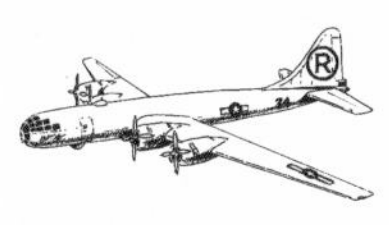

buccaneer (*buhk* . kuh . *neer'*) an unscrupulous adventurer, pirate, privateer, or freebooter owing allegiance only to self or a small band of thieves, usually seagoing along the Spanish-American coasts and among the Caribbean Islands. Seventeenth-century buccaneers preyed on the rich sea trade, often taking women and dignitaries as hostages to be redeemed for cash. The word is problematic and may stem from a West Indian or Brazilian term referring to a *boucan,* a curing frame or barbecue rack. In Chapter 1 of Joseph Conrad's *The Heart of Darkness,* the speaker typifies the buccaneer as reckless, greedy, and cruel.

buckboard a rough-riding, lightweight wagon topped by a single uncovered seat centered on slats or a spring plank that fit onto the double axle. The bucking ride resulted from the lack of a shock absorber. As late nineteenth-century transportation in America, the buckboard was commonly used for domestic chores such as ferrying passengers to a depot, church, and visits; as a hired vehicle to stores to carry groceries and parcels; or to and from mines or other outback business concerns. In Jack Schaefer's *Shane,* Ledyard, the trader, or peddler, delivers goods to the farm in a buckboard.

buckeye a horse chestnut, a large shiny nut native to the Balkans that can be ground into a tea to treat pneumonia in horses or settle an upset stomach in humans, or crushed into snuff for inhaling or into a healing paste for a poultice to soothe a swollen joint or relieve infection from a boil, hemorrhoids, external ulcers and lesions, or varicose veins. In a show of young love, Lightfoot pledges her friendship by giving Will Tweedy a buckeye in Olive Ann Burns's *Cold Sassy Tree.*

buckskin shoes faddish dyed slip-on shoes made from untanned sueded leather with a raised, fuzzy grayish-yellow nap on the surface. Originally made from deer, elk, or sheep, buckskin has been the leather of choice of frontier outfitters, glovemakers, upholsterers, harness-makers, and cobblers. In Lorraine Hansberry's *A Raisin in the Sun,* George Murchison looks like a flashy college clotheshorse in his white buckskin shoes.

Buddha (*boo'* duh) an honorific applied to Siddhartha Gautama (563–483 B.C.), an Indian prince who became an enlightened teacher and moralist. From Buddha evolved Buddhism, a philosophy of forbearance of earthly sufferings, nonviolence, and oneness with the sublime spirit. His name, which spread to China in the third century B.C., derives from the Sanskrit *to know* or *to awaken.* Buddha's likeness appears in many forms, but is usually dominated by a sublimely contented smile. In Pearl S. Buck's *The Good Earth,* O-Lan sews a gilt Buddha on the hat of her newborn son to show him off to her former master.

bulkhead a sturdy support wall or upright partition separating the inner portion of a ship into rooms or chambers. Derived from the Norse for *cargo head,* this fifteenth-century nautical term also applies to planes and barges. In addition to restraining the shift of cargo in rough seas, bulkheads help control flooding, contamination, or the spread of fire. A bulkhead is all that separates Leggatt, the captain's stowaway in Joseph Conrad's "The Secret Sharer," from detection by Captain Archbold, his pursuer.

bullboat a lightweight round boat made from buffalo hides stitched over a willow frame and sealed along the seams with tar or tallow. To propel the boat, two people rowed or poled it across short stretches of water. The pendant buffalo tail was attached to a log to serve as a tiller. Sacagawea, central figure in Scott O'Dell's *Streams to the River, River to the Sea,* spins helplessly in a bullboat because she tries to paddle it like a canoe. *See also* tiller.

bullroarer a ritual noisemaker formed out of a length of string or rawhide threaded through a disc or slat made of pottery, stone, wood, or bone. When swung about the head, the bullroarer creates a distinctive hum that is used in animistic ceremonies as a call to the gods. In Chinua Achebe's *Things Fall Apart,* set in precolonial Nigeria, the steady drone of the bullroarer summons the people to an unprecedented daylight assembly.

bulrushes any stiff grasslike, leafless water plant native to Europe and Asia, such as sedge, papyrus, or rush, that is cut, dried, and used in weaving and basketry. These sturdy vertical shoots, which grow up to three feet and end in spiky clusters of flowers, serve as breakwaters or decoration in pools and ponds. In Mark Twain's *The Adventures of Huckleberry Finn,* the title character listens to after-dinner readings from the Bible about "Moses and the bulrushers." *See also* rush; rush-light.

bulwark (*buhl'* wuhrk) the wall of a ship that extends above the decks and wards off high seas; also, a metaphor for a supporter or a strong, courageous person who defends weaker people. Entering English in the fifteenth century, the term derives from the German for *plank work.* In Herman Melville's *Billy Budd,* the title character advances past the bulwark to the forechains for his meeting with an informer.

bund earthwork or stone dikes or embankments that separate paddies or flooded fields; also, a causeway, quay, dike, or raised path in wetlands. During an attack in Maxine Hong Kingston's *Woman Warrior,* black irrigation water flows through broken bunds.

bung or **bunghole** a corked or sealed opening or spigot in a cask, barrel, or tun through which liquids are poured or emptied; also, the cork or stopper that seals a bunghole. A Dutch word that entered English in the fifteenth century, the term has changed little since its application to early containers. After the hurricane in Theodore Taylor's *The Cay,* Phillip tests for salt contamination in a keg by opening the bung and tasting the water. *See also* taproom.

bunting gaily colored flags, banners, or streamers in patriotic colors used to deck banquet halls, costumes,

hats, ball parks, stadiums, or parade floats on festive or commemorative occasions, for example, the Fourth of July, election day, Memorial Day, Flag Day, or Bastille Day. An eighteenth-century term, *bunting* may derive from an earlier word for *sift,* possibly referring to cloth used for sifting flour. In Joseph Conrad's "The Secret Sharer," Captain Archbold recalls covering the face of a corpse with a bit of bunting.

burgess (*buhr'* j's) a citizen, burgher, or freeman with voting rights; a landowner or member of the middle or merchant class. This thirteenth-century term derives from the Old English *burgh* or borough, the district in which the burgess lives. By extension, elected city council members are known as burgesses. In *The Mayor of Casterbridge,* Thomas Hardy refers to "placid burgesses" who have no fear of thieves.

burgher *See* burgess.

burka or **boorka** or **burqu** (*boor'* kuh) the Urdu word for a long, ample tunic or enveloping veil concealing all body parts and featuring a mesh panel to cover the face; the Indian equivalent of the Persian or Afghan chadar or the Turkish yasmak. Muslim women wear this obligatory modesty shield in Islamic countries to conceal themselves from the scrutiny of strangers, particularly unknown males. According to the Koran, concealment of female beauty preserves rigid chastity laws by protecting women from attack and by inhibiting men from impure thoughts arising from their response to female allure. In Ruth Prawer Jhabvala's *Heat and Dust,* midwives shield Olivia from public attention by enshrouding her in a burka and hustling her through the streets.

burrow a snug hole, excavation, refuge, or shelter; a segment of a rabbit warren or lengthy, interconnected series of subterranean passageways suitable for sleep, hibernation, or birthing chambers for underground animals. To guard against predator attack or accidental collapse of a lane, animals such as field mice, foxes, moles, voles, and rabbits dig emergency exits that open onto well-screened territory. Derived from the Middle English term for *mound, burrow* connotes nestly warmth and safety from bad weather and cold. In Richard Adams's *Watership Down,* General Woundwort supervises visitation of the local burrow, which he has turned into a concentration camp.

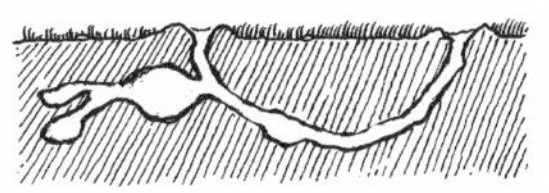

bushpilot an aviator who flies small planes to remote terrain inaccessible to land vehicles or who lands floatplanes on isolated bodies of water. The word derives from an American slang term dating to 1936. The bushpilot often conducts emergency or humanitarian missions, for example, delivery of medicines or vaccines, fighting forest fires, resettling wild animals in a suitable habitat, or search and rescue. Russel recalls the crash of a plane and the anger of the bushpilot in Gary Paulsen's *Dogsong.*

buskin a laced military boot consisting of a flat sole and leather ankle guard, sometimes padded with soft strips of swaddling or socks. In ancient Greek theater, tragic actors wore high-heeled buskins or cothurnus boots to give them added stature, a symbol of status or prestige. During the Middle Ages, hunters wore buskins to ward off cuts or snags during swift movement through thick brush. Titania refers to Hippolyta as a buskined Amazon in William Shakespeare's *A Midsummer Night's Dream.*

buttress (*buht'* trihs) a sturdy supportive structure of stone, wood, or brick slanting upward from the ground to brace or reinforce a wall. These supports, usually built at a perpendicular angle and inclined inward to connect with a beam or arch, are called flying buttresses, the typical supports of fourteenth-century architecture. In Sir Walter Scott's *Ivanhoe,* buttresses rise from the ground to brace and strengthen the sides of a tower.

butt-shaft a lightweight practice arrow directed at a butt, an absorbent mound, obstacle, or backstop behind a target or shooting range where arrows fall harmlessly and are collected and reused. Mentioned in William Shakespeare's *Romeo and Juliet,* the butt-shaft that pierces Romeo's heart flies from Cupid's bow, the stereotypical image of sudden infatuation.

C

cabaret (*ca* . buh . *ray'*) a bar, tavern, or restaurant offering live entertainment, for example, stage shows, instrumentalists, singing, and dancing. Derived from the seventeenth-century Picard term for *little room,* the word implies a lively, intimate nightclub. In *The Diary of a Young Girl,* Anne Frank looks forward to escaping her family's hiding place in the annexe and to returning to a life of cabarets, entertainment, and other familiar pleasures. *See also* annexe.

cabbala or **kabbala** (kuh . *bah'* luh) a collection of mystical interpretations of godhood, scripture, prophecy and visions, wisdom, numerology, and sacred mysteries. Derived from the Hebrew for *tradition,* the term covers occult practices of the Essenes or ascetic Jews from Jericho, which scholars systematized in the Zohar, a text composed in southern France and northern Spain during the twelfth and thirteenth centuries. Young Elie Wiesel in his autobiographical *Night* recalls learning cabbala lore from Moshe the Beadle and devoting himself to prayer and Judaic study.

cabriolet (*cab* . ree . oh . *lay'*) a light-framed, two-wheeled Italian-made carriage shaped like a shell and pulled by a brisk trotter. The cabriolet seated four passengers either open-air or under a convertible leather top; the Victoria version sported a platform at the rear for a footman or groom. Eventually, the term was shortened to *cab.* After receiving a disturbing letter from home, Victor, the title character in Mary Shelley's *Frankenstein,* hurriedly engages a cabriolet and departs from Geneva.

cacao (kuh . *kow'*) an evergreen tree native to the tropics that produces a valuable oval pod filled with up to forty reddish-brown fatty cocoa beans. After the beans are dried and roasted, they are ground into cocoa, which is blended with butter and flavorings and made into chocolate, mocha, and cocoa butter. In Alice Walker's *The Color Purple,* a letter from Nettie describes shady cacao trees everywhere and African workers returning home with their cacao buckets in their hands.

cache (kash) a hidden stash of supplies, ammunition, food, tools, valuables, or clothing that is lashed to a treetop or raised platform or buried in a root cellar or deep hole and concealed by careful replacement of topsoil, ash, litter, and sod to seal in food odors to keep out thieves or digging animals. In Gary Paulsen's *Dogsong,* Oogruk's food cache is situated on a platform on stilts with dogs tied beneath as guardians.

cadenza (kuh . *dehn'* zuh) a striking and sometimes improvised solo performance, aria, or flourish for voice or a single instrument that repeats or restates a crucial theme and precedes the conclusion of a musical performance or concerto. An early seventeenth-century musical term, the word derives from the Italian for *cadence.* Hugh Conway, protagonist of James Hilton's *Lost Horizon,* compares a pause for tea to a musical cadenza or virtuoso showpiece.

cadet (kuh . *deht'*) a junior office clerk or low-level noncommissioned recruit or trainee who enters military service or a local guard or police force to obtain basic instruction. An early seventeenth-century term, it derives from the Latin for *head.* The characters carrying the rank of cadet or beginner admire, emulate, and boost the ego of the title character in Edmond Rostand's *Cyrano de Bergerac.*

caesarian or **cesarean** (sih . *zar'* ee . uhn) **section** surgical removal of a fetus, often in emergency situations that require cutting the abdomen and uterine wall to resuscitate a frail or expiring infant or to separate it from a mother who is unable to delivery normally or whose life is in danger. Etymologists differ in explanation of the term, which legend dates to Egyptian healers in 3000 B.C., but applies to the birth of Julius Caesar; a more plausible derivation is from the Latin *caesum* or *cut.* The procedure reached Europe in the fifteenth century. Mary Donally, an Irish midwife, successfully performed the procedure in 1738, the first recorded application in Britain. In Ray Bradbury's *Fahrenheit 451,* vapid women discuss their reasons for preferring caesarian section to normal vaginal delivery of newborns.

caftan (*kaf'* tuhn) a Mediterranean overshirt or robe of cotton or silk with full sleeves and a sash or belt at the waist. The caftan can be worn alone or over trousers or a tunic; its uses vary from loose house garment to a gilt-edged ceremonial robe with matching fez and slippers. Alexander the Great shocked his Greek troops by adopting this Persian style, formerly worn by his enemy Darius. The main character of Chaim Potok's *The Chosen* bumps into a man in a black caftan who belongs to the Hasidic Jews, a conservative religious group.

cairn (kayrn) *See* barrow.

Cajun (*kay'* juhn) an ethnic group in Maine and the southern Louisiana wetlands and prairies who descended from French refugees fleeing anti-Catholic, anti-Gaelic persecution of the English in Acadia, Nova Scotia, in 1755. The term also refers to the Cajun-French patois; "chinka-chink" zydeco music; and spicy stews and dishes made from peppers, tomatoes, seafood, rice, and hot cayenne sauce. In Ernest Gaines's *The Autobiography of Miss Jane Pittman,* Jane lives amicably on the Charles River in a Cajun settlement.

cakewalk a semiserious processional, complex promenade, or humorous strutting dance in which the body is canted backward and the feet prance and corner around a precise square. A memorable dance figure in African-American lore, in the nineteenth century the cakewalk was an elimination contest with a cake or pastry as the prize for the handsomest, most intricate steppers. Tennessee Williams's *The Glass Menagerie* pictures Amanda Wingfield dressed in a yellowed voile gown and sash that she wore when she won the cakewalk at a cotillion in her girlhood.

calabash a hard-shelled gourd from the calabash or bottle tree or a dipper, ladle, or other hollowed-out, carved container used to store and serve liquids, soups, stews, and ceremonial foods or to be smoked as a pipe for tobacco. Derived from the Arabic term for *dry gourd,* the word entered English in the late sixteenth century. Tommo, protagonist of Herman Melville's *Typee,* attends the traditional Feast of Calabashes, a Polynesian holiday.

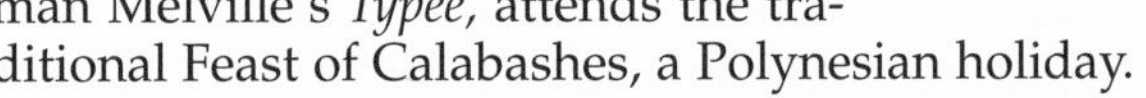

calèche (kuh . *lehsh'*) a dashing, high-bodied chaise or trap with raised driver's box and small-bodied shell seating four. The folding top covered only the rear seat; a platform at the rear carried parcels and luggage, and a metal step at the front enabled passengers to climb in at a small side door. In Bram Stoker's *Dracula,* as Jonathan Harker is carried aboard the Count's calèche into the wild countryside, wolves begin to howl.

calico a cheap, insubstantial, unbleached cotton cloth woven one over and one under and named in the late sixteenth century for Calcutta, India, from which it was imported. In the nineteenth century, coarse, narrow-gauge calico yard goods were heavily printed or figured on one side by a revolving, color-imbedded drum and used for lightweight aprons, curtains, hat bands, cloth-bodied dolls, house garments, or summer wear. Calico is commonly mentioned throughout literature. The mother of the bride-to-be in Jane Austen's *Pride and Prejudice* dictates orders for calico, muslin, and cambric.

calking *See* caulking.

callaloo or **calalu** (*ka* . luh . *loo'*) a member of a diverse family of tropical plants related to philodendron, dieffenbachia, arum, anthurium, and taro, some of which contain latex and provide starchy corms that yield a digestible food; also a stew of callaloo greens, onions, spices, and crabmeat. Hannah Gumbs, foster mother of the title character of Theodore Taylor's *Timothy of the Cay,* keeps her son well by serving him callaloo greens from the *dasheen* plant.

Calvary (*cal'* vuh . ree) the hill west of Jerusalem's outer wall on which Christ was crucified along with two thieves. The word derives from the Latin Vulgate translation of the Greek *Golgotha* or *the place of the skull.* Calvary, which may have been a cemetery or a skull-shaped outcropping, has become a metaphor for an ordeal, intense torment, or test of courage. In Martin Luther King's "Letter from the Birmingham Jail," the writer describes how Christ was crucified on "Calvary's hill" for a beneficial form of extremism or martyrdom similar to the civil rights marches that African-Americans organized; ironically, King himself suffered a similar assassination and martyrdom.

calypso (kuh . *lihp'* soh) a characteristic West Indian folk music composed of romantic, humorous, suggestive, and loosely rhymed lyrics and Creole dialect set to a syncopated beat echoed by strings and bongo or steel drums. The twentieth-century term, originating in Trinidad, remains untraced; conjecture pairs it with West African jump dancing and languages spoken by slaves who satirize local officials during Lenten Carnival street festivals. To Philip, the young protagonist in Theodore Taylor's *The Cay,* Timothy's voice epitomizes calypso with its soft, velvety, reassuring texture.

camas (*kah'* muhs) or **squamash** or **quamash** a star-flowered member of the lily family with grassy stems that grows wild in bogs, savannahs, and meadows. Also called bear grass or sweet grass, camas, a sacred plant, supplied Native American tribes with an edible onion-shaped tuber that could be steamed or cooked in loaves, traded, or made into fish poison, soap, or a soothing sedative. According to

Hal Borland's *When the Legends Die,* Tom Black Bull returns to the wilderness, where a bear tears up a camas patch.

cambric a fine-textured, slightly glossy, thin white cotton or linen used for starched ruffs, nightwear, slips, scarves, lining, baby clothes, collars, neck bands, and cuffs. Cambric can be boiled and bleached to restore its original freshness. The term currently applies to the heavy black voile that is tacked to the underside of upholstered furniture. The word derives from a Flemish term for Cambrai, France, and entered English in the mid-sixteenth century. Edgar wipes away tears with his cambric pocket handkerchief in Emily Brontë's *Wuthering Heights.*

camion (*kam'* yuhn or kam . *yohn'*) a World War II-era heavy-duty bus, truck, or dray that replaced the animal-drawn caissons and field wagons used during World War I to transport heavy artillery and ammunition. In Ernest Hemingway's *A Farewell to Arms,* weighty camions splash the infantry on muddy roads and bog down as rains make the surface slippery and impassable.

camomile *See* chamomile.

campanile (*kam* . puh . *nihl'* or *kam* . puh . *nih'* leh) a bell tower separate from a city hall, church, basilica, or abbey; a belfry, sometimes housing religious artifacts and sculptures or used by city officials to summon citizens to a meeting or to warn of danger, such as fire, flood, or military attack. Derived from the Italian *campana,* the term, entering English in the mid-seventeenth century, reflects the source of dependable metal from Campania, the region around Naples, Italy. In Ernest Hemingway's *A Farewell to Arms,* the protagonist, who is widely traveled, recalls a campanile in Caporetto.

camphor a white flammable crystal that gives off a pungent odor that repels insects. Dating to the fourteenth century, the term derives from a Malaysian name for the compound, which is made from the oil of the bark and leaves of the camphor tree and prized as a cure-all and valuable trade item. In Marjorie Kinnan Rawlings's *The Yearling,* among the essentials on the family's shopping list is camphor. Frontier families hung small camphor pouches about the neck to ward off colds; rubbed it on as a painkiller and antidote to skin rashes and heart problems; and mixed it into salves and liniment to ease gout, rheumatism, and sprains in both people and animals.

camwood or **cam wood** a tough, resilient West African redwood used chiefly as a dyeing agent; barwood, a hard, heavy, carveable product of Nigeria composed of dark fibrous inner layers streaked with charcoal black. Following tradition, a significant theme in Chinua Achebe's *Things Fall Apart,* a marriageable girl reddens her skin with camwood before decorating her limbs and trunk with patterns.

canasta a complicated Uruguayan or Argentine form of rummy requiring two decks and rewarding two pairs of partners who accumulate stacks of seven cards of equal value or mixed with wild cards. Named for the Spanish word for *basket,* which refers to the tray that contains discards, the term dates to the mid-twentieth century, when canasta clubs were first popular enough in the United States to displace bridge as a favorite game. J. D. Salinger's Holden Caulfield, protagonist of *The Catcher in the Rye,* wants to unwind after a fight with his roommate by playing canasta with Ackley.

candlefish the common name for the eulachon (*yew'* luh . k'n), a tiny, silver-scaled, oily smelt that thrives along the Pacific Coast of North America. Indians strung these small fish on a rush to be lighted as a candle. The heroine in Scott O'Dell's *The Island of the Blue Dolphins* stores candlefish in her living space so that she can have enough light to fashion a green cormorant-feather skirt during the dark days.

Candlemas a Roman Catholic and Episcopalian feast and procession of lights begun in the fourth century and held on February 2 to honor the purification of the Virgin Mary; in Eastern Orthodox churches, the feast commemorates Christ's presentation at the Temple 40 days after his birth. According to celebrants, the candles symbolize Christ as the light of the world. In Thomas Hardy's *Tess of the D'Urbervilles,* the title character anticipates heavy work in preparation for the Candlemas Fair.

Canis lupus (*kah'* nihs *loo'* puhs) the biological identification of the wolf, a predatory animal that runs in packs and preys upon other animals. Unlike the domesticated *Canis,* or dog, the wolf lives in wild northern stretches. Lieutenant Farley Mowat departs Ottawa by transport plane to solve the Canadian government's problems with *Canis lupus* in his nonfiction account of zoological field work in *Never Cry Wolf.*

canker a destructive green caterpillar, the larval stage of the geometrid moth, that feeds on tender shoots of fruit trees; the looper, inchworm, or measuring worm. Before leaving Denmark to return to school, Laertes, a friend of the title character in William Shakespeare's *Hamlet,* compares an insidious romance to a canker worm, which destroys the bud before it has an opportunity to blossom—a prefigurement of Hamlet himself, dead in his youth from a duel fought with poisoned swords.

cannel (*can'* n'l) **coal** a popular fireplace fuel that burns with a bright flame and gives off voluminous smoke; bituminous coal formed of prehistoric spores. This sixteenth-century term may refer to candle power, an apt description for so volatile a fuel. After lunch, Turkey's face glows red like cannel coal poured atop anthracite, as described in Herman Melville's "Bartleby the Scrivener."

canon an ecclesiastical law, code, regulation, or decree; dogma that ruled all people living in lands under Roman Catholicism and refused Christian burial to those who killed themselves. Beset by self-doubt and frustration, the title character in William Shakespeare's *Hamlet* wishes that canon law did not forbid suicide.

canteen (kan . *teen'*) a lunchroom, snack bar, or cafeteria at a school, hospital, or military base. Derived from the Spanish for *small corner,* the term denotes a place selling or serving light provisions or snacks to workers and villagers. In Sandra Cisneros's *The House on Mango Street,* latchkey children eat their school lunch in the canteen because they live too far away to return home for the noon meal.

caparisoned (kuh . *par'* ih . suhnd) **coursers** matched teams of horses wearing heavily adorned harnesses and saddles. Derived from a sixteenth-century Spanish term for *saddle cloth,* the word also refers to the polished metal discs, ribbons, insignia, and plumes that constitute parade dress for dray animals. In Charles Dickens's *Great Expectations,* Pip assures Mrs. Joe that Miss Havisham has a coach but no caparisoned coursers.

capital felony a serious crime, such as treason, murder, rape, kidnapping, armed robbery, or arson, punishable by execution. Derived from Latin for *head,* the term denotes a loss of the head as punishment. In Harper Lee's *To Kill a Mockingbird,* the speaker jokingly distinguishes between a misdemeanor, or minor crime, and a capital felony.

capo. *See* kapo.

capstan (*kap'* stan) a vertical axis in the form of windlass, spindle, post, barrel, shaft, spool, or rotating drum around which rope, cable, or chain is wound to ease the strain of pulling a heavy object, for example, a ship's anchor, lifeboats from moorings into position for launching, or barrels of water from a mine shaft. In Robert Newton Peck's *A Day No Pigs Would Die,* Rob's father uses a capstan as an aid to dragging a corncrib into place to make a pen for Rob's pet pig.

capstone the crowning or finish stone, slab, or shaped mortar placed at the head of a column, turret, or tower or laid along a brick or stone fence; a coping or finial that dresses a raw edge or conceals an inner hollow. Spying a fallen capstone, Madame Magloire deduces that a thief has climbed the wall in Victor Hugo's *Les Misérables.*

Capuchin (*kap'* yoo . chihn) an austere friar or monk following the example of Saint Francis of Assisi; a Franciscan. Named in the sixteenth century for the Italian word for the sharp-pointed cowls that obscured their faces, the Capuchins dedicated themselves to social work, counseling, ministry, and preaching and to care of the sick during plagues. A Capuchin priest in Edmond Rostand's *Cyrano de Bergerac* is sent to perform the marriage ceremony between Roxane and Christian, Cyrano's rival.

carabinieri (*kah* . ruh . bih . *nyeh'* ree) *sing.* **carabiniere** the Italian national police, who are under the command of the minister of defense and who take their name from cavalry soldiers armed with carbine rifles. In Ernest Hemingway's *A Farewell to Arms,* the carabinieri attempt to direct traffic during a slow-moving retreat through mud and rain. *See also* carbine.

carapace (*kar'* uh . pays) a hardened bony or horny shell that covers and protects the dorsal, or spine, side of a turtle, armadillo, crab, or other crustacean. In Ernest Hemingway's *The Old Man and the Sea,* Santiago, who exposes himself to sun, sea, hunger, and pain during his epic fishing expedition, observes that the turtles behave in exactly the opposite way—shutting their eyes so that they are completely carapaced against harm.

carbine (*kar′* been or *kar′* byn) a lightweight, short-barreled, smooth-bore rifle or musket with low velocity that is aimed from the shoulder. Until it was displaced by the M-16, the carbine was standard issue to mounted soldiers, glider pilots, tank gunners, paratroopers, police sharpshooters, or hunters or guerrilla forces in thickets and deep jungle. In Joseph Conrad's *The Heart of Darkness,* bearers for Mr. Kurtz carry his protective arsenal—a heavy rifle, two shotguns, and a carbine, none of which can ward off the assault of conscience that disturbs his dying moments.

carbolic acid an aromatic, corrosive, and poisonous antiseptic or disinfectant derived from coal tar and used in soap; phenol. It was discovered by the French in 1834; 30 years passed before Joseph Lister applied dressings soaked in carbolic acid to septic wounds. Paul Baumer, the protagonist of Erich Maria Remarque's *All Quiet on the Western Front,* dislikes the smell of carbolic acid in the field dressing station.

carborundum (kar . boh . *ruhn′* duhm) a trademark name for an abrasive blend of silicon and carbon that produces a hard, rasping surface for grinding, polishing, and refining rough surfaces. The term is a manufacturer's name for silicon carbide, made from clay and coke, manufactured by Edward Acheson and patented in 1893. Carborundum is an abrasive that coats emery paper for files, grinding tools, buffing cloths, and industrial sandpaper belts. In John Steinbeck's *The Grapes of Wrath,* Noah sharpens the ax on a carborundum stone before the family slaughters a pig.

carcinoma (*kar* . sih . *noh′* muh) a malignancy or cancer occurring on the epithelium or outer layer of flesh. Derived from the Greek term for *crab,* the word suggests cancer's aggressive tendency to spread to surrounding tissues. According to John Hersey's *Hiroshima,* post–atomic bomb damage to human tissue precipitated carcinomas of the reproductive organs, urinary tract, salivary glands, lungs, breast, thyroid, and stomach.

caribou (*kar′* ih . boo) a herd animal, similar to a deer, that is adapted to the arctic and subarctic tundra; also, reindeer that once provided the Inuit with meat and animal food. Marked by branching palmate antlers, the animal browses the tundra for mosses, which hunters cut out of carcasses and eat like delicacies because they lack access to vegetables. In *Never Cry Wolf,* Farley Mowat observes a herd of caribou heading for the high barrens in late June.

cariole or **carriole** (*kar′* ree . ohl) a small open two- or four-wheeled carriage similar to a calèche and seating no more than two passengers; a covered cart drawn by one horse. Jensine anticipates traveling by cariole from the village to the landing in Isak Dinesen's "The Pearls." *See also* calèche.

car man or **car-man** the driver of a dray, wagon, or hired cart who moves bundles and boxes; makes deliveries for local merchants or the mail service; or ferries passengers short distances within a city or to nearby depots, quays, and villages. In Herman Melville's "Bartleby the Scrivener," Ginger Nut avoids the burdensome and low-paid trade of his father, a car man.

carp a large-scaled bottom-feeding food fish related to goldfish that thrives in freshwater ponds and still pools as well as thick mud and polluted waters. Because of its prolific reproduction, the carp is standard stock in aquaculture and a favorite of sport fishers and pond owners. In Rudolfo Anaya's *Bless Me, Ultima,* the carp is a beautiful, magical fish that brings ill luck to anyone who hooks it.

carpetbag a sturdy, inexpensive purse-shaped travel bag, carryall, tote, valise, or hand luggage composed of a metal frame, shoulder strap, and sides and bottom made from patterned carpet scraps. In Mark Twain's *Life on the Mississippi,* passengers and salesmen carry carpetbags, or satchels, filled with personal items sufficient for a brief absence from home or stocked with wares for sale along the way.

carrefour (*kar′* uh . foor) a crossroads, junction, or intersection; also, a farmer's market, square, plaza, or piazza. Derived from the Latin for *four forks,* the term implies a meeting place for business or commerce. Lucetta, a blatant self-promoter and ambitious plotter, buys a house overlooking the bustle of the carrefour in Thomas Hardy's *The Mayor of Casterbridge.*

carronade (*kar* . uh . *nayd′*) a short-barreled, limited-range cannon that fired large-caliber shot from a warship. Common to British, French, and U.S. vessels from the late eighteenth century into the mid-nineteenth century, the carronade could fire a 30-pound ball. To hold off boarding parties in Paula Fox's *Slave Dancer,* Ned the Carpenter builds a platform for the carronade.

cartridge a form of ammunition for small arms; a cylindrical metal, cloth, or cardboard casing that houses both the propellant charge, primer, and projectile, bullet, or shot and prevents escaping gas from harming the shooter. Before a counterattack in Stephen Crane's *The Red Badge of Courage,* soldiers reach for all types of cartridges.

cash a general category of small copper coins of little value used throughout Asia; a Chinese tael (tayl), a copper coin with a square hole in the middle to accommodate a wire or string. Derived from the Tamil for *coin* by way of the Sanskrit term for a gold or silver weight, the word entered English in the late sixteenth century. A beggar asks Wang Lung, protagonist of Pearl S. Buck's *The Good Earth,* for a small cash, thus elevating the farmer to a slightly higher position among townspeople.

cassava (kuh . *sah'* vuh) another name for yucca or manioc; a tropical plant prized for its palmate leaves that are ground into silage, or winter feed, for livestock. Cassava tubers are boiled and eaten like sweet potatoes or grated, fermented into beer, or dried into a flour to thicken soups and desserts. Featured in Chinua Achebe's *Things Fall Apart,* cassava is an important Nigerian agricultural crop.

cassino or **casino** (kuh . *see'* noh) a simple card game derived from eighteenth-century rules and using one 52-card deck for two players or pairs of partners. The game requires players to match from their hands the four cards dealt on the board. Capturing a pair increases the point count toward the goal of 21. The characters in Jane Austen's *Pride and Prejudice* play quadrille and cassino.

cassock (*kas'* suhk) a fitted red or black cloak or coat with stand-up collar, tapered waist, and tight cuffed or plain sleeves worn either plain, sashed, or belted or topped with an alb, surplice, or cotta by a member of the clergy or a lay assistant. A seventeenth-century term, it derives from the Persian for *stuffed silk.* Meursault, the protagonist of Albert Camus's *The Stranger,* loses control of his emotions, grabs a priest by his cassock, and yells at him.

cast an impression of a human face or other body part made by forming a plaster coating over the skin and removing it after it hardens; a death mask. Such casts formed the working likenesses from which early sculptors made realistic images of famous people, for example, Abraham Lincoln. Shelved in Mr. Jaggers's office in Charles Dickens's *Great Expectations* are casts of executed criminals, whose features intrigue Pip on his first visit.

castor oil a yellowish, fatty tonic derived from the oil of castor beans that lubricates the digestive tract to aid digestion and elimination or is used to soften rough skin and calluses, make soap and embalming fluid, or purge the bowels of parasites. In Marjorie Kinnan Rawlings's *The Yearling,* Jody's family includes 50 cents worth of castor oil in their annual shopping list.

cat derived from the shortened form of Caterpillar, the trademark of a heavy-duty earth-moving bulldozer or belt- or chain-tread-driven tractor capable of moving boulders, reshaping terrain, pushing obstacles out of the way, and toppling buildings. In John Steinbeck's *The Grapes of Wrath,* the cat drivers "tractor out" Oklahoma farmers like the Joads, who are bankrupted and ruined by the Dust Bowl.

catafalque (*kat'* uh . falk) an elevated and sometimes ornate, canopied, or pall-draped dais, platform, or frame on which a coffin or slab is placed for the formal viewing of a corpse, especially a hero or a person of rank or royalty. The priest claims to have seen the Irish nationalist Parnell stretched out on a catafalque in James Joyce's *The Portrait of the Artist as a Young Man. See also* bier; pall.

catapult or **onager** a primitive piece of portable military artillery favored by the Roman army and imitated by their enemies. The catapult was ratcheted into position; then the windlass holding its tightened, twisted ropes, hair, or sinews was released to hurl a boulder, burning debris, or dart at a besieged town. While collecting money from Winston Smith for Hate Week, his neighbor Parsons apologizes for his son's indiscriminate use of a toy catapult against Smith in George Orwell's *1984.*

cataract an opaque thickening that obscures the lens over the iris and impedes vision or blinds the victim by limiting the amount of light that strikes the retina at the rear of the eyeball. To restore vision, a surgical procedure, first performed with a scalpel in 1748 and replaced by laser in 1979, removes the thickening and replaces it with a synthetic lens. A condition common in the elderly, cataracts limit mobility, handwork, and reading, but are readily cured with laser surgery. In Kawabata Yasunari's "The Jay," Yoshiko's grandmother is nearly blind from cataracts in both eyes.

catarrh (kuh . *tar'*) an inflammation of the mucous linings that causes the chronic, effusive discharge of watery mucus from the mouth, lungs, and nose. The term, dating to the fifteenth century, derives from the Greek for *downward flow.* The Reverend Arthur Dimmesdale, a frail minister who is constantly suffering ill health, stands at the window and risks catarrh and cough in Nathaniel Hawthorne's *The Scarlet Letter.*

catechism (*kat'* uh . kihzm) during pre-confirmation training, a rigorous list of memory work consisting of questions and answers beginning with the confirmand's name and proceeding to difficult definitions that summarize the faith, practice, and principles of Christianity. In Jeanne Wakatsuki Houston and James D. Houston's *Farewell to Manzanar,* Jeanne studies catechism under Maryknoll nuns, who hope to convert her to Catholicism against the will of her father, Ko.

cathead usually, the wood or iron beam that projects from the bow of a ship and from which the anchor is lowered and raised, usually with the aid of a capstan. Avi's *The True Confessions of Charlotte Doyle* lists the cathead as a protuberance from the bow of the *Seahawk.* In Maya Angelou's *I Know Why the Caged Bird Sings,* however, the word refers to large, irregularly shaped biscuits. *See also* capstan.

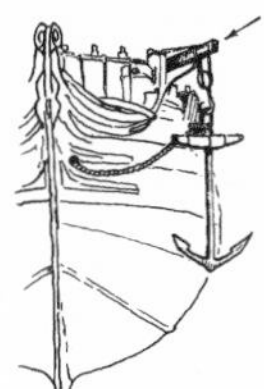

catheter a flexible tube that can be anchored in a body orifice, duct, or canal to empty fluids into a catch basin or plastic sac for examination, measurement, chemical study, or disposal. In the mental institution in Ken Kesey's *One Flew Over the Cuckoo's Nest,* Chief Bromden observes black orderlies taping used catheters to incontinent patients and deliberately ripping the tape off to cause pain.

catlinite (*cat'* lih . nyt) *See* pipestone.

cat-o'-nine-tails a whip created by attaching to a handle flexible three-to-four-foot strands of leather with knots, tacks, or burs tied at the ends that claw the flesh like cat's claws and wielded as a means of punishment, discipline, and permanent disfigurement. In Ernest Gaines's *The Autobiography of Miss Jane Pittman,* young Ticey reports to a Union officer that she has been beaten with a cat-o'-nine-tails.

cat's cradle an internationally popular children's game that involves the creation of an intricate web made of one circle of string or twine passed over and around the fingers, palms, and wrists of two hands forming figures such as a cup and saucer, steeple, church door, and swing. As a diversion, Purvis shows Jessie a cat's cradle in Paula Fox's *Slave Dancer.*

cat's face the wrinkling or disfigurement on a garment that results from faulty ironing of cottons, silks, or linens, particularly starched cloth, which firmly imprints the cat's face until the garment is rewashed. Maya Angelou, the autobiographer of *I Know Why the Caged Bird Sings,* recalls the cat's faces that appear on poorly ironed cloth.

cat's ladder *See* cat's cradle.

cat's-paw a slight breeze that ripples the surface of a lake or the sea; also, the menial who performs chores or runs errands for a ship's officer. To emphasize the difficulty of a river pilot's job, Mark Twain explains the difference in appearance between a sandbar and a cat's-paw on the river's surface in his autobiographical *Life on the Mississippi.*

caucus (*kaw'* kuhs) a serious discussion or private political meeting to select candidates or adopt a party platform and election strategy. Entering English in the early seventeenth century, this Algonquin word appears in the diary of Captain John Smith, a settler of New England. The satiric caucus race in Lewis Carroll's *Alice's Adventures in Wonderland* consists of running from any starting point and quitting when the Do-do calls, "The race is over!" *See also* parley; pow-wow.

caul (kawl) the amnion, the innermost of two membranes that surround and protect a fetus. Derived from the Irish word for *veil,* the term, which entered English in the fourteenth century, refers to a magical shred of human tissue that superstitious sailors purchased to protect themselves from drowning, just as the thin sac protects an unborn child in the uterus. According to superstition in James Hurst's "The Scarlet Ibis," children born with the caul intact on their heads are blessed with a piece of Jesus' nightgown.

caulking (*kawl'* kihng) a protective sealant or waterproofing forced into the seams, planking, knotholes, and joints of a boat, siding, roof, or jointed pipes to prevent seepage or in crevices, door frames, or windowsills to shut out drafts and moisture. According to his autobiography, *Narrative of the Life of Frederick Douglass,* the title character practiced the caulking trade, which involves pressing oakum and pitch or tar into a seam with a sharp blade. *See also* oakum; pitch.

cavalier a royalist and supporter of Charles I, the deposed king of England, who was beheaded and replaced by the Puritan Roundheads, led by Oliver Cromwell and his son Richard. The Commonwealth they established lasted from 1649 until the restoration of Charles II in 1660. The term, which derives from the French for *horseman,* implies a dashingly courageous political or military figure and was later replaced by *tory* or *loyalist.* In Sir Arthur Conan Doyle's *The Hound of the Baskervilles,* Sir Henry Baskerville identifies the lace-bedecked villain Hugo as a cavalier.

cay a small, sometimes waterless and nearly treeless island or reef composed of coral and sand and often unlisted on navigational charts. Derived from a Taino word for *shoal,* the term entered English in the early eighteenth century. Philip and Timothy take shelter on a low uncharted spit of land in Theodore Taylor's survival novel, *The Cay,* and its sequel, *Timothy of the Cay.*

cayuse (*ky'* yoos) a sturdy breed of wild, wiry ponies that prospered on the northern Pacific Coast Range under the cultivation, training, and breeding of a tribe bearing the same name. The term has expanded to include any rough-haired, spirited prairie or range pony. In John Steinbeck's *The Red Pony,* Billy Buck rides a hammer-head cayuse, an appropriate mount for a rough-edged farm laborer. *See also* mustang.

C.C.C. or **Civilian Conservation Corps** a social improvement program begun in 1933 by President Franklin Delano Roosevelt to employ 2.5 million idle men, who strengthened American infrastructure by building bridges and roads, digging firebreaks, and reforesting depleted and eroding slopes. In Maya Angelou's *I Know Why the Caged Bird Sings,* references to the C.C.C. give meaning to the hard times weathered by Mama Henderson and her general store, which sold clothing, tobacco, and lunch items to local workers.

cenotaph (*sehn'* uh . taf) a memorial or ceremonial marker placed over an empty grave or constructed in honor of a person buried elsewhere or one whose remains were not (or could not be) recovered, such as a person buried at sea or burned. The cenotaph in John Hersey's *Hiroshima* marks the site of the immolation of unsuspecting residents of Hiroshima, Japan, who were destroyed by an atomic bomb dropped by American forces on August 6, 1945.

censer (*sehn'* suhr) an ornately pierced or slotted covered metal container or diffuser that holds lighted incense formed of aromatic gum or spice. A celebrant swings the censer by a chain over worshippers during a Catholic mass or ritual. Smoke from a censer, which symbolizes prayers rising to heaven, engulfs the wedding of Marius and Cosette in Victor Hugo's *Les Misérables.*

centaur (*sehn'* tawr) a mythological monster born of Ixion and a cloud. The centaurs, who were native to Mount Pelion in Thessaly, combined the bodies of a horse with the torsos, heads, and arms of a human male and tended to live a wild, savage existence. Edith Hamilton's *Mythology* describes a noble centaur, the wise, good-natured Chiron, a sage, healer, and teacher of Aesculapius, Jason, and Hercules.

cesspool the underground trap, rock-lined pit, catch basin, or storage pond that holds the untreated solid wastes from an industrial or storm drain or household sewage pipe after surrounding soil, porous fill, or drain field has absorbed liquids. In John Steinbeck's *Of Mice and Men,* Lenny and George remain unemployed after digging a cesspool on their last job in Weed, California.

cestus (*sehs'* tuhs) *See* girdle.

chador (*chah'* duhr) *See* burka.

chaff the dry, flyaway outer covering of grain, including the dried calyx or husk, scales, stems, leaves, and other inedible debris that is removed during harvesting, winnowing, or threshing. O-Lan, a thrift-conscious wife, winnows and preserves the grain from chaff in Pearl S. Buck's *The Good Earth.*

chain gang an outdoor work team of male convicts fastened together by leg chains while they perform menial chores, particularly roadwork, digging ditches, cutting timber, or clearing brush. The purpose of chaining is to prevent escape while providing freedom of movement of arms and legs. Paul D describes the secret communication system and camaraderie of the members of a chain gang under the guns and whips of sadistic, sexually perverse overseers in Toni Morrison's *Beloved.*

chaise (shayz or chays) a fashionable, lightweight open pleasure or traveling carriage pulled by a single horse and seating two passengers who were protected during wind and bad weather by a folding top. In Jane Austen's *Pride and Prejudice,* the social standing and prestige of a visitor is determined by the use of a chaise over a less stylish conveyance, such as a pony-shay, wagon, or dog-cart. *See also* dog-cart.

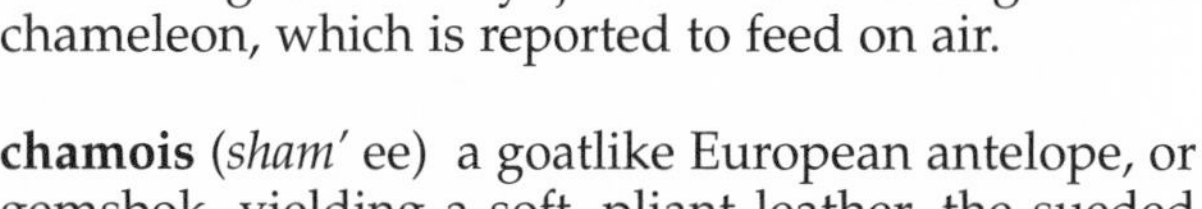

chalah or **challah** (*cha'* luh) a festival or ceremonial bread braided from long rolls of white yeast dough and glazed with egg white to form a hard, shiny crust over a light, tasty interior. Reuven and Danny anticipate eating the tuna fish, eggs, and chalah bread laid out on a Shabbat, or Sabbath, tablecloth in Chaim Potok's *The Chosen.*

chalice (*chal'* ihs) a goblet or ornate drinking cup; a ritual eucharistic vessel used to serve communion wine. In medieval lore, the Holy Grail was the chalice from which Christ drank at the Last Supper before his crucifixion. During a duel in William Shakespeare's *Hamlet,* the title character drinks from a poisoned chalice.

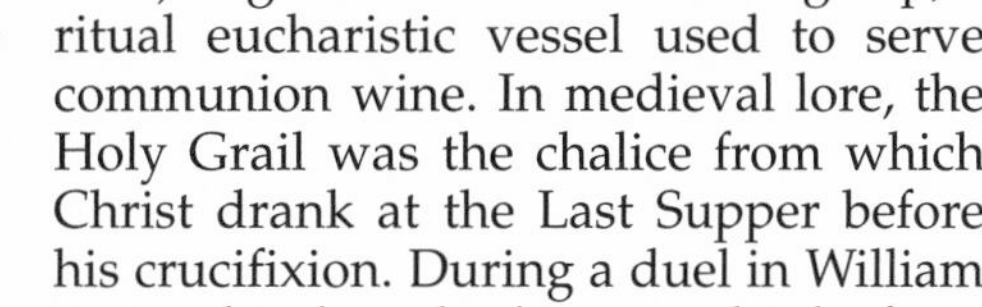

chalk scores a barkeep's tallies on a slate denoting unpaid drinks charged to the tab of regular customers; a crude record of credit to a store, pub, or eating establishment. In Charles Dickens's *Great Expectations,* Pip notices alarmingly long chalk scores at the Jolly Bargeman, indicating a generous policy toward credit accounts, foreshadowing his own debts.

chamberlain (*chaym'* buhr . lihn) a bedroom attendant, household steward, domestic manager, doorkeeper, hall guard, or valet who served royalty or nobility, particularly at night. The royal chamberlains in William Shakespeare's *Macbeth* awaken to find themselves recovering from a drugged drink, smeared with blood, and implicated in the murder of King Duncan, whom they were hired to guard.

chambray (*sham'* brih) a serviceable linen-finished gingham fabric native to Chambrai, France, which is woven of colored threads over white ones. Work shirts in John Steinbeck's *The Red Pony* are made of chambray. *See also* cambric; gingham.

chameleon (kuh . *meel'* yuhn) a small pop-eyed, long-tongued crested tree lizard that grasps branches with its curled prehensile tail. The chameleon is a feisty challenger capable of changing its skin tone to green, brown, or yellow to camouflage its appearance. The title character in William Shakespeare's *Hamlet* lightheartedly jokes about eating like a chameleon, which is reported to feed on air.

chamois (*sham'* ee) a goatlike European antelope, or gemsbok, yielding a soft, pliant leather, the sueded side of which is used for polishing automobile fenders and wheels, gun barrels, cutlery, and other metal objects; also, the polishing cloth itself. In Arthur Miller's *Death of a Salesman,* Willy orders his boys to use the chamois to clean the hubcaps when they simonize his car. *See also* simonize.

chamomile (*kam'* uh . meel) a bitter, apple-scented plant topped with daisy-shaped flowers and used as an emetic, a tonic, or an anti-inflammatory; a standard additive to herbal teas, decoctions, shampoo, bubble bath, facial mask, and soap. Sethe, protagonist of Toni Morrison's *Beloved,* is stained with the sticky juice of the chamomile stalk, an image suggesting seminal fluid after sexual relations with Paul D.

chancery (*chan'* suh . ree) a U.S. court of equity that settles matters of rights, property, liability, and ownership; also, the office of public records that files deeds, titles, and liens. As part of his job, the title character in Herman Melville's "Bartleby the Scrivener" copies in quadruplicate some documents from the High Court of Chancery.

chaps (shaps or chaps) removable leggings that are strapped or buckled across a rider's pants and laced across the back of the leg to ward off contact with brush, cactus thorns, or other forms of abrasion. Tom Black Bull, protagonist of Hal Borland's *When the Legends Die,* wears chaps to protect his legs while he rides rodeo broncs.

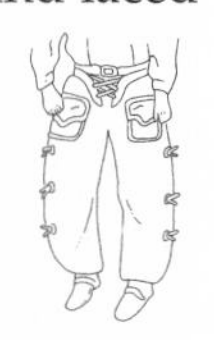

characters the 50,000 word-clusters or radicals in the Chinese written language. Before twentieth-century simplification, writers joined graphemes, or pictograms, to form abstract concepts. For example, as described in Amy Tan's *The Kitchen God's Wife,* the symbol for *mother* is topped by the symbol for *mouth* to create the verb *scold,* a verb that links concrete nouns to produce an abstract concept. Before character modernization, the burden of such complex memory work deprived many Chinese of literacy—only the rich had the money and leisure to be tutored in the entire written vocabulary. Today, more people learn Chinese

because the character base has been pared down to 2,000 units.

chesterfield a short-legged sofa, divan, or settee padded on the back, seats, and arms with ornate scrolling and buttoned upholstery, usually velvet. In Katherine Mansfield's "The Garden Party," Laura's mother moves the chesterfield to make room for the party.

cheval-glass a full-length framed mirror mounted on swivels that allow the mirror to be tilted in its metal or wood frame. The prefix *cheval* comes from the French for *horse,* referring to the frame upon which the glass "rides." The searchers of the laboratory in Robert Louis Stevenson's *The Strange Case of Dr. Jekyll and Mr. Hyde* locate a cheval-glass, which suggests that the scientist observed his metamorphosis from normality into a monstrosity.

chevron (*shehv'* ruhn) an inverted V; a decorative angled pattern common to pottery, ritual items, architecture, upholstery, and other textiles or a motif on an arm badge, bar, stripes, or sign of rank on the uniform of a firefighter, soldier, guard, or police officer. In Edmond Rostand's *Cyrano de Bergerac,* the title character pointedly warns his Gascon cadets that the next chevron added to their insignia will be blood red. *See also* cadet.

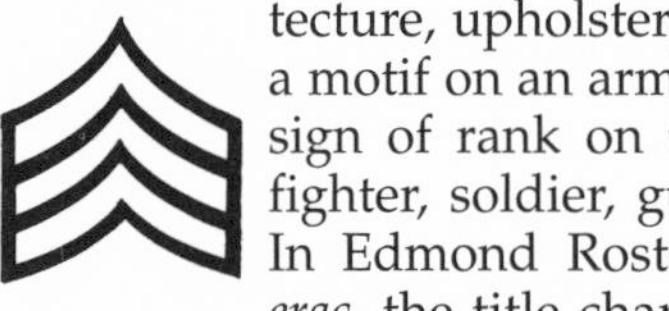

chifferobe or **chiffarobe** or **chifforobe** (*shihf'* fuh . rohb) a tall, bulky piece of furniture combining a wardrobe for hanging garments on one side with a chest of drawers and mirror on the opposite side; a useful wardrobe for older houses without built-in closets. In Harper Lee's *To Kill a Mockingbird,* a cast-off chifferobe is crucial evidence in the case against Tom Robinson, an accused rapist whom the victim asked to chop up the piece to dispose of it.

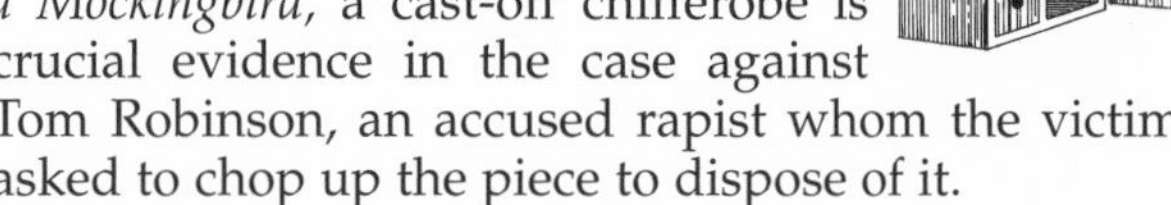

chiffonier (*shihf* . fuh . *neer'*) an eighteenth-century French term for a chest of drawers or cupboard with a sideboard top and back mirror. The chiffonier is used in a dining room to contain silver, linens, and other table items; in a bedroom, it holds jewelry, scarves, sweaters, and other folded items. The furniture in the dorm room of Holden Caulfield, protagonist of J. D. Salinger's *The Catcher in the Rye,* consists of a desk and chiffonier.

chignon (sheen . *yon'*) a stylized French twist or coil of hair arranged in a tight, sleek style that secures strands into a curving knot at the back of the head or the nape of the neck. Dating to the late eighteenth century, the term derives from the Latin for *chain.* In Jeanne Wakatsuki Houston and James D. Houston's *Farewell to Manzanar,* Jeanne tries to look sophisticated for the queen's court by arranging her hair in a chignon.

chilblain (*chihl'* blayn) an itchy irritation, sore, or ulceration that can occur in skin exposed to cold or impaired by poor blood circulation. Before the invention of knitting in the Middle Ages, woodcutters, hunters, and others who worked outdoors suffered infected, chapped skin because they had to expose their hands to do their jobs. In Charlotte Brontë's *Jane Eyre,* the children at boarding school develop chilblains from working outdoors without gloves.

chimera or **chimaera** (ky . *meer'* uh) a grotesque, fiery-eyed female monster created from the body parts of various animals: a snake's tail, goat's body, and lion's head and chest; metaphorically, an outlandish thought, dream, nightmare, vision, or fantasy. In Edith Hamilton's *Mythology,* Bellerophon flies away on Pegasus, his winged horse, to fight the fire-breathing chimera.

chimney-piece the hood, mantel, fireboard, or ornamental framing around a hearth or fireplace, often decorated with columns, entablature, scrolled wood, stucco bas-relief, crocheted doilies, felt, fringe, tassels, or needlework and topped with a mirror or pier-glass. John Tenniel, illustrator for Lewis Carroll's *Through the Looking Glass,* pictures Alice as climbing to the chimney-piece and pushing through into the reverse side of her reflection. *See also* bas-relief; pier-glass.

chimney sweep a person, usually a slender lad, who was dispatched down a flue to brush away loose soot to prevent chimney fires and to increase ventilation to the fire. Before 1842, children from a workhouse could be forced to take this job, which endangered life from falls, burns, and lung disorders. The plight of the chimney sweep is a focus in Charles Dickens's *Oliver Twist. See also* workhouse.

chinaberry a deciduous shade or ornamental tree of the mahogany family that is common in the southeastern United States. Because the tree has a stout trunk and perpendicular limbs and produces lavender flowers and clusters of hard green berries, it is a favorite of children, who climb the lower branches and use the unripe fruit in pea shooters or slingshots. In *I Know Why the Caged Bird Sings,* Maya Angelou recalls sitting in the shade of a chinaberry tree during her childhood.

chine (chyn) the intersection of keel and planking on a flat boat, which produces a spinelike angle like ribs joining a backbone; also the spine of an animal. In Thomas Hardy's *The Mayor of Casterbridge,* a drayman rolls a barrel along a chine to keep it from bumping against the horizontal planks beneath it.

Chinese New Year a significant 15-day Chinese celebration occurring between January 21 and February 19. The focus of the festival is repaying debts, cleaning house, and resolving differences of opinion to assure a peaceful new year. At the high point of a ritual week before the new year, housewives burn a picture of Tsao Wang, the hearth god who bans evil from the door. On New Year's Eve, visiting, feasting, gift-giving, fireworks, and calls of *kung-hsi fa-ts'ai* (*guhng'* shee *fat'* sy), or "Greetings and riches to you," precede parades marked by paper lanterns and dragon dancers. In Amy Tan's *The Kitchen God's Wife,* custom requires Winnie to make up with her friend during Chinese New Year.

chink a gap, crack, or aperture in a log wall where the edges of adjoining logs fail to meet. Chinking in crude, unfinished wood structures is usually caulked or filled with mud or plaster, but weathering can cause the fill to slip out of place and allow light, rain, and wind to enter. Tom and Huck peer through the chinks in a cabin in Mark Twain's *The Adventures of Tom Sawyer.*

chinoiserie (sheen . *wahz'* ree) elegant or imaginative painted scenes or gilt oriental patterns that ornament furniture or screens; also, the characteristic design or style of lacquerware, oriental pottery and ceramics, silk, wallpaper, tapestry, bronze or porcelain figurines, and other Asian bric-a-brac. Hugh Conway, protagonist of James Hilton's *Lost Horizon,* absorbs the tasteful beauty of chinoiserie in a Tibetan lamasery called Shangri-La.

chirography (ky . *rah'* gruh . fee) scrolled, ornamented script or handwriting; formalized or overly ornate calligraphy used on important documents, formal announcements, signs, or invitations. In "The Custom House," the speaker in Nathaniel Hawthorne's *The Scarlet Letter* locates the focus of his grim novel in an envelope decorated with chirography and, appropriately, secured with a red ribbon.

chivalry (*shih'* vuhl . ree) an idealistic moral, social, and religious code associated with medieval knights, who professed allegiance to the ideals of honor, nobility, kindness, charity, courtesy, gallantry toward women, fairness, and valor. Henry Clerval is well read in romance and chivalry, as opposed to the interests of his scientific friend Victor, the title character in Mary Shelley's *Frankenstein.*

chocolate pot a heated ceramic or metal kettle used to blend milk with mocha, brandy, vanilla, and other flavorings for chocolate, which is shaved into the liquid and stirred to melt the solid bits. When Juana and Kino come to request aid from the local physician in John Steinbeck's *The Pearl,* the doctor is enjoying refreshment from the chocolate pot and refuses to help their infant, Coyotito, who suffers from the bite of a deadly scorpion.

chokecherry or **chokeberry** a low-growing native American bush of the rose family that produces clusters of bitter red to purplish-black berries. In Gary Paulsen's *Hatchet,* Brian makes himself sick on gut cherries, which he later identifies as chokecherries, a favorite flavoring in Native American pemmican and stews, jellies, sauces, and wines.

cholera (*kah'* luh . ruh) a potentially fatal bacterial inflammation of the small intestine causing acute, debilitating cramps, chills, diarrhea, vomiting, and subsequent dehydration that can kill in two to seven days. Cholera runs rampant through areas where toilet and water sanitation standards are low, particularly among refugees. In Ernest Hemingway's description of an Allied retreat through mud and slush in *A Farewell to Arms,* 7,000 soldiers die of cholera.

chopine (shah . *peen'*) a woman's shoe extravagantly stilted or elevated at toe and heel, sometimes requiring the wearer to lean on a servant. Popular in southern Europe and England during the sixteenth and seventeenth centuries and worn as overshoes to cover slippers, the cork-soled chopine protected the wearer from dirty sidewalks, rainwater, and free-flowing sewage in city streets, particularly London, Madrid, and Venice. As the tragic hero in William

Shakespeare's *Hamlet* greets the all-male players who come to perform, he notes that one lad has grown the height of a chopine.

chop suey (chahp *soo'* ee) a popular Chinese takeout dish composed of chopped fish or meat mixed with rice, bean sprouts, and diced vegetables. Derived in the late nineteenth century from the Chinese for *odds and ends,* the term denotes the use of leftovers to flavor rice. In Tennessee Williams's *A Streetcar Named Desire,* Pablo suggests that the other poker players send out for chop suey so that the foursome can eat and continue the game.

chough (chuhf) a common cliff-dwelling jackdaw, or blackbird, with shiny blue-black plumage, a yellow bill, and red legs that Shakespeare mentions frequently to give the impression of an aggressive, meddlesome creature. In *A Midsummer Night's Dream,* Puck describes the noisy flight of a flock of choughs, a minor annoyance in the idyllic, romantic world of the forest.

chow-chow a vinegary, peppery relish made by grinding together cucumber, carrot, peppers, onions, and cabbage with a piquant canning liquid. In southern cuisine, chow-chow spices up bland meals of dry peas and beans and accompanies plain slices of pork or beef. Maya Angelou, in her autobiographical *I Know Why the Caged Bird Sings,* recalls the sharp flavor that chow-chow adds to pinto beans.

chromosome aberration (*kroh'* muh . sohm *ab* . buhr . *ray'* shuhn) a freakish or unpredictable variation, malfunction, or fault in the threadlike genetic material that determines heredity through patterned cell formation and distribution, for example, the extra chromosome that produces Down's syndrome or Tay-Sachs disease. In *Hiroshima,* author John Hersey reports that residents of Hiroshima and Nagasaki did not produce chromosome aberrations until 20 years after the atomic blasts that ended World War II.

chronicle a straightforward report, public record, daybook, or objective history or account of facts or events; a detailed chronological narration of highlights common to Europe in the post-Roman era, from the sixth to the twelfth century; also, in North America in the Walum Olum, a scroll depicting in icons the history of the Delaware Indians from the time they migrated from Russia across the Bering Land Bridge to what is now Alaska. *Chronicle* is a common name for a newspaper, as demonstrated in Sir Arthur Conan Doyle's *The Hound of the Baskervilles.*

chronometer (krah . *nahm'* ih . tuhr) a precise instrument for measuring time in any weather or temperature; a navigator's timepiece in a ship, submarine, airplane, or spaceship. The version invented by British physicist Charles Wheatstone in 1835 utilizes the degree of polarization of light to establish the time. Passepartout, the valet of the protagonist, Phileas Fogg, in Jules Verne's *Around the World in Eighty Days,* insists that his heirloom watch is an accurate chronometer.

chrysalis (*kry'* suh . lihs) the intermediate, or dormant, stage of an insect life cycle; a pupa that attaches to a limb or other permanent mooring by a pad of silk tissue. The title character in Lewis Carroll's *Alice's Adventures in Wonderland* predicts that the caterpillar will one day change into a chrysalis before becoming a butterfly.

chuck wagon an American slang term for a portable kitchen carrying provisions and utensils as well as first-aid materials and other necessities. The chuck wagon formed the center of temporary evening campsites, near mines, on cattle drives or ranches, and in lumber camps. In Jack Schaefer's *Shane,* the speaker is as tall as the backboard of his father's chuck wagon.

chum chopped fish and vegetable scraps, fish oils, and fish-house refuse used as bait or to attract fish to a seining operation. Father Ko Wakatsuki is arrested for espionage after carrying chum out to sea in Jeanne Wakatsuki Houston and James D. Houston's *Farewell to Manzanar;* in Ken Kesey's *One Flew Over the Cuckoo's Nest,* George describes candlefish as chum. *See also* candlefish.

chupatty or **chapatti** (chuh . *pah'* tee) a thin, unleavened disc of bread or cake flattened in the palms and baked on a griddle or heated oven stone. Derived from the Hindi term for *wheat cakes,* the word entered English during the early nineteenth century, when Indian cuisine became known in England. Hugh Conway compliments Chang on the unexpectedly satisfying breakfast of tea, pomelo, and chupatties in James Hilton's *Lost Horizon.*

church warden an elected layperson representing an Anglican congregation by addressing routine parish needs, legal matters, requests for charity, and local concerns in church council sessions. In Victor Hugo's *Les Misérables,* a church warden asks Marius to relinquish his specified seat.

chypre (*ky'* p'r) a yellow, heavy-scented, nonalcoholic sandalwood oil pressed from the roots and trunk of a small evergreen native to parts of Asia and Cyprus (for which it is named). Called *bois de santal* in French, chypre is a common base for candles, cosmetics, sachets, and soap. It is also used in folk remedies, ceremonial fans, boxes, carved screens, and incense to mask cremation odor in Buddhist rituals. Lenina, the *femme fatale* in Aldous Huxley's *Brave New World,* dabs herself with chypre.

cicada (suh . *kay'* duh) a large-winged, stout, chirping insect, the male of which rubs his hind legs against a wide membrane on the lower end of the torso to produce a persistent drone or buzz throughout the summer and early fall as a means of courtship, to acknowledge a change in the weather, or to frighten enemies. In his silent approach toward two gunmen, Kino, protagonist of John Steinbeck's *The Pearl,* hears the harsh rasp of cicadas and tree frogs.

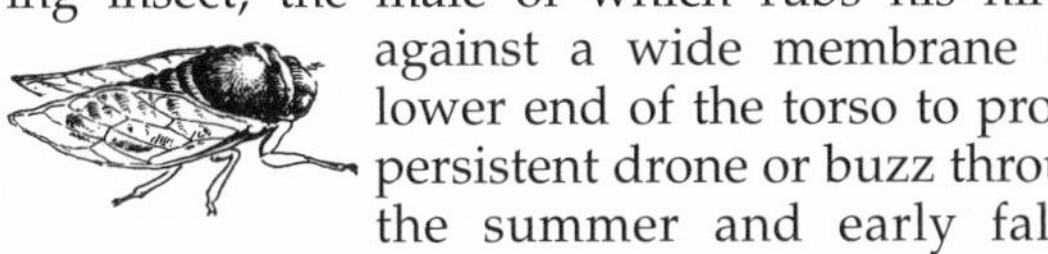

cirrus (*seer'* uhs) fleecy, silky, white high-altitude clouds formed in the troposphere into thin bands or patches of ice crystals; cirrus sometimes precede hurricanes and typhoons or follow jet vapor trails. Santiago, protagonist of Ernest Hemingway's *The Old Man and the Sea,* spies the wisps of cirrus clouds high above the cumulus heaps. *See also* cumulus.

civet (*sih'* viht) a long-torsoed, snouted carnivore related to the mongoose; the civet yields a musk scent from its anal glands that is prized as a perfume base or in soaps, aftershave, incense, and candles. In satiric jest, John calls for an ounce of civet in Aldous Huxley's *Brave New World.*

clabber a thickened or clotted cream or soured, curdled milk similar to yogurt that gathers around the dasher of a churn. Derived from *bonnyclabber,* an Irish term that spread to New England, the word refers to a farm treat of curdled milk blended with sweetener and cream and eaten as a dessert. In Toni Morrison's *Beloved,* Sethe learns long after her departure from her husband and from slavery that he watched her torment from a barn loft and smeared his mouth with clabber, an ambiguous reaction to his wife's humiliation.

clan a traditional interrelated group of tribe members claiming descent from a single ancestor, usually a prestigious male from whom the surname or tribal identity derives; a close-knit kinship or society carrying distinct obligations and taboos concerning support, intermarriage, and protocol, such as who sits at the head of the communal table and who decides the apportionment of an estate. Obierika complains to Okonkwo in Chinua Achebe's *Things Fall Apart* that white missionaries have destroyed clan solidarity.

the clap a vulgar name for gonorrhea, an inflammatory bacterial disease that can cause painful urination, swelling, blockage of the fallopian tubes, and sterility. Derived from a French term that means both rabbit warren and brothel, the word dates to the late sixteenth century, when there were no cures for the disease. In Samuel Beckett's play *Waiting for Godot,* Vladimir maligns a family named Pozzo by commenting that the mother had the clap.

clapboard (*klab'* buhrd) a stave or piece of structural lumber shaved thin on one edge and overlapped by the thick edge of the board directly above it to give texture to the finished outer wall of a frame house or to barrels, boats, or wainscoting. In Arthur Miller's play *The Crucible,* John Proctor yearns beyond the clapboard meeting houses of New England for European cathedrals.

clasp knife a large, thick-bladed folding pocketknife, jackknife, or hunting knife housing a single wide blade that is held open by a catch and used for utility chores such as cutting twigs, trimming cigars, or skinning game or scaling fish. Pap, the father of the title character in Mark Twain's *The Adventures of Huckleberry Finn,* suffers the DTs and threatens his son with a clasp knife.

claw-foot a decorative ferrule on a table leg that extends three fanciful eagle's talons around a glass or marble ball. One of the adornments of the Wingfield house in Tennessee Williams's *The Glass Menagerie* is a small claw-foot table and ivory chair typical of nineteenth-century decor.

claymore an antipersonnel land mine that hurls jagged fragments on detonation. The claymore was named for a two-edged Scottish broadsword and derives from the Gaelic for *sword.* The term entered English in the late eighteenth century. In Walter Dean Myers's *Fallen Angels,* Richie Perry sets claymores in the ground to halt infiltration by Viet Cong, who menace the camp perimeter at night.

clerical collar a stiff, upright collar or neckband fastened at the back and worn with a dark suit to indicate membership in certain sects or denominations of the Christian clergy, particularly Lutheran, Anglican, and Roman Catholic. In Alan Paton's *Cry, the Beloved Country,* the Reverend Kumalo wears a frayed clerical collar that underscores his poverty in service to God at a country parish.

clink British slang for a term in a jail, prison cell, brig, or lockup. Named for a prison in Southwark, England, the term came into use in the early sixteenth century. In Erich Maria Remarque's *All Quiet on the Western Front,* Paul Baumer and fellow hospital inmates are threatened with "clink" if they continue throwing bottles and making an uproar.

clog wood or wood-soled overshoes or carved sandals with upturned toes or working shoes elevated to protect farmworkers and tradespeople from mud; also, shoes worn by special dancing groups who make rhythmic noises from patterned steps. Called a *sabot* in France and a *geta* in Japan, the cheap, durable shoe appears around the world in varied forms, often with straps to tie it to the instep. The working-class citizens of the town in Thomas Hardy's *The Mayor of Casterbridge* wear simple clogs on their trips to town.

cloister (*kloy'* stuhr) a walled, covered colonnade, courtyard, or quadrangle; an enclosed garden or mall; a central space or atrium that is an architectural feature of a secluded society, such as the inmates of a college, university, cathedral, convent, monastery, or abbey; a barricade, restriction, or protection from distractions of the outside world. In William Shakespeare's *A Midsummer Night's Dream,* Theseus ponders Hermia's choice of marrying the man her father chooses or living her life in a cloister.

cloud chamber a receptacle containing supersaturated water vapor that reveals the tracks of charged ions, gamma rays, X-rays, protons, alpha or beta particles, or other subatomic particles; a radiation detector. Tillie looks forward to the experiment Mr. Goodman is going to conduct with a cloud chamber, an early twentieth-century invention, in Paul Zindel's play *The Effect of Gamma Rays on Man-in-the-Moon Marigolds.*

clout Indian an Indian who avoids European-American society by following ancient customs, including the wearing of a breechclout, which covers only the genitals. In Hal Borland's *When the Legends Die,* white cynics sneeringly refer to Native Americans in traditional dress as "clout Indians," an insult implying that wearing only a loin cloth and going bare-legged and bare-chested is a sign of uncivilized behavior or inferior socialization. *See also* breechclout.

clove hitch a knot consisting of two parallel hitches made in opposite directions and crossed at right angles; a builder's knot. The clove hitch is used to lash a line about a post, pole, spar, yard, or mooring cable. In Robert Louis Stevenson's *Treasure Island,* Ben Gunn refers to Jim Hawkins's predicament as a clove hitch, a common sailor's knot.

clubfoot a common deformity or malformation of the metatarsal arch or a curling of the ankle and/or heel or down-turned toes, either congenital in nature or caused by polio or spinal disease. Clubfoot is treated in infants with splints and casts; severe malformation may require surgery to tendons and ligaments. Homais, eager for fame, wants to try a new procedure to cure clubfoot in Gustave Flaubert's *Madame Bovary.*

clutch plates a coupling device activated by a spring that moves gears by means of the rotating disk of a drive shaft that engages a second disk on the transmission or drive shaft. Constant friction of these two disks, which are made of asbestos or a metal alloy, produces heat and wear that can deplete efficiency. Al is alert to sounds of the engaging clutch plates on the Joad family truck on the way from Oklahoma to California in John Steinbeck's *The Grapes of Wrath.*

C.M.E. Church the Colored Methodist Episcopal Church, a separatist sect that left the Southern Methodist Church in 1870 to devote itself to evangelism in Africa. By the time Maya Angelou mentions the group in her autobiographical *I Know Why the Caged Bird Sings,* members had altered their name to the Christian Methodist Episcopal Church.

coal box a low-speed German shell fired by a cannon known as the Black Maria. The coal box earned its name from the cloud of dense black smoke it released on detonation. Paul Baumer and other infantrymen discuss the sounds and idiosyncrasie of the coal box and various explosives and artillery in Erich Maria Remarque's *All Quiet on the Western Front.*

coalhole a coal cellar, compartment, or storage chamber built into the wall of a chimney or fireplace; also, a street-level entrance to a coal bin, chute, or storage chamber. In George Eliot's *Silas Marner,* the title character attempts to discipline his adopted daughter Eppie by shutting her in the coalhole.

coal scuttle a shallow, open metal bucket or lightweight pan or vessel with a handle or bail and a flanged lip that allows the user to dump coal into a fireplace or to stoke a stove without touching the coal. In Charles Dickens's *A Christmas Carol,* a renewed Scrooge orders Bob Cratchit to buy another coal scuttle so that the office will be better heated.

coal-whipper a dockworker who unloads coal from a barge by means of a container raised and lowered by pulleys. The bulk of the dockworker provides a counterweight to lift and lower the load. In Charles Dickens's *Great Expectations,* Pip describes the busy operation of the coal-whippers, who move measures of coal from barges onto deck.

cocaine (koh . *kayn'*) a potent, toxic alkaloid derived from coca, a shrub native to South and Central America and cultivated by Incas as a sacred plant. The leaves can be chewed or dried, ground, and dispensed as a local anesthetic to paralyze nerve endings or used illegally as a euphoric or stimulant that becomes dangerously addictive. In Alex Haley's *The Autobiography of Malcolm X,* the title character describes his experiences with cocaine, marijuana, and illegal alcohol during the early years in Harlem before he went to prison for burglary.

coccyx (*kahk'* siks) the thin, tapering triangular bone formed of four fused vertebrae at the bottom of the human spine. This delicate, semiflexible structure houses the end of the spinal cord. Derived from the Greek for *cuckoo's beak,* the term dates to the early seventeenth century. In Aldous Huxley's *Brave New World,* a radio station reports that John, the savage Zuñi, kicked reporter Primo Mellon in the coccyx.

cock a domestic rooster or gamecock bred for fighting in pairs in an enclosed arena until one of the two birds is mortally wounded. To enhance the lethal blows of the talons, promoters attach razors or metal spurs to inflict a quick kill. In Thomas Hardy's *Far from the Madding Crowd,* Bathsheba's husband, Sergeant Troy, wastes her money by gambling on matches of fighting cocks. In Ernest Hemingway's *The Old Man and the Sea,* Santiago tries to imagine the pain of a fighting cock's spur lodged in the heel.

cockade (kah . *kayd'*) a badge, rosette of ribbons, ornament, or insignia pinned to a cap or hatband; often worn by members of fraternal organizations or by the servants of royalty or of military officers. Derived from the Old French for *rooster* or *cackling,* this French Revolution–era term has become an emblem of rebellion. The rebels in Charles Dickens's *A Tale of Two Cities* wear a red, white, and blue cockade.

cocoyam (*koh'* kuh . yam) the edible starchy tuber of the taro plant, a member of the arum family that grows in the tropics and is eaten like potatoes, cooked into a paste or poi, or ground into flour, which can be mixed with water and fermented to make beer. In Chinua Achebe's *Things Fall Apart,* Okonkwo relegates the cultivating and harvesting of cocoyams to women.

coffer (*kahf'* fuhr) a wooden chest, decorative trunk, state treasury, or utilitarian strongbox; often a literal or symbolic repository of a family's or nation's fortune or monetary resources. A coffer is usually sealed against water or moths, for storing valuables, coins, ritual clothing, heirlooms, or keepsakes. Derived from the Greek for *basket,* the term, which entered English in the fourteenth century, is also applied to the church coffer, or poor box. In Homer's *Odyssey,* King Alcinous bids Queen Arete to present Odysseus a coffer containing fine clothing and a cauldron so the wanderer can wash his salt-encrusted skin and prepare for a spectacular banquet in his honor.

coffle (*kahf'* f'l) a line of slaves linked with chains at the ankle, wrist, waist, or neck and that travels as a unit to prevent escape. Derived from the Arabic for *caravan,* the term entered English in the late eighteenth century and was generally applied to a slavemaster's style of keeping order among slaves, most of whom understood no English. Paul D, protagonist of Toni Morrison's *Beloved,* recalls the humiliation of a chain gang linked like a slave coffle.

col (kahl) an elevated pass, or passageway, between mountain peaks; a depression among ridges in a mountain chain. Derived from the Latin for *neck,* the term is also described as a saddle, or gap, between summits or at either side of a rocky tor. Hugh Conway, protagonist of James Hilton's *Lost Horizon,* admires the col that overlooks Shangri-La.

cold frame *See* cucumber frame.

cold house a storage shed often constructed into the side of a hill to preserve perishable foods, particularly meat, milk, and eggs; a springhouse, usually built over a spring or creek to circulate cool air to prevent stored foods from spoiling. In Toni Morrison's *Beloved,* women store in the cold house the foods that would deteriorate in a heated kitchen or pie safe.

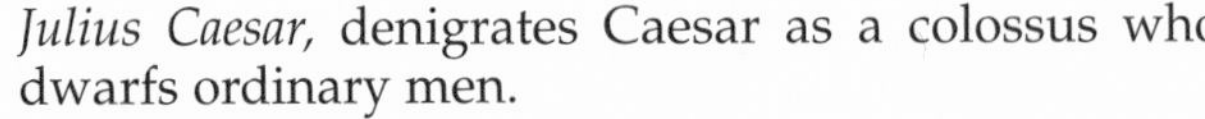

colic (*kah'* lihk) an acute abdominal spasm or paroxysm caused by the twisting, distention, or blockage of the intestine in either horses or human beings; a common bowel complaint in infants and children that is brought on by a change of diet or allergy to milk. The term *colic* derives from the Greek for *colon* and applies to hollow organs. Uncle Isom uses herbs to cure colic in Ernest Gaines's *The Autobiography of Miss Jane Pittman.*

collect (*kahl'* lehkt) a short prayer, invocation, or reading suited to the day or occasion on the Christian calendar, particularly communion. Derived from the Latin for *assemble,* the term applies to a standard part of Anglican or Roman Catholic liturgy preceding the reading of the *epistle.* At Lowood School, a setting in Charlotte Brontë's *Jane Eyre,* children assemble and repeat the collect at the beginning of each day.

colonnade (*kah* . luhn . *nayd'*) a graceful series of evenly spaced columns or supports for a portico or roof, sometimes raised to a double layer. The colonnade often defines an architectural perimeter enclosing a private grotto, fountain, public market, coliseum, cloister, or statue. The final scene between the title hero and Roxane in Edmond Rostand's *Cyrano de Bergerac* takes place in a colonnade, symbolic of Cyrano's punctual weekly visits to his old friend. *See also* cloister.

color sergeant the senior noncommissioned officer of an infantry brigade or battalion; also, a military official who protects, stores, displays, and carries into battle one of the group's collections of national, state, and company flags. When the color sergeant falters, Henry Fleming, protagonist of Stephen Crane's *The Red Badge of Courage,* grabs for the banner before it falls. *See also* battalion.

colossus (kuh . *lahs'* suhs) a gigantic, imposing statue of a muscular male figure. One of the seven wonders of the classical world, the Colossus at Rhodes, built by Chares of Lindus in 280 B.C., was a huge, awe-inspiring statue of Helios, the sun god. It stood watch over the harbor until its collapse during an earthquake in 225 B.C. Cassius, one of the conspirators in William Shakespeare's *Julius Caesar,* denigrates Caesar as a colossus who dwarfs ordinary men.

colours, the *See* color sergeant.

Colt's revolver the original handgun with a revolving chamber of ammunition that moves into place when the weapon is cocked; a six-shooter. The prototype, invented by Samuel Colt in 1836, gained popularity in 1846 when the army supplied six-shooters to American soldiers during the Mexican War. Favored by Texas Rangers, the Colt's revolver played a significant role in the settlement of the American West. By 1855, the Colt's arms works, which supplied the United States and Europe, produced more small arms than any other manufacturer in the world and made a strong commitment to helping the North defeat the South during the Civil War. Hal shoots Dub, an injured dog, with a Colt's revolver in Jack London's *The Call of the Wild. See also* pepper box.

coma a pronounced state of torpor or prolonged stupor, unresponsiveness to stimuli, or unconsciousness brought on by poison, anoxia, brain concussion or other trauma, shock, or disease, particularly epilepsy. In a comatose state, the patient fails to seek bodily comforts or nourishment and depends on intensive nursing care, usually augmented by machines to aid respiration, digestion, and excretion. In Gary Paulsen's *Dogsong,* Russel fears that Nancy's physical condition has deteriorated into a coma.

comfit (*kuhm'*. fuht) a candy or confectionery treat that contains a piece of licorice root, nut meat, seed, or dried fruit at the center and a coating of syrup over the surface; dating to the thirteenth century. Derived from the Latin for *completed,* the term entered English in the fourteenth century. In Lewis Carroll's *Alice's Adventures in Wonderland,* Alice reaches "in her pocket and [pulls] out a box of comfits" to award the animals who run in the caucus-race.

company or **battery** a military unit consisting of 150 soldiers and led by a captain. The combined strength of six or seven companies equals a battalion. Christian, Roxane's fiancé in Edmond Rostand's *Cyrano de Bergerac,* is a member of the hero's company of cadets. *See also* battalion; cadet.

compound (*kahm'* pownd) a fenced-in, cloistered, or walled-in area composed of numerous buildings, sheds, and residences; an encampment, zoo, training facility, mall, agora, or forum. In Chinua Achebe's *Things Fall Apart,* Okonkwo's family grows so large they live in separate dwellings within a single compound. *See also* cloister.

concertina (*kahn* . suhr . *tee'* nuh) **bed** a folding cot or couch that collapses, compresses, or folds like an accordion for storage when not in use; a hideaway or rollaway bed. According to Anne Frank's *The Diary of a Young Girl,* Margot sleeps on a concertina bed. *See also* opklap bed.

conch (kahnk or kahnch) a spiraled tropical seashell that houses an edible marine mollusk. Marked by a pointed end, opalescent lining, and flared outer edge, the conch, the symbol of the Greek god Triton, can be lopped off at the apex and used as a horn, which resonates a blast of air through its inner whorls and into a deep, sonorous tone. A key image in William Golding's *Lord of the Flies,* the conch, used to call an assembly, represents order and cooperation.

concierge (kon . *syehrj'* or kohn . see . *ehrzh'*) the multilingual manager or doorkeeper of a European-style hotel; the caretaker of a condominium or apartment complex; the superintendent, maintenance supervisor, or warden of a prison, castle, palace, or compound. Safe in Switzerland, Catherine Barkley and Frederick Henry follow the concierge to their room in a Montreux luxury hotel in Ernest Hemingway's *A Farewell to Arms.*

concubine (*kahn'* kyoo . byn) a bedroom slave, mistress, or an unmarried woman who cohabits with a man; a kept woman whose sole purpose is the sexual delight and satisfaction of her keeper; a secondary wife, usually of lesser social status than the primary wife. A status symbol for Wang Lung in Pearl S. Buck's *The Good Earth* is his ability to afford a concubine in addition to a wife and children. To the concubine in Amy Tan's *The Kitchen God's Wife,* life among favored wives forces her to accept a marriage proposal and elope, leaving her daughter behind to bear the family ignominy, devaluation, and harassment.

condensed milk a thick, sweetened milk product made from whole milk from which excess water is evaporated. Condensed milk is used to flavor coffee or tea and forms the base of certain types of cream pies, cake icings, puddings, flans, and fudge. In Ernest Hemingway's *The Old Man and the Sea,* Santiago takes his morning coffee from old condensed milk cans.

conduit (*kahn'* doo . iht) a pipe, tube, duct, or channel through which a stream or collected groundwater is directed or in which wires or cables are protected from dampness or traffic; a natural or excavated underground passage. Trapped in a cul-de-sac in Victor Hugo's *Les Misérables,* Jean Valjean tries to rescue himself and Cosette by climbing a delapidated conduit.

confinement pregnancy, lying-in, or the days preceding childbirth; an outdated euphemism for the final period of gestation when a woman was considered too heavy and awkward to show herself in public. In Frederick Douglass's autobiography *Narrative of the Life of Frederick Douglass,* Mr. Covey's concubine Caroline receives excellent care during her confinement.

confirmation (kahn . fuhr . *may'* shuhn) a climactic ritual according membership privileges to people who are joining a Christian church; the sacrament blessing young Christians, anointing with holy oil, or requiring the laying on of hands to confer God's grace. According to Rudolfo Anaya's *Bless Me, Ultima,* baptism and confirmation begin the process of salvation, but Christians do not reach a state of grace until they receive first communion, symbolically taking into their bodies the flesh and blood of Christ.

conjure (*kahn'* juhr) to cast a magic spell, to jinx or hex, to bewitch or charm; to summon a spirit or demon, or to overpower the will of a person by forcing the conjured one to perform acts at the command of the conjurer; to mesmerize and exploit a victim by supernatural incantation, voodoo, or application of a magic potion. In Arthur Miller's *The Crucible,* Reverend John Hale asks Mary if she is being conjured by someone in the courtroom.

conked head naturally curly or kinky hair that is straightened by application of congolene or homemade straightener. A product invented by Sarah Breedlove Walker, America's first black female millionaire, in 1910, hair straightener involved the application of a strong cream with a hot iron comb. In Alex Haley's *The Autobiography of Malcolm X,* the title character describes his friend Shorty applying Vaseline to Malcolm's ears and neck, combing a mixture of white potatoes, lye, and eggs through his hair, and then rinsing out the mixture with soap and water. In Lorraine Hansberry's *A Raisin in the Sun,* Walter admires a jazz musician with conked hair, a style that demonstrates a radical departure from traditional hairstyles for black men.

conquistador (kuhn . *kees'* tuh . dohr) *pl.* **conquistadores** a professional soldier of fortune, explorer, or military rogue from Spain or Portugal who traveled in the Western Hemisphere during the fifteenth century in search of glory, gold, or riches. The most notorious conquistadores—Hernán Cortés, Francisco Pizarro, Hernán de Soto, and Vasco Balboa—earned a reputation for brutalizing and slaughtering native peoples and looting the Aztec and Inca empires. In Rudolfo Anaya's *Bless Me, Ultima,* Antonio dreams of rough, rapacious adventurers who descended from the conquistadores.

consecrated candle a votive candle two to three inches tall that is lit in a place of worship and anchored in a small glass container near the altar to symbolize a wish, oath, thanksgiving, festal or commemorative anniversary, or prayer of consecration. In John Steinbeck's *The Pearl,* Juana lights a scrap of consecrated candle and examines Kino's bruised forehead.

conservatory (kuhn . *suhr'* vuh . toh . ree) a greenhouse or glass-topped sunroom in a home or museum where exotic plants are propagated and displayed; a hothouse for growing tropical plants, vines, or fruit trees that require a warm, moist atmosphere. In Charlotte Brontë's *Jane Eyre,* the willful Georgiana breaks off the buds of hothouse plants in the conservatory.

constellation (con . stuh . *lay'* shuhn) a conventional designation of one of 88 identifiable patterns or clusters of stars; a configuration of heavenly spheres joined by hypothetical lines to form the archer Sagittarius, the hunter Orion, Pegasus, Cassiopeia, Andromeda, the Gemini, Capricorn, Leo, and other imaginary figures bearing Latin names, based on a naming system derived by Ptolemy and completed during modern times with the discovery of more stars. In her *Mythology,* Edith Hamilton connects mythic stories with the formation of the Great Bear and the Lesser Bear, two familiar constellations commonly known as the Big Dipper and Little Dipper.

consumption (kuhn . *suhmp'* shuhn) tuberculosis or other contagious wasting diseases caused by a bacterium that is inhaled and incubated in the respiratory system. Infection, which may be delayed during a period of dormancy, ultimately depletes body tissue, develops nodules, or weakens an organ, particularly the lungs, brain, genitals, joints, or bones. In Henrik Ibsen's *A Doll's House,* Nora declares that Dr. Rank has consumption of the spine.

contrition, act of (kuhn . *trih'* shuhn) a humble gesture of remorse or regret for a personal fault or wrongful behavior; a penitent act or request for forgiveness that precedes a sincere change of heart; compunction to apologize or atone for a shameful or harmful act toward another person or group. In Herman Melville's *Benito Cereno,* Juan Robles, after being tossed overboard, manages to stay afloat long enough to make acts of contrition.

convolutions (kahn . voh . *loo'* shuhnz) **of the brain**

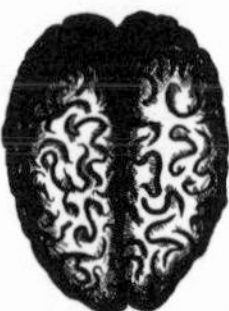

convex folds in the cranial tissue on the brain's surface; intricate curves, gyri, and inward whorls and valleys in the cortical tissue of the cerebrum. In Ray Bradbury's *Fahrenheit 451,* Granger claims that his grandfather's influence can be spotted in the convolutions of Granger's brain. In Daniel Keyes's *Flowers for Algernon,* deterioration in the mouse's brain convolutions predicts a similar decline in Charlie Gordon, the first human to undergo Dr. Strauss's experimental psychosurgery.

convoy (*kahn'* voy) a group of motor vehicles organized for maximum protection of a vital delivery; an armed escort of troops, planes, or ships to conduct civilians or merchants through hostile or dangerous territory; also, a group of vacationers, bikers, truckers, or motorcyclists traveling in a tight formation or single file. The term derives from the French for *accompany.* The Captain claims to have been a liaison officer of a British convoy in Alexander Solzhenitsyn's *One Day in the Life of Ivan Denisovich.*

convulsion (kuhn . *vuhl'* shuhn) an involuntary paroxysm or irregular contraction of muscles in the limbs; a cramp, spasm, or seizure; an unpredictable, violent contortion of the body accompanied by foaming at the mouth, biting of the tongue, and loss of control of the bowels or bladder; abnormal motor activity triggered by the nervous system as a result of hysteria, high fever, epilepsy, brain tumor, or other physical abnormality or disease. In Paul Zindel's *The Effect of Gamma Rays on Man-in-the-Moon Marigolds,* Tillie fears Ruth's tendency to have convulsions.

cooperage (*koo'* puhr . ihj) a workshop where workers called coopers make and sell barrels as well as repair wooden casks, tuns, tubs, and other objects requiring watertight connections of kiln-dried curved pieces of lumber or staves bound with hoops. Derived from the Greek for *cup,* the word, now preserved in the surname *Cooper,* entered English in the fourteenth century and refers to a trade dating to first-century Switzerland. In Conrad Richter's *The Light in the Forest,* the cooperage is the scene of a struggle between whites and True Son and Half Arrow that nearly results in a scalping.

cootie slang for body lice, a wingless insect that infests the head and pubic hair; a parasite feeding off the blood of a human host. Derived from a Malaysian term in wide use in the British military during World War I, this derogatory term entered English in the early twentieth century. Miss Caroline, the elementary school teacher in Harper Lee's *To Kill a Mockingbird,* recommends that Burris use strong soap to rid himself of cooties. *See also* crabs.

coppice (*kahp'* pihs) a harvested thicket, spinney, or a stand of trees that is carefully cut back and new growth pruned and tended to supply the woodkeeper with shoots and root suckers for weaving into wickets and fences, branches for tool handles, rudimentary trunks for firewood, and ash for pottery glaze and soap. This medieval system of husbandry, mentioned in Hermann Hesse's *Siddhartha,* Jane Austen's *Pride and Prejudice,* and Sir Arthur Conan Doyle's *The Hound of the Baskervilles,* was essential to the architectural method of wattle and daub, a weaving of branches into mats and plastering over the frame.

copse (kahps) *See* coppice.

copy-book a manual or handbook of samples for students to copy to learn the alphabet or to improve handwriting in both block and cursive styles. Colonial copy-books often contained aphorisms or paragraphs on a moral topic or verses from the Bible and were, therefore, considered dull, dry reading for children. In his autobiography, *Narrative of the Life of Frederick Douglass,* the author describes working in Master Thomas's copy-book as a means of improving his penmanship.

coracle (*kohr'* uh . k'l) a small, lightweight cup-shaped boat fashioned from a waterproof hide, canvas, or tarpaulin stretched over a sapling or wicker frame. The word, derived from the Welsh for *boat* and limited to the British Isles, entered English in the sixteenth century. Similar to the circular Indian bullboat, the coracle, which was large enough for five passengers, was oblong or round in shape and required special effort to keep its awkward shape moving forward. Paddlers or polers had to halt its natural inclination to spin, especially in rough waters. In Robert Louis Stevenson's *Treasure Island,* Jim Hawkins sets out in a crude coracle made of goatskin. *See also* bullboat.

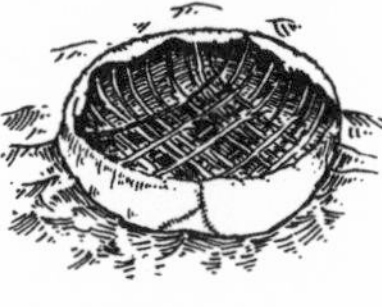

corded bedstead a slatless bed frame composed of a wooden rectangle topped by interwoven cord or rope passed through holes bored in opposite sides. Atop the cording lie the mattress, pillows, and other bedcoverings. When Telemachus prepares for bed in Homer's *Odyssey,* his nurse, Eurycleia, escorts him to his corded bedstead, hangs up his tunic, and latches the door for the night. *See also* rope bed.

cormorant (*kohr'* muh . ruhnt) a dark, long-necked, web-footed diving bird common to steep-sided seacoasts; originally, a sea raven. To satisfy its hunger and feed its young, the cormorant employs a sharp curved bill and expandable throat pouch in harvesting fish and crustaceans and can be trained to fish for human owners. In Scott O'Dell's *The Island of the Blue Dolphins,* which is set in the Catalina Islands off California, cormorants and gulls infest the rocky ledges.

corn crib or **corn cratch** an elevated rectangular enclosure or storage facility formed of slatted sides and bottom to ventilate drying corn and prevent mold until the kernels are shelled from the cob and ground for meal or animal feed. In Robert Newton Peck's *A Day No Pigs Would Die,* Rob's father uses a rope wrapped around a capstan and tied to Solomon the bull to pull a corn crib into place to serve as a pen for Rob's pig. *See also* capstan.

corn dodger deep-fried bread balls common to the cuisine of the southern United States. Dodgers are shaped from a stiff batter made with cornmeal, flour, eggs, sugar, and milk and cooked in oil; a hushpuppy, pone, or cake of cornbread. Jim feeds Huck corn dodgers, buttermilk, pork, cabbage, and greens during their sojourn on the Mississippi in Mark Twain's *The Adventures of Huckleberry Finn;* similarly, in John Steinbeck's *The Grapes of Wrath,* food is so scarce that Ma Joad is reduced to frying wads of cornmeal and water in lard and pan drippings. During the trek into Indian territory in Charles Portis's *True Grit,* Rooster packs a large bag of corn dodgers for trail food.

cornice (*kohr'* nihs) a horizontal decorative band or projection that crowns the top of a column, edifice, entablature, or wall. Derived from the Greek *corona,* the term names the ornamental molding that caps or frames the outside of a finished architectural structure or the upper edge of an inner wall. In the final scene of Thomas Hardy's *Tess of the D'Urbervilles,* Angel Clare and his sister-in-law gaze upward to the cornice of a tower, where prison officials raise a black flag on a staff to announce Tess's execution.

coronet (kohr . uh . *neht'*) a slender chaplet, crown, headband, or tiara made of metal and precious stones; a ceremonial wreath, circlet, or ring woven of flowers and vines to designate heraldic, royal, or noble rank. In William Shakespeare's *Julius Caesar,* Caesar's polite but unconvincing refusal of a coronet at a public ceremony worries his adversaries that he intends to supplant the Roman republic with a monarchy.

corps a major subdivision of an army, consisting of 100,000 troops; two corps plus about 25,000 support troops make up an army. The corps comprises divisions of various strengths ranging from 3,500 to 18,000 and is commanded by a lieutenant general. The term is also used to refer to a large group of people organized for a specific purpose; for example, in Alex Haley's *The Autobiography of Malcolm X,* Malcolm acknowledges the contribution to the local people of the 600 Peace Corps volunteers in Nigeria. *See also* army; division.

corral (kuh . *ral'*) a holding pen, stall, paddock, or enclosure that confines cattle, mules, llamas, or horses; also, a trap used in the capture of wild animals, such as prairie mustangs, or the place where wild animals are gentled or broken. From an elevated position on the corral, Bob catches his first glimpse of the title character in Jack Schaefer's *Shane.*

corrugated (*kohr'* ruh . *gay* . tihd) **iron** rigid galvanized iron sheets fortified, grooved, or strengthened by furrows and ridges in parallel rows and used as roofing. The alternation of wavy grooves increases the strength of this form of roofing because it prevents puddling of rainwater by channeling precipitation to the ground. Miss Sasaki is pinned by a fallen bookcase, plaster, and corrugated iron after the atomic bomb blast described in John Hersey's *Hiroshima.*

corset a stiff, confining, and unyielding undergarment bolstered by stays or boning and held in place by lacing or hooks and eyes and often finished with extended elastic bands to secure the tops of stockings. The corset was worn over a woman's torso from breasts to hips to support or conform the figure to the standards of fashion or propriety. The corset remained in vogue until 1914, when Mary Phelps Jacob patented her brassiere, hand-sewn from silk handkerchiefs and ribbon. According to Scout in Harper Lee's *To Kill a Mockingbird,* Aunt Alexandra was testy on Sundays because she wore a corset to recreate her former hour-glass figure by pinching in the waist, flaring out the posterior, and pushing her breasts "to giddy heights."

cosmology (kahz . *mah'* luh . gee) the study, theory, or philosophy of rules or conditions that define or control time, space, natural phenomena, and the dynamics of the physical universe as a whole; a world view. As in John Milton's *Paradise Lost,* the cosmology described in Arthur Miller's *The Crucible* calls for Satan to perform an active role opposite God in the perpetual duel for human souls.

cossack (*kahs'* sak) a member of a skilled equestrian paramilitary unit that served the expansionist aims of the Russian czars and guarded the frontier, or steppes, particularly the border of Poland. Before 1917, these freebooters, similar to the Japanese *ronin,* numbered around 4.4 million and lived a semiautonomous existence free of government control. The sixteenth-century term derives from the Turkish word for *adventurer.* In Chaim Potok's *The Chosen,* Reuven's father narrates the violent attack of mounted cossacks on Polish Jews.

cotter (*kaht'* tuhr) a pin, rod, wedge, key, or bolt that passes through a hole or channel to unite two parts of a harness or machinery; a split pin bent like a hairpin, then passed through holes in adjoining metal parts and flanged, or spread apart, at the ends to secure the connection. At the request of his father, Rob fetches the oxbow and cotter in Robert Newton Peck's *A Day No Pigs Would Die.*

cotterel (*kaht'* tr'l) a moveable iron crane, arm, hook or bracket on which to hang a kettle at a fireplace; the rotating bar that moves a cookpot over the flame or out to the hearth for easy stirring and serving. While thinking over a melody, Angel Clare notices that Tess's words keep time to the bubbling kettle hanging from the cotterel in Thomas Hardy's *Tess of the D'Urbervilles.*

cotton boll a tough, taloned pod bearing an oily seed and bursting when ripe to display puffs of cotton fiber. After the fibers are removed for use in textiles, the boll is crushed and blended into animal feed; the seed is ground and formed into cotton meal cakes to be processed further into soap, vegetable oil, margarine, or industrial lubricant. The pickers mentioned in Maya Angelou's *I Know Why the Caged Bird Sings* suffer fatigue and pain from repeated snags of their fingertips against prickly cotton bolls.

cottonwood a rapid-growing, showy member of the willow family common to stream banks and lowlands. Cottonwoods are used primarily for screening and decorative landscaping; the soft inner fiber is suitable for pulp or cheap lumber. In Mark Twain's *The Adventures of Huckleberry Finn,* Huck and Jim hide in a cottonwood thicket and wait until nightfall to move their raft.

couloir (kool . *wahr'*) a steep mountain gully, gorge, ravine, or pass. Derived from the French word for *slide,* the word entered English in the early nineteenth century and is a standard part of mountain climbing jargon. In James Hilton's *Lost Horizon,* Hugh Conway ponders the col and couloir of a prominent mountain slope as he takes pleasure in Shangri-La. *See also* col.

council house or **council lodge** a meeting house for the forest Indians of the northeastern United States. The council house served as a caucus site or meeting place for tribal leaders and spokespersons, who conferred to settle boundary disputes or determine intertribal matters. In Conrad Richter's *The Light in the Forest,* True Son's foster father forces the boy to the council house of the white settlers, who return him to Paxton Township and his parents, the Butlers. *See also* caucus.

counterpane or **counterpin** a heavy quilted bedcovering; an ornate spread decorated with raised figures; a coverlet or duvet stitched in a criss-cross pattern. An English word derived from the French for *embroidered quilt,* the word has been in use since the fifteenth century. In Edith Wharton's *Ethan Frome,* the title character and the family housekeeper, Mattie Silver, return from town and find Ethan's wife, Zeena, wrapped in a counterpane and standing at the door.

coup (koo) a military honor achieved after a Plains Indian stole the enemy's horse or touched his living body or corpse during battle. This harmless tap with a coup stick, wand, rattle, or bow offered a humane way of celebrating courage without dismembering a fallen enemy or causing needless deaths in intertribal warfare. In his autobiography, *Black Elk Speaks,* by John G. Neihardt, the narrator recalls a ritual coup for which a brave might be awarded an eagle feather as perpetual reminder of military service.

coupé (koo . *pay'* or koop) a closed two-door, four-seater automobile distinguished by a fold-down front seat to accommodate passengers in the back and by a high, rounded or sloped trunk. In F. Scott Fitzgerald's *The Great Gatsby,* a coupé lies in a ditch after one of Gatsby's lavish parties.

court an open square surrounded by rooms and a covered walkway; an atrium, quadrangle, or open-air chamber covered by a skylight or shaded with awnings. Wang Lung, the protagonist of Pearl S. Buck's *The Good Earth,* builds a separate court to house his concubine. *See also* cloister; colonnade; concubine.

courtier (*kor'* tyuhr) an attendee, staff member, aide, or ambassador at a royal court or palace; in a less flattering light, a hanger-on, flatterer, sycophant, or favor seeker. In Lewis Carroll's *Alice's Adventures in Wonderland,* courtiers who attend the King and Queen of Hearts are dressed in diamonds, symbolic of lavish court dress.

court-martial a military tribunal, hearing, or trial outside the jurisdiction of the civilian system of justice; a select group of officers who study evidence and decide appropriate penalties for infractions of military code committed by enlisted or commissioned personnel. According to Walter Dean Myers's *Fallen Angels,* soldiers in Vietnam who disobey official orders are subject to court-martial.

court-plaster strips of silk coated with glycerin, isinglass, and adhesive and used as a facial decoration, such as a beauty mark or fake mole; also, medicated adhesive strips used as bandages. Named for its popularity at court, this term entered English during the last quarter of the eighteenth century, when ornate fashions such as powdered wigs accentuated fantasy in personal dress. According to the railroad agent in Willa Cather's *My Antonia,* Wick Cutter leaves town with court-plaster stripped across his face. *See also* patch.

cowl a hood, often part of a caftan or anorak; a woman's linen or silk neck draping or high, loose-necked sweater worn to keep cold air off the neck and shoulders. Also, the face-obscuring uniform of religious orders who incline the head in prayer, thus veiling their features in the folds of the cowl. In Hermann Hesse's *Siddhartha,* the title character recognizes a monk in a yellow cowl as the Buddha.

cowpuncher American slang for a cowboy, herder, drover, rancher, or mounted farmworker who prods or drives cattle or horses over open range to market; a performer on the professional rodeo circuit; also, a buckeroo, gaucho, or *vaquero.* In Jack Schaefer's *Shane,* Joe assures his wife that the title character was at one time a cowpuncher.

cowrie (*kow'* ree) a glossy, finely grooved, egg-shaped shell of a sea mollusk shaped with a central rise leveling out to a flat bottom and serrated edge; a form of shell currency used in Nigeria, as mentioned in Chinua Achebe's *Things Fall Apart,* and in other African and Pacific Rim countries. In R. K. Narayan's "An Astrologer's Day," the main character carries a square of cloth and a dozen cowrie shells as professional equipment.

coxcomb (*kahks'* kohm) a conceited, overdressed male; a showy dandy, fop, or clotheshorse; a vain, pretentious show-off sporting fine clothes and overly refined mannerisms and accomplishments, particularly dance steps, table manners, or horsemanship. In Emily Brontë's *Wuthering Heights,* Hindley accuses Heathcliff of being an interloper and coxcomb.

coxswain (*kahk'* suhn) the steerer of a jolly boat or director of the rowers on a racing shell or scull; the senior petty officer of a submarine or ship. A Middle English term dating to the fifteenth century, the word indicates a *boat servant.* Mr. Israel Hands is the coxswain and principal crewman left on the ship in Robert Louis Stevenson's *Treasure Island* when Jim Hawkins creeps aboard.

crabs a slang term for a contagious type of body lice that infest body hair, especially in the pubic area during intimate relations. Crabs feed on human blood and cause intense itching, rashes, and skin irritation. Maya Angelou's mother questions her daughter about crabs in a mother-daughter discussion about sex in *I Know Why the Caged Bird Sings. See also* cootie.

cracker a derogatory term for an ignorant or illiterate southern white bigot, especially a smart-mouthed, boastful, or swaggering rural racist who often exacerbates local disharmony or brutalizes, menaces, or takes advantage of nonwhite neighbors. The title character in Gary Paulsen's *Nightjohn* has reason to fear entanglements with crackers because he breaks the law by teaching slaves to read and write.

cracklin' bread corn bread made from batter mixed with the crisp shreds of pig or goose skin that remain after lard has been rendered or the skin has been roasted. In Harper Lee's *To Kill a Mockingbird,* Calpurnia shows her affection for Jem and Scout, the son and daughter of her employer, Atticus Finch, by baking a pan of cracklin' bread.

crack-the-whip *See* pop-the-whip.

cradler a worker wielding a scythe equipped with a framework of long-tined forks perpendicular to the blade that cuts, catches, and lays in even windrows the harvested stalks of grain. After cradling, the dried grain is gathered into sheaves or shocks or baled. During the time that Paxton cradlers were harvesting grain, Indians stole Johnny Butler, the protagonist of Conrad Richter's *A Light in the Forest.*

crap game a dice game played by two or more throwers and observers who bet on the outcome of each throw. A score of 7 or 11 on the first throw wins the game and allows the shooter to continue; an immediate loss accompanies tallies of 2, 3, or 12. In his autobiography, *Black Boy,* Richard Wright claims that he had little interest in crap games played in the locker room after work.

cravat (kruh . *vat'*) an ornate lace or linen neckerchief, band, fichu, jabot, ascot, neckcloth, or scarf accentuated with an intricate knot, stickpin, or loose, flowing ends that were sometimes twisted or looped into a waistcoat or buttonhole; an item of men's neckwear that developed into the modern necktie. The French adopted this fashion accessory around 1650 from Croatian mercenaries, from whom the tie takes its name. In Mark Twain's *The Adventures of Tom Sawyer,* the superintendent who mounts the pulpit wears a fringed cravat as broad as a banknote.

crawdad slang name for a crayfish, a small, spiny, lobster-shaped crustacean that hides in mud or under rocks and ledges in freshwater streams and creeks. Equipped with meaty pincers, crawdads are prized as a delicacy, particularly in Creole cookery. In Robert Newton Peck's *A Day No Pigs Would Die,* Rob entertains his pig Pinky at the crawdad hole.

crèche (krehsh) the French term for the traditional miniature or live Christian tableau depicting the Holy Family—Joseph, Mary, and the infant Jesus—grouped in a farm or pasture setting in which the Christ Child, who is the central figure, sleeps in a manger or animal feed box; domesticated oxen, cows, and sheep along with shepherds and traveling sages follow a bright star and come to worship the child. In Margaret Atwood's *The Handmaid's Tale,* a public execution lights up with sunlight like a Christmas crèche, a paradox of the savagery to which a fundamentalist Christian society has sunk in its drive to exterminate undesirables while it breeds human young from devout parents.

Creole (*kree'* ohl) an American native, particularly from the Gulf states, who is born of mixed African, French, Portuguese, or Spanish descent; also, the cuisine, dance, style of dress, and patois spoken by Creoles. This eighteenth-century term, derived from the Portuguese for *person born in the colonies,* applies to numerous racial and cultural blends, usually including

French immigrants. In Ernest Gaines's *The Autobiography of Miss Jane Pittman,* Jane lives peacefully among her neighbors until a racist Creole, Albert Cluveau, murders her son. *See also* Cajun; pidgin.

crêpe-de-chine (*krayp* . duh . *sheen'*) literally, Chinese crepe, a soft, sheer or gauzy, silky material that drapes appealingly about the body in blouses, dresses, slips, gowns, peignoirs, hatbands, or scarves. When Nick meets Myrtle in F. Scott Fitzgerald's *The Great Gatsby,* she is dressed in crêpe-de-chine.

cress pungent, bitter green plants of the mustard family common to marshy or damp soil. High in vitamin C, rock cress, watercress, peppercress, and garden cress provide the tender sprouts, rounded leaves, and stems that are used in salads, in meat or cheese sandwiches, and as a garnish to roasted meat. In Pearl S. Buck's *The Good Earth,* fragrant bunches of cress are among the many herbs and vegetables sold at the farmer's market.

cresset (*krehs'* siht) a metal brazier, torch, or lantern mounted on a staff or set in a wall sconce; a vented basket or vessel holding oil, charcoal, wood, or other fuel and set ablaze along walkways, plazas, colonnades, and gardens to light night activities and processions. Derived from the Latin for *small lamp,* the term dates to the fourteenth century. Penelope's gluttonous suitors set up cressets to light their outdoor dances and entertainments in Homer's *Odyssey. See also* sconce.

cretin (*kree'* tihn) a person suffering profound retardation caused by severe hypothyroidism before birth and during the growth years. This endocrine imbalance produces coarse features, discordant voice, stunted growth, limited mental capacity, dystrophic limbs, low metabolism, and freakish body malformations. Vladimir and Estragon conclude that Lucky is a half-wit and cretin in Samuel Beckett's *Waiting for Godot.*

cribbage a one-deck card game for two to four players for which players keep score on a pegboard pierced with 4 rows of 30 holes each. Credited as an invention of the seventeenth-century Cavalier poet Sir John Suckling, the game may take its name from the Greek word for *reed basket.* In Jack London's *White Fang,* Bill, daunted by two weeks of 50-below weather, wishes he were at Fort McGurry playing cribbage.

crimping iron a heated metal rod with a latch that is used to grasp hair to make waves or curls; also, a silversmith's tool that produces wavy or regular parallel lines, corrugated folds, or fluting on metal surfaces. The crimping iron and solution designed to suit the hair of black women was designed and marketed by Madame Sarah Walker, the first black millionaire. After injuring his hand, the main character disdains to show his replacement how to hold a crimping iron in Esther Forbes's *Johnny Tremain.*

crinoline (*krihn'* oh . lihn) a bell- or oval-shaped petticoat, boned and hooped cage, or quilted underskirt made of coarse woven horsehair netting, cotton, or linen and stiffened with starch or supported by taped bands to line a hat or to support a heavily flounced ball gown, bustle, or train. Derived from the Latin for *hair linen,* the term reached the height of popularity in the mid-1800s. Although dressed in a crinoline and skirts, Jensine accompanies her husband up steep paths in Isak Dinesen's "The Pearls."

croaker sack *See* croker sack.

crockery basin the forerunner of the modern lavatory, a crockery basin or a shallow earthenware or porcelain pan or washbowl, often decorated with painted figures or filigree edging and fitted to a wooden rack or cabinet and mirror; a drainless lavabo that is filled from an outside source and emptied into a slop bucket after use. In Conrad Richter's *The Light in the Forest,* True Son, who was brought up by the Lenni Lenape, has to be taught to wash with soap and water from the crockery basin.

croker sack or **croaker sack** or **crocus sack** a loosely woven burlap bag that is sewn shut with loose stitches at the end to contain peanuts, turnips, sweet potatoes, and other produce on its way to market; a gunny sack tied about the waists or over the shoulders of field hands to hold fresh-picked cotton, vegetables, nuts, or fruit. In Harper Lee's *To Kill a Mockingbird,* Mr. Cunningham delivers croker sacks filled with hickory nuts to pay Atticus Finch for legal work.

Cro-Magnon (kroh . *mag'* nuhn or *ma'* nyuhn) a broad-faced, prehistoric nomad or cave dweller living in Europe during the Pleistocene epoch and distinguished from earlier hominids by their erect, bipedal posture, creation of cave art and religion, use of fire, and the invention of tools and weapons made from bone, tusks, and stone. Brian contrasts his crude attempts at fire-building with the skills of a Cro-Magnon in Gary Paulsen's *Hatchet.*

cross belt a white woven strip or band that crossed the chest and back over the uniform of the French soldier; a pair of transverse or X-shaped bandoliers or bandoleros. In Victor Hugo's *Les Misérables,* rebels mingle with other citizens by dressing in uniforms, cross belts, and shakos. *See also* shako.

croupier (*kroo'* pyay) the attendant to a faro dealer; the distributor of tokens and winnings at a gambling table or casino. Derived from the French for *horse's rump,* the word entered English in the early eighteenth century and implies that the croupier rides behind the saddle, or center of action. In Ken Kesey's *One Flew over the Cuckoo's Nest,* McMurphy plays the part of a croupier at his gambling table.

crown an obsolete British silver coin worth five shillings or one quarter pound, roughly three days' wages for an English day laborer in the mid-nineteenth century, who earned from seven to ten shillings per week. In Jorge Luis Borges's "The Garden of Forking Paths," the speaker finds a watch and chain, a crown, and a few shillings and pence among Captain Madden's possessions. *See also* shilling; half-a-crown.

crowning the appearance of the top of the fetus's head at the mouth of the vagina, or birth canal, during the final stage of a normal labor, signaling a normal presentation and imminent delivery. In Margaret Atwood's *The Handmaid's Tale,* the term carries ambiguous significance for the female infant, whose life will not be crowned with privilege or honor unless she is fertile and bears children for the fundamentalist-run state.

crucible (*kroo'* sih . b'l) a heavy earthenware, graphite, platinum, or porcelain vessel or melting pot capable of withstanding the high temperatures of an annealing furnace, which melts materials such as silver for belt buckles or hollowware. The crucible is shaped like a bowl or ewer with a handle or indentations for tongs and a spout or lip for pouring. In Esther Forbes's *Johnny Tremain,* Dove retaliates against Johnny's pride by setting him up for an accident with a faulty crucible, which spills molten silver on Johnny's hand and ends his apprenticeship to a silversmith. By metaphoric extension, Arthur Miller's play *The Crucible* depicts the test of courage and faith in a community that presses for the execution of suspected witches. *See also* annealing furnace.

crucifixion *See* Stations of the Cross.

crude oil raw, unrefined petroleum with the impurities (nitrogen, oxygen, and sulfur) that existed in its natural state while still in the earth. By heating oil to certain temperatures, the refiner extracts a pure product to be used for specific purposes, such as fuel oil, gasoline, diesel fuel, kerosene, lubricants, asphalt, and solvents. In Theodore Taylor's *The Cay,* the island of Curaçao is important to the Allies during World War II because the refinery there purifies oil and separates it into usable products and fuels to aid the war effort.

cruet stand a rack, base, or carrier fitted with glass vials, casters, or pitchers containing everyday table condiments, such as salt, pepper, oil, and vinegar, the latter two being liquids that must be shaken together to attain a blend. When served from a cruet stand, portions of each liquid are poured separately over salad or cooked greens. In Joseph Conrad's "The Secret Sharer," the steward polishes the cruet stand, a symbol of the captain and his stowaway, who represent the complementary sides of a single personality.

cruiser a fast-moving, light-armored sea vessel of 15,000 tons or less that is more maneuverable than a battleship because it carries less artillery. Introduced by the British in 1880 and replaced by the better-equipped destroyers in the late twentieth century after the development of missile warfare, the cruiser is able to remain at sea for long periods of time to collect information, scout, or raid; to engage land-based artillery in night battles; to precede a landing force onto the shoreline; and to blockade or capture enemy ships. In William Golding's *Lord of the Flies,* rescue comes to the boys in the form of a search team from an English cruiser.

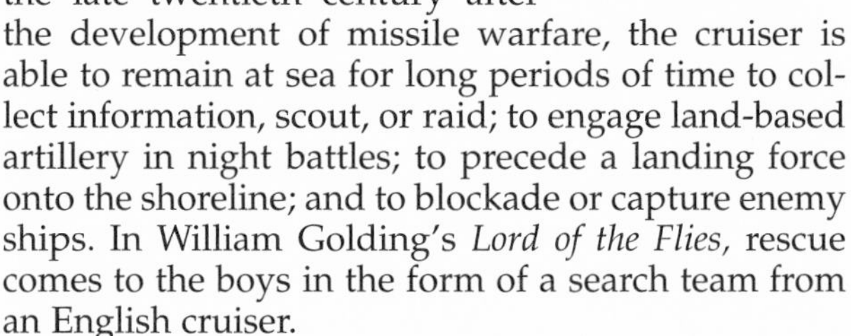

crusade an aggressive, protracted fight or lethal military expedition launched or sanctioned by a pope or religious hierarchy, grounded on high, idealized moral principles, and waged to further a cause or to attain some basic right or ownership, often to recover usurped church property, icons, or sovereignty. The term derives from the Latin word for *cross,* a prominent Christian symbol. The most memorable crusades in world history are the Catholic Church's costly drives against Islamic rulers of Jerusalem and Palestine in the eleventh, twelfth, and thirteenth centuries, during which troops carried with them a garrison of monks who served as medics. To Jurgis, protagonist in Upton Sinclair's *The Jungle,* the formation of a union to protect workers' interests is a holy mission synonymous with a religious crusade to recapture holy land.

cucumber frame or **cold frame** an enclosure planted with seeds and topped with a hinged glass or clear plastic lid to allow sun to warm the soil so that gardeners can get an early start on the spring growing season. As the days grow warmer, the lid is propped open to allow warm air to circulate over the seedlings to prevent disease or sun scald and to acclimate the sheltered plants. While Alice chases the White Rabbit in Lewis Carroll's *Alice's Adventures in Wonderland,* the rabbit falls through a cucumber frame. When the shepherd Gabriel woos Bathsheba in Thomas Hardy's *Far from the Madding Crowd,* he names a cucumber frame as one of the gifts his bride will receive.

cud (kuhd) the partially digested food from the paunch, or first stomach, of a cow, goat, sheep, deer, antelope, giraffe, camel, or other ruminant animal. The stomach, distended with the gas caused by fermentation, disgorges the mass, which the animal chews more thoroughly, then swallows again for further digestion in the last three stomachs. In George Orwell's *Animal Farm,* the animals gather round Old Major to hear about his great vision, with the cows contentedly chewing their cuds and the others finding comfortable spots on the straw.

cuddy (*kuhd'* dee) the sheltered alcove, closet, cupboard, galley, equipment or anchor locker, or small cabin under the poop deck at the stern, or rear, of a sailing vessel. The term, which entered English in the mid-seventeenth century, is obscure and may derive from the French for *shanty.* The captain in Joseph Conrad's "The Secret Sharer" serves dinner to a member of his staff in the lighted ship's cuddy.

cuirass (*kwih'* ruhs or kwih . *ras'*) a segment of snug-fitting leather or metal armor protecting the sternum, ribs, back, and midriff; a buckler, the forerunner of Roman chain mail. A contrast to the scarlet breast adornment and constant punishment of Hester Prynne, protagonist of Nathaniel Hawthorne's *The Scarlet Letter,* the burnished helmet, cuirass, greaves, and gorget of the governor's armor depict the removable covering Bellingham wore with pride during the Pequod War.

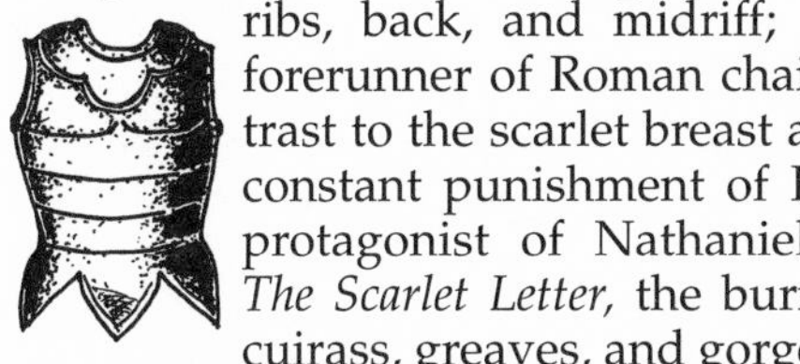

cul-de-sac or **cul de sac** a dead-end or blind alley; a thoroughfare that has only one exit. Derived from the French for *sack bottom,* the term entered English in the mid-eighteenth century. In Daniel Keyes's *Flowers for Algernon,* the mouse that parallels Charlie's rise and fall in intelligence suffers an ominous setback that becomes evident when he chooses the wrong passageway in the T-maze, enters a cul-de-sac, and suffers an electric shock. Thus, the result of the experimental brain surgery has itself reached a dismaying impasse. *See also* T-maze.

culling selecting the best from a variety of choices; discriminating quality specimens. Also, gleaning, winnowing, separating, or grading, as in the process of dividing types of lumber or wool according to use, for example, pulp paper and decorative paneling or pillow stuffing and fine sweaters. Derived from the Latin for *collect,* the word entered English in the thirteenth century; a later cognate implies the opposite—ejecting or casting out the worst or inferior members of the lot or killing the least promising of a herd or flock. While watching a poor out-at-elbows apothecary culling simples or herbs near Mantua in William Shakespeare's *Romeo and Juliet,* Romeo determines to bribe the man into selling him poison, which the drug-maker compounds out of dried vegetable matter. Thomas Keneally's *Schindler's List* uses the term in its later sense: SS officials cull the sickly, anemic, lame, or aged prisoners, then condemn them to gas chambers or mass killings. *See also* apothecary; SS.

cultivator a farm implement pulled by a dray animal or tractor that kills weeds, pulverizes stalks and limbs, and loosens soil to aerate a seedbed by dislodging stones, uprooting stumps, and breaking up clods and crust with a long-tined fork. An invention of the mid-nineteenth century, the cultivator, or drag harrow, consists of curved digger disks, spikes, or blades—either stationary, spring-loaded, or rotating—that reach between rows of seedlings to till the soil, encourage root expansion, and discourage run-off, which depletes the land of fertilizer and moisture. The title character in Jack Schaefer's *Shane* indicates that Ledyard, a shifty farm implement seller, is overcharging on the cost of the new cultivator.

cumulus (*kyoom'* yuh . luhs) a white, flat-bottomed, mounded cloud that expands upward from a low altitude in dense rounded masses, domes, or cauliflower shapes of condensed moisture as a result of unstable plumes of hot, moist air. Santiago, the protagonist in Ernest Hemingway's *The Old Man and the Sea,* studies the sprinkling of cumulus clouds, a phenomenon common to late afternoon that indicates a favorable wind for fishing. *See also* cirrus.

Cunard (koo . *nahrd'*) a famous British-based steamship line (officially the British and North American Royal Mail Steam Packet Company) founded by Samuel Cunard in 1840 for carrying mail and passengers between Liverpool and Boston or Halifax, Nova Scotia. By the next century, the Cunard had developed into a fleet of luxury liners. In F. Scott Fitzgerald's *The Great Gatsby,* Daisy Buchanan imagines that a bird on her lawn is an English nightingale that crossed the Atlantic Ocean on a Cunard liner.

cupola (*kyoo'* puh . luh) a vaulted ceiling, widow's walk, observation tower, or lantern- or onion-shaped domed structure atop an eave or ridgepole usually adorned with fancy woodwork, a weathervane, a brass ball, or lightning rod or decked with columns or trim matching the main structure below. In Edith Wharton's *Ethan Frome,* builder Andrew Hale jokes with Ethan about adding a cupola to Frome's farmhouse, an extravagance obviously far beyond Ethan's means or needs.

cupping a method of healing a patient by heating a glass cup and applying it to a wound to draw out diseased or superfluous blood or humors. As the air in the cup cools to room temperature, it contracts, creating a vacuum that draws out body fluids to fill the space. In wet cupping, the procedure is applied to lacerated or scarified flesh or to the site of a snakebite or scorpion's sting; in dry cupping, the treatment is applied to unbroken skin. In Charles Dickens's *David Copperfield,* a "cupper" is considered a more scientific practitioner than one who merely cuts and holds a basin to catch the blood flow.

curandera (*koo* . rahn . *deh'* ruh) *masc.* ***curandero*** a skilled female herbalist capable of conferring blessing and protection, applying folk remedies, or counteracting the evil spell of a *bruja,* the Spanish term for sorcerer or witch. In Rudolfo Anaya's *Bless Me, Ultima,* Gabriel's grandmother, the title character, is a wise, loving, and powerful *curandera* called *médic,* or healer, whom superstitious locals suspect of being a dangerous *bruja,* or witch. *See also bruja.*

curate (*kyoor'* iht) the assistant vicar, rector, curé, or clergyman who takes charge of parish duties, often involving teaching catechism or Christian education to youngsters. In Emily Brontë's *Wuthering Heights,* Hareton damns the curate in reply to Nelly's questions about his bad behavior and rude language.

curé *See* curate.

curricle (*kuhr'* rih . k'l) a heavy-yoked open two-wheeled chaise popular in the early to mid-nineteenth century and drawn by a matched pair of horses. The balance of heavy center pole and lightweight body rendered hazardous a conveyance that could easily tip over if the horses shied or bolted. As described in Jane Austen's *Pride and Prejudice,* the livery or coat of arms on the curricle denotes to Elizabeth the prestige of guests. *See also* chaise.

curry to use a metal-toothed comb or textured tool to groom, rub down, debride, or untangle the hide, mane, and tail of a horse, cow, dog, sheep, or other show animal. Also, to apply a currycomb or brush to a dirty, matted, or shedding pelt or to remove winter fur. In *Narrative of the Life of Frederick Douglass,* Mr. Covey's attack on Frederick Douglass occurs while the slave was currying a horse.

curteisye (*kuhr'* tuh. see) courtesy, graceful or exaggerated mannerisms, cooperation, homage, or refined table manners, gestures, posture, or behavior suited to the expectations of a monarch or nobility; respect, deference, or reverence for a court, legal body, or governmental session. Literally, the Anglo-Saxon version of the word means a kind of "Sunday manners," behavior expected of members of a royal court and their staff and visitors. Derived in the thirteenth century from the term for for *cohort* or *group,* the term is a doublet for *curtsy.* In the Prologue to Geoffrey Chaucer's *Canterbury Tales,* the narrator describes the knight as a true example of chivalry in that he projects the tenets of knighthood—curteisye, truth, and honor.

custom house an office or building where goods are weighed to determine the duty, tariff, or tax owed by the importer or exporter; the place where the port authority issues cargo stamps or declares ships free entrance or exit to or from the port. Pip, the protagonist of Charles Dickens's *Great Expectations,* makes a show of arriving and leaving from the wharf at the custom house so he can facilitate the escape of Abel Magwitch by packet boat. *See also* packet.

cutlass a heavy, broad-bladed machete or single-edged sword with a slightly curved blade measuring over two feet and a wide, ornate hand shield at the hilt to protect the fingers. The cutlass was issued to seamen on warships to be used during boarding or to ward off enemies. The term, taken from the Latin for *plowshare,* entered English in the late sixteenth century. In Mark Twain's *The Adventures of Tom Sawyer,* the title character fantasizes that he is the

Black Avenger of the *Spanish Main* with a "crime-rusted cutlass" at his side.

cutter a fast-moving rowboat or powerboat featuring a sleek hull, tapered bow, and lightweight arms; also, a lightweight one-horse, one-passenger sleigh built for speed or sport. Derived from the Old English verb *cut,* the term implies rapid movement through minor impediments toward a goal or port. Dennis Eady shows off his cutter to impress Mattie Silver in Edith Wharton's *Ethan Frome.*

Cyclops (*sy'* klahps) *pl.* **Cyclopes** (*sy'* kloh . pees) a member of a mythic race of barbaric, one-eyed giant cannibals who tended sheep and goats on isolated crags in Sicily and who stoked Mount Etna, the furnace in which they forged lightning bolts for Zeus, or who served as helpers of Hephaestus, blacksmith of the Greek gods. In Homer's *Odyssey,* Odysseus cannot resist the urge to taunt Polyphemus, a Cyclops who calls down punishment from heaven on the Greek sailor who tricked and blinded him.

cyclotron (*sy'* kluh . trahn) or **particle accelerator** a mechanical device divided into two conjoined D-shaped halves in which charged subatomic particles are accelerated into spirals by alternating currents within a magnetic field. Invented by Ernest Lawrence and Stanley Livingston in the 1930s, the cyclotron was crucial to the development of atomic power. In John Hersey's *Hiroshima,* a Japanese physicist, who owns a cyclotron and understands the principle of fission, fears that radiation will remain in the atmosphere after the detonation of the atomic bomb.

Cynthia a surname, epithet, or alternate name for Artemis, goddess of the moon, whom the Romans called Luna. The name derives from the Greek name for Mount Cynthus, a bare crag on the island of Delos, the birthplace of Artemis or Diana. As the title characters arise from their night of love in Act II of William Shakespeare's *Romeo and Juliet,* Romeo denies that the light is the dawn and claims that it is Cynthia, the playwright's personification of the moon and a satiric gesture in that Cynthia also symbolizes good fortune.

czardas or **csardas** (*chahr'* duhs) the Hungarian national folk dance for couples, influenced by Gypsy or Magyar rhythms and syncopation; the dance begins slowly and builds to dramatic leaps, whirls, and intricate patterns of steps. Derived from the Persian term for *vault*, the word entered English in the late nineteenth century, when nationalism inspired composers such as Franz Liszt and Frederic Chopin to re-examine and imitate folk melodies and dances. In Thomas Keneally's *Schindler's List,* the Rosner brothers maintain a facade of gaiety and celebration by playing a czardas for diners' entertainment.

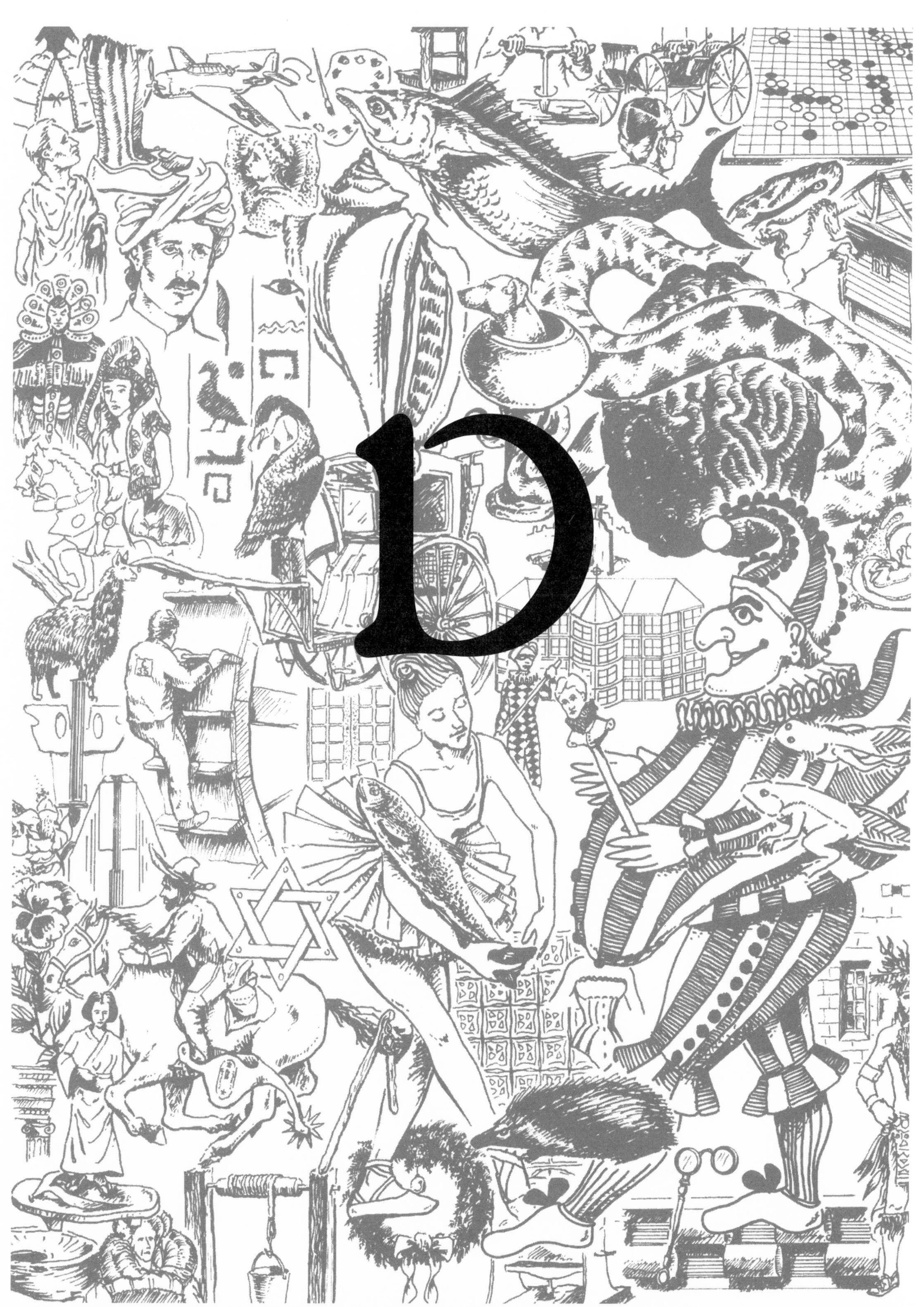
D

dace a general term for varieties of the swift, slender European freshwater darter, minnow, carp, creek chub, or goldfish common to ponds, home aquariums, and streams, where they swim in schools. While thinking of the Golden Country he recalls from a dream, Winston Smith, protagonist of George Orwell's *1984,* looks for dace in the stream.

daguerreotype (duh . *gehr'* roh . *typ*) a forerunner of modern photography. Invented in 1839 by Louis Jacques Mandé Daguerre, the daguerreotype differed from photos in the placement of iodide vapor on silver-coated copper plates rather than on glass. A common possession, the daguerreotype mentioned in Mark Twain's *Life on the Mississippi* captures the likeness of family members and replaces the expense and bother of sitting for an oil portrait.

daiquiri (*dak'* uh . ree) a cocktail named for a Cuban village consisting of light rum, citrus juice, and sugar that are shaken together with crushed ice. Holden Caulfield, protagonist of J. D. Salinger's *The Catcher in the Rye,* creates an impression of worldliness by claiming that, after scotch and soda, daiquiris are his favorite drink.

daisy cutter a World War I concussive, antipersonnel explosive mortar shell varying in size from 50 to 410 millimeters and designed to maim. Before impact, the daisy cutter flies low to the ground like a soccer ball, thus earning its name. The fuse ignites above ground level, showering shrapnel on a plane parallel to the ground and striking its human targets in the legs. According to experienced soldiers in Erich Maria Remarque's *All Quiet on the Western Front,* the daisy cutter emits a high-pitched whistle before detonation.

damask (*dam'* uhsk) a tightly woven, reversible twilled fabric of silk, wool, cotton, linen, or rayon used for table linens, upholstery, draperies, wall hangings, or fine garments. Ornamented with a lustrous, intricate raised pattern, often formed from applications of the same color warp on woof by coded punch cards fed by belt into a jacquard loom, damask takes its name from Damascus, Lebanon, the city where damask was made during the Middle Ages. In Victor Hugo's *Les Misérables,* Marius sees Jean Valjean walking with his daughter, who is simply but elegantly dressed in a black damask dress and mantle and is carrying an ivory-handled parasol.

dame school a private form of primary or nursery home schooling conducted by a female teacher for the benefit of young neighborhood children, who learned the alphabet by copying simple Bible texts. A forerunner of kindergarten, the dame school provided limited literacy to rural children from the sixteenth to the nineteenth centuries. With difficulty, the title character in George Eliot's novel *Silas Marner* parts with Eppie, his foster daughter, for two hours of instruction in reading at the dame school.

dandy a fastidiously groomed, well-dressed man given to exaggerated airs of fashion, elegant manners, or contrived, ostentatious pose or affectation; a fop, beau, or coxcomb; a clotheshorse such as Beau Brummel, a style-setter who influenced the wardrobe of other would-be beaux but was often the butt of jokes by servants and amused bystanders. Evolved from the Scottish nickname for *Andrew* into *jack-a-dandy,* an insult, the term appeared in English in the late eighteenth century. Pap Finn ridicules his son, the title character in Mark Twain's *The Adventures of Huckleberry Finn,* for sleeping in a bed and dressing like a dandy.

Daughters of the American Revolution or **D.A.R.** a prestigious historical society composed of "daughters" or female descendants of men who served with patriot forces during the American Revolution. Begun in 1890, the group answers to Congress through reports to the Smithsonian Institution and is known for preservation of noteworthy buildings, education for underprivileged children, promotion of patriotism, and high-quality genealogical studies of colonial America. Amanda Wingfield, the widowed matriarch of Tennessee Williams's *The Glass Menagerie,* misses the D.A.R. meeting to check on Laura's absence from secretarial school.

dauphin (doh . *fan'*) a ceremonial title (Dauphin de Viennois) marking the eldest son of the French king as heir and future regent; the prince's wife carried the title of *dauphine* (doh. *feen'*). The French word, referring to three dolphins on the royal coat of arms, remained in use from 1349 to 1830. One of a pair of con artists in Mark Twain's *The Adventures of Huckleberry Finn* claims to be Louis XVII, *dauphin* and son of Louis XVI and Marie Antoinette, who were executed on the guillotine during the French Revolution.

deadeye one of a pair of flat circular wooden disks or blocks encircled by iron bands and pierced with three holes through which ropes are threaded and secured. The connecting lanyard serves as the point where lines to shrouds or stays can be tightened or loosened. An ominous screen of deadeyes obscures the stranger who wants a conference with Billy Budd, title character in the novella of the same name by Herman Melville. *See also* backstay; shroud.

deadfall a weighty log, tree trunk, or elongated stone that is propped with a light stick and baited with meat, liver, or fish oil to lure prowling mammals. The hunter intends for the deadfall to crush, trap, or daze the animal, which becomes meat for the tribe. In William Faulkner's "The Bear," the narrator recalls the use of the deadfall in the early days of hunting in Yoknapatawpha County, Mississippi.

deadlights the shutters of brass, wood, or iron either outside or inside a ship that cover a porthole or cabin window to protect the glass from heavy weather or to obscure light to conceal the ship's presence during wartime. As used by Billy Bones, a colorful old sea dog in Robert Louis Stevenson's *Treasure Island,* deadlights serve as a metaphor for eyelids or sight.

dead march a solemn funeral march with a slow steady cadence, often accompanied by a rhythmic tattoo of snare drums and the sounds of horses' hooves or the footsteps of a cadre of honor guards on pavement; especially for military funerals. In the stage directions accompanying Arthur Miller's *Death of a Salesman,* a dead march follows the ignoble car crash that kills Willy Loman and precedes the final scene, the Requiem. *See also* requiem; tattoo.

decanter an ornamental clear, lead crystal, etched, frosted, or cut-glass bottle topped by a heavy glass or metal stopper and used to serve liqueur, wine, or brandy, often in glasses or tumblers that match the decanter. Huck is impressed when Tom and Bob pour bitters from a decanter and wish each other's health in a daily ritual described in Mark Twain's *The Adventures of Huckleberry Finn.*

decree an authoritative ordinance, announcement, law, or decision made by a ruling body or religious leader or council. In Sophocles' *Antigone,* the title character defies the decree of King Creon and obeys family ritual that requires rites and burial for her dead brother. In the Christmas story told in Luke 2:1, the Holy Family goes to Bethlehem after Caesar Augustus issues a decree calling for enrollment and taxation in each citizen's city of birth.

defile derived from the French for *march in a column,* a narrow, vertically restrictive gorge, mountain pass, or valley through which files of troops or explorers can march one at a time. The marooned English boys in William Golding's *Lord of the Flies* tramp through defiles during their initial study of island terrain, symbolically separating the boys so that each perceives the view as an individual rather than a group.

delirium tremens or **d.t.'s** a violent nervous twitch accompanied by weakness, convulsions or seizures, garbled speech, rapid pulse and respiration, sweating, anxiety, visions, hallucinations, or nightmares caused by chronic, excessive alcohol or barbiturate abuse or by withdrawal from drinking. In advanced cases, delirium tremens can extend sporadically over a few days or several weeks and can be fatal if the victim is not treated for shock and dehydration. Pap, Huck Finn's father, has reached the stage of alcohol-induced d.t.'s on the day he tries to kill his son in Mark Twain's *The Adventures of Huckleberry Finn.*

demijohn a globular, narrow-necked, 3- to 10-gallon liquor bottle or glass or earthenware jug that is covered with an outer wicker basket and lifted by a woven handle. The term, which derived by folk etymology from the French for *Dame Jeanne,* was first used in the early nineteenth century. During hunting season, Major de Spain and General Compson drink from tin cups filled from the demijohn in William Faulkner's "The Bear."

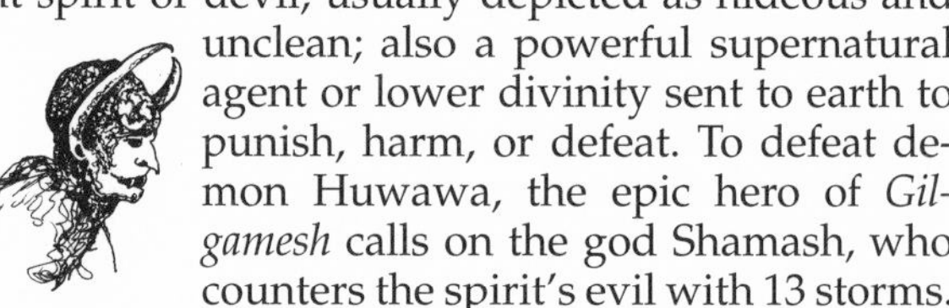

demon a distressingly evil, cruel, wicked, or malignant spirit or devil, usually depicted as hideous and unclean; also a powerful supernatural agent or lower divinity sent to earth to punish, harm, or defeat. To defeat demon Huwawa, the epic hero of *Gilgamesh* calls on the god Shamash, who counters the spirit's evil with 13 storms.

derby the American equivalent of a bowler, a fashionable round hat in brown, black, or gray felt with a stiff, domed top and narrow curved or rolled brim made popular in the mid-nineteenth century as a daytime replacement for the formal top hat or stovepipe hat. Named in honor of William Bowler, a haberdasher, the hat was popularized in France as a *melon.* Brown, the British villain in Joseph Conrad's *Lord Jim,* is known for his stylish bowler hat. In Olive Ann Burns's *Cold Sassy Tree,* Will Tweedy's father receives a derby hat from New York.

derrick (*dehr'* rihk) a tall vertical framework, hoist, crane, or lift dating to Egypt and India about 1500 B.C. Named for a sixteenth-century hangman in Tyburn, England, the term at one time referred solely to a gallows. The derrick is anchored to a firm base and extends an adjustable beam or telescopic boom that drops a rope or cable from pulleys to raise heavy loads, for example, from barges to quays or loading ramps. The derrick operator pivots the boom toward the place where the load is to be lowered and deposited. In Esther Forbes's *Johnny Tremain,* dock workers use a derrick to unload cargo from ships to the wharf. *See also* block and tackle.

dervish (*duhr'* vihsh) a Sufi, a devout Muslim who takes vows of asceticism, chastity, and poverty. To achieve spiritual heights, he abandons his rational self in howling, chanting, and a controlled, rhythmic dance or whirl to express through ecstasy or trance his oneness with Allah. Derived from the Persian for *beggar,* the term entered English in the late sixteenth century. As used in Charles Dickens's *A Tale of Two Cities,* the word implies a frenzied twirling, an image conveying political gyrations in the days preceding the French Revolution. *See also* Allah.

Deutsche mark or **Deutschmark** (*doy'* chuh . mahrk) the monetary unit of Germany after the abandonment of the Reichsmark at the collapse of Hitler's empire in the mid-1940s. The Deutsche mark is abbreviated DM and equals 100 pfennigs. In *Zlata's Diary,* the editor indicates that inflation during the siege on Sarajevo had raised the cost of a can of meat to 50 Deutsche marks.

devilfish a wide-bodied manta ray whose whip-length tail and extended hornlike pectoral fins suggest the body markings of a devil. Common to the warm surface waters and shallows of the sea, the manta ray, or stingray, was named for the Spanish for *mantle,* a shape suggested by its angular, flat body. In Scott O'Dell's *The Island of the Blue Dolphins,* Karana anticipates the juicy white meat of the devilfish, which is difficult to spear.

dewlap a flaccid fold of skin that hangs or dangles loosely from the throat or neck of an animal, bird, or person, usually elderly; pendulous wattles. Puck, the mischievous fairy in William Shakespeare's *A Midsummer Night's Dream,* brags that he teases and tricks old ladies by making them dribble their ale onto their dewlaps.

dhoti (*doh'* tee) a loosely wrapped loincloth passed between the legs from front to back and tucked into the waist. From early times into the twentieth century, the dhoti has been the informal dress of Hindu men. According to Ruth Prawer Jhabvala's *Heat and Dust,* modern men of India embrace modern ways by giving up the traditional white dhoti and dressing in business suits.

diablerie (dee . *ahb'* luh . ree) sorcery, witchcraft, black magic, gris-gris, or consorting with demons or Satan; sin, wickedness, mischief, devilment, or other metaphysical practice not condoned by the church as normal or acceptable to God. While having her fortune told by Mother Bunches, the title character of Charlotte Brontë's *Jane Eyre* claims that there is diablerie in the air. *See also bruja;* demon.

diaphragm the stiff, dome-shaped sheet of muscle and connective tissue that separates the chest from the abdomen. Because it contracts and forces air into the lungs, the diaphragm is crucial to respiration as well as to excretion, coughing, sneezing, hiccupping, weeping, laughing, vomiting, and giving birth. Using the force of his diaphragm, Ralph, the protagonist in William Golding's *Lord of the Flies,* produces a deep sound from the conch shell that calls the marooned children to an organizational meeting.

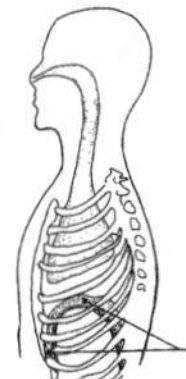

dice cup a round, cup-shaped box or receptacle for shaking dice before throwing them. The purpose of the dice cup is to assure a fair throw and to inhibit the replacement of fair dice with loaded or weighted dice. In Edmond Rostand's *Cyrano de Bergerac,* during a lull in fighting, the cadets rattle the dice cups. *See also* crap game.

Dilantin (dy . *lan'* tihn) the trade name for a drug that suppresses seizures, especially epilepsy. A patient in Ken Kesey's *One Flew Over the Cuckoo's Nest* hides his Dilantin capsule because he dislikes the drug's side effects; Chief Bromden, a victim of paranoia, suspects the medication contains transistors.

dimity (*dih'* muh . tee) sheer, plain-woven cotton fabric with raised checks or stripes. Dimity is a serviceable cloth that is easily starched and used in bed linens, draperies, hangings, upholstery, pillows, linings, and women's dresses and undergarments. Derived from the Greek for *double thread,* the term entered English in the sixteenth century. Beneath the bed's dimity tester, or canopy, the title character in Thomas Hardy's *Tess of the D'Urbervilles* spies a sprig of mistletoe.

dim sum small, hot, and spicy hors d'oeuvres, pastries, snacks, or light refreshments; small servings of sliced meat, rice balls, and steamed dumplings filled with minced meat and vegetables. Derived from the Cantonese for *heart spot,* the term entered the vocabulary of American cuisine after World War II. In Amy Tan's *The Kitchen God's Wife,* the bakery near Waverly Place specializes in Chinese baked goods and dim sum.

Dionysiac (*dy* . oh . *nee'* see . ak) ecstatic, sexual, lascivious, or free of inhibitions, restraint, or discipline. After the style of Dionysus, the Greek god of wine and fertility, orgies or processions conducted in frenzied, Dionysiac style involved blatant sexuality in costume, gestures, jokes, songs, and chants. In commentary accompanying *The Crucible,* Arthur Miller notes that Puritan leaders hoped to crush witchcraft and Dionysiac frolics. *See also* Bacchic rite.

dirk a short, straight dagger or small sheath knife without a hilt; often concealed in a boot, waistband, or jacket for use as personal protection in hand-to-hand combat or street fighting where there is no room for brandishing a sword. In Avi's *The True Confessions of Charlotte Doyle,* a crewman advises the heroine to keep a dirk under her mattress as protection from some unnamed menace.

discus a flat metal, wood, or stone circle or thick-centered plate that is whirled at a target zone in track-and-field contests of strength, control, and accuracy. One of five events in the Olympic pentathlon, the sport derives from an earlier version in which athletes stood on a pedestal and whirled in a tight circle to gain momentum and speed for the release, which was enhanced by a push from the fingertips. Odysseus, hero of Homer's *Odyssey,* proves his mettle to the Phaeacians by whirling the discus far beyond their preliminary throws.

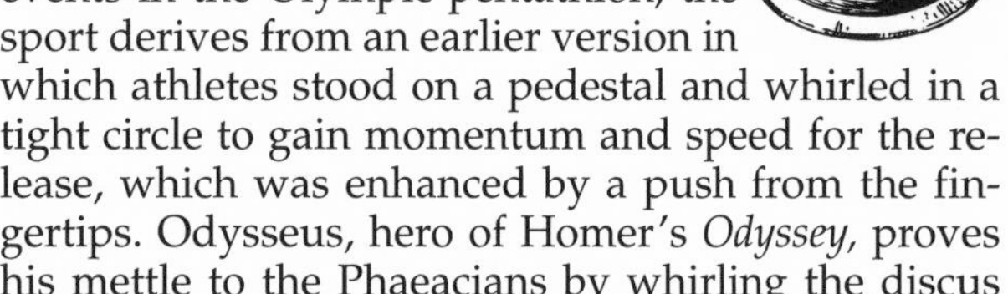

distaff (*dihs'* taf) the split stick, rod, or staff to which is tied a hank of flax, tow, or wool to be pulled out in small increments and spun into thread. In early times, the distaff was held in the hand; after the invention of the spinning wheel, it was attached to the wood frame to free the hands. A symbol of womanly domesticity, the distaff has come to refer to females, who, from early times, were responsible for making thread to weave cloth for towels, sheets, wall hangings, clothing, ritual garments, and other household items made from fiber. In Homer's *Odyssey,* like other Mediterranean women, Helen, queen of Sparta, seats herself at her distaff and wheeled sewing basket.

Distinguished Service Cross or **DSC** a prestigious U.S. Army medal (second only to the Congressional Medal of Honor) featuring a gold cross centered with an eagle and attached to a blue ribbon edged in thin stripes of red and white. The DSC is awarded for outstanding heroism in combat or against an armed enemy. According to his records, McMurphy, the protagonist in Ken Kesey's *One Flew Over the Cuckoo's Nest,* received the Distinguished Service Cross for leading escapees from a Communist prison camp in Korea.

ditty bag a small bag pulled shut with a string tie; a carryall for needles and thread, buttons, and toilet articles. The origins of this naval term, which dates to the mid-nineteenth century, are obscure; it may derive from *dutty,* a coarse, unbleached calico. In Herman Melville's *Typee,* Toby and Tom jump ship carrying their ditty bags, which contain personal items such as tobacco and a change of shirts. *See also* reticule.

divi-divi (*dihv'* ee . *dihv'* ee) a shallow-rooted, flowering tropical tree of the pea family that yields a 3-inch curled pod rich in tannic acid that is used in dyeing. The word, which entered English in the early nineteenth century, may derive from an Arawak Indian term. While living on the island of Curaçao, Phillip, protagonist of Theodore Taylor's *The Cay,* loves the divi-divi trees, which lean to leeward because strong Caribbean winds force them in that direction. The image foreshadows Philip's testing during a hurricane while he is marooned on an uncharted cay. *See also* cay.

divining rod or **dowsing rod** a forked branch or stick of rowan, ash, yew, or hazel that is held by the outer tips and aimed away from the body during a search for water, valuable ore, buried treasure, or a missing object. When the rod approaches its goal, it points down and pulls the arms of the diviner toward the discovery. The King, one of two sharpers who accompany Jim and Huck in Mark Twain's *The Adventures of Huckleberry Finn,* has used a divining rod in one of his many con games. *See also* hebona; yew.

division a segment of an army composed of air power, armored vehicles and tanks, artillery, cavalry, engineering corps, two auxiliary or field headquarters, ground support of mechanized and light infantry, main headquarters, paratroopers, and signal corps. The standard arrangement of 15 divisions per army, with about 15,000 men per corps, is led by a major general. In Stephen Crane's *The Red Badge of Courage,* rumors float down to the men in the field from division headquarters that the army is soon moving out. *See also* army.

dixie a large military field cooking pot or soup kettle divided into halves. The top served as a beverage holder; the bottom held food. In honor of the Confederate South, the British referred to the bottom as the "dixie." In Erich Maria Remarque's *All Quiet on the Western Front,* Ginger adds meat and fat to a dixie filled with beans.

djinn (jihn) *pl.* **djinni** or **jinni** a benevolent, supernatural spirit from Islamic lore who helped and protected human masters; also, one of a pair of spirits who alternately tempted and scolded the human he attended. A djinn could take on any shape to work the will of the person or god who summoned him. The term entered English in the seventeenth century; the djinn often appeared in literature dressed in Arabian silks and turbans as well as myriad disguises, for example, in Rudyard Kipling's *Just So Stories,* where the djinn superintending deserts travels in a cloud of dust.

DNA or **deoxyribonucleic** (dee . *ahk'* see . *ry* . boh . noo . *klay* . ihk) **acid** the double helix, or intertwined ladder, bonded from nucleic acids that carries and transmits a coded message that replicates living tissue, the basis of heredity. Jing Mei, a character in Amy Tan's *Joy Luck Club,* fears that DNA may impel her to behave in stereotypical Chinese fashion.

do-do a stubby-winged, flightless gray-blue bird of the pigeon family common to the Indian Ocean island of Mauritius until its extinction around 1790. Waddling its turkey-shaped body on broad talons, the do-do used its curved bill to hunt for food. In Lewis Carroll's *Alice's Adventures in Wonderland,* the do-do proposes that Alice join the caucus race, a meaningless contest that helps to dry her wet clothing.

dog-cart a one-horse two-wheeled pleasure cart consisting of two benches back to back with space underneath for parcels or freight. The vehicle was originally designed to convey hunting parties and their hounds, who rode in a cage under the seat. Sherlock Holmes, master detective in Sir Arthur Conan Doyle's "The Adventure of the Speckled Band," startles Helen Stoner by deducing from the mud splashes on her clothing that she arrived in a dog-cart.

dog irons andirons; metal supports that hold flammable material in a fireplace. The term blends the word *andirons* and its synonym, *firedogs.* Huck, protagonist of Mark Twain's *The Adventures of Huckleberry Finn,* is impressed by the Grangerfords' wealth, particularly the massive dog irons capable of holding a large log.

dogvane a makeshift weathervane composed of a cork and feathers suspended on a thread from a short stick placed on the gunwale near the helmsman's post to point the direction of the wind. In Herman Melville's *Moby-Dick,* Captain Ahab uses the dogvane and compass to help him locate the white whale.

dogwatch one of two two-hour periods of guard duty aboard a ship between 4:00 and 8:00 P.M., the application of which maneuvered the arrangement of watches to seven, an odd number that caused a natural rotation of seamen. As described by Herman Melville in *Billy Budd,* the dogwatch was a melancholy time around twilight when sailors on duty tend to feel sad, mournful, or uneasy.

doily a protective or ornamental paper or linen napkin, placemat, or cloth placed on a tray or sideboard, beneath a dessert dish, and on the arms and backs of couches and chairs. When used in drawers or gift boxes, doilies are often edged with lace, tatting, or crochet and scented with lavender or rosewater. In Moss Hart and George S. Kaufman's *You Can't Take It with You,* Alice complains that she would like a more predictable family and a standard home with doilies on the furniture. *See also* antimacassar.

doldrums (*dohl'* druhmz) a band of windless calm; squalls; or light, unpredictable breezes that typify stagnated sailing weather near the equator between the northern and southern trade winds. Derived from the Anglo-Saxon for *foolish,* the term entered English in the early nineteenth century. To the crew immured in the blockhouse in Robert Louis Stevenson's *Treasure Island,* the inactivity is as unpleasant as the doldrums. *See also* trades.

dolichocephalic (*doh'* lih . koh . sih . *fa* . lihk) a narrowing of the skull, a descriptive term of interest to nineteenth-century phrenologists, who studied the shape and texture of the skull for clues about personality, behavior, and intelligence. Dr. Mortimer asks for a closer examination of dolichocephalic traits on the skull of Sherlock Holmes, renowned detective in Sir Arthur Conan Doyle's *The Hound of the Baskervilles. See also* parietal fissure; phrenology.

dolphin an intelligent small-toothed whale approximately six feet long and marked by gray to black skin and a long snout. In Roman decor, the dolphin was a frequent figure in wall paintings, pool mosaics, and edgings because it symbolized benevolence and luck. Graceful and playful, dolphins are a favorite of animal trainers, who keep them in saltwater pools for display at marine circuses. In the myth of Arian, a singer and poet in Edith Hamilton's *Mythology,* sailors try to rob and drown the boy, who sings so plaintive a tune that a dolphin rescues him and ferries him safely to shore. *See also dauphin.*

domino a costume composed of a long-sleeved hooded cloak or voluminous cape worn with a black full or half mask. To conceal the face, head, and shoulders, the domino served as a disguise for a masquerade ball, procession, or carnival. For the evening's performance in Henrik Ibsen's *A Doll's House,* Helmer wears a domino and Nora an Italian costume.

dominoes a competitive game played with 28 ivory, wood, bone, or plastic bars divided into halves, either blank or dotted on each half with from one to six spots. In play, dominoes must be aligned with pieces on the board that exhibit matching patterns of spots. In Joseph Conrad's *The Heart of Darkness,* Marlowe and the other passengers on board the yacht fail to begin their game of dominoes and listen instead to Marlowe's narrative about Mr. Kurtz.

don a tutor, college professor, distinguished expert, fellow, department head, or respected staff member at Oxford or Cambridge who was marked by an academic robe or gown, hood, and cap. Hugh Conway, linguist and unflappable intellectual leader in James Hilton's *Lost Horizon,* is said to have served as an Oxford don after World War I.

doodlebug an American slang term for the larva of the ant lion, which digs a conical hiding place in the sand where it extends its serrated jaws to trap and devour ants and other insects. To lure a doodlebug to the surface, children stir in the hole with a stick while they chant, "Doodlebug, doodlebug, you'd better come out. Your house is on fire and your children will burn." To learn his future, Tom, protagonist of Mark Twain's *The Adventures of Tom Sawyer,* questions a doodlebug.

dormer window a gabled or peaked window set upright in the top floor of the house and projecting from a sloped or mansard roof. Before scaling the convent wall to save Cosette from their pursuer, Jean Valjean, protagonist of Victor Hugo's *Les Misérables,* looks up at the dormer windows across the street and finds them barred, thus leaving him only one way to escape a cul-de-sac.

dormouse a soft, furry nocturnal European, African, or Asian rodent resembling a bushy-tailed squirrel or chipmunk. The dormouse lives in trees, stores fat in its rounded body, and hibernates in winter. In Lewis Carroll's *Alice's Adventures in Wonderland,* the dormouse—which derives its name for the Latin for *sleep*—demonstrates the author's love of puns by sleeping through the beginning of the Mad Hatter's tea party.

dorsal fin the fin that projects from the spine of a mammal or fish and stabilizes the body against currents, storms, attackers, or passing vessels. At the entrance of Kingcome Inlet in Margaret Craven's *I Heard the Owl Call My Name,* Mark sees the dorsal fin of a whale and learns that whales often leap from the water to knock barnacles from their bodies.

dose of salts a quantity of mineral salts to serve as a strong laxative, cathartic, or purge to cleanse the bowels of impurities. After Mr. Covey severely beats Frederick Douglass, author of *Narrative of the Life of Frederick Douglass,* Master Thomas administers a dose of salts but refuses to rescue the slave from further violence.

double-dutch rope a rope-skipping game requiring two ropes of equal length turned by two players simultaneously in opposite directions while a third player leaps into the path and jumps both whirling ropes. In Sandra Cisneros's *The House on Mango Street,* Esperanza recalls the rhymes chanted by girls jumping double-dutch rope, a children's game requiring speed and coordination.

double entendre (*doob'* luh awn . *tahn'* d'r) a simple, innocent, droll, or ambiguous statement that intentionally conveys a second meaning, implication, or connotation, usually scurrilous, risqué, suggestive, or indecent. Bailey Junior, Maya Angelou's much-loved brother in *I Know Why the Caged Bird Sings,* demonstrates his wit with *double entendres.*

doublet (*duhb'* liht) a short, tight vest or sleeved jacket worn by men from the fourteenth to the eighteenth century; a forerunner of the suit coat or jacket.

Designed to fit under chain mail, the doublet developed into a popular garment ornamented with braid, slashed or puffed sleeves, drawstring waists, peplums or skirts, and tabs. William Shakespeare mentions doublets on characters in *Romeo and Juliet* and *Hamlet* and, because sartorial accuracy was not significant in his day, also in *Julius Caesar.*

doubloon (duh . *bloon'*) a Spanish or Spanish-American gold coin called a *double pistole* and worth 4 escudos or about $15. Mentioned in Robert Louis Stevenson's *Treasure Island,* Alexandre Dumas's *The Count of Monte Cristo,* and Herman Melville's *Benito Cereno,* the doubloon attests to the importance of Spain in fifteenth- and sixteenth-century trade, especially that originating in the New World.

dowsing rod *See* divining rod.

doxology (dahks . *ah'* loh . gee) a short hymn opening a Christian worship service offering honor, glory, and praise to God; a formal liturgical thanksgiving beginning "Praise God from whom all blessings flow," "Glory be to the Father," or "Glory to God in the highest." To ease the tension of the arrival of mourners in Mark Twain's *The Adventures of Huckleberry Finn,* someone begins singing the "doxologer."

drachma (*drahk'* muh) an ancient Greek silver coin worth 6 obols, each valued at $5. The word, which also refers to a standard of weight, derives from the Greek for *fistful.* In Act III, Scene II, of William Shakespeare's *Julius Caesar,* Mark Antony reads to the mob from Caesar's will, which pledges every man 75 drachmas, a sum worth about $30 per citizen, or two weeks' wages to the average worker.

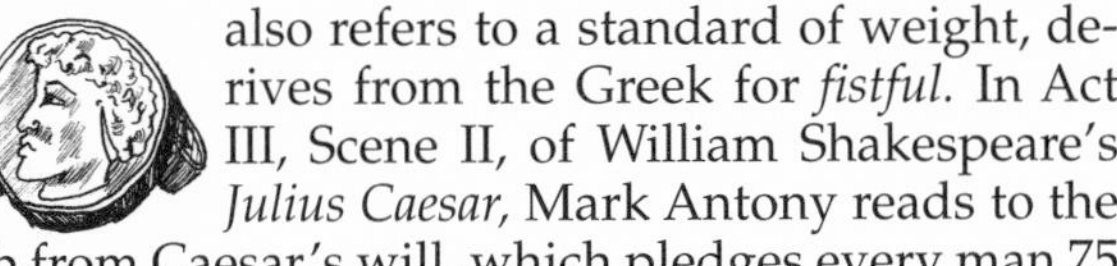

the dragon a symbol of the Ku Klux Klan, a racist fraternal organization fomenting hatred and violence. Ruled by the Grand Dragon, the Klan, begun in 1866 by Nathan Bedford Forrest in Pulaski, Tennessee, rose to its height during the 1920s and has experienced resurgences during periods of black pressure for civil rights. In a metaphoric passage in Toni Morrison's *Beloved,* the dragon swims the Ohio River each night to satiate its desire for black blood.

dragoon a heavily armed horse soldier of the seventeenth and eighteenth centuries in France, Prussia, and the United States; also, the short musket or carbine carried by a dragoon—a fiery weapon that gave the soldier his name. In Victor Hugo's *Les Misérables,* the dragoons served during the Napoleonic wars as both cavalry and infantry.

dram a liquid measure equal to .0625 ounces. In William Shakespeare's *Romeo and Juliet,* the protagonist pays a Mantuan apothecary a high price—40 gold pieces—for illegally dispensing a dram, or dose, of poison so that Romeo can return to his wife's tomb and commit suicide. *See also* apothecary.

dramshop a barroom or saloon where measured shots of whiskey are sold; a cheap bar offering little more than quick drunkenness. In Upton Sinclair's *The Jungle,* to avoid pursuers, Jurgis steers clear of gamblers and dramshops.

draught (draft) a swallow, mouthful, portion, or dose of medicine. In Mary Shelley's *Frankenstein,* the doctor administers to Robert Walton a soothing draught to help him rest. In the plural, the term denotes the game of checkers, which takes its name from the act of dragging or drafting game pieces over the board. In Joy Adamson's *Born Free,* Africans play *bau,* a form of draughts.

dregs residue or sediment that remains when a glass is emptied of liquid or a decanter is tilted to pour away the liquid; waste, grounds, or foreign matter that remains at the bottom when a cup is emptied. The duped farm animals in George Orwell's *Animal Farm* watch through the windows as the self-important tyrant pigs drain mugs to the dregs, the same behavior that Farmer Jones, their human master, once displayed before the rebellion.

dressing case a decorative and often monogrammed lidded box, hand luggage, or carryall fitted out with bottles for scented water and lotion and slots for toilet articles, hairbrush, and comb. The protagonist in Charlotte Brontë's *Jane Eyre* completes the redecorating of Moor House, her cousins' residence, and sets out new dressing cases on the toilet tables for Diana and Mary.

dressing gown a light robe, kimono, burnoose, negligee, or loose wrapper worn during pregnancy or for lounging or recuperating from illness; also, a protective gown, or peignoir, literally *combing gown,* worn over formal wear during the arranging of the hair or application of makeup. In Franz Kafka's *The Metamorphosis,* Gregor is accustomed to seeing his languid father lying back in a dressing gown rather than dressed for business.

driving-band the soft metal band or ring around the shell of a cartridge or explosive from a cannon; the

collar that the rifling on a gun barrel engages to set the shell in motion. To replace earlier metal ball and timber projectiles, Wilfred Stokes, an engineer for the English army, invented three-inch mortar shells for the World War I–vintage howitzer. In Erich Maria Remarque's *All Quiet on the Western Front,* treasure-hunting soldiers foolishly endanger themselves by going out at night looking for the valuable copper driving-bands of spent shells.

dropsy an obsolete medical term for edema or swelling; an accumulation of fluid in the tissues and body cavities. The word dates to the thirteenth century and derives from the Greek for *water.* In Luigi Pirandello's *A Breath of Air,* the old man suffers from hardening of the arteries, bad heart, weakened kidneys, and dropsy, which requires periodic draining of fluids from his abdominal cavity.

drover a cowboy, cowpuncher, *vaquero,* herder, or drover of cattle or sheep; also, a trader or dealer in livestock. On their way past Chicago's famous holding pens for cattle depicted in Upton Sinclair's *The Jungle,* Jurgis and Elzbieta pass the drovers and stockmen who move vast numbers of animals to the stockyards for sale and slaughter.

drumhead court a wartime court-martial conducted in battle dress in the field or on the deck of a ship; a summary trial hurriedly set up on the flat side of a drum in lieu of a table to punish traitors, deserters, or others who obstruct the movement, function, or safety of armies or ships' crews. The title character in Herman Melville's *Billy Budd* receives a sentence of hanging after the drumhead court finds him guilty of striking and killing an officer.

drummer a slang term referring to a traveling salesperson or demonstrator of products such as bicycles or farm implements. The term originated from the use of a drum to summon customers or draw attention to a product or commodity. The woman who seduces Willy Loman in Arthur Miller's *Death of a Salesman* makes a pun on his trade by calling him "drummer boy."

drunk tank a large prison cell, detention center, or holding pen where drunks are incarcerated until they are bailed out or appear before a magistrate for sentencing or fining. An unnamed girl in Rudolfo Anaya's *Bless Me, Ultima* fears that both Narciso and Andrew will be thrown into the drunk tank if they summon the sheriff.

D.S.O. the Distinguished Service Order; a white cross suspended from a green ribbon edged in red; a medal awarded to outstanding commissioned officers in the British army, navy, or air force for uncommon valor during combat. Hugh Conway, the protagonist of James Hilton's *Lost Horizon,* won a D.S.O. while fighting in France during World War I.

ducat *(duhk'* iht) a gold coin common to many European countries during the Middle Ages and the Renaissance. The term derives from the Latin *leader,* whose picture adorns the coin. In William Shakespeare's *Romeo and Juliet,* the protagonist pays the apothecary 40 ducats for an illegal act—dispensing a dram of poison.

duck-weed a family of tiny, stemless aquatic herbs or flowering plants of the Arales family that float near or on the top of a freshwater pond or stagnant pool and oxygenate the water; green pond scum, which is eaten by ducks. In Erich Maria Remarque's *All Quiet on the Western Front,* Albert and Paul submerge themselves in a pond covered with duck-weed to avoid detection.

dudeen or **dudheen** (doo . *deen'*) the Irish term for a straight-stemmed, small-bowled clay pipe used for smoking tobacco; a briar. In Samuel Beckett's *Waiting for Godot,* Pozzo complains to Vladimir that he has lost his dudeen.

dudgeon (*duh'* juhn) an obsolete term for boxwood, a type of wood used to make flutes, chess pieces, inlaid boxes, and the haft, handle, or hilt of a dagger; by extension, the term applies to the weapon itself. The word derives from the Dutch for *stave.* In his hallucinatory vision of a dagger dripping clots of blood, the title character in William Shakespeare's *Macbeth* notes both blade and dudgeon.

duenna (doo . *ehn'* nuh) a companion, chaperone, governess, or mature female relative who takes charge of, accompanies, or supervises the behavior of young unmarried women. A Spanish or Portuguese title or designation of respect and authority, the term derives from the Latin for *mistress* and dates to the early seventeenth century. When Roxane appears at the theater in Edmond Rostand's *Cyrano de Bergerac,* her duenna takes a seat behind her.

dugout the earliest and most primitive form of boat or canoe, formed of a trunk that is flattened on one side, then burned or hollowed out with an adze or scraper on the other side to form a hollow. In shallow water, the dugout was propelled by poling. In Joseph

Conrad's *The Heart of Darkness,* Kurtz, an ivory dealer, travels upriver in a dugout manned by four African paddlers. *See also* adze.

dugs teats, breasts, or udders. This Old English term for *nipple* dates to the early sixteenth century and is considered vulgar when applied to human mammary glands. The shepherd dog in John Steinbeck's *Of Mice and Men* has the long, pendulous dugs characteristic of a lactating female who suckles a litter of pups.

dumb-waiter a wheeled receptacle or cabinet containing shelves in which dishes of food can be kept at serving temperature and free of insects. In more elaborate settings, the dumb-waiter—literally a "mute servant"—is an elevator bearing serving containers from a lower floor to an upstairs dining area. In Charles Dickens's *Great Expectations,* Pip arrives at Mr. Jaggers's table and finds a dumb-waiter alongside well stocked with bottles, decanters, and dishes of fruit for dessert. *See also* decanter.

dun a bill collector or person authorized to collect payment from a debtor; an aggressive written request or demand for restitution or a threat of a bad credit rating or reclamation or repossession of property. In Herman Melville's "Bartleby the Scrivener," a dun arrives at the office to press for payment of a bill owed by Nippers, the lawyer's clerk.

dunce cap a cone-shaped cap that lazy or inferior students were forced to wear as a form of punishment, ridicule, or humiliation. The student, wearing the dunce cap marked with a *D,* often perched on a stool at the front of the class or in a corner facing the wall as an added deterrent to behavior problems or poor study habits. Scout, protagonist of Harper Lee's *To Kill a Mockingbird,* notes that her brother, Jem, learns by the "half Dewey decimal–half dunce-cap method."

dupe (dyoop) the victim of a hoax or scam; a fool or innocent who is easily tricked, gulled, manipulated, or led astray. Derived from French for *hoopoe bird,* the term dates to the late seventeenth century and recalls a character in Aristophanes' satiric *The Birds.* In Mark Twain's *The Adventures of Tom Sawyer,* the title character's friends feel like dupes after trading their tickets to Tom, who earns a Bible from Mr. Walters.

dust devil a small whirlwind stirring up a spiral of dust, debris, leaves, and sand. As an explanation of her defiance of Albert, whom she calls Mr., Celie, protagonist in Alice Walker's *The Color Purple,* claims that a dust devil flew into her mouth and forced her to take a firm stand against her husband's persistent abuse.

dustman a servant or household or government employee who removes refuse from dustbins or garbage cans; a trash collector. In George Bernard Shaw's *Pygmalion,* Eliza's father, the independent, smart-mouthed dustman Alfred P. Doolittle, surprises his daughter when he gives up bachelorhood.

dutch oven a heavy cast-iron kettle or pot on legs with tight-fitting convex lid. The dutch oven can be suspended by its handle over a flame, heaped with hot coals, or settled directly onto coals for slow cooking. In camp at the coon hunt, Grandpa, Father, and Billy eat a meal of fried potatoes, side meat, and corn bread cooked in a dutch oven in Wilson Rawls's *Where the Red Fern Grows. See also* streak-a-lean.

dynamo (*dy'* nuh . moh) a generator that converts mechanical energy into electricity. A turbine, sometimes powered by water, coal, gas, oil, or nuclear energy, rotates a conductor in a magnetic field to produce voltage, which passes through carbon brushes to storage batteries. In George Orwell's *Animal Farm,* Snowball declares that the animals can produce labor-saving electric current by building a windmill to power a dynamo.

dysentery (*dihs'* ihn . teh . ree) a potentially fatal intestinal disease causing shock and nutritional depletion from extensive loss of blood and electrolytes from persistent diarrhea and vomiting. Amoebic dysentery results from the ingestion of parasitic amoeba in contaminated water or food or from swallowing water while swimming in unclean waters. In Erich Maria Remarque's *All Quiet on the Western Front,* the soldiers believe that dysentery causes a regular round of casualties.

E

eagle a slang term for an American $10 gold coin with a unique concave image of an eagle on the reverse side rather than the customary convex or bas-relief. In a late-night gambling scene in Mark Twain's *Life on the Mississippi,* Backus punches up the bidding with an eagle, followed by a raise of an eagle plus $10. *See also* bas-relief.

earl the oldest English hereditary title that was conferred on chieftains during the feudal period with accompanying rights to property and income; a low-ranking nobleman or member of the English peerage who rates above a count, viscount, baron, and thane but below a marquis, or marquess, and duke. Colonel Fitzwilliam, a character in Jane Austen's *Pride and Prejudice,* believes that the younger son of an earl should be accustomed to self-denial because he is on the far end of the line of inheritance. *See also* title.

earlocks a ritual or ceremonial curl or traditional tendril hanging in front of the ear. In Chaim Potok's *The Chosen,* Danny observes the black caftan, fur hat, beard, and earlocks of a Hasidic Jew, a member of a devout mystical sect. *See also* Hasidic Jews.

eave the projecting roofline, or edge of the roof, that overhangs a wall and channels water to the ground or through an eave trough to a downspout. In Sir Arthur Conan Doyle's *The Hound of the Baskervilles,* the maiden in the upstairs room escaped Sir Hugo by climbing down the ivy on the walls and departing along the edge of the eaves.

éclair (ay . *klayr'*) a tubular shell of choux, or puff pastry, filled with pudding, custard, or whipped cream and topped with icing, usually chocolate. While the Savage visits his mother in a terminal ward of the hospital in Aldous Huxley's *Brave New World,* visiting children who have come to the hospital to learn about death receive éclairs from their teacher.

eddy a vortex, drift, or circular current in water, smoke, or air caused by a forceful stream or conflicting current moving counter to the main channel. A Norse word entering English in the fifteenth century, the word is a synonym for *whirlpool.* During a rainy summer in Pearl S. Buck's *The Good Earth,* the moats overflow into channels marked by swirls and eddies.

effigy (*ehf'* fuh . gee) a dummy, model, likeness, or symbolic portrayal on a tombstone, marble slab, or effigy mound; a crude image or caricature that becomes the focus of local hatred or ridicule and is subjected to contempt before being hanged or burned. To express political distaste for the traitor Goldstein, citizens of Oceana burn him in effigy in George Orwell's *1984. See also* skimmity-ride.

eiderdown (*ay'* duhr . down) the soft, fine breast feathers of an eider, a large northern marine duck. Eiderdown is prized as light, fluffy, but warm stuffing for vests, jackets, pillows, comforters, duvets, bolsters, sleeping bags, and quilts. Each night, Anne Frank's sofabed is made up from sheets, pillows, and an eiderdown from Mr. Dussel's bed, as described in *The Diary of a Young Girl.*

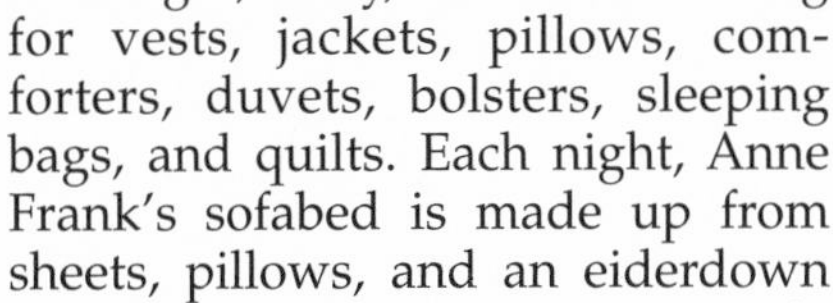

ejector (ee . *jehk'* tuhr) a mechanism in a breech-loading firearm that shucks an empty shell or spent cartridge from the bore or firing chamber after the charge is fired. While cleaning his pistol, Carlson, a farmworker in John Steinbeck's *Of Mice and Men,* snaps the ejector, an ominous sound prefiguring the death of Lennie, a retarded killer, who is ejected from society. *See also* breech-loader.

elder an elected governing official of the session in the Presbyterian church and other denominations; a deacon, church leader, presbyter, or teacher chosen on the basis of age, wisdom, experience and, over much of history, gender. In Maya Angelou's *I Know Why the Caged Bird Sings,* the Reverend Thomas, the presiding elder who graces Mama Henderson's table for Sunday dinner, prays until fat congeals on the food and then eats the best parts of the chicken.

electrocardiogram or **EKG** literally, an electric picture of the heart, the chart, tracing, printout, or pattern on the screen of the oscilloscope produced by the electrocardiograph, a diagnostic tool attached to electrodes pasted on the body. The EKG, invented in 1903 by Dutch physiologist Willem Einthoven and improved in the early twentieth century by English clinician Sir Thomas Lewis, records the rhythm of electrical impulses with each beat of the heart and locates irregularities, or arrhythmias. An electrocardiogram of Father Takakura locates an abnormality, one of many physical ailments or malfunctions caused by radiation described in John Hersey's *Hiroshima.*

electroencephalograph or **EEG** literally, an electric picture of the brain, a diagnostic machine that attaches to the head with paste-on electrodes to record electrical activity in the brain, which is recorded on a chart, tracing, or printout. Invented in 1924 by German psychiatrist Hans Berger from studies of Einthoven's electrocardiograph, the EEG can detect the presence of a tumor as well as states of excitement, seizure, brain damage, sleep, coma, and retardation. The staff in Ken Kesey's *One Flew over the Cuckoo's Nest* study patients' brain activity with an electroencephalograph.

elements in Eastern lore, all earthly things are made up of a blend of metal, water, fire, wood, and earth. In Lu Hsun's "My Old Home," the speaker rejoices at the choice of a husband whose horoscope indicates that, of the five elements, he lacks earth. In Greek lore, Empedocles theorized that all things are made of unique blends of four elements—fire, air, earth, and water. Based on the study of alchemy, doctors applied this combination of elements to balancing inequalities in the body's four humors, said to derive from yellow bile, blood, black bile, and phlegm and to determine temperament, behavior, and stamina. In William Shakespeare's *The Tempest,* Prospero notes the importance of the four elements of human behavior.

elf-bolt flint arrowheads or spear points that folk tales describe as the weapons of elves. In a dreamy state, Catherine Linton, the protagonist of Emily Brontë's *Wuthering Heights,* pictures Nelly picking up elf-bolts on the moor.

ell an obsolete cloth or string measure dating to the Middle Ages and still used on the Isle of Jersey. An ell equals 45 inches or 1.14 meters; the Scottish ell, which is shorter, equals 37.2 inches. In Holland and Belgium, only 27 inches or 3/4 yard equal an ell. In William Shakespeare's *Romeo and Juliet,* Mercutio contrasts the size of an inch and an ell.

embryo the state of human or animal prenatal growth marked by development of primitive organs. The embryo follows the zygote stage, when the fertilized egg implants itself in the uterine wall. In the eighth week, the embryo becomes a fetus with fully viable organs and systems. Derived from the Greek for *swell,* the term entered English in the mid-sixteenth century. The Bokanovsky Process, a key innovation in Aldous Huxley's *Brave New World,* turns one embryo into 96 clones.

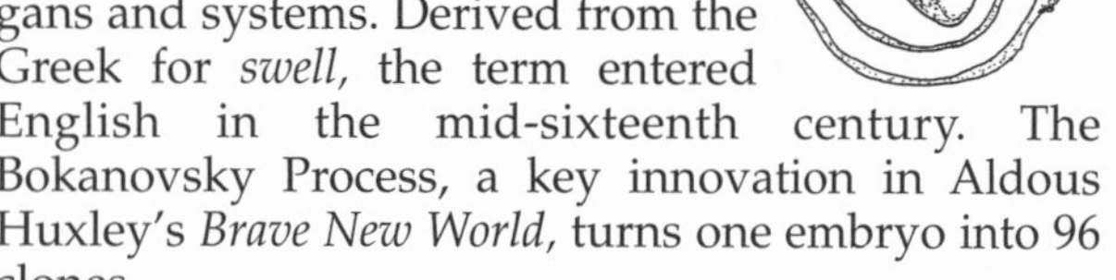

emetic (ee . *meht'* ihk) a substance or medicine that induces vomiting; an antidote to poisoning, such as ipecac, that disgorges unabsorbed poisons before they can pollute the bloodstream. After Emma, protagonist of Gustave Flaubert's *Madame Bovary,* swallows the emetic, she begins to vomit blood. *See also* ipecac.

Empire (ahm . *peer'*) **gown** a severely plain, high-waisted gown consisting of puffed sleeves; a bodice, or spencer, to the bottom of the bust; and a tubular skirt, often overlayered with gauze, silk, or tulle and falling from the bustline straight to the floor. The Empire gowns worn by the fashionable New Orleans ladies described in Kate Chopin's "The Awakening" mimic the style worn by women in Napoleon's court. *See also* spencer.

endgame or **end game** the concluding stage of a bridge game or chess match when the number of game pieces or cards has been reduced to the final face-off; a showdown or final battle of wits or skill. Waverly Jong, the chess whiz in Amy Tan's *The Joy Luck Club,* realizes the need for patience, strategy, control, and foresight during the endgame.

ensign (*ehn'* sihn) an emblem, standard, or heraldic banner; a distinctive badge of rank or loyalty, national or military insignia, colors, or flag, which is valued as a symbol or representation of honor or allegiance. Charlie Marlowe, the narrator in Joseph Conrad's *The Heart of Darkness,* recalls coming upon a French man-of-war whose ensign drooped during the heat of battle. *See also* escutcheon.

entailment a limitation or restriction on the inheritance of property to a specific line or succession of heirs as a means of assuring that the land or building will remain within the family of the original owner. Entailment is a major motivating factor to Max's murder of his adulterous wife, the title character in Daphne du Maurier's *Rebecca.* Scout asks Mr. Cunningham about his entailment, a legal matter that Atticus Finch manages in Harper Lee's *To Kill a Mockingbird.*

enzyme (*ehn'* zym) one of a number of complex proteins that act like catalysts at body temperature by binding to other molecules to trigger or accelerate internal processes or reactions such as digestion of the lactic acid in milk products. The biochemical term, which entered English in the late nineteenth century, derives from the Greek for *yeast.* In an unseemly academic squabble in Daniel Keyes's *Flowers for Algernon,* Dr. Strauss claims that his psychosurgery and enzyme-injection patterns influenced the project more than Dr. Nemur's theories have.

epaulet or **epaulette** (*ehp'* uh . *leht*) one of a pair of ornamental shoulder decorations in the shape of a fringed plate, band, loop, strap, buttoned tab, swirl of soutache, or other trim on a coat, dress, or shirt; a braided shoulder adornment to indicate rank on armor or a military dress uniform as well as the daily wear of guards, doorkeepers, train conductors, pilots, firefighters, and police officers. After the wedding of Cosette and Marius in Victor Hugo's *Les Misérables,* an usher in colonel's epaulets escorts them from the church.

épergne (ay . *puhrn'*) an ornate, branching metal centerpiece for table or sideboard. The épergne contains movable dishes to display a mix of fruit, sweetmeats, glass or marble objects, or flowers. At Satis House, the home of Miss Havisham in Charles Dickens's *Great Expectations,* Pip finds spiderwebs cloaking the long unused épergne that was meant to highlight her wedding banquet.

ephah (*ee'* fuh) an ancient Hebrew dry measure equal to 37 quarts, or slightly more than 9 gallons or a bushel. Originally Egyptian, the term entered English in 1611, the year that the King James Bible was published. In the biblical book of Ruth, the title character feeds herself and her mother-in-law Naomi by gleaning behind reapers in Boaz's fields and winnowing enough barley to make an ephah of grain. *See also* winnow.

ephemeris (eh . *fehm'* uh . rihs) an astronomical handbook, almanac, table, or guide that sets the limits for charting horoscopes to predict how the ephemerides, the orbital positions of planets, satellites, and comets at a particular time, will influence a person's behavior, temperament, and destiny. In William J. Lederer and Eugene Burdick's *The Ugly American,* Colonel Hillandale ingratiates himself with superstitious people by bringing his ephemeris and log tables.

epitaph an inscription, commemorative verse, citation, valediction, or brief statement on a grave, monument, or tombstone that honors the dead; a short literary composition that summarizes the philosophy or accomplishments of the deceased. In Lorraine Hansberry's *A Raisin in the Sun,* Mama asks Beneatha if she has written her brother's epitaph to indicate that he has sealed his fate.

epitome (ih . *pih'* toh . mee) an embodiment, quintessence, summation, model, or representation; the symbol of an abstract idea, quality, characteristic, ideal, or belief. In "The Bear," William Faulkner refers to the animal as the epitome of nature and of a time before the wilderness was tamed, when the bear roamed free of human predators.

epode (*ehp'* ohd) the third and most metrically original segment of the Pindaric ode, which is composed of strophe, antistrophe, and epode; a serious lyrical conclusion or summary statement to the two segments that precede it, which the chorus sings on stage while standing in formation. In Sophocles' *Antigone,* the epode stresses that the title character faces death decreed by her implacable uncle, King Creon. *See also* antistrophe; strophe.

Epsom (*ehp'* suhm) **salts** magnesium sulfate, a bitter crystalline salt used as a laxative or in solution for soaking inflamed body parts to draw out poisons causing swelling, pain, or itch. Celie, the protagonist of Alice Walker's *The Color Purple,* bathes in milk and Epsom salts to help her sleep. *See also* dose of salts.

equinox (*ee'* kwih . nahks) the date when the sun crosses the celestial equator, equalizing the length of day and night. In the Northern Hemisphere, the vernal equinox occurs on March 21 and the autumnal equinox on September 22 or 23, varying every eight revolutions for leap year; the dates reverse for the Southern Hemisphere. About the time of the equinox, the days are so short that the title character in Thomas Hardy's *Tess of the D'Urbervilles* must work by candlelight.

equipage (e . *kwih'* pihj) the carriage, harness, decorative brass, horses, and servants needed for a journey or formal parade; the furnishings, trappings, or necessities for a ceremonial procession or retinue that is held to display the wealth, power, and prestige of the participants. In *A Tale of Two Cities,* Charles Dickens reports that the traveler journeying from London to Paris met with rough roads and bad equipage.

escritoire (*ehs'* krih . twahr) a dainty, sometimes elegantly scrolled chest, portable lapboard, secretary, desk, or table with a hinged top drawer that can be raised or let down to form a writing desk. Inside are cubbies and shelves to accommodate stamps, stationery, ink, pens, blotter, personal items, and correspondence. In Charles Dickens's *David Copperfield,* Uriah Heep sits at an escritoire, where he keeps accounts.

escutcheon (ehs . *kut'* chuhn) a shield-shaped badge, ornamental plate, entablature, or emblem featuring a flanged or fluted edge and bearing an insignia or coat of arms as a display of honor or prestige, often conferred by royalty and inherited by succeeding family members. In Charles Dickens's *A Tale of Two Cities,* the Monsignor takes care to protect the good name indicated by the emblem on his escutcheon. *See also* ensign.

esker (*ehs'* kuhr) a long, narrow winding ridge or causeway of stratified layers of boulders, gravel, sand, or other sediment carried by a stream of melted runoff either above or under the rim of a stagnant glacier; a channel deposit quarried for gravel or sand. Derived from the Irish for *ridge,* the term entered English in the mid-nineteenth century. An esker overlooks zoologist Farley Mowat's observation post on the bay in *Never Cry Wolf,* where he records information about the local flora and fauna.

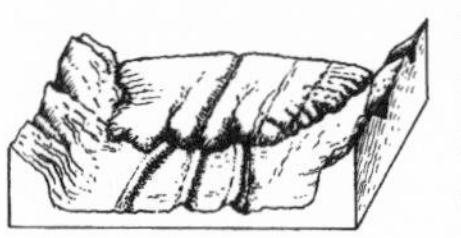

esplanade (ehs . pluh . *nahd'*) a sloping, open walkway or promenade, either paved, grassed, or graveled, to be used as a bike path or pedestrian concourse through a park or along a boulevard, quay, or shoreline. At the esplanade alongside the Conservatory, Jean Valjean, the protagonist of Victor Hugo's *Les Misérables,* conducts Cosette out of the carriage and through the streets.

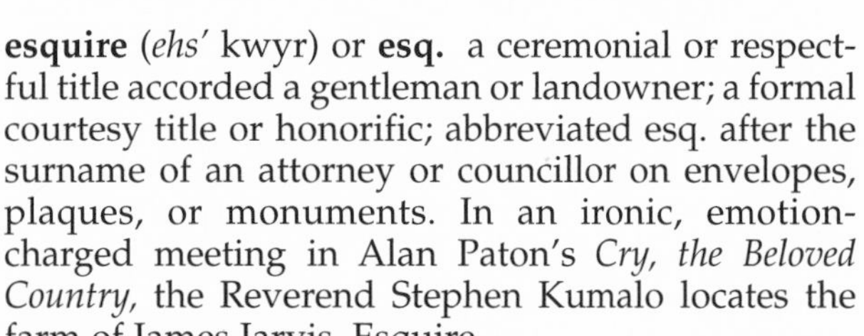

esquire (*ehs'* kwyr) or **esq.** a ceremonial or respectful title accorded a gentleman or landowner; a formal courtesy title or honorific; abbreviated esq. after the surname of an attorney or councillor on envelopes, plaques, or monuments. In an ironic, emotion-charged meeting in Alan Paton's *Cry, the Beloved Country,* the Reverend Stephen Kumalo locates the farm of James Jarvis, Esquire.

EST or **electroshock therapy** the use of low levels of electric current passed by electrodes through the brain of a sedated patient for a fraction of a second to treat depression or mental instability; also, electroconvulsive therapy. A technician in Ken Kesey's *One Flew Over the Cuckoo's Nest* suggests administering EST to a patient who is already sedated with Seconal. *See also* Seconal.

estuary (*ehs'* chuh . *wer* . ee) the wide V-shaped conjunction of a river or freshwater stream with ocean tides; a firth, tidal inlet, fjord, coastal river valley, or arm of the sea that penetrates the shore and tempers saltwater with fresh. An estuary is often a tidal flat, marked by sandbars, river-borne debris, clay, and organic matter that nurtures valuable stocks of shellfish and crustaceans in the brackish water. In the opening scene of Joseph Conrad's *The Heart of Darkness,* the *Nellie* crosses from the Thames estuary into the sea, a symbolic passage illustrating the moral crossover that dooms Kurtz and his ilk for their despoliation of Africa, its resources, and its people.

étagère (*a* . tah . *zhayr'* or *eh* . tuh . *zhehr'*) an open, backless wall unit or suite of shelves atop a cabinet or enclosed base. Sometimes built completely of glass and lighted with concealed bulbs, the étagère is a decorative piece of furniture intended as a focal point to display collected items, books, or a mix of art objects and memorabilia, including photos and souvenirs. A mid-nineteenth century term, the word derives from the French for *stage* or *scaffolding.* The Helmers' home, the setting for Henrik Ibsen's *A Doll's House,* contains an étagère, a piece of furniture intended to display knicknacks and art objects. The unit suggests the affectation and pretense that Helmer projects to the outside world.

eulachon (*yoo'* luh . kuhn) *See* candlefish.

eunuch (*yoo'* nuhk) a man who has had his genitals removed; a nonthreatening, unsexed overseer or guard of a harem or residence of royal or upper-class girls and women. In Mary Renault's *The Persian Boy,* the story of Bagoas, the eunuch servant to Alexander the Great, begins with a brutal castration.

evangelist (ee . *van'* jih . lihst) a revivalist, missionary, or preacher of the gospel or Christian doctrine; a zealous, melodramatic, or emotional proselytizer or converter of non-Christians to orthodox faith. The work of the evangelist in helping nonbelievers attain salvation is usually accompanied by testimonials of sin, acts of contrition, prayers for intercession, and baptism. At the conclusion of Upton Sinclair's *The Jungle,* Jurgis learns about sin and redemption from a Chicago evangelist. *See also* contrition, act of.

evil eye the gaze or penetrating stare of a potentially malicious person possessing supernatural powers, such as a medium, witch, or sorcerer, who can overpower the will and force a victim to perform evil deeds. Often, the evil eye is associated with vengeance and can be avoided only by prayers and rituals, magic chants and potions, or the wearing of an amulet. In Sandra Cisneros's *The House on Mango Street,* Elenita, the witch woman, urges Esperanza to avoid the evil eye and to return on

Thursday for another psychic reading. *See also bruja; curandera.*

ewer (*yoo'* wuhr) a wide-lipped pitcher or vase-shaped water carrier with a handle and a flanged spout. The ewer is often paired with a decorative washbasin and fitted into a mirrored cabinet for use in a bedroom or private suite. A nobleman pulls a prank on Christopher Sly, a drunken beggar in William Shakespeare's *The Taming of the Shrew,* by having his staff transport Sly to rich surroundings and to provide him with such princely personal service as rosewater, a ewer of rinse water, and a drying cloth.

excise (*ehks'* syz) a tax, tariff, license, import duty, or customs charge on the manufacture, transportation, distribution, or use of a product, such as liquor, cigarettes, or gold jewelry; a levy, toll, or fee for a privilege, for example, parking a vehicle or vessel, crossing a causeway into a private reserve, or residing in a historic district. Derived from the Old French for *assess,* the term dates to the fifteenth century. In Charles Dickens's *David Copperfield,* the title character claims that his domestic situation has been so poorly managed that he must have paid an extravagant portion of the nation's excise tax on spices to unscrupulous dealers who overcharged him.

excommunicate to deprive of acceptance by a Roman Catholic or, less frequently, Anglican church ruling body; to exercise ecclesiastical or parish authority to deny the rites of the church, such as baptism, marriage, confirmation, confession, last rites, or burial on sacred ground. Also, to depose, eject, expel, sentence, curse, or damn. Derived from the Latin for *out of participation,* the term entered English in the fifteenth century. According to the title character in Charles Dickens's *David Copperfield,* he is weary from a long day at a tedious parish trial during which the Consistory of the Anglican assembly temporarily excommunicated a baker for refusing to pay a paving charge.

exordium (ehg . *zohr'* dyuhm) an introductory or kick-off speech or treatise; a discourse meant as a preface, foundation, or inauguration. A Latin term for *beginning,* the word entered English in the last quarter of the sixteenth century. On the first day of the school term in Charles Dickens's *David Copperfield,* the title character and his schoolmates listen to the menacing exordium spoken by Tungay, who threatens to lash all who deviate from school regulations.

expiation (*ehks* . pee. *a'* shuhn) an act of atonement, propitiation, or ceremonial cleansing; a purification rite, peace offering, or penance that compensates for a wrong or achieves forgiveness for sin. Also, reparation, redress, or amends for a misdeed. A formal religious rite meant to atone for guilt, the late sixteenth-century term derives from the Latin for *appease by means of sacrifice.* In Sophocles' *Oedipus Rex,* King Creon explains to the title character that the pollution that afflicts his realm must be cleansed with an act of expiation or blood atonement.

eyrie or **eyry** or **airie** or **airy** (*ayr'* ee or *eye'* ree) the grass-, moss-, and leaf-lined, cup-shaped nest of twigs and branches up to 5 feet long built by an eagle, osprey, hawk, or other large bird of prey. These birds prefer a lofty crag, cliff, ledge, or tall tree as a safe place to raise their young, which remain helpless and vulnerable to predators for an extended period. At the height of the pivotal battle in J. R. R. Tolkien's *The Hobbit,* Bilbo spies eagles from northern eyries in flight to rescue his party.

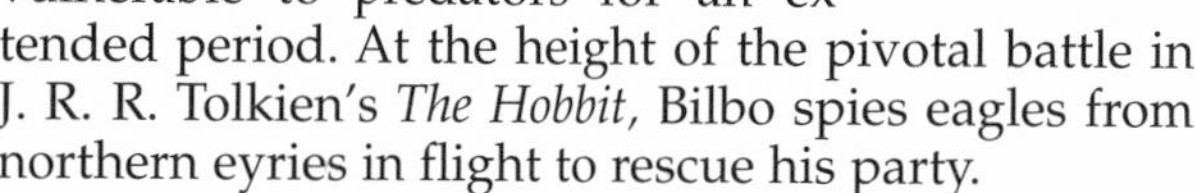

F

façade (fuh . *sahd'*) the false or superficial front or outward appearance of a building; an impressive or ornate surface treatment that is added to a plain wall to enhance its architectural appeal, to modernize or blend with surroundings, or to conceal damage or deterioration. In Amy Tan's *The Joy Luck Club,* Lena St. Clair recalls that her family moved to an old apartment building that was brightened on the outside with a renovated façade of stucco.

factotum (fak . *toh'* tuhm) a general servant, employee, majordomo, aide, or assistant who manages a wide variety of tasks and services; a jack-of-all-trades or custodian. Derived from the Latin for *do all,* the term dates to the mid-sixteenth century. A female servant at The Pure Drop in Thomas Hardy's *Tess of the D'Urbervilles* is a factotum, who also serves as groom and ostler. *See also* ostler.

faggot or **fagot** (*fag'* g't) a bundle of twigs, branches, sticks, kindling, or split pieces of firewood that are tied together for ease in transporting and selling; a network of branches used to fill ditches or to create a loosely fortified barrier. In Toni Morrison's *Beloved,* slave catchers light faggots under Six-O to roast him alive.

fakir (fuh . *keer'* or *fay'* kuhr) a wandering Muslim or Hindu beggar, peddler, or ascetic who whirls in religious ecstasy, makes a display of enduring the pain of self-mutilation or physical hardship, performs magic, or works miracles to impress an audience. Entering English in the early seventeenth century, the term derives from the Arabic for *poor man* or *mendicant.* In Jules Verne's *Around the World in Eighty Days,* rescuers watch fakirs, dotted with oozing wounds, whirling around a statue of the love goddess in preparation for a suttee, the public burning of a widow on her husband's funeral pyre. *See also* suttee.

false front a switch, fall, or wiglet of tendrils that enhances or augments a bouffant hairstyle, tucks in beside a hat or head covering, or covers a bald spot, injury, or scar. In Charlotte Brontë's *Jane Eyre,* Mrs. Brocklehurst makes a grand appearance before her husband's students at Lowood by displaying a velvet shawl trimmed in ermine and a false front of French curls.

falsetto (fahl . *seht'* toh) a forced or unnaturally high head tone that carries a male singing or speaking voice into a boyish, shrill, or effeminate range, often for comic effect or as a form of mockery; a sound produced in the treble range above the normal speaking voice by relaxing the thyro-arytenoid muscle that parallels the vocal cord. In Hal Borland's *When the Legends Die,* a boy ridicules Tom Black Bull by piping in falsetto, "My name is Bear Meat."

familiar any animal—especially an owl, snake, cat, toad, hedgehog, or bat—that serves as assistant or companion to a witch or sorcerer during the commission of evil or sacrilegious acts or as a sacrifice during devil worship. Some folklore describes the familiar's diet as human blood or breast milk. Suckling left "witch marks" that were displayed in court trials as evidence against defendants accused of witchcraft. In Elizabeth George Speare's *The Witch of Blackbird Pond,* local people label a cat as the familiar of Hannah Tupper, an isolated and unwanted elderly Quaker suspected of black magic.

fanfare an effusive, attention-getting flourish of trumpets, French horns, or other brass musical instruments, often welcoming royalty, accompanying the arrival of dignitaries, or announcing an important event on a battlefield or in a jousting ring. In Edmond Rostand's *Cyrano de Bergerac,* Comte de Guiche interprets a joyous fanfare as proof that French reinforcements are arriving at a critical point in the battle. *See also* flourish; sennet.

fanlight a semicircle of clear or colored glass over a front door or across an entranceway. The fanlight admits filtered sunlight into a foyer or hall; patterned colors on the floor often complement oriental rugs, chandeliers, sconces, or other decorations. In Margaret Atwood's *The Handmaid's Tale,* the contrast of red and blue panes in the fanlight heightens the antipathy between the Handmaid, wearing a red uniform, and her rival, the mistress of the house, dressed in blue.

fanning wheat *See* winnow.

faquir *See* fakir.

fardel (*fahr'* d'l) a burden, bundle, faggot, or heavy load; in the religious sense, a sin, suffering, moral dilemma, or cumbrous emotional baggage or unconfessed wickedness that impedes spirituality or contentment. The word derives from an Arabic term. In William Shakespeare's *Hamlet,* the title character, while pondering suicide, asks why anyone would deliberately burden himself with a fardel. *See also* faggot.

farden *See* farthing.

faro (*fay'* roh) **dealer** a gambler or cardsharp who presides over faro, a game in which players bet on the outcome of the next draw from the dealer's box, from which the dealer slides cards one at a time. An eighteenth-century term, it derives from the phonetic spelling of *pharaoh,* an Egyptian ruler pictured on the backs of the cards. In Jack London's *White Fang,* the faro dealer owns Cherokee, a bulldog who refuses to loosen his grip on the neck of his opponent.

farol (fuh . *rohl'*) a portable lantern that contains a small tank of oil and a moveable wick that can be cranked up or down by an adjusting dial or knob to increase or decrease the intensity of the flame or to extinguish the lantern. A removable glass globe, which must be wiped clean of soot to permit maximum glow, shields the light from wind and humidity. The word is Spanish for *lantern.* In Rudolfo Anaya's *Bless Me, Ultima,* Antonio's father fumbles with the farol as he tries to respond to the messenger at the door.

farrago (fuh . *rah'* goh) a mishmash, jumble, blend, or hodgepodge; gibberish; a confusion of words or thoughts. Derived for the Latin term for *mixed grain,* the word entered English in the early seventeenth century. Dr. Lanyon, who is at a loss to explain the farrago in Henry Jekyll's letter, hurries to confer with Dr. Jekyll's butler in Robert Louis Stevenson's *The Strange Case of Dr. Jekyll and Mr. Hyde.*

farrier (*fayr'* ree . uhr) a blacksmith and forerunner of the veterinarian, who treats animals for infestations of parasites or minor cuts, doses them with simple remedies, attends difficult births of colts and calves, and puts shoes on horses and mules. At the local pub, the farrier in George Eliot's *Silas Marner* receives respect from locals for his medical expertise and practical wisdom.

farrow (*far'* roh) a piglet or a litter of pigs; also, the act of giving birth to piglets. When the title character in William Shakespeare's *Macbeth* asks witches to summon a prophetic image, a witch blends in the blood of a female pig who has eaten her nine farrow, an ominous image of savagery and atavism.

farthing (*fahr'* thing) or **farden** a virtually worthless coin or mite valued at a quarter of a penny in the old British monetary system. Derived from the Old English term for *a fourth,* the word entered English before the twelfth century. In Fyodor Dostoevsky's *Crime and Punishment,* Marmelodov rants on about poverty, complaining that his daughter cannot earn even 15 farthings a day at respectable forms of labor.

farthingale (*fahr'* thin . gayl) a canvas petticoat inset with one or more wicker hoops a few inches below the waist to hold the skirt at a distance from the body, thus emphasizing a small waist and causing a graceful sway of the fabric. Farthingales took either a drum shape with straight fall of cloth or a bell form that expanded the skirt gradually to a wide flounce at floor level. In William Shakespeare's *The Taming of the Shrew,* Petruchio plans to return to his father-in-law's house in splendor, with his wife decked in jewels and wearing a farthingale.

fascinator (*fa'* sih . *nay* . tuhr) a lightweight netted, crocheted, tatted, or lace head scarf, often worn loosely thrown around the neck, knotted at each end, and weighted with a bead or bauble to keep it from slipping off. As Mattie dances the Virginia reel with Denis Eady in Edith Wharton's *Ethan Frome,* the title character studies the girl's cherry-colored fascinator, a symbol of her intense allure.

fascism (*fash'* izm) a belief in the strong, brutal central control of government that quells public involvement and opposition by stifling freedom of speech and civil rights. Robert Jordan, explosives expert and protagonist in Ernest Hemingway's *For Whom the Bell Tolls,* joins Pablo's guerrilla band to counter fascism in Spain by blowing up a bridge.

Fata Morgana (*fah'* tuh mor . *ga'* nuh) a mirage, or refractive illusion, native to the Strait of Messina between Sicily and mainland Italy that causes the horizon to appear in an elongated double reflection, both below and above the object. The phenomenon, which takes its name from Morgan le Fay, the lurking sorceress of Arthurian legend, results from a warm air mass overspreading chilled air at the water's surface. As the *Pequod* sinks in Herman Melville's *Moby-Dick,* the glimmer of its masts in the distance suggests the "castles in the air" illusion of the Fata Morgana.

fathom (*fa'* thuhm) an obsolete unit of linear measure equaling 6 feet or 1.8256 meters; common to the nautical measure of ropes, chains, soundings, and depths before the metric system and sonar replaced it. The term derives from the Old English word for *embrace* because it represents the side-to-side measure of a man's outstretched arms. In one of the most famous songs from William Shakespeare's plays, Ariel, the sprite in *The Tempest,* sings "Full fathom five thy father lies."

faun (fawn) in Roman mythology, a lustful rural wood spirit, prophet, and follower of Faunus, the god of herders and pasturing animals. The faun, which resembles the satyr, has almost an entirely human male body and the ears, tail, and cloven feet of a goat. In Edith Hamilton's *Mythology,* Evander explains that the arrival of Saturn on earth cleared the land of fauns and satyrs and made a suitable human dwelling. *See also* satyr.

feather the oars to reduce drag on a small boat by angling the blade of the oar edgeways rather than vertically to combat choppy conditions, as though dipping the widest part of a feather in the water. In Ernest Hemingway's *A Farewell to Arms,* Frederick Henry, the protagonist, does not have to feather the oars as he rows toward Switzerland because he is moving with the wind rather than against it.

fee sheet a voucher, expense account, or ruled daily log that a traveling employee submits to an employer to obtain reimbursement for food, lodging, mileage, supplies, and incidentals purchased as a part of a field assignment or job. In Charles Portis's *True Grit,* Mattie Ross helps U.S. Marshal Rooster Cogburn fill out his fee sheets in neat, logical chronological order.

feist (fyst) or **fyce** a small, aggressive cur; a slick-haired, contentious mongrel trained to hunt bears. Derived from the Middle English term for *break wind,* the word entered English in the late eighteenth century as *fisting hound,* a combative dog that attacks animals far beyond its capacity to capture or subdue. In Marjorie Kinnan Rawlings's *The Yearling,* Penny doubts that Perk, the family feist, is a true bear-dog.

felloe (*fehl'* loh) or **felly** the arced segment of wheel rim that separates two spokes. In the opening scene of Thomas Hardy's *The Mayor of Casterbridge,* the dewy grass bears the marks of the felloes of carts driven by gypsies and showmen on their way to the Weydon-Priors fair, suggesting the parts of the circle that make up Henchard's rise and fall.

felon a criminal, traitor, murderous villain, or otherwise wicked, reprehensible person guilty of a serious or capital crime, such as arson, rape, murder, sedition, kidnapping, or armed robbery. In the autobiographical *Narrative of the Life of Frederick Douglass,* the title character claims that a slave owner is a felon by nature of owning other human beings.

fen 0.01 or 1/100 of a yuan, the basic monetary unit of China (which was the equivalent of an American half-dollar during the 1930s), or 0.1 or 1/10 of a *jiao,* a Chinese dime. In Amy Tan's *The Kitchen God's Wife,* Winnie's mother-in-law is so greedy and suspicious that she insults a trusted servant over 10 fen, or a penny, which she expected as change from her purchase. *See also* yuan.

fender a low, decorative metal screen or frame opposite the hearth rug enclosing the outer rim of an open fireplace to keep hot coals from popping or tumbling onto the floor. The fender is often the spot where people prop wet shoes to dry or warm cold, damp feet. When Alice writes a letter to her right foot in Lewis Carroll's *Alice's Adventures in Wonderland,* she addresses the envelope to "Hearthrug, near the Fender. (with Alice's love)."

fenian movement (*fee'* nee . uhn) a secret anti-Anglican, anti-British terrorist or revolutionary society among Irish Catholics in Ireland and the United States, centered in Catholic communities in Boston, New York, and Baltimore, who seek the overthrow of British rule on Irish soil. The term derives from the legendary Irish warrior cult of the second and third centuries, which was named for the hero Fionn or Finn. In James Joyce's *A Portrait of the Artist as a Young Man,* Mr. Casey's explosive table conversation introduces the argument against Catholicism for the bishops' dishonor of rebels and for his pulpit denunciation of the fenian movement.

fennel (*fen'* n'l) an edible, aromatic licorice-flavored cooking herb of the carrot family. Fennel seeds are prized in a tea for their soothing effect on a queasy stomach and as a cure for flatulence, sore eyes, and chest colds. In her madness, Ophelia, girlfriend of the title character in William Shakespeare's *Hamlet,* offers herbs and flowers that bear symbolic meaning, especially fennel for flattery, columbine for faithlessness, daisies for falsehood, violets for faith, and rue for repentance.

ferule or **ferrule** (*fehr'* ruhl) the protective or reinforcing metal tip at the end of a walking stick or a teacher's cane, which is used to strike unruly students; a metal ring used to join two sections of cane or two slender wooden dowels or to connect a handle of a paintbrush to the bristles. Derived from the Latin word for *iron,* ferule entered English in the early seventeenth century. In Herman Melville's *Moby-Dick,* Captain Ahab breaks off the ferrule of his ivory prosthetic leg and must lean on Starbuck.

festoon (fehs . *toon'*) a looped, curved, or draped chain, strip, ribbon, garland of flowers, greenery, or yard goods or bunting in patriotic or seasonal colors used to adorn clothing, walls, staircases, and door frames; also, the carved or painted likeness of a festoon on wood or plaster moldings. In Joseph Conrad's *The Heart of Darkness,* vines enshroud the silent African jungle in festoons. In the ominous red room in Charlotte Brontë's *Jane Eyre,* the bed is liberally draped and festooned with hangings, which both adorn the furnishings and protect sleepers from light and drafts. *See also* bunting.

fetters ankle chains, restraints, bindings, or shackles on the feet. Often connected by a chain to manacles or handcuffs, fetters impede the free range or escape of animals, slaves, or prisoners. Entering English before the twelfth century, the term derives from the Old English for *foot.* On a tour of Newgate Prison, Pip, the protagonist of Charles Dickens's *Great Expectations,* spies fetters hanging from the wall. *See also* ball and chain; coffle.

fez (fehz) *pl.* **fezzes** a brimless, flat-topped cone hat worn by Muslim men of the Mediterranean Rim and signifying the national dress of Turks until the beginning of the twentieth century, when Turkey became a republic. The fez is made of felt—usually wine-red, black, or blue—decorated with a black silk tassel on top that hangs below the bottom rim. Named for the town of Fez, Morocco, the term entered English in the nineteenth century. Enamored of romantic touches in music and art, Emma, protagonist in Gustave Flaubert's *Madame Bovary,* enjoys the fezzes and sabers of Turkish costumes.

fiacre (fee . *ah'* kruh) a small, boxy four-wheeled hackney chariot or hired carriage drawn by two or four horses. Derived from the Irish Saint Fiacre, patron of the poor, the coaches were for hire at the Hotel de Saint Fiacre in the Rue Saint Antoine in Paris; the term entered English in the seventeenth century. In Victor Hugo's *Les Misérables,* the family in the garret look forward to the arrival of the philanthropist, who displays his wealth by riding in a fiacre.

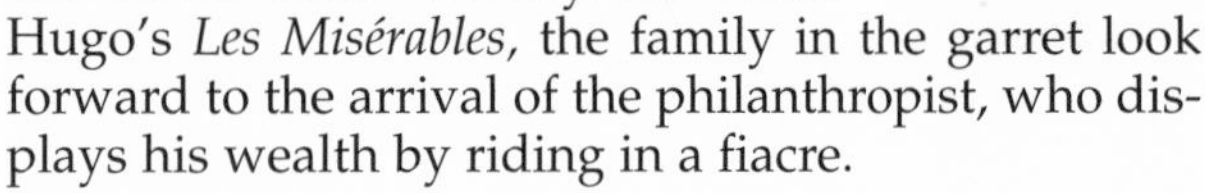

fibula (*fih'* byoo . luh) a slender pin, buckle, or decorative clasp similar to a safety pin, used in ancient Rome to fasten a robe, tunic, cape, or stole, especially in a fashionable clutch or mingling of draped materials at the shoulder. In *The Mayor of Casterbridge,* Thomas Hardy notes how frequently Roman skeletons are found in the English town, often interred with a brooch or fibula to fasten funereal dress.

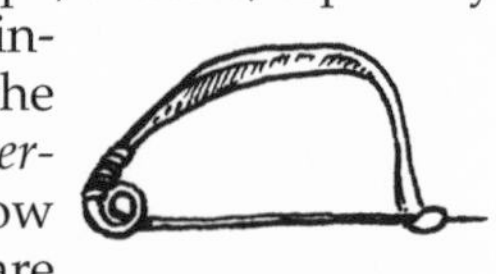

fiend (feend) an inhumanly evil, diabolical, or monstrous spirit; a superhuman devil; malevolent demon; or cunning, cruel, or wicked enemy; a synonym for Satan. Entering English before the twelfth century, the term derives from the Sanskrit for *scorn.* The narrator in Nathaniel Hawthorne's *The Scarlet Letter* blames the Fiend for damning Hester Prynne with a constant reminder of her sin.

fiesta (fee . *ehs'* tuh) among Spanish and Latin American Catholics, a Christian feast day celebrating a religious holiday or honoring a saint with gala processions, dancing, games, commemorative foods, tableaus, and merriment. Derived from the Latin for *feast,* the term entered English in the nineteenth century. In John Steinbeck's *The Pearl,* Kino, a poor man who works hard and earns little, recalls a fiesta when he ate an enormous number of cookies.

filaments (*fihl'* uh . mehntz) the frail, poison-charged tentacles, or tendrils, that trail as far as 50 meters below the body of the Portuguese man-of-war to entrap and paralyze prey. In Ernest Hemingway's *The Old Man and the Sea,* the iridescent Portuguese man-of-war, which is common in the Gulf Stream, trails its filaments harmlessly among tiny fish but can inflict a painful sting on human flesh.

filigree (*fih'* lih . gree) intricate, fanciful openwork or embellished designs decked with jewels and plaited, intertwined, or woven in wire or delicate metal strips or soldered to the surface of jewelry, Christmas ornaments, or wall decorations. A nineteenth-century term, *filigree* derives from the Latin for *wired grains.* In Fyodor Dostoevsky's *Crime and Punishment,* Raskolnikov murders a pawnbroker with an ax, steals a leather pouch, but rejects crosses and an image in filigree.

finger bowl a dainty bowl or shallow saucer filled with scented water, herbs, and fragrant petals and offered by a servant or placed at a table setting for washing or rinsing the fingertips, usually after the last course of a meal. In Willa Cather's *My Antonia,*

Mr. Cutter angers his wife by smashing a finger bowl that she had decorated with painted flowers.

fingerling the immature stage in the life of a trout or salmon, when the fish is still slender, without evidence of the sturdy body of an adult; a minnow or parr. In Margaret Craven's *I Heard the Owl Call My Name,* Jim points out the stages of the salmon's life and stresses that the fingerling swims to its destiny out of the river and into the sea, a foreshadowing of the dying priest's fate among the Kwakiutl.

finger post one of a set of directional signs at a junction or crossroads that lists a town and the distance to it. The finger post is shaped and painted to resemble a projecting arm and hand and points a finger in the appropriate direction. After accidentally killing Wildfire, his brother's horse, Dunstan Cass, the villain in George Eliot's *Silas Marner,* sets off in search of the Rainbow Inn in the direction pointed out by the finger post.

firebrand a mischief-maker or contentious rebel; an agitator, malcontent, or inflamer of passions concerning commerce, land ownership, or war. Also, an inciter to riot, revolt, or combat with authorities; a rabble-rouser, usurper, or supplanter of a rightful ruler or heir. In Victor Hugo's *Les Misérables,* Jean Valjean describes himself as an unredeemed firebrand after his condemnation to the galleys.

firebreak a plowed strip of land, moat, cleared perimeter, or other natural obstacle set up as a precautionary barrier and intended to stop the spread of a forest, grass, or prairie fire. In Willa Cather's *My Antonia,* the firebreak was plowed beyond the hedge on Grandfather's farm.

firedrake (*fyr'* drayk) a mythic fire-breathing dragon that holds a central place in Teutonic literature, usually because it hovers over a hoarded trove of treasure and because it can extend eternal life to mortals who eat its heart or drink its blood. In *Beowulf,* the epic hero rules peacefully for 50 years until a firedrake flying by night begins to ravage the mead hall and its occupants.

fire drill a sharpened stick or root fitted to a groove in a plank and twirled between the hands or by a bowstring, which is wrapped around the upright and pulled like a starter cord. The resulting spark from the friction ignites tinder, for example, leaves, bark, moss, wood chips, rushes, or dried dung. Visitors to a Zuñi reservation in Aldous Huxley's *Brave New World* observe the Native American method of lighting a fire with a fire drill.

fitchew (*fiht'* choo) or **fitch** an obsolete name for a skunk or European polecat; a slender, carnivorous beast of the weasel family that preys on domestic fowl. Dismayed by Lenina Crowne's immodest behavior, John the Savage, the victim in Aldous Huxley's *Brave New World,* labels her a fitchew, a word he learned from reading William Shakespeare's plays.

five-pound note paper money worth five pounds, a British denomination of currency. In George Orwell's *Animal Farm,* Frederick pays Napoleon for lumber with five-pound notes. *See also* pound.

Five-Year Plan the economic plan for gradual development of socialized industry, trade, agriculture, and internal improvements in the U.S.S.R., the first beginning in 1928 and ending in 1933. In Moss Hart and George S. Kaufman's *You Can't Take It with You,* Mr. Kolenkhov, the immigrant ballet master, predicts that the third Five-Year Plan will be as disastrous as the second.

fixing ceremony a ritual washing of a corpse with soap or herbal preparations, stopping of body orifices, dressing in a shroud, winding-sheet, or funeral garb, and arrangement of limbs, expression, gesture, and hair preceding presentation to mourners. As mentioned by Toni Morrison in *Beloved,* the corpse is "fixed," or forced into shape, before rigor mortis makes the joints and muscles too stiff for placement. *See also* winding-sheet.

flagellation (flaj . ihl . *lay'* shuhn) hitting, whipping, flogging, or beating with a scourge made from a handle attached to loose strands of leather, hemp, or rope that are knotted and/or studded on the ends with nails, burs, or metal tips that rip and tear, leaving thick scars and sometimes killing the victim. In William Lloyd Garrison's preface to *Narrative of the Life of Frederick Douglass,* he mentions the inhuman treatment of slaves, who endure thumb screws, flagellation, shackles, and other torments at the hands of cruel masters.

flagged path a paved walkway composed of odd-shaped flat flagstone, split striated stone, or slate that is often placed in a meandering, asymmetrical pattern in a garden or at the entrance of a house. The speaker in Edith Wharton's *Ethan*

Frome enters the Widow Hale's house by passing between paired Norway spruces and following the flagged path to the portico.

flagon (*flag'* uhn) a large, often pot-bellied metal or pottery pitcher with a handle, spout, and hinged lid. The flagon, which dates to the fifteenth century, held several servings of liquid and retained the temperature of chilled ale or cider or hot wine punch or holiday wassail, a Christmas favorite; the container was designed for easy pouring at the table by servants or seated diners or for use as a communion or ceremonial vessel. In Esther Forbes's *Johnny Tremain,* Cilla runs to the cellar for a flagon of cold ale. *See also* tankard; wassail.

flail a wooden or leather threshing tool composed of a solid handstaff attached by thong to a loose or jointed swingle or beater that is used like a whip against stalks of grain. The flail gave place to more efficient mechanical threshers in the nineteenth century. Before winnowing or separating grain from chaff in Pearl S. Buck's *The Good Earth,* workers beat the stalks with flails to knock loose the grain heads from lightweight husks and stalks.

flak jacket a heavily padded bulletproof vest or jacket meant to protect the major body organs from bullets, shrapnel, or concussion. An acronym derived from the German ***Fl**ieger**a**bwehr**k**anonen* or *flier defense cannon,* the term entered English in the late 1930s. In *Zlata's Diary,* Zlata Filipovic writes that the flak jacket is a necessary torso protector for civilians and news reporters who cross war zones to take photos, to deliver messages or confer with people on the opposite side, or to secure water, food, or medical care.

flambeau (flahm . *boh'*) *pl.* **flambeaux** a flaming torch made from dried timber dipped or soaked in pitch or from multiple waxed wicks plaited into a single stem. The flambeau could be carried to light the way for a night procession or hunt or, as described by Charles Dickens in *A Tale of Two Cities,* be positioned in an iron sconce and angled from the wall to throw light on a path, doorway, or steps. *See also* candlefish; rushlight; taper.

flamethrower a portable antipersonnel assault gun and backpack that hurls a stream of burning fuel into open hatches, bunkers, or trenches. Introduced by the German army in 1915, the simple flamethrower evolved into a mobile, tank-mounted weapon by World War II, for which scientists at Harvard invented a new destructive gel called napalm, a lethal defoliant composed of gasoline and soap. Young German soldiers in the trenches in Erich Maria Remarque's *All Quiet on the Western Front* fear rumors of flamethrowers.

flank one of the ends of a line of infantrymen; one of the lateral extremes or wings of battle formation, whether foot soldiers, mobile artillery, or cavalry. Julius Caesar utilized the two-horned flanking attack called the *cornu,* or horn, from the inward curve of opposite ends toward the center, allowing no escape for the enemy. In Ernest Hemingway's *A Farewell to Arms,* Frederick Henry ponders how the flank would lose its best men if it were turned on a mountain slope to face gunfire from the enemy below.

flask a small, flat pocket container featuring a screw-on cap suitable for use as a cup or measure for liquor or hot drinks; a cleverly designed container intended to conceal alcohol in a pocket, walking stick, book, or other hiding place. As he recalls in his autobiographical *Black Boy,* Richard Wright was only a preschooler when men bought him drinks at the bar or gave him swallows from flasks on the street.

flatbed *See* skiff.

flatcar a topless, sideless railroad car with attachable side bars, posts, and end pieces to accommodate odd-shaped loads, such as stacked logs or heavy machinery. In Yoko Kawashima Watkins's *So Far from the Bamboo Grove,* the fleeing women hide under a tarp covering a flatcar loaded with lumber.

flax fibers from the stem of the flax plant that are soaked, extracted, cleaned, combed, and spun into linen thread. Woven into cloth used for sheets and ceremonial garments, flax was revered in ancient Egypt and Greece for its pure white color and graceful drape. As mayor, Jean Valjean, protagonist in Victor Hugo's *Les Misérables,* supports a flax-spinning factory as well as plants producing jet and tulle.

flint a hard, dark-colored silica or fine-grained quartz that strikes sparks when hit against steel. Early cigarette lighters required frequent replacement of flint as the striker wore down the original flint. In Ernest Gaines's *The Autobiography of Miss Jane Pittman,* the title character treasures a flint rock and a lump of iron given in trust by Big Laura, who was killed by slave-catchers, leaving behind an orphaned toddler.

flintlock a firearm dependent on the spring action of the trigger, which caused the hammer to strike the flint, which in turn created a spark to ignite the powder in the priming pan, fire the main charge, and propel the ball from the bore. Invented by Marin le Bourgeois in the early seventeenth century, the flintlock musket, which was easy to load and cheap to manufacture, remained in use for two centuries before it was replaced by the percussion lock. The desperate rebels forming ranks in Boston in Esther Forbes's *Johnny Tremain* treasure any old flintlocks, squirrel guns, and fowling pieces that will help them beat off the Redcoats. *See also* match; musket.

flip a blended or whipped beverage composed of beer, whiskey, or cider and sugar stirred together with milk, beaten eggs, spices, or flavorings in a tankard and heated by plunging a red-hot poker into the mix. At a grim supper with his family, Pip, the protagonist of Charles Dickens's *Great Expectations,* eats roast fowl and drinks a flip.

flivver *(flihv'* vuhr) a cheap, insubstantial vehicle, usually old and unreliable; a jalopy, frequently sporting mismatched bumpers, used parts, and a noisy engine or muffler. An American slang term of indeterminate origin, the word dates to the first days of the automobile culture. In Zora Neale Hurston's *Their Eyes Were Watching God,* migrant field hands arrive in flivvers for the picking season.

flock bed a homemade mattress, casing, or ticking stuffed with inferior wool scraps, cotton tufts, ends of yard goods, discarded clothing, shredded upholstery or curtains, linen waste, cleaning rags, and other odds and ends. George Eliot notes in *Silas Marner* that the country people around Raveloe often hoard money in their flock beds. *See also* tick.

flocked decorated with short, fuzzy pulverized fibers formed into a raised textured pattern as decoration for wallpaper, upholstery, book jackets, or coverlets. Offred, the protagonist in Margaret Atwood's *The Handmaid's Tale,* sleeps in a bed covered by a chaste, white flocked spread, ironically suggesting fuzzy lambs and innocence beneath the spot where the previous handmaid hanged herself on a ceiling light fixture.

floorwalker a roving manager or overseer of a department store or factory who supervises employees; keeps order; assists clients; surveys the condition and cleanliness of machinery and facilities; and prevents waste, theft, or damage. The Grand Duchess boasts that Uncle Sergei will advance to the job of floorwalker in Moss Hart and George S. Kaufman's *You Can't Take It with You.*

florin *(flohr'* ihn) a guilder or gulden, the monetary unit presently worth 100 cents in Holland, Surinam, and the Netherlands Antilles. Originally named *fiorino* for the embossed lily on one side, the florin, first minted in the mid-thirteenth century, was common currency throughout Europe. In *The Diary of a Young Girl,* Anne Frank comments that because a pound of coffee has risen in price to 80 florins ($22.40 in the late twentieth-century economy), citizens are tempted to trade on the black market. *See also* gutter.

flourish a lengthy, ostentatious, or ornamental trumpet call preceding a processional to announce or draw attention to prestigious guests, nobles, or royalty. In William Shakespeare's *Julius Caesar,* the playwright purposely leaves the arrival of the key dramatis personae until Scene 2, when a flourish accompanies the entrance of the title character and other dignitaries to the holiday course. *See also* fanfare; sennet.

flue a pipe, channel, duct, or shaft; a subway tunnel. Also, the conduit by which air enters a chimney and smoke exits. After work, Guy Montag, protagonist of Ray Bradbury's *Fahrenheit 451,* leaves the fire station and takes a subway, which glides down a lubricated flue. Because *flue* usually applies to chimneys or steam pipes, the author deliberately compares the shaft to heat, smoke, or steam, all of which impinge on the firefighter's job.

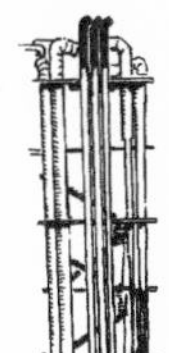

flukes the spread wings or horizontal triangular lobes or fins of a whale's tail, which the animal displays in full width as it sounds and slaps the surface while diving headfirst to the bottom of the sea. In Herman Melville's *Moby-Dick,* Captain Ahab calls for the lowering of boats after he sights the flukes of the white whale. *See also* breach.

flutter mill a child's toy or model of a vertical waterwheel that rotates as the current strikes horizontal paddles or baffles; a flutter wheel or paper windmill. In Marjorie Kinnan Rawlings's *The Yearling,* Jody adjusts his flutter mill, which he builds out of twigs and palm leaves. In Robert Newton Peck's *A Day No Pigs Would Die,* Rob entertains his pet pig Pinky by building a flutter wheel, which he centers on two forked uprights.

fly a light, maneuverable one-horse carriage, hackney chariot, stagecoach, or hired cab, often found at depots, quays, shopping malls, theaters, and hotels. In Charles Dickens's *David Copperfield,* the title character returns a dropped horse cloth to a fly driver and asks directions to the home of his aunt, Betsy Trotwood. *See also* hackney chariot.

flying buttress *See* buttress.

flying fish a small saltwater surface-feeding fish with a slim, tapered body and succulent meat; a specialty either fried or broiled and served with lime at Caribbean breakfasts. The flying fish opens its chest and forked tail fins and leaps across the surface of the sea in a single smooth gliding motion. In Ernest Hemingway's *The Old Man and the Sea,* Santiago wrestles with his catch and eats raw slices of flying fish to keep up his strength.

flying jib one of a set of triangular sails attached to the foremast stays or extended booms and angled parallel with the bowsprit. While playing pirate, the boys in Mark Twain's *The Adventures of Tom Sawyer* call out the position of the flying jib. *See also* bowsprit.

flyman driver of a hired hackney chariot or fly; a cabman, deliveryman, or hireling. In Thomas Hardy's *The Mayor of Casterbridge,* after leaving Michael Henchard to contemplate the significance of her address, Elizabeth-Jane waves politely to the flyman. *See also* car man; fly.

fo'c'sle *See* forecastle.

fodder dry, coarsely chopped stems, leaves, sorghum heads, corn ears, hay, or straw placed in stalls, racks, or mangers to feed domestic animals—sheep, horses, cattle, or goats—especially during the winter. In *Narrative of the Life of Frederick Douglass,* the writer reports that, during fodder saving time, Mr. Covey drives the laborers past midnight.

foetal (*fee'* tuhl) **posture** or **fetal position** a body placement sometimes preceding sleep that curves the spine outward in a convex arc as the limbs draw inward to the abdomen and the head drops toward the chest, thus mimicking the position of unborn mammals. In Samuel Beckett's *Waiting for Godot,* Vladimir sings a repetitive lullaby as Estragon draws into a foetal posture and tries to sleep.

foil a long, slender, flexible fencing sword with a four-sided blade that tapers from the hand guard to a lethal point that is covered by a rounded knob to prevent injury during sporting events; an épée. In J. D. Salinger's *The Catcher in the Rye,* Holden admits that the fencing team forfeited the match because he left the foils and other equipment on the subway.

folio (*foh'* lee . oh) a large sheet or leaf of paper folded once to form a four-page or two-leaf document or advertising spread. The term derives from the Italian for *fold.* In Herman Melville's "Bartleby the Scrivener," the speaker notes that his copyist works for four cents a folio, which equals 100 words.

Follies an elaborate stage show, vaudeville performance, or dance revue composed of glamorously costumed and posed set pieces in which participants sing, dance, play musical instruments, perform gymnastic stunts, or act in tableaus or skits. In F. Scott Fitzgerald's *The Great Gatsby,* the single dancer beginning the evening's entertainment is rumored to be an understudy for the lead in the Follies.

fontanel or **fontanelle** (*fahn* . tuh . *nehl'*) a sensitive membrane or tissue that covers gaps in the incomplete juncture of the parietal bones of an infant's skull; one of the six "soft spots" in a baby's cranium. To the confusion of the title character in John Gardner's *Grendel,* the dragon disparages the thumb, fontanel, and technology as poor examples of human advancement.

food stamps a stamp or trading coupon issued monthly by the Food and Nutrition Service of the U.S. Department of Agriculture either free or at reduced rates to impoverished, homeless, or disabled people as a form of currency, or scrip, redeemable only in food stores for edible commodities, excluding household needs, cleaning supplies, alcohol, cigarettes, and other nonfood items. Initiated in 1964, food stamps are a method of hunger relief that formed an integral part of President Lyndon Johnson's vision of the Great

Society. In Toni Cade Bambara's "Blues Ain't No Mockin' Bird," a photographer and crew receive a chilly reception when they inquire about the food stamp program.

foo foo or **fufu** a traditional African dish composed of mashed yams that are eaten as a side dish, sweetened or spiced as an appetizer, or rolled into balls and added to broth or stew as dumplings. In Chinua Achebe's *Things Fall Apart,* a generous serving of foo foo is expected at ritual feasts, family gatherings, and community festivals as a display of wealth and hospitality.

foolscap (*foolz'* kap) a standard 13-by-8-inch sheet of writing paper. Derived for the watermark featuring a jester in cap and bells, the term entered English in the early seventeenth century. In Sir Arthur Conan Doyle's *The Hound of the Baskervilles,* Sherlock Holmes inspects a warning letter written on a folded sheet of foolscap.

fool's gold iron or copper sulfide or pyrite, a bright yellow striated mineral that glitters in its natural crystalline state, deceiving inexperienced gold prospectors with its luster. An unimpressed pearl dealer compares Kino's oversized pearl to fool's gold in John Steinbeck's *The Pearl.*

footpad a thief, brigand, spy, informer, or mugger on foot. Entering English in the seventeenth century, this colloquial term refers to highwaymen who prey on pedestrians, particularly those traveling alone after dark or on deserted stretches of road. On his way to Soho in Charles Dickens's *A Tale of Two Cities,* Mr. Lorry depends on Jerry Cruncher to ward off footpads.

foot-washers an American slang term referring to members of a fundamentalist subsect of Baptists who imitate Christ's humility before his disciples on Maundy Thursday (three days before Easter Sunday) by carrying towel and basin from member to member and performing a ritual rinsing of bare feet. Note that the ceremony has been observed in Eastern and Roman Catholic services as well as Lutheran, Anabaptist, and other Protestant denominations. Scout, the opinionated speaker in Harper Lee's *To Kill a Mockingbird,* compares the fervent foot-washers to the Devil.

forceps (*fohr'* sehps) tongs or pincers used to grasp or manipulate small objects such as gears or minute parts of a watch, to assist in dissection or the repair or removal of the teeth, or to remove bits of shrapnel or other debris from a wound. A standard medical tool, *forceps* derives from the Latin for *to take warm* and entered English in the early seventeenth century when British male midwife Peter Chamberlen used a homemade device for delivering babies. The major who examines Frederick Henry's wounds in Ernest Hemingway's *A Farewell to Arms* waves his forceps by way of greeting.

forebitts forward beams bolted to a ship's deck as a place to attach cables or secure rigging. *See also* bitt.

forebraces the ropes, cables, or wires that attach to each end of the front yard and are used to rotate the boom to take advantage of changes in the direction of prevailing winds. As the speaker of Joseph Conrad's "The Secret Sharer" takes firm command of his ship, the crew stands at attention by the forebraces and awaits orders, a symbolic acknowledgment of the change of leadership.

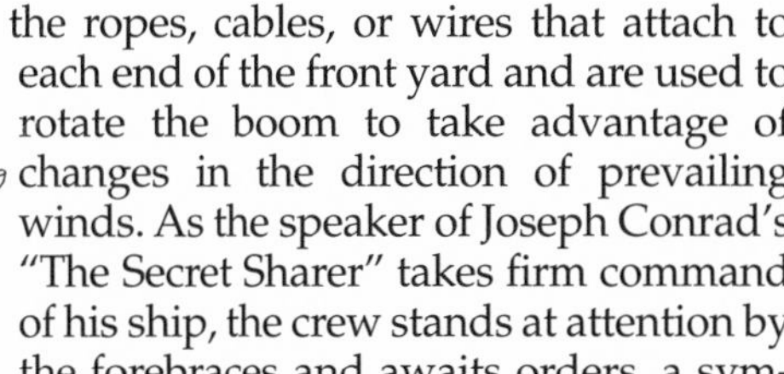

forecastle or **fo'c'sle** (*fohk'* s'l or *fork'* s'l) the raised deck located in the front of early merchant vessels that serves as living, exercise, and relaxation space, and sleeping quarters for a ship's crew. In Herman Melville's *Billy Budd,* the protagonist's comments correspond to those of the veterans in the forecastle.

forechains a platform alongside the aft chains and the shrouds of a ship where the leadsman stands to cast the weighted line into the water to determine its depth. The protagonist in Herman Melville's *Billy Budd* goes to the forechains to receive an ominous warning from an unidentified source.

forelock the upper portion of a horse's mane that hangs under the headstall between the ears and over the forehead. Jody, protagonist of John Steinbeck's *The Red Pony,* is so pleased to own a horse that he curries, braids, unbraids, and recurries its forelock. *See also* curry; headstall.

foretop a sentry post on a platform atop the front mast, from which to spot companion vessels, enemy ships, whales, a rocky coastline, or the approach of bad weather. In Herman Melville's *Billy Budd,* the title character serves as foretopman. In Avi's *The True Confessions of Charlotte Doyle,* the title character proves herself seaworthy by climbing to the foretop and safely descending.

foreyard the yardarm holding the topmost sail on the mainmast. In Herman Melville's *Billy Budd,* the title character is hanged from the foreyard, from which position the crew gets a good view of the proceedings that they remember well and record in verse.

Formalin (*fohr'* muh . lihn) the trademark name for a 40 percent solution of formaldehyde, methanol, and water that undertakers, biologists, or other scientists use as an embalming fluid, disinfectant, or preservative of tissue samples. As he records in *Never Cry Wolf,* Farley Mowat is nearly overcome by the smell of Formalin in the chief's office.

foundry a factory producing cast metal, which is formed from heated ores that are poured into a sand or clay mold, cooled, then removed by separating the mold into two halves. While looking for work, the protagonist in Charlotte Brontë's *Jane Eyre* learns that most job openings come from the needle factory, the foundry, or farms—none of which suits her talents.

four o'clocks perennial flowers producing three-foot stems and prolific yellow or fuchsia blossoms that open during daylight and close in late afternoon. In Toni Morrison's *Beloved,* Denver shuts down her emotions like a four o'clock after a schoolmate asks about the murder of Beloved, Denver's baby sister.

fox pieces fox furs attached head to tail in a line forming a shrug, scarf, or shoulder decoration, often added to an afternoon dress or light suit. The skins, popular in the 1920s and 1930s, were treated and displayed so that their legs hung down and their fake eyes, noses, and nails were polished to contrast with the soft colors of the pelt. In Tennessee Williams's *A Streetcar Named Desire,* Blanche DuBois puts on airs with her fake jewelry, frilly dresses, and fox pieces. In Pearl S. Buck's *The Good Earth,* Wang Lung pulls a Western lady in his rickshaw and wonders about the fox pieces draped about her shoulders.

fox-trot a standard ballroom dance in two-four or four-four time that develops elaborate patterns and simpler slides and variations from a basic box step. Popularized by Vernon and Irene Castle in 1912, the fox-trot gained popularity as a major showpiece in the Ziegfeld Follies. In F. Scott Fitzgerald's *The Great Gatsby,* Nick is surprised to see Jay Gatsby dancing a graceful, sedate fox-trot with Daisy Buchanan. *See also* Follies.

frame house a simple box-shaped house framed at the sides, top, windows, and doors from wood beams and covered with clapboard siding or shingles. In the floating two-story frame house in Mark Twain's *The Adventures of Huckleberry Finn,* Jim warns Huck not to look at the face of the murdered man, who Huck later learns was his father, Pap Finn. *See also* clapboard.

franc the basic unit of currency in France, Belgium, Luxembourg, Switzerland, and numerous African nations that were once French colonies. The franc, which was named for the king of France, equals 100 centimes, or pennies. On the way to his post on the Congo River, Marlowe, the protagonist in Joseph Conrad's *The Heart of Darkness,* hears the Swedish captain muttering about the kinds of work people perform for a few francs per month.

Franklin car a veteran, medium-sized open touring sedan built in the early 1900s featuring raised steering wheel, running boards, front and rear button-back seats, and brass headlights and carriage lights. In Olive Ann Burns's *Cold Sassy Tree,* Mr. Blakeslee reports that, during his trip to New York, his new wife, the former Miss Love Simpson, forced him to ride in a Franklin car.

Franklin stove a cast-iron, free-standing stove invented by Benjamin Franklin to replace the less efficient fireplace and hearth by locating the source of heat away from the wall, yet keeping fumes, smoke, and hot coals safely inside folding doors. The use of metal baffles, or inner honeycombs, improves the draw, radiates heat more evenly, and prevents overheating; the top can be used for cooking or heating water. At the uninviting rear entrance to the Radley house in Harper Lee's *To Kill a Mockingbird* stands a squat Franklin stove.

free association a psychological method of studying individual neuroses by encouraging a patient to speak spontaneously on any subject or to connect a simple term to the first thought that springs to mind. In Najib Mahfouz's "The Happy Man," a blatantly happy man tries to discover the root cause of his inappropriate joy by seeking psychoanalysis, which requires lengthy sessions of uncensored free association of words and images from the conscious mind to reveal repressed or subconscious causes of his strange mental malady.

Freedom Beero an approximation of the term Freedman's Bureau, created by Congress on March 3, 1865, and extended the following year (despite the veto of

President Andrew Johnson) as the Bureau of Refugees, Freedmen, and Abandoned Lands, under the leadership of Commissioner Oliver Otis Howard. Newly freed slaves (numbering four million) settled 40-acre parcels on abandoned plantations or found work for hire. In addition, the bureau supplied emergency fuel, shelter, and clothing and promoted due process, civil rights, education, health care, and aid for black Civil War veterans until 1872, when the poorly funded bureau was disbanded and its agents let go. When Ned and Jane, the protagonists in Ernest Gaines's *The Autobiography of Miss Jane Pittman,* first hear of the "Freedom Beero," they learn that Yankees are traveling south to work for the federal government to improve the lives of former slaves.

Freemasonry a fraternal organization founded in 1717 in London, based on the medieval workmen's guild and dedicated to honor, civic responsibility, fellowship, charity, and service to the brotherhood. Masons, including the American lodges founded in 1730 in Philadelphia, use secret hand signals to identify themselves to fellow members and perform rituals honoring skilled professionals. A women's auxiliary, the Eastern Star, was founded in 1876. In Sir Arthur Conan Doyle's "The Red-Headed League," detective Sherlock Holmes recognizes the Mason's pin worn by a stranger.

French doors or **French windows** a pair of glass-paned or glazed doors hinged at the far right and left so that they open at the center between rooms or onto a balcony or view from an outside wall. Danny, the protagonist in Chaim Potok's *The Chosen,* describes his father's office as windowless with curtained French doors on one side.

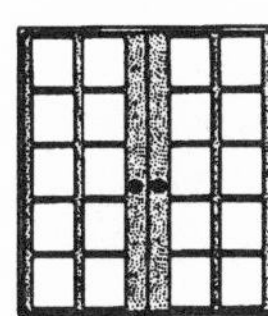

French hose or **trunk hose** tight knee socks that rose above the bottom of equally tight pants. French hose evolved into tights—a single garment formed of joined stockings that stretched to the waist. In William Shakespeare's *Macbeth,* the porter makes a joke about a tailor stealing from French hose, implying that the dishonest tailor skimped on the client's fabric.

French seams an enclosed seam that strengthens the garment, involving shallow stitching on the outside that is then pulled to the inside and resewn; also, the double stitching of two pieces of fabric by turning under the raw edges and resewing them. In Maya Angelou's *I Know Why the Caged Bird Sings,* Mama Henderson pulls her granddaughter's dress up to demonstrate to Mrs. Flowers the sturdiness of the armholes finished in French seams to secure sleeves firmly to the bodice.

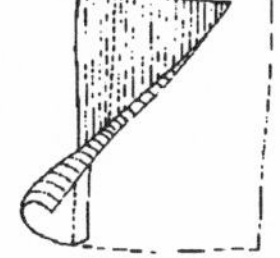

fresco (*frehs'* koh) a style of artwork popular from ancient Crete to the present in which watercolors are applied to wet high-calcium lime plaster. The pigments form a permanent bond with the wall or ceiling, but because they penetrate the damp surface, they are slightly paler than paint on canvas or paper. Derived from the German word for *fresh,* the term entered English in the mid-sixteenth century. At the villa serving as a makeshift hospital in Ernest Hemingway's *A Farewell to Arms,* Frederick Henry admires a fresco.

freshet (*frehsh'* iht) a tumultuous gush of freshwater over rocks or in a stream bed; also, the overflow of rain or melted snow. In *Walden,* author Henry David Thoreau describes how lumber from Maine forests travels at no charge to the sawyer on a freshet, by which it floats downstream to the buyer.

fret narrow metal bar, ridge, or band on the fret board or finger board of a guitar, mandolin, banjo, autoharp, or other stringed instrument that guides the placement of the fingers into the chords. While learning music from Hortensio in William Shakespeare's *The Taming of the Shrew,* Bianca grows frustrated with the study of frets and bashes Hortensio with her lute, thus illustrating the pun on fret, which also means *to be peevish* or *ill-tempered.*

fricassee (frihk . uh . *see'* or *frihk'* uh . see) to fry or stew pieces of fish, fowl, lamb, veal, or beef and serve with a roux or white sauce made from flour stirred into meat stock or pan drippings. Dating to the sixteenth century, the term derives from Latin for *crack* and *fry.* The ingenuous speaker in Jonathan Swift's "A Modest Proposal" suggests that impoverished parents sell their children, who can be boiled or fricasseed.

frieze (freez) in classical architecture, a long, horizontal band ornamented with a sculpted pictorial relief or a repeated painted motif or design (such as leaves, rosettes, waves, crosshatching, or abstract shapes) above a row of columns and below the cornice. Derived from the Latin for Phrygia (an ancient land now known as Turkey), the term dates to the mid-six-

teenth century. When Banquo and Duncan arrive at the castle in William Shakespeare's *Macbeth,* Banquo notes that a martin is building a nest where there is no projecting frieze.

frigate (*frih'*guht) a sleek, medium-sized boat featuring three masts and square sails. During the eighteenth and nineteenth centuries, the frigate was used for speedy travel and reconnaissance, raiding, cruising, or escort rather than for combat. In Herman Melville's *Billy Budd,* the *Bellipotent* serves in place of a frigate as a scout, or information-gathering ship.

frock (frahk) the combined skirt and bodice of a girl's or woman's dress; a simple day dress or house attire. Derived from the Old High German, the term is a generic word for *dress* and at one time applied to a loose garment worn by male or female toddlers. The protagonist of Mark Twain's *The Adventures of Tom Sawyer* spies a frock, but wilts in disappointment because the wearer is not Becky Thatcher, his new love.

frock coat a nineteenth-century double-breasted, knee-length man's dress or suit coat fitted at the top and flaring to a gathered or full skirt with a vent at the back. Usually worn unbuttoned, the frock coat, which was typically black or gray wool, served as formal business attire for a professional man. In Avi's *The True Confessions of Charlotte Doyle,* Mr. Grummage, who escorts the heroine to the ship, is well dressed in a frock coat.

frond fan a single paper or sturdy fiber fan flared at the upper end, attached to a thin pasteboard or wood strip handle and wafted before the face as a means of cooling. In the early twentieth century, American companies gave away cheap frond fans as enticements to customers. In Jerome Lawrence and Robert E. Lee's *Inherit the Wind,* the frond fans used by observers of the Scopes trial display advertisements for a local funeral home.

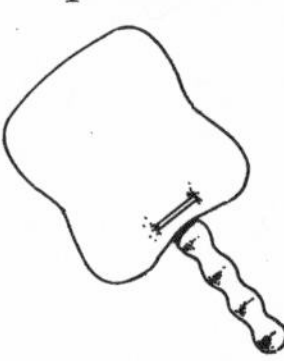

fugue (fyoog) a temporary, stress-induced loss of conscious control of actions, which the victim cannot recall after the symptoms subside; a psychological episode causing extreme distress and loss of awareness of identity. In Daniel Keyes's *Flowers for Algernon,* Charlie Gordon records in his symptom log his fugues of amnesia.

fulcrum (*fool'* kruhm) the contact point between a lever and a supporting frame or resting point; the prop or base on which the lever pivots to raise a weighty object on the end opposite the pressure point, as with an oar in an oarlock. Dating to the seventeenth century, the term comes from the Latin for *prop.* In William Golding's *Lord of the Flies,* Ralph uses his hand as a fulcrum to unearth the conch shell.

funeral rites in ancient Greece, an obligatory ceremony performed by a family member or friend to release the soul of the deceased into repose in the underworld. Consisting of the sprinkling of oil and wine and the placement of a coin in the mouth or on the eyelids to pay the soul's passage across Acheron, one of the four rivers that separate the land of the dead from the land of the living, these rites preceded burial or cremation. In Sophocles' *Antigone,* the title character earns a death sentence for disobeying her uncle Creon's ban on funeral rites for her brother, an enemy of the state.

funnel the flue, vent pipe, or flare-ended shaft that protrudes from a steam-driven ship to emit smoke and unburned particles; a smokestack. Derived from the Latin for *pour,* the term entered English in the fifteenth century. In the last stage of his journey, Phileas Fogg, eager to win the bet that launches Jules Verne's *Around the World in Eighty Days,* spies the *Henrietta,* an iron-hulled ship with a funnel, off New York's Battery.

furmity (*fuhr'* mih . tih) or **frument** a wholesome cooked cereal or wheat-flour porridge or wheat germ boiled in milk or whey and seasoned with honey, sugar, cinnamon, and other spices. Under the influence of a basin of rum-laced furmity, Michael Henchard sells his wife, Elizabeth-Jane, to a sailor in Thomas Hardy's *The Mayor of Casterbridge.*

furze (fuhrz) a prickly, dense evergreen bush of the legume family that produces a fragrant yellow blossom and black pods. Also called gorse or European ulex, furze is common to the poor soil of heaths, plains, moors, or barrens. In George Eliot's *Silas Marner,* Molly, who is drunk on laudanum, uses a furze bush as a pillow, falls asleep in the snow, and dies.

fusillade (*fyoo'* sihl . lahd) a sustained assault or barrage; a burst of simultaneous or repeated discharge of firearms or other weapons. Dating to the early nineteenth century, the term derives from the French for *shoot.* The arrival upstream of Marlowe's boat in Joseph Conrad's *The Heart of Darkness* precipitates a spirited fusillade of arrows and spears from Congo warriors lying in ambush.

fustian (*fuhs'* chuhn) a napped twill or corduroy woven of cotton over flax or linen. A common fabric for blankets or jackets during the Middle Ages, the time-consuming process of weaving and trimming or singeing fustian originated in ancient Egypt. While searching for seasonal harvesting work, Michael Henchard wears a fustian vest adorned with horn buttons in Thomas Hardy's *The Mayor of Casterbridge*.

fusuma (foo . *soo'* mah) a pocket door, sliding panel, or partition in a Japanese house. Made of lightweight paper edged with bamboo or wood splints, the panel, which equals the height of the room, slides along a pair of parallel grooves or tracks in the floor and ceiling. In *So Far from the Bamboo Grove,* when Yoko Kawashima Watkins and her sister petition a Buddhist monk to pray for their mother's soul, he rudely slams shut the fusuma.

futon (*foo'* tahn) a sleeping pad stuffed with cotton that serves as a seat when rolled or folded into thirds or as a mattress when spread on the floor on a bed frame. In *So Far from the Bamboo Grove,* Yoko Kawashima Watkins is asleep on a futon when a messenger awakens her and her family to warn them that the Russians have landed in Korea.

fyce *See* feist.

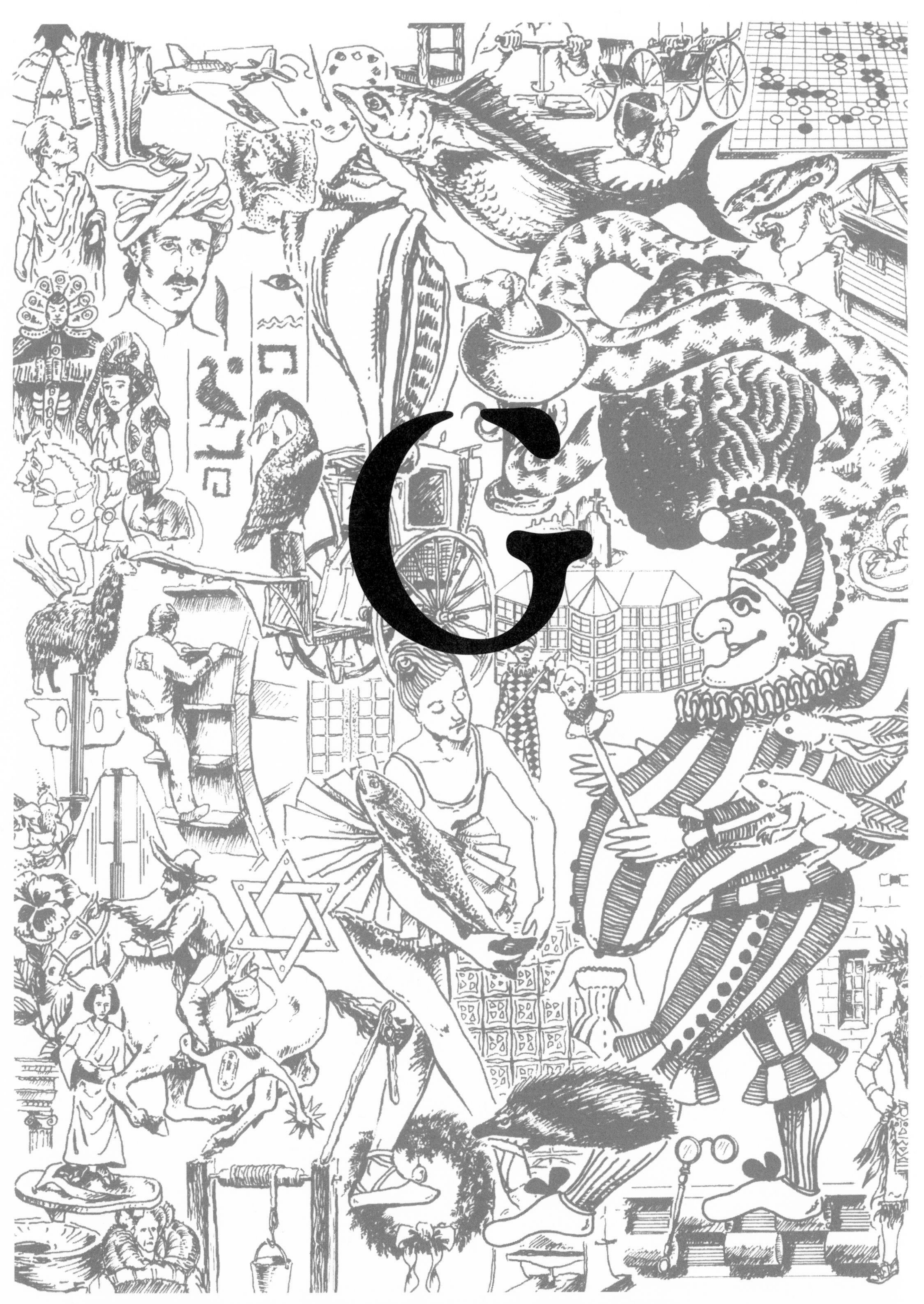
G

gable a vertical triangular endpiece or ornate projection from the ridgepole at the juncture of a pitched roof and its supporting walls or over a protruding door or window casement. In Nathaniel Hawthorne's *The House of the Seven Gables,* Colonel Pyncheon acquires the land for his ornate family manse by helping to condemn the rightful owner, Matthew Maule, who is executed for witchcraft.

gad-fly a horsefly, botfly, or other nettlesome insect that goads, annoys, or stings large animals, particularly cattle. The parasitic fly enters the host's mouth when the animal licks larvae from its pelt. After hatching, the gad-fly robs the animal of nutrients and ruins both meat and hide. In Edith Hamilton's *Mythology,* the invidious Hera sends a gad-fly to plague Io, who is unable to rest or eat without torment. *See also* bots.

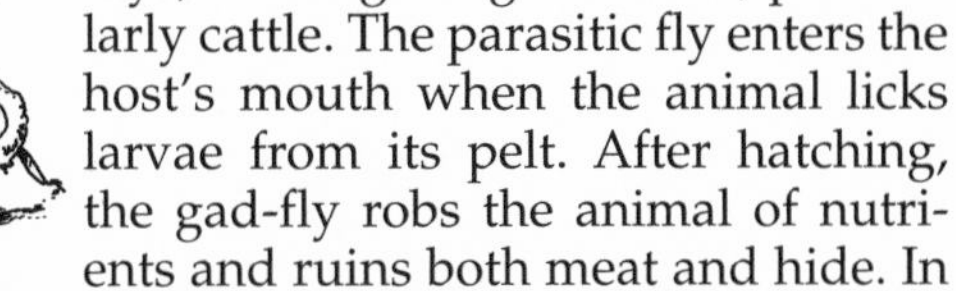

gadroon (guh . *droon'*) a fluted, beaded, puckered, arced, or reeded decorative edge, embellishment, notching, or molding on fine silver. Derived from the French for *crease,* the term evolved into a general term to name any type of adorning edge. In Esther Forbes's *Johnny Tremain,* silversmiths use the gadroon, relief, repoussé, and carving to stylize fine tableware. *See also* crimping iron; repoussé.

gaff a diagonal spar or half-sprit that attaches to a mast to hold erect the slanted side of an irregular fore-and-aft sail, such as a snow mast. In Gabriel García Márquez's "The Handsomest Drowned Man in the World," delighted villagers make a litter from masts, gaffs, and rigging to carry a corpse from the beach. *See also* snow mast.

gaiters canvas, cloth, or leather leggings worn by both men and women. Gaiters, which protect and support ankles and calves, reach from the arch of the foot above the ankle nearly to the knee. Men's gaiters are paired with nankeens, or short breeches, to cover the leg. An unannounced visitor wearing gaiters and a frock coat and bearing a riding crop bursts into Sherlock Holmes's residence in Sir Arthur Conan Doyle's "The Adventure of the Speckled Band." In George Orwell's *Animal Farm* Mollie accepts sugar from a man decked out in checked pants and gaiters.

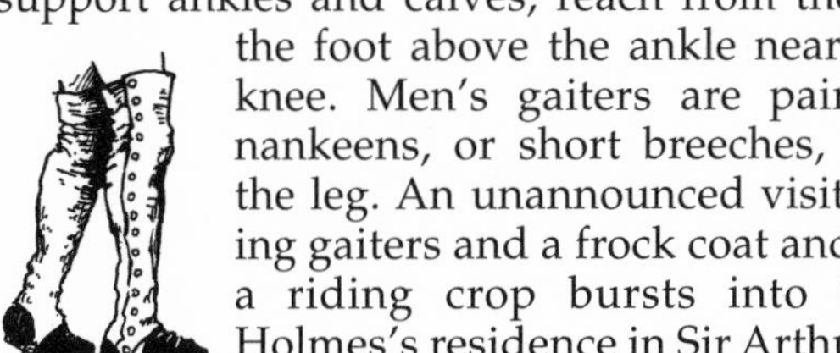

gale a wind strong enough to sway trees and inhibit people from walking. A stronger gale can destroy buildings and force vehicles off the road. The Beaufort scale, named for Sir Francis Beaufort and ranging from 0 to 12, ranks the varying degrees of gale in the upper end of hazardous weather, from 8 to 11, with winds of approximately 40 to 70 miles per hour. In Mary Shelley's *Frankenstein,* Walton reports in a letter to his sister that gale winds are welcome because they are warmer than expected.

gallery a long, narrow, intimate upstairs porch or verandah cantilevered from an outside wall, protected by a railing, balustrade, and overhang, and sometimes partially enclosed by siding, shades, or slatted blinds or overgrown with vines for privacy. In Tennessee Williams's *A Streetcar Named Desire,* Blanche DuBois finds, on her arrival in New Orleans, rickety outside stairs, ornamented gables, and galleries as a dominant architectural motif.

gallipot (*gal'* lih . paht) a small ceramic or glazed earthenware container used by pharmacists for containing or dispensing salve or medicine. Derived from Middle English in the fifteenth century, the term became slang for *chemist* or *apothecary.* In Conrad Richter's *The Light in the Forest,* Dr. Childsley uses a gallipot as a catch basin when he bleeds True Son's feet.

galluses (*gal'* luhs . sihz) suspenders or elasticized braces, often gaily decorated with stitchery, braid, or lettering. Galluses attach or button to the front of trousers and pass straight over the shoulders to similar mooring at the back or cross midway down the back and continue to the waistband. The defense attorney in Jerome Lawrence and Robert E. Lee's *Inherit the Wind* makes a joke at the prosecuting attorney's expense by revealing that he purchased his purple galluses in Weeping Water, Nebraska, the prosecutor's hometown.

gangline a cable, towline, or trace that forms the central connection between pairs of harnessed sled dogs and the front beam of the sled. The swing dogs, who take the center position, are attached to the gangline by neck lines and tug lines at their front and rear. The single dog at the front is called the lead dog; the pair nearest the sled are the wheelers. In *Dogsong,* author Gary Paulsen takes possession of a used sled, gangline, and harnesses. *See also* gee-pole.

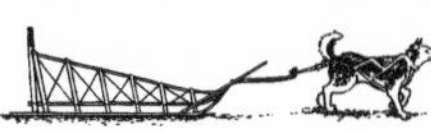

gangplank a moveable platform, ramp, or footway striated with cleats or wooden laths or strips that enables passengers and porters to board and disembark from a ship or steamboat. In Mark Twain's autobiographical *Life on the Mississippi,* the landsman is in charge of positioning the gangplank for the best shore access and passenger safety.

garland in ancient Greece, a ritual bouquet, wreath, festoon, or chaplet of braided or interwoven evergreen branches wound with white wool and given to the gods during a formal request for divine intervention or succor. In Sophocles' *Oedipus,* suppliants at the shrine of Pallas Athena bear garlands on behalf of the townspeople, who are ravaged by plant blight and plague.

garret the unfinished area or partitioned, unceilinged rooms that lie beneath a sloping roof or gable. A fourteenth-century term for *defend,* the word also names an attic or storage area. In Guy de Maupassant's "The Necklace," the loss of the borrowed jewels and Madame Loisel's resultant poverty force her to give up dreams of grandeur and to seek lodging in a garret.

garrison a localized body of troops or permanent militia staffing a fortress or fortified command post established to guard a town or other populated area. From the French word for *protect,* the term entered English in the fifteenth century. In Erich Maria Remarque's *All Quiet on the Western Front,* Paul Baumer regrets that his unit is sent back to the garrison to fetch equipment.

garter an elastic band, tie, or belt around the knee, lower thigh, or upper leg that holds up hosiery or on the upper arm to anchor shirtsleeves; also, a traditional bit of lace adorned with bows and rosettes and worn about the legs of brides, dancing girls, or prostitutes. In the glare of the sun, Ralph, the protagonist of William Golding's *Lord of the Flies,* removes stockings and garters, then sheds the rest of his clothes and stands naked as he surveys the tropical surroundings.

gateleg table a table that can be expanded by raising hinged leaves at the side and propping them on a swing-out frame. Designed in the sixteenth century, the gateleg table has remained popular, even though the apparatus is awkward and the table less sturdy than the more common four-legged type. In George Orwell's *1984,* the antique dealer offers to rent Winston a room with a gateleg table, which needs some repairs on the hinges.

gauge cock (*gayj'* kahk) a primitive valve, faucet, spigot, or spout that measures the force of a head of steam arising from a furnace or boiler. The gauge cock is a safety feature designed to open and release steam and/or hot water if pressure reaches a force greater than pipes or cauldrons are set to maintain. As Mark Twain's title character in *The Adventures of Tom Sawyer* paints at a fence, he pretends to pilot a steamboat and to test the gauge cocks.

gauntlet (*gawnt'* leht) a trial or ordeal requiring a contender to run a narrow, perilous course lined on both sides by enemies shouting, threatening assault, lashing with whips, hurling rocks, or promising certain death. The boat in Joseph Conrad's *The Heart of Darkness* threads its way up a gauntlet, with African natives hurling spears from both banks of the river. Also, (in the plural) silk, velvet, or kidskin gloves for men or women that extend a flared cuff of fringe, tassels, and embroidery to the forearms; the protective gloves worn by armored warriors. In Nathaniel Hawthorne's *The Scarlet Letter,* Pearl admires Governor Bellingham's suit of armor complete with chain mail, gauntlets, and sword.

gavotte (guh . *vaht'*) a lively peasant round dance in four-four time popularized in the seventeenth century by residents of Dauphiné, France, and later in the ballets of Lully and in Bach's suites. Named for Alpine settlers, the dance replaces the sliding steps of the more sedate minuet with skipping and exaggerated lifts of the feet and with kisses between partners. In James Hilton's *Lost Horizon,* Conway enjoys watching a Chinese musician play a gavotte on the harpsichord.

gazelle (guh . *zehl'*) a grass-eating ruminant antelope living in herds in its native Africa or Mongolia. Decked with graceful horns, the gazelle is famous for its handsome markings, swiftness, and beautiful hide. The epic *Gilgamesh* describes Enkidu as a wild man who stalks the grasslands alongside gazelles.

gazette (guh . *zeht'*) a newspaper, court journal, or in-house newsletter serving as a public calendar of events by publishing bulletins or announcements of common interest, especially promotions, financial transactions, and public

National Gazette.

honors. Entering English in the early seventeenth century, the term derives from the Italian for a Venetian halfpenny, which was the cost of the single news sheet. Serving as Roxane's gazette up to the moment of his death, the title character in Edmond Rostand's *Cyrano de Bergerac* dispenses items of gossip from the French court.

gee a command to a horse, dog, or mule team to move on, speed up, or turn to the right; the opposite of *haw,* which directs the team to stop, slow down, or move toward the left. These directions entered English in the seventeenth century, but are of unknown origin. In Gary Paulsen's *Dogsong* and *Winterdance,* the musher calls a soft gee when he wants the lead dog to guide the team into a slight right-hand turn.

gee-pole a slender shaft or dowel on the gee, or right, side of a dogsled that is used for steering. Beginning mushers can get the feel of the team by moving to the front of the sled, straddling the towline, and holding on to the gee-pole while calling commands to the team. In Jack London's *The Call of the Wild,* Hal, a novice musher, grasps the gee-pole in one hand and his whip in the other as he sets out with an overloaded sled. *See also* gangline.

geisha (*gay'* shuh) a well-trained Japanese female entertainer who sings, dances, plays musical instruments, and converses with male guests or clients; a professional hostess who provides a refined, relaxed, congenial atmosphere for after-hours business meetings. Derived from the Japanese for *art person,* the term entered English at the end of the nineteenth century and has since been misconstrued as a synonym for *prostitute.* In Jeanne Wakatsuki Houston and James D. Houston's *Farewell to Manzanar,* Jeanne shows more interest in emulating American cheerleaders than in learning odori or becoming a Japanese geisha. *See also* odori.

gelding a male animal that loses its reproductive powers when its testicles are removed by rubber-banding or through surgery that neuters, castrates, or emasculates. In Charles Portis's *True Grit,* Mattie recognizes that her father was cheated when she observes that the breeding stock he bought is composed of gelding ponies.

gematriya or **gematria** (*geh* . muh . *tree'* yuh) a formal study of facts, Jewish ritual, or biblical interpretation by the application of numerology, a mystical cabbalistic system that assigns numbers to each letter of a word. The sum of each phrase denotes whether the phrase is positive or negative in meaning or value. In Chaim Potok's *The Chosen,* Danny's father embarrasses him by conducting a gematriya in front of Reuven, Danny's guest. *See also* cabbala.

genie (*jee'* nee) *See* djinn.

genocide (*jeh'* noh . syd) the deliberate, systematic extermination of people because of race, ethnicity, nationality, or religious or political affiliation through massacre, repeated pogroms, or enforced sterilization or birth control. In Thomas Keneally's *Schindler's List,* Oskar, the title character, realizes that the Nazi party intends to obliterate Jewish communities through genocide. *See also* holocaust; Nazi; SS.

gentry (*jehn'* trih) a class or caste set above or apart from others by virtue of prestige, rank, birth, wealth, or manners and refinement; the elite or aristocracy. In Emily Brontë's *Wuthering Heights,* Mrs. Linton asks Ellen to set a place for the gentry to dine apart from Heathcliff, who is a common peasant too coarse to sit at the table.

geomancer (*gee'* oh . *man* . suhr) a diviner, fortune-teller, or skilled practitioner of I Ching, cabbala, or the like who is sometimes blindfolded before tossing grains of soil, sticks, bones, pebbles, marbles, or gemstones into the air. The geomancer studies the pattern or angle of their fall for clues to the future or for auspicious placement of buildings or the digging of wells. Other methods of geomancy include reading tea leaves or studying ink blots, runes, or random dots. The shapes the geomancer discerns have meanings, such as the following: a square indicates protection; a swastika, profit; a diamond, a trade or deal; X-shapes, love affairs; and wavy lines, a voyage. In Pearl S. Buck's *The Good Earth,* a geomancer helps Wang Lung select a propitious day three months hence for O-Lan's funeral.

gestalt (guh . *stahlt'* or guh . *shtahlt'*) a formal study of the patterns and interrelations of behaviors, responses, perceptions, and other human reactions to stimuli. When applied to education psychology, the study of gestalt (a branch of psychology founded by Max Wertheimer in 1912) helps to explain why some people are driven to complete a problem or task and why some answers seem to come in a flash of completing the pattern. In Daniel Keyes's *Flowers for Algernon,* Charlie Gordon studies all forms of psychology, including gestalt.

Gestapo (gish . *tah'* poh) the 50,000 elite secret police forming a division of Hitler's Schutzstaffel, or SS, which served as his personal bodyguard and state security officers from the mid-1930s until 1945. In Thomas Keneally's *Schindler's List,* the title character bribes the Gestapo hierarchy with lavish gifts of liquor, cigarettes, delicacies, entertainment, and valuables. *See also* SS.

geta or **gaeta** (*geht'* uh) a bright-colored wooden-soled thong sandal for street or yard wear. The geta fastens to the foot by a cord or velvet strap that passes between the big toe and the second toe. As an overshoe, the geta, worn over tabi socks, may raise the foot four or more inches from the ground. In Yoko Kawashima Watkins's *So Far from the Bamboo Grove,* Yoko and her sister settle in a geta factory. *See also* clog; tabi.

ghee (gee) a cooking oil or flavoring common in India and Pakistan. Ghee is made from butter from cow or buffalo milk that is melted, boiled, and strained, or clarified, then used for frying or served over rice and vegetables. In William J. Lederer and Eugene Burdick's *The Ugly American,* Americans plan to encourage Asian farmers to raise cattle and sell their milk in the form of ghee, which does not spoil as easily as fresh milk.

ghetto a small, restricted section of a city with limited industrial or commercial opportunity; a self-contained community of ethnic or religious minorities, particularly blacks, gypsies, refugees, religious or social outcasts, lepers, or Jews. In Elie Wiesel's autobiographical *Night,* Nazis created a ghetto in Sighet, Hungary, in 1939 with walls, guards, traffic barriers, and barbed wire and set Jewish officials over its governance until residents could be shipped to crematoria or work camps. *See also* holocaust; Nazi; SS.

gibbet (*jihb'* biht) a gallows or stanchion consisting of an upright post and cantilevered arm used for hanging a condemned felon and displaying the corpse for a period of public edification to remind potential criminals of the degradation and finality of punishment. In Jonathan Swift's "A Modest Proposal," to end the waste of lives on the gibbet, the speaker proposes selling children for profit.

giblets (*jihb'* lihts) the edible internal organs of poultry or game fowl including head, neck, kidneys, cock's comb, pinions, skinned feet, liver (minus the gall bladder), heart, and gizzard, which are often roasted inside a whole bird or diced and added to stuffing, soup, sauce, or gravy. Entering English in the fifteenth century, the term derives from the Walloon for *rabbit stew.* In Pearl S. Buck's *The Good Earth,* Wang Lung notes that he was used to a simple diet in his native land and not the chicken, goose giblets, and vegetables of the city.

gig a light two-wheeled sporting carriage set on resilient springs. An elaborate conveyance, the gig dates to the seventeenth century and spawned numerous versions, including the buggy, shay, fly, and trap. In Charles Dickens's *A Christmas Carol,* Scrooge observes his playmates from childhood approaching a Christmas party in gigs and farm wagons.

gilt (gihlt) a young female pig (from four to six months, depending on the breed) that has shown signs of estrus or sexual maturity but has not been mated; also, a fertilized female pig that has not produced a litter of piglets. In Robert Newton Peck's *A Day No Pigs Would Die,* Rob's pig Pinky, a squealing gilt, tries to elude Samson, a lusty boar.

gimbal (*gihm'* buhl) a stabilizer consisting of two concentric rings mounted at right angles to each other on a bearing or pivoting base. The object (particularly a ship's lamp, stove, compass, or chronometer) mounted at the center of this mechanism remains constant regardless of the movement of the outer frame. A late eighteenth-century term, it derives from the Latin for *double ring.* According to the speaker in Joseph Conrad's "The Secret Sharer," his quarters are lighted by lamps mounted on gimbals.

gingerbread ornately or gaudily scrolled and gilded woodwork, wrought iron, and other forms of ornamentation forming the finer points of the porches, fences, gates, screen doors and upper decks on late-Victorian houses and fancy steamboats. This nineteenth-century term derives from the baked sweet or cookie that was often gilded with edible paint. Mark Twain recalls in his autobiographical *Life on the Mississippi* the gingerbread that adorns the pilothouse of a riverboat.

gingham (*gihng'* uhm) a plain over-and-under weave in cotton cloth, which is unprinted, but is often woven with strands of contrasting colors to produce decorative edging, stripes, checks, or plaids. The seventeenth-century term derives from the Malay word for *striped cloth.* In Charlotte Brontë's *Jane Eyre,* the title character is so provoked with her fiancé's insistence on silk finery for her wedding dress that she makes a mock serious threat to be married in a gingham frock.

ginseng (*jihn'* sehng) **root** a wild plant of the Panax family that bears a fan-shaped leaf, red berries, and an aromatic root. Ingested from powder, tea, or chewed stem, ginseng, a valuable trade commodity, is a key palliative in Chinese herbal pharmacopoeia. For over a thousand years, ginseng root has been prized as a tonic to increase mental and physical capacities and to invigorate the aging. Named for the human shape of its root, the term derives from the Chinese for *manlike.* In Amy Tan's *The Kitchen God's Wife,* an herb shop around the corner from Winnie's flower shop sells ginseng.

gipsy *See* gypsy.

girdle a close-fitted cloth garment, tasseled cord, leather belt, obi, or wrapped sash worn around the torso, usually at, below, or above the waist or at an angle from waist to hip, often securing to the body a loincloth, ornament, cross, spindle, purse, keys, mirror, or dagger case; a cestus. The sixteenth-century term was derived from the Greek for *embroidered,* which denotes a ceremonial or nuptial belt worn by a bride as an outward avowal of virginity or purity. In Charles Dickens's *Great Expectations,* Miss Skiffins's symbolic act of removing her girdle and laying it on the table represents her intention to maintain a platonic or nonsexual relationship with Mr. Wemmick until their marriage.

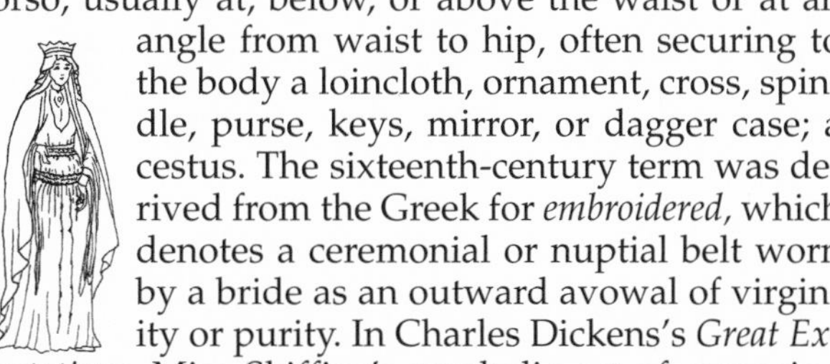

Gladstone (*glad'* stohn or *glad'* stuhn) a flexible-sided portmanteau, or hand luggage, composed of a rigid rectangular frame covered with cloth or leather and divided into equal halves. The style was named in 1889 to honor William Ewart Gladstone, England's four-term prime minister during the latter portion of Queen Victoria's reign. Holden Caulfield, protagonist in J. D. Salinger's *Catcher in the Rye,* admires his Gladstones as a mark of prestige or good taste.

glazier (*glay'* zhuhr) a maker, cutter, fitter, or repairer of glass. A fourteenth-century term, it derives from Middle English for *glass.* In Thomas Hardy's *The Mayor of Casterbridge,* Billy, the glazier, holds a prominent place among other working men who frequent the inn. In Toni Morrison's *Beloved,* the job of replacing a broken window is called "glazing."

gleeman *pl.* **gleemen** an itinerant minstrel or professional singer, usually performing unaccompanied; a jongleur or reciter of verse. Derived from the Middle English for *male singer,* the term entered English in the thirteenth century and appears to have been common throughout the Middle Ages. In Nathaniel Hawthorne's *The Scarlet Letter,* the author notes that the sober Puritans countenanced none of the entertainment of gleemen or jugglers that audiences loved in Elizabethan England. *See also a cappella.*

G-man an agent or officer of the Federal Bureau of Investigation. A short form of *Government man,* the slang version dates to the mid-1920s, when G-men, under the supervision of J. Edgar Hoover, earned a romanticized reputation for fighting crime. In Moss Hart and George S. Kaufman's *You Can't Take It with You,* Penny cringes at a raid by G-men investigating their printing operation.

goatee (goh . *tee'*) a slender tuft of chin hair trimmed to a narrow point; a beard shaped to resemble that of a male goat. Popular in the mid-nineteenth century, the goatee returned to popularity after such notable people as General George Armstrong Custer began sporting well-trimmed facial hair. In Alex Haley's *The Autobiography of Malcolm X,* when Malcolm X was assassinated, blood spurted from his goatee. *See also* Vandyke.

goblet a deep-sided, footed, or stemmed glass or metal crater, bowl, or drinking cup without handles; a decorative ceremonial chalice, often grouped in sets with a matching ewer and serving tray. A fourteenth-century term, it derives from the Celtic word for *cup.* Jason, a Greek hero in Edith Hamilton's *Mythology,* pours a libation from a goblet into the sea. *See also* ewer; libation; loving cup.

goh or **go** a board game for two players. Resembling chess and depicting battle strategy, goh was introduced in Japan in A.D. 735 and taught in military school to improve students' command of reasoning. Goh is played on a grid divided into 361 squares with 180 white and 181 black markers, which players place at intersections in clusters or chains; an opponent may capture markers by surrounding them. Jeanne Wakatsuki Houston and James D. Houston's *Farewell to Manzanar* recalls the old internees squatting together outdoors for a game of goh or hana. *See also* hana.

goiter (*goy'* tuhr) an enlarged thyroid gland that swells from the top of the sternum to the front of the neck base and against the windpipe as a result of hyperthyroidism or other endocrine imbalance, tumor, or enzyme or iodine deficiency. Untreated goiter causes choking, difficulty in swallowing, and distended veins. In Robert Newton Peck's *A Day No Pigs Would Die,* Rob becomes an instant hero by reaching into the throat of a choking cow to extract a goiter.

gonococcus (*gah* . nuh . *kahk'* kuhs) a spherical, parasitic bacterium, or germ, that produces gonorrhea, an acute, highly contagious inflammatory venereal disease that can lead to sterility, pain and scarring in the urinary tract, or arthritis in adults and to conjunctivitis in infants born to infected mothers. Classified in 1889 by its discoverer, Albert Neisser, the bacterium takes its name from the Latin for *semen seed.* At Estragon's request in Samuel Beckett's *Waiting for Godot,* Vladimir yells "Gonococcus! Spirochete!" In Ernest Hemingway's *A Farewell to Arms,* Rinaldi reports that the Italian army suffers jaundice, chilblains, gonorrhea, and soft chancres. *See also* spirochete.

Good Friday the commemoration of Christ's crucifixion at Golgotha, which follows Palm Sunday and Maundy Thursday and precedes Easter Sunday; since the thirteenth century a moveable feast that occurs after the full moon on or following March 21 on the Christian calendar. Before first confession, the confirmands in Rudolfo Anaya's *Bless Me, Ultima* experience fasting, prayer, and a dismal Good Friday. *See also* Calvary.

gorget (*gohr'* jiht) a circular piece of neck decoration or armor formed of shell, pottery, slate, wood, or metal. Pierced at each side, the gorget, which is a standard part of Native American armor, is threaded on a thong and worn around the neck to ward off wounds to the throat. Among cuirasses, breastplate, and a helmet, Nathaniel Hawthorne in *The Scarlet Letter* lists the gorget as a part of the armor displayed in Governor Bellingham's mansion.

gorgon (*gor'* guhn) one of three winged, snake-haired, scaly bodied, and brass-handed daughters of Ceto and Phorcys, sea deities of early Greek mythology; also, an ugly, horrifying, or predatory female. The term derives from Greek for *blazing eyes* because these monsters (Euryale, Steheno, and Medusa) possessed a dreadful look that turned enemies to stone. In Edith Hamilton's *Mythology,* Perseus outsmarts and defeats the gorgon Medusa by watching her through a brass mirror and cutting off her head, which he carries as a trophy. *See also* aegis.

gorse (gors) *See* furze.

Gospel (*gahs'* p'l) the Christian doctrine of redemption and resurrection; the teachings and evangelism of Christ and his twelve apostles as contained in the first four books of the canon New Testament, written by Matthew, Mark, Luke, and John. Derived from the Old English for *good news,* the term entered English before the twelfth century. In Arthur Miller's *The Crucible,* Reverend John Hale questions Elizabeth Proctor about her faithfulness to the Gospel, which becomes a test of her innocence of witchcraft.

gout (gowt) a chronic, disfiguring form of arthritis of the hands, feet, or knees. Gout afflicts the joints because of the body's inability to metabolize uric acid, which turns to painful chalky stones that impede movement. In *Silas Marner,* author George Eliot associates the rich diet and indulgences of the upper class as causes of gout and apoplexy, which were less likely to strike the poor.

governess-cart a round, open-topped two-wheeled tub cart pulled by a single horse. The governess-cart featured two facing seats along the sides of a bucket-shaped frame covered with wicker. A small gate offered access at the rear. In George Orwell's *Animal Farm,* Muriel and Benjamin use a governess-cart to haul stones to build a windmill.

Goy *pl.* **Goyim** or **Goys** a Gentile or non-Jew; also, an insult or disparaging term applied to a non-Jewish person or nation. Jews condemned Goys for idolatry, which prevented them from seeing the true God. Entering English in the mid-1800s, the term derives from a general Hebrew term for *people.* In Chaim Potok's *The Chosen,* Reb Saunders grows explosively angry at the suggestion that Goyim inhabit the Holy Land alongside devout Jews.

grace period an extension of time beyond a due date when an insurance bill, tax, mortgage, lien, credit card payment, or other monetary or legal obligation may be paid or a set of requirements met, such as a car inspection, return of borrowed library books or videos, or immunization, without penalty, fine, cancellation, reduction in status, or loss of coverage. In Arthur Miller's *Death of a Salesman,* Linda Loman reminds her husband, Willy, that he must pay the insurance premium, which is overdue and has entered the grace period.

graft thievery, extortion, bribery, blackmail, influence peddling, or other unscrupulous behavior or abuse of office to acquire money or power. Of uncertain derivation, the term entered English in the second half of the nineteenth century. As reported in *Black Boy,* Richard Wright plots with a girl in the movie theater box office in a graft scam to steal part of the owner's proceeds by reusing tickets.

gramme or **gram** a metric measure of mass equal to a cubic centimeter of water. The term is abbreviated *g* and equals 0.035 ounce. In Aldous Huxley's *Brave New World,* Lenina Crowne escapes the squalor of the Zuñi reservation by taking six half-gramme tablets of *soma,* a soporific that frees her from anxiety.

granary (*gray'* nuh . ree) a storehouse, barn, grange, or silo used for storing threshed wheat, shelled corn, winnowed rice, or loose heads of other grains. In medieval times, the granary stood in the inner bailey of a castle to protect stores from fire or theft. Entering English in the sixteenth century, the term derives from the Latin for *grain.* In Thomas Hardy's *The Mayor of Casterbridge,* Donald Farfrae opens his own granary and drives rival Michael Henchard out of business. *See also* grange.

grange (granj) a farmhouse, residence, homestead, or agricultural or livestock outbuilding, such as a barn, storage shed, silage bin, sheepcote, or silo. The occupant, owner, or farmer of a grange is called a granger. In Charlotte Brontë's *Jane Eyre,* St. John Rivers abandons the grange and returns to the parsonage. In Charles Portis's *True Grit,* late in her relationship with Rooster Cogburn, Mattie learns that he has gone to Wyoming to harass nesters and grangers.

granny glasses old-fashioned small-lensed eyeglasses set in a thin metal frame. In the mid-nineteenth century, granny glasses were worn to create the modish appearance of an outdated fashion in eyewear. During the 1960s and 1970s, granny glasses became a symbol of the anti-establishment counterculture. In Maxine Hong Kingston's *Woman Warrior,* the mother, dressed in granny glasses and shawl, sits at her daughter's bed and advises her on treatment for colds.

graphite (*gra'* fyt) a gray, shiny form of carbon occurring in nature in striated crystals. Graphite is used in pencils, coatings and lubricants, crucible steel, paint and polish, spectroscopes, nuclear reactors, and electrical conductors. Before subduing McMurphy with electroshock treatment in Ken Kesey's *One Flew over the Cuckoo's Nest,* attendants squeeze graphite cream onto his temples as a conductant, then apply the electrodes.

greatcoat a man's voluminous overcoat, topcoat, or surtout that was constructed of sturdy material, often waterproofed and fitted with a collar that could be turned up and fastened with toggle and loop to protect the inner garments from rain. In Sir Arthur Conan Doyle's "The Red-Headed League," Sherlock Holmes's client withdraws a folded paper from an inside pocket of his greatcoat.

Great Spirit the Native American animistic god of the universe who governs all human events and reveals his presence through nature. Also called Manitou or the All-Father, the Great Spirit, who is wedded to the All-Mother, or earth, symbolizes the oneness of all things. As he lies weakened with illness and despair, True Son, protagonist in Conrad Richter's *The Light in the Forest,* feels deserted by the Great Spirit.

greave (greev) an inflexible shin guard or plated leg armor worn below the knee and attached to the knee guard and foot covering as a part of a suit of armor or as protection during athletic events. Derived from the French for *shin,* the term entered English in the fourteenth century. In Nathaniel Hawthorne's *The Scarlet Letter,* Hester and Pearl pass a suit of armor in Governor Bellingham's palace complete with greaves, gorget, helmet, and cuirasses.

greengrocer a retail stallkeeper at a farmers' market or mall or a neighborhood seller of fresh items, including fruits, vegetables, herbs, and flowers and sometimes eggs, clotted cream, and local cheeses. In Anne Frank's *The Diary of a Young Girl,* Margot reports to her sister that the greengrocer has sold the family 19 pounds of green peas, which they must shell for dinner.

grenadier (*grehn* . uh . *deer'*) a soldier belonging to the Grenadier Guards, an elite cadre of British riflemen distinguished by tall fur hats, or shakos, and belonging to a regiment that protects the royal household. Although the term originally applied to those soldiers assigned to lob grenades, the designation passed to other military regiments overseeing various duties. In Thomas Hardy's *Far from the Madding Crowd,* a folk song romanticizes over the "tall grenadier," a figure suggested by the handsome, conceited Sergeant Troy. In *Around the World in Eighty Days,* Jules Verne describes his focal character, Phileas Fogg, as seated in an armchair with his feet close together like a grenadier. *See also* shako.

griffon or **griffin** or **gryphon** (*grihf'* fihn) a mythical beast with the head, wings, and forepaws of an eagle and the torso, hindquarters, and tail of a lion. A religious symbol derived from Greek mythology and featured on the gates of Oxford University, the blended beast represents the dual nature of Christ, a divinity born of woman. In Lewis Carroll's *Alice's Adventures in Wonderland,* the Gryphon takes Alice to meet the Mock Turtle.

grille a decorative room divider, visor, grating, automobile radiator screen, or vent cover; a metal framework of parallel bars, crosshatching, or other geometric shapes that admits sound, light, and air, but prohibits entry, keeps out insects and rats, or shields privacy. In Ray Bradbury's *Fahrenheit 451,* Guy Montag hides his cache of illegal books behind the grille in his home.

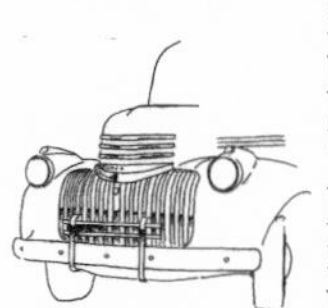

Grim Reaper a caricature symbolizing death. Carrying a scythe in one ghostly hand, the figure, usually depicted as a skeleton or a skeletal head swathed in a hooded cloak, appears to grin as he and the New Year's baby stroll among the living and look for victims. In Tennessee Williams's *A Streetcar Named Desire,* Blanche insists to Stella that the Grim Reaper had taken residence near Belle Reve, their family home.

grisette (gree . *zeht'*) a young female worker or shopgirl who moonlights as a prostitute. Named for the cheap gray fabric of her dress, the term appeared in English in the early eighteenth century. In Victor Hugo's *Les Misérables,* a grisette notices the white hair and proud posture of Jean Valjean on his frequent walks with his foster daughter on the public promenade.

gristmill a water-powered mill consisting of a wheel that turns a shaft and rotates a grinding wheel over a bottom stone. The miller pours rough grain into grooves to produce cornmeal or flour, depending on the space left between the wheel and the bottom stone. Derived from the Anglo-Saxon term for *grind,* the term originated before the twelfth century. In Olive Ann Burns's *Cold Sassy Tree,* Will Tweedy, the focal character, passes the gristmill built on the Hudson River by his great-grandfather in 1850.

groats (grohts) a twelfth-century term for hulled grain that is ground or crushed into a coarse meal for cooking into a thick, bland gruel or hot cereal akin to grits. The prison kitchen in Alexander Solzhenitsyn's *One Day in the Life of Ivan Denisovich* produces bowls of cooked groats for breakfast. *See also* gruel.

grog (grahg) rum and hot water mixed with sugar, lemon, or other flavorings; a common drink associated with sailors and shore pubs, called grog shops. The term derives from the grogram cloak worn by Admiral Edward Vernon (1684–1757), who earned the sobriquet "Old Grog" for weakening his mariners' rightful daily portion of rum by diluting it with hot water. In James Michener's *Hawaii,* the grog seller in Lahaina fails to compromise the stiff principles of the Reverend Abner Hale, a local missionary and devout teetotaler.

grotto (*graht'* toh) a dugout, cave, or cavern; a sheltered entranceway, ornamental retreat, or an arched recess or alcove in a wall. Entering English in the early seventeenth century, the term derives from the Latin for *crypt.* Waverly Jong reports running to the safety of a grotto entrance of the China Gem Company in Amy Tan's *The Joy Luck Club.*

grout (growt) thin mortar, plaster, or filler applied to gaps or regular spaces between tiles, paving stones, molded façades, or brick or at the juncture of wall and ceiling. In Judith Guest's *Ordinary People,* Conrad comments that, after his brother's death, his mother insisted that the bathroom tile be regrouted to remove the blood. *See also* façade.

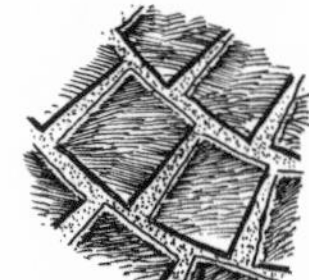

gruel (*groo'* uhl) a thin, watery, cooked cereal, such as oatmeal, porridge, or farina boiled in milk or water and fed to invalids or babies or served to unruly or mutinous prisoners or wayward children as punishment. Mr. Lockwood's gruel grows cold as he listens to the history of Heathcliff, the wild gypsy boy who captures the heart of Catherine Earnshaw in Emily Brontë's *Wuthering Heights. See also* groats.

Grumman (*gruh'* muhn) one of 9,836 fighter planes built for the U. S. Navy by Grumman Aircraft Corporation, including the Avenger, the Wildcat, and the Hellcat. The Avenger TBF-1, which remained in use from 1940 to 1955, was a seven-seat monoplane with a radial engine and accommodation for night attack and radar avoidance. In John Hersey's *Hiroshima,* survivors huddled in Asano Park fear that Grummans are coming to strafe the city. *See also* strafe.

grunion (*gruhn'* yuhn) a slender, silver marine fish native to the waters off California. Also called "silversides," the grunion migrates to the beach at night during high tide to burrow tail first into the sand to lay eggs. When the eggs hatch, tides carry the next generation out to sea. In Jeanne Wakatsuki Houston and James D. Houston's *Farewell to Manzanar,* the Wakatsuki family works together to grab or net the plentiful fish for a late-night feast.

gryphon *See* griffon.

guano (*gwah'* noh) a palm grown in the Western Hemisphere that supplies the inhabitants with fronds for thatching and roofing their beach dwellings. In Ernest Hemingway's *The Old Man and the Sea,* Santiago lives in a hut made from the budshields of the guano palm, which grows on the island of Cuba.

guerilla or **guerrilla** (guh . *rihl'* luh) fighters, insurgents, or infiltrators who harass the enemy by stealing supplies, making surprise raids, sabotaging machinery and artillery, or hindering troop movement by blowing up bridges, roads, and airstrips. Derived from the Spanish for *war,* the term describes the actions and intent of the main characters in Ernest Hemingway's *For Whom the Bell Tolls.*

guilder (*gihl'* duhr) or **gulden** a Dutch or German gold coin that evolved into the basic currency of the Netherlands, Surinam, and Dutch colonies in the Antilles. The term, which dates to the fifteenth century and is abbreviated *G,* is derived from the Dutch for *golden.* According to Anne Frank in *The Diary of a Young Girl,* a Dutch newspaper announced in March 1943 that, in an effort to halt the black market, authorities declared 500- and 1000-guilder notes invalid, but accepted them for taxes along with the owner's explanation of their origin.

guillotine (*gee'* yuh . teen) the French device created to provide the state a system of humane public executions. An angled blade dropped quickly and heavily against the neck, severing the head, which fell into a basket. Louis XVI and his wife, Marie Antoinette, were guillotined January 21, 1793, after the self-absorbed royal couple bankrupted the French treasury and precipitated the French Revolution. Charles Dickens's *A Tale of Two Cities* describes graphic guillotine scenes, near which Madame Defarge sits at the base of the device to observe each decapitation and log the name of the victim. In Albert Camus's *The Stranger,* Meursault comments that the guillotine kills discreetly and efficiently.

guinea (*gih'* nee) a gold coin featuring an elephant motif and commonly referred to as a shiner. The guinea was minted for the convenience of the Company of Royal Adventurers, an English trading firm on the Guinea coast of Africa. In circulation from 1663 to 1813 as a domestic coin in England, the guinea was worth 21 shillings, or one pound one shilling. In Charles Dickens's *David Copperfield,* David lists traveling expenses from London to Dover of a half-guinea, or ten shillings and sixpence. *See also* shilling.

Gulf Stream a warm, swift current in the Atlantic Ocean. Forming in the Yucatan Channel in the Gulf of Mexico, it passes through the Florida Straits, hugs the Carolina shore at Cape Hatteras, and flows to the Grand Banks off Newfoundland. Approximately 150 feet wide and 2,600 feet deep off the coast of Miami, Florida, the stream has been the focus of voluminous marine study, but its exact parameters and influences remain a scientific puzzle. As the setting for portions of Ernest Hemingway's *The Old Man and the Sea,* the Gulf Stream demonstrates its rich lode of fish and birds.

gum lac (guhm lak) a wine-colored gelatinous resin obtained from a sticky substance exuded by insects in Madagascar that hardens when heated. In Victor Hugo's *Les Misérables,* Jean Valjean uses gum lac and turpentine to make jet for costume jewelry, belt buckles, and combs, thus cutting the manufacturer's costs for materials from 4 francs per pound to 30 sous. *See also* sou.

gunny sack a term derived in the mid-nineteenth century from the Punjab name for a coarse fabric. The speaker in Rudolfo Anaya's *Bless Me, Ultima* follows the title character across the prairie in search of healing herbs and roots, which they will put in a gunny sack. *See also* croker sack.

gunwale (*guhn'* 'l) the upper edge of a projecting wall of ship's timbers, planking, or finished boards surrounding the top level of decking on a boat or ship. Named for the *gun wall* or ledge that supported cannon, the term entered English in the fifteenth century. In Margaret Craven's *I Heard the Owl Call My*

Name, Jim and Mark struggle with a pump organ, which they balance on the gunwales of their boat before loading it on canoes.

gypsy or **gipsy** or **rom** a member of a clannish, nomadic European race thought to have immigrated from Egypt or India during the 1300s. Also called Romanics, these dark-skinned wanderers have been the object of race discrimination and stereotyping as pickpockets, beggars, fortunetellers, and horse- or child-stealing vagabonds. They have survived on the ragged edge of society as virtual pariahs and were the object of Nazi genocide during World War II. In Emily Brontë's *Wuthering Heights,* Mr. Earnshaw creates a stir by bringing home a gypsy boy to rear. *See also* genocide; holocaust.

H

hack a hired cab. *See* hackney chariot.

hackamore (*ha'* kuh . mor) an adjustable slip noose or bitless rope bridle that passes across the nose of a horse during the breaking and training process. Corrupted from a Spanish term for *halter,* the word appeared in English in the mid-nineteenth century. Billy Buck, the hired hand in John Steinbeck's *The Red Pony,* promises to save tail hair from Gabilan and to braid Jody a hackamore.

hackles (*ha'* k'lz) erectile hairs on a dog's neck that rise and bristle when the animal is challenged or threatened. Applied to human beings, the term refers to the prickly sensation that sweeps over the neck as part of the physical response to anger or fear. In Conrad Richter's *The Light in the Forest,* True Son feels his hackles rise when he hears insults directed at his Lenni Lenape father, Cuyloga.

hackney chariot or **hackney coach** a hired two-wheeled four-seater carriage with fold-down top. The hackney chariot is drawn by a single trotter called a hackney, which was named for a village that has since become a borough of London. In England, hackneys remained the most popular form of hired coach until the creation of the safer, more comfortable hansom cab in the 1830s. Pip, the protagonist of Charles Dickens's *Great Expectations,* travels from the Temple in a hackney chariot. *See also* hansom cab.

Haganah (hah . guh . *nah'*) the Jewish underground militia, a defense group of 70,000 men and women formed in 1921 to mobilize Palestinian Jews in an effort to create a new Zion as a permanent Jewish homeland. Haganah, whose name is derived from the Hebrew for *defense,* assisted the British in setting up the state of Israel in 1948, then altered its aims and purpose to that of a national defense corps. According to Alex Haley in *The Autobiography of Malcolm X,* after World War II, the Jews kept close tabs on neo-Nazis through Haganah, their intelligence agency.

haint (haynt) an American dialect term for a ghost, poltergeist, or malevolent house spirit that annoys the tenants of a building by disturbing the peace, terrifying guests, tapping windowpanes and banging doors, overturning containers, causing drafts, or smashing fragile objects. Derived from a nonstandard southern pronunciation of *haunt,* a Germanic word for *home,* the demands and caprices of the haint in Toni Morrison's *Beloved* alarm visitor Paul D and influence the novel's themes and action.

hair ball a clump of hair that collects in the stomach or bowels of an animal that licks its fur, especially during shedding of the outer coat. When these masses form an obstruction, they can be coughed up or eased with a lubricant such as mineral oil to pass them through the intestines. In Mark Twain's *The Adventures of Huckleberry Finn,* Jim uses a hair ball obtained from the fourth stomach of an ox to work magic.

hair-guard a small lanyard or loop woven from strands of human hair and attached to a pocket watch. As a gesture of devotion, the hair-guard represented the attention and concern of a sweetheart for her beloved. After dumping purse and watch before the Commissioners in a gesture of bankruptcy in Thomas Hardy's *The Mayor of Casterbridge,* Michael Henchard withdraws the hair-guard plaited for him by Lucetta.

Hajj or **Haj** or **Hadj** (hahj) a prayerful religious journey to Mecca where pilgrims pray, walk seven times around the central column, and kiss the Ka'ba, the sacred black stone of the holy mosque, during Dhu'l Hijja, the twelfth month of the Muslim calendar. As described in Alex Haley's *The Autobiography of Malcolm X,* the Hajj, or religious pilgrimage, is a once-in-a-lifetime obligation performed by devout, healthy, and debt-free Muslims, who thenceforth bear the title or honorific of *Hajji.*

halberd (*hahl'* buhrd) or **halbert** or **halbard** a medieval cleaving or stabbing weapon composed of an ax head and double-edged spear point mounted on the end of a 6-foot pike. After the introduction of firearms to warfare, the halberd remained in use primarily as a ceremonial weapon of an honor guard, such as the Swiss soldiers who protect the entrance to the Vatican. In Nikolai Gogol's "The Overcoat," Akaky, the protagonist, mutters to himself and accidentally bumps into a watchman armed with a halberd.

half-a-crown two and one-half shillings, or one-eighth of a pound, in the old British monetary system, written 2s. 6d. In Joseph Conrad's *The Heart of Darkness,* Marlowe interrupts his narration with a scurrilous implication that his listeners perform tricks for "half-a-crown a tumble." *See also* crown; pound; shilling.

half gainer a pivoting dive requiring a forward plunge interrupted by a spiral and backward flip that takes the diver head first into the water and facing the board. Holden Caulfield, protagonist in J. D. Salinger's *The Catcher in the Rye,* dislikes Al Pike's drawing attention to himself by performing half gainers.

half-guinea *See* guinea.

half-hitch a simple sailor's knot; a looped rope or strap about a spar or pole with the loose end passed through the loop to cinch it in place when the rope is tightened. In John Steinbeck's *The Red Pony,* Billy Buck, a hired farmworker, is capable of lassoing a steer, getting a half-hitch on the horn, and dismounting.

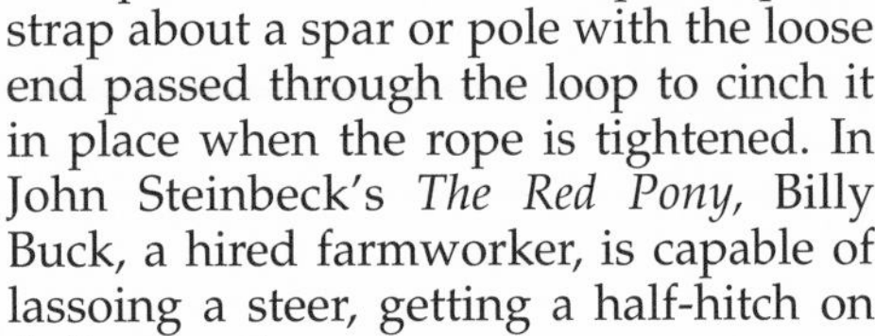

half nelson a wrestling hold in which the attacker's arm passes under the arm of the opponent and the attacker's hand grasps the back of the opponent's neck. In Rudolfo Anaya's *Bless Me, Ultima,* Horse humiliates the protagonist by grabbing him around the neck in a half nelson.

hallucination (huh . *loo* . sih . *nay'* shuhn) a compelling delusion, apparition, or vision that the brain perceives as real. Derived from the Greek for *wander,* the term, which entered English in the early seventeenth century, names a mental aberration resulting from damage to the brain or nervous system, from schizophrenia, or from the ingestion of hallucinogenic drugs. In Daniel Keyes's *Flowers for Algernon,* Dr. Strauss believes that Charlie is at the stage of adolescence when sexual thoughts can produce panic and hallucinations. *See also* psychosis.

halter a rope noose, rawhide strap, or leather bridle or head harness composed of noseband and throatlatch attached to a circlet on an animal's head behind the ears and extending around the upper jaw. The halter or lead, which was essential to the evolution of plow and wagon, allows a person to manage a horse or other domestic animal or fasten it to a restraint or plow harness or to a second animal, as with a team harness. Entering English before the twelfth century, the term derives from Anglo-Saxon. In desperation to escape the Dust Bowl and agricultural ruination, farmers in John Steinbeck's *The Grapes of Wrath* sell halter, hames, and harness for small change and apply their gains to cheap trucks and cars that will take them to part-time work in California. *See also* hames; headstall.

halyard or **halliard** or **haulyard** (*hal'* yurd or *hal'* yuhd) a rope, wire, cable, or tackle used to hoist or lower a sail, yard, spar, or flag. Derived from the Middle English for *haul yard,* the term entered English in the fourteenth century. As the epic hero Odysseus prepares to return to Ithaca in Homer's *Odyssey,* Calypso provides him with sailcloth, which he attaches to halyards and sheets.

hamatsa (huh . *maht'* suh) a ritual initiation dance performed by prestigious members of the Kwakiutl, a tribe native to Washington State and the Vancouver area. The hamatsa dancers, dressed in red cedar bark, perform a staged display of magic in the form of faked cannibalism. In Margaret Craven's *I Heard the Owl Call My Name,* mourners bury the dead in a spot where they are safe from the ravenous hamatsa.

hambone frill an ornamented edging or fluted or pleated collar of stiffened cotton, horsehair, or voile worn as an embellishment on a somber robe or vestment. The term derives from the English custom of decorating the exposed bone of a baked ham or leg of lamb. Shortly after the plane crash that precipitates the action in William Golding's *Lord of the Flies,* choirboys dressed in ankle-length black cloaks and sporting crosses, black caps, and hambone frills at the neck turn into a pack of hunters.

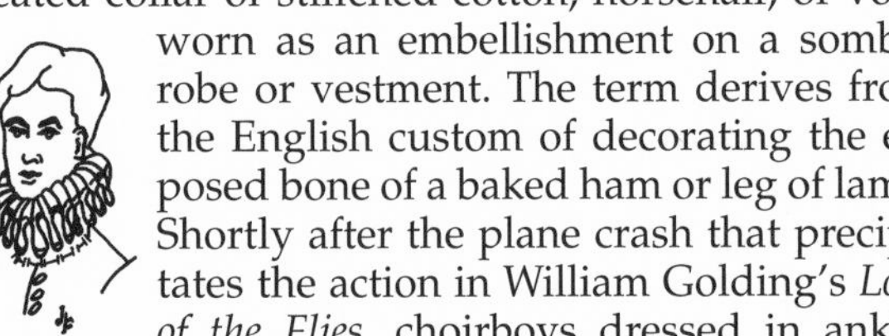

hames a pair of curved iron or wood support pieces similar to a horse collar that fit the neck and shoulders of a draft animal and attach to the traces, which are sometimes decorated with bells. One of the key innovations of the Middle Ages, hames expedite work and travel by preventing a harness from strangling the animal. In their haste to migrate out of the Dust Bowl, Oakies in John Steinbeck's *Grapes of Wrath* sell halters, collars, and hames they once used on their plow horses.

hammer-cloth a serviceable canvas or cloth covering the box seat of the stagecoach driver and concealing tools and gear. On his journey to Jaggers's office in London, Pip, protagonist of Charles Dickens's *Great Expectations,* boards the stagecoach, noting the ragged condition of the hammer-cloth.

hana (*hah'* nuh) a Japanese card game played with cards decorated with flowers. Jeanne Wakatsuki Houston and James D. Houston's *Farewell to Manzanar* describes how men in detention camps passed the time with games of goh or hana. *See also* goh.

handspike a crude wooden peg, tool, or lever tipped or covered with iron used for scoring wood, grappling, or catching hold of a ledge, metal collar, or flanged edge. While working for ship builders at Fell's Point, the autobiographer of *Narrative of the Life of Frederick Douglass* describes men armed with stones, bricks, and handspikes who attack him and break his nose.

hansom cab a two-wheeled hired carriage with a high, enclosed body, a double-paneled front entrance that folded back to admit passengers, and a seat for the driver on top or at the rear. To confer with passengers, the driver spoke through a trapdoor in the roof. The hansom, named for English inventor Joseph Hansom in the 1830s, remained in service for decades as London, New York, and Boston's most serviceable cab. In Sir Arthur Conan Doyle's *The Hound of the Baskervilles,* Sherlock Holmes and Dr. Watson pursue a hansom cab containing a bearded spy.

hant *See* haint.

harelip a congenital cleft or fissure of the upper lip, which may be pitted or split vertically into halves and may accompany a cleft palate. The malformation, which occurs during the early gestation of the fetus in one out of a thousand births, requires reconstructive surgery to join the two segments, usually during early infancy. In William Shakespeare's *A Midsummer Night's Dream,* a prayer over the newlyweds asks that their children be born healthy and free of harelip. In Mark Twain's *The Adventures of Huckleberry Finn,* Huck avoids mentioning Joanna Wilks's harelip even though he is constantly aware of it.

harem (*hayr'* 'm) according to strict Muslim tradition, a secluded, closely guarded compound or quarters that derives from the Arabic for *sanctuary;* also, the people who populate or dwell in a harem. The physical harem comprises a courtyard and suites where female family members, wives, mistresses, and concubines under the guard of eunuchs and other servants are kept free of prying eyes from the outside world. While discussing the life of Solomon with Jim, Huck, the protagonist in Mark Twain's *The Adventures of Huckleberry Finn,* attempts to explain the purpose of a harem. *See also* eunuch.

harlequin (*hahr'* lih . kwihn) a masked clown, buffoon, or tricky servant in English comedy and pantomime wearing parti-colored tights, pantaloons, and a jerkin of patchwork or diamond-figured material and carrying a baton or slapstick. Derived from the *commedia dell' arte,* or street theater of Italy, this stock figure was originally called *arlecchino,* a favorite pose for maskers during carnival season. In Charlotte Brontë's *Jane Eyre,* Rochester's insistence on dressing Jane in finery convinces her that she will look as ridiculous as a harlequin.

harmattan (*hahr* . muh . *tan'*) a sharp, dry wind or dust storm arising on the Sahara and blowing onto the Atlantic coast of West Africa during the winter months, obscuring visibility for planes and land travelers. In Chinua Achebe's *Things Fall Apart,* Okonkwo's fame as a tribal leader and entrepreneur grows like a brush fire in a harmattan.

harmonium (hahr . *moh'* nee . uhm) a small organ console with a keyboard attached to a set of reeds graduated in size to produce a pitched sound when air from a bellows passes over them. Introduced in 1818 in Austria, the instrument remained popular in parlors and chapels until the 1930s. In Edith Wharton's *Ethan Frome,* a harmonium player and fiddlers provide music for the church social.

harpoon (hahr . *poon'*) a barbed fish gig, dart, javelin, leister, or spear used by fishers of seagoing tribes. Strong enough to be used against lobster, salmon, dolphin, and larger catch, the traditional Polynesian, Eskimo, Nootka, Athapascan, or Kwakiutl harpoon ends in three prongs, which may fasten to a toggle or crosspin that pivots or turns inward to hold the target and may be tied to a buoy or sinew for quick location and retrieval. Modern harpoon guns pass an electric charge along the line to the catch. In Gary Paulsen's *Dogsong,* the author tells of a fisherman who sang to whales and made them swim toward his harpoon. *See also* toggle point.

harpsichord (*hahrp'* sih . kord) a musical instrument resembling a piano containing two keyboards and quills or leather plectra that pluck the double strings. Popular from the sixteenth to the eighteenth century, the harpsichord was a forerunner of the pianoforte. Hugh Conway, protagonist in James Hilton's *Lost Horizon,* is infatuated with a Chinese harpsichord player.

Harpy one of three winged monsters from Greek mythology that bore the face and torso of a woman and the wings and brass claws of a vulture. According to Edith Hamilton's *Mythology,* during Jason's voyage aboard the *Argo,* Harpies befouled or snatched the food of King Phineus, pressing him to the brink of starvation.

harrow a heavy, iron-toothed farming implement pulled by horses or tractor over rough land to loosen and remove branches, weeds, debris, and stones. The harrow is also helpful in breaking up clods, leveling soil for planting, and covering seeds. In more recent models, spring-loaded tines or teeth, devised in 1869 by David L. Garver, bent away from anything strong enough to break the tool. The late nineteenth-century models had discs attached to axles; these harrows sliced through earth, but flipped out of the way of rocks that could break them. Snowball, an idealistic pig in George Orwell's *Animal Farm,* dreams of a time when the windmill will produce electricity to power plows, reapers, and harrows and spare dray animals much drudgery.

Hasidic (huh . *sihd'* ik) **Jews** *pl.* **Hasidim** zealous observers of Jewish tradition and ritual; also, seekers of purity and goodness. Evolved in the second century B.C. from Jews repelled by the excesses of Hellenes, the ascetic Hasidim (literally, *the righteous ones*) demonstrated their piety and austerity by avoiding modern behaviors and wearing ritual curls, black garb, and severe black hats. In Chaim Potok's *The Chosen,* Danny describes how local Hasidic Jews follow his devout father. *See also* earlocks.

hasp a rectangular hinged metal strap or plate pierced with a slot that fits over a staple or projecting metal keeper. The plate is secured in place by a peg, bolt, or bar that fits into the staple or by a padlock that prevents the plate from slipping off the staple. Departing from their home, Wang Lung and his family fasten the hasp and seek relief from famine in another town in Pearl S. Buck's *The Good Earth.*

hauberk (*haw'* buhrk) a snug, sleeved tunic or coat of chain mail with a turned-up collar to protect the neck and chin. Invented by the Romans from flexible metal links to replace ancient forms of armor plating, this protective costume was common in the twelfth through the fourteenth century, when firearms rendered them obsolete. In the final clash of opposing forces, Dain, a warrior in J. R. R. Tolkien's *The Hobbit,* leads fighters garbed in knee-length hauberks and flexible metal hose.

haversack a satchel or carryall for provisions, which hikers, mountain climbers, and soldiers bear on straps over the shoulders or across the upper back. Derived from the German for *oat sack,* the term originally named the knapsack of feed for horses. In Stephen Crane's *The Red Badge of Courage,* soldiers carry food and personal items in their haversacks.

hawk-bill a 100-pound, yellow or brown plated sea turtle common to warm waters of the tropics and valued for tortoiseshell, a natural material carved into hair ornaments, combs, eyeglass frames, belt buckles, and costume jewelry. In Ernest Hemingway's *The Old Man and the Sea,* Santiago prefers green sea turtles and hawk-bills to the feisty loggerheads.

hawker a noisy, aggressive peddler, vendor, tinker, or street seller of services, goods, or produce from a barrow or pushcart or the back of a truck, van, or car. The hawker earns a reputation for boisterous, aggressive sale or promotion of services such as shoe mending by calling to passersby and holding up for inspection samples of wares or evidence of services, such as sharpened knives, mended kettles, leather goods, or resale items. Outside Lucetta's residence in Thomas Hardy's *The Mayor of Casterbridge,* the farmers, dairymen, merchants, and hawkers fill the carrefour on market day. *See also* carrefour.

hawse-hole (*hawz'* hohl) the opening in the bow or forecastle of a ship through which cables, anchor chains, stabilizing ropes, or hawsers are threaded to the outside. In Herman Melville's *Benito Cereno,* the American captain notes that Don Benito, an obviously effete aristocrat, did not get his sea training at the hawse-holes by doing mundane ship's duty. *See also* forecastle.

hawser a thick rope, chain, or cable used for towing, mooring, or stabilizing the buffeting of a ship at dockside or along a jetty or quay. The hawser is tied to a post, bitt, or bollard, a sturdy mooring spool. A standard term from the beginning of Middle English, the word appears to have derived from the French for *hoist.* At Billingsgate in Charles Dickens's *Great Expectations,* Pip passes through stacks of rusted chain and hemp hawsers. *See also* bitt.

hawthorn a rugged shrub or spiny tree that each spring produces white flowers resembling apple blossoms. The leaves and clusters of ruddy berries were prized by nineteenth-century herbalists as a cardiac depressant and a palliative for high blood pressure. In

F. Scott Fitzgerald's *The Great Gatsby,* Daisy, a lover of beauty, admires the fragrance of hawthorn.

haymow a pile or stack of hay that is dried in the sun and then covered with a tarp or canvas to keep it safe from mold and tight against wind; a hayrick. Also, a storage shed or loft where loose hay is stored and forked down into hanging feed racks for foraging animals. When Leo visits the title character of Willa Cather's *My Antonia,* he chooses to sleep with the boys in the haymow.

hazel a deciduous bush of the birch family producing scraggly yellow flowers, edible nuts, and leaves, bark, and twigs used in the production of an astringent called witch hazel. The connection with witches derives from the use of forked hazel limbs as divining or dowsing rods. Alongside hazel bushes and streams filled with dace, Winston Smith, protagonist of George Orwell's *1984,* names the field the "Golden Country." *See also* divining rod.

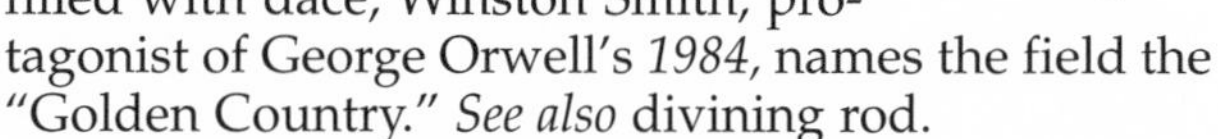

head cheese ground pork brain, tongue, liver, heart, hooves, and other edible animal parts, which are boiled, chopped, mixed with spices, drained, and molded into a jellied brawn, cheese, or loaf or forced into casings for sausage. In Toni Morrison's *Beloved,* Stamp Paid eats a piece of Ella's head cheese to demonstrate good will.

headline the mooring rope, hawser, chain, or cable that secures the prow of a boat or ship to a mooring buoy or upright post, bollard, or beam on a wharf or to a cleat on the rear of a towing barge. Also, the headline enables the pilot to swing the stern around by pulling the ship against the headline. While playing riverboat pilot, the title character in Mark Twain's *The Adventures of Tom Sawyer* calls for headline and spring-line. *See also* hawser; spring-line.

head rag a scarf, bandanna, or scrap of recycled clothing or toweling used to tie up hair, cool the neck, absorb sweat, keep hair from falling into food, or protect the hair of a person who is cleaning or whitewashing a ceiling, rafters, railings, sconces, or a chandelier. In Zora Neale Hurston's *Their Eyes Were Watching God,* to humble and control his wife, Jody forces her to conceal her beautiful hair with a head rag while she works at the neighborhood store.

headset a framework or lightweight flexible band that clamps to the head to support or contain a voice transmitter or microphone and either one or two earpieces or receivers for use with a two-way radio, ship-to-shore communication system, switchboard, telephone, or cassette or CD player. In Gary Paulsen's *Hatchet,* the passenger removes the headset from the dead pilot and tries to locate help before the Cessna runs out of fuel.

headstall a part of a bridle or halter that crosses a horse's head both above and below the ears to balance the bit between the teeth and spread the pull of the reins evenly over the head. Jody, the protagonist in John Steinbeck's *The Red Pony,* assembles brow band, headstall, and other tack used to harness Gabilan, his pony.

heath (heeth) an expanse of nonarable, acid wasteland featuring shallow-rooted evergreen shrubs, sandy or rocky soil, fetid bogs, and a thin cover of peat or humus; a barren or moor. Also, the wiry plants that cover a heath. Derived from Old Welsh for *unplowed turf,* the term dates to the eleventh century and forms the root of *heathen,* an unchurched dweller of a wasteland. The setting of Thomas Hardy's *The Return of the Native* depicts the interconnected lives of residents of windy, desolate Egdon Heath. Likewise, Emily Brontë's *Wuthering Heights* features a wild setting and a brooding gypsy named Heathcliff. *See also* heather; moor.

heather (*heh'* thuhr) low-growing, spiky erica; a creeping shrub or evergreen producing branching stems; overlapping leaves; feathery heads of small fragrant white, mauve, yellow, or purple bell-shaped blooms; and nectar, which can be distilled into a liqueur or beer or steeped into a tonic or tea. The dried stalks and roots are used for making bridal bouquets, dye, antivenin, diuretics, sedatives, and cough medicine as well as thatch or roofing, matting, brooms and brushes, briarwood pipes, basket materials, animal bedding, and fuel. While wandering over heather, the title character in Charlotte Brontë's *Jane Eyre* expects to die of hunger and exposure. *See also* heath; moor.

hebona (*heh'* buh . nuh) or **ebonen** or **hebonen** taxine, a toxic alkaloid juice kin to morphine and strychnine. Obtained from the yew, a poisonous coneless evergreen shrub or tree yielding scaly bark, flat two-toned needles, and red berries, hebona causes red welts on the skin. When ingested, it halts the respiratory system and impedes circulation by causing heart arrhythmia. In William Shakespeare's *Hamlet,* the ghost reports that his brother Claudius poured hebona in the victim's ear to kill him and steal his throne and wife. *See also* yew.

hecatomb (*hehk'* uh . tohm) a public ritual begun in ancient Greece and Rome by which worshippers propitiate the gods with the slaughter of a hundred (or a great number of) cattle and the offering of choice pieces of organ meat, sinew, and fat on the altars. The term derives from the Greek for *a hundred cattle. Hecatombaion,* the first month of the Greek civic calendar, which fell in July to August, became the popular month for these extravagant sacrifices. Athena, a significant Olympian goddess in Homer's *Odyssey,* seeks protection for Telemachus by offering prayers and a grand hecatomb to Poseidon, god of the sea.

hedgehog small, shy nocturnal animal of Africa, Asia, and Europe featuring a pointed snout, rotund, spiny body, and sharp claws with which it digs for insects; the European equivalent of the North American porcupine. In Anglo-Saxon style, this fifteenth-century term derives from the juncture of two simple nouns, hedge and hog. As Titania, Queen of the Fairies in William Shakespeare's *A Midsummer Night's Dream,* readies herself for sleep, the attendant fairies bid the relatively harmless hedgehog, newts, and other nuisances to depart and leave their mistress in peace.

hedgerow a length of shrubbery, trees, or shaped bushes used as a fence, border, privacy screen, windbreak, boundary marker, or containment for livestock. To create a nearly impermeable hedge, gardeners or farmers interweave branches of a blend of plants to create a dense horizontal growth that approaches a work of art in texture, fragrance, and color. In Richard Adams's *Watership Down,* Hazel warns a mouse of danger by addressing him in the lingo of the hedgerow, which is the home and habitat of small animals.

heeler or **ward heeler** a derogatory slang term for a representative, errand-runner, or agent of a political machine or precinct boss, who extends favors such as employment opportunity and protection from the police and bureaucrats to people who vote for and support key politicians who keep the boss in power. In a working-class bar, Jurgis, protagonist of Upton Sinclair's *The Jungle,* meets heelers from both parties and admires the style of Buck Halloran, a Democrat.

hello-girl or **hello-central** a switchboard operator during the early days of telephones when calls had to be placed through a central dispatcher, who was usually female. Mark Twain has Hank, the protagonist of *A Connecticut Yankee in King Arthur's Court,* name his child Hello-Central after the hello-girl Hank loved in Hartford. In Olive Ann Burns's *Cold Sassy Tree,* Will Tweedy dislikes the way people class milliners with hello-girls and other low-level workers.

helmsman the pilot or steerer of a ship, who stands on deck or in the pilot house and follows the directions of the navigator and turns the wheel to direct the rudder in a set direction, which is given in degrees. Before the invention of the wheel, the helmsman occupied a position below deck and moved the whipstaff to activate the rudder. In Joseph Conrad's "The Secret Sharer," the unnamed captain alarms the helmsman by stealing up to have a look at the compass.

hemistitch or **hemistich** (*hehm'* ih . stihtch) half of a line of poetry, which may precede or follow a caesura, or pause, in rhetorical expression or stand alone as an incomplete or defective line. Ragueneau, a literate cavalier in Edmond Rostand's *Cyrano de Bergerac,* insists that the caesura belongs between two hemistitches rather than left dangling in mid-line, as the Greek derivation of the term implies.

hemlock a lacy wildflower that resembles Queen Anne's lace with its flattened, umbrella-shaped spread of flower clusters. Unrelated to the hemlock tree, the poisonous hemlock gained historical fame as the substance used to execute Socrates. Likewise, the lethal association of the word can be found in the name of the Hemlock Society, a California-based organization that advises people on ways to commit suicide to escape pain or severe handicap. In Dr. Martin Luther King's "Letter from a Birmingham Jail," he compares accusations against him to the situation in Athens where citizens blamed Socrates for courting the toxic cup of hemlock that killed him.

Henry rifle a single-shot breech-loading rifle. Mattie Ross, protagonist of Charles Portis's *True Grit,* identifies Tom Chaney as a cruel-mouthed man armed with a Henry rifle. *See* Martini-Henry.

heptarchy (*hehp'* tahr . kee) a seven-part rule or confederacy, specifically the Anglo-Saxon alliance made up of seven kingdoms—East Anglia, Essex, Kent, Mercia, Northumbria, Sussex, and Wessex—from

A.D. 449 to 828. In *The Adventures of Huckleberry Finn,* Mark Twain's title character explains royal rogues to Jim and includes Saxon heptarchies among the notorious.

herald a messenger, ambassador, announcer, or runner who bears daily dispatches and other mundane communications, official edicts, tournament challenges, invitations, proposals of marriage, or proclamations to heads of state and to rural or isolated areas outside the reach of a centralized government such as a castle, citadel, or stronghold or to armies in the field. As she tells the story of King Laius's entourage in Sophocles' *Oedipus,* Queen Jocasta mentions a herald who witnessed the pivotal event that killed the king and ended the plague.

herbal medicine according to the *Pen Tsao,* a Chinese pharmacopoeia, and other written documents dating to eighteenth-century China, healers depended on freshly gathered or dried roots, berries, leaves, stems, or fruits of wild plants to cure disease and as tonics to restore internal balance and energy. Through a holistic treatment of acupuncture and moxa burning, healers extended the power of such herbs as ginseng root, hemp, dogbane, opium poppy, rhubarb, aconite, licorice, camphor, angelica, ginger root, and ephedra. In Amy Tan's *The Kitchen God's Wife,* Winnie intends to treat her daughter's multiple sclerosis with the aid of herbal medicine. *See also* arnica; ginseng root; moxa.

hermaphrodite (huhr . *ma'* froh . dyt) an animal or person who exhibits the reproductive organs (penis, testes, labia, vagina) and secondary sex characteristics (breasts, curves, musculature, beard) of both male and female. The term derives from a Greek myth about the son of Hermes and Aphrodite who couples with the nymph Salmacis and becomes bisexual. In early adolescence, Maya Angelou, in the autobiographical *I Know Why the Caged Bird Sings,* wonders how hermaphrodites manage simple body functions and how they decide which gender suits them. The image epitomizes the teenager's ambivalence toward her own sexuality and toward the perplexity common to her peers.

hernia (*huhr'* nyuh) the rupture or entrapment of an organ or connective tissue through an abnormal fissure, such as a tear in the internal wall of the body. A miserably painful condition, hernia can lead to shock, strangulation of an organ, internal infection and bleeding, and gangrene. In *Zlata's Diary,* Zlata Filipovic worries that, because her father suffered a hernia, there is no one to carry water to the family's apartment.

heroin (*heh'* roh . ihn) a bitter, odorless crystalline narcotic, analgesic, and sedative derived from opium that can addict abusers psychologically to the euphoric states it produces. Derived from the Greek for *hero,* the term was a trade name for a soporific drug distributed by Friedrich Bayer & Company in 1898. As Alex Haley notes in *The Autobiography of Malcolm X,* a runner can earn $100 a day from the sale of cocaine or heroin, but must know how to avoid the narcotics squad.

herring clouds a colloquial term describing a sky striated with long rows of clouds like blinds partially shading a window. During the flight of Kino and Juana from pursuers in John Steinbeck's *The Pearl,* a sky striped with herring clouds creates a series of light and dark moments as the moonlight is alternately revealed and occluded, producing an ominous setting for the novel's falling action. *See also* cirrus.

hessian bag (*heh'* shuhn) a sturdy sack made of coarsely woven white jute, hemp, or burlap; a gunny sack or croker sack. In Joy Adamson's *Born Free,* she describes making crude toys from hessian bags stuffed with inner tubes and swung from tree limbs like oversized cat toys to keep the lions occupied. *See also* croker sack.

hex a curse, spell, or verbal charm uttered by a conjurer against an enemy or victim to induce passion or to cause humiliation, loss, pain, misfortune, death, or damnation; a jinx or hoo-doo. Derived from the Middle English for *crone* or *witch,* the term dates to the mid-nineteenth century. To bolster his courage, the title character in John Gardner's *Grendel* shouts a hex on any lurking stalker.

heyoka (hay . *oh'* kuh) a male visionary and healer of the North American Plains tribes whose contact with the spirits caused him to act and speak backward, for example, mounting a horse with his back to the animal's head, wearing his clothes inside out and his hair long on one side, waving goodbye as he approaches a gathering, and saying "I'm sorry" to an adversary. According to Black Elk in John Neihardt's *Black Elk Speaks,* after the sacrifice of a dog, 30 painted heyokas carrying silly gimmicks perform slapstick comedy.

hieroglyphics (*hy* . roh . *glih'* fihks) an ancient Egyptian system of pictographic writing invented by the priestly caste. Hieroglyphs employ drawings or carvings representing a verbal sound, syllable, sign, idea, abstraction, or word; characters recorded on

Egyptian monuments, tombs, tablets, drawings, and scrolls. Derived from the Greek for *holy script,* the ornate lettering evolved about 3000 B.C. into an alphabet of over 600 characters. With the aid of the Rosetta Stone, Jean Champollion was the first European to decipher this early form of picture writing. In Willa Cather's *My Antonia,* Jake and Otto travel by train and talk with a worldly conductor whose cuff buttons are decorated with hieroglyphics.

highball a tall glass holding liquor or whiskey and soda or carbonated water over ice; a cocktail or mixed drink. Derived from a railroad term for an open-road signal (literally, a ball raised as a go-ahead signal), the drink dates to the late 1890s and demonstrates a lighthearted attitude toward public consumption of alcohol. In J. D. Salinger's *The Catcher in the Rye,* Mr. Antolini sips a highball while he discusses erudite philosophy with Holden.

highboy a tall chest of drawers or tapered chest-on-chest mounted on a stand or legs, banded with moldings at the juncture of top and bottom sections. A home showpiece, the highboy was decorated with brass fittings or hardware and topped with an elaborate cornice. The term derives from the French for *high wood.* The highboy is called a tallboy in England. In Thornton Wilder's *Our Town,* a Boston buyer of secondhand furniture offers Mrs. Gibbs $350 for an antique highboy.

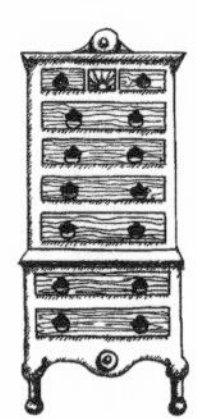

high road an easily navigated thoroughfare, turnpike, or main path, course, or roadstead; a highway elevated to provide maximum runoff of rain and melting snow to facilitate safe passage of vehicles and dray animals in heavy traffic and during bad weather. Hale's daughter in Arthur Miller's *The Crucible* embarrasses her family by standing on the highroad and flapping her arms as though she were trying to fly.

highscreen seat a tall-backed wooden seat, bench, or settle placed near a fireplace or between an entranceway and hearth to provide maximum warmth and to block drafts from an open door at the rear. The entry of the title character to the Rainbow Inn in George Eliot's *Silas Marner* is obscured by the highscreen seats and causes the patrons to think they have seen a ghost. *See also* settle.

high yellow or **high yaller** an American slang term or pejorative referring to a person of mixed African background who has a light complexion. Originating in the 1920s, the term is the equivalent of *mulatto* or *octoroon.* According to Alex Haley's *The Autobiography of Malcolm X,* at the age of 15, Malcolm travels with a fast cosmopolitan crowd and mixes with black and brown girls as well as high yellows and whites.

hilt the handle of a tool, knife, sword, dagger, spear, or jousting lance. Made of materials ranging from plain wood to carved bone, ivory, cast iron, or steel, the hilt is often shielded or basketed to protect the user's hand or to shield the arm from splatters of blood. After stabbing a pig in William Golding's *Lord of the Flies,* Jack asks to borrow Ralph's knife to make a nick in the hilt of his spear to commemorate the first kill.

hippogriff or **hippogryph** (*hihp'* poh . grihf) or **hippogriffin** a mythical beast with the wings, talons, and head of an eagle or griffin and the body and hindquarters of a horse. A literary creation of Ariosto and other writers of the European chivalric tradition, the term dates to the mid-seventeenth century and demonstrates the creation of a classical hybrid based on the winged Pegasus and named for the Greek for *horse* and the Latin for *griffin.* The title character in Esther Forbes's *Johnny Tremain* rides Goblin, a horse easily spooked by flapping laundry on the line, which appears as menacing as a hippogriff.

hipster a slang term for a modish male fashion plate or coxcomb; a stylish, in-the-know jazz-age fop, dandy, or clotheshorse. A corruption or adaptation of *hep,* meaning *up-to-date,* this evolving street term was common in the early 1940s. According to Alex Haley's *The Autobiography of Malcolm X,* the title character buys flashy zoot suits, pegged pants, and shoes popular with hipsters.

Hitler Youth or **Hitler Jugend** a compulsory movement established in Germany in 1920 by Baldur von Schirach, who organized youth into uniformed marching cadres meant to spread Nazi propaganda and to provide information gleaned by young spies to enhance and further the aims of Hitler's Third Reich. After a free-for-all ends the winter carnival in John Knowles's *A Separate Peace,* Finny refers to his schoolmates as "Hitler youth." *See also* holocaust; Nazi; SS.

hoarding (*hohr'* dihng) a security wall, billboard, privacy screen, or fence erected around a construction site and used by advertisers and propagandists as a likely spot to hang or paste up handbills, movie posters, and political campaign information. Derived from the Old English for *conceal,* the term entered

English in the first quarter of the nineteenth century. In his yearning for a normal life, Paul Baumer, protagonist in Erich Maria Remarque's *All Quiet on the Western Front,* idolizes a girl featured on a poster attached to the hoarding.

hoarhound or **horehound** (*hohr'* hownd) candy, tea, cough syrup, or throat lozenges made from the musky, bitter juice of an aromatic mint named for its white bristly surface. Prized by Hippocrates, the Greek father of medicine, hoarhound recurs in herbal lore as a palliative for infertility and an antivenin, purgative, and lactation stimulant. In Olive Ann Burns's *Cold Sassy Tree,* Grandpa treats Will Tweedy and Mary Toy to peppermint and hoarhound candy while he takes a stiff drink of whiskey.

hob a casing, projection, or shelf built around the inside perimeter of a fireplace, where cooks kept plates, kettles, casseroles, and pans hot and stored extra peat or dried firewood and damp tinder. Dating to the sixteenth century, the elusive term appears to have evolved from *hub* and refers to a lump of clay. In Charles Dickens's *A Christmas Carol,* Scrooge is warming a pan of gruel on the hob when the ghost of his former partner appears.

hobble to tie, fetter, strap, or fasten the feet of an animal to regulate its gait during training or to prevent it from kicking or wandering away. This Germanic term, which entered English in the fourteenth century, names an early twentieth-century fashion called the hobble skirt, whose hemline, narrowed at the ankles, made it difficult for the wearer to walk. On the ride south into New Mexico in Hal Borland's *When the Legends Die,* Tom and Red hobble the horses for the night before making camp.

hobby-horse a wicker prop fitted over a human body and used on stage or in a public arena to represent a humorous mounted figure in a morris dance, skit, mummery, parade, or pantomime; also, a child's plaything consisting of a horse's head on a pole. In William Shakespeare's *Hamlet,* the title character recites a line from a popular ballad ridiculing Puritans who objected to the use of the hobby-horse in May Day celebrations.

hob-nail a short stud, nail, or peg with a broad, thick head and used to reinforce the sole of a work shoe, brogan, or boot. Derived from the Middle English for *peg,* the term dates to the late sixteenth century. Tom Joad, an ex-con returning from prison and dressed in prison-issue clothing in John Steinbeck's *The Grapes of Wrath,* wears new work pants, a chambray shirt, and hob-nailed shoes with half-circles on the heels to protect them from wear.

hoe cake or **johnnycake** a flat, thin cake of salted corn bread baked or fried in a skillet, on a flat rock, or possibly on the blade of a hoe and carried by field workers or travelers. Originally known as journey cake or ash cake in the mid-eighteenth century, the food kept well and could be softened in milk or vegetable broth after it hardened. Before deserting her husband, Janey, protagonist of Zora Neale Hurston's *Their Eyes Were Watching God,* places a plate over a pan of hoe cake and overturns it to settle the bread on the dish, a symbolic act suggesting her own intention to overturn her life.

hogan (*hoh'* gahn) the Navaho name for a one-room, dome-roofed building or residence made of pine logs stacked horizontally into a six- or eight-sided matrix 6 feet high, then topped with brush and gravel, and finished with mud, clay, or adobe. Built to blend with the surrounding growth and arroyos, the hogan has no windows; its only openings are a smoke hole and a front door that faces east. In Scott O'Dell's *Sing Down the Moon,* Chief Old Bear exits his hogan to greet the visiting cavalry, little realizing that Colonel Kit Carson will use these troops to force the Navaho on the Long Walk. *See also* adobe; arroyo.

hogshead a large waterproof barrel, tun, or cask used to transport, contain for fermentation, or store from 100 to 140 gallons of liquid, particularly beer, cider, or wine. The term, which is of uncertain derivation, gave its name to a measure of 63 gallons. In Mark Twain's *The Adventures of Tom Sawyer,* Huck sleeps in a hogshead in the lumberyard. *See also* bung; cooperage.

hoist a mechanical lift, crane, block and tackle, or other apparatus used to raise heavy or cumbersome objects and swing or move them to another location, especially at quayside where barges and boats are loaded and unloaded. Entering English in the early sixteenth century, the term probably originated from the Low German term for *raise.* During the Boston Tea Party, the title character of Esther Forbes's *Johnny Tremain* hears the squeak of the hoist that patriots use to lift bales of tea

over the ship's side and drop them into Boston Harbor to create a gesture of defiance to Tory tax collectors.

holloware or **hollow-ware** (*hahl'* loh . wayr) voluminous or heavy tableware, including salvers, bowls, ewers, serving vessels, vases, kettles, and pitchers, as opposed to flatware, the general term for eating utensils. At one time, Ephraim Lapham, the aged instructor of the title character in Esther Forbes's *Johnny Tremain,* produced quality silver holloware for Boston's wealthiest citizens.

holocaust (*hoh'* loh . *cawst*) a widespread destruction, mass murder, slaughter, or massacre of people or animals, usually by fire. Derived from the Greek for *completely burnt,* this Old Testament term entered English in the thirteenth century and refers to religious sacrifices on an altar. When capitalized, the term refers to the killing and cremation of six million Jews and millions of others, including Slavs, Poles, Gypsies, Seventh Day Adventists, political dissidents, homosexuals, and the mentally or physically handicapped or deformed, by Hitler's SS throughout Europe during World War II. Although Jews were not the only group targeted, the Nazi focus on their extermination led to the death of over 70 percent of Europe's prewar Jewish population. The methods of murder included shooting, hanging, garrotting, poisoning, forced labor, starvation, epidemic, euthanasia, exposure, medical experiment, bombing, and gassing with Zyklon B. Thomas Keneally's *Schindler's List* depicts the dedication of one industrialist to saving Jews from the Holocaust. *See also* genocide; Hitler Youth; Nazi; pogrom; SS.

holograph (*hoh'* loh . graf) a document, letter, deed, affidavit, or testament, all copies of which are written individually by the hand of the author—not a carbon copy; an authentic work, contract, or will written by the testator. Derived from the Greek for *wholly written,* the term entered English in the early seventeenth century. In Robert Louis Stevenson's *The Strange Case of Dr. Jekyll and Mr. Hyde,* Mr. Utterson studies Dr. Jekyll's will, a holograph leaving all possessions to Mr. Hyde.

holystone (*hoh'* lee . stohn) a chunk of soft sandstone used for scrubbing, scouring, or buffing wooden decks and stairs, which were drenched in seawater and bleached white by the sun. The term derives from sailors' practice of stealing headstones from graves. They laughingly divided them by size, calling small stones prayer books and larger ones Bibles. In Avi's *The True Confessions of Charlotte Doyle,* after the heroine becomes a sailor, she takes her turn caulking and smoothing the deck with holystones. *See also* caulking.

homburg (*hahm'* buhrg) a soft felt hat with a high crown dented from back to front with a curved, stiff brim and matching ribbon or braid at the base. Named for its manufacturer in Homburg, Germany, the hat, a favorite of England's Prince Albert during the second half of the nineteenth century, became a mark of the distinguished, well-groomed man or woman. Oskar Schindler, the focal character of Thomas Keneally's *Schindler's List,* maintains his reputation as a well-dressed businessman by sporting a topcoat and homburg.

homeboy American slang term for a visitor or new acquaintance who shares membership in a gang or student body or residence in a neighborhood or town. Dating to the 1920s, the term underwent a change in the 1990s, when it came to mean a rap performer or singer in a rap group. In Alex Haley's *The Autobiography of Malcolm X,* Shorty acknowledges Malcolm's acceptance among the in-crowd by calling him "Homeboy."

homespun plain, coarse, loosely woven cloth of undyed wool, linen, flax, thistledown, or blended fibers to be used for sacks, casings, house dresses, tunics, shirts, toweling, or curtains; the cheapest, least adorned yard goods, usually of uneven texture and color. Dating to the seventeenth century, the term denotes the role of the housewife in producing thread or yarn for the home loom. In Marjorie Kinnan Rawlings's *The Yearling,* the family's annual list of purchased goods includes 6 yards of homespun. *See also* croker sack; hessian bag; huckaback.

hominy (*hah'* muh . nee) *See* posole.

hoo-doo a late nineteenth-century term derived from the Hausa word for various types of conjury, black magic, or hex. Also, to curse with misfortune or ill luck; to damn, jinx, or repay an enemy with dire consequences. The title character in Ernest Gaines's *The Autobiography of Miss Jane Pittman* tries to save her husband from injury or death by seeking the advice of a woman skilled in hoo-doo or black magic. *See also* hex.

hoodwinked capped or blindfolded, as with a trained bird of prey that is kept at bay by pulling a hood over its eyes; also, deceived or tricked by a deliberate ruse, misinformation, imposture, or disguise. A seventeenth-century fowling term, the word derives from

Old English for *guard.* Benvolia refuses to hoodwink Cupid, the god of infatuation, in William Shakespeare's *Romeo and Juliet.*

hookah (*hoo'* kuh) an ornate Oriental water pipe consisting of a bowl, a series of flexible, interlacing tubes, and a mouthpiece. The water filters and cools the substance being smoked, which could be tobacco, hashish, marijuana, or hemp. Derived from the Arabic for *water urn,* the term entered English in the mid-eighteenth century. Considered a curiosity, the hookah was often displayed among collections of objects of Oriental origin. In Lewis Carroll's *Alice's Adventures in Wonderland,* Alice finds the philosophical caterpillar peacefully sitting on a mushroom and puffing on a hookah.

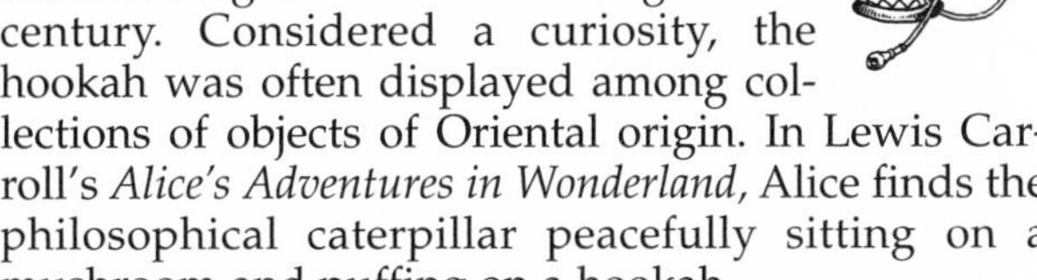

hookworm the larva of a nematode or parasite that lives in excrement and burrows under human or animal skin. The hookworm migrates through the circulatory system to the intestines, where it thrives on blood and mucus. Symptoms include itching, lung inflammation, anemia, cramps, diarrhea, malaise, and weakness and can lead to death. Elsa, the lioness in Joy Adamson's *Born Free,* grows languid from an infestation of hookworm she contracted on a trip to the coast of Kenya.

hoopstick a short dowel or baton, part of the equipment used in the game of rolling a hoop on the ground. To keep the hoop upright, the player watches for rocks or an uneven course and levels the moving circlet with frequent touches and adjustments of the stick. In Mark Twain's *The Adventures of Tom Sawyer,* the title character trades his hoopstick for a blue ticket so he can win a Sunday school prize.

hops a vine of the hemp family featuring bitter white or greenish cones that form the basis of ale, malt liquor, or beer. Native American healers use soporific hops in sedatives, tonics, and analgesics. In John Steinbeck's *The Red Pony,* Billy treats Jody's horse for the strangles by mixing bran and hops with turpentine and carbolic acid to form a pungent, healing steam.

hornpipe a lively jig or folk dance for a solo performer, danced primarily with hands on hips and weight balanced on one foot with much switching from right to left in time to rousing nautical tunes played on a Celtic fife. The hornpipe is often associated with Scots or sailors and was used by slavers as a means of exercising African captives on deck during the voyage from Africa to the auction block. In George Eliot's *Silas Marner,* dancers take a break while the youngest of Squire Cass's sons executes a hornpipe. In Paula Fox's *Slave Dancer,* Jessie must play his pipe to help slaves survive the debilitating journey over the Atlantic Ocean to Cuba.

hospice (*hahs'* pihs) a religious house, nursing home, refuge, or monastic hall that provides shelter, lodging, and food for the homeless and medical attention for the terminally ill. Derived from the Latin for *host,* the term entered English in the early nineteenth century and appeared in the hospice movement in 1967 from the formal initiative of Dr. Cicily Saunders to help the dying live out their time in dignity and relative comfort. Angel Clare and his sister-in-law Liza-Lu arrive near a tower and hospice on the day of Tess's execution in Thomas Hardy's *Tess of the D'Urbervilles.*

hourglass a primitive timepiece or chronometer such as an egg timer. The hourglass is formed from two glass or plastic globes, chambers, or bulbs, one on top of the other, joined in the middle to allow the slow trickle or leak of granules, liquid, or mercury from top to bottom, the passage of which determines the time elapsed. An early sixteenth-century hybrid term, it derives from the Latin for *hour* and Old English for *glass.* To please Becky Thatcher, with whom he flirts during class in Mark Twain's *The Adventures of Tom Sawyer* by drawing pictures on his slate, the protagonist sketches her portrait with a flattering hourglass figure, rounded head, and fanlike hands. *See also* chronometer.

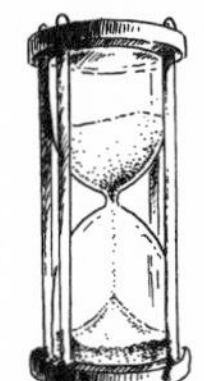

howdah (*how'* duh) a canopied box seat or pavilion with side rails, tassels, and ornate padded interiors that provides shelter, comfort, and dignity for one or two passengers on an elephant or camel. Derived from the Urdu for *litter,* the term entered English in the late eighteenth century. In India, Phileas Fogg, protagonist of Jules Verne's *Around the World in Eighty Days,* travels unsteadily aboard a jostling, rolling howdah on an elephant's back.

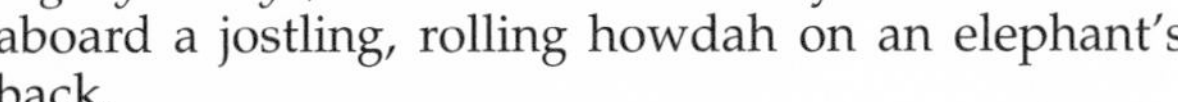

huckaback (*huhk'* uh . *bak*) a durable, roughly woven toweling made of absorbent linen, cotton, homespun, or blended fibers to be used as kitchen towels or cleaning cloths. The term, of uncertain origin—

possibly *hugaback* or *hugabag*—dates to the late seventeenth century. In Edith Wharton's *Ethan Frome,* Zenobia accuses Mattie Silver of stealing a huckaback towel. *See also* homespun.

huckleberry a tangy North American blueberry growing on a low shrub found in marshes and woods in acid soil. Native Americans prized the berry as the source of a purple dye and in pies and jams; herbalists prescribed it as a diuretic and palliative to cure infections in the mouth and urinary tract. In "Civil Disobedience," Henry David Thoreau joined a group of friends and picked huckleberries when he was released from jail.

Huey (*hyoo'* ee) the workhorse helicopter during the Vietnam War that landed and removed troops from fire zones and hauled the dead and wounded to aid stations. In Walter Dean Myers's *Fallen Angels,* soldiers use flares to identify their locations so that Huey pilots can drop in close and get out without harm. For extra protection, a door gunner strafes the area while men are pulled aboard.

Huguenots (*hyoo'* guh . nahts or *hyoo'* guh . noh) French Calvinist Protestants or members of the French Reformed Church who had been converted by Swiss missionaries. Persecuted in the sixteenth and seventeenth centuries, the Huguenots formed a militant defiance of Papist laws. After extensive slaughter, they escaped the rule of Catholic kings by emigrating. While explaining her French heritage to Mitch, Blanche DuBois, the melodramatic protagonist of Tennessee Williams's *A Streetcar Named Desire,* claims that her family were Huguenots.

hulks abandoned, dismantled, wrecked, or unseaworthy naval, cargo, or transport vessels stripped of their masts, rigging, and gear; anchored in calm waters; and used as temporary prisons for convicts being shipped to a distant penal colony, such as Australia. In Charles Dickens's *Great Expectations,* the escape of a convict from the Hulks is the main event and precipitating factor to the novel's action because it brings together Abel Magwitch and Pip, his foster son and heir.

hunting frock a durable, waterproof winter tunic with fringed sleeves made of deerskin, often with full-length leggings and topped by a bandolier slung across the chest to hold a powder horn, skinning knife, or other hunting gear. True Son, protagonist in Conrad Richter's *The Light in the Forest,* angers his aunt by appearing at the table in hunting frock and leggings.

hurdle a wooden sledge, crate, or framework on which traitors and other condemned prisoners were hauled to the place of execution. The twelfth-century term appears to derive from the Indo-European word for *door.* In Capulet's tirade in William Shakespeare's *Romeo and Juliet,* he threatens to drag Juliet on a hurdle to Saint Peter's Church for her wedding to Paris, whom she declines to marry because she is already wed to Romeo.

hurdy-gurdy a boxed instrument, lute-shaped wheel fiddle, or lap symphonia used by performers in churches and festivals and by street beggars, who play a keyboard at the same time that they turn a crank to activate a wheel that strikes the strings. The term, which entered English in the mid-eighteenth century, imitates the instrument's plinking sound. As Jean Valjean searches for Petit Gervais in Victor Hugo's *Les Misérables,* he describes him as a ten-year-old boy traveling with a marmot and hurdy-gurdy.

hurricane deck the light upper deck at the top of a passenger steamboat; the observation deck on which stands the wheelhouse, from which the pilot observes the course and watches for any obstacles or changes in the weather. In Mark Twain's *The Adventures of Tom Sawyer,* the title character fantasizes that he stands on the hurricane deck of a riverboat and gives orders to his crew.

hussar (huh . *zahr'*) a light-armed cavalry officer or scout, especially from Croatia or Hungary; a dashing fifteenth-century European military figure in fancy, bright-colored formal attire composed of short military jacket decorated with gold braid, loose pelisse or dolman coat hanging from the left shoulder, cylindrical hat or busby, and shiny black boots with tassels at the top. Derived from the Serbian term for *pirate,* the word entered English in the mid-sixteenth century. The title character in Alexander Solzhenitsyn's *A Day in the Life of Ivan Denisovich* reflects on his wife's job painting carpets with the figure of a hussar in a troika. *See also* troika.

hydrant a freeze-proof device that has a handle to activate valves that lift water from a well, main, or pipe and discharge it from a spout. Unlike the municipal fire hydrant, the home, orchard, or farm version resembles a manual pump and often attaches to irrigation lines. A yard hydrant is the chief source of water for Granny's house in Richard Wright's autobiographical *Black Boy,* where the title character fills his empty stomach to keep it from rumbling during school.

hydrocephalus (*hy* . droh . suh . *fa'* luhs) or **hydrocephaly** a congenital brain deformity or abnormality caused by obstruction or infection in which spinal fluid collects, enlarges the cranium, and damages or atrophies brain tissue. Other symptoms include crossed eyes, vomiting, and stiffness or weakness of the limbs. This seventeenth-century term derives from the Greek for *water head.* McMurphy, the protagonist in Ken Kesey's *One Flew Over the Cuckoo's Nest,* listens to Harding's explanation of the flaccid movements of a young patient suffering from hydrocephalus.

hydroplane (*hy'* droh . playn) a lightweight, propeller-driven seaplane fitted with floats or pontoons so that it can skim or land on water. After inviting his neighbor Nick to join him on his new hydroplane, Jay Gatsby, title character in F. Scott Fitzgerald's *The Great Gatsby,* introduces himself and invites Nick to one of Jay's many all-night parties.

hydrotherapy (*hy* . droh . *theh'* ruh . pee) the treatment of mental or emotional disorders by immersing patients in water or applying water to the body externally at varied pressure, coverage, and temperature from showerheads or rows of jets capable of narrowing to needle-fine streams or opening to deluges. The speaker of Ken Kesey's *One Flew Over the Cuckoo's Nest* notes that drugs have replaced labor-intensive hydrotherapy treatment.

hypochondria (*hy* . poh . *kahn'* dree . uh) a form of depression marked by morbid obsession with health or a persistent fear, anxiety, or suspicion of disease or body malfunction. Derived from the Greek for *below the breastbone,* the term reflects a belief that the disease centered in the upper chest. Fyodor Dostoevsky, author of *Crime and Punishment,* introduces Raskolnikov as a tense, overwrought young man whose self-absorption verges on hypochondria.

hypothesis (hy . *pah'* thih . sihs) the unproved or tentative supposition or assumption that becomes the foundation for a series of empirical studies, experiments, arguments, or rational discussions that will prove or disprove the original theory. From studying the decline of the mouse, the title character in Daniel Keyes's *Flowers for Algernon,* Charlie Gordon deduces that Dr. Strauss's original hypothesis about the curative powers of psychosurgery and hormone treatment is flawed.

hyrax (*hy'* raks) a short, brown, mouselike mammal common to Africa and the Middle East with a stubby body, short limbs and tail, and flat, hooflike nails. The rock- or tree-dwelling hyrax lives primarily on plants, but also digs for grubs and worms. Joy Adamson's concern for her dying hyrax foreshadows her involvement in returning Elsa the lioness to the wild in *Born Free.*

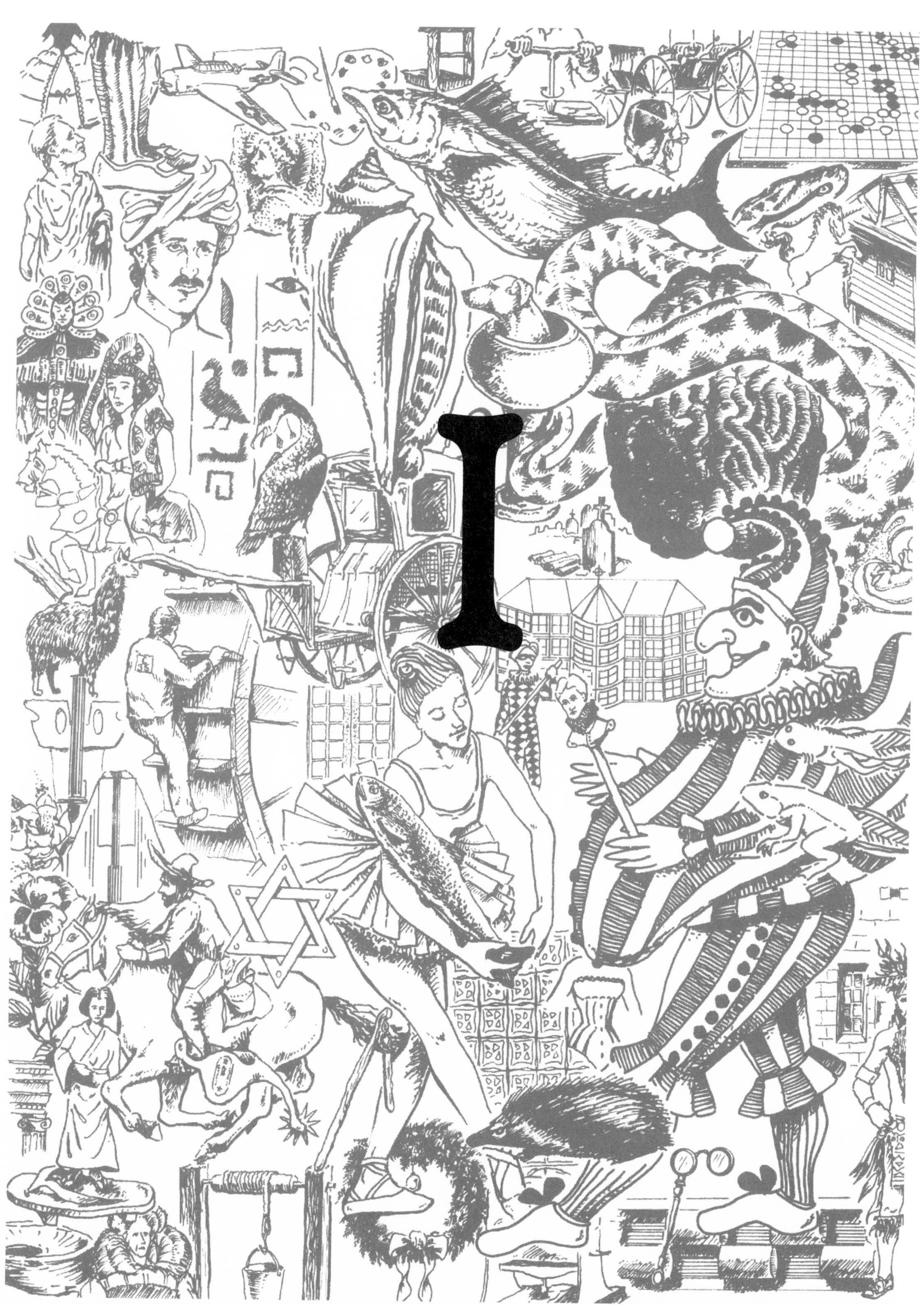
I

icon or **ikon** (*i'* kahn) a sacred picture or image of the Virgin Mary, Christ, or a revered saint; in Byzantine art, a venerated wooden panel edged with gilt and depicting sacred objects or scenes common to the worship or shrines of members of the Eastern Orthodox religion. While surveying the quarters of the moneylender, Raskolnikov, the protagonist of Fyodor Dostoevsky's *Crime and Punishment,* notes cleanliness, order, and a display of piety in a small light burning before a religious icon.

id (ihd) the abstract concept of primitive, instinctual human drive; an unconscious psychic energy that habitually demands physical satisfaction of hunger, thirst, sexual release, and other basic needs. Derived from the Latin for *it,* the term is crucial to an understanding of Dr. Sigmund Freud's three-part self, which consists of drive, conscience, and the conscious self or personality. During a counseling session with Dr. Strauss, Charlie Gordon, protagonist in Daniel Keyes's *Flowers for Algernon,* makes angry wordplay on the id, ego, and superego.

ideograph (*ih'* dee . oh . *graf*) a graphic character, sign, or symbol composed of pictorial representation of an idea or object; a unit of language or logogram that does not represent the word by sounds, such as a universal highway sign, ¥ (yen), or ¶ (paragraph). In Maxine Hong Kingston's *Woman Warrior,* the speaker compares the outstretched wings of a bird to the Japanese ideograph for *human. See also* characters; hieroglyphics; seal.

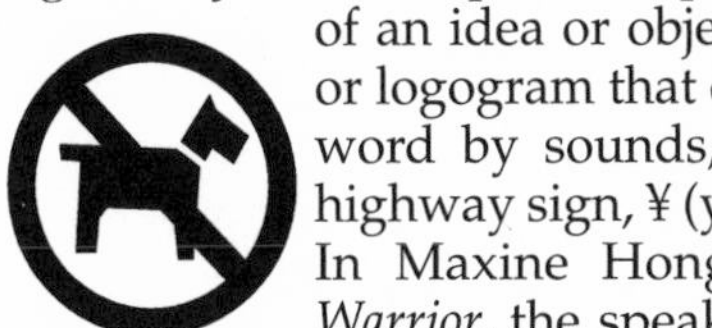

ides (idz) the fifteenth of the month or, in a generalized interpretation, the middle of the ancient Roman lunar-solar calendar, which began with March (in honor of Mars, the Roman patron god) and was divided into the kalends, or beginning; the nones on the fifth or seventh; and the ides on the thirteenth or fifteenth. The remaining days counted backward to the kalends of the next month, the last day being the eve of the kalends. In William Shakespeare's *Julius Caesar,* a soothsayer bids the title character to "beware the Ides of March."

Iditarod (i . *deet'* uh . rahd) Alaska's official 1,200-mile sled-dog race, begun in spring 1973. Commemorating the 1925 run of Leonhard Seppala, who followed a swampy trail out of Anchorage to deliver diphtheria serum to Nome, the race carries a purse of $100,000 distributed among the top 20 participants, who also earn stipends from commercial sponsors. Gary Paulsen's *Dogsong* and *Winterdance* describe his preparations for and participation in the Iditarod.

ignis fatuus (*ihg'* nihs *fah'* too . oos) the ghostly phosphorescent light that springs from the methane gas caused by decomposed organic matter. Also called the will-o'-the-wisp or jack-'o-lantern, the *ignis fatuus* sometimes hovers over a marsh or fen. Derived from the Latin for *foolish fire,* the term entered English in the mid-sixteenth century. Willing herself to return to sense from the folly of self-deception, the title character of Charlotte Brontë's *Jane Eyre* describes as an *ignis fatuus* her dream of a romance with her employer, Mr. Rochester.

I.H.S. a Latinate monogram depicting a misreading of the first three letters of *Iesous,* the Greek spelling of Jesus. The initials appear in elaborate embroidery on clerical and church choir vestments, altar cloths, book covers, and writings and on carved pulpits, doors, coffins, and collection boxes and plates. Dolly Winthrop, an ignorant neighbor of the title character of George Eliot's *Silas Marner,* pricks her cake with I.H.S., but has no idea why the letters are holy or valuable.

impress to coerce, compel, or recruit a crew member, fisherman, or professional mariner 18 years or older from a private vessel into military service aboard a navy vessel; to shanghai, levy, seize goods or cargo; or force into public or military service on land or sea vagrants or people of questionable character. Begun in the sixteenth century, this heavy-handed method of staffing naval operations ended in 1835; during World War I and II, England replaced impressment with a more orderly draft law calling for compulsory public service while the country was at war. The focus of Herman Melville's *Billy Budd* is the result of an act of impressment against the main character, who, ironically, is forced from the merchant ship *Right of Man* and assigned as foretopman of the *H.M.S. Bellipotent.*

incubus (*ing'* kyoo . buhs) *pl.* **incubi** a devil or demon that lusts after and preys upon sleeping women; an evil supernatural seducer who causes witches to have unspeakably perverted sexual relations—for example, bestiality, fellatio, or sodomy—with Satan. Derived from the Latin for *recline upon,* the term dates to the thirteenth century. In Arthur Miller's *The Crucible,* Reverend John Hale claims to have a book describing incubi and succubi. *See also* succubus.

indentures or **indenture** (ihn . *dehn'* chuhr) a contract or other binding document requiring a worker, bondsman, or apprentice to accept the patronage of a master, employer, or artisan for a prescribed number of years (usually seven) in exchange for obedience to prearranged rules and a rigorous schedule of work and study. In Charles Dickens's *Great Expectations,* Pip's indentures make him Joe's apprentice blacksmith, a dirty job that shames and disgusts Pip. *See also* apprentice.

Indian-head a U.S. penny designed in 1859 with a bas-relief of an Indian princess on the front and, on the back, the words "One Cent" framed by a laurel circlet, which the mint replaced with an oak wreath and shield the next year. The cent piece remained in production until 1909. In 1908, engraver Bela Lyon Pratt designed an Indian-head $5 piece with a male profile in war bonnet and surrounded by stars and the word "Liberty" at the top. The reverse side features an eagle and the inscriptions "In God We Trust" and *"E Pluribus Unum,"* the Latin phrase for "one out of many." Scout and Jem, the young protagonists in Harper Lee's *To Kill a Mockingbird,* find two Indian-head pennies in a hole in their neighbor's tree.

indictment (ihn . *dyt'* muhnt) a formal legal document, accusation, or statement charging a person with a crime or offense; a bill of indictment. Drawn up by the prosecuting attorney, the charge is presented to a grand jury. From the Latin for *speak against,* the term entered English in the fourteenth century. In Albert Camus's *The Stranger,* Meursault perceives himself as a witness at the reading of his own indictment. In Richard Wright's *Native Son,* Bigger's indictment indicates that he has already confessed his guilt.

indigo (*ihn'* dih . goh) a shrub of the pea family that produces a blue dye from fermented leaves. Introduced to South Carolina shortly before the American Revolution, indigo, a labor-intensive crop tended at first by slaves, led the dye market until 1900, when synthetic coloring replaced it. Sethe's mother, as described in Toni Morrison's *Beloved,* works such long hours in the indigo fields that she barely knows her daughter.

ingot (*ing'* uht) molten materials, especially precious metals, cast into a standardized shape, usually a bar or block, for ease in tabulation, storage, and transport. Derived from the Middle English for *poured in,* the term dates to the fourteenth century. In Alexandre Dumas's *The Count of Monte Cristo,* Edmond Dantés opens a chest stacked with ingots and heaped with diamonds, rubies, and pearls.

injunction a court order or authoritative command protecting or guaranteeing a complainant's rights by halting an offensive, prejudicial, or harmful action or by forcing the cessation of a specific act or requiring an act to be performed, such as promotion or enrollment at a school. In a graphic passage from Upton Sinclair's *The Jungle,* Bubbly Creek serves as a grease pit for the waste and filth from a meat packer until an entrepreneur begins harvesting blocks of congealed fat from the surface to sell as lard. The workers halt his project with a court injunction and adopt his money-making scheme, thereby profiting from their own pollutants.

inkhorn a portable bottle, flask, or desk-top vessel made of horn and used for storing ink; a version of the inkpot. A fourteenth-century term, the word derives from the era of the quill pen (which was dipped into writing fluid) and was replaced by the fountain pen (which contained a reserve of ink). During the formative months of the American Revolution, Sam Adams, one of Boston's most influential patriots, sits before his papers and inkhorn in Esther Forbes's *Johnny Tremain.*

inkpot a small bottle or stoppered vial containing ink. A standard feature of offices, school desks, and home escritoires, removable inkpots usually fit into a depression or slot on the upper lefthand corner of the writing surface. Anne Frank, the autobiographer of *The Diary of a Young Girl,* recalls that she received a fountain pen, but school authorities forced her to use pen and inkpot during class. *See also* inkhorn.

Inns of Court private hotels catering to the legal profession and serving as the seat of English law since the Middle Ages; four clusters of buildings—Lincoln's Inn, Gray's Inn, Inner Temple, and Middle Temple—housing the four legal societies that dominate the training, examining, and acceptance of attorneys and solicitors to the bar and govern the education of stewards, accountants, bookkeepers, and other students of commerce. In Charles Dickens's *Great Expectations,* Pip and his roommate rent an apartment at the Inns of Court but have no intention of becoming lawyers.

i'noGo tied (*ihn'* uh . goh . *tahk*) an Inuit amulet or lucky charm strung on a thong and worn at the wrist, neck, ankle, or waist as a protection from harm or evil or an assurance of good fortune or divine protection. The term is a Upick phrase meaning "house of the spirits." In Jean Craighead George's *Julie of the Wolves,* Miyax wears an i'noGo tied made of seal fur and blubber by the shaman of Nunivak Island. *See also* amulet; shaman.

inquest an official inquiry by a court or coroner concerning a suspicious, violent, or sudden death; a formal fact-finding hearing or examination of evidence following the preliminary investigation of a crime. From the Latin for *inquire,* the term dates to the thirteenth century. Bigger, the protagonist in Richard Wright's *Native Son,* dominates Chicago headlines after he faints at the inquest into a murder he unintentionally committed.

intercalary (ihn . tuhr . *kal'* uh . ree) **month** a correction of the ancient Chinese lunar-solar calendar that divides 360 days into 12 months. The remaining five days of the solar year are collected into a thirteenth month, which is added to the calendar every four or five years to agree with the solar year. Derived from the Latin for *proclaim among,* the term indicates the role of priests in establishing a regular accounting of days. In Lu Hsun's "My Old Home," the speaker describes Jun-tu as a person his own age who was born in the intercalary month and was named "Intercalary Earth."

ipecac (*ihp'* ih . kak) an alkyloid emetic used as an antidote for poisoning by causing the victim to regurgitate lethal substances from the stomach before they enter the bloodstream; also, a potion used by Indian healers to treat sore throat, amoebic dysentery, intestinal parasites, or lymphatic disease or as a ritual purge or annual religious purification. Derived from dried roots harvested from a viny shrub found in Central and South America, the term originated in the Tupi language and was one of the indigenous herbal cures that Indians introduced to European doctors. In William J. Lederer and Eugene Burdick's *The Ugly American,* insurgents intend to cripple the Japanese army by putting ipecac into their food.

ironclad the generic name for nineteenth-century shallow-draught military vessels sheathed along the hull or covered in iron or steel armor plating. The *Monitor* and *Merrimac,* the most famous American ironclads, first battled on March 6, 1862, at Hampton Roads, Virginia. In Irene Hunt's *Across Five Aprils,* which is set in the North during the Civil War, Jethro ponders the role of ironclads at the battle of Fort Henry, a Confederate stronghold captured by Union forces.

Iron Cross a Prussian-German military decoration established in 1813 by Frederick William III as a reward for bravery on the battlefield. The black Maltese cross is edged in silver with crossed swords and a cluster of oak leaves at the center of the black-and-white-edged red ribbon above. During Paul Baumer's leave in Erich Maria Remarque's *All Quiet on the Western Front,* he meets his German master, who declares that all young soldiers deserve the Iron Cross.

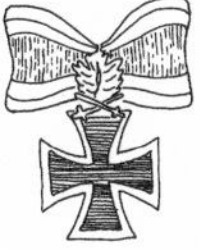

isinglass (*i'* zihn . *glas*) a semitransparent gel used in the manufacture of jelly, glue, sizing, waterproofing, and solvents. Derived from the Dutch for *sturgeon bladder,* this mid-sixteenth-century term indicates one source of the whitish substance that was also made from sheets of mica and waste matter from slaughterhouses. In *The Jungle,* author Upton Sinclair notes that the meat industry processes hooves, hide, hair, and bone into shoe blacking, gelatin, and isinglass.

Islam (*ihs'* luhm or ihs . *lahm'*) a fast-growing, influential monotheistic religion begun by the seventh-century prophet Muhammed (A.D. 570–632), a follower of the god Allah; also, Muslims, who trace their scriptural origins to Abraham and his son Ishmael. Islam flourishes in many African and Asian nations, where the faithful study the Koran in the original Arabic. Today there are more than one billion Muslims, a fivefold increase since the turn of the century. Derived from the Arabic for *submission,* the term entered English in the early nineteenth century. According to Alex Haley's *The Autobiography of Malcolm X,* members of the Black Muslims embraced Islam as a positive influence on black behavior and a boost to the solidity and influence of the black family.

issei (*ee'* say) immigrants from Japan; also, a Japanese immigrant who entered the United States after 1907 under a law making newcomers from Japan ineligible for citizenship. Derived from the Japanese for *first generation,* the term entered English in the 1930s. In Jeanne Wakatsuki Houston and James D. Houston's *Farewell to Manzanar,* the issei suffer serious loss during the Japanese internment of World War II because they are the older family members whose loyalties are torn between their new land and their ancestral home, where relatives still live. *See also* nisei; sansei.

Ivy League the prestigious coterie of eight northeastern colleges and universities—Brown, Columbia, Cornell, Dartmouth, Harvard, Princeton, University of Pennsylvania, Yale—that comprise the traditional leaders in United States education, values, sports, fashion, and scholarly research. Except for Cornell, the Ivy League predates the Revolutionary War. Alex Haley in *The Autobiography of Malcolm X* characterizes whites in Harlem as Ivy Leaguers.

J

jack a device powered by a hand crank, clockspring, or winding key that turns a spit over a fire; a mechanical rotisserie or barbecue skewer. The title character of George Eliot's *Silas Marner* uses a key and string to suspend meat over a hearth fire because he doesn't own a jack.

jackal (*jak'* uhl) a nocturnal wild dog that hunts in packs, eats all forms of meat—living or dead—and is thought to hunt prey for lions; metaphorically, an ill-famed lackey who does the dirty work from which a superior profits or takes credit. In *A Tale of Two Cities*, Charles Dickens refers to Sydney Carton as the jackal because he performs the drudgery and preparatory footwork necessary to Mr. Stryver's courtroom presentations. Metaphorically, Sydney is the jackal to Mr. Stryver's lion.

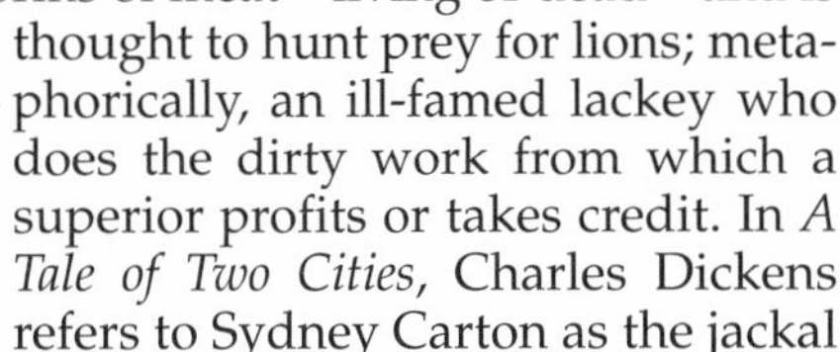

jackboots sturdy, square-toed military boots favored by the cavalry in the seventeenth and eighteenth centuries and made of a weighty, high-gloss black leather hardened with pitch to protect the foot during travel in bad weather. Detailed with an instep flap and high, square heels, jack-boots reached to the thigh or were cuffed at mid-thigh. They were revived by the Nazis in the 1930s. As the stagecoach approaches Paris in Charles Dickens's *A Tale of Two Cities,* figures shod with clomping jackboots add to an ominous, prerebellion atmosphere. *See also* bootlegging.

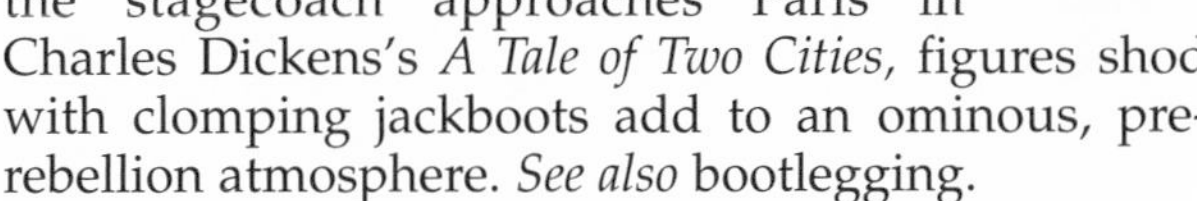

jack-o'-lantern a will- 'o -the -wisp or fluctuating glow over marshy ground; a mystical glow attributed to the decomposition of swamp humus, which produces combustible methane gas. Jim, the runaway slave in Mark Twain's *The Adventures of Huckleberry Finn,* watches for Cairo, the gateway to the free states and the end of slavery; Huck notes that Jim's outcries are wasted on the glimmer of jack-o'-lanterns or lightning bugs. *See ignis fatuus.*

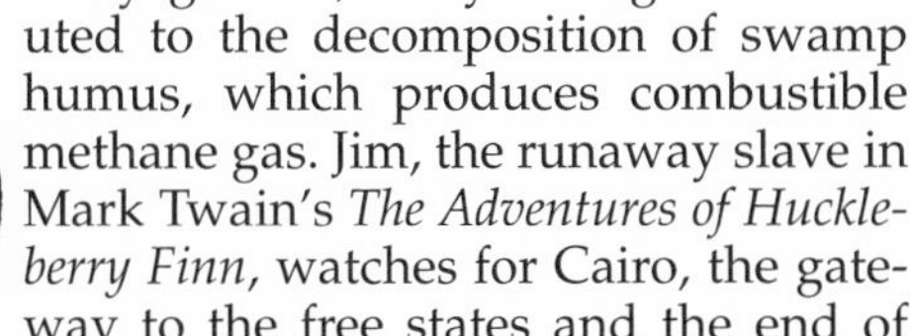

jacks a coordination game in which the player bounces a small rubber ball and tries to toss and retrieve a group of six-pointed metal or plastic game tokens called jacks or jack rocks. At each stage of the game, the toss is made more difficult by maneuvers such as throwing them with the palm and catching them on the back of the hand before the ball hits the ground. In Maya Angelou's *I Know Why the Caged Bird Sings,* Maya and Louise cement their friendship over jacks, hopscotch, and confidences.

jack-towel a loop of coarse huckaback or napped toweling on a roller that is pulled down to dry so that the next user can have an unused or dry segment. In Charles Dickens's *Great Expectations,* Joe urges Pip to pad his backside with the jack-towel so he won't feel the smack of Tickler, Mrs. Joe's disciplinary rod. *See also* huckaback.

jaeger (*yay'* guhr) a dark, long-tailed predatory or robber sea bird native to the mossy tundra and known to destroy other birds' nests and to chase or victimize kittiwakes and terns until they drop their prey or collapse; a skua. Derived from the Dutch for *hunter*, the term entered English in the early nineteenth century. In Jean Craighead George's *Julie of the Wolves,* Miyax recognizes the jaeger, which feeds on carrion, and follows it to a fresh caribou kill.

jalousie-blinds (*jah'* luh . see) flexible latticed window shades with horizontal sloping slats or overlapping louvers fitted into a frame. The slats can be directed against rain or sun or turned upward to receive ventilation and filtered light without sacrificing privacy. Derived from the French for *jealous*, the term entered English in the mid-eighteenth century. The Monseigneur's château in Charles Dickens's *A Tale of Two Cities* maintains privacy by shutting out prying, envious eyes with jalousie blinds.

jampani (dzahm . pah . *nee'*) a bearer of a jampan, an Indian sedan chair supported by two bamboo poles and carried on the shoulders of four servants. In Rudyard Kipling's "Miss Youghal's Sais," jampanis and other servants play knucklebones until they are called into service.

jasmine *See* jessamine.

jaundice (*jawn'* dihs) a liver disease resulting in yellow eyes and skin, indigestion, and malaise. Jaundice results from a bile duct obstruction or the inability of the liver to filter bilirubin from the blood. Derived from the Latin for *greenish yellow*, the term dates to the fourteenth century. Rinaldi, an Italian officer in Ernest Hemingway's *A Farewell to Arms,* notes that there are more cases of jaundice at the military hospital than shell wounds like those of Frederick Henry.

jerk to cure meat by slicing it into strips, soaking in salt water, and drying in the sun or over a slow fire. Derived from a Quechua term in the mid-nineteenth century, it refers to a Native American method of preserving fish or meat and the Caribbean style of meat preservation by wrapping slices of flank meat in allspice leaves and cooking over a low flame. The meat shed in Marjorie Kinnan Rawlings's *The Yearling* contains smoked alligator and a haunch of jerked venison, which is used to feed the dogs.

jerkin (*jur'* kihn) a sleeveless vest or jacket, close-fitting over a tunic, tabbed at the shoulder, and reaching to the hips. Common to the sixteenth century, the jerkin was usually made of leather but might also be fashioned from coarsely woven cloth, unfinished hide, or suede. In Jonathan Swift's *Gulliver's Travels,* Lemuel Gulliver describes his upper garment as a buff-colored jerkin.

jerry can a flat-sided World War II military-style five-gallon container used to store gasoline or water. The term derives from the 1930s and 1940s, when the Allies nicknamed their German enemies "jerries." In *Zlata's Diary,* Zlata Filipovic worries that her disabled father can no longer carry jerry cans, which residents of Sarajevo use to transport water to their homes and businesses.

jessamine (*jehs'* suh . mihn) or **jasmin** or **jasmine** a heavily fragrant ornamental climbing shrub of the olive family distinguished by tubular yellow or white flowers and tapered green leaves. Although producing a deadly poison, in small doses extract of jessamine can also serve as a sedative, analgesic, and antispasmodic. Sherlock Holmes, investigator in Sir Arthur Conan Doyle's *The Hound of the Baskervilles,* detects Beryl's jessamine perfume on letter paper.

jet a soft black lignite that is buffed to a high polish and used in the making of costume jewelry, belt buckles, buttons, ornaments, eyeglass frames, and trinkets. Derived from the Greek name for a town in Asia Minor, the term entered English in the fourteenth century. Jean Valjean, protagonist of Victor Hugo's *Les Misérables,* revives the industry of a French village by introducing a cheap method of manufacturing jet. *See also* gum lac.

jetty (*jeht'* tih) a pier, wharf, quay, or breakwater serving as a landing point, protective wall, or bulwark around a harbor to deflect the tide or current, or an egress or landing for passengers boarding or leaving a riverboat or ship. This fifteenth-century term, akin to *eject* and *project,* derives from the Latin for *throw.* Marlowe, narrator of Joseph Conrad's *The Heart of Darkness,* recalls that a jetty extended from the bank on which the company headquarters was built.

jewelblock a block attached to an eyebolt through which is laced the halyard that keeps a sail fully extended across a yardarm; also, the block from which a noose is suspended in a shipboard execution. In the ballad "Billy in the Darbies" at the conclusion of Herman Melville's *Billy Budd,* the speaker compares the hanged corpse to a jewelblock suspended from a yardarm, thus elevating Billy above the accusation of murder and an ignoble demise.

jew's harp or **juice harp** a common percussion instrument dating to ancient Europe and Asia. The instrument is made from metal or bamboo and gives off twangy sounds when held between the teeth. As described in Maya Angelou's *I Know Why the Caged Bird Sings,* the player vibrates the stem of the jew's harp against teeth, tongue, and jaw and uses muscle control to vary the sounds and rhythms.

jib one or more triangular sails set at an angle from the bowsprit to the mainsail. Of unknown derivation, the term dates to the mid-seventeenth century. By studying the two jibs and mainsail of the schooner *Hispaniola* in Robert Louis Stevenson's *Treasure Island,* Jim realizes that the ship is unmanned and moving at the wind's will.

Jim Crow laws laws or statutes requiring segregation in schools, courtrooms, train cars, theaters, restaurants, steamboats, barbershops, and hotels. This mid-nineteenth-century term derives from a prancing figure in Thomas Rice's minstrel show, which featured a white performer in blackface and rags pretending to be the stereotypical lighthearted, subservient darky. In his autobiographical *Black Boy,* Richard Wright declares that southern legislatures enacted the Jim Crow laws to keep black people from bettering themselves through access to public facilities, schools, better jobs, housing, and transportation.

jinni (*jee'* nee) *See* djinn.

joint-stool a lowly piece of furniture composed of a seat with a folding back supported by three or four legs; a milking or utility stool. The term is related to the Middle English word *joiner*, which is a synonym for *carpenter*. In Nathaniel Hawthorne's *The Scarlet Letter*, the protagonist, Hester Prynne, compares the governor's bondsman to a commodity on a par with an ox or joint-stool.

joist a framing timber or one of a series of parallel beams to which a builder nails flooring and ceiling panels. This fifteenth-century term derives from the Latin for *lying down*. When Janie fires at Tea Cake in Zora Neale Hurston's *Their Eyes Were Watching God*, her shot knocks him down while his simultaneous fire hits the joist above her.

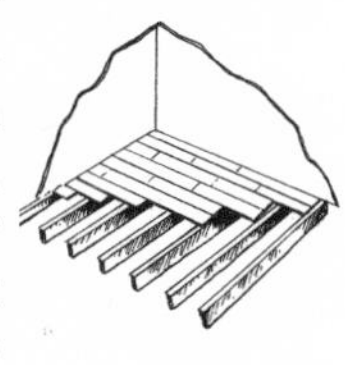

jolly-boat *See* yawl.

Jolly Roger a black banner featuring a white skull and crossed bones underneath to indicate that the ship was a privateer and observed no national loyalties; a pirate flag, possibly a poor imitation of an Austrian banner centered with a double eagle, the imperial crest. In the staging instructions for Tennessee Williams's *The Glass Menagerie*, a ship and Jolly Roger appear on a screen as Tom explains to Laura that he prefers adventure to a deadend job as a warehouse clerk.

jook or **juke** a black-owned restaurant or roadhouse, bordello, gambling or dance hall, honky-tonk, or house of questionable reputation; often rowdy and given to violent outbursts out of vengeance or jealousy. Derived from the Bambara or Gullah for *disorderly* or *wicked*, this southeast American slang term dates to the 1930s and was applied to the jukebox. In Zora Neale Hurston's *Their Eyes Were Watching God*, Janie grows restive and jealous when Tea Cake does not come around and assumes that he is hanging around a jook.

jota (*hoh'* tuh) the Spanish name for the letter *J*, which derives from the Greek *iota*, the smallest letter in the alphabet, which looks like a lower case *i* without a dot over it. Santiago, protagonist in Ernest Hemingway's *The Old Man and the Sea*, pronounces "John J. McGraw" as "John *Jota* McGraw."

journeyman a day worker, mechanic, or experienced apprentice in the second stage of indenture who assists a master artisan or tradesman for a day's wage rather than for room and board. Derived from the French for *day*, the term entered English in the fifteenth century. When forced by a master to display his burned hand, the title character in Esther Forbes's *Johnny Tremain* presents the pathetic limb with a flourish before journeymen and female customers. *See also* apprentice; indentures.

juba (*joo'* buh) a rhythmic, joyful West African dance, jig, or frolic involving complex parallel movement of feet and rhythmic hand clapping, knee tapping, and thigh slapping. Performed during plantation celebrations, the juba may have influenced such lively, uninhibited American dances as the Charleston and Black Bottom. Mark Twain's autobiographical *Life on the Mississippi* pictures the performance of a juba on the levee where the steamboat docks.

jubilee (*joo'* buh . lee) a time of rejoicing and shouting; also, a religious folk tune or Negro spiritual. Derived from the Old Testament description of the blast of the ram's horn announcing the new year and the freeing of Hebrew slaves from Egyptian masters, the term appears to have entered slave language as an act of emancipation precipitating the end of slavery. In the worship scene in Harper Lee's *To Kill a Mockingbird*, the Finch children wonder how Zeebo can lead the singing of "Jubilee" when there are no hymnals.

jugular (*jyuh'* guh . luhr or *jyoo'* guh . luhr) one of several trunk veins of the neck that funnel most of the blood flow from the cranium and face directly to the heart. This sixteenth-century term derives from the Latin for *yoke*. In Wilson Rawl's *Where the Red Fern Grows*, Little Ann springs to Old Dan's rescue as the mountain lion searches for Dan's jugular vein and an instant kill.

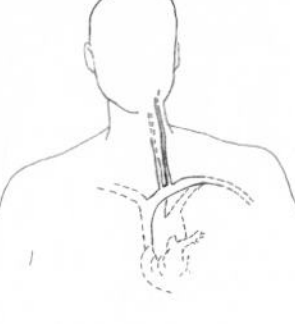

juice harp *See* jew's harp.

juju (*joo'* joo) a hex, black magic, ban, taboo, or evil spell created, governed, or enforced by a charm, idol, personal or house fetish, amulet, or other object invested with supernatural powers by a conjurer or root doctor. This nineteenth-century term appears to derive from the Hausa for *toy* or *evil spirit*. Maya Angelou's autobiographical *I Know Why the Caged Bird Sings* describes Mr. Taylor's ghost story, which causes Maya to think of haunts, banshees, juju, and voodoo. *See also* hex; hoodoo.

juke joint *See* jook.

jumbi or **jumbie** or **jumby** (*dzoom'* bee) a West Indian term for an evil presence, jinx, departed spirit, or poltergeist that threatens harm, makes mischief, or causes mysterious joint and muscle aches, swelling, or fever. Derived from the Kikongo for *fetish,* the term entered English in the nineteenth century. In Theodore Taylor's *The Cay,* Phillip Enright fears that Timothy will harm Stew Cat to rid himself of *jumbi* or ghosts.

jump the broom an African American folk marriage consisting of simple vows of loyalty followed by a leap over a broomstick. Because slaves could not enter into legal contracts, such as a formal betrothal or marriage, the jump-the-broom ceremony served as an unofficial, nonbinding recognition of a marital union and its offspring. The title character in Ernest Gaines's *The Autobiography of Miss Jane Pittman* becomes Joe's wife after they jump the broom before witnesses.

juniper a fragrant, low-growing evergreen shrub yielding scraggly bark, prickly needles, aromatic oil, and blue or gray-green berries used by Native Americans to make roofing shingles, firewood, diuretics, palliatives for indigestion, green dye, beads, or cooking spice. In Rudolfo Anaya's *Bless Me, Ultima,* Antonio's boyhood home lies on a juniper-covered hill, which becomes the herb hunting ground of Ultima, a respected *curandera. See also bruja; curandera.*

junk a flat-bottomed Chinese or Javanese sailing ship with a high stern deck, square bow, deep rudder, and from one to three masts fitted with trapezoidal sails made of a stiff matting strengthened with bamboo slats. Derived from the Javanese for *ship,* the term entered English in the early seventeenth century as European sailors acquired experience with the Orient. In Jules Verne's *Around the World in Eighty Days,* the *Rangoon* steams toward the *Carnatic* through a flotilla of fishing boats, sampans, and junks. *See also* sampan.

junta (*hoon'* tuh) a self-appointed governing body, council, administrative board, or commission; a military coterie or usurper who seizes control of a country by *coup d'etat,* then rules autocratically. Derived from the Latin for *yoke,* the term entered English in the early seventeenth century. In *The Crucible,* playwright Arthur Miller notes that the unified group that arrived on the Mayflower had been supplanted by splinter groups ruled by a narrow fundamentalist junta.

jutka (*juht'* kuh) a one-horse buggy common to southern India that is hired as a taxi; a hackney chariot. Derived from the Hindi for *lurch,* this term entered English in the late nineteenth century, the height of the British colonial period. Against the uproar of cars and swearing jutka drivers in R. K. Narayan's "An Astrologer's Day," the astrologer ponders the deal offered by a potential client. *See also* hackney chariot.

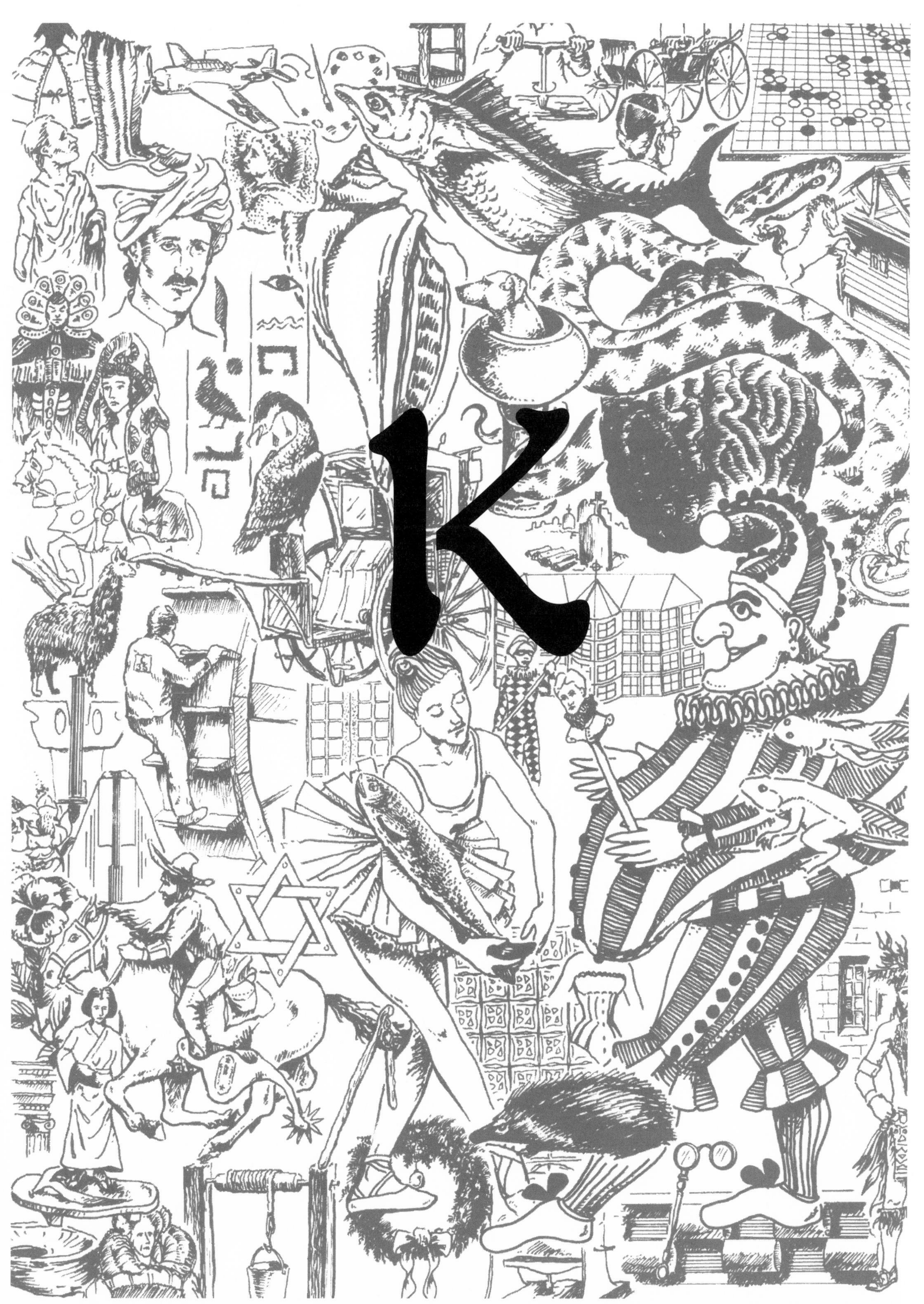
K

kabbala *See* cabbala.

kabuki (kuh . *boo'* kee) a melodramatic or comic form of traditional Japanese court drama, odori dance, and pantomime evolved from puppetry and performed on a shallow stage by male actors and acrobats wearing stark makeup, wigs, and brilliant costumes. Accompanied by traditional No drums, samisen, bells, and flute, the stylized scenes may be farcical, realistic, historical, mythic, or epic. Introduced in 1603, classical kabuki drama remains popular. Entering English in the late nineteenth century, the term derives from Japanese for *art of singing and dancing.* Mentioned in Jeanne Wakatsuki Houston and James D. Houston's *Farewell to Manzanar*, kabuki theater consists of posturing, song, and dance. *See also* odori; samisen.

kaddish (*kah'* dish) a traditional Jewish doxology or prayer for peace of unknown authorship. A paean to God, the words are recited at burials, during memorial services, and on subsequent anniversaries of the death. This early seventeenth-century term, derived from the Aramaic for *holy,* is a unifying text expressing the hopes of all Jews for the prosperity of Israel. Akiba Drumer, a character in Elie Wiesel's autobiographical *Night,* asks that other death camp inmates say kaddish in his honor, but the survivors are so wrapped up in day-to-day hazards that they forget their promise to the condemned man.

kaffir or **kafir** (*ka'* fuhr) a pejorative term for a non-English speaking black South African, particularly a Xhosan. Entering English in the late eighteenth century, the term derives from the Arabic for *infidel* or *nonbeliever.* In Doris Lessing's "No Witchcraft for Sale," local kaffirs attest to the skill of bush healers and herbalists like Gideon who draw on native African plants to cure snake bite.

kaleidoscope a tubular viewing instrument that rotates two mirrors joined along their long sides or a piece of shiny aluminum bent at a 45, 60, or 90 degree angle in a tube to reflect a random pattern of colored glass shards, beads, or tinsel into a symmetrical pattern. Invented in 1825 by David Brewster, the device derives its name from hybrid Greek for *look at beautiful shapes.* In George Orwell's *1984,* a dystopian satire, workers in the fiction department of the Ministry of Truth spin out plots for their novels on large kaleidoscopes.

kapo (*kah'* poh) or **capo** a prisoner chosen by the prison authorities to process, supervise, discipline, or spy on other prisoners. Derived from the Latin for *head,* the term also names a boss or leader in the Mafia hierarchy. Significant disciplinary agents in Elie Wiesel's *Night,* kapos in the concentration camp at Auschwitz are capable of sadism and cruelty that exceeded that of the vicious Gestapo. *See also* Gestapo; holocaust; Nazi; SS.

karma (*kahr'* muh) a Buddhist or Hindu concept of fate resulting from good or bad behaviors in a former life or from choices or intentional wrongdoing in a current life that produce an evil destiny in a later incarnation as payment for sin. Entering English in the early nineteenth century, the term derives from the Sanskrit for *work* or *action.* In Amy Tan's *Joy Luck Club,* Lena St. Clair insists that her relationship with Harold does not demonstrate bad karma.

kasha or **kache** (*kah'* shuh) a mush or porridge of buckwheat groats, semolina, cracked wheat, or other hot grain cereal fried in butter or oil, covered in boiling water, and baked until a crust forms. Kasha is also rolled flat and fried like pancakes. In Russia, kasha is served with meat, cheese, or mushrooms or is added to a stew or soup. Wracked by hunger, the title character in Alexander Solzhenitsyn's *One Day in the Life of Ivan Denisovich* dreams of former times at home, when he had milk, meat, potatoes, and pots of kasha. *See also* groats.

kayak (*ky'* ak) a slender, shallow, 10–25-foot-long canoe seating one or two persons, often back to back. Invented about 800 B.C., this lightweight, silent, maneuverable craft consists of a bone or wood frame covered in caribou or seal hides. The user or users are often sealed into the oval, watertight opening to shut out wind and water; they propel the kayak with double-ended paddles. Derived from an Inuit term, *kayak* dates to the mid-eighteenth century. In Gary Paulsen's *Dogsong,* a stranger visiting an Arctic village might sing of a misadventure with a kayak in which the hunter nearly drowned while hunting a walrus.

keel-hauling a naval practice, dating to the fifteenth and sixteenth centuries, of punishing a sailor by tying him to a rope, tossing him overboard, and dragging him from the bow along the keel or center joint of the underside to the stern. This barbaric disciplinary measure could result in bruises, hypothermia, shark attack, or drowning. In Robert Louis Stevenson's *Treasure Island,* Morgan admits to Long John Silver that he and Black Dog were discussing the practice of keel-hauling.

keep the innermost and safest segment of a castle; the thick-walled dungeon or living quarters of the owners, who are guarded by sentries posted at corner turrets or towers. The term, as applied to a medieval castle, entered English before the twelfth century and derives from an Anglo-Saxon term for *look.* Jonathan Harker notes to his client in Bram Stoker's *Dracula* that the Carfax estate looks like part of a keep.

keeping room an antiquated term for the parlor, library, or sitting room, the most formal part of a home or inn, where tea is served and visitors enjoy a warm fire, good company, and pleasant conversation. Baby Suggs, a central character in Toni Morrison's *Beloved,* retreats to her bed in the keeping room, recedes into senility, and dies. *See also* keep.

kelp a long, feathery seaweed or tangleweed composed of undulating reddish or olive-brown streamers. Folk healers use cooked kelp in soups and as a poultice or wrap for arthritic joints. Derivatives from kelp are used in mineral tonics, cough medicines, skin creams, and purgatives. The term, of unknown origin, dates to the Middle English of the fourteenth century. In the setting of Scott O'Dell's *The Island of the Blue Dolphin,* the isolated island lies off the coast of California and is surrounded by a kelp bed.

kendo *(kehn'* doh) a bladeless, ceremonial form of dueling with bamboo swords or staves held in a two-handed grip. A competitive sport resembling fencing, kendo requires the use of masks, gloves, and chest and abdomen padding. Derived from the Japanese for *sword skill,* the term names a ritual, bloodless samurai training and entered English in the 1920s, a half century after the demise of the warrior class. Jeanne Wakatsuki Houston and James D. Houston's *Farewell to Manzanar* indicates that children who grew up in American internment camps could choose from ordinary school activities as well as traditional Japanese needlework, judo, and kendo.

kerseymere (*kuhr'* see . meer) a coarse, low-knapped ribbed wool twill woven in narrow widths for use in hosiery. Entering English in the Middle Ages, the term may have derived from the village of Kersey, Suffolk, or from a corruption of *cashmere.* The blue jacket, kerseymere leggings, and black whiskers on mounted effigies humiliate Lucetta, a victim of public ridicule in Thomas Hardy's *The Mayor of Casterbridge.*

kewpie doll (*kyoo'* pee) the trademark name of a smiling female doll with short skirt, chubby cheeks and limbs, curly bobbed hair, and wide, innocent eyes. Because kewpie dolls are frequently awarded as carnival prizes, they carry the aura of tawdry, poorly made trinkets. The term appears to derive from *Cupid,* the Roman god of love, and dates to the 1920s. In John Steinbeck's *Of Mice and Men,* Susy speaks disdainfully of Clara's brothel and her kewpie doll lamp.

keystone a wide-topped stone, often decorated or carved, that wedges into the top of a curved arch or vault and holds the structure in place by virtue of gravity, which pulls down on the keystone, thus forcing the other stones into position. As an adjective, the term describes a *sine qua non,* or central supporting element or argument, and applies to central figures, concepts, or principles. In *White Fang,* Jack London describes Jim Hall's grudge against Judge Scott and Jim's opinion that the judge was a keystone of injustice.

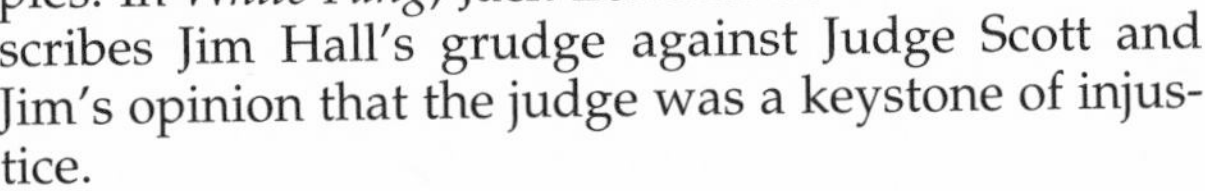

kimch'i or **kimchee** (*kihm'* chee) a traditional Korean pickle or condiment made from cabbage spiced with garlic, ginger, and red pepper and fermented underground in a round earthenware crock or jar; the national dish of Korea. During the snowstorm in Yoko Kawashima Watkins's *So Far from the Bamboo Grove,* the Kim family and their Japanese visitor enjoy a meal of steamed rice and spicy kimch'i.

kimono (kuh . *moh'* noh) a long, loose unisex robe or dressing gown with wide sleeves and sash. The kimono is a traditional costume that the Japanese adapted from a Chinese garment during the third century B.C. Formed of a double layer of material, the overlapping edges of the robe fold back into a high quilted collar that matches or contrasts with the inner lining of the sleeves and lapels. Derived from the Japanese for *thing to wear,* the term entered English in 1898. Yoshiko admires the fit of her kimono in Kawabata Yasunari's "The Jay."

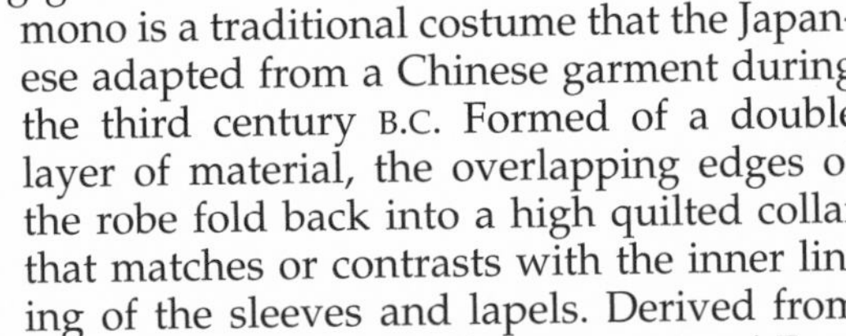

king's evil *See* scrofula.

kirkyard a walled enclosure that protects the privacy and sanctity of a church and its outbuildings. Derived from the Old English for *churchyard,* the term applies to an inner series of paths, gardens, and above-ground crypts, often those of church founders or significant figures in parish history. Villagers in Emily Brontë's *Wuthering Heights* are surprised that

Catherine Linton's grave is in a corner of the kirkyard rather than in the chapel or among the graves of her family or the Linton family.

kite a member of the hawk or falcon family with white head and underside, hooked beak, and dark forked tail and pointed wings; a notorious scavenger bird. The kite is capable of gliding gracefully, but is known as a sharp-eyed predator intent on swooping down on snails, its usual food, as well as on lizards, bats, rabbits, and the eggs of other birds. In William Shakespeare's *Macbeth,* after learning that assassins have slain his wife, children, and servants, Macduff cries out in anguish and calls the king a hell-kite.

kiva (*kee'* vuh) an underground, typically round ritual chamber used by the Pueblo, Zuñi, or Hopi Indians in the southwestern United States as a men's worship area to propitiate the gods for rain, good health, healthy children, tribal cohesion, and victory over attackers. The kiva followed a pattern of construction from the time of the ancient Anasazi—a hole in the floor to symbolize earth's birth canal, a fire pit, niches to hold sacred rattles and prayer sticks, and wall decorations featuring religious iconography. Preceding the snake dance, the chamber was a storage pit for collected snakes, which were fed, purified, and sprinkled with meal or pollen before being released during the August ceremony. In Aldous Huxley's *Brave New World,* Lenina Crowne sees a Zuñi Indian emerging from a kiva, which is off limits to female visitors.

Klan *See* Ku Klux Klan.

knacker (*nak'* uhr) a buyer of aged, injured, or sick animals that are slaughtered and processed into soap, glue, fertilizer, or pet food. Entering English in 1812, the term derives from a slang term for *harness-maker* or *saddlemaker*. The prophet Major, a venerable 12-year-old boar in George Orwell's *Animal Farm,* predicts that Boxer will suffer the ignoble death common to farm horses—Jones will sell him to the knacker to be boiled into dogfood for the foxhounds.

knapsack (*nap'* sak) a bag made of canvas, leather, nylon, or other waterproof material featuring long buckled flaps and side pockets and fitted with shoulder straps to the back of a hiker or soldier to carry food, gear, and personal items. Derived from the German for *bite sack,* the term dates to the seventeenth century. In Stephen Crane's *The Red Badge of Courage,* soldiers cheer a young girl who stops a thieving soldier from loading his knapsack onto her horse and riding away.

knave a low-born menial, unprincipled person, or deceitful rascal. In the standard pack of 52 playing cards, the knave is the jack or lowest of the three court cards, after the king and queen. Derived before the twelfth century, this Old English word refers to a *boy* or *underling*. In Charles Dickens's *Great Expectations,* Estella considers the word "jack" a vulgarism for "knave."

knickers (*nihk'* uhrs) or **knickerbockers** loose-fitting or gathered short breeches that fasten below the knee with a strap, buckle, or fitted band, which made them popular men's wear during the 1920s for light sports, particularly hiking or bicycling. Named for Diedrich Knickerbocker, a pen name for American author Washington Irving, the sporty pants date to the 1880s. Leper, the outcast and school misfit in John Knowles's *A Separate Peace,* stalks the wild in knickers and puttees. *See also* puttee.

kohlrabi (kohl . *rah'* bee) a nutty, sweet, fleshy, globular vegetable that grows above ground and produces green stems and leaves from the green or purple body of the plant, which can be peeled, boiled, steamed, and added to soup or stew or eaten raw in salads. Derived from the Latin for *cabbage turnip,* the term entered English in the early nineteenth century. The inmates of the annexe in Anne Frank's *The Diary of a Young Girl* eat whatever is in season, meal after meal, whether peas, salsify, kohlrabi, or beets.

kolach (*koh'* lash) a bite-sized tart or pie filled with fruit and served as a savory, a fruit-topped dessert. Derived from the Czech for *wheel,* the term entered the United States in the early 1900s during a wave of eastern European immigration. In Willa Cather's *My Antonia,* Nina and Jan point to the canning jars filled with spiced plums that their mother uses to make kolaches.

kola nut the brown, bitter, caffeine-rich fleshy seed pod of a tropical shrub or tree native to West Africa and used in the making of diuretics, stimulants, and cola drinks. Derived from the Malinke word *kola,* the term entered English in the mid-nineteenth century. At official gatherings of men in Chinua Achebe's *Things Fall Apart,* the host serves alligator peppers or kola nuts as condiments or hors d'oeuvres, which are chewed to relieve hunger, fatigue, and malaise. *See also* alligator pepper.

kolkhoz or **kolkos** (kohl . *kahz'*) a collective farm operated by the Soviet state to meet a set of predetermined objectives that are mandated by a state bureaucracy. Derived from the Russian for *household farm*, the term entered English in the 1920s, after the fall of the czarist government and the rise of Communism. In Alexander Solzhenitsyn's *One Day in the Life of Ivan Denisovich*, the title character learns from his wife's letters that young people have grown disillusioned with work on the kolkhoz.

kopek or **copek** or **kopeck** (*koh'* pehk) a bronze or copper coin worth 1/100 of a ruble, the central monetary unit of Russia and its satellite nations. Named for the Russian lance borne by Ivan IV, the term entered English in the late seventeenth century. Because Petrovich, in Nikolai Gogol's "The Overcoat," charges too few kopeks for tailoring, his wife begs customers for a few more coins to cover the cost of his work. *See also* ruble.

Koran or **Qur'an** (kuh . *rahn'* or koh . *ran'*) the poetic sacred text and supreme authority of Islam, representing Allah's, or God's, commands as revealed to Mohammed through a vision of the angel Gabriel in A.D. 610. The 114 suras, or chapters, composed in Arabic, comprise both philosophical and practical advice to the faithful, who recite the opening chapter five times daily as a prayer to the almighty. Because Muslims consider the Koran to be God's actual words, the text is believed too subtle and too holy to be translated into other languages. Derived from the Arabic for *reading*, the term entered English in the early seventeenth century. While serving a prison sentence for housebreaking in Alex Haley's *The Autobiography of Malcolm X*, Malcolm studies the Koran, which restores his balance and offers him positive values and goals. *See also* Allah; Islam.

kosher (*koh'* shuhr) or **kasher** conforming to the sanitation and dietary standards of processing and preparation derived from Leviticus 11 and Deuteronomy 14, which require that fish and domestic animals—poultry, cows, sheep, goats—have their throats slit, their carcasses drained of blood, certain nerves and muscles removed, and no dairy and meat products mixed or touched by the same utensils. According to orthodox Jewish ritual, meat must be slaughtered by an approved butcher; no pig or pork may touch or contaminate the meat. Kosher products, including traditional pickles, wine, and other nonmeat items, are sanctioned by a rabbi as wholesome and suitable for Jews to sell, serve, or eat. Derived from the Hebrew for *proper*, the term entered English in the mid-nineteenth century. Visitors to the meat processing plant in Upton Sinclair's *The Jungle* see neat packages stamped by the kosher rabbi as consumable by orthodox Jews.

koto (*koh'* toh) a long zither fitted with 13 silk strings that stretch over moveable bridges resting on an oblong sound box. This traditional Japanese instrument, which evolved from other Asian stringed autoharps and lutes, stretches horizontally on floor or table while the player plucks a melody using thumb, index finger, and middle finger or an ivory plectrum, or pick, and shapes the tones by applying pressure with the other hand. In Yoko Kawashima Watkins's autobiographical *So Far from the Bamboo Grove*, performances for the war wounded include singing, dancing, and koto playing.

kowtow (*kow'* tow) to perform a traditional act of obeisance by kneeling, leaning forward, and touching the forehead to the ground out of submission, respect, homage, or fealty; also, to fawn, grovel, or defer to one's betters. Derived from Beijingese for *knock the head*, the term entered English during the early nineteenth century. An-Mei Hsu, a focal character in Amy Tan's *The Joy Luck Club*, learns that her mother honored her deceased husband by kowtowing in a Hangkow pagoda; she promised to refrain from harsh opinions and hoarding wealth and to maintain a balance of life elements.

kraal (krahl) a walled South African village composed of huts and a common paddock surrounded by a picket fence or stockade to protect livestock. Derived from the Portuguese for *enclosure* or *corral*, the term entered English as a doublet—kraal and corral—in the early eighteenth century. In Doris Lessing's "No Witchcraft for Sale," Gideon, the Farquar family cook, is content in the compound and never asks to return to his native kraal.

kroner or **kronur** or **kronor** (*kroh'* huhr) or **kronen** *sing.* **krona, krone** the monetary unit of Iceland, Norway, Sweden, and Denmark, which is equal to 100 øre. Derived from the Scandinavian for *crown*, the term entered English in the late nineteenth century when the gold and silver coins were also circulated in Austria and Germany. In 1884, the captain of the *Amager* offers a monthly wage of four kroner to the title character of Theodore Taylor's *Timothy of the Cay.*

kudu or **koodoo** (*koo'* doo) a large, curly-horned herbivorous antelope found in the mountains and plains of eastern and southern Africa and identified by its shaggy beard and dark pelt marked by white stripes. Derived from a

Khoisan, Xhosan, or Afrikaans term, the word entered English in the late eighteenth century. In *Born Free*, Joy Adamson describes Mount Marsabit in Kenya as the home of kudu, lions, rhinos, and buffaloes.

Ku Klux Klan (koo kluhks klan) a lawless group of white supremacist vigilantes who require secret oaths before a burning cross and allegiance to a central board that assigns sheet-draped members to humiliate, harrass, terrorize, rape, or kill blacks, homosexuals, socialists, union leaders, Jews, Catholics, Muslims, Asians, and nonwhite immigrants. Justified by an illogical melange of biblical and historical lore glorifying Aryan stock, this male-dominated racist group began as an outgrowth of poor whites' frustration with the end of slavery during the Civil War. Formed in 1866 in Pulaski, Tennessee, by General Nathan Bedford Forrest, the first Imperial Wizard, the Klan enjoyed brief revivals during the civil rights marches and demonstrations for gay rights. In Maya Angelou's *I Know Why the Caged Bird Sings*, a local uproar over a suspected sexual insult to a white woman provokes Ku Klux Klansmen, or night riders, to harass black men.

kukri (*koo'* kree) a sword or knife curving into a flared, double-edged blade at right angles to the hilt. The kukri became famous as the signature weapon of the Nepalese Gurkha soldier. The term entered English in the late nineteenth century. In Bram Stoker's *Dracula*, Jonathan Harker makes an incomplete swipe at the Count with a kukri knife, slashing open his coat.

kulak (*koo'* . lak) a prosperous land owner, trader, proprietor, or farmer in czarist Russia preceding the Communist takeover in 1917. Kulaks were then reclassified as exploiters and bullies of the serf class. Entering English in the late eighteenth century, the term is Russian for *fist* or Estonian for *cheapskate*. According to eyewitness accounts by the gang boss in Alexander Solzhenitsyn's *One Day in the Life of Ivan Denisovich*, both kulak and proletarian suffered the same persecution.

L

labboard *See* larboard.

Labyrinth (*la'* buh . rihnth) a tangle of interconnecting hallways or winding subterranean passages, cul-de-sacs, baffles, and optical illusions intended to befuddle a trespasser; an intricate, tortuous maze. Also, a garden hedge shaped into a maze intended to amuse visitors. Described in Edith Hamilton's *Mythology* as the fearful dwelling of the half-man, half-bull Minotaur, the Labyrinth of Crete, built by the inventor Daedalus as a lair for the fearful beast, was the site of multiple annual human sacrifices until Theseus followed Princess Ariadne's advice, tied a ball of string to a column, and threaded his way into the dark, where he killed the Minotaur and returned victorious.

lackey or **lacquey** a footman, valet, or uniformed body servant; also a menial or toady who performs disreputable jobs at the command of a scheming master who wishes to remain anonymous. Derived from the Middle French for *servant*, the term entered English in the early fifteenth century. In sardonic self-deprecation in Edmond Rostand's *Cyrano de Bergerac*, the title character disparages his own death, an ignoble ambush inflicted by a lackey wielding a log of wood.

lacquer (*lak'* uhr) a high-gloss resinous wood finish, shellac, or varnish applied to fine, fragile Oriental furnishings to produce a hard, smooth surface; a focal point of chinoiserie, which became popular in Europe after traders entered Asian markets. To Wang Lung and O-Lan, protagonists in Pearl S. Buck's *The Good Earth*, the mark of elegant living includes silks, carved tables, painted scrolls, and lacquered boxes.

lacquey *See* **lackey.**

Lady Day March 25, a sacred day honoring the angel's annunciation to the Virgin Mary; also, the end of the first quarter of the fiscal year, when quarterly installments on loans were due. The remaining three pay periods ended on Midsummer Day (June 24), Michaelmas (September 29), and Christmas Day (December 25). In Thomas Hardy's *Tess of the D'Urbervilles*, the farmer teases the title character about believing his vow of love and expecting a written guarantee that extends to Lady Day. *See also* Good Friday; Michaelmas.

lagoon a stable shallow lake, quiet pond, tidal pool, or trapped body of brackish seawater isolated from ocean encroachment by a coral atoll, sand barrier, limestone rock, sediment, or topography restructured by volcanic eruption or shift in the ocean floor. Dating to the late seventeenth century, the word is an Italian corruption of the Latin for *small lake*. The lagoon is the setting of the opening chapter of William Golding's *Lord of the Flies*, in which children swim naked in blue depths as warm as bath water.

lamasery (*lah'* muh . *seh* . ree) a monastery or spiritual retreat where monks of the Tibetan or Mongolian Buddhist tradition live in quiet pursuit of religious goals (celibacy, moderation, obedience) and tasks, namely, meditating, training novices, and translating Buddhist scripture into Tibetan. Derived from the Persian for *inn*, the term entered English in the mid-nineteenth century. The major setting of *Lost Horizon*, James Hilton's utopian classic, focuses on the relaxed atmosphere of an Asian lamasery somewhere in the Himalayas.

lamp bowl a primitive form of light derived from floating a wick of absorbent moss, rush, twists of cotton, bark, plant fiber, or pith in a flammable liquid, such as melted animal fat, tallow, oil, or other combustible substance, which is contained in a stone or shell bowl or saucer. In Gary Paulsen's *Dogsong*, the lamp bowl contains a yellow fat that serves as fuel.

lancet (*lan'* siht) a sharp-pointed, two-edged surgical probe used to slice open boils and abscesses, excise tumors, make incisions, or perform mole or splinter removal and other minor operations. In Bram Stoker's *Dracula*, Lucy Westenra reports being unnerved by the way that Dr. Seward toyed with a lancet.

Land Rover the trade name of a British four-wheel drive, cloth-topped vehicle similar to the American Jeep and preferred by travelers in unpredictable driving conditions and extremes of weather and temperature. The all-terrain vehicle driven in Joy Adamson's *Born Free*, the Land Rover carries heavy, cumbersome loads and performs well in wet and dry terrain over rock, mud, and sand.

langosta (lan . *goh'* stuh) or **langouste** a spiny marine crustacean native to the Caribbean Sea and distinguishable from the more common lobster by its heavy antennae, carapaced body, leathery tail, and small front claws or pincers. This early nineteenth-century term derives from the Latin for *locust*, which the langosta resembles in its flexible body armor. During Phillip's five-month marooning in Theodore Taylor's *The Cay*, the boy fishes for langosta, which he roasts over an open flame.

lapis lazuli (*lap'* ihs *la'* zuh . lee) a semiprecious blue stone composed of a blend of sulfur, silica, sodium, and aluminum. Ranging from opaque to translucent, the blended elements contrast the basic azure with streaks, highlights, and metallic spangles. Formerly the base of ultramarine paint, the substance serves primarily as a gemstone. A fifteenth-century blended term, it derives from the Latin for *stone* and the Arabic for *sky blue*. Enkidu, the epic figure in *Gilgamesh*, blesses the harlot and wishes for her sparkling stones, including carnelian and lapis lazuli.

lapwing a migratory crested plover common to grassy turf, marshes, and moors throughout Europe, Asia, and Africa. Marked black and white, tipped with wing spurs, and identified by a shrill cry, the bird produces brown eggs and feeds its young on insects. The Old English term derives from *leapwink*, a description of the odd motions characteristic of lapwings. In Emily Brontë's *Wuthering Heights*, Catherine Linton's fevered state causes her to fret over a collection of feathers of the lapwing, which Heathcliff promised not to harm.

larboard port or left, the naval term that is the opposite of starboard, the right side of a ship. A fourteenth-century term, the word derives from the Middle English for *loading side*, the point at which cargo enters a ship. While learning the trade of shipbuilding, the author of *Narrative of the Life of Frederick Douglass* learns a coded system of markings with L standing for larboard, S for starboard, A for aft, and F for forward.

lariat pin the loose end of a noose, lasso, tether, or riata that fastens around the neck of a herd animal. By pulling the pin, the roper, or cowboy, slides the slack end through the loop and tightens the noose around the animal's throat, thus gaining a better hold on the struggling animal. In Willa Cather's *My Antonia*, Mrs. Shimerda pulls up the lariat pin while trying to maneuver a balky cow into a dark cave.

laryngoscope (luh . *ring'* uh . *skohp*) a mirrored device or rod that passes through the mouth and into the throat to give a better view of the larynx, or voice box, that contains the folded, muscular vocal cords that vibrate to produce human speech. In George Bernard Shaw's *Pygmalion*, among the devices in Professor Higgins's vocal laboratory is a laryngoscope.

lateen sail a narrow triangular sail invented by Arab traders around the second century A.D. Attached to a slanted yardarm, the sail moved easily with the wind and increased maneuverability, thus boosting commerce, travel, and cultural exchange. After escaping prison in a sack, Edmond Dantes, protagonist of Alexandre Dumas's *The Count of Monte Cristo*, spies the lateen sail of a Genoese ship and correctly deduces that the vessel carries pirates.

lath a thin strip of wood used as a framework for tile roofing or plaster, bound into a row for window blinds, or crossed into trellises or lattices. After placing her dead infant in a shawl and closing the deal box, the protagonist of Thomas Hardy's *Tess of the D'Urbervilles* makes a cross of two laths, binds them with flowers, and places them near a marmalade jar of blossoms on the unhallowed grave.

lathe (lay~~th~~) a horizontal carving machine that rotates wood, ivory, or metal while pressing knives, sharpened blades, or grinding wheels at predetermined points to create a pattern or to shape a component of furniture or carpentry, such as a table leg or spindle. An early seventeenth-century term, the word derives from Middle English for *rotating stand*. In Thomas Keneally's *Schindler's List*, Levartov returns to his lathe to make hinges after witnessing Amon's murder of a youth claiming to be a metalworker.

latigo (*lat'* ih . goh) the strap or cinch that tightens or fastens a saddle into place around the girth of a horse or mule. A late nineteenth-century term, it derives from the Spanish for *thong*. As a warning to a beginning rodeo rider in Hal Borland's *When the Legends Die*, Red orders Tom Black Bull to check latigos and cinches himself before risking his life in the ring.

latrine poles (luh . *treen'*) adjustable timbers that lie across a communal open sewer pit and form a removable, reusable framework that supports the buttocks in the absence of toilet seats. Through these poles, attendants can pour earth or lime to mask or deodorize the sewage. In Erich Maria Remarque's *All Quiet on the Western Front*, soldiers perch on the latrine poles to enjoy a smoke, conversation, and shared reading of the mail.

lattice (*lat'* tihs) a decorative structure formed of crisscrossed wood or metal laths, rods, or bars and placed over a window, grate, or wall as a support for vining plants or a semipermeable shield against sun or wind; a façade, network, grille, or privacy screen. After hearing the Reverend Arthur Dimmesdale's outcry in Nathaniel Hawthorne's *The Scarlet Letter*, Mistress Hibbins, a suspected follower of Satan, thrusts her head through the lattice and gazes upward. *See also* lath.

laudanum (*lawd'* nuhm) a common bedside sedative, sleeping potion, and painkiller made of a 1 percent solution of opium or 10 percent solution of morphine and alcohol. Laudanum, a term originated by Paracelsus in the sixteenth century possibly from the Latin for *resin*, was distilled from the cistus plant and was administered to patients in tincture or liquid form. It was frequently prescribed to soothe a fretful infant and also formed the base of perfume. In Harriet Beecher Stowe's *Uncle Tom's Cabin*, Cassy recalls how she gave her child laudanum and held him close. In George Eliot's *Silas Marner*, Molly Farren overdoses on laudanum and freezes to death outside the door of the title character, who adopts her orphaned toddler.

laurel (*lah'* ruhl) a fragrant evergreen featuring long, tapered leaves, white flowers, and purple or black berries; bay leaves or branches twisted into a corona as a symbol of honor. Laurel is a source of cooking oil and flavorings and a base for perfumes and pharmaceuticals. As Creon approaches the priest in Sophocles' *Oedipus*, the celebratory laurel sprigs on Creon's head suggest that he bears encouraging news about the plague that is decimating Thebes.

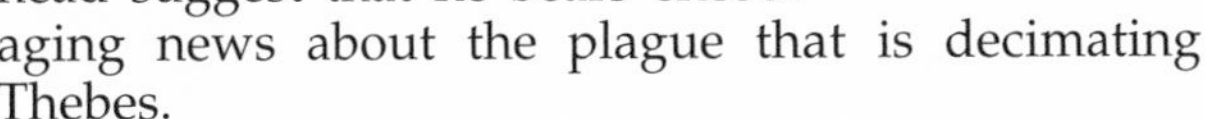

layette (lay . *eht'*) a coordinated set of clothing, towels, linens, blankets, tweezers, scissors, diaper pins, oils, powder, and other items to outfit an infant or equip a newborn's nursery. Derived from the Middle English for *load*, the term entered English in the mid-nineteenth century. In Alex Haley's *The Autobiography of Malcolm X*, the title character is surprised when a waitress he barely knows gives him a layette for his child.

leader a short length of gut, lightweight cord, wire, or invisible nylon monofilament that fastens a hook to fishing line. Often prethreaded to the hook, the leader saves the fisher time in readying lines for service and may disguise the presence of the heavier line. In Ernest Hemingway's *The Old Man and the Sea*, Santiago hates the thought of losing his leaders and hooks if the great fish breaks his line.

league an inexact unit of land measure derived from a Roman mile and varying from 2.4 to 4.6 miles, but generally equaling about 3 miles, or 4.8 kilometers. In *Gilgamesh*, the title character and Enkidu travel 50 leagues, or 150 miles, a day, stopping only once for food and resting briefly at night.

leech a flat, segmented aquatic worm approximately one inch long that is commonly found in ponds, streams, and creeks. The leech attaches its flat mouth to fish, wading birds, turtles, or mammals; anesthetizes the point of contact; and sucks nourishment through a mouth tube inserted into the host's flesh. The use of leeches to draw out contaminated blood from a bruise, tumor, or wound became so common in the nineteenth century that doctors themselves were known as leeches. In Scott O'Dell's *Streams to the River, River to the Sea*, Captain Clark wishes for the healing leeches that are common in the east but rare on his journey over the Missouri River.

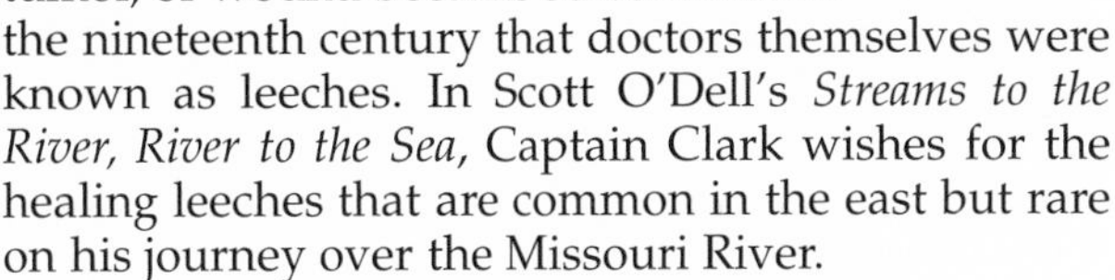

leeward (*lee'* wuhrd or *loo'* ard) *See* alee.

legend an inscription or title, often forged in bas-relief on a coat of arms, seal, button, plaque, medal of honor, or coin, for example, "In God We Trust" on coins minted in the United States and "For Valour" on the Victoria Cross. In F. Scott Fitzgerald's *The Great Gatsby*, the title character displays to Nick a military decoration bearing the circular legend *Montenegro, Nicholas Rex;* the back bears an engraved honorarium for valor.

leggings fringed leg coverings shaped of deer or other soft hide and laced tight against the skin with babiche, thongs, or cord to protect a hiker or rider from cold, snow, or scratches from brush or cactus. Some waterproof leggings attach to moccasins to protect the feet from snow or water. As Conrad Richter describes in *The Light in the Forest*, True Son's refusal to give up his hunting frock and leggings causes consternation in his aunt, who insists that he abandon his Lenni Lenape ways and live like whites. *See also* hunting frock.

lemming a stubby-tailed Arctic rodent kin to voles and mice that breeds heavily in tundra and grasslands. Large populations of lemmings frequently migrate in a mad, misguided rush into danger or certain death as they attempt to swim a wide body of water in search of food. The wolf that Farley Mowat observes in *Never Cry Wolf* is drawn to a lemming colony, where traps await.

Lenni Lenape or **Leni Lenape** (*leh'* nee leh . *nah'* pee) a tribe more commonly known as Delaware; a populous agricultural tribe known for establishing a strong offense against white settlers in the Delaware Valley. As is characteristic of tribe names, the term Lenni Lenape means *true men.* True Son, protagonist of Conrad Richter's *The Light in the Forest,* is proud of his Lenni Lenape heritage.

lentil (*lehn'* tihl) a protein-rich flat pea native to southwest Asia that became a staple in the human diet in prehistoric times. The nutritious, digestible lentil is a standard addition to soups and stews, can be ground into flour, and is recommended for pregnant and lactating women, invalids, and children. The stalk and leaves are suitable for fodder. During cross-examination in Arthur Miller's *The Crucible,* Abigail testifies to Reverend John Hale and the court that a small frog jumped into the lentil soup.

leprosy (*lehp'* ruh . see) a disfiguring bacterial infection of the skin and nerves that creates lesions or thickens the epidermis, causing pallor, nodules, numbness, deformity, and eventual paralysis and atrophy. Currently called Hansen's disease, leprosy has connoted terror and loathing since ancient times, even though casual contact is not sufficient to spread the infection. Entering English in the fourteenth century, the term derives from the Greek for *peel.* During a discussion of white colonists in Chinua Achebe's *Things Fall Apart,* Machi makes a pun on "leprosy," which his tribe calls "the white skin."

leucotomy (loo . *kah'* toh . mee) *See* lobotomy.

levee (*leh'* vee) an artificial quay, seawall, dike, ridge, or earth embankment wide enough to accommodate traffic and high enough to protect low-lying neighborhoods and fields from massive flooding. Derived from the French for *raise,* the term entered English in the late seventeenth century. As Mark Twain describes the village levee in *Life on the Mississippi,* it serves as storage platform for freight until the boxes, casks, and bundles can be moved to the stone wharf and onto a steamboat or barge.

liaison (*lee'* uh . *zahn* or lee . *ay'* zahn) an arrangement, bond, exchange of information, intercommunication, or cooperative effort intended to establish better relations between warring parties, military powers, nations, or governments. Dating to the mid-eighteenth century, the term derives from the Latin for *tie.* In Ernest Hemingway's *A Farewell to Arms,* Rinaldi intends to have a liaison officer arrange an English medal for Frederick Henry.

libation (ly . *bay'* shuhn) a ceremonial sacrifice involving the pouring or spilling of wine or olive oil to honor or propitiate a divinity at a shrine, altar, or grave. Entering English in the fourteenth century, the term derives from the Greek for *pour.* The title character in Sophocles' *Antigone* willfully breaks her uncle Creon's law by pouring a ritual libation for her brother and covering his corpse with dirt.

libido (lih . *bee'* doh) the instinctive drive or desire for sexual gratification and release of sexual tension found in normal human beings; an inborn urge. A significant concept in psychoanalytic terminology of the early twentieth century, the word derives from the Latin for *satisfy* or *please.* Charlie Gordon demonstrates his departure from an unnatural state of immaturity when surgery ends his mental retardation and awakens his libido in Daniel Keyes's *Flowers for Algernon.*

lighter (*ly'* tuhr) a flat-bottomed boat or skiff used to ferry goods, such as crates, barrels, and chests, from ship to shore. The fourteenth-century term, derived from Old English for *lightweight,* names a simple barge or light craft employed by harbor workers to transfer heavy or bulky items. In *The Diary of Samuel Pepys,* the author describes how people escaping the London fire of 1666 piled their possessions on lighters and hurried them down the Thames River, out of reach of the great disaster.

limbo (*lihm'* boh) a traditional, but unsanctioned Roman Catholic concept locating an unspecified site, holding pen, or spiritual condition forced upon the souls of unbaptized infants, pagans who died before Christ's birth, and other worthy innocents who bear original sin and have not earned acceptance into heaven. Entering English in the fourteenth century, the term derives from the Latin for *boundary.* In Rudolfo Anaya's *Bless Me, Ultima,* Antonio and his family pray to the Lady of Guadelupe, a holy figure in limbo surrounded by the babies who take the form of cherubs.

limekiln (*lym'* kihl) a furnace that converts limestone or chalk deposits, shells, and other forms of calcium carbonate into lime. The term, which entered English in the thirteenth century, appears to be an Old English version of the Latin for *cooker* or *kitchen.* In Charles Dickens's *Great Expectations,* Orlick sends an unsigned note bidding Pip to meet him at the limekiln near the sluice-gate.

link a hand-held torch made of tow or light wood and soaked in pitch for lighting a path, cavern, shadowy glade, or streets before cities provided lightposts. Derived from the Greek for *lamp,* the term entered English in the early sixteenth century. In *A Christmas Carol,* Charles Dickens depicts runners carrying links volunteering to accompany carriages down alleys to light the way through the fog. *See also* rush-light.

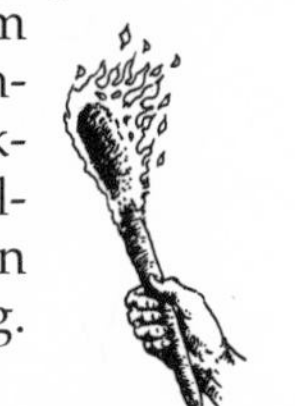

linotype (*ly'* noh . typ) a trademark name for a machine invented by Ottmar Mergenthaler in 1886 comprising a keyboard attached to a revolving drum or matrix that composes lines of words or symbols on metal strips, bars, or slugs for use on a printing press. In Harper Lee's *To Kill a Mockingbird,* Scout notes the rare Sunday morning when a local issue takes Mr. Underwood from his linotype, on which he composes all of Maycomb's news.

linstock (*lyn'* stahk) a staff or rod with a slit or forked tip used to touch lighted tinder to the firing mechanism of a cannon while the holder of the rod stands safely out of the way of the cannon's recoil. Dating to the late sixteenth century, the Dutch term means *matchstick.* While investigating writings on the wall of a cell, Defarge, a key player in the revolt in Charles Dickens's *A Tale of Two Cities,* exchanges his linstock for the turnkey's crowbar.

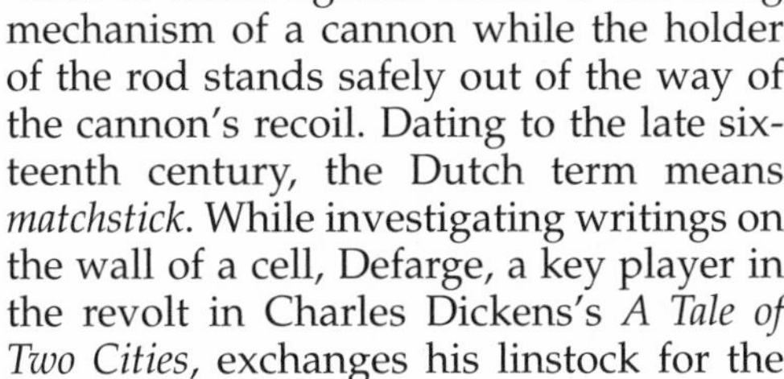

lintel (*lihn'* t'l) in primitive architecture, such as Stonehenge, a horizontal beam or timber that spans or heads two supporting stones or side beams of a colonnade, door, or window. Entering English in the thirteenth century, the term evolved from the Latin for *boundary.* In Homer's *Odyssey,* Odysseus admires the silver posts and lintel in the door to Alcinous's palace. In J. R. R. Tolkien's *The Hobbit,* Bilbo Baggins locates a set of stairs that lead to a peculiar door that has no post, lintel, or keyhole.

lithograph (*lihth'* oh . graf) an inexpensive print, copy, image, or reproduction made by placing blank paper over an inked engraving or etched plate. Entering English in the late eighteenth century and popularized by Eugene Delacroix, Theodore Gericault, and others of the Impressionist school of art, the term derives from the Greek for *stone writing,* a metaphoric reference to the flat zinc or limestone plate from which the print is taken. After the animals turn out Mr. Jones in George Orwell's *Animal Farm,* they file silently into the parlor and marvel at the looking glass and the lithograph of Queen Victoria over the fireplace.

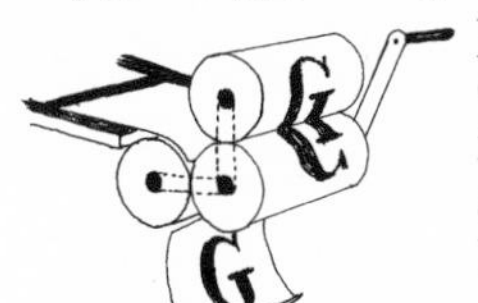

live oak a hardy, medium-sized evergreen, southern hardwood tree valued for its tough bark, ample shade, timber for shipbuilding and paneling, and sweet acorns, which are processed into hog feed. As described in Marjorie Kinnan Rawlings's *The Yearling,* the live oak, or *Quercus virginiana,* which doesn't shed its leaves, symbolizes resilience and dependability.

liver spot a harmless tan or brown patch of darkened pigmentation called melanin appearing on sun-damaged skin of elderly people. Forced to read to Mrs. Dubose, whose snow-on-the-mountain camellia he maliciously destroyed, Jem, protagonist in Harper Lee's *To Kill a Mockingbird,* recoils from the old lady's liver spots and gnarled hands.

liver wing according to nineteenth-century culinary custom, a special tidbit formed of the right wing tucked under the liver of a poached or roasted fowl. Departing from his former surly treatment of Pip in Charles Dickens's *Great Expectations,* Mr. Pumblechook, aware of the boy's inheritance, cultivates a close friendship by serving him choice bits of tongue and the liver wing.

livery a distinctive servant's uniform or outfit worn by a retainer or company hireling, such as a bank guard, gate attendant, or hotel doorkeeper. Livery is often decorated with a family coat of arms or traditional colors, mock-military epaulettes, braid, fringe, soutache scrolls, insignia, a company emblem, and a double row of metal buttons. Dating to the fourteenth century, the term derives from the Latin for *free* and applies to the freemen who work for a feudal lord. In Franz Kafka's "The Metamorphosis," Gregor's father, dressed in livery, struts before lodgers.

llanero (yah . *ner'* oh) *fem.* ***llanera*** a plainsman, pioneer, squatter, or settler of the plains in northern South America; a herder, drover, or keeper of livestock. Derived from the Spanish for *plain,* this seventeenth-century term sets the place and outlook of the characters in Rudolfo Anaya's *Bless Me, Ultima,* which takes place on a treeless grassland outside a southwestern U.S. town among poorly educated *llanero* families.

loadstone or **lodestone** a piece of magnetite or vein of iron oxide, an abundant rock or metal ore that has natural polarity or attractive powers of magnetism.

In Charles Dickens's *A Tale of Two Cities*, Tellson's Bank becomes the metaphoric loadstone that draws people to the source of wealth for a deposed ruling class of plutocrats and moneyed aristocrats.

lobotomy (loh . *bah'* toh . mee) a form of psychosurgery that passes a cutting tool through the whites of the eye to sever the nerves that connect the thalamus and the forward lobes of the brain as a means of calming uncontrollable schizophrenics and obsessives; also called prefrontal lobotomy or leucotomy. Lobotomy and leucotomy fell into disuse during the 1950s when drug therapies proved less traumatic and less likely to destroy the personality. In Ken Kesey's *One Flew over the Cuckoo's Nest*, a fellow patient notes that electroshock, leucotomy, and lobotomy have benefited chronic psychotics.

lockjaw a colloquial name for tetanus, an acute bacterial disease that derives from deep puncture wounds contaminated by soil or animal dung infested with the bacilli. Tetanus, which causes convulsions, headache, skeletal rigidity, and spasms or contractions of the chewing muscles, can be prevented by inoculation. On the opening pages of Olive Ann Burns's *Cold Sassy Tree,* Will Tweedy is grieving for Bluford Jackson, his best friend, who died of lockjaw only ten days after an accident involving firecrackers.

lodestone *See* loadstone.

loincloth a primitive form of dress that employs an unstitched, often undyed length of cloth as a wrap around the hips with a loose knot at the front or side to hold it in place. While preparing himself for a life of self-denial, the title character in Hermann Hesse's *Siddhartha* gives away all his clothing except for a loincloth and cloak and prepares himself for fasting, meditating, and begging. *See also* breechclout; dhoti.

loophole a slender vertical slit breaching a wall or defense tower to let in light and air and to provide access for firing small arms. In a castle, the inner side of a loophole often opens into an embrasure or niche wide enough for a bowman to stand and aim at an approaching enemy. In the setting of Robert Louis Stevenson's *Treasure Island*, the stockade is loopholed to accommodate musket fire. *See also* musket.

lorgnette (lohr . *neht'*) a pair of spectacles popular in the nineteenth century that fit over the bridge of the nose and are held in place by a handle at one side. Users seated in the boxes of theaters magnify the sight lines to the stage and scan the audience to study the escorts and costumes of patrons or to flirt with a person in a distant box or seat. The term derives from the French for *squint;* a word of a similar derivation—*lorgnon*—names a pair of short-handled spectacles or a monocle. While a clerk escorts Emma and Leon through a chapel in Gustave Flaubert's *Madame Bovary*, Emma peers about through her lorgnette as though she wants to learn about church architecture from the guided tour.

loss of face humiliation, disgrace, or embarrassment; a diminution of respectability, dignity, or prestige through poor behavior or deliberate affront by an enemy, business competitor, or political rival. In Amy Tan's *The Kitchen God's Wife*, avoiding loss of face results from following tradition and rituals, as with the practice of opening gifts in private to conceal disappointment and thus the embarrassment of both receiver and giver.

lottery a form of gambling by which a city, state, or nation issues tickets to be sold for a nominal price. A winning ticket or tickets are drawn at random and prize money or gifts awarded to the holder. Numbers are often displayed in shop windows or announced over radio or television. Derived from the Old English for *lot*, this sixteenth-century term is also the root of *lotto*, a form of gambling resembling bingo. In Sandra Cisneros's *The House on Mango Street*, Papa holds a lottery ticket and dreams of owning a spacious house.

lotus or **lotos** (*loh'* tuhs) a pond or freshwater lily common to Asia, Africa, and Australia and popular in ancient times. The lotus displays large pink blossoms centered among wide floating leaves. In Pearl S. Buck's *The Good Earth*, the butcher uses a dried lotus leaf as wrapping paper for an order of beef; also, Wang Lung's concubine is named Lotus, an alias chosen to suggest delicacy and natural beauty.

lotus pose or **position** a cross-legged sitting position in which the feet tuck under the thighs of the opposite legs. An integral part of yoga meditation, the pose symbolizes creative powers and enhances concentration by assembling the head, shoulders, and hips into a tight balance. In Ruth Prawer Jhabvala's *Heat and Dust*, Chid sits for hours in the lotus pose chanting a mantra and fingering his prayer beads.

louis d'or (*loo* . ee . *dohr'*) a gold coin of France discontinued after the revolution of 1795 and reissued as a 20-franc piece after the revolution. Derived from the French for *golden louis*, the term dates to the mid-seventeenth century and refers to Louis XIV, France's flamboyant Sun King. In Victor Hugo's *Les Misérables*, as his enemy Javert watches, Monsieur Madeleine tries to tempt a volunteer to lift the wagon from a priest by raising the offer of 5 louis d'ors to 20. *See also* franc.

love-feast a gathering of Christians or a shared meal displaying communal affection and unity of purpose. Often following a seasonal service, particularly Christmas Eve Mass, the loosely structured love-feast encourages informal conversation and reception of visitors and potential members. In the autobiographical *Narrative of the Life of Frederick Douglass,* the author comments that Rigby Hopkins, a notorious slave-driver, presents the picture of piety at prayer meetings and love-feasts.

loving cup an ornamental or ceremonial wine bowl or goblet with two or more handles used for communal drinking among friends, at a banquet or religious ritual, or between adversaries who wish to make a public display of unity by sharing the same container; also, a featured prize at a sporting event or beauty contest. After the birth of Stella's baby in Tennessee Williams's *A Streetcar Named Desire*, Stanley Kowalski offers champagne to his sister-in-law Blanche and suggests they make it a loving cup.

low relief *See* bas-relief.

lozenge (*lah'* zihnj) a cylindrical, trapezoidal, or rectangular stone laid horizontally alongside a standing headstone marked with a surname to indicate a grave of a family member. Charles Dickens's opening scene in *Great Expectations* reveals the graves of Pip's parents and his five brothers, whose deaths are marked by engraved stone lozenges.

luge (loozh) a narrow racing sled about four feet long used in competitive sports over an icy expanse of turns and loops; a toboggan seating one or more riders in a supine position and guided by a captain holding a hand rope and steering with the feet. At the arrival of the protagonists in Switzerland in Ernest Hemingway's *A Farewell to Arms*, border officials try to interest Frederick Henry and Catherine Barkley in the sport of luge.

Luger (*loo'* guhr) trade name of a German small-bore semiautomatic pistol capable of ejecting a spent shell and reloading. Named for inventor and engineer George Luger (1849–1923), the firearm was used by the German military during World War I and remained competitive with newer small arms during the mid-twentieth century. In John Steinbeck's *Of Mice and Men*, Carlson's firing of the Luger to euthanize Candy's old dog prefigures Lenny's execution.

lugger (*luhg'* guhr) a small two-masted ship rigged with a square lugsail set crossways on an upper yardarm. Owners prefer the lugger for fishing and coastal trade; smugglers and pirates rely on the boat for rapid strike and flight. Because Supervisor Dance learns that there is a lugger in Kitt's Hole, he saves Jim Hawkins and his mother from murderers in Robert Louis Stevenson's *Treasure Island.*

lumbago (luhm . *bay'* goh) a generalized folk diagnosis of backache indicating a slipped spinal disc or debilitating muscular rheumatism or arthritis of the sacral area. Entering English in the late seventeenth century, the term derives from Latin for *loins.* While the title character in Edith Wharton's *Ethan Frome* considers how to approach Mr. Hale, a lumber client, for payment, Mrs. Hale reports that her husband is down with lumbago in his back, on which she has placed a plaster.

Lupercal a fertility festival honoring Lupercus, god of shepherds, and propitiating the gods for a year of plenty and healthy births of children and livestock. The holiday, derived from the Latin for *wolf*, falls on February 15 on the ancient Roman calendar. In the opening scene of William Shakespeare's *Julius Caesar*, the citizens of Rome gather on the streets to watch the race that is a focal point of the Feast of Lupercal, during which men clad in goatskins run the course, striking Calpurnia and other barren women with flicks of their whips, a symbolic method of breaking the curse of sterility.

lute a stringed instrument similar to a guitar with a pear-shaped sounding box and fingerboard strung with 6 to 13 pairs of strings and bent back at a 275 degree angle to accommodate tuning pins. The lute, which has been popular since the Middle Ages, derives from the Moors and gets its name from the Arabic for *wood*. A graceful

instrument, it is plucked or bowed like a fiddle rather than strummed. During evening performances of lute music and singing, Wang Lung, protagonist in Pearl S. Buck's *The Good Earth*, sits drinking tea, enjoying prosperity, and relaxing from farm work.

lyceum (ly . *see'* uhm) a community enlightenment program organized in the nineteenth century to provide readings, lectures on the arts and sciences, concerts, debates, musical performances, and other entertainments and cultural events and to foster museums and libraries. Begun in Millbury, Massachusetts, by Josiah Holbrook and supported by Susan B. Anthony, Henry David Thoreau, Ralph Waldo Emerson, Oliver Wendell Holmes, Nathaniel Hawthorne, Charles Dickens, William Makepeace Thackeray, William Lloyd Garrison, and Daniel Webster, the lyceum presaged the Chautauqua and other adult education programs and quickly spread across New England. In Henry David Thoreau's "Civil Disobedience," the essayist objects to a tax supporting the clergy and notes that ministers do not support the lyceum.

lymph a yellowish fluid that flows through vessels and ducts to the bloodstream to manufacture antibodies and cleanse tissues of bacteria and foreign matter. At the neck, underarm, and groin, lymphatic junctions filter infection, which may cause the nodes to swell and become feverish and sore. Derived from the Greek for *water sprite*, the term entered English in the late seventeenth century and names a major system of the body. In John Steinbeck's *The Pearl*, the scorpion bite on Coyotito's shoulder extends a red swelling to a hard lymphatic mound.

lynx (lingks) a solitary wildcat or bobcat found in Europe, Asia, and northern North America. Named for the Greek for *white* and marked by a mottled pelt of black-tipped fur, tufted ears, and short tail, the lynx prowls at night and feeds on small mammals by climbing rocks and springing on its prey. In *White Fang*, Jack London describes a deadly battle between a she-wolf and a lynx; the she-wolf overcomes the lynx, but lies near death for days until her wounds heal.

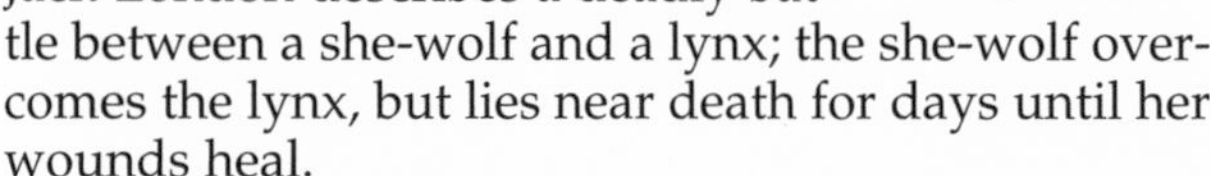

lyre a small, flat stringed instrument similar to a harp or cithara and formed of a square wooden or tortoiseshell sound box, two side arms, and a bridge strung with gut. Made famous in the Bible by David, who was a master of lyric performance, the lyre was held in the hand or slung from a neck strap at chest level. In eastern Mediterranean countries, wandering poets strummed the lyre with a plectrum to mark the beat of recitations or chants. During the Middle Ages, the lyre was bowed like a lute or fiddle to produce the sweet sounds consistent with love lyrics. Edith Hamilton's *Mythology* describes how Orpheus, a master poet and singer, charms the gods of the Underworld by singing sad love songs in honor of his dead bride. In his honor, the lyre became *lyra*, a heavenly constellation. *See also* lute.

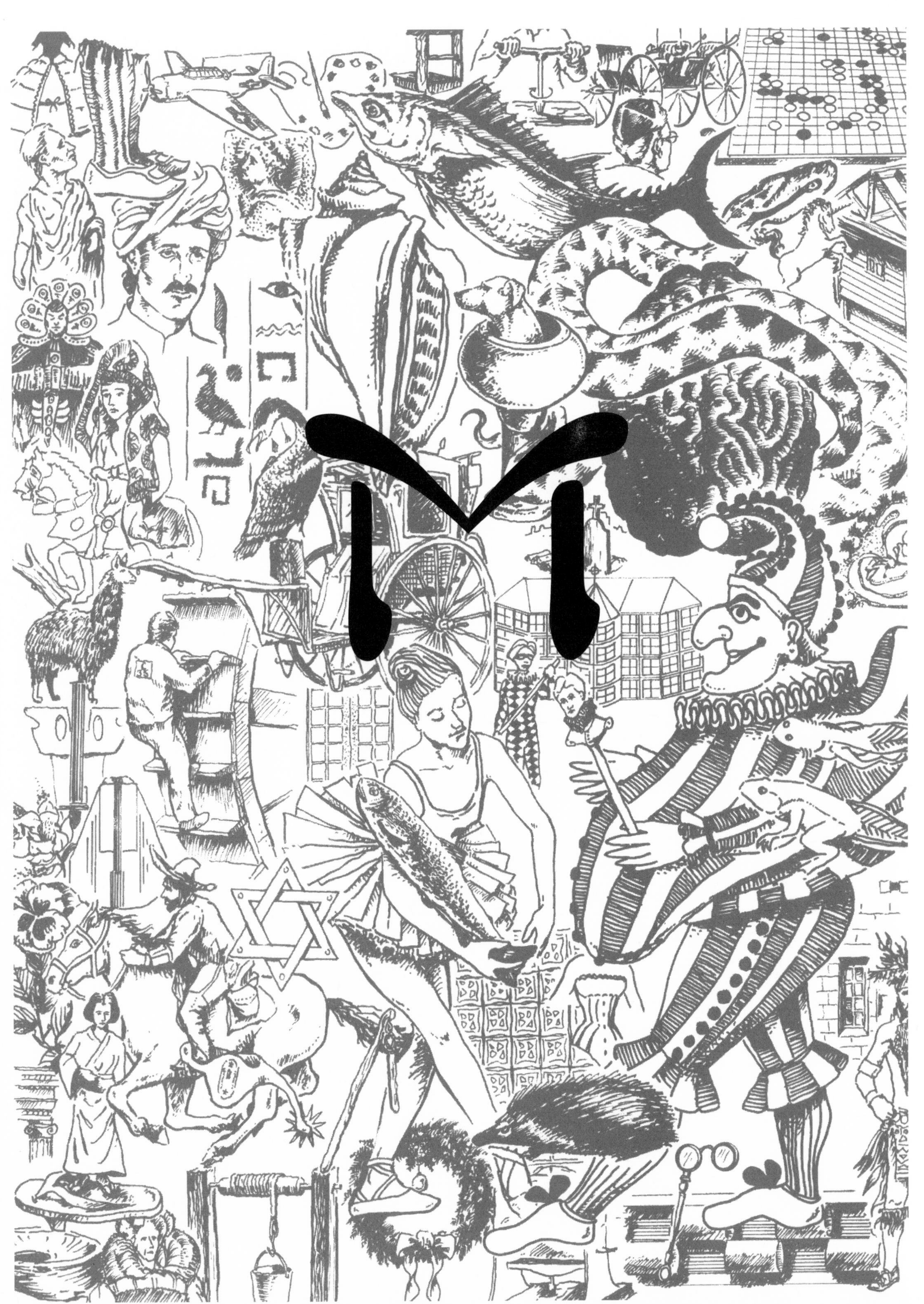
M

macaroon (*mak'* uh . roon) a sweet, chewy, toasted cookie or biscuit made of almond paste, vanilla, egg white, and coconut and topped with a bit of candied cherry or a nut. Invented in Italy in the early seventeenth century and named from the Greek for *barley*, the macaroon became so popular, it was mass produced. In Henrik Ibsen's *The Doll's House*, Nora nibbles at macaroons concealed in her pocket, demonstrating the childlike guile that her husband Thorvald attributes to her.

machete (muh . *sheh'* tee) a broad-bladed cutlass or utility knife with a curved blade and simple wooden hilt. The machete is an all-purpose tool or weapon in Africa, the Caribbean, Hawaii, the Philippines, and the Americas and is used for self-protection, clearing underbrush or vines, or for harvesting sugarcane, tobacco, corn, sorghum, pineapples, coconuts, and other crops. Entering English in the early sixteenth century, the term derives from the Latin for *mallet*. Okonkwo, protagonist of Chinua Achebe's *Things Fall Apart*, uses a machete for slicing seed yams and as an executioner's weapon when he kills his foster son.

mackinaw (*mak'* ih . naw) a thick, woolly blanket or short double-breasted jacket, often in bright plaid or stripes; the traditional napped lumberjack's coat. Entering English in the early nineteenth century and derived from an Ojibwa word for *turtle* or *flatboat*, the word is linked to Mackinac, a Michigan trading post, and refers to government-issue blankets distributed to Native Americans. A mackinaw keeps Billy's father warm and dry during a long, tedious mule ride in Wilson Rawls's *Where the Red Fern Grows.*

mackintosh or **macintosh** (*mak'* ihn . tahsh) a lightweight waterproof fabric coated with rubber; also, a generic term for raincoats and hooded capes made of mackintosh. Named for Charles Macintosh, the Scots inventor who patented waterproofing in 1823, the mackintosh, or "mack," was a favorite of early motorists, who suffered rain, mud, and fumes while traveling in open cars. In Jules Verne's *Around the World in Eighty Days*, Phileas Fogg insists on traveling around the world with a minimum of luggage: carpetbag, stout shoes, traveling cloak, and mackintosh.

macramé (*mak'* ruh . *may*) a style of knotting or interlacing threads, cord, or rope with square or hitch knots into a lacy, fringed artwork, geometric design, mask, window covering, screen, pot hanger, purse, hammock, swing, or other shape. A mid-nineteenth century skill that was popular with sailors and was revived during the 1970s as a hobby or craft, the word derives from the Arabic for *coverlet* or *towel*. While contemplating a divorce from Ted in Amy Tan's *The Joy Luck Club*, Rose Hsu Jordan ponders a macramé wall hanging, a symbol of the coarsely woven threads of her failing marriage. *See also* netting.

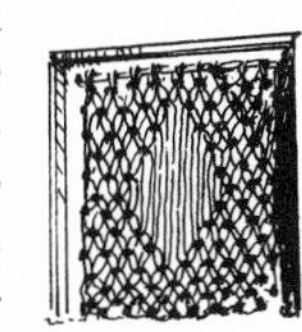

maelstrom (*mayl'* struhm) an Arctic whirlpool 5 miles wide and 20 fathoms deep near the island of Moskenaes off the west coast of Norway that the fiction of Jules Verne and Edgar Allan Poe describes as inescapable and powerful enough to pull ships into its center and destroy them with its swirling turbulence; also, a metaphor for fatal emotional confusion or agitation. Entering English in the late seventeenth century, the term derives from the Dutch for *whirling stream*. The white whale in Herman Melville's *Moby-Dick* creates a maelstrom by swimming round and round the *Pequod* until it sinks, leaving only one witness alive to tell of Ahab's obsession.

Maenad (*may'* nad) a madwoman in ancient Greek lore who followed Dionysus or Bacchus, the god of wine, and participated in uninhibited forms of nature worship; a wild, frenzied, or drunken Bacchante capable of murdering an infant, suckling serpents at their breasts, and participating in sexual orgies with satyrs. According to Edith Hamilton's *Mythology*, the Maenads roved the wilds crying, waving ivy-decked wands, and giving way to delusions, religious fanaticism, and an excess of passion. One of their victims was Orpheus, whom they tore to bits for rejecting their dedication to sexual ecstasies in Dionysius's honor. *See also* Bacchic rite; Dionysiac.

magazine the cylinder or storage chamber of a pistol or firearm that holds extra rounds of ammunition to be fed one by one into the firing chamber; also, a storage shed, supply depot, or protected room in a fort or ship relegated to powder, ammunition, or explosives. Entering English in the late sixteenth century, the term derives from the Arabic for *storehouse.* After buying a pistol and holster, Frederick Henry, the protagonist in Ernest Hemingway's *A Farewell to Arms*, fills the magazine and claims to be leaving for the front.

maharajah or **maharaja** (*mah* . hah . *rah'* juh) the Hindu ceremonial title accorded a state potentate, sovereign prince, or king in India. The maharajah's wife or consort is known as the maharani or maharanee; the maharajah is the superior of a rajah, or local chief. This honorific, which dates to the late seventeenth century, derives from the Sanskrit for *great king*. The hijacked plane in James Hilton's *Lost Horizon* was built for a maharajah and donated to help the four escapees flee an uprising in India.

mah jong or **mah-jongg** (mah . *zhong'*) a nineteenth-century Chinese game similar to a blend of dominoes and rummy and played by four people. Instead of a deck of cards, mah jong utilizes dice, racks, and 144 tiles or squares that are marked with pictographs of seven suits—circles, bamboo, characters, winds, dragons, seasons, and flowers. To win, a player must capture four sets and a pair. Mah jong became popular in America during the 1920s and delights the Joy Luck Club, the title group in a novel by Amy Tan.

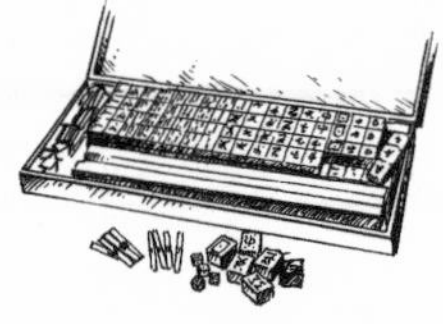

maidenhead a mucous fold, membranous fringe, or septum that rings or occludes the inner vestibule of the vagina and forms a minor barrier to the initial act of intercourse; the hymen, which supposedly attests to purity, innocence, and constancy by proving a woman's virginity. Entering English in the thirteenth century, the term derives from Middle English for *maidenhood* and persists throughout a lengthy history of folk belief that women owe their husbands virginal bodies unclaimed by former lovers. Juliet's nurse, a ribald, outspoken family servant of the Capulets, swears by her maidenhead in a comic scene from William Shakespeare's *Romeo and Juliet.*

mairie (*may'* ree) the French term for town hall or civil office building and office or residence of the mayor, the chief executive office of a town or borough. Derived from the Latin for *major*, the term indicates the growth of town bureaucracy that accompanied the decline of the feudal system and the rise of cities. In *Les Misérables*, Victor Hugo describes Cosette, Marius's bride, as lovely both at the *mairie* for the signing of the marriage certificate and later at the sacred ceremony in the chapel.

malingerer (muh . *ling'* uhr . uhr) a person who evades work, military duty, or other responsibility by pretending to be ill or incapacitated or by feigning weakness or exaggerating symptoms to prove the existence of a disease; a shirker. Derived from the French for *sickly*, the term entered English in the early nineteenth century. Gregor Samsa, protagonist in Franz Kafka's "The Metamorphosis," fears that the insurance doctor will label him a "healthy malingerer" for reporting his bizarre transformation into a cockroach. In Alexander Solzhenitsyn's *One Day in the Life of Ivan Denisovich*, prisoners who report to the infirmary are suspected of being malingerers.

malt a general term for sprouted barley or other cereal grain steeped in water in a revolving drum until it sprouts rootlets and undergoes a softening of the outer hull. Malt is dried in an oven and distilled into malt liquor, brewed into beer or ale, or fermented into vinegar. This eleventh-century term derives from the Old English for *melt*. To the attentive Elizabeth-Jane in Thomas Hardy's *The Mayor of Casterbridge*, Solomon Longways describes Henchard's wheat as so rough that it looks like malt and produces a thick bottom crust on loaves of bread.

mammoth (*mam'* muhth) a tusked mammal resembling a shaggy, reddish-brown elephant and ranging in height to 15 feet. The mammoth, which cave painters feature for its size, majestic form, and value as a source of ivory and meat, flourished during the Pleistocene Epoch in the tundra of Asia, Europe, North Africa, and North America before becoming extinct about 2000 B.C. In Gary Paulsen's *Dogsong*, Russel notes that the dancer doesn't just imitate the mammoth; he *becomes* the mammoth.

Mandarin (*man'* duh . rihn) **Chinese** the predominant language of Asia, Mandarin is spoken from China south and west to Vietnam, Tibet, Thailand, Laos, and Burma. The territory is so large that Mandarin differs from other Chinese dialects like a foreign language and was at one time valued as the language of scholars and clerics, court officials, or the elite. Derived from the Sanskrit for *adviser*, the term entered English in the late sixteenth century. In Amy Tan's *The Kitchen God's Wife*, Pearl's mother speaks Wu, or Shanghaiese, a coastal branch of Mandarin Chinese.

mandrake *See* May apple.

mangel-wurzel (*mang'* uhl *wuhr* . z'l) a large-rooted yellow or orange root vegetable of the beet family grown as food for livestock. Dating to the mid-eighteenth century, the term derives from the German for *beet root*. The jubilant rebel animals of George Orwell's *Animal Farm* sing "Beasts of England," an anthem looking forward to a time of plenty, including lots of mangel-wurzels.

manger (*man'* juhr) a long free-standing trough, creep feeder, or open feed box attached to the wall of a barn, feeding station, shed, or stable where livestock come to feed off grain, fodder, or loose hay or to lick a salt block. Entering English in the fourteenth century, the term derives from the Latin for *chew*. In John Steinbeck's *Of Mice and Men*, Jody's pony tries to remove the headstall from his head by rubbing it against the manger.

mangle laundry equipment consisting of adjustable rollers turned with a crank to guide wet laundry through a rigorous squeezing process preceding hanging on a line to dry or stretching on a frame. The same process through a heated mangle produces wrinkle-free clothing. The mangle is a common household item prized by Mrs. Sparsit in Charles Dickens's *Hard Times*.

mango an aromatic, peach-flavored tropical fruit with an oval shape, thick peel, and tart orange flesh that is sliced from a central stone and served as a topping, condiment, or dessert. The fruit is common to Asia and Africa. The term, which entered English in the late sixteenth century, derives from the Tamil word for the fruit. The presence of a ripe mango at dinner suggests the unlikely warmth and fertility of Shangri-La, the Himalayan setting of James Hilton's *Lost Horizon*.

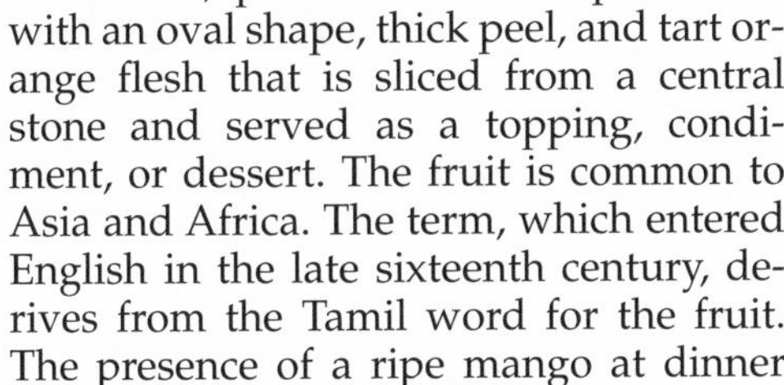

mangrove (*mang'* grohv) a tropical evergreen shrub or tree common to coastal waters, springing from a mass of thick air roots, and thriving in sprawling, tangled thickets. One variety, the red mangrove, supplies juice for dye and wood for railroad ties, fence posts, rafters, and charcoal. With a prefix derived from the Taino word for the plant, this hybrid term entered English in the early seventeenth century. The fearful contortions of mangroves springing from fetid black waters dismay Marlowe, protagonist of Joseph Conrad's *The Heart of Darkness*.

manioc *See* cassava.

manor an estate or major parcel of land consisting of a central home for the owner; a walled compound enclosing barns, silos, storage sheds, and domestic animals; and outlying cultivated fields, orchards, woodlots or copses, and gardens. Derived from the Latin for *dwell*, the term applies primarily to the feudal domain of a lord, his family, retainers, tenants, and hirelings. The domestic animals in George Orwell's *Animal Farm* claim rights to Farmer Jones's manor house. *See also* copse.

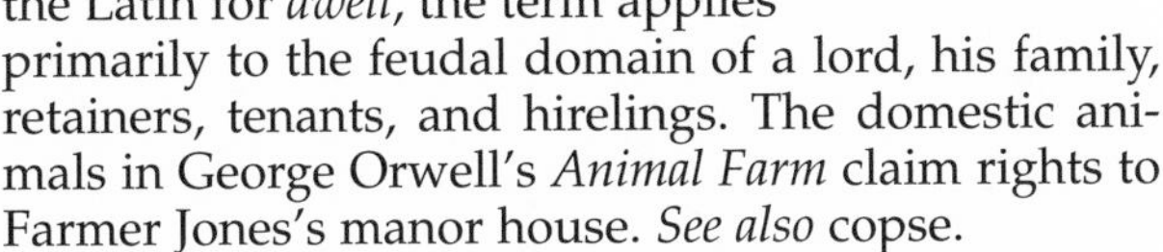

man-o'-war or **man-of-war** a generic term indicating a battleship or armed vessel designed for combat at sea. In *Narrative of the Life of Frederick Douglass*, the title character works in the Baltimore shipyard of Mr. William Gardner, who hurries to complete a contract for two man-o'-war brigs. *See also* brigantine.

mantilla (man . *tee'* yuh) an ornate white or black lace scarf, veil, or ritual head covering framing the face and draping about the shoulders. Dating to the mid-nineteenth century, the term derives from the Spanish for *blanket*. Among Hispanic Catholics, it was once the height of fashion in Spanish couture; the mantilla is worn as a head covering for brides, often attached to a high comb to lift it above the head. In Erich Maria Remarque's *All Quiet on the Western Front*, when Marja Lewandowski visits her husband in the military hospital, she wears a beribboned, bridelike mantilla, suggesting that the purpose of her visit is to claim her marital rights.

mantle a voluminous draped outer garment or sleeveless cloak worn by men and women in ancient Rome for warmth, as a mark of dignity or social station, and to conceal the head and face. A standard term in European fashion vocabulary, the word derives from the Latin for *hand* because the buttonless garment was anchored by one hand. Mark Antony makes a moving speech in William Shakespeare's *Julius Caesar* by referring to the occasions on which Caesar wore the mantle that now covers his riddled, blood-stained corpse.

manzanilla (*man* . zan . *ee'* yuh) a type of chamomile or heath common to the American southwest and brewed into a tea to cure colic, flatulence, nausea, and intestinal complaints. This traditional herb of the *curandero* or *curandera* derives its name from the Spanish for *apple*. In Rudolfo Anaya's *Bless Me, Ultima*, Antonio learns that Ultima treated Leon with manzanilla. *See also curandera;* herbal medicine.

marchpane (*march'* payn) or **marzipan** candy, biscuit, sweetmeat, or confectionery treat made of a dough consisting of sugar and ground almonds that is formed into imaginative shapes such as fruit, vegetables, shells, birds, flowers, or petits fours, and then baked and painted with food coloring. Before the Capulets' party in William Shakespeare's *Romeo and Juliet*, the servants look forward to large servings of marchpane.

Mardi Gras (*mahr'* dee *grah*) the traditional carnival celebration occurring on Shrove Tuesday—preceding Ash Wednesday, the first day of Lent—with a gaudy display of costumes, processions, floats, mummery, and royal courts. In Louisiana, Brazil, and the Caribbean, the carnival season is the height of an annual orgy of merrymaking, feasting, and drollery. The French for *fat Tuesday,* the term implies that Christians have only one day to indulge themselves before undergoing the self-denial demanded by a devout observance of Lent. In Tennessee Williams's *A Streetcar Named Desire,* Stanley Kowalski humiliates his deluded sister-in-law by calling pathetic her attempt at dressing up a Mardi Gras costume. *See also* Good Friday.

marimba (muh . *rihm'* buh) a percussion instrument shaped from rosewood planks or bars like the keys of a xylophone, which are positioned atop individual resonating chambers in a framework resembling a keyboard and played with rubber mallets or hammers by one to four performers. The instrument has a range of four to four and one-half octaves. The term, which entered English in the nineteenth century, derives from an African word for *thumb piano.* Early Congolese marimbas used tuned gourds as resonators, a construction style carried by African slaves to Central America. In the late nineteenth century, Sebastian Hurtado evolved a Guatemalan version with membrane-covered wooden boxes replacing gourds. Later models were factory-produced with metal resonators. At Gil's Furniture, the speaker in Sandra Cisneros's *The House on Mango Street* listens to a music box that sounds tinkly like marimbas.

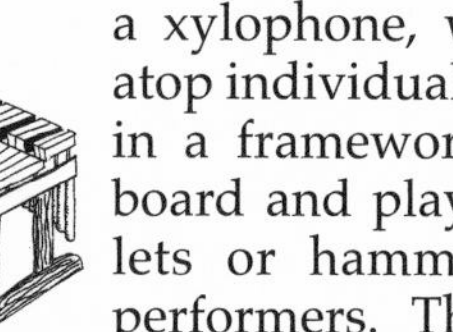

mark SEE Deutsche mark.

mark twain a knot on a weighted measuring line that the leadsman lowers into a waterway to determine a safe depth for riverboat passage. One mark is a fathom, or six feet; two marks is a reassuring twelve feet. When Mark Twain describes the call of the leadsman to pilot Horace Bixby in *Life on the Mississippi,* he explains the derivation of his now world-famous pen name from a navigation term that indicates safety.

marlin (*mahr'* lihn) a large, dramatically colored marine fish related to the sailfish. The marlin's markings include a dark blue tapering to silvery-blue on the underside, a long upper bill or spear, and extensive dorsal fin. The sport fish is a favorite for preservation and wall display. Santiago, protagonist in Ernest Hemingway's *The Old Man and the Sea,* describes the loving devotion of a male marlin who remains beside the female after she is hooked and leaps high above the water to see her body landed aboard the boat.

marlinspike or **marlinespike** (*mahr'* lihn . *spyk*) or **marlingspike** a sharp, wood-handled iron awl or pick used to separate strands of rope, wire, or cable for splicing. Derived from the Dutch for *binding line,* the term entered English in the early seventeenth century. In his explanation of his nervous response to the afterguardsman in Herman Melville's *Billy Budd,* the title character knows his rights in claiming expertise of the foretop and the use of the marlinspike.

marquee (mahr . *kee'*) a tent or pavilion erected to shelter guests, performers, or attendees at an outdoor social occasion or commercial venture, such as a wedding reception, musicale, art exhibit, or auction. Entering English in the late seventeenth century, the term derives from the French for *marchioness.* As a work crew sets up a marquee in Katherine Mansfield's "The Garden Party," the lawn takes on a temporary air of festivity that contrasts with the somber tone of the nearby funeral.

Marseillaise (*mahr'* say . ez) the stirring French national anthem, composed by Rouget de Lisle in 1792 before the beginning of a war with Austria. The hymn takes its name from the singers, who were patriots from the southern French city of Marseilles. At the end of a pro-labor speech in Upton Sinclair's *The Jungle,* Jurgis trembles and thrills to the majesty of *La Marseillaise.*

marshal a police officer, constable, or peace officer similar to a sheriff who is charged with controlling prisoners and inflicting punishment dictated by a court or magistrate. Derived from the Old High German for *horse servant,* the term entered English in the thirteenth century. In the United States it evolved into the title of a federal officer who enforces federal laws and mandates, for example, Marshal Rooster Cogburn, a bounty hunter in Charles Portis's *True Grit.* At the height of multiple accusations in the court scene of Arthur Miller's *The Crucible,* Reverend Hale calls for the marshal to bring irons, presumably to shackle prisoners.

martingale a strap or lead rope attached from a pack animal's girth, passing between the front legs, and splitting into halves, each of which fastens to the reigns or noseband to prevent the animal from rearing its head. In Victor Hugo's *Les Misérables,* Jean Valjean leads Valvert, his implacable stalker, out of the wine shop by a martingale, then cuts the ropes and sets Valvert free.

Martini-Henry or **Henry rifle** a single-shot breech-loading magazine rifle, an 1871 union of Von Martini's firing mechanism and Benjamin Tyler Henry's design firing a .577/.450-inch reduced-caliber cartridge. In the brief battle scene in Joseph Conrad's *The Heart of Darkness,* the helmsman, against Marlowe's orders, opens the shutters of the pilot house to fire the Martini-Henry at attacking Africans and dies before his master's eyes. *See also* breech-loader.

masker or **masquer** a masked or disguised participant at a masquerade ball, especially one who attends without an invitation or one who wishes to flirt

without revealing his or her identity. Entering English in the mid-sixteenth century, the term derives from the Italian for *false face.* In William Shakespeare's *Romeo and Juliet,* youthful maskers look forward to attending the Capulet party incognito.

Mason's apron a ceremonial garment bearing the Freemason emblem, which is tied about the waist of a member during secret rituals. Mattie Ross, protagonist of Charles Portis's *True Grit,* reports that she did not attend the burial of her father, whom Yarnell, the family retainer, shipped home by train and interred in his Mason's apron. *See also* Freemasonry.

masque (mask) a medieval spectacle, game, or ceremony in which masked figures or mummers celebrate a holiday, wedding, or festival by processing silently through the streets. In the Elizabethan and Jacobean eras, masques, which honored nobility, featured excessive costuming and scenery in a series of extravagant musical tableaux, allegorical dramas, or plotless skits derived from mythology or legend and designed to please court tastes and interests. At the conclusion of a triple wedding ceremony in William Shakespeare's *A Midsummer Night's Dream,* Theseus invites his bride and the two young couples to pass the three hours before bedtime in dancing and masques. *See also* domino; harlequin.

massif (mas . *seef'*) a compact arrangement of interconnecting mountains or an elevated plateau unsuited to agriculture, but rich in timber; also, a fault-block mountain forced upward by tension or pressure in the earth's crust. Hugh Conway, protagonist in James Hilton's utopian *Lost Horizon,* takes pleasure in the miniature Eden that lies at the heart of an encircling massif.

master-at-arms a warship's police officer, disciplinarian, jailer, or peacekeeper; also, a petty officer who serves as light arms instructor, nicknamed "jaunty" or "janty." Entering English in the mid-eighteenth century, the title derives from the Latin for *magister* or *teacher.* In Herman Melville's *Billy Budd,* to determine whether the title character is on duty in the foretop, Captain Vere checks with the master-at-arms.

match a twist of cord or wick forced into the hole in the firing mechanism of a matchlock rifle to ignite the charge in the pan. Derived from the Latin for *lamp wick,* the term entered English military vocabulary in the mid-sixteenth century. As the attack commences in Edmond Rostand's *Cyrano de Bergerac,* Carbon calls for soldiers to light their matches in preparation for firing. *See also* flintlock; linstock; musket.

match safe a metal repository for kitchen matches to keep them dry and prevent them from accidentally igniting. Some vertical models contain a small slot at one end to dispense the matches one at a time. In Edith Wharton's *Ethan Frome,* Zeena implies that her housekeeper, Mattie Silver, has stolen a match safe.

matins (*mat'* 'ns) or **matin** a religious service of praise and devotion held in early morning, the first canonical hour; also, morning prayer. This fourteenth-century term derives from the Latin name for the goddess of the dawn. Jack Merridew, the choirmaster and chief of the hunters in William Golding's *Lord of the Flies,* has no mercy on a boy who faints at matins in front of the lead chanter.

matrix (*may'* trihks) a biological term for a complex of blood-rich tissue in which a zygote or embryo nestles during its early growth period; also, a general term for uterus or womb. Derived from the Latin for *mother,* the term carries extra significance in Margaret Atwood's *The Handmaid's Tale,* a dystopic novel about state-mandated conception. As the birth of Angela approaches, the handmaids smell the matrix and draw near to encourage the mother.

mausoleum (*maw* . soh . *lee'* uhm) a large stately burial vault or above-ground tomb, usually of stone or marble. The mausoleum of Abraham Lincoln in Springfield, Illinois, contains a walk-in vestibule, quotations, and bas-relief. The grandeur of other examples is enhanced by statuary, entablature, or an obelisk along with engraving or bronze nameplate, dates, and a suitably noble or flattering description of the deceased. Entering English in the Middle Ages, the term, which names one of the Seven Wonders of the World, derives from Mausolus, a fourth-century B.C. Persian ruler of Halicarnassus (modern Turkey). After discussing happiness with Clarisse McClellan, Guy Montag, protagonist of *Fahrenheit 451,* returns to his empty marriage and a bedroom as cold and unwelcoming as a mausoleum.

maxim (*maks'* ihm) a short, pithy statement of truth; a self-evident aphorism, axiom, proverb, concise precept or truism, or succinct statement of principle. The term, derived from the Latin for *greatest,* entered English in the mid-sixteenth century. In George Orwell's *Animal Farm,* Snowball, a leader of the rebels against Farmer Jones, condenses the Seven Commandments into a single antihuman maxim: "Four legs good, two legs bad."

May apple or **mayapple** or **mandrake** a perennial spring herb of the North American barberry family once valued as a cure for deafness and as an insect or crow repellent. A name dating to the eighteenth century, the May apple, which has a poisonous forked root, is identified by its lobed leaves, white blossoms, and yellow fruit, which forms a base for jams and condiments. In Conrad Richter's *The Light in the Forest,* True Son tries to locate the root of the May apple to commit suicide and avoid returning to his white parents.

maze *See also* Labyrinth; T-maze.

mazel tov (*mah'* zuhl tahf) an interjection expressing blessings, congratulations, best wishes, or good luck. Derived from the Hebrew for *good star,* the term, common to weddings, commendations, or other auspicious occasions, entered English in the mid-nineteenth century. In Daniel Keyes's *Flowers for Algernon,* Charlie Gordon cringes as bar patrons jeer mocking cries of "mazel tov" after a retarded busboy drops a load of glassware.

mazurka (muh . *zuhr'* kuh) a lively, rhythmic sixteenth-century Polish folk dance for couples who link arms or strike poses with their hands on their hips. The mazurka displays improvisation and complex patterns of sliding steps, stamping, heel tapping, twirls, and hops with emphasis on the second and third beats of a three-beat measure. Named for Mazury, an area in northeast Poland, the term entered English in the early nineteenth century. It became an instrumental focus of composition by Frederick Chopin and Peter Ilyich Tchaikovsky. Essie, who aspires to become a ballerina, promises to dance a mazurka for Mr. Kirby in the closing lines of Moss Hart and George S. Kaufman's *You Can't Take It with You.* In Tennessee Williams's *A Streetcar Named Desire,* a plaintive, earthy mood arises from strains of the Varsouviana, a nineteenth-century modification of the mazurka.

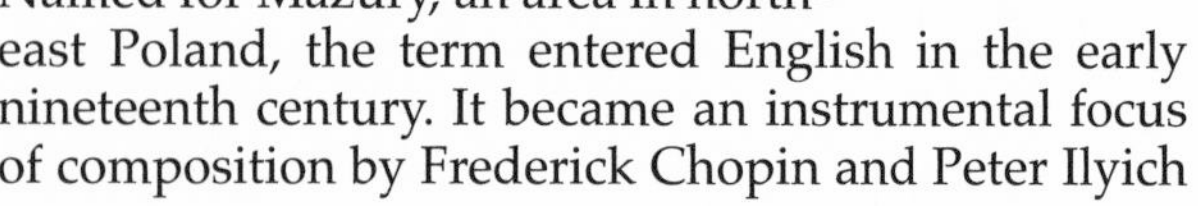

mead (meed) a pale golden fermented drink composed of honey, malt, yeast, spice, fruit juice, and water that was used as a magic elixir and battlefield tonic and restorative and as a ceremonial toast to honor fallen Viking heroes. Mead was drunk from bone cups or carved horns by leaders who bet on which imbiber could swallow the most mead in one draft. Predating the twelfth century, the term may derive from the Sanskrit for *honey* or the Greek for *wine.* In Edith Hamilton's *Mythology,* the Norse hero Odin endangers himself by stealing from the Giants the entrancing mead, a liquid that turned drinkers into poets. *See also* malt; meadhall.

meadhall a high-vaulted gathering place for Viking heroes and nobles for feasts; celebrations of epic deeds; and retellings of the stories of Odin, the trickster who took the giant Suttung's mead, revered by Teutons as the drink of the gods. The focal setting of the epic *Beowulf* and John Gardner's *Grendel,* the meadhall evoked the pride and camaraderie that derived from recitations of folk tales and heroic verse.

meccano set (meh . *kan'* noh) the British version of the American Erector set, a sophisticated building toy that encourages the creation of engineering models such as bridges, towers, vehicles, and moveable engines out of reusable metal beams, connectors, screws, and nuts. Derived from the Greek for *machine,* the trademark entered English in the early twentieth century. In Ruth Prawer Jhabvala's *Heat and Dust,* the Nawab, a victim of colonialism, orders a shooting gallery, hockey equipment, meccano sets, and a piano, all Western pastimes that remain in storage because no one in his palace knows how to use them.

medicine man a tribal shaman among North American Indian tribes who treated illness, trained young braves, interpreted visions and dreams, and called on the gods during dangerous or distressing times. Using rattles, drums, or bells, the medicine man treated illness by overpowering its evil and forcing it from the sufferer's body. According to an oral autobiography, John Neihardt's *Black Elk Speaks,* the title character becomes a medicine man after strange bouts of illness and visions indicate that he can communicate with the spirit world.

melodeum (muh . *loh'* dee . uhm) or **melodeon** a small keyboard instrument producing reedy sounds from the current of air sucked in by a foot-operated bellows; a cabinet organ similar to a harmonium and popular for use in homes and churches. An invention of the late nineteenth century, the melodeum takes its name from the Greek for *tune*. At the funeral in Mark Twain's *The Adventures of Huckleberry Finn*, a musician tries to coax suitable music from a colicky melodeum borrowed for the somber occasion.

memsahib (*mehm'* sahb) a respectful title or honorific from India's colonial period that is applied by Indians to prestigious European women, such as the wives of government officials. A hybrid term derived from the Anglo-Indian *ma'am* and the Arabic for *master*, the word suggests the syncretism that arises from the melding of two cultures. As a part of her social role as *burra memsahib* in Ruth Prawer Jhabvala's *Heat and Dust*, Mrs. Crawford inspects the newcomers and their bungalow.

Merchant Seamen the official designation of the crew of the United States Merchant Marine, the commercial fleet that is composed of registered passenger liners, tankers, coastal vessels, and cargo carriers. Laura's brother Tom, who runs away from a warehouse job to join the Merchant Seamen in Tennessee Williams's *The Glass Menagerie*, continues to love and dream of his delicate sister, who remains under the control of Amanda Wingfield, their domineering mother.

merengue or **meringue** (muh . *ring'* gay) a Creole ballroom dance for couples originated in Haiti and the Dominican Republic and popularized throughout Hispanic countries and the Caribbean. Punctuated with timely sways of the hip, the merengue emphasizes syncopated rhythms and the stylized drag of the leg. In Sandra Cisneros's *The House on Mango Street*, preteen girls who are just discovering their hips practice jumping rope and dancing to the merengue beat.

merino (muh . *ree'* noh) a heavy-fleeced sheep native to the Spanish by way of North African Moors that produces a fine, soft grade of wool worsted or knitting yarn used in hosiery, silky underwear, and other high-quality garments. Merino can be dyed to look like cashmere or expensive fur or blended with cotton for a lighter-weight fabric. The term, entering English in the early nineteenth century, perhaps derives from the Merins, a Berber tribe. In Edith Wharton's *Ethan Frome*, the main character realizes that his wife is dressed for travel because she is wearing her good brown merino.

mesa (*may'* suh) a tableland, butte, or steep-sided hill with a level top that looks down on a canyon or gorge or across plains. An eighteenth-century term, the word derives from the Latin for *table.* Shaped by the current of a prehistoric river and cooled by desert winds, the mesa, a favorite landmark in the southwestern United States, is the site of the Zuñi reservation in Aldous Huxley's *Brave New World. See also* bluff bank; palisade.

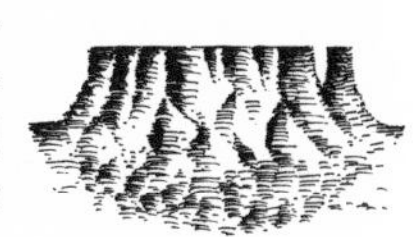

mescal (mehs . *kal'*) or **mezcal** a small bean or disc from the agave, aloe, or maguey plant (as it is named in the ancient Nahuatl language). Mescal buttons are dried and chewed as a stimulant, cooked as a vegetable, fermented into a drink, administered as an antispasmodic, or eaten as a hallucinogen in lengthy prayer services among desert Indian tribes. The resulting trance or vision from mescal consumption is a significant contrast to the use of *soma*, a major tranquilizer for Popé and Linda, village outcasts in Aldous Huxley's *Brave New World. See also* peyote.

mesmerism (*mehz'* muhr . izm) a form of hypnotism, spellbinding, or desensitization to pain resulting from the influence of a mesmerist, hypnotist, or psychotherapist over a willing subject. Derived from its practitioner, Franz Anton Mesmer, a German physician, in 1784, the term precedes the psychopathology of Jean Charcot and Dr. Sigmund Freud, who soothed or eased distraught patients through hypnotic trance. The Duke and the King consider a joint effort at patent medicine selling, acting, mesmerism, and phrenology in Mark Twain's *The Adventures of Huckleberry Finn. See also* phrenology.

mesquite (meh . *skeet'*) a large family of prickly shrubs or plants in the pea family and common to the deserts of the southwestern United States. A useful plant, mesquite attracts honeybees and provides forage for livestock and seeds and berries for food, ointment, dye, and glue. Mesquite flour can be made into dumplings, hot cereal, desserts, thickeners for soup, and beer. The milieu of Rudolfo Anaya's *Bless Me, Ultima* is desert land covered with juniper, mesquite, and yucca.

Messiah (muh . *sy'* uh) a savior, warrior, liberator, champion, or leader of oppressed peoples, as predicted by the prophet Isaiah in the Old Testament and identified as Jesus Christ in the New Testament. Derived from the Aramaic for *anointed one,* the term dates to Jewish antiquity. In Elie Wiesel's autobiographical *Night,* the situation among Jews in concentration camps grows so desperate that they predict that the long-awaited Messiah is coming.

mess kit a compact or nested cooking and eating container fitted with utensils and used in the field by campers and soldiers, who take charge of washing and storing their own gear. Internees in Jeanne Wakatsuki Houston and James D. Houston's *Farewell to Manzanar* receive mess kits like those issued to soldiers.

metaphysics (*meh* . tuh . *fih'* ziks) the basis of knowledge; the study of where matter came from, how the universe was made, and how human intelligence can comprehend the immensity of nature. Entering English in the mid-sixteenth century, the term derives from a title by Aristotle. In William Shakespeare's *The Taming of the Shrew,* Tranio advises his master Lucentio to speak on mathematics and metaphysics only if he feels he can give a good impression of his knowledge.

miasma (my . *as'* muh) a poisonous, noxious, toxic, or infectious vapor or exhalation arising from the decaying or putrefying plant and animal matter in a swamp, fen, quagmire, or bog. A late seventeenth-century term, it derives from the Greek for *pollute.* The doctor from Lancaster County in Conrad Richter's *The Light in the Forest* believes that Indians die in large numbers from the pollutants found in miasmas.

Michaelmas (*mih'* kuhl . muhs) September 29, celebrated in the Catholic Church as the Feast of Michael the Archangel and observed in the British Isles during the Middle Ages as the end of the third quarter of a fiscal year, when quarterly payments on loans were due. The other three pay days were Lady Day (March 25), Midsummer Day (June 24), and Christmas Day (December 25). In Emily Brontë's *Wuthering Heights,* Cathy Linton grows pensive after Michaelmas because she must exercise but misses her father's companionship. *See also* Good Friday; Lady Day.

microfilm photographic film used for the preservation of lengthy texts or periodicals in tiny portions that can be accessed through magnification on microfilm readers. A technology dating to the 1930s, microfilm has been largely supplanted by microfiche, computer disks, and compact disks, which are capable of storing much more in a smaller space and of reproducing color and sound. Microfilm is often used to store data or documents in a fireproof vault or underground depository to protect information during war or from fire, industrial espionage, or theft. Granger explains to Guy Montag, protagonist in Ray Bradbury's *Fahrenheit 451,* that the book people chose to memorize texts rather than trust their chosen works to microfilm.

middleman a trader, intermediary, agent, jobber, or dealer who purchases goods, raw materials, or commodities from a producer, such as a mine owner, drover, or farmer, then transports, packages, and sells them for profit to a consumer or retailer who often lives at a distance from the products' source; a profiteer, entrepreneur, investor, distributor, or go-between. In Pearl S. Buck's *The Good Earth,* Wang Lung hesitates to approach the Old Lord on business without employing the services of a middleman. In the purchase of Lotus, Wang Lung's "middleman" is a woman.

militia (muh . *lish'* uh) a local fighting force raised from nonmilitary populations and kept on call during emergencies. The purpose of a militia is to supplement or undergird a professional army. During the 1770s, local militiamen in colonial New England, called minutemen, stood ready in case of attack by British Redcoats. Henry David Thoreau, in his famous essay "Civil Disobedience," rails against the citizen's loss of individuality under the control of soldiers, the militia, jailers, constables, and other military types.

millet (*mihl'* liht) a long-spiked, drought-resistant cereal grass resembling cattails and cultivated worldwide for flatbread, porridge, beer, hay, birdseed, or forage. Derived from the Greek for *grain,* the term dates to the fifteenth century; the grain itself has been domesticated since the Stone Age. In Edith Hamilton's *Mythology,* Venus requires Psyche to separate a heap of millet, poppy, and wheat seeds.

mill house cheap, flimsy housing provided free or at low rent by a factory owner to entice landless or homeless workers to live in the mill village, remain loyal to their jobs, and depend on the good will of the mill hierarchy, who maintains a close watch on workers' lives and behavior. Lightfoot, Will Tweedy's friend in Olive Ann Burns's *Cold Sassy Tree,* lives in a mill house that he describes as better than most, but still unadorned and depressing.

mill-weir *See* **weir**.

mince pie a hot tart, deep-fried sweetmeat, or deep, top-crusted pie filled with finely chopped meat, fat, or suet blended with sugar, spice, rum or brandy, candied citrus peel, nuts, raisins, currants, and chopped apples, oranges, pineapple, or other fruit. While observing Christmas past in Charles Dickens's *A Christmas Carol*, Ebenezer Scrooge watches his old friends dancing and eating roast, cake, and mince pies washed down with beer.

minstrel (*mihn'* str'l) a white actor, singer, instrumentalist, or dancer wearing blackface, patched costumes, and white gloves and performing stylized clownish antics, impersonations, comic patter, and repartee that mimicked the stereotypically superstitious, simple-witted "pickaninny" or "darky." After the Civil War, black performers formed their own minstrel troupes that perpetuated faulty, sentimental glimpses of plantation life and smoothed over the anguish of slavery with pleasing banter and buffoonery. Mark Twain's *Life on the Mississippi* recalls the ambitions of local children to join a Negro minstrel show, a forerunner of vaudeville. *See also* Jim Crow laws.

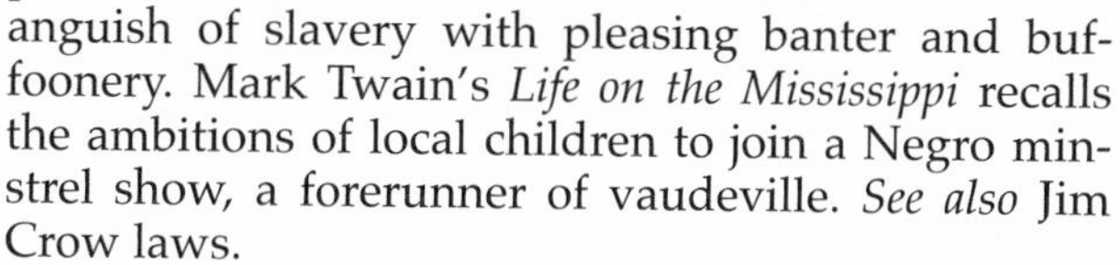

minuteman *See* militia.

miraculous Virgin a local Catholic shrine in Loreto, a town on the eastern coast of southern Baja California. Pilgrims come to be blessed or healed by a statue of Nuestra Señora de Loreto, established by Padre Juan Maria Salvatierra in a mission on October 25, 1697, and severely shaken by earthquake, after which the chapel and tower were rebuilt. The Museo de Las Misiones de Baja California contains sacred manuscripts detailing the significance of the miraculous Virgin. On his way to the capital city to sell his giant pearl, Kino, focal character in John Steinbeck's *The Pearl*, takes the path that leads north to Loreto, the shrine of the miraculous Virgin.

miso (*mee'* soh) a protein-rich puree, soup, or sauce that is a staple in Japanese cuisine. Miso is made from cooked or fermented soya, rice malt, or barley; salt; and water. Over a fire near the warehouse, Ko cooks a scanty meal of miso soup from rice and water in Yoko Kawashima Watkins's *So Far from the Bamboo Grove*.

mizzen-top or **mizen-top** (*mihz'* z'n . *tahp*) the upper tip of the third or sternward mast on a three-masted ship. A fifteenth-century term, the word derives from the Latin for *middle*. The title character in Herman Melville's *Billy Budd* performs so well that Lieutenant Ratliffe considers appointing him captain of the mizzen-top as a replacement for the Dansker, an aging, less agile sailor.

moat (moht) a water-filled ditch, trench, canal, or encircling stream used as a protective barrier around a manor, town, zoo enclosure, or the rampart of a fort; also, a lake, sluiceway, or irrigation pond alongside planted fields. Derived from the Middle English for *hill*, the term entered English in the Middle Ages. Equality 7-2521 spies the Golden One kneeling in a moat in the field she tends in *Anthem*, Ayn Rand's dystopian fable.

molasses a viscous brown syrup boiled from raw sugar, beets, or sap crushed from sorghum stalks. The bottom grade, blackstrap, is a brown-to-black, strong-flavored liquid that is used in fodder for winter feeding of livestock or as a base for making rum. Blackstrap was once the mark of the poorest southerners, who ate it on bread, grits, or rice when there was nothing else to flavor a bland diet. A late sixteenth-century term, the word derives from the Latin for *honey*. In his autobiography, *Narrative of the Life of Frederick Douglass*, the author describes how masters cured slaves of stealing molasses by making them eat a quantity large enough to cause sickness. *See also* sorghum.

molly apple *See* May apple.

Molotov (*mah'* luh . tahv) **cocktail** a homemade incendiary bomb or crude antitank grenade composed of a breakable jar or bottle filled with a flammable liquid and stoppered with a rag wick. The user lights the fuel-soaked wick and lobs the cocktail at a target. Named for a Soviet statesman, the term entered English in the early days of World War II. In William Dean Myers's *Fallen Angels*, soldiers joke about making Molotov cocktails from insect repellent.

Molotov flower basket a container loaded with a cluster of smaller explosives that spread over a wide range when the basket explodes. A weapon dating to World War II, the Molotov flower basket was designed as an antipersonnel weapon meant to injure, maim, or incapacitate. Dr. Fujii, one of the subjects of John Hersey's *Hiroshima*, surmises that the bomb blast that leveled the city must have been a Molotov flower basket. *See also* Molotov cocktail.

moly (*moh'* lee) in Greek mythology, a magical white-flowered, black-rooted perennial, possibly a healing herb or bulb such as rue, cyclamen, garlic, golden allium, or squill. The colors, similar to the Oriental concept of yin/yang, suggest a symbolic plant combining the opposing forces of good and evil. In Homer's *Odyssey,* Odysseus receives moly from Hermes, messenger of the gods, who helps the seafarer to recover a luckless party of sailors whom the enchantress Circe has transformed into swine. *See also* yin/yang.

momzer or **momser** or **mamzer** (*mahm'* zuhr) *pl.* **momzerim** a scurrilous Hebrew term denoting bastardy, illegitimacy, or the offspring of an incestuous relationship. Of Ashkenazi origin, the term can carry a twist of wry humor, implying that the momzer is a shrewd or wily character or trickster. After the batter intentionally collides with the second baseman in Chaim Potok's *The Chosen,* Sidney calls the batter a momzer.

monocle (*mah'* nuh . k'l) a single eyeglass held in place by the muscles of the eye socket. When not in use or when replaced by a lens of a different strength for close or distant vision, the monocle fits into a vest or coat pocket with its strap on the outside for quick retrieval. Fashionable for men in the early nineteenth century, the monocle was replaced by double-lens pince-nez glasses; for theater and sporting wear, the myopic turned to the lorgnon or lorgnette. A hybrid term, the word derives from the Greek for *one* and the Latin for *eye.* In Elie Wiesel's *Night,* the notorious Dr. Josef Mengele sports a monocle and carries a baton as he examines concentration camp internees to determine who is strong enough to work and who must die. *See also* lorgnette; pince nez.

monolith (*mah'* noh . lihth) a single huge, impressive rock, obelisk, or rough-hewn block of stone used in early architecture as a marker or column; a menhir, often set with others in a circle to mark an outdoor temple or worship center. A mid-nineteenth century architectural term, the word derives from the Greek for *single stone* and refers to the unshaped or crudely carved uprights of Stonehenge. In a letter to Sherlock Holmes in Sir Arthur Conan Doyle's *The Hound of the Baskervilles,* Dr. Watson reports the grim charm of the moors with their craggy monoliths. *See also* lintel.

monstrance a gold or silver container or receptacle in which the host or consecrated wafer is stored during the act of consecration that precedes communion or the Eucharist; also, a glass-covered shrine or case on a stand holding for public display and veneration a holy relic, such as a garment, hair, or bone fragments of a saint. A fifteenth-century term, the word derives from the Latin for *show.* The parochial school students in James Joyce's *A Portrait of the Artist as a Young Man* wonder if a miscreant has dared to steal a monstrance to sell.

Montenegro (*mahn* . tuh . *nay'* groh) a Serbo-Croatian republic in southern Yugoslavia founded in the twelfth century and bordered by Albania, the Adriatic Sea, and the Dinaric Alps. Named for Monte Nero, the Black Mountain, the republic encompasses 5,333 square miles. In F. Scott Fitzgerald's *The Great Gatsby,* Nick learns that the title character earned a military award from Montenegro for valor during World War I.

moochie or **mooche** or **moochi** (*moo'* chee) or **peckin'** a lively dance invented in black jooks and roadhouses during the early 1900s in which couples bobbed heads and pecked at each other's neck while grinding hips to erotic ragtime. Similar to its successors—the shimmy, Charleston, and ballin' the jack—the moochie encouraged extravagant, rhythmic self-expression and formed the basis for later inventions, notably the camel walk, truckin', shag, suzi-q, Lindy hop, and jitterbug. Duke Ellington's "The Mooche," written in 1929, was popularized by his orchestra's widespread performances. As described by Shug Avery in Alice Walker's *The Color Purple,* Albert could dance the moochie for an hour. *See also* jook.

moon cake a Chinese New Year's treat made from pork fat, sugar, and rice flour, which is kneaded and flattened into round white cookies resembling the moon. In Maxine Hong Kingston's *The Woman Warrior,* holiday diners eat long noodles and moon cakes, the same confection that O-lan makes to celebrate the New Year after the birth of her first son in Pearl S. Buck's *The Good Earth.*

moonstone a pearly, milky-blue, silvery, or iridescent semiprecious gemstone; a lustrous, translucent feldspar with a silica sheen; also opal, one of the June birthstones. When Guy Montag, protagonist of Ray Bradbury's *Fahrenheit 451,* peers down at Mildred, he sees moonstones in place of eyes because she has taken an overdose of a sleeping potion and is near death.

moor a grassy, infertile tract of peaty wetland relatively free of shrubs and trees; a barrens, fen, wasteland, or heath characteristic of the British Isles; also, an uncultivated tract preserved as shooting grounds for small game, grouse, or pheasants. In Gothic settings, such as Charlotte Brontë's *Jane Eyre* and Sir Arthur Conan Doyle's *The Hound of the Baskervilles,* moors provide a misty, dismal, or spooky atmosphere. *See also* bracken; heath; heather.

moose-bird a crested gray Canadian jay, kin to the raven, crow, and magpie; the whisky jack or gray-jay. The moose-bird eats seeds, grubs, and insects; builds a compact round nest; and, like the mockingbird, is known for its ability to imitate the calls of other birds. In Jack London's *White Fang,* the pup cuffs a moose-bird and gets a peck on the nose.

morocco (moh . *rahk'* koh) a fine, soft leather covering featuring a delicate pebbly grain and used for books, picture frames, and other collectors' items. Originally, morocco was a flexible, durable goatskin or lambskin tanned rust-red with sumac and used for making shoes, bags, purses, luggage, whips, and gloves. An early seventeenth-century term, it derives from the country in northwestern Africa. In John Steinbeck's *The Red Pony,* Jody's father gives him a pony and a saddle covered in morocco leather.

morphine (*mohr'* feen or mohr . *feen'*) a bitter, crystalline alkaloid emetic, painkiller, and narcotic extracted from the sticky sap of the immature seed case of the opium poppy and converted into codeine or heroin, a more potent form. Synthetic versions used in hospitals are dispensed under the labels Demerol or Methadone. Isolated in 1806 by Friedrich W. A. Sertürner, a German chemist, the drug was named for Morpheus, the Greek god of sleep. It is useful for surgical and terminally ill patients or people experiencing chronic pain; however, its euphoric, depressive effect is addictive. When Jurgis locates Marija in Upton Sinclair's *The Jungle,* her pallor and fragility give evidence of addiction to morphine.

mortice or **mortise** (*mohr'* tihs) a rectangular slot, groove, or hole cut to receive the tenon, or tab, at the end of a piece of lumber or stone to produce an interlocking or dovetailed joint or to receive a rope or pin. In Abraham Lincoln's "The House Divided" speech delivered after the Dred Scott decision of 1857, Lincoln refers to the tight mortice and tenon joints that frame a sturdy building, a metaphor for the kind of nation he envisions for the future.

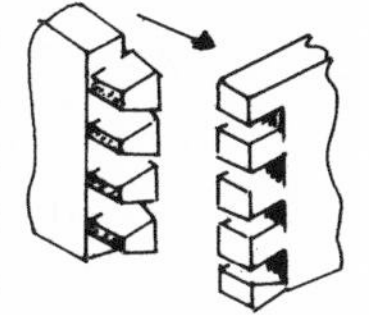

Mosaic (moh . *zay'* ik) **Law** the Ten Commandments, or decalogue, revealed by Yahweh to Moses on Mount Sinai and held sacred and binding by Jews and Christians. Enumerated in Exodus 20 and Deuteronomy 5, these ethical laws were all-inclusive governers of human behavior and are recorded on two stone tablets. They direct followers to honor God, make no graven images or blaspheme; observe the Sabbath; and refrain from killing, stealing, adultery, giving false testimony, coveting others' possessions, and dishonoring parents. After prayer in Mark Twain's *The Adventures of Tom Sawyer,* Aunt Polly delivers a sermon on Mosaic Law from Mount Sinai.

mosque (mahsk) a hall or covered area used by Muslims for prayer, readings from the Koran, or public worship. The mosque may also house libraries, halls of justice, lecture rooms, and refuges offering political asylum. Derived from the Arabic for *place of prostration,* the term entered English in the early eighteenth century. After his break with the Black Muslims in Alex Haley's *The Autobiography of Malcolm X,* the title character forms the Muslim Mosque, Inc., in Harlem. *See also* Allah; Hajj; Koran.

mosquito bar a weighted bar, bamboo, or ledge attached to mosquito netting, a gauzy, semipermeable curtain, with ropes or ties. In areas where malaria, dengue fever, and other insect-borne disease is prevalent, the mosquito bar unrolls or drapes over a bed, sleeping porch, hammock, or crib to hold the fabric in place in breezy weather and to keep insects from entering at the lower edge. Madame Antoine lets down the mosquito bar after Edna Pontellier falls asleep in Kate Chopin's *The Awakening.*

Mother Hubbard a loose, shapeless housedress, work dress, tunic, or gown shaped like a muumuu with square neck attached to gathered, unbelted folds that hang straight or flared and provide room for easy movement. Named for a character in a Mother Goose rhyme, the term entered English in the late nineteenth century and describes a floor-length garment that missionaries forced newly converted Pacific island women to wear in place of topless grass skirts. In John Steinbeck's *The Grapes of Wrath,* Tom, newly returned from prison, sees his mother dressed in a Mother Hubbard so old that the colored flowers have turned gray.

mountebank a seller of fraudulent medicines, tonics, cures, and nostrums; a hawker, alchemist, vendor, or quack who pretends to be a doctor or pharmacist. The term, which entered English in the late sixteenth century, describes the behavior of a con artist or huckster who stood on a bench and shouted, gestured, or demonstrated the effects of a product to persuade passersby to purchase or sample wares.

Thenardier accuses Monsieur Leblanc of being a mountebank for pretending to be penniless in Victor Hugo's *Les Misérables.*

mourners' bench a front church pew or section reserved for troubled people who pray for deliverance from illness, debt, worry, alcohol or drugs, wayward children, guilt over past misdeeds, and other personal problems. As mentioned in Maya Angelou's *I Know Why the Caged Bird Sings*, the mourners' bench placed these sufferers in front of other worshipers, who could observe their grief and join them in prayer.

mouth harp *See* jew's harp.

mow (moh) a grain heap, pile of straw, cornshock, or haystack; a lean-to, loft, or shed for storing grain sheaves, hay, straw, or fodder. Derived in the early Middle Ages from the Old Norse for *heap*, the term describes a method of drying and preserving grain before the advent of balers. True Son, protagonist of Conrad Richter's *The Light in the Forest*, leads Half Arrow to a mow where he has hidden a bearskin, rifle, meal, lead balls, and powder.

moxa (*mahk'* suh) the leaves of mugwort, also known as artemisia or wormwood, that herbal healers burn in a treatment called moxibustion, which combines with acupuncture to deliver pain relief to energy points distributed throughout the body. Practitioners of Asian herbal medicine, as described in Amy Tan's *The Kitchen God's Wife*, use moxibustion as a curative, soothing therapy, muscle relaxant, or cauterizing agent. *See also* acupuncturist; herbal medicine.

Mrunas black people, or African or Caribbean Negroes, who were often classified by the pejorative maroons or marinies. A variant spelling of maroon, the term derives from the Spanish *cimarron*, a wild horse that escapes a corral. In the late nineteenth century, a gang of Jamaican maroons terrorized owners and overseers of sugar plantations. Mrs. Merriweather, one of the ladies gathered for missionary study in Harper Lee's *To Kill a Mockingbird*, tells Scout about the pathetic Mrunas.

M-16 the standard issue air-cooled, 7.6-pound weapon of the Vietnam War, a .223 caliber automatic or semiautomatic rifle fed by a 20- or 30-round detachable magazine and gas operated. Named Model 16, the abbreviated term has appeared in military literature and film since the 1970s. In Walter Dean Myers's *Fallen Angels*, soldiers polish the barrels of their M-16s with carbon tetrachloride to remove corrosion. *See also* magazine.

muff a soft tube of fur or padded velvet, silk, or other decorative cloth into which girls or women thrust their hands to keep them warm and dry. A sixteenth-century invention, the muff was briefly carried by men as well as women; by the eighteenth century, the muff became an elegant female item of fashion, often suspended from the neck by a braided silk cord and decorated with beading, smocking, ribbons, ruching, lace, or feathers. After a terrifying mishap with a bull, Elizabeth-Jane returns to the barn to fetch Lucetta's muff in Thomas Hardy's *The Mayor of Casterbridge.*

mufti (*muhf'* tee) unofficial or civilian clothing worn by military personnel, police, or clergy who choose to be out of uniform or ritual dress, either as a disguise, for traveling incognito, or in violation of regulations. Entering English in the early nineteenth century, the term derives inexplicably from the Arabic for *Muslim jurist*. Nurse Ferguson in Ernest Hemingway's *A Farewell to Arms* recognizes that Frederick Henry is in mufti for illicit reasons.

muktuk (*muhk'* tuhk) or **maktak** a light, nutty, sweet blubber found beneath the hide of a beluga or baleen whale. Eskimo preparers slice the delicate fat, soak it all summer in seal oil, then eat it cooked or frozen. An Inuit term, it entered English in the early nineteenth century. Oogruk, a key figure in Gary Paulsen's *Dogsong*, asks Russel for muktuk, which the villagers lack because they haven't killed a whale in a year.

mulatto an equal mix of white and black races, usually Caucasian and Negro; also, the first generation sired by mixed parentage. Depending on point of view (Caribbean, Cajun, European, or South American), the term can be either a pejorative, racial slur, status symbol, or elitism. Derived from the Latin for *mule*, the term entered English in the late sixteenth century. In Zora Neale Hurston's *Their Eyes Were Watching God*, Janie applies *mulatto* as a pejorative description of rice, a blend of plain and wild varieties sometimes known as "dirty rice."

mull to blend heated cider, ale, or fruit punch with sugar, whipped egg white, flavorings, and crushed aromatic spices. Spiced drinks were often heated by plunging a hot poker into the ewer or individual mugs. A questionable derivation of this term is the Latin for *soften*. At the Earnshaw house in Emily Brontë's *Wuthering Heights*, polished silver tankards await the pouring of mulled ale for holiday guests. *See also* flip; tankard.

mullion (*muhl'* yuhn) a decorative upright, slender bar tracery, ornate column, or vertical divider in a glass window or screen, particularly those in Gothic style. A mid-sixteenth-century architectural term, the word may derive from the Old French for *middle.* Baskerville Hall, the setting of Sir Arthur Conan Doyle's *The Hound of the Baskervilles,* gleams in the distance from light through mullioned windows.

multiple sclerosis (skluh . *roh'* sihs) or **MS** a debilitative nerve disease that results from depletion of myelin, the fatty insulation that pads the outer surface of nerves. MS, which is often triggered by infection or trauma during the victim's young adulthood, results in loss of sensation and balance, weakness, impaired vision, paralysis, and mental breakdown. According to Amy Tan's *The Kitchen God's Wife,* Pearl hopes to live a normal life but realizes that multiple sclerosis can quickly progress to lethal proportions.

mumbledypeg or **mumbletypeg** (*muhm'* duhl . dee . *pehg*) or **knifey** a game of skill requiring the player to flip an open pocket knife, clasp knife, or jackknife handle up into the ground or at a target, such as a log, wood, or the space between bare toes. Entering English in the early seventeenth century, the term derives from the removal of the knife from a target with the teeth. In Maya Angelou's *I Know Why the Caged Bird Sings* and Laurence Yep's *Dragonwings,* children enjoy games of mumbledypeg.

Murphy bed *See* opklap bed.

muscadine a thick-skinned, speckled wild grape or raisin either greenish-gray or tan and native to North America; also, a James grape. In Europe, a musk-flavored muscatel used to make sweet, strong-bodied wine. Albert Cluveau, the murderous Cajun racist in Ernest Gaines's *The Autobiography of Miss Jane Pittman,* seems harmless as he shares coffee with Jane and buys buckets of figs, pecans, and muscadines from local children, yet remains adamant about killing Jane's son in retaliation for educating blacks.

musette (myoo . *zeht'*) a small canvas or leather shoulder bag or knapsack carried by soldiers, hikers, cyclists, and travelers as a container for food, tobacco, and personal items. A fourteenth-century term, the word derives from the French for *bagpipe* because of its resemblance to a small musical instrument. Frederick Henry has his rucksack and two musettes packed aboard a train from Turin to Milan in Ernest Hemingway's *A Farewell to Arms.*

muskeg (*muhs'* kehg) a fen or swamp composed of standing puddles, decaying plant matter, and moss; also, a crater or bowl-shaped depression that fills with water-logged debris resembling peat or sphagnum moss. An early nineteenth-century term, the word derives from the Cree or Ojibwa term for *swamp.* In *Never Cry Wolf,* Farley Mowat tracks an animal across the boggy, chocolate-colored muskeg.

musket (*muhs'* kiht) an antique, lightweight, smoothbore shoulder rifle, such as a flintlock or matchlock, used by infantrymen. The musket was charged with gun powder and loaded with a lead ball or similar projectile, which the user fired from the shoulder at an average of four shots per minute and a range of 100 yards. The term derives from the Latin word for *housefly* and entered English in the late sixteenth century. In Jonathan Swift's *Gulliver's Travels,* Lemuel Gulliver compares the Lilliputians' tiny bread loaves to musket balls. In Esther Forbes's *Johnny Tremain,* militiamen scramble for squirrel guns, muskets, or any other weapon to defend themselves from the Redcoats. *See also* bayonet; flintlock; match.

mustang a short, wild, hardy, mixed-breed horse native to Mexico and the southwestern United States; a bronc, cayuse, or surefooted, sturdy cow pony, introduced to North American Indians by Spanish conquistadores and adaptable to desert terrain. A nineteenth-century word, the term derives from the Latin for *mixed.* Mattie Ross, the protagonist in Charles Portis's *True Grit,* sets out to settle her father's deal with a wily livestock agent selling Texas mustangs. *See also* cayuse.

mustard gas a lethally corrosive dichloro-diethyl sulfide poison introduced by the Germans against French and Canadian forces at Ypres near Flanders, Belgium, April 22, 1915, mustard gas altered international warfare. The gas depletes fluid from the blood by searing the alveoli, which are tiny pouches in the lungs. Watery discharge overwhelms the lungs, drowning the victim. As described in Erich Maria Remarque's *All Quiet on the Western Front,* the oily gas sinks into low-lying trenches and attacks exposed flesh. Soldiers fleeing the gas emerged from foxholes into the direct line of fire of machine guns, the most lethal weapon of World War I.

musulman or **musselman** or **mussulman** (*muhs' suhl . muhn*) an internee in a concentration camp who becomes withdrawn and flaccid after exhaustion, hunger, and work reduces all hope of survival and increases the likelihood of selection for the gas chambers and crematory. Derived from the Persian for *Muslim,* the term evolved in Nazi death camps during the late 1930s. In Elie Wiesel's *Night,* internees recognize which musulmen will be exterminated because they are useless, dying of malnutrition or dehydration, or infected with disease. *See also* holocaust.

muzzle the projecting jowls, nose, snout, or elongated part of the face of an animal, especially a horse, mule, or dog. Derived from Middle Latin for *snout,* the term entered English in the fifteenth century. When he recognizes that men intend to demolish the mill with blasting powder, Benjamin, a donkey in George Orwell's *Animal Farm,* wisely nods his muzzle as though he knows from experience what to expect.

myrtle a low-growing, richly scented evergreen; also the plant that scented the Garden of Eden. Mentioned in Edith Hamilton's *Mythology,* myrtle is the plant from which festal crowns are woven as honoraria for contest winners and insignia for dignitaries and honored guests. *See also* laurel.

N

naphtha (*naf'* thuh) a petroleum solvent and byproduct boiled from coal tar and made into degreasers, rubber and dry cleaning solvent, paint, varnish, and coarse, aromatic soap. Derived from the Persian for *bitumen,* the term entered English in the late sixteenth century and gained recognition in 1819 for turning rubber into a waterproofing solution for rainwear, overshoes, expedition gear, tents, and awnings. The speaker in Sandra Cisneros's *The House on Mango Street* describes Nenny as the dark brown color of the last bit of naphtha laundry soap. *See also* mackintosh.

naturalization papers the preliminary paperwork leading to application for citizenship. The U.S. Naturalization Law, introduced in 1790, requires a naturalized citizen to obtain lawful entry, remain five years, be of worthy character, understand rudimentary English, know the fundamentals of the Constitution, and reside for six months in the district in which application is made. A nightwatchman encourages Jurgis and other immigrants to take out naturalization papers in Upton Sinclair's *The Jungle.*

nave the central body or seating area of a cruciform, or cross-shaped, cathedral extending between aisles from narthex or lobby to the choir screen. The term, which entered English in the late seventeenth century, derives from the Latin for *ship* because the rafters look like the beams of a hull and remind worshippers that Christ promised to make his followers "fishers of men." At a significant moment in the rivalry between Mayor Henchard and Donald Farfrae in Thomas Hardy's *The Mayor of Casterbridge,* Henchard enters Farfrae's entertainment tent, which is sturdily built within the overlapping branches of trees like the nave of a cathedral.

nawab (nuh . *wahb'*) or **nabob** or **nob** a male member of India's privileged or noble class; an Indian lord or provincial governor. Also, an elite, princely Muslim. From the Urdu for *deputy,* the term entered English in the mid-eighteenth century, often with derogatory or unflattering racial implications. Ruth Prawer Jhabvala's *Heat and Dust* pictures the nawab as an unprincipled opportunist and bandit who seduces the wife of an English colonial officer by flattering her vanity and relieving her boredom as a forgotten wife in colonial India.

Nazi (*naht'* see) the German National Socialist party, a racist, totalitarian hegemony begun by Hitler in 1920. The oppressive party, which set out to exterminate individual rights, rose to supreme power in the period 1933–1945. Using heavy-handed fascist measures, the Nazis created a tight authoritarian domination over Germany and its subject states. Derived from *Nationalsozialist,* the shortened form was first used in 1930. In Thomas Keneally's *Schindler's List,* the title character predicts that the fall of the Nazi party will put Heinrich Himmler, Hitler's strongest supporter, behind bars. *See also* genocide; holocaust; SS.

neckcloth *See* cravat.

necromancer (*nehk'* roh . *man* . suhr) a wizard, sorcerer, or magician who studies forbidden lore, practices black magic, and communicates with the dead; a conjurer who predicts the future. Hybridized in the early sixteenth century, the term derives from the Greek for *black* and Latin for *divination.* In J. R. R. Tolkien's *The Hobbit,* Gandolf warns Bilbo Baggins to avoid the route to the south, which passes by the necromancer's black tower.

negus (*nee'* guhs) a hot punch made of watered port wine or sherry, sugar or honey, citrus juice, nutmeg, and other spices. Named for Francis Negus, an English army colonel, the term entered English in the mid-eighteenth century. When Mrs. Fairfax welcomes the title character of Charlotte Brontë's *Jane Eyre* to her new job as governess, she calls on Leah to pour Jane a cup of negus and make some sandwiches.

nereid *See* nymph.

nester a farmer, granger, or homesteader who disrupts the open grazing system and stirs up animosity with cattle ranchers by planting crops and fencing in livestock; a squatter who takes over an abandoned farm or cultivated land without securing formal permission, claim, title, or deed. In Charles Portis's *True Grit,* Mattie Ross is dismayed to learn that Rooster Cogburn has hired on with stockmen to harass and dispossess nesters and grangers. *See also* grange.

nether (*neh'* thur) **world** the land of the dead, often depicted as a murky, bottomless abyss of indescribable dimensions and atmosphere; the underworld or infernal regions; the place of everlasting torment for the damned, often depicted as Hades or hell. Derived from the Sanskrit for *down,* the term dates to the early Middle Ages. In *Gilgamesh,* Enkidu promises to bring up from the nether world the drum and drumstick that fell through a hole.

netting making mesh or coarse network from cord, rope, hemp, or thread for use as snoods and hair nets, shawls, window hangings, hammocks, or fish seines. Netted reticules displayed an external decorative netting revealing the bright color of a silk lining. The

netter used a shuttle to pass the material through the openings and to form decorative knots, often in contrasting colors. A sixteenth-century term, the word derives from the German for *seine.* Elizabeth-Jane possesses some skill in netting but has received little formal education in Thomas Hardy's *The Mayor of Casterbridge.* See *also* macramé.

neurasthenic (*noor* . as . *thee'* nihk or *nyoor* . as . *thee'* nihk) fatigued, irritable, debilitated, frail, or mentally drained by emotional unrest and psychosomatic illness, particularly headache, worry, joint pain, and nervousness. A mid-nineteenth century psychological term, the word originated from the Greek for *weakened nerves.* In Tennessee Williams's *A Streetcar Named Desire,* Blanche DuBois speaks in a neurasthenic voice robbed of life by exhaustion.

neurosis (nyoo . *roh'* sis) *pl.* **neuroses** a mental disorder or dysfunction marked by stressful, but not necessarily debilitating symptoms, including depression, anxiety, tension, hypochondria, malaise, phobia, sexual dysfunction, or mild instability. In Najib Mahfouz's "The Happy Man," the patient laughs when he recalls how the doctor used free association to reveal the patient's neuroses. *See also* psychoanalyst; psychosis.

newt (noot or nyoot) a small, orangy-red salamander marked by long, flat tail and spotted back. Considered harmless, the newt can be poisonous to animals that swallow it. Entering English in the fifteenth century, the term combines *an ewt,* an Old English name for the semiaquatic animal common to rocky streambeds and riverbanks. As Queen Titania sinks in slumber in William Shakespeare's *A Midsummer Night's Dream,* the hovering fairies shoo away hedgehogs, newts, and other obnoxious pests.

nib the split or honed end of a quill pen; a metal pen point, such as the varied and interchangeable styles of pen tips used in calligraphy. Also, the point of a fountain pen. A mid-sixteenth-century Norse term, the word appears to mean *beak.* Harry Butler scratches entries in his account book with the rough nib of a quill in Conrad Richter's *The Light in the Forest. See also* quill.

night bucket *See* slop jar.

nightcap a stocking cap or banded bonnet tied under the chin and worn by men or women to keep the head warm in unheated hallways and lavatories and drafty bedrooms. Charles Dickens's *Oliver Twist* refers to a particular nightcap worn by a condemned prisoner, which a guard pulls over the felon's face before the execution—a permanent state of night.

night-soil collectors sewage workers who remove human excrement from covered containers, cesspools, or privies and haul it away in wheelbarrows to be used on planted fields. In Amy Tan's *The Kitchen God's Wife,* protagonist Winnie Louie concludes that the Burmese method of composting sewage for fertilizer spreads cholera, dysentery, and typhoid fever.

nimbus (*nihm'* buhs) shortened form of cumulonimbus, a low-hanging gray or gray and slate-toned thundercloud that appears like heaps of lumpy, rounded, thick masses from 1 to 3 miles above sea level; the nimbostratus. The nimbus, which does not hide the sun completely, precedes drizzle, rain, sleet, or snow. Entering English in the early seventeenth century, the term derives from the Latin for *cloud.* In Sandra Cisneros's *The House on Mango Street,* children lie on their backs and study types of cumulus clouds and nimbus, the rain cloud.

nine men's morris a shepherd's game popular in Europe during the Middle Ages. Played like tic-tac-toe on a pattern of three concentric squares linked by several intersecting lines laid out on the lawn or village commons, the participants must get three markers or stones in a row. The term derives from *Moorish* and resembles the morris dance, a ritual folk dance common to court masques. In William Shakespeare's *A Midsummer Night's Dream,* Queen Titania promises weather so bad that it will spoil the nine men's morris field.

Nirvana (nuhr . *vah'* nuh) the Hindu concept of heaven or mystical cosmos; the goal of an earthly cycle of births, deaths, and reincarnations. Nirvana, a Sanskrit term meaning *blowing outward,* is the merger of self with the universe through yielding or giving in to the unending flow of suffering and joy, which ultimately merges into pure energy. The unity of self with otherworldliness relieves the soul of its yearnings. A transcendent state, nirvana requires that the seeker realize the true simplicity of the divine. By locating the individual path to oneness with the universe, the seeker abstains from sensuality, pride, and emotion and welcomes eternal truth as past, present, and future lose their meaning. At the outset of their search for a transcendent state, the title character in Hermann Hesse's *Siddhartha* doubts that he and his friend Govinda will achieve Nirvana.

nisei (*nee'* say) first-generation Americans born of emigrant Japanese parents. Derived from the Japanese for *second generation,* the term entered English in the late 1920s. Jeanne Wakatsuki Houston and James D. Houston's *Farewell to Manzanar* describes the attitudes and difficulties of Jeanne and other Japanese-American children who are born to issei parents, but who must cope with American lifestyles. *See also* issei; sansei.

nob *See* **nawab.**

noddy a general term for sea bird. Derived from a pejorative English word for *fumbling,* the term entered English in the early sixteenth century and applies to a bird so unalert that it can be caught by hand. In Herman Melville's *Benito Cereno,* the noddy perched on the *San Dominick*'s ratlines symbolizes the slipshod condition of a once noble vessel. *See also* tern.

noggin a small mug, cup, flagon, or drinking vessel; also, a bartender's container that measures a gill or a quarter of a pint. Of Gaelic origin, the term dates to the mid-seventeenth century and has mutated from a term denoting the head of a drunkard to a generic word for *head.* In Robert Louis Stevenson's *Treasure Island,* Mr. Bones breaks Dr. Trelawny's orders and demands that Jim bring him a "noggin o' rum."

nonce-rules (nahns) regulations created on the spur of the moment or for a limited period of use; impromptu or temporary legalities that suit the occasion and are therefore virtually meaningless. A medieval term, the word *nonce* is kin to *once.* In John Gardner's *Grendel,* the dragon ponders the continual scheming of the human mind to create new sets of nonce-rules.

non-com (*nahn'* kahm) a subordinate, noncommissioned officer of low rank in the army, air force, or marines; one who earns the rank of sergeant rather than receive it through privilege, wealth, favoritism, nepotism, or appointment. The abbreviated term entered English in the late nineteenth century. The lieutenant in Erich Maria Remarque's *All Quiet on the Western Front* is more understanding of the soldiers because he is a non-com who came up from the ranks.

nonnette (nahn . *neht'*) a novice, beginner, neophyte, female postulant, or new entrant into a religious order or convent. Entering English in medieval times, the term originated in the feminine form of the Latin for *monk.* Because the title character in Charlotte Brontë's *Jane Eyre* gazes demurely downward and remains serious and unobtrusive, Rochester thinks of her as a nonnette. *See also* novice.

Nordic of or relating to Scandinavian, Germanic, or Northern European peoples in general; Aryan. Derived from the Old English for *north,* the term entered English in the late nineteenth century when philosophers justified colonialism, European domination over dark-skinned people, as a natural right of Nordic people, who had supposedly evolved quicker wits and refinement from their origins in cool climes. Tom Buchanan is obsessed with the survival of the Nordic race in F. Scott Fitzgerald's *The Great Gatsby. See also* Aryan.

normal school a two-year training academy or college to prepare high school graduates to become teachers for elementary schools. Named for the French *école normale,* the term dates to the mid-nineteenth century and prevailed in the United States until the 1930s. Lady Jones, teacher of the local elementary school for black children in Toni Morrison's *Beloved,* was chosen to attend a Negro normal school in Pennsylvania because she had light skin.

nosegay a small bundle of blossoms mixed with herbs and pungent greenery and wrapped in tissue to protect the hands and clothes from staining; a colorful, fragrant lapel bouquet, posy, or boutonnière worn in a man's top coat or suit coat. The court officials in Charles Dickens's *Great Expectations* carry nosegays to overcome the body odor of prisoners and to ward off disease, particularly typhus or "jail fever."

nouveau riche (*noo* . voh . *reesh'*) *pl.* ***nouveaux riches*** a prejorative term referring to vulgar, tasteless, flashy people who have recently acquired wealth, but have none of the graces or manners of people who have always enjoyed a genteel lifestyle and have no reason to show off their money or position. A visitor to Sherlock Holmes in Sir Arthur Conan Doyle's *The Hound of the Baskervilles* comments that, in the days of the *nouveaux riches,* it is refreshing to find humbled nobles who are willing to work hard to restore the good name of their families.

novena (noh . *vee'* nuh) an intense Roman Catholic ritual or devotional; a public or private prayer addressed to the Virgin Mary or the saints over a period of nine consecutive days as a petition for grace, a favor, or intercession in an urgent matter, such as healing or making a difficult decision; as thanksgiving; or as a preparation for a feast, saint's day, or celebration, such as Pentecost. A standard ritual since the mid-nineteenth century, the word derives from the Latin for *nine* and represents the nine days that Christ's disciples waited and prayed for the coming of the Holy Spirit, as described in Luke 24:49 and Acts 1:4. The observance also reflects the ancient Roman nine-day period of mourning. The priest in James Joyce's *A Portrait of the Artist as a Young Man* urges Stephen to say a novena to his patron saint to help him find a suitable vocation.

novice (*nah'* vihs) a convert, postulant, or probationer in a religious house who is contemplating lifelong vows of chastity, poverty, and obedience as the bride of Christ; a young nun or sister who has just entered a Roman Catholic convent. Derived from the Latin for *new*, the term originated in the Middle Ages. Blanca, a spirited young woman in Isabel Allende's *The House of the Spirits*, threatens to enter a convent as a novice rather than submit to a marriage proposal from the Count, a pompous elitist and poseur.

numbers runner an agent of small-time criminals or racketeers who collects money from people who bet on a lucky number in a daily lottery drawn from the stock quotation or other posted numerals. In Maya Angelou's *I Know Why the Caged Bird Sings,* Maya and Bailey Junior see their first street criminals and numbers runners in St. Louis during a visit to their mother.

nymph (nihmf) a semidivine nature goddess, sprite, nereid, or minor deity of mountains, streams, hills, or trees; one of the lovely young beauties or personifications of nature in Greek literature who are often the quarry of lustful satyrs. A term entering English in the fourteenth century, it originated from the Greek for *bride.* Book I of Homer's *Iliad* pictures Hera's jealousy of the winsome sea nymph Thetis, who petitions Zeus to intervene on behalf of her son Achilles. *See also* satyr.

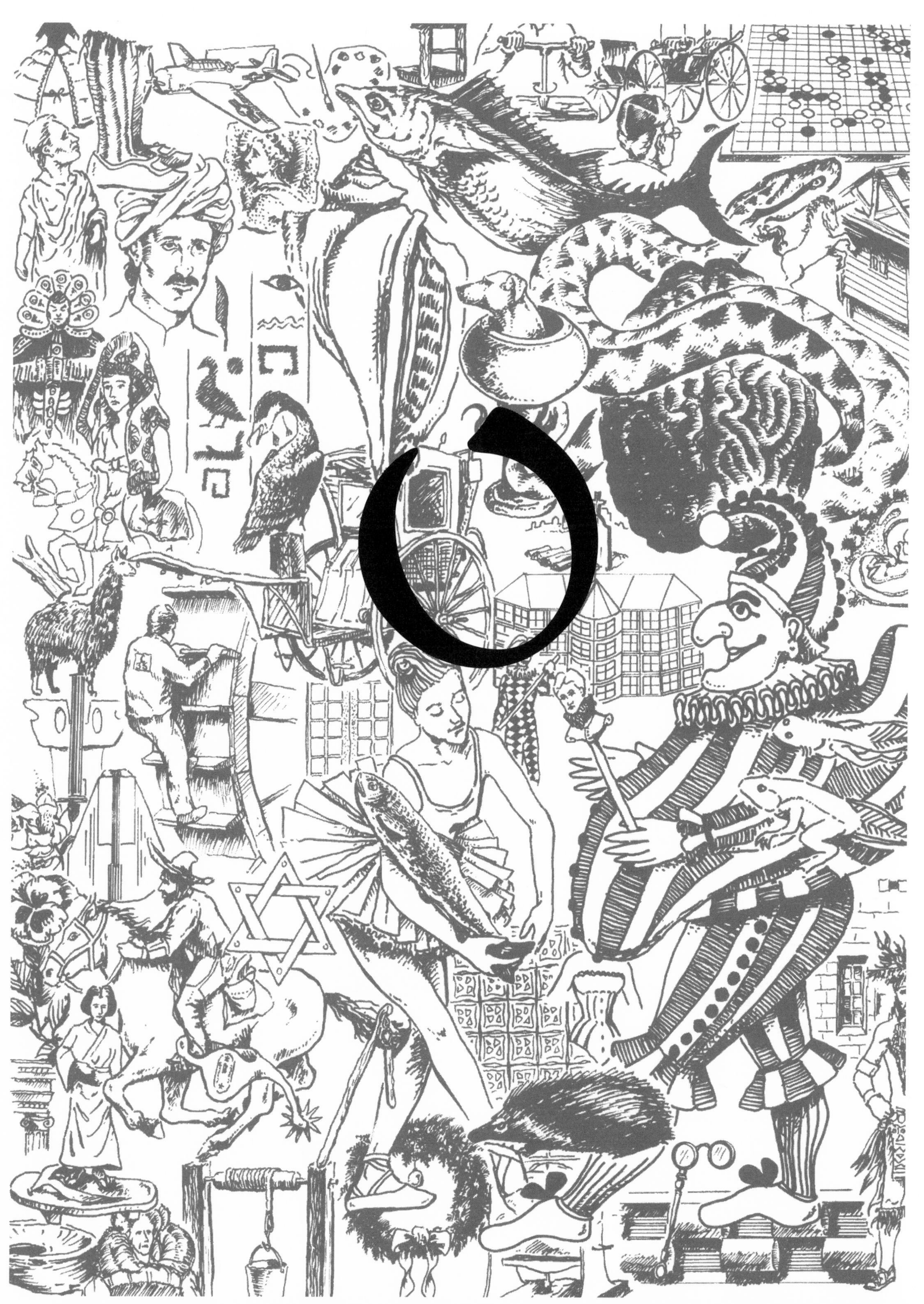

oakum (*oh'* kuhm) waste fibers recycled from discarded rope or cording that are untwisted, soaked in tar, and used to fill cracks and stop leaks in a boat before additional caulking is applied. Oakum was also valued in naval infirmaries and military aid stations as lint or packing to stop hemorrhaging from deep wounds. Entering English in the Middle Ages, the term originated from the Anglo-Saxon term for *comb out*. In Herman Melville's *Benito Cereno,* picking and sorting oakum—the lowliest, dirtiest, and most repetitive work—is assigned to black slaves. *See also* awl; caulking.

oarlocks paired U-shaped staples or lashings on a boat's gunwale where oars are anchored between thole pins and operated by the rower like levers to lift water and propel the vessel either forward or back; rowlocks. Entering English in the eleventh century, the term reflects the Anglo-Saxon tendency to form technical terms from two common words, in this case *oar* and *lock*. On his appearance at Odysseus's hall in Homer's *Odyssey,* the suitors mock Telemachus and suggest selling his guests into slavery by putting in "vessels with many oarlocks" and rowing them to Sicily, presumably to a Mediterranean slave market. *See also* thole pin.

obi (*oh'* bee) the Igbo term for a segment of a Nigerian compound or a thatch-roofed hut suitable for a single occupant, particularly a wife of lower status than the head wife. Also, a Japanese term for a broad cummerbund or sash, often of contrasting color from the kimono or traditional robe it binds or belts. In Chinua Achebe's *Things Fall Apart,* the obi is a single dwelling in Okonkwo's compound. In Kawabata Yasunari's "The Jay," Grandmother looks intently at Yoshiko's kimono and obi. *See also* compound; kimono.

obsidian (uhb . *sih'* dee . uhn) a green-black, gray, red, or clear volcanic silicate turned to a compact glassiness suitable for use in jewelry, mirrors, ritual blades, utility knives, skinning tools, and weapon points. In ancient times, obsidian items were valuable trade items in many parts of the world, particularly among many Native Americans. The vitreous substance bears the name of its mythic Greek discoverer, Obsius. In Aldous Huxley's *Brave New World,* the wrinkled old Indian's face resembles an obsidian mask.

occipital bone (ahk . *sihp'* pih . tuhl) the convex bone at the lower rear of the skull through which the spinal cord passes. The strong plate protects the cerebellum and medulla oblongata; the two bony lumps at each side help the neck bone to move freely. From the Latin for *against the head,* the term entered English medical vocabulary in the mid-seventeenth century. Yearning for revenge against the man who killed his father, the title character in Alexandre Dumas's *The Count of Monte Cristo* longs to pass the blade of the guillotine between the killer's trapezius and occipital bone. *See also* trapezius.

odori (oh . *doh'* ree) a graceful Japanese dance performed with stylized gestures by women wearing traditional floor-length dress. An essential part of kabuki theater since 1603, the odori, akin to pantomime, calls for intense body control and use of the fan as a major prop. Ko, the adamant father in Jeanne Wakatsuki Houston and James D. Houston's *Farewell to Manzanar,* agrees that his daughter may be carnival queen if she registers for odori lessons. *See also* geisha; kabuki.

ofay (*oh'* fay) a pejorative or denigrating term for a Caucasian, or the white race, and its idiosyncrasies and foibles, for example, racist attitudes, patriarchy, and condescension toward nonwhites. An African-American slang term originating in the 1920s, the word, possibly from West African dialect, is of questionable derivation. In Lorraine Hansberry's *A Raisin in the Sun,* Beneatha refers to white slang as "ofay," indicating that it is inappropriate in a black household.

oilcloth or **oilskin** cotton or napped flannel fabric coated with oil, wax, clay, pigment, paint, silicone, or resin to waterproof it for use in tablecloths, shelf liner, curtains, hats, raincoats, and raingear for sailors and fishers; oilskin. A late eighteenth-century process, oilcloth remains popular for picnic cloths and ground cloths. As the hurricane approaches the Everglades in Zora Neale Hurston's *Their Eyes Were Watching God,* Tea Cake orders Janey to cut a piece of oilcloth in which to wrap their important papers to keep them dry. In Robert Louis Stevenson's *Treasure Island,* Jim Hawkins discovers Billy Bones's packet, kept safe in oilskin. *See also* mackintosh; sou'wester.

omnibus (*ahm'* nih . buhs) a horse-drawn public transportation coach carrying 8 to 16 passengers and covering a set route. Originating in Paris in 1662, the conveyance bears a Latin name meaning *for all.* The omnibus remained popular in Europe and America until the age of the gasoline-powered bus. The omnibus door opened at the rear; seats extended along the left and right sides. The driver's seat was

on top. In F. Scott Fitzgerald's *The Great Gatsby,* the title character uses his Rolls Royce as an omnibus to ferry partygoers to his Long Island estate.

one-eyed jack one of the four trios of face cards or court cards consisting of king, queen, and jack, or knave. Called the one-eyed jack because the face is depicted in profile, revealing only one eye, the picture at one time was the jack of clubs, the lowest face card in value. It represented Sir Lancelot, the knight and friend of King Arthur and the seducer of Arthur's wife, Queen Guinevere. During a card game at the Kowalski flat in Tennessee Williams's *A Streetcar Named Desire,* Pablo calls for the one-eyed jack to be a wild card.

open sesame (*seh'* suh . mee) the magic incantation or password that opens the door to the robbers' cave for Ali Baba in the Arabic tale "Ali Baba and the Forty Thieves." Also, a means of obtaining something inaccessible or hidden. In Arthur Miller's *Death of a Salesman,* Willy Loman predicts that his numerous business alliances will guarantee an "open sesame" for his two sons. Maya Angelou repeats the magical phrase in *I Know Why the Caged Bird Sings.*

opium den a refuge for opium users where attendants supply a couch or bed, an opium pipe, and privacy. In Jules Verne's *Around the World in Eighty Days,* Detective Fix seduces Passepartout with wine and opium in an attempt to deter his pursuit of Phileas Fogg. According to Verne, opium is a "despicable vice" rigorously outlawed by the Chinese government, but alluring to rich and poor, who die within five years from horrible contortions and agony. After observing the effect of addiction on the House of Hwang in Pearl S. Buck's *The Good Earth,* Wang Lung uses opium to rid himself of an unwelcome, prying sister-in-law.

opklap bed (*ahp'* klahp) a fold-up bed fastened to a wall. When not in use, the bed lifts from the foot and rotates on a hinge at the floor to fit against the curtained wall like shelving. The term derives from the Dutch for *fold-up.* In *The Diary of a Young Girl,* Anne Frank describes the use of the opklap bed, a version of the Murphy bed, which was a popular spacemaker in the 1920s.

oracle (*ohr'* uh . k'l) a prediction or prognostication. Also, the priestess of Apollo, called the Pythia, who sat on her perch at Delphi over a fissure in the earth, inhaled escaping fumes, and babbled in loose, ambiguous phrases the answer to a petitioner's question, such as how to regain health, end a plague, win a war, or find a worthy wife. In Homer's *Iliad,* an oracle predicts that Paris, the son of King Priam and Queen Hecuba, will be a torch that will cause Troy's destruction.

orderly a messenger or agent who transmits military orders; also, a valet, servant, or army corporal or sergeant who performs personal errands and domestic affairs for a superior officer. Because orderlies often wait in antechambers to learn the outcome of important conferences, they are privy to battle strategy and other concerns vital to soldiers. The tall soldier in Stephen Crane's *The Red Badge of Courage* gets third-hand gossip from an orderly at headquarters about troop movement, which will soon put the blue-coated regiment in the line of fire of the grays.

ordinand (*ohr* . dih . *nand'*) a postulant or candidate for the priesthood, ministry or holy orders, which an ecclesiastical superior confers through ordination, one of the seven sacraments of the Church. Also, a priest-in-training awaiting ritual consecration through the laying on of a bishop's hands, anointing of the hands with oil, acceptance of the chalice and paten or plate, Holy Communion, and public vows of obedience. At the beginning of Margaret Craven's *I Heard the Owl Call My Name,* a doctor confides to the bishop that Mark, the young ordinand assigned to the Kwakiutl village of Kingcome, is dying and will not survive more than three years.

øre (*uhr'* uh) *pl.* **øre** a Norwegian or Danish penny or 1/100 of a krone, or krona; a coin similar to the Swedish öre. Originating in the early seventeenth century, the term derives from the Latin for *gold.* In 1884, the 14-year-old title character of Theodore Taylor's *Timothy of the Cay,* who lives on Curaçao, a Dutch island off Venezuela, earns a few øre for delivering parcels. *See also* kroner.

origami (*ohr* . uh . *gah'* mee) the craft of folding sheets of tissue into shapes of animals, flowers, buildings, or geometrics for use as gifts, decorations, mobiles, or curiosities. Derived from the Japanese for *folded paper,* the term entered English in the mid-twentieth century and has remained a popular activity or artistic expression. The speaker in Maxine Hong Kingston's *The Woman Warrior* devotes much paper to her aunt—not to make origami figures but to write memories and reflections.

osier (*oh'* syuhr) the willow; a tree common to river banks that yields bark used in fever-reducing medicines similar to aspirin and pliant branches for weaving into baskets, trays, travois, and hanging bridges.

Originating in the Middle Ages, the term is Latin for *river bed.* The bridge in Thornton Wilder's *The Bridge of San Luis Rey* is a century-old osier span woven by Incas about 1600 to save the long overland route that winds from the mountains to Lima, Peru.

OSS or **Office of Strategic Services** a spying or information-gathering network dispatched by the United States behind enemy lines from 1942 to 1945; a forerunner of the Central Intelligence Agency. In William J. Lederer and Eugene Burdick's *The Ugly American,* unassuming OSS agents the size and physical build of Asian people infiltrate an area menaced by Japanese forces.

ostler (*ahst'* luhr) or **hostler** the attendant, groom, or stablekeeper at an inn or posting-house who takes charge of transportation by making temporary repairs to frayed harnesses, cleaning wagons and carriages of mud, and feeding and bedding down horses, mules, or oxen for the night. Dating to the Middle Ages, the term originated from the Anglo-Saxon for *hostel,* a hotel or wayside inn. In Charles Dickens's *Great Expectations,* Estella feels compelled to tip the waiter, ostler, and chambermaid. *See also* posting-house.

Our Father a recitation of the Paternoster or Lord's Prayer as a penance or petition for help from God. Use of the term dates to the late nineteenth century; the first two words of Christ's prayer as given in Matthew 6:9–13 and Luke 11:2–4 became a substitute title for "The Lord's Prayer." To propitiate God's help in catching a fish, Santiago, protagonist in Ernest Hemingway's *The Old Man and the Sea,* says ten Our Fathers and ten Hail Marys to help him overcome his 40-day string of ill luck, a symbolic figure paralleling Christ's 40 days in the wilderness.

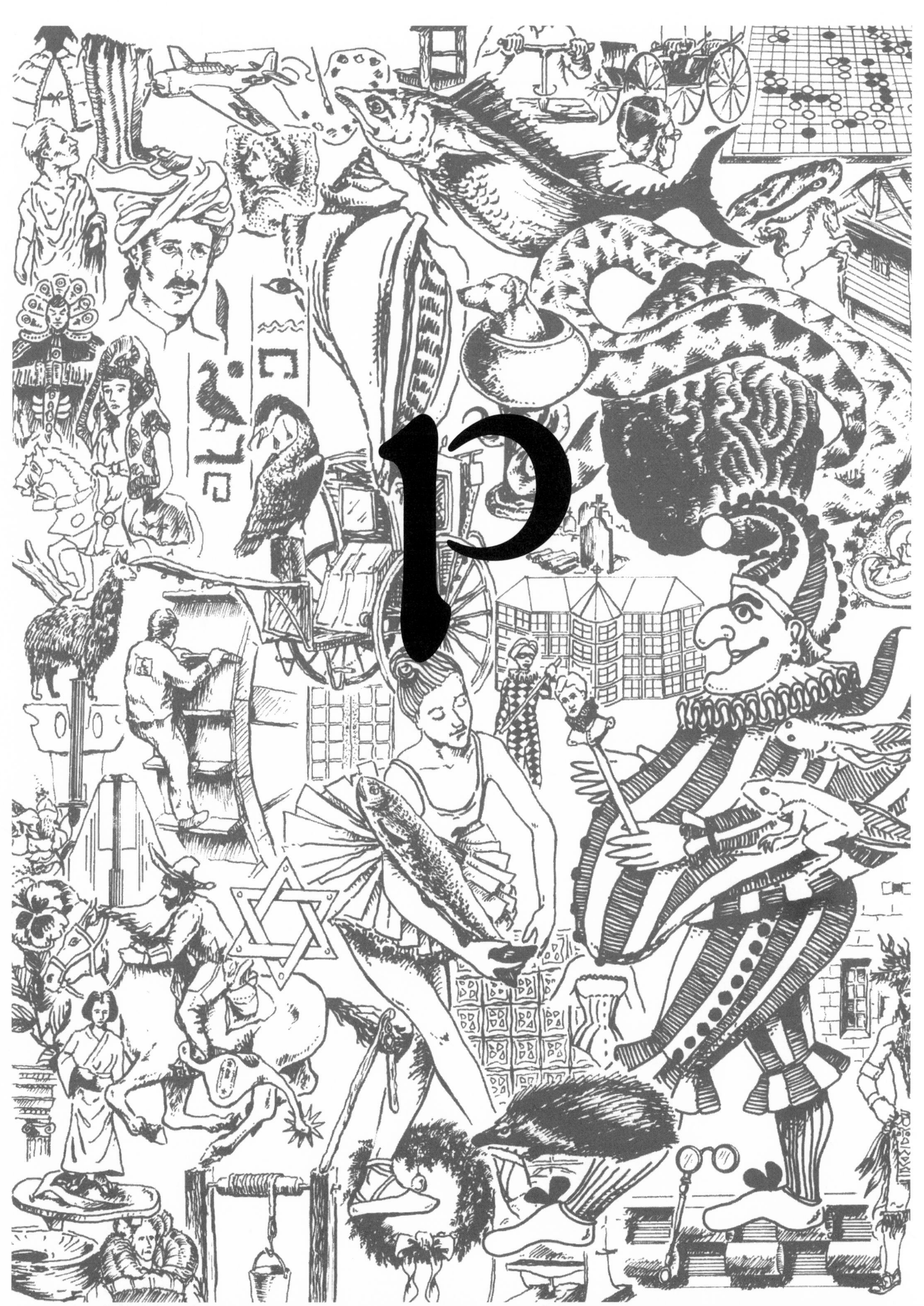
P

packet a coastal or river steamer or sternwheeler that follows a standard route between two ports or over a series of small wharves, warehouses, and seaside inns and carries freight, mail, and passengers. A common term in the nineteenth century, it originated from the French *pacquebot*. The packet in Charles Dickens's *A Tale of Two Cities* is a regularly scheduled boat, which Abel Magwitch aims to board in his abortive escape. *See also* stagecoach.

paddle box a fender or casement enclosing the upper portions of side wheels or stern wheels on a riverboat. The paddle box prevents curious children from falling into the apparatus, inhibits splashes and spurts of lubricant on passengers' clothing, and preserves the aesthetics of the boat's grace and outward appearance by concealing the driving mechanism. In his autobiographical *Life on the Mississippi,* Mark Twain describes the painted rays that top the name of the boat on the paddle box.

paddock (*pad'* duhk) or **parrock** a small fenced-in pasture or enclosure adjacent to a barn or training compound and reserved for grazing, exercising, saddling, grooming, showing, and trading fine horses. Originating from the Anglo-Saxon for *enclosure,* the term dates to the early seventeenth century. The devious Napoleon, a villainous tyrant in George Orwell's *Animal Farm,* converts the livestock's paddock into a field to be plowed for barley.

paddy wagon a police car or armored van used to round up rioters, prostitutes, or tipplers from the streets, to take suspects into custody, or to transport prisoners to jail or from jail to prison. A 1930s slang term, it derived from the Hibernian name *Patrick* and illustrates the stereotype of the Irish drunk. In a description of her shameful past in Tennessee Williams's *A Streetcar Named Desire,* Blanche DuBois tells how rowdy soldiers stood under her window and called her name until the paddy wagon hauled them to jail.

paean or **pean** (*pee'* uhn) a somber chant, hymn, shout, or song of rejoicing, exultation, victory, or thanksgiving; a triumphal anthem, encomium, or invocation to a divinity. Derived from a Greek name for *Apollo,* the god of healing, this late sixteenth-century term once named the odes sung by a chorus to Apollo alone, then generalized to any song of praise. The general in Stephen Crane's *The Red Badge of Courage* is so pleased with his men's battlefield courage that he feels the urge to utter a paean.

pagoda (puh . *goh'* duh) a pyramidal temple comprising several stories, each progressively smaller and either square or polygonal. Pagodas are capped by terraces branching out into symmetrical projecting roofs or curving eaves that are marked with finials or ornaments at each level. Found primarily in Asia, the pagoda serves as a temple complex, memorial or shrine, worship center, tomb, or repository for religious relics. It is also built in miniature as a garden decoration or symbol of proportion. From the Persian for *temple idol,* this architectural term is widely applied to any building with upturned edges along the roof, for example, the state capitol in Raleigh, North Carolina. As the unnamed captain scans the horizon in Joseph Conrad's "The Secret Sharer," the only identifiable landmark he sees is the Paknam Pagoda.

paint *See* pinto.

paisano (py . *zah'* noh) or **paisan** *pl.* **paisanos** or **paisans** a peasant, civilian, friend, fellow citizen, or compatriot; an informal form of address or expression of endearment or recognition to an acquaintance, coworker, or comrade, particularly in Spain, Sicily, Corsica, or Italy. In use in English since the mid-nineteenth century, the term derives from the Spanish for *countryman*. In Maya Angelou's *I Know Why the Caged Bird Sings,* the speaker wonders how her pedantic schoolgirl Spanish sounds to the paisano ear.

palanquin (*pa* . luhn . *keen'*) a covered or enclosed sedan chair, divan, or litter seating one occupant and carried by two or four bearers, who shoulder the two horizontal poles on either side of the coach. Derived from the Bengali for *bed,* the term entered English in the late sixteenth century. The palanquin serves as a private conveyance through a crowd; as a seat of honor for nobility or revered persons; or transport for the infirm, handicapped, or injured. In Jules Verne's *Around the World in Eighty Days,* Phileas Fogg hires a palanquin for Aouda and escorts her to a hotel.

palette (*pal'* iht) a thin oval board, tablet, or disk on which an artist mixes pigments or oil paints for immediate use with brush or palette knife. The palette has a hole to accommodate the thumb to ease strain on the hand. Derived from the Latin for *spade,* the term entered English in the late eighteenth century. Penny Sycamore prepares palette, brushes, and paints for work on the portrait of a discus thrower on one of her artistic evenings in Moss Hart and George S. Kaufman's comedy *You Can't Take It with You.*

paling (*pay'* lihng) a picket fence or safety or privacy enclosure composed of upright slats or strips of wood pointed at one end and wired or nailed together and attached to upright posts to align them; also, a barrier against sand along a dune or beach or a protective wall against drifting snow. Glad of an opportunity to be outdoors, Elizabeth and her sister ride along the paling of Rosings Park in Jane Austen's *Pride and Prejudice*.

palisade (*pal* . ih . *sayd'*) a tall row of wood or iron palings or guard rails surrounding a fortification. Usually sharpened at the upper end, the palisade may be paired with a moat to keep out attackers or infiltrators. A late-sixteenth-century term, the word derives from the Latin for *pole*. At night, Doctor Trelawny leaves the blockhouse, crosses the palisade, and sets out to see Ben Gunn in Robert Louis Stevenson's *Treasure Island.*

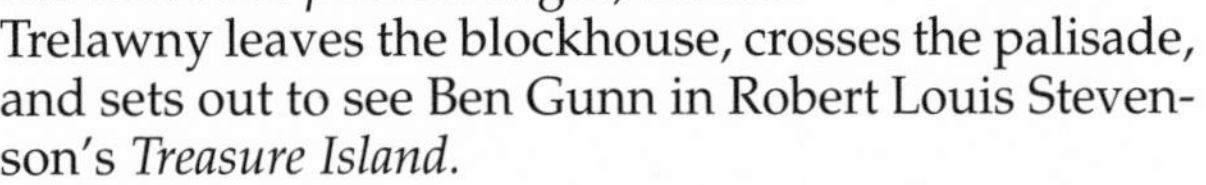

pall (pawl) a rich black, white, or purple velvet or brocaded cloth often inscribed with religious symbols such as I.H.S., a cross or crown, or the alpha and omega. The pall can be spread over an altar, communion table, floor, catafalque, casket, or hearse or draped over a commemorative cross during Holy Week. This fourteenth-century term derives from the Latin for *cloak* and symbolizes royalty or immortality. In Jack London's *White Fang,* the descent of night in the Arctic seems like a pall. *See also* Good Friday; I.H.S.

palma christi (*pahl'* muh *krihs'* tee) the 12-lobed leaf of the castor oil plant, a poisonous foliage shrub 30 to 40 feet high that yields an oil used for lamps, varnish, or household lubricants and soaps. Palma christi served as embalming fluid in ancient Egypt and as a purgative or skin balm among herbalists and folk healers. A pre–twelfth-century term, the name derives from the Latin for *palm of the hand* and the Greek for *Christ.* In Zora Neale Hurston's *Their Eyes Were Watching God,* Janie binds palma christi leaves about Nanny's head to soothe a "sick headache."

palmer a medieval religious traveler or seeker of healing, inspiration, or vision who wore crossed palm fronds to indicate completion of a pilgrimage to the Holy Lands; also, a journeyman monk under the vow of poverty who migrated to various shrines and wore the palm as a symbol of mortality and of the palm-decked processional of Christ and his disciples into Jerusalem. The Prologue to Geoffrey Chaucer's *Canterbury Tales* pays tribute to palmers from distant places who travel to holy shrines. *See also* Hajj.

palmetto (pal . *meht'* toh) a hardy, low-growing tree of the palm family common to the Caribbean wilds and subtropical United States that provides wood for fencing or fuel. The fibrous fronds are used to thatch roofs or to weave into mats, visors, fans, hats, baskets, trays, room dividers, and sunshades. In Marjorie Kinnan Rawlings's *The Yearling,* Jody uses palmetto branches to fashion a flutter mill. *See also* flutter mill.

pampas (*pam'* puhs) *sing.* **pampa** the flat, sparsely populated savanna, open grassland, veld, or plains of South America reaching from the Andes Mountains to the Atlantic Ocean. Traditionally, the gauchos, or herders, of the pampas raise dairy and beef cattle, sheep, goats, and horses and farmers raise wheat, corn, and flax. Derived in the early eighteenth century from the Quechuan for *prairie,* the term is usually written in the plural. As mentioned in Luigi Pirandello's "A Breath of Air," the herdsman grows rich on the pampas and salt marshes of La Plata, Argentina. *See also* veld.

pannikin (*pan'* nih . kihn) a tin drinking cup, military food container used in the field, or tray molded from a single piece of metal to provide separate compartments of varying sizes and shapes to accommodate meat, vegetables, dessert, or bread. An early nineteenth-century term, the word is a diminutive form of *pan*. In the institutional cafeteria in George Orwell's *1984,* Syme and Winston Smith empty their pannikins of an unidentified and unappetizing pinkish stew.

panoply (*pan'* oh . plee) an army equipped with a full, impressive array of weaponry, armor, and trappings necessary for infantry and cavalry. From the Greek for *all armor,* the term entered English in the early seventeenth century to indicate either a ceremonial appearance or the psychological effect of a fighting force ready for combat. In Sophocles' *Antigone,* the chorus sings of the foe that galloped in full panoply against Creon's kingdom.

panpipes a musical wind instrument formed from a rank of lightweight reeds or tubes made from metal, wood, or clay; the syrinx. The panpipes are graduated in height and vented with slots at the side; they give a melodious tone when breath is blown into the open ends.

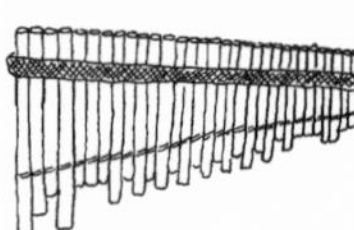

Played like a harmonica either as a serious musical instrument or child's toy, the panpipes carry a mythological connection to Pan, the goat-footed god. In a letter to the banker in Anton Chekhov's "The Bet," the prisoner refers to his reading experiences of songs of sirens and the "pipes of Pan."

pansy (*pan'* zee) a staple, low-growing garden, edging, or windowbox annual of the viola family featuring five bright or particolored daisy-shaped petals radiating from a velvety core set on a stocky stem in a nest of rounded leaves. Derived in the late Middle Ages, the term reflects the French for *thought*. In William Shakespeare's *A Midsummer Night's Dream*, the pansy appears indirectly as love-in-bloom, the valuable herb that Ariel fetches and squeezes out a magic potion to cast love spells at his master's bidding. In Mark Twain's *The Adventures of Tom Sawyer,* Amy Lawrence passes from Tom's heart after the new girl, Becky Thatcher, tosses him a pansy over the fence.

pantaloons a seventeenth- or eighteenth-century style of blousy or baggy breeches reaching to the ankles, where they tied with ribbons or buttons or fastened with stirrups over socks. During the French Revolution, patriots wore pantaloons as a uniform, thus earning the name of *sans culottes* or "trouserless." Poorly dressed in black pantaloons, yellow coat, and old hat, Jean Valjean, protagonist of Victor Hugo's *Les Misérables,* became known as a beggar who shared his alms with others.

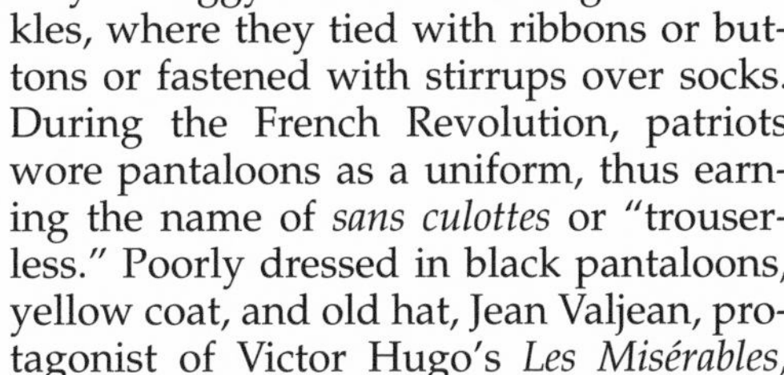

panzer (*pan'* zuhr) or ***panzerdivision*** a unit of a German division of heavily armored vehicles, especially tanks, that Hitler's forces concentrated in tight ranks for quick strikes of intense shelling and deadly accuracy. Entering English during World War II, the term evolved from the Latin for *belly.* Reuven, the protagonist in Chaim Potok's *The Chosen,* listens to news of an Allied victory over a German panzer attack.

papaw or **pawpaw** *See* papaya.

papaya (puh . *py'* uh) the long, bulbous, pulpy yellow fruit of the papaya, or custard apple, tree. Like yams, papayas can be baked or boiled whole, pickled, or crushed and pureed into sherbet, pudding, jam, and jelly. As a cash crop, the papaya also yields papain for coagulants and meat tenderizer and milk for latex. In Sandra Cisneros's *The House on Mango Street,* Rafaela evades her husband's lock on the door by leaning out the window to drop a shopping bag on a string in which children place the papaya juice and coconut they bought for her at the store.

papier poudre (*pahp'* yay *poo'* d'r) a stack of thin sheets of one-inch-square rice paper coated with face powder. Used in the nineteenth century when makeup was forbidden for decent women, the sheets could be rubbed over the face for a quick touch-up of oily skin or blemishes, then discarded or hidden in a pocket, purse, or reticule. The reference to *papier poudre* in Margaret Atwood's *The Handmaid's Tale* reminds the reader that forbidden pleasures often came from France or had a French name. *See also* reticule.

parapet (*pa'* ruh . peht) a low protective wall or railing surrounding a mansion, platform, roof, pier, balcony, or compound or lining either or both sides of a bridge; also, a crenellated edge around the outer defensive wall of a fort. A late sixteenth-century term, the word derives from Latin for *shield the breast*. In Thomas Hardy's *The Mayor of Casterbridge,* Elizabeth-Jane, in the role of Lucetta's companion, contemplates moving into High-Place Hall, an imposing downtown building with a Palladian façade and parapet. *See also* façade

parasol (*pa'* ruh . sahl) a portable folding sunshade or canopy—derived from the Latin for *sunshield.* The frame is formed of metal, wooden, or bamboo ribs and handle covered in silk, paper, parchment, or cotton. A dainty device in comparison with an umbrella, the parasol is often made of material matching a dress, coat, or ensemble and trimmed in lace, fringe, tassels, or delicate stitchery and is used by female dancers and stage performers as a prop. In Fyodor Dostoyevsky's *Crime and Punishment,* Raskolnikov, the protagonist, is appalled to see a young girl weaving drunkenly in the sun without a parasol. *See also* odori.

paregoric or **paregorick** (*pa* . ruh . *goh'* rihk) a blend of alcohol, camphor, and opium flavored with anise, honey, and benzoic acid that soothes pain, coughing, menstrual cramps, and diarrhea by lessening abdominal spasms. Derived in the mid-nineteenth century from the Greek for *calm the assembly*, the term names a narcotic that is still in use, but falls under the category of controlled substances. In Marjorie Kinnan Rawlings's *The Yearling,* the Forresters add paregoric to their regular shopping list as a medical necessity.

parietal (puh . *ry'* uh . t'l) **fissure** the central joint of the cranium that runs from forehead to the rear of the head and connects the sides and top of the skull. The term derives from the Latin for *wall.* In Sir Arthur Conan Doyle's *The Hound of the Baskervilles,* James Mortimer expresses an interest in phrenology and asks to trace the parietal fissure of Sherlock Holmes's skull. *See also* dolichocephalic; phrenology.

pari-mutuel (*par* . uh . *myoo'* choo . `l) a syndicated gambling hall, booth, or counter at a race track or street office where persons placing bets may win a proportional first, second, or third place—called win, place, or show—minus a commission paid to the operators. A late nineteenth-century term, it evolved from the French for *shared risk.* Catherine Barkley and Frederick Henry, protagonists in Ernest Hemingway's *A Farewell to Arms,* entertain themselves by betting at the pari-mutuel.

Paris green copper aceto-arsenate, a deadly bright blue-green powder used as a vivid paint pigment, fungicide, insecticide, wood preservative, and protectant for ship hulls. In James Hurst's "The Scarlet Ibis," Doodle's unnamed brother leads him to a loft where a casket lies under a film of Paris green, a home remedy that kills rats; the poison and casket foreshadow Doodle's imminent death.

parish a township, administrative district, community subdivision, or congregation of a church or diocese, which fall under the authority of a civil or ecclesiastical bureaucracy and pay the wages of town officials or the stipend of a parish priest in the Roman Catholic or Anglican church. Derived from the Greek for *alongside a dwelling,* the term entered English in the fourteenth century. Mr. Tanimoto, a character in John Hersey's *Hiroshima,* grows weary from the cares and demands of his parish.

parka a one-piece pullover anorak, shirt, or jacket with loose sleeves and hood, made of fish skin, seal intestine, or caribou hide, that Eskimo and Arctic travelers oiled and softened to keep pliant. Derived from the Samoyed dialect, the term refers to a unique garment capable of shutting out cold air and trapping a layer of body heat inside. Hunters often shaped parkas out of warm skins with the fleece on the inside and added an extra lining of long fur around the edge of the hood; women attached an inside strap to hold an infant against the torso. As Gary Paulsen describes in *Woodsong,* the musher has to keep the parka pulled tight against the virulent winds blowing along the Yukon River.

parley (*pahr'* lay) a military conference, powwow, huddle, council, political debate, argument, negotiation, or disputation; a summit meeting or exchange of information between enemies that is guaranteed by truce, armistice, prisoner exchange, or mutual peace accord. Dating to the late sixteenth century, the word replicates the French for *speak,* which derives from the Latin for *speech.* The Russian Captain Orlov, a ruthless seal hunter, conceals murderous intent against the islanders by asking for a parley with Captain Chowig in Scott O'Dell's *The Island of the Blue Dolphins. See also* caucus; liaison.

paroquet (*par'* oh . keht) or **parakeet** a member of numerous species of small nomadic parrots native to warm climates, with hooked beak, tapered body, long tail, and white, blue, violet, gray, or yellow feathers; a budgerigar or other pet bird capable of repeating memorized sounds. A sixteenth-century French term derived from the name *Peter,* the word was also spelled *parrakeet.* Once they pass Fort Pitt, Half Arrow and True Son spy a noisy flock of bright-colored paroquets flying overhead in Conrad Richter's *A Light in the Forest.*

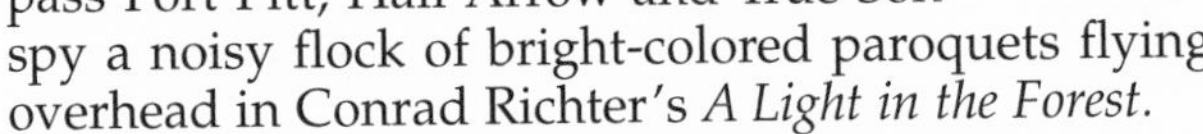

parrain (pahr . *rehn'*) the Louisiana patois term for godparent or sponsor, who attends an infant's baptism or confirmation and agrees to serve in place of the child's parents if they die or are incapacitated, unavailable, or negligent in nurturing or educating the child in religious faith. Unable to accept the racial distinction between himself and Timmy, his black half-brother in Ernest Gaines's *The Autobiography of Miss Jane Pittman,* Tee Bob refuses to listen to his *parrain,* Jules Reynard, and kills himself.

parry (*par'* ree) to counter or ward off a direct attack by sidestepping a dueling sword or turning it aside; to evade, elude, or disengage a charging enemy or an accuser. From the Latin for *prepare,* this late seventeenth-century term is fencing jargon for a deft, subtle motion of the wrist or arm that deflects or renders harmless an energetic lunge or sword thrust of an opponent. In a verbal exchange with Christian, the title character in Edmond Rostand's *Cyrano de Bergerac* claims to parry the thrust and surprises onlookers by refusing to engage his tormenter in a duel.

Parsee or **Parsi** (*pahr'* see) a member of a small body of Zoroastrian mystics native to India, including some of the nation's most prestigious and successful families. An early seventeenth-century corruption of *Persian* from the Greek for *people of Persis,* the name applies to Middle Eastern religious refugees who settled in Bombay in the late seventh century and practiced a religion that emphasizes the triumph of good over evil. In Herman Melville's *Moby-Dick,* Fedallah, a Parsee, predicts that Captain Ahab will know neither hearse nor coffin after his death.

particle accelerator *See* cyclotron.

partisan (*pahr'* tih . zihn) a late sixteenth-century spear or ceremonial halberd, bill, or pike carried by a doorman or gatekeeper at a palace or civic building or during formal processions of office. The partisan possesses a broad blade with one or more lateral wings on a six-to eight-foot wooden shaft, sometimes decorated with a tassel, medallion, or coat of arms. Derived from the Latin for *political party,* the term evolved into a name for the person who takes sides in a local forum or political debate. In the fracas that begins Act I, Scene I of William Shakespeare's *Romeo and Juliet,* peace officers call for clubs, pikes, and partisans to halt the eruption of street violence.

partridge a plump, compact game bird with short tail and speckled feathers that camouflage the bird among rocks and low brush. The plucked carcass is roasted whole and served either whole or sliced. Because the meat is difficult to digest, cooks truss and roast it in Madeira wine or marinade, stuff it with savory filling, or serve it in aspic or a terrine. To her daughters, Mrs. Bennet, the high-strung mother in Jane Austen's *Pride and Prejudice,* pronounces the partridges a success with Mr. Darcy.

partridgeberry the common name for two wild plants prized by herbalists: One, a member of the madder family, is a creeping vine that forms red berries favored by grouse and used to accelerate labor and birth; the second, the wintergreen plant, bears white blooms and shiny green leaves that healers mix in salve to ease arthritis or sciatica. During a dramatic moment in Nathaniel Hawthorne's *The Scarlet Letter* when Hester Prynne and Arthur Dimmesdale meet for private conversation, Pearl gathers partridgeberries that resemble drops of blood.

passado (pas . *sah'* doh) a single thrust of the sword coordinated with a forward movement of the back foot; a lethal lunge or dramatic, aggressive opening move in a duel. Derived from the Latin for *passage,* the term entered English in the early sixteenth century. Mercutio baits Tybalt to make the opening passado in the fatal sword fight in William Shakespeare's *Romeo and Juliet.*

Passover or **Pesach** or **pasch** a significant Jewish holiday that commemorates the Jews' departure from Egypt, where they had been held as slaves of the Pharaoh. This mid-sixteenth-century term derives from the night the Hebrews fled bondage after the Angel of Death passed over those houses whose door posts were smeared with lamb's blood and spared the lives of the firstborn, who were marked for death. Near the end of Chaim Potok's *The Chosen,* Danny's family invites a guest to Seder, a Passover dinner ritual that celebrates the exodus of Moses and his followers from captivity. *See also* Rosh Hashanah.

patch a bit of black silk or court plaster shaped in a symbolic or creative design to conceal a facial flaw or to mimic a mole or beauty mark as an accent to the lip, eye, jawline, shoulder, or cleavage. In eighteenth-century England, partisans demonstrated their loyalties by patching with emblems designating Whig or Tory loyalty. In *The Diary of Samuel Pepys,* the author notes women's overuse of patches and pasty-white makeup, which were favorite cosmetics in the mid-seventeenth century. *See also* court-plaster.

patch box a covered compartment to the right of the stock of an eighteenth-century central European flintlock rifle. The patch box—originally of curly maple with a sliding lid, then later of brass or iron with a hinged top—stored flint, tools, and extra patches for use in loading. These weapons and their makers migrated to the United States during the settlement of Pennsylvania and the move west. In Conrad Richter's *A Light in the Forest,* Kate accuses True Son of stealing a rifle with a broken patch box and rust on the brass fittings. *See also* flintlock.

pateroller (*pat'* uh . *rohl* . luhr) a rustic pronunciation of *patroller,* one of a network of slave state border guards, security inspectors, and bounty hunters who trailed and captured runaway slaves to earn a reward for returning them to their masters. In Ernest Gaines's *The Autobiography of Miss Jane Pittman,* paterollers attack the fleeing slaves, kill Big Laura, a conductor on the underground railroad, and leave Jane to care for Ned, Laura's orphaned son. *See also* underground railroad.

patron (*pay'* truhn) a wealthy or prestigious supporter or sponsor of the arts; a benefactor who provides a stipend, living quarters, an annual salary, supplies, or a studio for an artist. Also, a person who champions or protects an artist who is out of favor with the populace, royal court, or church. In Edmond Rostand's *Cyrano de Bergerac,* the title character disdains the system of patronage that would compromise his honest expression of opinion and art.

patrón (puh . *trohn'*) the Spanish name for the overseer or superintendent of agricultural laborers or timber cutters; also, a gang boss, proprietor, chief officer, landlord, or captain of a fishing boat. From the Latin for *father,* the term indicates the position of the official as supervisor of underlings, such as migrant workers or peons. In Isabel Allende's *The House of the Spirits,* the *patrón* originally holds total power over his enslaved workers but gradually loses control of the younger generation, who study the concepts of Karl Marx.

patten (*pat'* t'n) a platform overshoe, clog, or sandal with a high arch and a wooden or metal sole used to raise the heel and the ball of the foot from dirt or debris on pavement, dirt paths, cobbles, or around wash or dye tubs; also, a thong worn in a Turkish bath. A fourteenth-century term, the patten, worn by men and women, derives from the French for *paw.* In Thomas Hardy's *Tess of the D'Urbervilles,* milkmaids wear pattens to keep their feet from miring in barn muck.

pax (paks) a period of respectful silence when one person has the attention of others during a discussion, caucus, or conference; a truce or cease-fire during wartime to accommodate a parley. Latin for *peace,* it entered English during the fourteenth century. Pursued by Jack Merridew's atavistic hunters, Ralph, the protagonist of William Golding's *Lord of the Flies,* longs to return to more amicable days when he could call "pax" and preside over a civilized meeting of the marooned boys. *See also* caucus; parley.

pea-coat or **pilot jacket** or **reefer** a double-breasted, hip-length coat of a heavy, cheap grade of dark blue wool and fitted with patch pockets and a sturdy lining for maximum warmth in gale weather. Originally favored by sailors and longshoremen because of its convenient length and named for the Dutch for a coarse fabric woven of recycled fiber, the popular topcoat was adapted for civilians and remained in demand as a driving jacket or complementary cold-weather topping for jeans. As Pip surveys his benefactor in Charles Dickens's *Great Expectations,* Abel Magwitch, the former convict escaped from the Hulks, takes a pipe from his pea-coat and fills it with standard issue naval tobacco.

peat a spongy, fibrous flammable fuel sliced by hand from acidic, carbonized, or decayed moss, roots, and other vegetable matter in bogs, fens, bayous, estuaries, moors, and swamps and dried in clods or harvested mechanically and pressed into low-grade anthracite blocks or briquettes for use in stoves and fireplaces. From his wife's letters, the title character in Alexander Solzhenitsyn's *One Day in the Life of Ivan Denisovich* learns that young Russians are escaping the bureaucracy of collective farms and working independently in peat fields.

peckerwood a pejorative term applied in the American South to shiftless, dishonest white riffraff or despicable rural folk. The obscure derivation suggests that the word derives from a regional tendency to reverse two-part words—for example, "peckerwood" for "woodpecker"—or from the worthless, denuded trunks of dying trees in which insects burrow. Woodpeckers are drawn to "peckerwood," from which they hammer out slugs for food. At the height of family tension over the proposed move from the ghetto, Mrs. Johnson in Lorraine Hansberry's *A Raisin in the Sun* alarms her neighbors with news of a racially motivated bombing that she blames on Chicago's no-count peckerwoods.

pedal pushers a youthful female fashion in tapered or tight pants that extended to mid-calf length and were worn with blouses, halters, or tie-up shirts for active sports, bicycling, beach walking, and outdoor work during the early 1950s; also called clam-diggers or toreadors. Maya Angelou recalls the faddish pedal pushers she wore during a long-anticipated visit to Daddy Bailey's trailer in her autobiography, *I Know Why the Caged Bird Sings.*

pedicab a three-wheeled taxi containing an enclosed, canvas-topped seat for up to three passengers and pedals, sprocket, and chain used by the seated driver to power the cab. Propelled like a tricycle, the pedicab replaced the bulkier rickshaw in the mid-twentieth century. In Amy Tan's *The Kitchen God's Wife,* Helen rescues Winnie from wartime chaos by stealing a pedicab and arms Winnie with a stick to beat off rioters.

pemmican (*pehm'* mih . k'n) a Cree term for traveler's cakes or emergency stores consisting of minced fish or meats mixed with marrow, nuts, suet or fish oil, molasses, flour, dried berries, and other flavorings and stuffed like sausage into animal intestines or links. Because pemmican is dried like jerky, it stores easily and provides quick energy with little preparation. In Scott O'Dell's *Streams to the River, River to the Sea,* Running Deer asks Sacagawea to stockpile enough pemmican for a long journey.

penance (*pehn'* uhns) a voluntary sacramental act of hardship, self-abasement, humiliation, mortification, devotion, or sacrifice imposed by a priest during confession to free a sinner from retribution in purgatory for evil or sacrilegious acts and to precede absolution, or cleansing the soul of wrongdoing. A fourteenth-century term, it derives from the Latin for *penalty.* On the day that Hester Prynne begins wearing her badge of shame in Nathaniel Hawthorne's *The Scarlet Letter,* Reverend Arthur Dimmesdale, her lover, accepts a self-imposed private penance performed in secret in his closet with a scourge.

penny post a nineteenth-century postal system that, for a penny each, dispatched letters or parcels routed no more than 10 miles out from London or any other point of departure. In *Walden,* the author, Henry David Thoreau, declares that the penny post never brings him news worth reading.

Pentateuch (*pen'* tuh . took or *pen'* tuh . tyook) *See* Torah.

Pentecost (*pen'* tuh . cahst) the Jewish harvest festival of Shavuoth that coincides with the Christian feast commemorating the arrival of the Holy Spirit in the form of harmless tongues of fire hovering over the heads of Christ's disciples; a religious event celebrated on the seventh Sunday after Easter; Whitsuntide. Derived from the Greek for *fiftieth day,* the term entered English before the twelfth century. In Nathaniel Hawthorne's *The Scarlet Letter,* the Reverend Arthur Dimmesdale reports that his congregation looks to him for guidance as though he were imparting a tongue of Pentecost. *See also* Good Friday.

penthouse a sloped-roof shed, porch, free-standing outhouse, lean-to, canopy, awning, or pavilion annexed or attached to a building at front or side or covering a walkway or an arcade between two businesses. A hybrid word from the Latin for *hang* and the Old High German *house,* the term dates to the thirteenth century. In the rag shop beyond a penthouse in Charles Dickens's *A Christmas Carol,* Scrooge observes the ignoble bargaining over his belongings after his death, as depicted in the third phantom's vision of a Christmas in the near future.

pepper box a small English percussion pistol featuring a revolving cluster of five or six barrels, each loaded individually. A common personal weapon of the mid-nineteenth century, the name derives from the similarity between the circle of barrels and the perforated end of a pepper shaker. The pepper box inspired Anson Chase, gunsmith for Samuel Colt, who invented the modern revolver in 1831. Rooster Cogburn, a U.S. Marshal in Charles Portis's *True Grit,* suggests that Mattie Ross give up her Colt's dragoon and arm herself with a five-shot pepper box. *See also* Colt's revolver.

perambulator (puhr . *am'* byoo . *lay* . tor) or **pram** a baby buggy or carriage composed of a hooded shell fitted with mattress and padded bumpers and resting on a four-wheeled frame propelled from behind like a handcart by a pedestrian pushing against the horizontal handle. Some perambulators were ornately decorated with lace, ribbons, and a family crest painted on the side. As German troops evacuate a village in Erich Maria Remarque's *All Quiet on the Western Front,* they meet fleeing refugees, some with belongings stacked on perambulators.

percale (puhr . *kayl'*) a tightly woven, lightweight, sheenless Indian cotton used for sheets, curtains, upholstery lining, shirts, and dresses. Derived from the Persian for *rag,* the term dates to the mid-nineteenth century, when English traders were profiting from cheap imported colonial goods. Janie, protagonist of Zora Neale Hurston's *Their Eyes Were Watching God,* serves as her husband's ornament by wearing wine-colored silk ruffles in the presence of local women dressed in simple calico and percale. *See also* calico; chambray.

percussion-cap a small paper or metal bubble or ball enclosing fulminating powder that is placed in a percussion chamber and struck by a hammer to ignite a spark that explodes a charge of gunpowder; a detonator. To entertain himself and his friend Joe Harper during class, the title character in Mark Twain's *The Adventures of Tom Sawyer* extracts a tick from a percussion-cap box and propels it over the desk with a pin.

periscope (*per'* ihs . *kohp*) an optical viewer invented in the early twentieth century by Simon Lake for use on submarines. The periscope consists of a tube or cylinder fitted with mirrors or prisms aligned to display the view above to the user below, who looks through an adjustable eyepiece. By holding a periscope above the line of normal vision, the viewer can remain concealed or can extend the range of vision over obstructions such as walls, crowds, or brush, or, in the case of a submarine's periscope, over water. While making a biological survey, Farley Mowat, author of *Never Cry Wolf,* sets up a periscopic telescope on a tripod so he can observe animals without being seen.

peristyle (*per'* ih . styl) a courtyard, marketplace, cloister, private garden, or atrium surrounded by columns; a covered walkway or colonnade. Derived from the Greek for *columns around,* the term applies to a variety of styles of architecture that enclose a space with an elaborately designed perimeter. On arrival in Japan, Passepartout, the quick-witted valet of Phileas Fogg in Jules Verne's *Around the World in Eighty Days,* observes a neat marketplace and residences opening on pleasant peristyles. *See also* colonnade; compound; court.

peritoneum (*pehr* . ih . toh . *nee'* uhm) the sturdy, smooth membrane or sac that encircles, warms, and supports the inner abdominal and pelvic cavity and encases the intestines and stomach. By stretching to accommodate body rhythms, the peritoneum acts as a protective barrier and a smooth, viscous surface against which organs can expand, contract, and reseat themselves during digestion, exercise, and other body functions. Derived from the Greek for *stretched around,* the term entered English in the fifteenth century. In the bottling room of the hatchery in Aldous Huxley's *Brave New World,* neatly cut squares of sow's peritoneum are whisked by conveyor into containers that house and nurture fetuses until they are ready to be decanted.

periwig (*peh'* ree . wihg) or **peruke** a full, cascading shoulder-length wig worn by men during the seventeenth and eighteenth centuries. For formal or professional wear, periwigs were ordinarily parted in the middle and ranged from simple loose styles to ornate ringlets, waves, and curls. For sport or relaxation, they were tied at the nape into a neat club or pigtail. While instructing an acting company on how to present the evening's entertainment, the title character in William Shakespeare's *Hamlet* derides a stage stereotype—the periwigged actor who overemotes.

permafrost (*puhr'* muh . frahst) the layer of soil below the surface in polar regions and at high altitudes that remains frozen; the soil above the permafrost may become soggy in summer as certain plant liquids thaw. A portmanteau word formed by the merger of *permanent* and *frost,* the term dates to the mid-twentieth century. In Jean Craighead George's *Julie of the Wolves,* the title character digs beneath the permafrost to store food for the winter where her wolf friends will not find it.

peruke *See* periwig.

peseta (puh . *say'* tuh) a silver coin that is the basic monetary unit of Spain and Andorra. The peseta, a term derived from the Latin for *weight,* is worth 100 centimos. Grandpa Sycamore, a purveyor of trivia in Moss Hart and George S. Kaufman's *You Can't Take It with You,* comments that a Nicaraguan can mail a letter to the United States for 2 pesetas.

peso (*pay'* soh) a common monetary unit or gold or silver coin in Latin America, Mexico, Cuba, the Dominican Republic, or the Philippines. The peso is equal to 8 Spanish reals, 100 Uruguayan centesimos, or 100 Mexican centavos, or cents. In Isabel Allende's *The House of Spirits,* 50 pesos from the *patrón* sets up Transito with shoes, dress, permed hair, perfume, and a ticket to a better life. *See also patrón.*

petcock a valve, faucet, or spigot that controls the flow or drainage of liquid or gas from a container or cylinder. A petcock also regulates or tests the pressure in a boiler, steam pipe, or radiator. Derived in the mid-nineteenth century, the term stems from the French for *small valve.* While Catherine Barkley is in labor in Ernest Hemingway's *A Farewell to Arms,* the attending physician opens and closes the petcock to control the flow of anesthesia to ease her pain.

petit four (*peh* . tee *fohr'*) pl. **petit fours** or **petits fours** a bite-sized piece of pound or sponge cake, macaroon, shortbread, or a biscuit that is iced and decorated with colored toppings such as marzipan and served as finger food at receptions, as desserts, or in paper doilies in a gift box. A late nineteenth-century term, it derives from the French for *small oven.* In the Poet's Bakery in Edmond Rostand's *Cyrano de Bergerac,* regular customers seat themselves among mounds and trays of brioches and petit fours.

petrel (*peht'* r'l) any of a large family of round-billed, gull-like diving seabirds that nest on shore and feed on plankton, small fish, and bits of waste from ships or wharves. Because the birds skim the surface of the ocean, they earn their name from a corruption of *Saint Peter,* who walked on water. Timothy, an experienced seaman in Theodore Taylor's *The Cay,* determines the nearness to shore by observing boobies and petrels diving for flying fish.

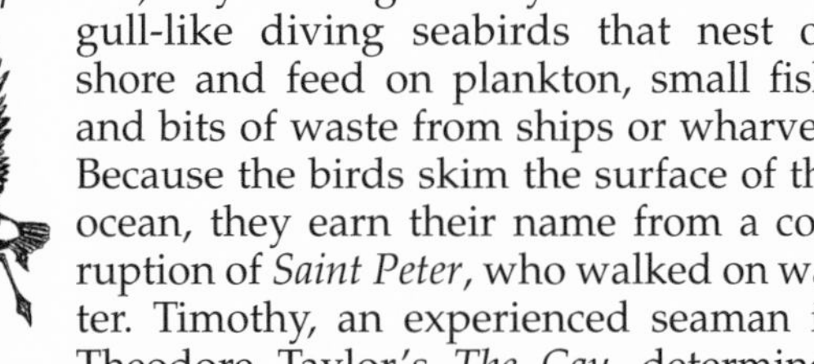

pewter a lustrous silvery gray metal alloyed from tin and either antimony, bismuth, copper, lead, or brass. Pewter grows dark with age and is easily molded into eating utensils, serving bowls, altarware, trays, ewers, tankards, and urns. A trade item from early Chinese, Egyptian, and Roman history, pewter is of unknown derivation. On her arrival, Isabella Linton, wife of Heathcliff in Emily Brontë's *Wuthering Heights,* studies the dusty pewter and general neglect while Mr. Earnshaw paces the floor and ponders his foster son's marriage.

peyote (pay . *oh'* tee) or **peyotl** a cactus native to the southwestern United States that yields a button or knob chewed by worshippers in a visionary ritual. The hallucinogenic shoot, which can also be consumed in tea, produces stimulating phantasms and whirling patterns. According to N. Scott Momaday's *The Way to Rainy Mountain,* peyote rituals include prayers, ritual servings of peyote buttons, all-night singing, prayer, and baptism. Aldous Huxley's *Brave New World* describes a similar trance resulting from the ritual ingestion of peyote. *See also* mescal.

phaeton or **phaethon** (*fay'* uh . t'n) a stylish lightweight, topless, four-wheeled carriage pulled by two horses and capable of carrying two passengers and a light stack of baggage on the rear axle. The phaeton was frequently the vehicle of choice for female drivers. During Mr. Bennet's private conversation with Mr. Collins in Jane Austen's *Pride and Prejudice,* Mr. Collins praises Miss de Bourgh's beauty and comments that she often drives by his residence in her pony-drawn phaeton.

Pharisee (*fayr'* uh . see) a member of a rigid, self-righteous, influential Hebrew sect of the period from 500 B.C. to A.D. 100. In outraged response to evidence of ecumenism, or blending of worship styles with other religions, the Pharisees required strict adherence to biblical law and traditional ritual according to their own interpretation. Derived from the Hebrew for *separate,* the word dates to the early Middle Ages. In Maya Angelou's *I Know Why the Caged Bird Sings,* Reverend Taylor preaches a pointed sermon about the Pharisees, who made a show of praying aloud in public, but the message is lost on Sister Monroe, who gave a vigorous testimony the previous Sunday.

phenylketonuria (*fee* . n'l . *kee* . tuh . *nyoo'* ree . uh) or **PKU** a birth defect that causes brain damage, neurological dysfunction, epileptic seizures, and progressive retardation because of a lack of tyrosine, an enzyme that oxidizes phenylalanine, an amino acid that is a natural digestive by-product of metabolized sugar. As explanation of Charlie's phenylketonuria in Daniel Keyes's *Flowers for Algernon,* Professor Nemur suggests that it resulted from a maverick enzyme, defective gene, radiation, or virus.

phial (*fy'* uhl) a small cylindrical or square glass bottle or vial stoppered with cork, a screw-on cap, or glass obelisk or sealed with wax. A phial often contained medication, perfume, cosmetics, or an herbal preparation or potion. From the Greek for *drinking cup,* the term dates to the fourteenth century. Before freezing to death during a drugged stupor, Molly Farren loses hold on her toddler and flings aside an empty laudanum phial in George Eliot's *Silas Marner.*

philippic (fuh . *lihp'* pihk) a bitter or harsh invective, vitriolic tirade, personal denunciation, or verbal attack; a pointed political harangue delivered from a public pulpit and intended to turn popular opinion against a public figure or to humiliate or degrade a candidate or enemy. Derived from Demosthenes' orations defaming Philip of Macedon, the word entered English in the late sixteenth century. After the death of the tall soldier in Stephen Crane's *The Red Badge of Courage,* Henry Fleming raises his fist to deliver a philippic, but mutters only, "Hell."

phoenix (*fee'* nihks) a mythical bird of the Arabian desert depicted in ancient eastern Mediterranean lore, mosaics, needlework, murals, insignia, crests, and paintings. The one-of-a-kind phoenix lives its 500-year life span, then climbs onto a funeral pyre and sets itself aflame. From its ashes springs a worm that develops into a new phoenix decked in radiant red, purple, and gold plumage. The act of regeneration symbolizes the immortality of the soul, as evidenced by the presence of the phoenix among Christian Christmas ornaments. In Jorge Luis Borges's "The Garden of Forking Paths," the narrator enters a vast library decorated with a bronze phoenix and a Persian vase. In John Hersey's *Hiroshima,* the phoenix comes to symbolize the rejuvenation of the bombed-out city.

phosphate (*fahs'* fayt) a bubbly soda fountain drink, or "flip," composed of fruit-flavored syrup, a small quantity of phosphoric acid, and soda water. Popular in the early years of the twentieth century, the soft drink fell from popularity with the advent of brand-name drinks available in glass bottles, particularly Coca-Cola. Recovering from a near collision with a runaway wagon in Thornton Wilder's *Our Town,* Emily orders a strawberry phosphate from Mr. Morgan, the counter clerk. *See also* flip.

phosphorescence (*fahs* . fohr . *ehs'* sihns) emitting a murky light without producing heat or combustion; a luminescence generated by the excitation of atoms, as demonstrated by marine plankton, angler fish, jellyfish, squid, and plants as well as fireflies, oscilloscopes, lasers, television screens, toys, signs, and watch dials that glow in the dark. A late eighteenth-century term, the word derives from the Greek for *bearing light.* At a deep well in the Gulf Stream, Santiago, protagonist in Ernest Hemingway's *The Old Man and the Sea,* observes the phosphorescence of seaweed.

phrenology (freh . *nah'* loh . gee) a short-lived pseudoscience that proposed that the study and measurement of the curves and anomalies of the skull revealed data about the brain, intellect, appetites, race, and ethical and moral beliefs. Derived from the Greek for *mind study,* the term was popularized in the early nineteenth century. The Duke in Mark Twain's *The Adventures of Huckleberry Finn* earns a dubious living from mesmerism, acting, and phrenology. In Toni Morrison's *Beloved,* Sethe recoils from the overseer's study of her physical traits and head size and shape in his pursuit of phrenology. *See also* dolichocephalic; parietal fissure.

phylactery (fuh . *lak'* tuh . ree) a small leather cube or case housing passages of scripture written on parchment and strapped with a leather thong to the forehead, left forearm, or middle finger of devout Jewish men during morning weekday prayers. Derived from the Greek for *charm* or *amulet,* the term, a synonym for the Hebrew *tefillin,* describes an outward show of obedience to a commandment in Deuteronomy 9:18 that requires worshippers to wear signs of piety on the hand and between the eyes. While Elie Wiesel hovers over his phylacteries in prayer in his autobiographical *Night,* shouts from German troops force Jews into the street.

piaster (pee . *as'* tuhr) or **piastre** a hundredth of a pound, the basic monetary unit of Egypt, Sudan, Syria, Turkey, and Lebanon; also a small coin in Vietnam in the early twentieth century. Derived from the Latin for *plaster,* the term dates to the late sixteenth century. As mentioned in Walter Dean Myers's *Fallen Angels,* the South Vietnamese piaster was worth a penny in 1968, at the height of the Vietnam War.

piccalilli (*pihk'* kuh . *lihl* . lee) minced vegetables bottled with a vinegar sauce spiced with mustard, turmeric, and hot pepper and used in East Indian cuisine as a traditional condiment to accompany bland vegetables and sliced meats. The term, which entered English in the mid-eighteenth century, may reflect a combination of *pickle* and *chili* or a diminutive of *pickle.* For his birthday, Dussel, one of the people hiding in the annexe in Anne Frank's *The Diary of a Young Girl,* receives wine, a book, and a jar of piccalilli.

pice (pys) or **paisa** *pl.* **pice** or **pies** or **paise** a nearly worthless coin equal to one-fourth of an anna or one-sixty-fourth of a rupee, the chief monetary unit of India, Nepal, and Pakistan. Derived from the Hindi for *paisa* and the Sanskrit for *foot,* the term dates to the early seventeenth century. In Rabindranath Tagore's "The Artist," Govinda thinks of wealth in terms of pice, which are the concrete representation of Kuvera, the Hindu god of wealth; in R. K. Narayan's "An Astrologer's Day," the seer charges 3 pies per question in a consultation.

pickaback or **pickpack** or **piggyback** transported on the shoulders or back. When applied to the movement of a human, the term implies that the weight of the burden's torso is borne on the carrier's back or that the human burden sits on the carrier's shoulder, with the chest leaning on the back of the carrier's head and the arms and legs hanging down to the carrier's chest. An alternative is the fireman's carry, which involves slinging a fallen or unconscious victim over the head and shoulders of the carrier, who secures a pendant arm and leg in the hands to steady the load. A mid-sixteenth century term, it appears to have derived from childish gabble or echo words. Because of the victim's physical weakness, Father Kleinsorge evacuates Mr. Fukai pickaback to the East Parade Ground in John Hersey's *Hiroshima.*

pickaninny or **piccaninny** (*pihk'* uh . *nihn* . nee) an offensive reference to a small black or Australian aboriginal infant or child. Derived from the Portuguese for *tiny child,* the term appeared in the mid-sixteenth century during the burgeoning of the American slave trade as a racist pejorative or patronizing and dehumanizing diminutive. In Willa Cather's *My Antonia,* Miss D'Arnault is alarmed by the sight of Samson, a blind pickaninny, leaning his face toward the sun.

picket a handful or small detachment of soldiers serving as escorts or guards at an outpost or camp periphery to ward off surprise attack, theft, or sabotage; also, a police officer in a garrison. Taken from the French *picquet,* this late seventeenth-century term appears in Stephen Crane's *The Red Badge of Courage* as Henry draws near the battlefield and finds one group of pickets firing lackadaisically at enemy pickets.

pidgin (*pihd'* jihn) a makeshift blend or creative adaptation of local languages developed by traders and merchants for business purposes, among sailors and longshoremen of different nationalities, or among children at play. The word derived in the early nineteenth century from the Chinese for *business.* Pidgin often develops into creole, the colloquial language of an area or country. In Theodore Taylor's *Timothy of the Cay,* slaves from 25 tribes incorporate bits of English to create a pidgin language of their own reflecting elements of their original language groups.

pieces of eight pesos, a type of silver coin widely circulated during the eighteenth and nineteenth centuries and usually spoken of in the plural; early Spanish silver dollars, the standard currency worth 8 reals. Also called a portrait dollar, the coin carried the likeness of a king or head of state. In Robert Louis Stevenson's *Treasure Island,* Long John Silver's parrot cries "Pieces of eight!" *See also* peso.

pieman a maker and seller of pies and fruit or meat tarts, which were layered in a sturdy wicker basket or carryall and covered with a cloth to keep out insects and debris as the pieman hawked perishable wares in the marketplace, at a street gathering or festival, or door-to-door. The pieman follows the hearse, which is driven by a chimney sweep through a rowdy crowd, including Jerry Cruncher, a seedy grave robber, in Charles Dickens's *A Tale of Two Cities.*

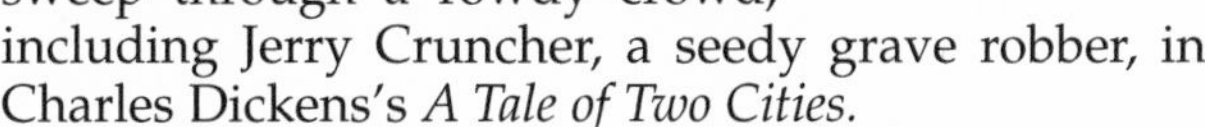

pier (peer) a wall, pillar, buttress, pilaster, or brick column made of masonry, wood, stone, or steel to support a portico, bridge span, or wall between two openings. The word, which entered English in the early seventeenth century, derives from the Latin for *rock.* In Thomas Hardy's *The Mayor of Casterbridge,* Elizabeth-Jane hides behind a brick pier from footsteps that turn out to be Michael Henchard on a visit to Lucetta.

Pierce-Arrow a veteran medium-sized touring sedan built in the early 1900s featuring a folding canvas top, fold-down windshield, front and rear button-back seats, and brass headlights and carriage lights. In James D. Houston and Jeanne Wakatsuki Houston's *Farewell to Manzanar,* Ko Wakatsuki learns to drive a Pierce-Arrow sedan while living in Idaho; in Olive Ann Burns's *Cold Sassy Tree,* Mr. Blakeslee reports that during his trip to New York he purchased a Pierce-Arrow, which will arrive by train.

pier-glass or **pier mirror** a long mirror set in the supporting pier between two windows; also, a decorative convex round mirror resembling a fish eye and producing a distorted reflection. In Margaret Atwood's *The Handmaid's Tale,* the curved pier glass contributes to the ambiguity of the setting, where concern for the production of offspring can result in the handmaid's execution if she proves infertile or incapable of bearing the Commander's child. *See* pier.**pies** *See* pice.

Pig Latin a systematic form of jargon or oral cipher popularized by children in the 1930s as a secret code. To spare Maya's tender feelings in Maya Angelou's *I Know Why the Caged Bird Sings,* Daddy Bailey refers to the victim of kidnapping by inverting the order of first letter and remaining letters—"indlay ergbay ildrenchay" for "Lindbergh children."

pignut a European root tuber or umbel of the carrot family and relative of the poisonous hemlock; the earthnut or hognut, which is used as a flavoring for alcoholic beverages and as an herbal remedy for stomach or intestinal pain, stimulation for a weak heart, and antispasmodic for muscle cramps. As the pirates dig for buried gold in Robert Louis Stevenson's *Treasure Island,* Long John Silver predicts that they will find pignuts.

pigtail tobacco a plaited hank, strand, twist, or roll of tobacco that is tucked into a pocket and bitten or cut into bite-sized pieces. A late seventeenth-century term, it applies to cheap chewing tobacco common to workers and sailors, an inferior grade for smoking in a pipe or rolling into cigars or cigarettes. After Bill's death in Robert Louis Stevenson's *Treasure Island,* Jim Hawkins searches his pockets and finds thread, needles, a thimble, coins, and pigtail tobacco chewed at the end.

pike a spike or honed point on the end of a long stave, shaft, spear, or stick; a primitive weapon used to parry the blows of an opponent. Dating to the early sixteenth century, the term may derive from the Latin for *woodpecker* or the Anglo-Saxon for *pickax.* In Charles Dickens's *A Tale of Two Cities,* executioners display the heads of guillotined officials on pikes high above the mob as a warning of vigilante justice against aristocrats and monarchists.

pilcher (*pihl'* chuhr) a rare late sixteenth-century term for a scabbard or sheath for a knife, dagger, bayonet, or short sword. Derived from the Latin for *pelt,* the term may have described a crude belt of untanned hide. Mercutio makes harsh jests against the King of Cats as he plucks his sword from its pilcher in William Shakespeare's *Romeo and Juliet.*

piles (pylz) a crude term for hemorrhoids, a protruding varicose vein or vascular tumor causing pain, swelling, dilation, and itching in the anus. Derived from the Latin for *ball,* the term usually occurs in the plural. In Rudolfo Anaya's *Bless Me, Ultima,* Antonio helps the *curandera* dig plants that cure burns, arthritis, bloody flux, sores, colic, and piles.

pillbox a concrete and steel gun emplacement usually low to the ground and perforated with small slits bristling with the barrels of machine guns or light antitank artillery aimed by guards standing behind the sturdy walls; also, a fortified underground outpost or picket. As Offred walks through Gilead for daily grocery shopping in Margaret Atwood's *The Handmaid's Tale,* she passes pillboxes guarded by machine-gunners. *See also* picket.

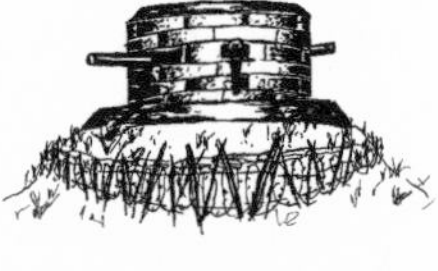

pillion (*pihl'* yuhn) an elongated saddle padded at the rear to accommodate a second rider or to steady luggage; a cushion atop a saddle cloth that attaches to the back of a saddle. From the Gaelic for *couch,* the term entered English in the early sixteenth century. Before Squire Cass's New Year's party in George Eliot's *Silas Marner,* female guests arrive with their escorts on pillions and enter the Red House to change into holiday party gowns and dancing shoes.

pillory (*pihl'* loh . ree) a wooden frame in a public place in which a public offender is confined in a wearying, humiliating position, usually with head, feet, and hands locked into position straight from the torso and forced to endure the catcalls, remonstrances, and hurled refuse and stones of passersby. A medieval term of questionable origin, the word may derive from the Latin for *pillar.* In Nathaniel Hawthorne's *The Scarlet Letter,* Hester Prynne carries her infant and follows the beadle to her place of punishment opposite the town church on the platform before the pillory where local miscreants are punished.

pilothouse a small structure on the top deck of a steamboat that houses the compass, wheel, and navigational devices. From the vantage of the pilothouse, the steersman or helmsman watches the river for snags and sandbars and guides the boat toward safe waters. Aboard a wrecked steamboat below St. Louis in Mark Twain's *The Adventures of Huckleberry Finn,* Huck notes to Jim that the texas and pilothouse are all that remains of the original structure. *See also* texas.

pinafore a low-necked, sleeveless garment, bibbed apron, wrap-around overdress, or jumper tied or pinned to the front of the dress of a child or worker to keep splashes and grime from soiling the garment underneath. A late eighteenth-century term, it derives from the English phrase *to pin to the front.* On Jane's first summons to Mrs. Reed's sitting room, the title character in Charlotte Brontë's *Jane Eyre* obeys Bessie by removing her pinafore and washing her hands.

pince nez (*pans'* nay) eyeglasses that stay in place without temple pieces because of the springy metal that fits across the bridge of the nose. Popular around the mid-nineteenth century, "pinch nose" glasses replaced the monocle and lorgnette. Professor Willard of the state university, wearing a pince nez on a satin ribbon, steps to the front of the set to read information about the area in Thornton Wilder's *Our Town.* *See also* lorgnette; monocle.

pinch bug the slang term for a beetle equipped with two forward pincers armed with barbs and hooked tips, as found on the longhorn beetle, stag beetle, or scavenger beetle. In Mark Twain's *The Adventures of Tom Sawyer,* the title character entertains himself during a church service by watching a poodle dog toy with a pinch bug.

pin money incidental cash for traveling or shopping; the weekly stipend granted by a husband to his wife for private expenditure on clothing and personal items. A late seventeenth-century term, the phrase may derive from the habit of careful travelers and shoppers of pinning bank notes or paper money to the inside of their clothing to prevent loss and foil pickpockets. Mrs. Bennet, in Jane Austen's *Pride and Prejudice,* marvels at the jewels, wealth, and pin money which Elizabeth will receive when she marries Mr. Darcy.

pinochle (*pee'* nuh . k'l) a variety of two-deck card games for two, three, or four players that award points for creating combinations of ace, king, queen, jack, ten, nine, and trumps. Derived from the French *binocle,* the game ends when a player or partnership reaches 1,000 points. After McMurphy's arrival at the hospital in Ken Kesey's *One Flew over the Cuckoo's Nest,* he arouses interest in lethargic fellow inmates by replacing pinochle with poker.

piñon or **pinyon** (*peen'* yuhn) a pine tree common to the Rocky Mountains that yields a pine nut valued by Native American cooks. Piñon nuts, which can be easily stored, transported, and traded, are added to stews, salads, or breads or toasted for snacks. As thickeners for soup, they provide fat and protein; they also serve as a base for ointments and salves. In Rudolfo Anaya's *Bless Me, Ultima,* the *curandera* burns fragrant pine wood in the stove while she treats Antonio's ailing uncle.

pinto or **paint** the small, patch-coated pony that is also named the calico, skewbald, or piebald. A mid-nineteenth century term, it derives from the Latin for *painted.* A dependable animal, the pinto earned a place in history as the mount of choice for Pony Express riders. In Scott O'Dell's *Sing Down the Moon,* three Indian captives plot their escape by tethering pintos as ready transportation back to the Navaho villages of Four Corners.

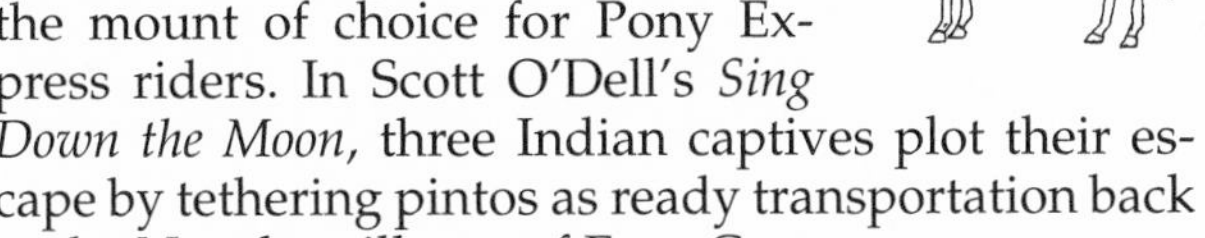

pipes *See* panpipes.

pipestone a soft, carveable red, gray, or brown clay capable of withstanding high temperatures. Quarried by several Native American tribes on neutral ground in Minnesota, pipestone became a valuable trade item for making cookware, utensils, serving dishes, arrow straighteners, and stems and bowls for calumets or ceremonial pipes; also called catlinite, steatite, soapstone, or talc. In N. Scott Momaday's *The Way to Rainy Mountain,* the speaker recalls that the dirt floor was the reddish color of pipestone.

pirogue (*pee'* rohg) or **piragua** a low, weighty dugout or canoe sometimes steadied by an outrigger. The pirogue, usually carved or burned from a single tree trunk, carries freight and passengers and is poled or paddled from island to mainland or across a bay, sound, or bayou or asea for fishing. Derived from the Caribe for *dugout,* the term entered English in the early seventeenth century. In Kate Chopin's "The Awakening," Robert asks Madame Pontellier if she is fearful of traveling back to the cabin by a tipsy pirogue.

pirouette (pih . roo . *weht'*) a formal turn in ballet requiring that the dancer stand on the ball of one foot, push off with the opposite foot, and maintain momentum and control while balancing the body upright for one or a series of full whirls. From the French for *spinning top,* the graceful dance step dates to the mid-seventeenth century. Essie, a self-styled ballerina in Moss Hart and George S. Kaufman's *You Can't Take It with You,* practices her pirouettes in the living room.

pistole (pees . *tohl'*) a slang designation of several European coins, including the French Louis, the Spanish 2-escudo coin, or the Scottish 12-pound coin. Shortened from the Italian *pistolet,* the term entered English in the late sixteenth century as a pun—literally *small daggers and shields,* which describes the pictures on the coins. After banishing his rebellious son Marius in Victor Hugo's *Les Misérables*, Monsieur Gillenormand orders his daughter to send him 60 pistoles per month, but never to mention his name again. *See also* Louis.

pitch a thickly viscous brownish-black residue resulting from the distillation of natural materials, especially coal tar, asphalt, petroleum, turpentine, or pine sap. Pitch is used as a waterproofing agent for roofing, boat hulls, pipe coating and insulation, and pavement; it is also used in cough syrup. It is the source of pitch oil, a crude lamp fuel. The hero of *Gilgamesh* uses kiln-heated bitumen pitch to caulk the hull of his new boat. *See also* caulking.

pitched ceiling an angled or raked ceiling parallel to a roof that follows the slope of the eaves of an upstairs room, garret, or attic. The windows of Grandma Baby's house in Toni Morrison's *Beloved* are set in a pitched ceiling rather than a wall; thus, they open upward and outward toward the sky.

PKU *See* phenylketonuria.

placard (*plak'* uhrd) a notice, advertisement, poster, or billboard posted on a wall or fastened to a post, fence, wall, or stick; also, a sign or plaque posted in a public place, such as an intersection or the exterior of a civic center. A sixteenth-century term, it derives from the French for *plate.* On the daily hunt for jobs, the Joad family in John Steinbeck's *The Grapes of Wrath* fall prey to the misleading handbills and roadside placards advertising for workers and promising unlikely wages and benefits in a time when many unskilled workers were competing for few jobs.

placenta (pluh . *sehn'* tuh) an oval organ rich in blood and nutrients to which the embryo of a warm-blooded animal attaches by the umbilical cord during gestation in the womb to draw nourishment and oxygen from its mother's blood. The placenta separates from the uterus and is discharged after birth. Developing instantly from water animal to land animal, the newborn animal relies on breathing and digestion for survival. Derived from the Greek for *flat,* the term entered English in the late seventeenth century. In Laura Esquivel's *Like Water for Chocolate,* Rosaura's placenta grows so firmly to her uterus that both organs are removed during Esperanza's birth; thus Rosaura can have no more children.

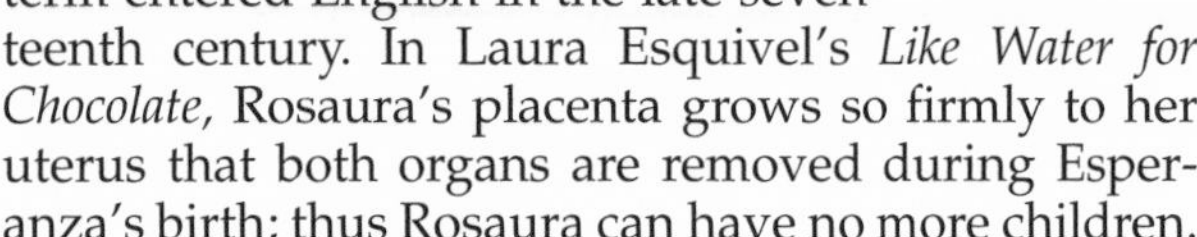

plaister *See* poultice.

plankton (*plangk'* tuhn) passive microscopic aquatic plants and animals that drift with the wind at night on the surface of currents and waves in both fresh and salt water and then collect at sunrise below the surface, where fish graze on them. Derived from the Greek for *wanderer* or *drifter,* the term entered English in the late nineteenth century. Santiago, protagonist in Ernest Hemingway's *The Old Man and the Sea,* studies the flight of seabirds and welcomes the appearance of plankton at the ocean's surface as signs of abundant fish in the waters below.

plantain (*plan'* t'n) a large family of woody herbs distinguished by rough ribbing on their leaves and a vertical spike projecting far above the collar of greenery at ground level, which is mentioned in William Shakespeare's *Romeo and Juliet* as a cure for bleeding. In Chinua Achebe's *Things Fall Apart,* Okonkwo enjoys having his wife serve him a meal of roast plantain, a starchy fruit that resembles a green banana and grows in clusters at the top of a 10- to 30-foot tree. The tropical plantain, named by the Arawak Indians, can be boiled, ground, fried, roasted, or fermented into beer and its leaves cooked as a green vegetable.

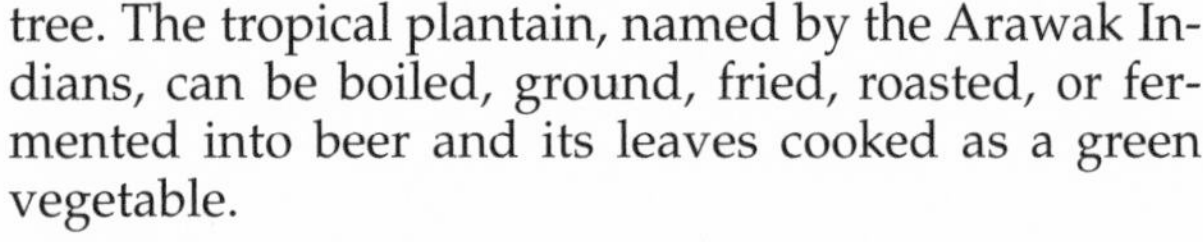

plaster *See* poultice.

plateau (pla . *toh'*) a period of stasis or leveling off of a graph, progress chart, or learning curve, indicating that the subject's performance remains stable, neither progressing nor regressing. Named for Belgian physicist J. A. F. Plateau, the term derives from early twentieth-century educational psychology, which sought to account for ups and downs in a normal learning curve. On April 8, Charlie Gordon, protagonist of Daniel Keyes's *Flowers for Algernon,* records in his diary that his teacher believes he has reached a learning plateau.

platonic (pluh . *tah'* nihk) businesslike, amicable, but not romantic; an idealistic or spiritual characteristic lacking amorous or sexual desires, intentions, or behaviors. Derived from Plato, the Greek philosopher, the term entered English in the mid-seventeenth century. While trying to maintain a platonic relationship with his teacher, Charlie Gordon, protagonist of Daniel Keyes's *Flowers for Algernon,* suffers nightmares. *See also* neurosis.

platoon (pluh . *toon'*) a subdivision of a squadron or troop of 40 soldiers led by a lieutenant. Derived in the mid-seventeenth century from the French for *ball,* the term applies more loosely to police work conducted by a group or handful of agents on foot patrol or fellow members of a watch or assigned duty. As Javert and a platoon of five or six men approach in Victor Hugo's *Les Misérables,* Jean Valjean fears that he will be arrested and parted forever from Cosette.

plebeian (pluh . *bee'* uhn) a member of the lowest social class of freedmen or Roman citizens, a person undistinguished by education, refinement, prestige, rank, or culture. From the Latin for *commoner,* the term entered English in the early sixteenth century. In a pro-suffrage speech in New York in 1873, Susan B. Anthony compares the disenfranchised female citizen to a serf, slave, or plebeian.

pleurosis (ploo . *roh'* sihs) an inflammation of the pleura, the heavily lubricated double membranes that encapsulate the lungs and line the thorax. A fifteenth-century term, it derives from the Greek for *rib.* Laura Wingfield, the handicapped daughter in Tennessee Williams's *The Glass Menagerie,* recalls how a schoolmate pronounced "pleurosis" as "blue roses."

plinth (plinth) the boxy, unadorned foundation, bottom, base, or block segment of a pedestal, pier, column, or decorative support for a wall or parapet. From the Greek for *tile,* this architectural term dates to the early seventeenth century. Mistreated, snubbed, or ignored by well-dressed Londoners awaiting transportation in George Bernard Shaw's *Pygmalion,* Eliza, a flower girl, withdraws to a plinth, where she sorts her trampled violets and waits for the rain to stop.

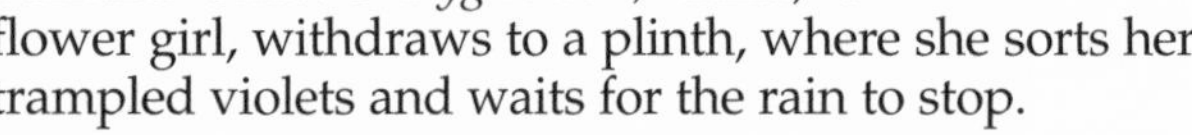

ploughshare or **plowshare** (*plow'* shayr) the lower pointed cutting edge of a plow that slices the soil and forces it up the moldboard and over so that the resulting clod is uprooted and overturned. From the Old English for *plow shear,* the term took its present form in the late medieval period and names one of the era's major contributions to civilization; the English moldboard, invented by Joseph Foljambe, was patented in 1720. In Sophocles' *Antigone,* the chorus extols the dominion of humanity over the earth, which an ox team subdues by pulling the ploughshare.

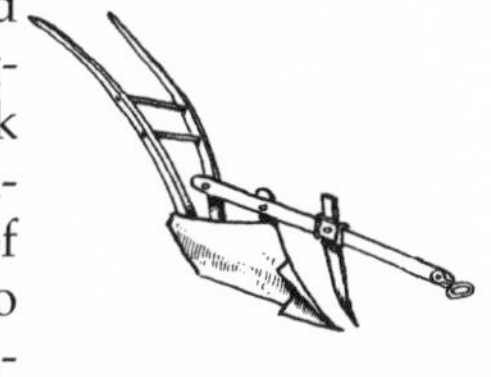

plumb line a cord or line attached to a lead weight called a plumb bob; a standard construction device. To determine the exact vertical of a building project, the user suspends the apparatus and follows the direction of the line indicated by the pull of gravity on the weight. Derived from the Latin for *lead,* the term entered English in the fifteenth century. While laying blocks in Alexander Solzhenitsyn's *One Day in the Life of Ivan Denisovich,* the title character gathers hatchet and wire brush to clear the ice and then assembles plumb line, bricklayer's gavel, and a yardstick.

pneumatic (nyoo . *mat'* ihk) **tube** a suction channel attached to a vacuum system in which currents of compressed air or gas dispatch objects along the tube toward a receptacle, disposal center, or holding tank. In George Orwell's *1984,* rewriters of history at the Ministry of Truth insert small documents into a small pneumatic tube and larger ones in a larger orifice, both of which lead to a furnace for instant incineration of unacceptable material or scraps of waste paper.

pocket-torch a portable flashlight or hand-held lamp given to soldiers as part of the regular allotment of government-issued military equipment. During the night, Detering, a trench soldier in Erich Maria Remarque's *All Quiet on the Western Front,* switches on his pocket-torch to observe a rat swinging on his portion of bread, which he suspended from a wire to keep it safe.

pock-marked defaced, spotted, or blemished by depressions, craters, or scars resulting from the pustules or infected eruptions of sebaceous cysts, wens, chicken pox, smallpox, acne, tumors, or other diseases or conditions that disfigure or pit the skin. Derived from pre–twelfth-century Dutch, the term indicates a small pocket or dent. When considering the choice of a wife, Wang Lung, protagonist in Pearl S. Buck's *The Good Earth,* concludes that a poor farmer has no need for a beauty, but he rules out any woman with pock-marked skin or a malformed lip.

pogrom (*poh'* gruhm) an organized massacre, destruction of property, terrorism, carnage, genocide, or antipersonnel assault on a community. A Yiddish term applied to the anti-Semitic violence condoned in czarist Russia during the early twentieth century, the word names vigilante-style punishment or retribution often surreptitiously or openly sanctioned by authorities and targeted at an unwanted or persecuted ethnic or minority community, particularly Jews or Gypsies. In response to the veiled warning Oskar gives Stern in Thomas Keneally's *Schindler's List,* Stern concludes that the SS is about to launch a pogrom against the Jews. *See also* holocaust; SS.

poi (poy) **See** cocoyam.

poke or **pokeweed** a common perennial weed producing tender green shoots in early spring and developing into tall, red-stemmed succulent plants. The poisonous purplish-black berries are spread by birds' ingestion of seeds, which they excrete. When picked and lightly blanched, the first leaves, called poke salad, make a tasty green vegetable. Native Americans made the seeds into ink and dye and grated and boiled the root into a purgative. After a lean winter, Jody, protagonist of Marjorie Kinnan Rawlings's *The Yearling,* digs into poke greens seasoned with pork fat, enjoys a dish blended from turtle meat, and ends his meal with sweet potato pone. *See also* pone.

pole a long, slender wood or cylindrical bamboo shaft or rod used to push, steady, or maneuver tipsy loads on a boat, canoe, pirogue, barge, or raft, especially in shallows such as a bayou, creek, or stream or over low falls. Derived in the eleventh century from the Latin for *stake,* the term is akin to *paling* and *impale.* As True Son cries piteously for help from the approaching whites in Conrad Richter's *The Light in the Forest,* the men use poles and oars to creep cautiously toward him and call to him to swim toward their boat. *See also* bayou; pirogue.

pole star Polaris, the North Star at the end of the constellation Ursa Minor, the Little Dipper, which is 680 light-years from earth; a whitish yellow light that is a fixed celestial point to which earth's northern axis points. Derived from the Latin for *fixed,* the term has permeated sailing lore since the eleventh century, when the star's variance of one degree from true north caused no serious navigational error to explorers of the Northern Hemisphere; today, pilots, sailors, and astronauts depend on more sophisticated computational methods. Confucius's *The Analects* compare a just ruler to the pole star, a fixed light to which lesser stars pay homage. Likewise, the title character in William Shakespeare's *Julius Caesar* describes himself as constant as the pole star, a guiding light to lesser men.

pomatum (poh . *may'* tuhm) a perfumed ointment or dressing used in styling hair, beards, and mustaches; pomade that coats the rough, scaly surface of the hair shaft and causes it to adhere and form into a smooth contour, wave, or curl. Derived from the Latin for *apple,* this mid-sixteenth-century term implies the sweet, natural fragrance of fruit, from which hair oil was originally made. Marmeladov, an alcoholic in Fyodor Dostoevsky's *Crime and Punishment,* confesses to protagonist Raskolnikov that he has stolen and spent for drink his daughter's money for clothes, shoes, pomatum, and other personal items.

pomegranate (*pahm'* gra . niht) a rounded fruit from an ornamental tree common to the Mediterranean. The fruit is filled with acidic, red encapsulated seeds and coated with a leathery tan rind. The fruit is fermented and blended in grenadine, a strong red flavoring for beverages and desserts; the bark is used in medicines and was once thought to purge the body of envy and greed. From the Latin for *seeded apple,* the term entered English in the fourteenth century. In Amy Tan's *The Joy Luck Club,* six months before her death, Jing-Mei Woo's mother gave her daughter a lobed jade pendant resembling a pomegranate, which some interpret as a fertility symbol.

pomelo (*pahm'* uh . loh) a shaddock, a 10- to 20-pound pear-shaped citrus fruit, the *Citrus grandis* or *Citrus maxima,* which is native to Malaysia and Polynesia and resembles a grapefruit or pompelmous with its thick rind, pale yellow pulp, and tart juice. The term, which derives from the Dutch, entered English in the mid-nineteenth century. In James Hilton's *Lost Horizon,* kidnapped arrivals discuss their plight at Shangri-La while Hugh Conway enjoys a breakfast of chupatties, pomelo, and tea.

pommel (*pahm'* m'l) the knob, saddlebow, or rounded protuberance on the front end of a saddle.

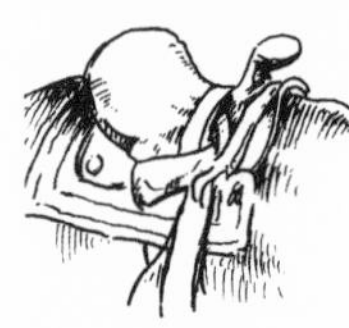

Derived from the Latin for *apple,* this fourteenth-century term describes the globular shape of the grip, which is both ornamental and practical. Tom Black Bull, rodeo champion in Hal Borland's *When the Legends Die,* uses a familiar method of controlling a bucking horse—he allows his body to unite with the jolting movement by tightening his knees below the pommel and letting the reins go slack.

pone (pohn) a flat cake of cornbread, usually baked in a skillet, but also on a flat stone or the blade of a hoe or shovel. Humble forms of unleavened pone are made from water and meal; tastier recipes call for shortening, baking powder, salt, and other flavorings, such as grated cheese, corn, or toasted slivers of pork rind. In literature set in colonial times or in the outback, especially Marjorie Kinnan Rawlings's *The Yearling,* pone is a handy food to wrap and store for travel and can be sliced and layered with butter, mashed beans, or strips of bacon.

poniard (*pahn'* yuhrd) a slender dirk or dagger consisting of hilt and a three- or four-sided blade; a lightweight personal weapon worn in a scabbard or sheath at the waist and attached to a belt or bandolier for easy access. The multisided stab wound from such a weapon requires more stitches and heals more slowly, leaving a thick scar. While explaining the complicated six-pass duel between the title character and Laertes in William Shakespeare's *Hamlet,* Osric notes that King Claudius has put up six barbary horses as a wager against Laertes' poniards, sheaths, and other goods. *See also* dirk; scabbard.

pontoon bridge a floating bridge built on barrels or inflatable tanks. Usually a temporary structure constructed by the military for easy troop and equipment transport, as with the construction the Persians used for Xerxes' invasion of Greece. The pontoon bridges of harbors and inlets swing wide to allow passage of tall ships, barges, and other commercial and passenger traffic. At the pontoon bridge in Punda, Phillip and other citizens cheer the British tanker steaming its way out of Curaçao's harbor in Theodore Taylor's *The Cay.*

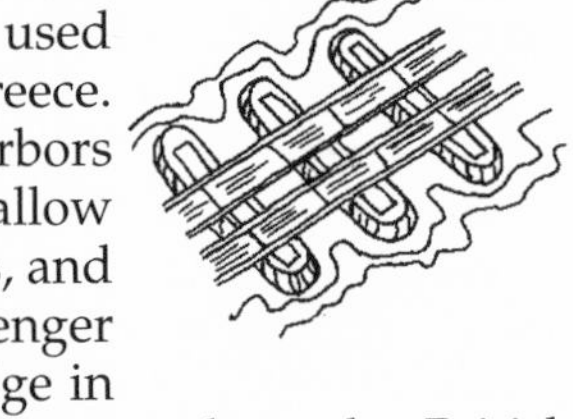

pony drag a canvas or rawhide travois; an A-shaped framed, wheelless conveyance common to the Plains Indian horse culture. The pendant strip was dragged on the ground to transport parcels, domestic goods, and sick, injured, or aged people. In John Neihardt's *Black Elk Speaks,* the aged seer recalls that he became so ill in boyhood that his family had to carry him in a pony drag.

poop deck the highest deck, which is located at the rear of the ship and gives a commanding view of the rigging and the remaining upper decks. The English term derives from the Latin word *puppis* or stern. The poop deck offers a clear view of obstacles and the horizon to the young unnamed captain in Joseph Conrad's "The Secret Sharer." Ironically, he looks to the rear rather than forward to the unprecedented events that are about to alter his view of himself and his role as captain.

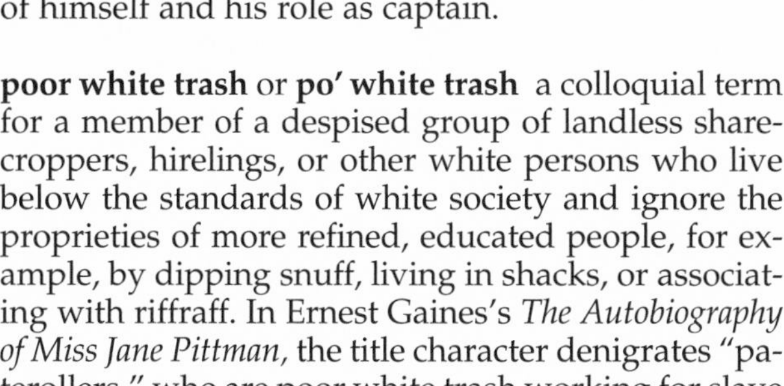

poor white trash or **po' white trash** a colloquial term for a member of a despised group of landless sharecroppers, hirelings, or other white persons who live below the standards of white society and ignore the proprieties of more refined, educated people, for example, by dipping snuff, living in shacks, or associating with riffraff. In Ernest Gaines's *The Autobiography of Miss Jane Pittman,* the title character denigrates "paterollers," who are poor white trash working for slave masters for a bounty, or fee, to recover runaways. *See also* pateroller; peckerwood.

poppet (*pahp'* piht) a doll, hand or finger puppet, or marionette, often with jointed limbs; also, a human effigy decked with human hair or constructed from wax or stuffed cloth stuck with pins or thorns. Witches or sorcerers employ these crude figurines to harm or cast spells on the person represented or to mark a path or area where outsiders are forbidden. Derived from the Latin for *doll,* this fifteenth-century term has fallen into disuse. Mary Warren's gift of a homemade poppet to Elizabeth Proctor results in serious court inquiry and implications of sorcery in Arthur Miller's *The Crucible.*

pop-the-whip or **crack-the-whip** a rowdy race or speed game played by ice skaters who join hands and follow the leader in rapid swirls and reversals of direction that gather momentum and put strain on the last member or members, who comprise the tip of the "whip" and who usually lose hold and fall. In the autobiographical *Black Boy,* Richard Wright's aunt, a teacher in a parochial school, delights in seeing her nephew hurt in cruel games of pop-the-whip.

porch in classical architecture, a decorative portico, porte cochère, colonnade, or cloister roofed over a series of symmetrical columns to provide a shelter against harsh weather, a shaded outdoor walkway, or a gathering spot; a graceful addition to an otherwise lackluster rectangular building. Entering English in the fourteenth century, the term derives from the Latin for *port.* After solidifying their plan to lure Brutus into an assassination plot, Cassius sets off on a stormy night to meet with unnamed conspirators at Pompey's Porch in William Shakespeare's *Julius Caesar. See also* porte cochère.

porphyry (*pohr'* fuh . ree) a hard red or purple igneous rock imbedded with variable amounts of red or white feldspar, quartz, or fine crystal. Porphyry is easily cut into ornate shapes and polished for use in architectural detail, serving dishes, vases, jewelry boxes, or costume jewelry. From the Greek for *purple,* the term entered English in the fifteenth century. During his walks about the club at Savile Row, Phileas Fogg, protagonist of Jules Verne's *Around the World in Eighty Days,* admires the domed gallery supported by red porphyry Ionic columns.

porringer (*pohr'* rihn . juhr) a shallow metal or ceramic dish or bowl, often with one or two sculpted or pierced handles. The porringer holds broth, soup, stew, porridge, gruel, or one-dish meals and is often placed on trays served to invalids; also, a cereal bowl from which infants and toddlers or handicapped people are fed. From the French for *soup,* the term entered English in the early sixteenth century. When the haberdasher presents Kate with a new cap in William Shakespeare's *The Taming of the Shrew,* Petruchio scorns its curves, which he declares were shaped on a porringer.

portage (*pohr'* tihj) the conveyance of a pirogue, canoe, dugout, or boat by hand overland from one waterway to another in order to skirt or avoid dangerous shoals, whitewater, sandbars, rapids, or cascades. Shortened from *porterage,* this fifteenth-century term derives from the Latin for *carry.* According to Scott O'Dell's *Streams to the River, River to the Sea,* Sacagawea observes the crew of the Lewis and Clark expedition conducting frequent portage of canoes from one stream to another.

portcullis (pohrt . *kuhl'* lihs) a crosshatched or grated gate or latticework composed of pointed iron bars or wood slats forming a screen that is suspended by block and tackle or rope and windlass and lowered on a grooved slide or track to inhibit passage through an entrance gate, drawbridge, or tunnel. From the Latin for *entrance filter,* this fourteenth-century term names a standard architectural defense mechanism of medieval castles. Before

a daring escape by water in a barrel, Bilbo Baggins, protagonist in J. R. R. Tolkien's *The Hobbit,* notes that the stream he is about to enter can be shut off by a portcullis that descends all the way to the streambed.

porte cochère (pohrt . koh . *shehr'*) the French term for *coach door,* which names a spacious covered passageway, interior courtyard, shelter, carport, or lighted carriage port through which vehicles pass to allow passengers to alight or enter a residence, colonnade, or building in safety and comfort. On his arrival to his master's porte cochère, the central dog in Jack London's *White Fang* suffers attacks by a collie and a charging deer-hound.

portfolio (pohrt . *foh'* lee . oh) an ample, two-sided, flexible leather, stiffened canvas, or cardboard case for transporting, protecting, collecting, or flattening art prints, sketches, documents, photos, loose papers and brochures, manuscripts, drawings, maps, or music. An early eighteenth-century Latin term meaning *page carrier,* the portfolio usually folds in the middle and ties on its outer ends for ease of storage. In the early period of her employment, the title character of Charlotte Brontë's *Jane Eyre* sends her portfolio to Mr. Rochester, presumably so that he can display her artistic talents to his guests.

portieres (pohr . *tyerz'*) curtains, strings of beads, netting, or drapes suspended over a doorway, portico, alcove, or inner room that give the illusion of a dividing wall, prevent drafts, or shut out unwanted light or insects; also, a room divider or screen that turns a large room into smaller units, such as a parlor, dining area, or bedroom. From the French for *doorkeeper,* the term entered English in the mid-nineteenth century. The humble setting of Tennessee Williams's *The Glass Menagerie* consists of inner rooms made semiprivate by portieres. *See also* alcove.

portmanteau (pohrt . *man'* toh) a large, stiff-sided carrying case, traveler's suitcase, or folding piece of luggage hinged in the middle and opening flat into two units similar to the modern two-suiter. From the French for *cloak carrier,* the term dates to the mid-sixteenth century. The monster in Mary Shelley's *Frankenstein* discovers a leather portmanteau from which he obtains books and teaches himself to read.

Portuguese man-of-war or **man-o'-war** a translucent, pastel-hued tropical marine animal kin to the jelly fish composed of a floating, gas-filled air sac, or bladder, and a crimped crest or sail above and underwater streamers as long as 165 feet. Underneath the bubble body lie poisonous cysts, polyps, or stinger cells that paralyze prey, then devour and digest them. While rowing his fishing boat, Santiago, protagonist in Ernest Hemingway's *The Old Man and the Sea,* looks down in the Sargasso weed and observes small fish swimming harmlessly among the filaments of a poisonous Portuguese man-of-war, which floats on the ocean surface like a bubble.

posole (poh . *soh'* lay) a southwestern vegetable also called hominy, a popcorn-shaped cereal grain from which grits are ground. A common dish described in Antonio's family's holiday menu in Rudolfo Anaya's *Bless Me, Ultima,* posole is made of dried yellow or white corn kernels that are soaked in oak ashes or lye, thoroughly rinsed, then cooked and seasoned with meat drippings or served with milk.

posset (*pahs'* siht) a soothing evening or bedtime drink or sleeping potion made from hot, sweetened, and spiced curdled milk, ale, wine, or cider. Perhaps derived from the Latin for *hot drink,* the term entered English in the Middle Ages. Before the murder of Duncan in William Shakespeare's *Macbeth,* Lady Macbeth serves the door guards a drugged posset so that Macbeth can easily gain entrance to the king's chamber and commit murder without being observed.

postboy *See* postilion.

postern (*pahs'* tuhrn) a small, plain side or back entrance, gate, stile, or secret escape that stands apart or out of sight of the main entrance of a fort, castle, or manse; a private entrance or back door used for deliveries or mundane domestic traffic. Derived from the Latin for *behind,* the term entered English in the Middle Ages. After an unidentified visitor ignores Heathcliff's curses, grabs a lantern, and pushes through the postern to escape foul weather in Emily Brontë's *Wuthering Heights,* Joseph stops milking and sets the dogs after the intruder. *See also* stile.

postilion or **postillion** (poh . *stihl'* yuhn) a rider or postboy who mounted the lead horse of a driverless stagecoach or postchaise to guide the vehicle from one posting-house or waystation to another. From the Italian for *mail station,* the term entered English in the early seventeenth century. In Charles Dickens's *A Tale of Two Cities,* during the early days of the French Revolution, the postilion applies the whip to start the team moving on the way from the beleaguered city of Paris. *See also* posting-house.

posting-house or **post-house** a sixteenth- or seventeenth-century waystation, hostel, or inn where rental horses were available to travelers who needed to change teams and to postilions who needed to replace lame dray animals or frayed harnesses; a place to secure food, lodging, fodder, or fresh mounts. In Charles Dickens's *A Tale of Two Cities,* the coach stands free of horses while the new postilion completes the trade of a new team for the old. *See also* postilion.

post office book recording device for a British savings plan that allows depositors to leave fixed sums of money in personal accounts at post offices, where clerks indicate the amount and accrued interest with stamps that can be exchanged for the equivalent amount of currency. In Alan Paton's *Cry, the Beloved Country,* Reverend Stephen Kumalo carries a post office book worth 10 pounds, which he and his wife were saving to buy a stove.

post with post a medieval relay or circuit postal system similar to the pony express that passes along documents, official decrees, parcels, and packets of letters to individual riders who cover a customary route before changing horses and returning to the opposite end of the circuit. When the title character of William Shakespeare's *Macbeth* receives word of his promotion to Thane of Cawdor, the news travels by post with post.

potassium cyanide (poh . *tas'* see . uhm *sy'* uh . nyd) a white alkali crystalline salt used as an insecticide, fumigant, or virulent poison. For self-protection, Farley Mowat, the biologist author of *Never Cry Wolf,* packs guns, ammunition, and "wolf getters"—devices that shoot potassium cyanide into the mouths of wolves that come too close.

potlatch or **patshall** (*pat'* shuhl) a traditional dance and banquet of the Bella Coola, Puyallup, Tsimshian, Nootka, and Haida tribes of the Pacific Northwest. A host initiates the gathering each winter to welcome a new baby, christen a building, initiate a youth into a tribe, honor the dead, settle a squabble, or extend personal prestige through the distribution of elaborate gifts of blankets, shell jewelry, and copper ornaments. Outlawed by Canadian authorities in 1921, the Kwakiutl potlatch that Margaret Craven describes in *I Heard the Owl Call My Name* continued in secret after being disguised as a Christmas rite or held in a remote location.

potpourri (*poh* . puhr . *ree'*) a musical medley, diverse sampling, or combination of melodies; any mixture, hodgepodge, or grab-bag of items. Also, a blend of fragrant herbs, leaves, flowers, and spices used in sachets, room fresheners, and drawer and luggage linings. From the French for *rotten pot,* the term entered English in the early seventeenth century. Mattie Silver, the servant girl in Edith Wharton's *Ethan Frome,* has few skills, including reciting verse, trimming a hat, and playing a potpourri from *Carmen.*

Potter's Field the public burial ground of criminals, unidentified corpses, miscreants denied by their families, and paupers or charity cases from the workhouse interred at community or parish expense. Named for the cemetery mentioned in Matthew 27:7, the term implies ignominy or shame for the person who ends up in an ignoble graveyard. In the final chapter of Victor Hugo's *Les Misérables,* Jean Valjean lies buried under an unreadable inscription in a tomb in Potter's Field, beyond the fashionable monuments of Paris's prestigious Père Lachaise. *See also* workhouse.

pottle (*paht'* t'l) a small tankard; also, an open straw carton or basket woven of wood slats or splints to hold fragile fruit such as berries or tomatoes that require a framework to ward off bruising and free movement of air to inhibit mold and decay. On Pip's first day in London in Charles Dickens's *Great Expectations,* his roommate returns late from Covent Garden market with two bags and a pottle of strawberries, a gesture of courtesy, welcome, and good will.

poultice (*pohl'* tihs) a soft, hot, moist dressing, plaster, or bandage made from a leaf, hide, cloth, or piece of sterile gauze that is coated with salve, medication, or a peppery concoction and placed over a wound or over an ailing organ of a sick person, particularly the throat or lungs. For example, a mustard plaster on the chest of a pneumonia victim raises the body temperature, kills fever, relieves painful breathing, and loosens phlegm because of the increased circulation of blood. In Nikolai Gogol's "The Overcoat," the doctor orders a poultice but indicates that Akaky Akakievich cannot survive more than a day or two.

pound the major unit of English currency. Until the introduction of decimal currency in Britain in 1971 it consisted of 20 shillings; since that date 100 pence have made up a pound. In Charles Dickens's *David Copperfield,* the impecunious Mr. Micawber relies on a mere 20 pounds per year to keep up a large family; David, who is apprenticed to Spenlow and Jorkins, receives a generous 90 pounds per year plus room and board. In Avi's *The True Confessions of Charlotte*

Doyle, set in 1832, 6 pounds pays passage aboard a merchant brig from Liverpool to Providence, Rhode Island. *See also* crown; guinea; shilling.

powder horn a flask, carrying case, or carton for storing and carrying gun powder. The receptacle, which was common in the seventeenth and eighteenth centuries, is made from the tip and shaft of a cow or ox horn that is sealed at the bottom with a piece of wood or metal or a scrap of hide and fitted with a shoulder strap or bandolier that could be fastened to the musket when not in use. The tip is sliced open to be used as a pouring spout for charging a muzzle-loading rifle. To keep the powder dry, the horn is sealed with a cap, rag, or plug. Before stealing Ben Gunn's boat, Jim Hawkins, the protagonist of Robert Louis Stevenson's *Treasure Island,* arms himself with rifle, powder horn, and bullets.

powhiterash *See* poor white trash.

pow-wow a formal convention, caucus, inter-tribal gathering, or ceremony, sometimes extended to include craft shows, dancing, shooting and wrestling matches, trick riding, and feasting. Adopted into English from Algonquin, the term now refers to a conference or serious discussion. In Stephen Crane's *The Red Badge of Courage,* Henry Fleming describes the cluster of artillery as a grim pow-wow. In contrasting usage, the speaker in Mark Twain's *Life on the Mississippi* typifies a noisy uproar as a pow-wow. *See also* caucus; parley.

praetor (*pree'* tuhr) in ancient Roman government, one of two annually elected magistrates, civil justices, trust officers, or judges, who were increased in number to eight by the first century B.C. because of civic demands on the court system. The praetor ranked below a consul in public prestige; the post was considered a necessary step in a politician's rise through civilian ranks to top position. In William Shakespeare's *Julius Caesar,* Cassius instructs Cinna to leave a piece of propaganda in the praetor's chair where Brutus is sure to find it.

praetorian (pruh . *toh'* ree . uhn) **guard** an elite body guard stationed in Rome and assigned to surround, protect, or accompany generals and, in the time of Caesar Augustus, to shield the Roman emperor from harm or assassins, particularly during public functions and in times of civic unrest. By the time of Claudius's accession to the throne, the powerful praetorian guard selected him to succeed the deranged Caligula. Professor Faber reminds Guy Montag, protagonist in Ray Bradbury's *Fahrenheit 451,* that books are like Caesar's praetorian guard—they constantly remind the mighty and prestigious of their mortality.

praline (*prah'* leen) a crisp candy made from almonds, pecans, or peanuts boiled in vanilla and molasses or sugar, cooled to harden the mixture, and then coated with chocolate. According to tradition, Louis XIII christened the confection in honor of the duc de Praslin (1598–1675). Because of his sexual dalliance with Eva, Lena punishes Jimmy, the child selected to lead the blacks to freedom in Ernest Gaines's *The Autobiography of Miss Jane Pittman,* then joins the other doting women who reward the boy with hugs and pralines.

prayer stick or **keetaan** in the animistic faith of Hopi, Kickapoo, Navaho, Pueblo, and other Native Americans of the southwest, a wand, hollow reed, ceremonial baton, or dowel often stuffed with corn pollen, feathers, or stones. The prayer stick enhances the act of prayer or ritual chant. Sometimes scored, painted, or edged with feathers, the prayer stick, like the one described in Aldous Huxley's *Brave New World,* symbolizes the sanctity of Zuñi communication with the spirit world.

precentor (prih . *sehn'* tuhr) derived in the early seventeenth century from the Latin for *chanting before,* the term is the formal title of the choir leader at a church service or the choirmaster or music cleric of a cathedral; in a synagogue, the cantor or leader of the congregation's liturgical responses. During a quarrel between Ralph and Jack Merridew about a fainting choirboy in William Golding's *Lord of the Flies,* Jack recalls that the same singer passed out on the precentor at matins. *See also* matins.

prefect (*pree'* fehkt) the head administrator or a high official of a state, province, or department. Derived from the ancient Roman civil post of governor of a foreign city or province, the term applies to various levels of power and responsibility in European bureaucracy. On the recommendation of the prefect in Victor Hugo's *Les Misérables,* Father Madeleine is appointed mayor. *See also mairie.*

press an upright shelved pantry, cupboard, clothes chest, bookcase, or wardrobe, often featuring small compartments above or below. An imposing piece of furniture designed to keep safe important objects or garments, the press was often built into a recess in a wall or designed free-standing on legs. As illustrated in Toni Morrison's *Beloved,* garments were hung in a press or chifforobe because nineteenth-century houses contained no closets. *See also* armoire; chifferobe.

prie-dieu (pree . *dyuh'*) *pl.* ***prie-dieux*** a low desk, ledge, or shelf for prayer books or Bible; a kneeling rail for studying devotionals, resting the head or forearms during meditation, and saying prayers. Derived from the French for *pray God,* the private prayer bench was a common sight in bedrooms, alcoves, or other private places in eighteenth-century homes. In Gustave Flaubert's *Madame Bovary,* the title character has a fleeting memory of her girlhood and of nuns praying at the *prie-dieu.*

primer (*prih'* muhr) originally, a textbook or prayer book that introduces a child to the alphabet and the rudiments of phonics, spelling, and reading along with the basics of religious dogma; an elementary reader, anthology, or introduction to a course of study. A fourteenth-century term derived from the Latin for *first,* the work originated in a period when religion and education were taught simultaneously through repetition of homilies, Bible verses, and moral advice, for example, "An idle mind is the Devil's workshop." By age three, Pearl, daughter of Hester Prynne in Nathaniel Hawthorne's *The Scarlet Letter,* knows well the *New England Primer* and the first column of the Westminster Catechism.

primipara (pry . *mih'* puh . *ruh*) a medical designation for a woman giving birth for the first time. The contrasting term—multipara—indicates to ambulance attendants, nurses, and admitting staff that the woman in labor has undergone more than one birth and is likely to advance to delivery more quickly than does a primipara. At age 37 during her first pregnancy, Offred's mother recalls a medical chart listing her an "aged primipara" in Margaret Atwood's *The Handmaid's Tale.*

prioress (*pry'* uh . rihs) a nun, deputy abbess, or mother superior in charge of the administration and community outreach of a religious house, such as a priory, abbey, or convent. Derived from the Latin for *coming before,* the term dates to the fourteenth century and is the feminine equivalent of *prior.* The gardener at the priory in Victor Hugo's *Les Misérables* introduces Jean Valjean as his 50-year-old brother and Cosette as Valjean's granddaughter; the prioress accepts the two suppliants and admits Jean as the priory's assistant gardener.

prism (prihzm) a solid piece of glass or crystal that admits light through a triangular segment and separates its rays into their basic colors; also, a decorative bauble, luster, pendulum, or ornate appendage added to a light fixture or sconce or hung as a light-catcher in a window as a means of spreading refracted light about a room. The term, derived from the Greek for *sawed,* entered English in the sixteenth century. As firemen chop and smash their way into Guy Montag's house in Ray Bradbury's *Fahrenheit 451,* the sound of crashing prisms and Mildred's mutters blend with Professor Faber's questions about what is happening to Guy.

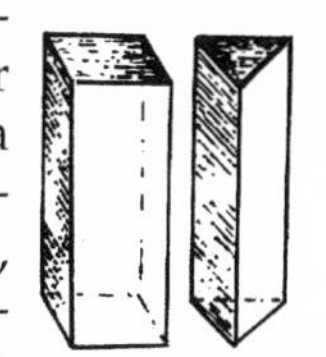

probate (*proh'* bayt) assessment of a will or other legal document by a judge or legal official to ascertain its validity, authenticity, and substance; also, the official designation of the genuine will and testament of a deceased person and the granting of inheritors of certified rights and dispersals stated in the document. From the Latin for *prove,* the term entered English in the fifteenth century and serves as a final assessment of a person's intent concerning who should receive all worldly goods, money, stocks, bonds, and other properties and entitlements. In a telegram to Mattie Ross in Charles Portis's *True Grit,* Lawyer Daggett indicates that he wants to hurry her father's will through probate and discuss important business that Mattie's mother is incapable of handling.

proboscis (proh . *bahs'* kuhs) an elongated trunk, nose, mouth or breathing tube, flexible snout, or other prominent facial organ through which an organism breathes, sucks, or ingests fluids from plants or other sources of food. From the Greek for *feed forward,* the term entered English in the late sixteenth century. Through a telescoping proboscis in Ray Bradbury's *Fahrenheit 451,* the mechanical hound injects numbing agents—procaine or morphine—into its victims. *See also* muzzle.

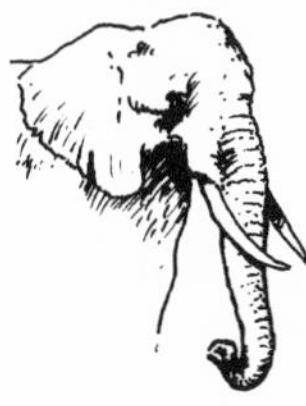

proclamation (*prah* . kluh . *may'* shuhn) a formal or public reading of an official edict, order, ban, denunciation, decree, manifestation, or announcement from a king, emperor, president, mayor, ruling body, or head of a business, university, or other public institution. One of the most famous proclamations in American history is the Emancipation Proclamation, drafted in 1862 and executed as of January 1, 1863, by which President Abraham Lincoln declared all slaves in the Confederate states free. After a presentation of this proclamation in Ernest Gaines's *The Autobiography of Miss Jane Pittman,* the master announces that he will retain any former slaves who are willing to work but that he lacks the cash to pay wages.

protocol (*proh'* tuh . kahl) a formal study and adherence to ceremony, ritual, and courtesy, particularly toward the local expectations of correct behavior, propriety, and precedence among foreign people, visitors, or outsiders. Among the duties of a protocol officer are the arrangements for introductions, seating at conferences and state dinners, attendance at state weddings and funerals, and correspondence concerning the rank and privilege of people in both friendly and enemy nations. In William J. Lederer and Eugene Burdick's *The Ugly American,* Prince Ngong serves the nation as protocol officer by smoothing meetings and state occasions for political leaders and diplomats.

provost (*proh'* vohst or *proh'* voh) a member of a military police detail; an aid to the provost marshal, who supervises military police, heads a military camp, and takes charge of prisoners awaiting court-martial or a military tribunal. Derived from the Latin for *placed in charge,* this term, which entered English in the eleventh century, centers on control and authority. On the march to the aid station in Stephen Crane's *The Red Badge of Courage,* Henry Fleming and his unnamed companions pass provost officers and escorts accompanying wounded officers.

psoriasis (suh . *ry'* uh . sihs) derived from the Greek for *an itching skin disease,* this dermatological term names a noncontagious chronic inflammation of the nails and the skin on the knees, elbows, scalp, chest, lower back, and buttocks. Possibly hereditary, psoriasis is marked by unsightly lesions, dry, white scaly patches, itching, mild surface bleeding, topical infection, and the formation of thickened plaque. There is no known cure; treatment may require scraping, rubbing with steroid cream, or coating with coal tar and exposure to ultraviolet light. To cover up for Beatrice, who often keeps her daughter Tillie out of school in Paul Zindel's *The Effects of Gamma Rays on Man-in-the Moon Marigolds,* Ruth tells the principal that Beatrice is terminally ill with gangrene, ringworm, psoriasis, and leprosy. *See also* leprosy.

psychoanalyst (*sy* . koh . *an'* uh . lihst) a mental health worker who treats emotional disorders by applying methods evolved from the findings of Dr. Sigmund Freud, an influential Viennese physician of the late nineteenth and early twentieth centuries. Treatment requires lengthy patient analysis through questioning about early childhood perceptions and relationships; study of recurrent dreams, repressed feelings, and overt conflicts that cause neurotic reactions and behaviors; or hypnosis. After numerous failures in private schools and an adverse reaction to his brother's death, Holden Caulfield, protagonist in J. D. Salinger's *Catcher in the Rye,* receives treatment from a psychoanalyst at a clinic near Hollywood, California.

psychopath (*sy'* koh . path) a mentally and emotionally unstable, antisocial person driven to bizarre behaviors, sexual perversion, demand for instant gratification of desires, violence, addiction to drugs, disorderly and impulsive acts, and an inability to feel remorse or to learn from experience how to control these episodes. McMurphy, an inmate remanded to a mental institution for evaluation of violent behavior in Ken Kesey's *One Flew over the Cuckoo's Nest,* questions the doctor about the nurse's written comment that he is a psychopath.

psychosis (sy . *koh'* sihs) a severe mental disorder or personality fragmentation, possibly the result of brain damage, tumor, or drug addiction. Psychosis may manifest itself in extreme disorientation, loss of contact with reality, delusions, hallucinations, imaginary voices, violent behaviors, and general inability to live, work, or maintain normal relationships with family and friends. The captain in Ray Bradbury's *The Martian Chronicles* implies to Hinkston that the best way to deal with the psychosis plaguing immigrants from Earth is by convincing them that their new home *is* Earth. *See also* neurosis; psychoanalyst.

psychosurgery (*sy* . koh . *suhr'* juh . ree) brain surgery intended to lessen seizures or aggression, to free the patient from intense pain, to enhance thinking processes, and to control asocial or antisocial behavior, in cases involving criminal or sexual violence. In an argument with Dr. Strauss in Daniel Keyes's *Flowers for Algernon,* Dr. Nemur claims that his advances in psychosurgery and enzyme injections will one day become standard practice in the treatment of mental retardation.

ptarmigan (*tar'* mih . guhn) a sturdy herbivorous bird of the grouse family that adapts to the colors of the wild, from speckled brown feathers in summer to white in winter. The ptarmigan thrives in the wilds, barrens, tundra, moors, and wastelands and is a natural prey to wolves, owls, and foxes. Derived from the Greek spelling of the Gaelic for *croak,* this pseudo-Greek term entered English in the late seventeenth century. As his understanding of life in the Yukon becomes less civilized, Buck, the dog protagonist in Jack London's *The Call of the Wild,* becomes adept at snatching a ptarmigan from the nest, cadging chipmunks, or grabbing fish.

pub the colloquial name for a public house; an inn, hotel, bar, taproom, or tavern. Managed by a publican or barkeep, a pub offers limited lunch and dinner menus while specializing in beer, ale, liquor, mixed drinks, and light snacks such as popcorn, peanuts, pickled eggs, or chips. A place of camaraderie in many parts of Europe and the United States, a pub may offer music, dancing, games of cards or darts, or pinball machines. After witnessing a bombing and a bloodless hand in a gutter, Winston Smith, protagonist in George Orwell's *1984,* turns into an alley and enters a pub where proles drink, argue, and relax from their toils.

pueblo (*pweh'* bloh) a dense community formed of interconnected, flat-topped rooms and suites built of stone or adobe and rising level at a time atop a mesa or against a butte. Derived from the Latin for *people* and serving as a community lifestyle since 6000 B.C., the elevated pueblo provides inexpensive housing and protection from rain, snow, or enemy attack. The pueblo setting of Aldous Huxley's *Brave New World* depicts the use of ladders as a means of moving supplies of water and food up the steep grade of a Zuñi pueblo. *See also* adobe; kiva; mesa.

pukka or **pukkah** or **pucka** (*puhk'* kuh) quality, A-one, or first-rate; genuine, firm, reliable, sure, solid, founded, established, or authentic. In describing clothing or behavior, the term indicates propriety or social acceptability. Also, in description of danger or disease, it denotes an extreme, severe, or life-threatening experience. Derived from the Hindi for *solid,* the term entered English in the late seventeenth century and appears to be derived from the Greek for *cook.* While discussing the arrival in Shangri-La by sedan chair with bearers for the baggage in James Hilton's *Lost Horizon,* Rutherford deduces that it was a pukka expedition.

pulley a grooved wheel or set of wheels through which passes the rope, belt, cable, or chain of a winch to lift heavy or awkward loads; a rotating device that transmits power to lighten the load pulled by a block and tackle. Dating to the fourteenth century, the term, which names one of the world's simplest tools, derives from the Greek for *axis.* Sitting innocently in the hay barn under a mechanical forklift suspended from a pulley in John Steinbeck's *Of Mice and Men,* Lennie passes his Sunday afternoon petting a puppy, oblivious to the doom that awaits him. *See also* capstan.

Pullman a railroad parlor coach or sleeping car containing overhead storage compartments, small sinks or water fountains, and facing sofas or upholstered lounges and upper cantilevered shelves that can be made up into lower and upper berths or sleeping compartments. Bearing the patronym of the inventor, George M. Pullman, the term names an elegant, comfortable way to travel in the late nineteenth century. From an elderly Pullman porter, Malcolm X gets a railroad job selling snacks, a departure from Boston heartily approved by his sister in Alex Haley's *The Autobiography of Malcolm X.*

pulque (*puhl'* kay) a common beverage in the southwestern United States and Central America made from the fermented juice of the maguey or agave plant. At one time, Aztecs sanctified pulque as a holy drink given them by their feathered god, Quetzalcoatl. Derived from the Nahuatl for *decomposed,* the term entered English in the late seventeenth century as Europeans made more frequent contact with desert Indians. For breakfast, Kino and Juana, the main characters of John Steinbeck's *The Pearl,* eat corn cakes dipped in sauce and enjoy a drink of pulque.

pump originating in the seventeenth century, a simple low-heeled or heelless court shoe for men or women, usually low-cut along the vamp, undecorated, and lacking strings, ties, or lacing. Because the pump grips the ball of the foot, it is suitable for gymnastics or dancing. Modern versions primarily for women have elevated the heel to medium or high while maintaining the classic cut and uncluttered lines of the early model. In William Shakespeare's *A Midsummer Night's Dream,* Bottom is eager to thread ribbons through pumps to get on with the evening's entertainment.

puncheon (*puhn'* chuhn) a roughly dressed timber, trunk, wood slab, or log split and left raw on the underside, but polished or smoothed on the flat side for use on a roadbed or under rails or as a door port, root or mine support, bench, trestle table, stave, or shelf. A medieval term, it derives from the Latin for *puncture.* Will Tweedy takes comfort from seeing his mama and grandmother sitting on a sawmill puncheon to hear his Friday recitation in Olive Ann Burns's *Cold Sassy Tree.*

punchinello (*puhn* . chih . *nehl'* loh) or **pulchinello** or **punch** a comic, long-nosed, hunchbacked figure dressed in motley colors, including a ruffled collar, patched or parti-colored suit, and matching cap with a peak and a bell on the end. Derived from troupes of street performers that developed into the Italian *commedia dell' arte,* Punchinello is the forerunner of Punch, the aggressive mate in Punch and Judy puppet shows. Ragueneau, friend of the title character in Edmond Rostand's *Cyrano de Bergerac,* describes the man's plume, sword, and punchinello ruff, above which rises a magnificent nose.

punkah or **punka** (*puhn'* kuh) the Hindi word for a late eighteenth-century fabric- or canvas-covered frame or fan woven from a palmyra leaf. Common to southern India and Pakistan, the punkah swings down from the ceiling by rope or cord and pulley operated manually by a servant. In Ruth Prawer Jhabvala's *Heat and Dust,* pulling the punkah is lowly work performed by servants or children, but use of the invention is considered necessary in colonial British homes to stir the air and keep flies and dust from spoiling meals.

punt a long, square-nosed, flat-bottomed boat or skiff used in shallow water and propelled by a pole. From the Latin for *bridge,* the term dates to the eleventh century and describes a common form of transportation down a stream or creek or pleasure-boating on a private lake or inland waterway. Hyzenthley, a doe rabbit in Richard Adams's *Watership Down,* warns Hazel that the punt may not clear the bridge when it drifts downstream and may become lodged in the supports. *See also* poling.

purgatory (*puhr'* guh . toh . ree) from the Latin for *purifying,* a medieval Roman Catholic concept of limbo, a spiritual waiting period or intermediate segment of the afterlife. The deceased, who died without completing their atonement for sins, live apart from God. During this temporary period of anticipation or yearning, unpurified souls await cleansing and atonement before attaining grace and entering heaven. To ease the unrest of those who wait in limbo, mourners on earth offer prayers of sanctification and release. Before Antonio's first communion in Rudolfo Anaya's *Bless Me, Ultima,* he attends catechism class and hears Father Byrnes question Rita about souls that reside in purgatory because the person died without gaining forgiveness for venial sins.

purple heart a military award to casualties that George Washington commissioned in 1782. Revived in 1932, this medal features a purple ribbon edged in white and suspended from a horizontal bar. The pendant—a gold heart centered in black with a gold bust of George Washington facing left—is topped by a small white shield banded with two red bars and an upper row of three stars. To the side are two stylized olive branches, symbolizing peace. Given to characters in Walter Dean Myers's *Fallen Angels,* the purple heart is the only national military commendation that does not feature red, white, and blue or shiny metals.

purser (*puhr'* suhr) literally, the "pursekeeper," a ship's financial officer, treasurer, or paymaster, who maintains accounts of purchases, legal papers, cargo, and the issuance of tickets to passengers. A salaried member of the captain's staff, the purser earned a commission from the issuance of food allotments and the collection and disbursal of freight. After the unaccountable rise of Billy Budd's corpse at the end of the noose, the purser in Herman Melville's *Billy Budd* questions the surgeon about spasms or other physical explanations of the phenomenon.

purslane (*puhr'* slayn) a common salad green or pot herb in the portulaca family. Purslane is also planted in hanging baskets and in sunny beds as a showy plant bearing yellow rosettes and reddish, succulent stems. As proof of the ease with which a person can obtain savory food, Henry David Thoreau describes in *Walden* a dinner of boiled purslane, a savory wildflower that he serves with salt.

puttee a gaiter or legging laced or strapped to the lower leg or strip of cloth or leather wrapped around the foreleg for support and protection from snakebite, thorns, or insects. Derived from the Sanskrit for *wrappings,* the term entered English during the late nineteenth century and is usually written in the plural. Wearing a deer-stalker hat, green puttees, and knickers, Leper, the misfit in John Knowles's *A Separate Peace,* stalks through snow on skis looking for a path through the woods, a symbolic search that foreshadows his mental deterioration. *See also* gaiters; knickers.

pylon (*py'* lahn) a tall metal structure, pillar, column, or post supporting high-tension electric or telegraph wires; a vertical guide or tower laying out a landing path or approach for aircraft; also, traffic cones marking a race course for bicycles or cars. Derived from the Greek for *gate,* the term dates to the mid-nineteenth century. The migrating rabbits in Richard Adams's *Watership Down* fear passing under the humming wires strung from pylons until Fiver assures them they will not be harmed.

python (*py'* thahn) a family of mighty, nonvenomous diamond-headed snakes from Australia, Africa, or Asia that crush by encircling their prey in multiple constricting coils. In the opening passages of *Fahrenheit 451,* in which Guy Montag exults in the power of holding the great python-like firehose in his hand and watching it destroy books, Ray Bradbury introduces a serpentine image prefiguring the hose that sucks out an overdose of barbiturates from Mildred, who despairs and tries to kill herself.

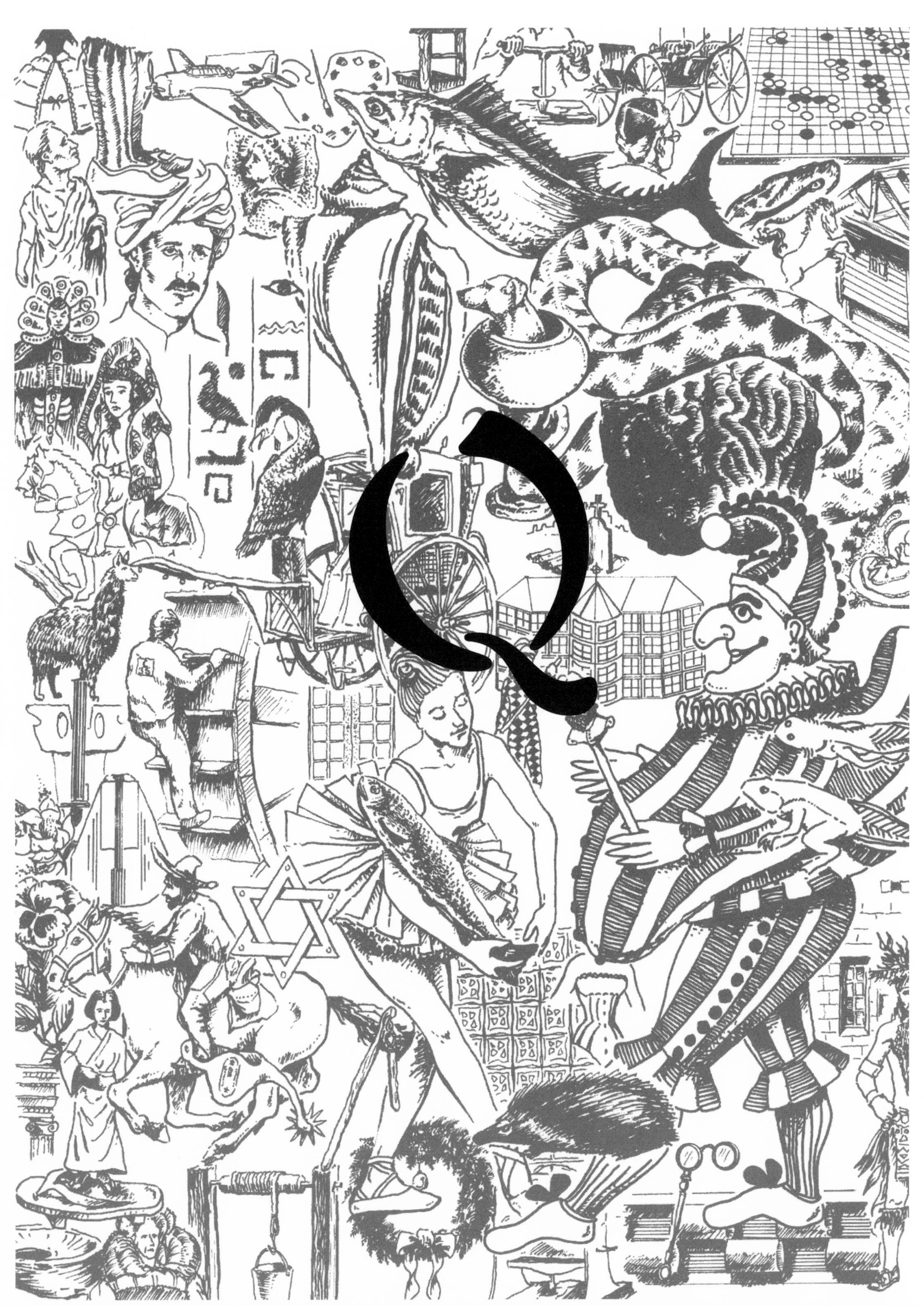
Q

quadrant (*kwahd'* ruhnt) a fifteenth-century navigational tool shaped like a quarter of a circle delineated from 1 to 90 degrees connected to a movable index or radius, suspended plumb line, and sight and used to measure elevation, angles, or altitude of a planet or sighting the pole star; also, similar tools used by surveyors, astronomers, and engineers to determine correct position or coordinates. In Herman Melville's *Moby-Dick,* Captain Ahab becomes so impatient to find the white whale that he tramples his quadrant. *See also* plumb line; pole star; sextant.

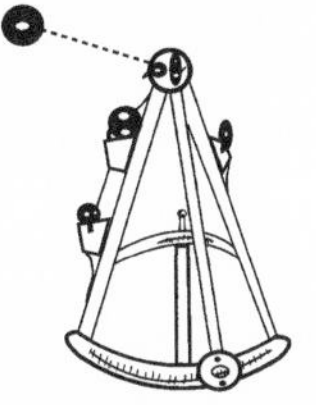

quadrille (kwah . *drihl'*) a graceful, complicated dance resembling square dancing or the Virginia Reel in which four couples act out five intricate figures or sets. The French term, dating to the late nineteenth century, also applies to the music that accompanies the dance, usually in two-four or six-eight rhythm. In Lewis Carroll's *Alice's Adventures in Wonderland,* the Mock Turtle crows to Alice, "You can have no idea what a delightful thing a Lobster-Quadrille is!"

quagmire (*kwag'* myr) a late sixteenth-century term of unknown origin denoting wet, mucky ground covered in sucking mud that yields to pressure and pulls at the feet like quicksand; a fen, marsh, or swamp. Sherlock Holmes contemplates tracking a killer across a peat bog pitted and fouled with quagmires, weeds, and decaying water plants in Sir Arthur Conan Doyle's The *Hound of the Baskervilles.*

quai or **quay** (kee) derived from the Old French for *landing strip,* a concrete or stone wharf, breakwater, or pier constructed parallel to a river or shore and used for loading or unloading ships or receiving passengers; a projection marking the boundaries of a bay or harbor. Also, a public walkway built along a reinforced riverbank, levee, or dike. A downcast man standing on a deserted quai attracts the attention of a policeman in Heinrich Böll's "My Melancholy Face."

quamash (*kwah'* mash) *See* camas.

quarry (*kwahr'* ree) an open excavation site, pit, or rich lode from which stone, limestone, marble, or slate is removed by cutting or chopping into blocks or blasting free. A fourteenth-century term, the word derives from the Latin for *square.* In Mark Twain's *The Adventures of Huckleberry Finn,* the title character follows a prominent set of tracks coming up from the quarry and pausing at the stile. *See also* stile.

quarter deck the portion of the upper deck between the aftermast and the ship's stern. The traditional domain of the captain or officer on watch, the quarter deck provides the captain a command post or private promenade; also, the spot from which the navigator makes sightings or where the boatswain and warrant officers come for directions or official announcements. In Herman Melville's *Billy Budd,* Claggart, a wily manipulator and poseur, stands like a suppliant on the quarter deck waiting to get Captain Vere's attention.

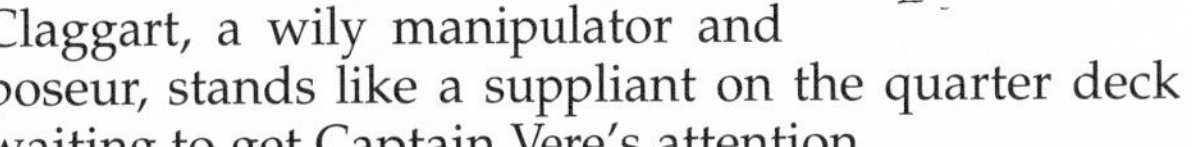

quartermaster the ship's officer in charge of stowing equipment in the hold; coiling and nesting cables; or attending to the upkeep of lines, lead, and log. The army quartermaster attends to billeting; assigning quarters; and packing and distributing food, utensils, tents, bedding, uniforms, camping gear, and items necessary to a bivouac or encampment. In Erich Maria Remarque's *All Quiet on the Western Front,* the lieutenant comments that the quartermaster takes such care with foodstuffs that they seem like his personal property rather than the rations for the whole army.

quarters the eighteenth- and nineteenth-century colloquial southern term designating the living area of slaves on a plantation or in a work camp. Often located near the "big house" and adjacent to the barn, paddock, and kitchen gardens, the quarters were situated close enough to white owners and overseers to allow constant surveillance, strict discipline, and easy access to house slaves. Before leaving to fight in the Civil War, the master in Zora Neale Hurston's *Their Eyes Were Watching God* returns to the quarters for one last sexual union with Nanny, his black mistress.

quartier (kahr . *tyay'*) a district of a city; an area, parish, or community having distinct characteristics, such as Little Italy in New York or Chinatown in San Francisco, where residents tend to share similar social class, religion, culture, or ethnic background. The small tourist center near Jackson Square in New Orleans, Louisiana, still carries the European designation of "French Quarter." Mayor Madeleine gets Fauchelevant a job as gardener in the Quartier Saint Antoine in Paris in Victor Hugo's *Les Misérables.*

quay *See* quai.

queue (kyoo) a line of people waiting to register, enter a restaurant, or buy tickets or a line-up of taxis or other vehicles at an airport or in front of a theater or kiosk. Derived from the Latin for *tail,* the term entered British English in the mid-eighteenth century, but remains virtually unknown in American English. In Aldous Huxley's *Brave New World,* gammas, the segment of the population with the lowest mentality, stand in queues at the tram stop like obedient domestic animals.

quick lime or **quicklime** a common name for calcium oxide or unslaked lime, a white caustic substance used in mortar and construction and in the making of glass, cement, brick, and aluminum. A practical use for quick lime is covering carrion or human waste in an outhouse to conceal odor and discourage insects. After the hurricane devastates the Muck in Zora Neale Hurston's *Their Eyes Were Watching God,* emergency relief crews ready the bodies for identification and burial and cover the rotting remains with quick lime to prevent contagion, hasten decomposition, and mask the smell of decaying flesh.

quicksilver or **quick silver** an Old English name for mercury, a heavy liquid element used in thermometers, barometers, dental fillings, and batteries. Because of its bright metallic flash, the term meaning "living silver" became the common word for mercury. When the ferry approaches shore in Mark Twain's *The Adventures of Huckleberry Finn,* Huck realizes that the authorities are performing a superstitious rite—releasing loaves of bread containing quicksilver on the surface of the river to locate his drowned corpse.

quid (kwihd) a wad or portion of chewing gum or tobacco cut bite-sized to fit on the tongue or in the cheek of the user; also, a slang term for a gob of spit. From the Old English for *cud,* the term dates to the early eighteenth century. As Israel Hands lies dying on the deck of the *Hispaniola* in Robert Louis Stevenson's *Treasure Island,* he asks Jim Hawkins to cut one last quid from his plug of tobacco. *See also* cud.

quill (kwihl) a pen with a separate point or nib attached; also, the Middle English term for the shaft of the tail feather of a goose, peacock, or other large bird. The hollow end is sharpened, split, and dipped into ink to be used as a writing tool. Harry Butler, the father of the main character in Conrad Richter's *The Light in the Forest,* figures his accounts in a ledger with a scratchy quill pen. *See also* inkpot; nib.

quilt frame an adjustable quadrangular frame made of wooden lathes on which quilters peg a base sheet on which to sew quilt scraps or pieces. Because the frame is light and set up waist high, quilters can pull chairs to the edge and reach under and over to arrange pieces; tie knots and execute intricate needlework, such as feather stitches, French knots, or satin stitches; and secure the outer layers to the batting. In Alice Walker's *The Color Purple,* Celie reports by letter to Nettie that she enjoyed setting up a quilt frame on the porch and working with Sofia on a coverlet.

quinine (*kwy'* nyn) a bitter colorless alkaloid derived from Native American pharmacopoeia, manufactured as "Countess powder" or "Peruvian bark" from the bark of the cinchona tree and used to control malarial fever and pain and to halt heart arrhythmia. Samuel Hahnemann determined the use of quinine in the 1790s and evolved a system of homeopathy from its reaction in the body. In Tennessee Williams's *A Streetcar Named Desire,* Blanche DuBois concocts a romantic death fantasy in which she collapses from eating an unwashed grape and dies in spite of the captain's administration of a dose of quinine.

quintal (*kwihn'* tuhl) a hundredweight, or, in the United States, 100 pounds. The British quintal equals 112 pounds. In the late twentieth century, the metric quintal has come to mean 100 kilograms or 220.46 pounds. Derived from the Latin for *hundred,* the term entered English in the Middle Ages. During the blockade of Boston Harbor in Esther Forbes's *Johnny Tremain,* the citizens of Marblehead send quintals of fish to keep their neighbors from starving.

quire (kwyr) a Middle English term derived from the Latin for *four,* the word referred originally to 24 sheets of writing paper or one-twentieth of a ream. It now means 25 sheets of the same weight, size, and stock. In the Baxters' shopping list in Marjorie Kinnan Rawlings's *The Yearling* is a half quire of paper.

quirt (kwuhrt) a riding crop or whip consisting of a wood, ivory, or bone grip with wrist guard attached to a lash braided from rawhide. A mid-nineteenth century Mexican-Spanish term for a fourth of a mule team, it derives from the Latin for *four.* Tom Black Bull, the protagonist of Hal Borland's *When the Legends Die,* makes peace with school by braiding leather and later finds his handmade quirt for sale in a local shop window.

quisling (*kwihz'* lihng) a turncoat or traitor. Derived from the surname of Vidkun Abraham Quisling, a Norwegian politician and fascist military leader who collaborated with the Nazis from 1933 through World War II, the term preserves the dishonorable deeds of a Nazi premier who was tried and executed for treason in 1945. In Corrie ten Boom's *The Hiding Place,* the National Socialist Bond refers to a consortium of Dutch quislings who spy on fellow citizens and aid the SS in rounding up and shooting Dutch Jews. *See also* holocaust; Nazi; SS.

quoits (kwoyts) a medieval game similar to horseshoes in which a player stands at a designated spot and tosses flat six- to nine-pound circlets of metal, wood, rubber, or rope at an iron peg or hob in the ground or deck of a ship and attempts to land the circlet on, over, or near the mark; also, ring-toss. Relying on his skill at skipping stones or throwing quoits, Bilbo Baggins throws at a menacing spider and kills it before it can attack Bombur in J. R. R. Tolkien's *The Hobbit.*

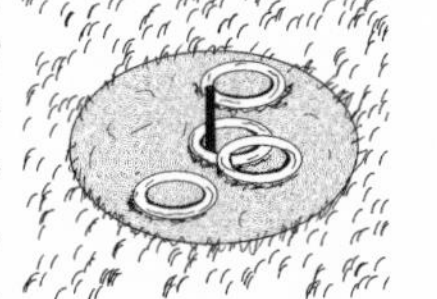

quonset (*kwahn'* siht) or **quonset hut** an open warehouse, longhouse, or storage building created by fastening preformed pieces of corrugated metal insulated with cellulose over semicircular trusses on a steel frame. Named for Quonset Point Naval Air Station, Rhode Island, and similar to the British Nissen hut, the buildings date to 1941 and were often found on military bases, along wharves, or in storage yards. In Jean Craighead George's *Julie of the Wolves,* Julie and Pearl go to the quonset to share a Coke with two straws.

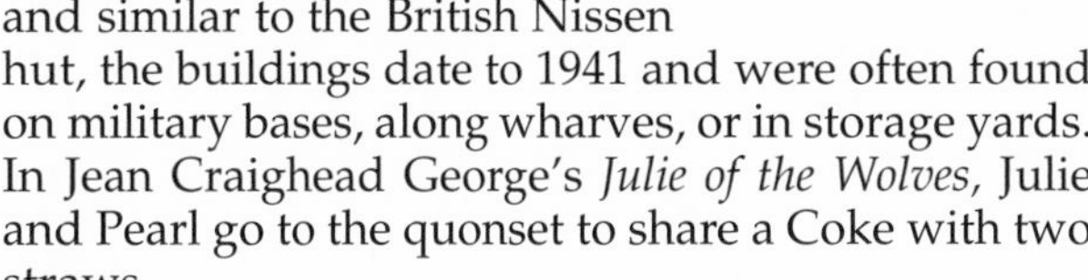

Qur'an *See* Koran.

R

raffia or **raphia** (*raf'* fyuh) soft, pliant, buff-colored material derived from a coarse stalk or broad fibrous leaf from the Madagascar palm. Raffia is woven into baskets, trays, twine, mats, sunshades, hats, cloth, and novelty goods. Derived from the Malagasy term for the palm plant, the word entered English during the height of the importation of raffia items during the late nineteenth century. In Chinua Achebe's *Things Fall Apart*, the *egwugwu*, a masked figure wearing a smoked raffia costume, terrorizes the Nigerian villagers.

rafter the parallel sloped beams of a pitched or raked roof on which shingles, thatch, or tile is laid; the framework of a loft or roof. Derived from Old Norse, the term entered English in the eleventh century. Trapped in a locked cabin while his father goes on an extended drunk in town, Huck, the title character in Mark Twain's *The Adventures of Huckleberry Finn*, searches between the rafters and roof clapboards and locates the remains of a rusty saw, with which he cuts his way clear to freedom and sets in motion a plot implicating Pap Finn in a nonexistent murder. *See also* clapboard.

ragout (ra . *goo'*) a general term for a hearty meat stew dating to the seventeenth century and derived from the Latin for *taste*. Ragout consists of small pieces of fish, meat, or chicken browned in oil, garnished with herbs, and cooked with dried beans or other vegetables in a thick, pungent stock, roux, tomato sauce, or gravy. The finished dish can be served as a main dish or used as a filling for meat pies. In his tongue-in-cheek satire, "A Modest Proposal," Jonathan Swift suggests that Londoners follow a plan suggested by a "very knowing American" and raise children to be sold for meat to serve as a ragout or fricassee. *See also* fricassee.

rajah or **raja** (*rah'* juh) a nobleman or chieftain from India or the East Indies; also, a Hindu aristocrat or a Malay magistrate or Javanese chieftain, overlord, or civil authority serving a king, who is often differentiated from underlings by the honorific *maharajah* or *great king*. Derived from the Sanskrit for *prince*, the term entered English in the sixteenth century. In Jules Vernes's *Around the World in Eighty Days*, hero Phileas Fogg decides to risk his life against a rajah's guards to free a young woman from being burned alive in a ritual suttee. *See also* suttee.

Ram the spring sun at the vernal equinox, around April 11. Arising in Aries, the Latin name for the first sign of the Zodiac, this first house of the 12 celestial signs is marked by friskiness and aggressiveness. A self-motivated astrological figure, Aries tends to dominate with sharp retort to any who try to interfere. In Geoffrey Chaucer's "Prologue to the Canterbury Tales," the author asserts that the season of "Aprille" is ruled by the sun and the Ram.

Ramadan (*rah'* muh . dahn) derived from the Persian for *hot*, the term names an ascetic 30-day religious commemoration of Muhammed's divine revelation during the ninth month of the Islamic calendar. Healthy celebrants—excluding the aged or menstruating, pregnant, or nursing women—observe the occasion with dawn-to-dusk fasting, one of the five pillars of Islam. Ramadan requires abstention from dining, smoking, bathing, and sexual pleasures and devotion to prayer and reading from the Koran. The end of the ritual fast brings shared meals and camaraderie among the faithful. On the voyage in search of the white whale in Herman Melville's *Moby-Dick*, Queequeg observes Ramadan.

rampart (*ram'* puhrt) a protective heap or mound of earth, rocks, or debris that encircles a fortification or castle as a means of stemming direct frontal attack by an invasive force; also, a reinforced parapet, permanent defense berm, or bulwark with a crown or roadway capping the crest. The term, which entered English in the early Middle Ages, comes from the Latin for *front preparation*. In the military clash that serves as the focus of Francis Scott Key's "The Star-Spangled Banner," observers take pride in the gallant flag, which they can see beyond the ramparts. *See also* battery; parapet.

ramrod a metal pole topped with a wooden block used for pressing a charge down the muzzle of a front-loading firearm or cannon. To fire the gun, the user forced a lighted match down the touchhole to set off the compacted powder. Also, the rag- or bristle-ended tool that cleans the barrel of a muzzle-loader. While Carbon calls for matches, ramrods, and charges in Edmond Rostand's *Cyrano de Bergerac*, Cyrano and Roxane attend the dying Christian. In Stephen Crane's *The Red Badge of Courage*, Henry Fleming remarks on the clang of ramrods forced into hot, smoky barrels as soldiers reload.

rapier (*ray'* pyuhr) a light, sharp-tipped, two-edged sword with a cup-shaped hand guard on the hilt. Originating in the sixteenth and seventeenth centuries, the rapier was common in the Renaissance as a weapon of choice for self-defense or dueling. Of unknown origin, the term describes a long, lithe weapon known for lightning speed; it could pare an opponent's flesh or do fatal damage to major organs by slicing or thrusting into the torso. Jody, the protagonist in John Steinbeck's *The Red Pony*, admires the golden-basketed hilt of an antique rapier that an elderly Gitano carries with him.

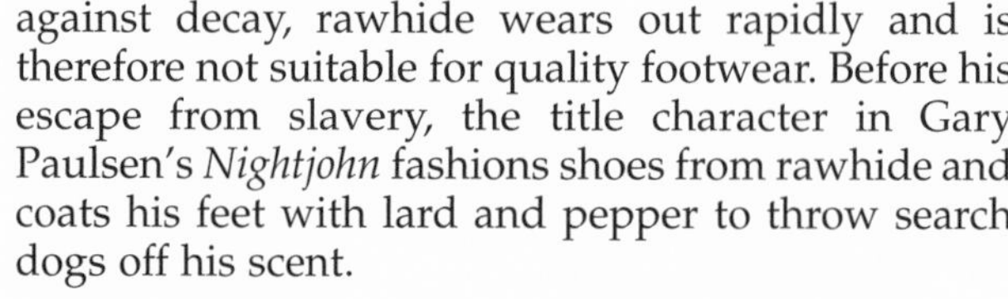

ratchet-drill a drill operated by a mechanism composed of interlocking teeth. Set at an angle, the teeth—extending from rotating metal circles or from a circle of teeth engaging a moveable bar or pawl—force the device into one direction to prevent an unexpected reverse. From the Old High German for *distaff*, the term entered English in the late eighteenth century. While crew members repair a steamboat, Marlowe, protagonist in Joseph Conrad's *The Heart of Darkness*, makes himself useful by handing workers wrenches and a ratchet-drill.

ratline a wide rope ladder or tarred hemp attached to the shrouds and woven horizontally into a series of steps, rungs, or squares suitable for several people to climb simultaneously while boarding a ship or climbing the rigging on a mast of a square-rigged ship. From the Middle English for *cording*, the term entered English in the fifteenth century. In Avi's *The True Confessions of Charlotte Doyle*, the heroine climbs the ratlines and makes her way to the top of the mainmast to prove that she is worthy of being called a sailor.

rattan (ruh . *tan'*) the flexible, jointed cane rod carried by a master-at-arms to symbolize the role of disciplinarian. Shaped from the stem of a tropical climbing palm, the round stem, which is tough, pliant, and solid enough to be woven into wicker chairs and cables, is also capable of delivering a blow sharp enough to lay open flesh. Carrying his rattan as a symbol of his office, the vigilant Claggart, the antagonist in Herman Melville's *Billy Budd*, observes Billy accidentally spilling his soup and returns to make a caustic comment. *See also* master-at-arms.

rawhide untanned cowhide that displays a rough edge and is used in making whips, quirts, luggage, upholstery, belts, bindings, or other rough leather goods. Because the untanned area is not protected against decay, rawhide wears out rapidly and is therefore not suitable for quality footwear. Before his escape from slavery, the title character in Gary Paulsen's *Nightjohn* fashions shoes from rawhide and coats his feet with lard and pepper to throw search dogs off his scent.

RCMP *See* Royal Canadian Mounted Police.

recorder a slender European wind instrument dating to the twelfth century. The recorder, carved from ivory, bone, or wood and often preferred by wandering street musicians and children learning the rudiments of music, was equally popular for court ensembles and soloists. Played with the fingers blocking holes in the cylinder, the recorder resembles a flute or flageolet and makes a reedy sound. At breakfast, while his grandmother grills him about being out too late, Conrad, protagonist in Judith Guest's *Ordinary People*, escapes mentally by following a melody played on a recorder.

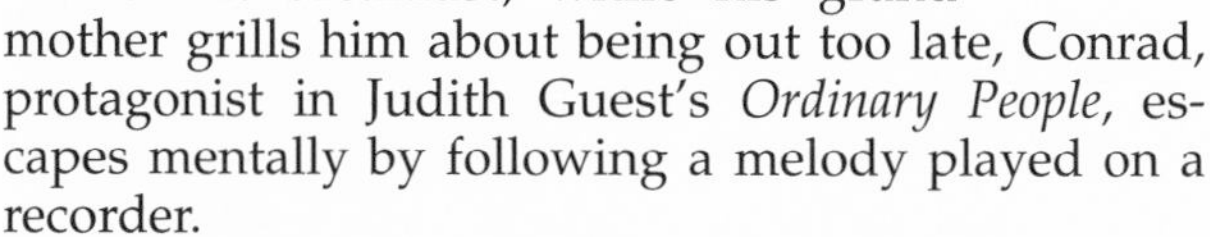

rectory (*rehk'* tuh . ree) the home or quarters provided an Anglican minister, clerk, or priest within the parish served; a manse or parsonage. Also, the tithes that accompany supervision of a parish. In a letter to Mr. Bennet concerning a disagreement, William Collins, a character in Jane Austen's *Pride and Prejudice*, asserts that Lady Catherine de Bourgh is responsible for helping him gain assignment to a remunerative rectory. *See also* parish.

red egg ceremony a jubilant celebration of the birth of a child, particularly a male, whose arrival brings good luck to the baby and the family. As described in Pearl S. Buck's *The Good Earth*, the distribution of red eggs to villagers indicates that Wang Lung, the protagonist, has fathered a son. Similarly, to Lindo Jong, a character in Amy Tan's *The Joy Luck Club*, the red egg ceremony honors month-old babies, who receive their given names during the good luck ritual.

reef to climb onto a yardarm to secure sails from damage by heavy gales. Also, an encircling barrier of rocks, coral, or debris that lies near the surface along the shoreline of a hazardous approach to an island, bay, or harbor. Usually marked with buoys, a reef is suitable for outriggers, pirogues, and other shallow-bottomed boats that often approach ships beyond the reef to barter for trade goods and rum. In Joseph Conrad's "The Secret Sharer," the unnamed captain steers close to the reef to allow Leggatt, his stowaway, to jump overboard and swim to shore. In James Michener's *Hawaii*, the local royal family at

Lahaina, Hawaii, navigates the shark-infested waters beyond the reef to welcome ships carrying missionaries, among whom is their son.

reel a whirling, spirited Celtic folk dance performed by couples facing each other or arranged in lines with men on one side and women on the other preceding more elaborate figures, particularly partnering and intertwining, later mimicked by the American square dance. Derived from a Norse term for *weave*, the word dates before the twelfth century. As the title character in Edith Wharton's *Ethan Frome* watches the young people enjoying a church social, he is dismayed to see Denis Eady lead Mattie Silver in a final reel.

refinery a factory, distillery, or processing apparatus for purifying oil, sugar, liquor, ore, or other goods by removing solids, gases, debris, or crude particles; separating components; or altering the basic structure as with an acid bath or application of heat or steam to produce reliable, high quality products such as table sugar, light rum, zinc, acetylene, or gasoline. In Theodore Taylor's *The Cay* and *Timothy of the Cay*, the presence of a Dutch petroleum refinery makes the island of Curaçao a target for German U-boats.

Regents a battery of comprehensive tests administered to high school students by the education department of New York state to determine competency in academic subjects. Created by the Board of Regents, which established free public education for residents in 1754, the test has served other states and private and parochial schools as a model of academic testing. In Arthur Miller's *Death of a Salesman*, Bernard summons Biff to join him in studying for the Regents test even though Biff feels certain that he has already been accepted at the University of Virginia on the basics of athletics.

regiment one of usually three military units in a division; a brigade numbering around 5,000 soldiers. A regiment of ground troops is composed of three battalions, batteries, or companies and is led by a colonel. As Henry Fleming watches the motionless regiment on the other side of the river in Stephen Crane's *The Red Badge of Courage*, he envisions a fearful dragon with bulging eyes. *See also* army.

Reich (ryk) the German term for the state or commonwealth. Derived from the German for *realm*, the term received renewed prominence during World War II, when the Nazi Third Reich threatened to topple and supplant the governments of much of Europe. Preceding German states included the First Reich, or the Holy Roman Empire, and the Second Reich, the German Empire set up by Otto von Bismarck in 1871. In Thomas Keneally's *Schindler's List*, the title character, Oskar Schindler, observes the diabolical workings of Hitler's fascist Third Reich to annihilate undesirables and create a pure Aryan race. *See also* holocaust.

reichsmark (*ryk'* smahrk) or **RM** the name of the German mark, abbreviated RM, that was the national unit of currency from 1925 to 1948, when it was simplified to *mark*. During World War II, Oskar Schindler, the protagonist in Thomas Keneally's *Schindler's List*, paid unskilled laborers a daily wage of 6 RMs and skilled workers 7.5 RMs.

relief a form of raised, molded, carved, stamped, or sculpted artwork projecting from a solid or plane surface and decorating a frieze, entablature, coin, or sculpture. Suggesting realistic three-dimensional depiction, relief possesses height and width, but only mimics depth, as depicted on aristocratic homes, crests, and seals in Charles Dickens's *A Tale of Two Cities*. Also, an American slang term for public assistance, entitlements, or welfare payments. In Richard Wright's *Native Son*, Mrs. Thomas fears that the relief checks will stop if Bigger doesn't cooperate by looking for a job. *See also* bas-relief; food stamps; repoussée.

repatriation return to one's native or birth country for a resumption or restoration of residence, allegiance, and citizenship. Derived from the Latin for *country*, the term implies nationality rather than racial or religious ties. In the autobiographical *Farewell to Manzanar*, Jeanne Wakatsuki Houston and her mother and siblings fear that men like Ko Wakatsuki will remain in prison until the U. S. government releases them for repatriation in Japan.

repoussé (ruh . *poo'* say) a pattern, relief, or edging beaten, hammered, shaped, or extruded from the back side of thin metal into a raised figure, ornamented band, or edging on the front of fine silverware, for example, on signet rings, lockets, tea services, trays, family crests, royal seals, serving dishes, or tankards. Literally *pushed back* in French, the term entered English in the mid-nineteenth century. As Esther Forbes describes in *Johnny Tremain*, Ephraim Lapham and Paul Revere are famous for quality silver, often decorated with figured relief or repoussé.

requiem (*reh'* kwee . uhm) a service, hymn, poem, recitation, dirge, chant, mass, or similar musical composition sung to honor a dead person. Derived from the ecclesiastical Latin for *rest*, the term is a part of the prayer *Dona eis requiem, Domine,* or "Grant them eternal rest, Oh Lord." The term is echoed by the abbreviated epitaph R.I.P., the Latin *Requiescat in Pace,* or "May he/she rest in peace." In Arthur Miller's *Death of a Salesman*, the author entitles the final act "Requiem" in honor of Willy Loman's poignant, ignoble death.

reticule (*reh'* tih . kyool) a cloth, meshwork, or velvet draw-string handbag, carryall, or needlework holder that fastened to the wrist and contained important items such as coins, comb, makeup and cologne, handkerchief, smelling salts, needles and pins, dance slippers, and sachets of dried herbs and petals. Derived from the Latin for *net*, the term entered English in the early eighteenth century, when such bags were popular. In Avi's *The True Confessions of Charlotte Doyle*, the proper, English-educated heroine carries a reticule and trunk aboard the *Seahawk*. See also netting; *papier poudre*.

reveille (*re'* vuh . lee) a bugle or drum call for troops, sailors, or crew members to assemble; also, a wake-up alarm, signal, or voice command for campers, garrison inmates, or prisoners to arise and prepare for formation, roll call, breakfast, or the business of the morning. From the Latin for *watch,* the term entered English in the mid-seventeenth-century from the French version meaning *get up*. The first word in Alexander Solzhenitsyn's *One Day in the Life of Ivan Denisovich* is *reveille*, the warder's 5:00 A.M. banging noise meant to awaken prisoners in the Siberian gulag.

Revelation (*reh* . vuh . *lay'* shuhn) the twenty-seventh book of the canon New Testament and the sixty-sixth, or last, book of the Protestant Bible, often attributed to St. John the Divine, who supposedly coded the work to hide his prediction that the Roman Empire was teetering on the edge of doom. Couched in swirling, terrifying symbol, the book describes the coming of righteousness to a wicked planet, the redemption of the good, and the abandonment of those who defy God's laws. In a symbolic gesture of finality to a disloyal gang of scoundrels, Long John Silver, pirate leader in Robert Louis Stevenson's *Treasure Island*, tosses Jim Hawkins a circle cut from the last page of the Bible, from Revelation 22:15, proclaiming that outside God's city "are dogs, and sorcerers, and whoremongers, and murderers, and idolaters, and whosoever loveth and maketh a lie."

revolver *See* Colt's revolver.

rhesus (*ree'* suhs) **monkey** an approximately two-foot-tall southeast Asian macaque; a long-tailed monkey that makes an agreeable pet. Researchers favor the rhesus monkey in medical, emotional, and psychological studies and in space travel as a means of determining how similar circumstances would affect human subjects. Named for the Latin for the mythical king of Thrace, the monkey is the source of the term Rh-factor, a quality of blood cells that causes strong antigens to reject incompatible transfusions. At a meeting of scholars in Daniel Keyes's *Flowers for Algernon*, Charlie Gordon grows angry at the triviality of a detailed study of reaction time in the rhesus monkey.

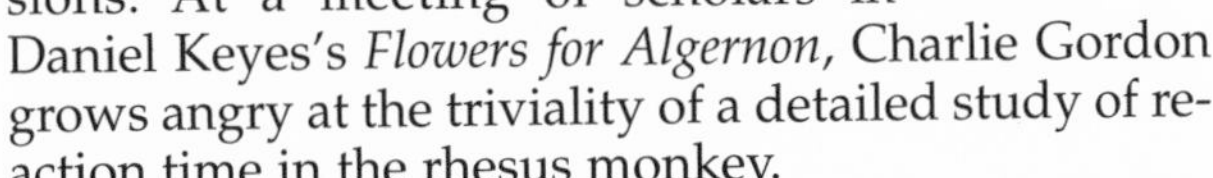

rheumy (*roo'* mee) describing an unattractive flow of watery mucus from the eyes, mouth, or nose; a condition often associated with poor health, alcoholism, or old age; chronic rhinitis. A fourteenth-century term derived from the Greek for *discharge*, the word originally applied only to tears. Still working two years after retirement age, Boxer, the stout mare with rheumy eyes in George Orwell's *Animal Farm,* will probably be forced to work until death.

riata or **reata** (ree . *ah'* tuh) a lariat or lasso created by forming a sliding loop in one end of a rope to be used in restraining animals during training or moving from barn to paddock; also, a picket line for mules, burros, or horses. From the Spanish for *retied*, the term served as the name of the ranch setting of Edna Ferber's *Giant*. In the farm setting of John Steinbeck's *The Red Pony*, a riata is a necessary tool for working with unbroken horses and cattle.

rick a haystack, bundle, or thatched heap of corn or grain left to dry in the open air or covered with tarps or layers of burlap. A Middle English farm term, the word entered English before the twelfth century. Tied with a bit of string or vine, a rick is easier to move than loose armloads of dried grain. A run of bad luck forces Michael Henchard, protagonist in Thomas Hardy's *The Mayor of Casterbridge*, to sell grain in ricks still in the field and thus unexamined for quality. In *Far from the Madding Crowd*, also by Hardy, Gabriel Oak saves the swirling grain by guying ricks to the ground with pegged tarps for protection from wind and rain.

rickshaw or **ricksha** (*rihk'* shah) or **jinriksha** a primitive conveyance common to Japan, China, and parts of southeast Asia. The rickshaw typically consists of a covered cab and a pair of leader poles extended to the front between which the puller ran while grasping a pole under each arm. Derived from the Chinese for *person power*, the term entered English in the late nineteenth century. While working for low wages in a city to the south of his land, Wang Lung, protagonist in Pearl S. Buck's *The Good Earth*, pulls a rickshaw and hides from soldiers seeking conscripts for the army.

ride on a rail an example of frontier vigilantism by which local people gain revenge against flimflam artists, seducers of young girls, disreputable preachers, mountebanks, and other rascals by tying the victim's hands and feet to a rail and carrying them like trussed pigs through town for general merriment and ridicule. A more dangerous version of this rough horseplay is the use of tar and feathers, which could lead to severe burns or death. After parting with the Duke and King in Mark Twain's *The Adventures of Huckleberry Finn*, Huck recognizes the two con artists being ridden out of town on a rail. *See also* mountebank; tar and feather.

ridge pole a central timber at the top of a tent or the horizontal beam of a store, church, house, or barn frame to which the apex of the rafters attach. A late eighteenth-century term, it derives from the Middle English for *back*. In Henry David Thoreau's *Walden*, he tells time by listening to whippoorwills calling from the ridge pole of his residence from 7:30 until 8:00 each evening.

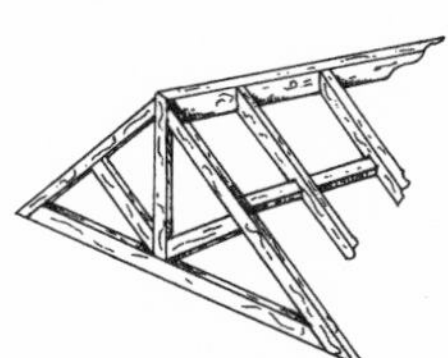

riding crop derived from the Anglo-Saxon for *head of a plant*, a riding crop is composed of a wood or leather-covered metal handle or stock, straight rod, and leather loop on the end and is used to hold back branches or briars or to prod deceased prey to be certain that it is dead. Because of the decorative, ostentatious nature of most riding crops, they enhance affectation and are often marked with initials or crests, as is the case with Godfrey Cass's crop, which is found with his brother's corpse at the bottom of a quarry in George Eliot's *Silas Marner*. Kneeling near the window, the title character in Thomas Hardy's *Tess of the D'Urbervilles* fails to hear the approach of a visitor until he touches the window pane with his riding crop.

riding light an established arrangement of night lights for ships riding at anchor to display their presence to passing water traffic. On a trawler or freight vessel not in service, two red lights mark the highest point. On a sailing vessel, the top and bottom left of the mast are marked with red lights; the right side of the mast shows a green light. The escapee in Joseph Conrad's "The Secret Sharer" explains that he jumped ship and swam toward the riding light.

rime (rym) frozen mist or atmospheric moisture; hoarfrost resulting from freezing water droplets that collect on cold objects, particularly metal. Dating before the twelfth century, the word also names fuzzy clumps of ice crystals that accumulate on the windward side and coat buildings, trees, and rocks. In Truman Capote's "A Christmas Memory," Buddy recalls rime as one of the signs of the approaching holiday, when he and his elderly cousin delivered homemade fruitcakes to their friends.

ringlet a tress, spiral, or lock of hair curled naturally into a springy vertical column or coated with hair-setting solution and wrapped around a heated curling iron; also, an artificial lock or curl attached to a hairpin and inserted in place around the face or neck or tucked in with the rest of an upswept coiffure to give the impression of carefully curled hair. On arrival at the home of her deceased aunt, the title character in Charlotte Brontë's *Jane Eyre* marvels at the fashionable black dress and blond ringlets that adorn her cousin Georgiana.

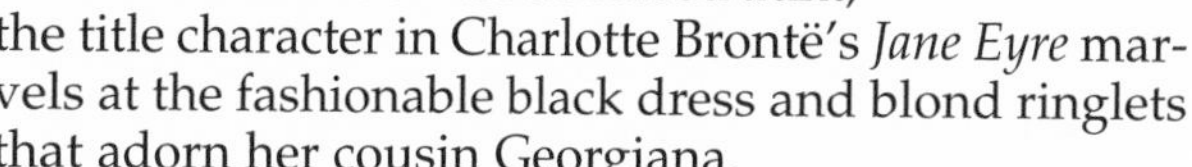

R.I.P. *See* requiem.

Rippers a humorous reference to Jack the Ripper, the signature on the letters of an unknown killer who murdered and surgically mutilated seven prostitutes in London's East End from August 7 to November 10, 1888. In the years since the killing stopped, writers and movie makers have proposed numerous theories on who committed the atrocities and managed to elude Scotland Yard and vigilant English bobbies. On a terrifying night as Mama Henderson and her granddaughter wait for Bailey Junior in Maya Angelou's *I Know Why the Caged Bird Sings*, Maya doubts that the Bluebeards and Rippers will get a scream from her daring brother. *See also* Bluebeard.

riser the vertical backstop or upright back wall of a stair or step that attaches at right angles to the horizontal tread, which is often carpeted to conceal or muffle noise of foot traffic. As his father approaches his room, Rob, the protagonist in Robert Newton Peck's autobiographical novel *A Day No Pigs Would Die*, identifies his father's step by the thump of his boots against the risers.

rivet (*rih'* viht) a short metal bolt, pin, or fastener that passes through aligned holes to connect two metal plates or beams or to secure the opposite ends of a sheet that is shaped into a cylinder, especially in the construction of a steam pipe, metal sleeve, or water conduit. After the rivet sinks to the head, the shank end is beaten flat on the opposite side to assure a close fit, for example, on an airplane wing, truck body, or molded chimney insert. The term, derived from Middle English, entered the language in the fifteenth century. Marlowe, the protagonist in Joseph Conrad's *The Heart of Darkness,* grows restless in camps along the Congo River as he waits for a packet boat to deliver the rivets to repair his steamer.

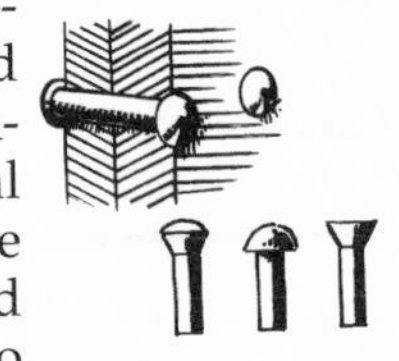

roadhouse a semirespectable roadside nightclub, inn, hotel, tavern, or restaurant providing food, alcoholic beverages, and noisy entertainment; a honky-tonk or gambling parlor; often the site of illicit behavior, fights, drug trafficking, and prostitution. The behavior of the party-goers grows so intense, noisy, and vulgar in F. Scott Fitzgerald's *The Great Gatsby* that Gatsby's neighbor Nick thinks of the mansion as a roadhouse.

roadstead a protected shoreline or offshore anchorage less accommodating and sheltered than a harbor where ships tie up. Passengers and crew take a jolly boat or tender to travel from ship to shore or to ferry small amounts of cargo or luggage. Santiago, the title character in Ernest Hemingway's *The Old Man and the Sea*, dreams of the harbors and roadsteads of the Canary Islands.

roadster a fashionable, youthful canvas-topped coupe or convertible seating two or three people. Some roadsters of the early twentieth century sported luggage racks, expensive wire-rimmed wheels, and trunks that opened outward to create a rumble seat to hold additional passengers. In F. Scott Fitzgerald's *The Great Gatsby*, Jordan Baker provides Nick with descriptions of the days when Daisy Buchanan wore white, drove a white roadster, and entertained young men in her family's home in Louisville.

roasting ear unshucked young, tender corn in the milk stage that is boiled, steamed, or roasted on a grill or open fire; also, corn that is peeled back to the stalk, salted and seasoned with butter and paprika or pepper, then rewrapped in the husk and secured with string for cooking. Billy, the protagonist of Wilson Rawls's *Where the Red Fern Grows*, earns extra money selling fishermen huckleberries, fresh vegetables, and roasting ears.

roasting jack a vertical device attached to the upper front of a fireplace to hold a joint of meat. The apparatus was wound up like a clock or music box to turn slowly so that the spitted meat cooked evenly on all sides and the fat dripped harmlessly into the fire. At Wemmick's home in Charles Dickens's *Great Expectations*, Pip finds Wemmick's aged father comfortably seated before a hearth where a small ornament indicates where a roasting jack could be placed.

rockaway a lightweight four-wheeled shay or carriage with a solid canvas or leather top and undraped sides. Common in the United States, the rockaway, which was developed in the mid-1800s, was frequently used as a hired carriage at depots and quays and in city centers. In Herman Melville's "Bartleby the Scrivener" and Kate Chopin's "The Awakening," characters travel by rockaway, a term that suggests the feeling of motion compounded by a light frame and absence of sides to silence vibration and street noise and keep out dust.

rococo (roh . *koh'* koh or roh . koh . *koh'*) or **rocaille** a fanciful style of decor detailing homes, churches, hotels, theaters, and business façades of the early eighteenth century with swirling, asymmetrical embellishments, entablature, foliage, shells, and scrolls; also, overly stylized, ornamented, or flowery literature, music, wallpaper, landscaping, window treatment, or artwork. The term derives from the French for *pebbly.* In Ray Bradbury's *The Martian Chronicles*, a spaceship lands on a neat lawn before an ornate house decked in rococo swirls.

Romanesque (*roh* . muhn . *ehsk'*) a simply ornamented but solid architectural style evolved in the eleventh and twelfth centuries in imitation of the massive barrel vaults, patterned masonry, thick walls, piers, arcades, and arched doors and windows of buildings designed in ancient Rome and Byzantium. In the buildings occupied by the Eyes in Margaret Atwood's *The Handmaid's Tale*, Offred walks

past Romanesque archways and wonders if Luke is held prisoner behind the old-fashioned façades.

rookery (*rook'* uh . ree) an eighteenth-century term for a nesting box or an aviary designed to house rooks or crows; also, a breeding spot for colonies of birds that people often cultivated to control flying insects or an adornment for a flower bed, orchard, or vegetable garden. On the arrival at Thornfield, the title character of Charlotte Brontë's *Jane Eyre* spies the contrast of a three-storied gentleman's manor and the rookery in the background, a symbolic connection suggesting the black sins that peck away at Rochester's domain.

root doctor a slang term for an herbalist, healer, or practitioner of naturopathy, gris-gris, voodoo, obeah, or home remedies; also, a shaman, witch doctor, *curandera*, mountebank, huckster, or traveling seller of fraudulent nostrums and patent medicine. As Jody grows weaker and more desperate in Zora Neale Hurston's *Their Eyes Were Watching God,* he reverses his former scorn of root doctors and summons a healer to his bedside. *See also curandera;* mountebank; shaman.

rope bed a homemade Chinese lattice-framed bed using crisscrossed hemp rope as cheap, adjustable bedsprings; a cradle, lounge, or hammock attached to a box frame supported by four corner uprights. On top of the matrix lie stuffed bolsters, a mattress, or folded quilts to form a sleeping space. As the hemp stretches, it is tightened or replaced with stronger material to hold the mattress level. William Portis's *True Grit* pictures the portly Rooster Cogburn attempting to rest in Chen Lee's rope bed, which is unsuited to Rooster's gangly body. *See also* corded bedstead.

Rorschach (*rohr'* shahk) or **Rorschach test** a projective personality and intelligence analysis of mental function and integration. The psychometrist's diagnosis derives from the viewer's interpretations or perceptions of a series of shapeless, untitled inkblots. Named for Swiss psychologist Dr. Hermann Rorschach in 1927, the Rorschach test is one of the psychological studies of Charlie Gordon, protagonist in Daniel Keyes's *Flowers for Algernon.*

rosary (*roh'* suh . ree) derived from the Latin for *rose,* a reference to the purity of the Virgin Mary, this set of prayer beads evolved in the fourth century from simple pebble counting. The ritual consists of five sets of decades, each representing meditations or devotional aves or salutations, each preceded by the Lord's Prayer, or Paternoster, and concluded with a praise to God the Father, or Gloria Patri. At each set of 13 beads, the worshipper commemorates an event or mystery in the lives of the Virgin Mary or Christ or makes a petition for grace. In Rudolfo Anaya's *Bless Me, Ultima,* Antonio's family reserves the sala for novenas and rosaries to protect his brothers away at the war. *See also* Our Father.

rosemary a pungent antispasmodic herb prescribed for indigestion, cough, and pain. The bush consists of prickly gray-green leaves on stalks topped with a panicle of blue blossoms. From ancient times, rosemary has been a symbol of remembrance and, for practical reasons, was sprinkled about foul-smelling sickrooms during outbreaks of plague to conceal the odors of death and dying. It appears in Ophelia's mad scene in William Shakespeare's *Hamlet* and in *Romeo and Juliet,* when Friar Laurence encourages the weeping family to dry their tears, cease mourning for a failed wedding, and deck Juliet's corpse with rosemary, as was the Renaissance custom.

Rose of Sharon one of the many names for the althea bush, a common shrub of the hibiscus or mallow family producing jagged leaves and curled lavender, rose, or white buds centered with a long sepal. As a textual reference to the Virgin Mary or Christ, the beloved, in the Song of Solomon 2:1, the name symbolizes pure sacrifice. In John Steinbeck's *The Grapes of Wrath,* the young husbandless character bearing the name Rosasharn, who was recently delivered of a stillborn child, offers her breast milk to an elderly dying man.

Rosh Hashanah or **Rosh Hashana** (rahsh huh . *shah'* nuh) the Jewish New Year, celebrating the anniversary of the creation of the world and observed, beginning the eve of the first day of the month of Tishri, for one day by reform Jews and two days by other Jews. Literally *head of the year* in Hebrew, this solemn holiday, marked by blasts on the shofar, or ram's horn, calls each worshipper to wake up to ways to better his or her life. Thus begins a ten-day period of self-examination and repentance culminating in Yom Kippur. As part of custom, special foods are eaten, including apples dipped in honey, indicating a desire for sweetness in the coming year. In his autobiographical *Night,* Elie Wiesel recalls his posture of rebellion against God for deserting the Jews: Elie defies the traditional observance of Rosh Hashanah.

rotogravure (*roh* . tuh . gruh . *vyoor'*) or **roto section** the process by which a sheet of stamps or brightly colored magazine copy is printed by a cylindrical copper drum; also, the colored insert in a daily newspaper or special Sunday edition, usually of higher quality than the rest of the newspaper. In Harper Lee's *To Kill a Mockingbird*, the children find little adornment except a banner proclaiming God's love and a rotogravure of Leigh Hunt's *The Light of the World*.

rouble *See* ruble.

rouleau (roo . *loh'*) a paper cylinder wrapped around coins in pre-counted lump sums to reduce the necessity of tabulating them a second time. The term is derived from the French for *little roll.* As reported in a flashback, the doctor attending a dying woman in Charles Dickens's *A Tale of Two Cities* rejected payment, which consisted of a rouleau of gold coins.

roundabout an early nineteenth-century term for a short, tight man's jacket, sometimes worn with a long-sleeved shirt topped by a voluminous collar reaching to the cap of the shoulders and adorned at the throat with a loose cravat. After a thorough wash, the title character in Mark Twain's *The Adventures of Tom Sawyer* allows his cousin Mary to button his roundabout and turn down his collar.

round hand a bold, vertical masculine form of handwriting that contrasts with the lighter, more graceful running hand, or longhand, used by women; a style of calligraphy favored for handwritten invitations and formal social correspondence. In Thomas Hardy's *The Mayor of Casterbridge*, Elizabeth-Jane admits to Lucetta that she can write only round hand instead of the more ladylike script, a type of calligraphy that was taught to genteel women of the nineteenth century.

roundhouse a block of cabins housing passengers or the infirmary on the quarter-deck or upper deck of eighteenth- and nineteenth-century sailing ships. The name derives from the fact that the crew can walk around the area. After remodeling provides the *Hispaniola* with an expanded companionway as large as a roundhouse to house the captain and the older men, Jim Hawkins is delighted to receive a berth in the after-part of the main hold in Robert Louis Stevenson's *Treasure Island.*

round robin a circular piece of paper or petition containing the signatures of conspirators pledged to a plot or mutiny against a ship's officers. The circular nature dooms all signers equally on paper that has no top or bottom and hence no ranking of the signatures. Anyone caught signing such a crude incriminating declaration faced death by hanging. On her arrival aboard the *Seahawk* in Avi's *The True Confessions of Charlotte Doyle*, Captain Jaggery warns the title character to report to him if she sees a round robin circulating among the crew.

rowel (row'l) a jagged rotating wheel attached to a crossbar on a spur. When a rider digs boots into a horse's side, the pointed ends of the rowels prod the animal's sides, sometimes piercing tender tissue. From the Latin for *wheel*, the term denotes a standard part of cowboy equipment that some wearers sport for the metallic flash and the jingling sound that the rowels make when the wearer walks on hard surfaces. In a fit of anger, Tom Black Bull, protagonist in Hal Borland's *When the Legends Die*, gouges a bronc with the dull rowels of his spurs and rides the animal to an ignoble death from a punctured lung.

Royal Canadian Mounted Police the RCMP or Mounties, Canada's national police who have supervised criminal matters in the provinces since 1873. Historically, the Mounties, similar to the U.S. Federal Bureau of Investigation, have aided in the settlement of the Canadian west, served as a link between the lower provinces and northern native tribes, assisted in the building of the Canadian Pacific Railway, and overseen the Yukon gold rush of 1890. In modern times, RCMP horse patrols have added an espionage division, sea and air surveillance, and tracking dogs. In legal matters involving identifying and burying the dead in Margaret Craven's *I Heard the Owl Call My Name*, the RCMP has the final word.

Royal Unicorn a mythic one-horned animal that is a central figure on the official seal of Great Britain. Because of its uniqueness and grace, the unicorn appears on notable artwork, crests, and religious icons around the world. In Thomas Hardy's *The Mayor of Casterbridge*, Lucetta, wife of Mayor Donald Farfrae, admires his square-linked gold chain of office, which resembles a similar neck adornment on the Royal Unicorn, a symbol of masculinity and power.

ruble or **rouble** (*roo'* b'l) the standard unit of Russian currency, divided into 100 kopecks. Derived in the mid-sixteenth century from the Russian for *piece*, the term indicates a circle cut from a silver bar. In Nikolai Gogol's "The Overcoat," the bureaucrat is pleased with his job and its annual salary of 400 rubles. *See also* kopek.

rubric (*roo'* brihk) from the Latin for *red*, a heading, instruction, guide, rules, or directives to the priest or liturgist for punctilious performance of rituals outlined in a prayer book, hymnal, missal, or Psalter. In the mid-twentieth century, the Roman Catholic Church amended the rubric to include reasons for each detail of ecclesiastical ceremony. In Charlotte Brontë's *Jane Eyre*, Eliza devotes herself to a rigid schedule that includes embroidering an altar cloth and reading from the Anglican liturgical guide, *The Book of Common Prayer*, which she calls her "rubric."

rucksack (*ruhk'* sak) a canvas or leather backpack, knapsack, or shoulder bag worn across the back and attached to the shoulders by loops, thus leaving the hands free for other tasks. Derived from the German for *back bag*, the term, which entered English in the mid-nineteenth century, names a common form of carryall borne by soldiers, travelers, hikers, and mountain climbers. After packing a rucksack with empty wine bottles, Miss Campen, a character in Ernest Hemingway's *A Farewell to Arms*, asks the porter to present the bottles to the doctor as evidence of the patient's disobedience of hospital rules; as a result, Frederick Henry loses his leave.

rudderhead the top portion of the rudder shaft to which the tiller attaches. A fourteenth-century Anglo-Saxon term for *paddle*, the word names the metal or wood device at a ship's stern that alters direction when the helmsman varies the position of the tiller. In a tense scene from Robert Louis Stevenson's *Treasure Island*, Jim stashes raisins, cheese, and pickled fruit behind the rudderhead before giving a drink of brandy to Israel Hands, his wounded adversary.

rue (roo) a common green perennial that produces clusters of yellow daisylike blossoms at the top of three-foot bracts. In the sixteenth and seventeenth centuries, rue served as an antivenin and treatment for internal poisoning and was gathered into nosegays as an air freshener, vermin killer, and antibacterial in hospitals, churches, and law courts. In her famous mad scene in William Shakespeare's *Hamlet*, Ophelia hands out real or imaginary herbs and flowers to onlookers, offering rue—the herb of grace—to herself and probably Queen Gertrude as a token of remorse, contrition, or repentance.

ruff a stiff, circular decorative collar made of pleated or frilled muslin or linen. The ruff extended several inches outward from the neck and often matched similar attachments at the wrist. A sixteenth- and seventeenth-century adornment whose name derives from the Middle English for *crumpled*, the ruff, favored by both men and women, is a notable feature on portraits of Queen Elizabeth I. In Nathaniel Hawthorne's *The Scarlet Letter*, sumptuary laws forbid ostentatious clothing, but authorities continue to deck themselves in ruffs, embroidered bands, and ornate gloves, symbols of pride that the outcast Hester Prynne sews as a means of supporting herself and her child.

rune (roon) an individual character, symbol, or cipher in any Anglo-Saxon, Germanic, or Scandinavian alphabet, usually carved on wood or stone rather than inscribed with ink on paper or parchment. Runes, employed from the third to the thirteenth centuries, exhibit crude lettering based on Greek or Roman writing. The term derives from the Old English word for *mystery* or *magic signs*. In *Beowulf*, the poet sings of sword hilts "carven in cunning runes, set forth and blazoned," a reminder that unlettered people considered reading a hidden art, reserved mainly for priests and sages.

runnel (*ruhn'* l) a liquid course, rivulet, or channel, such as a stream, brook, or creek. Derived from the Anglo-Saxon for *run*, the term entered English before the twelfth century. Simon, the doomed mystic in William Golding's *Lord of the Flies*, stares at the pig's head while runnels of sweat course his face, drawing flies that feed off the salty liquid. Symbolically, the pouring sweat prefigures Simon's burial in the sea's salty depths after the tide sweeps his corpse from the sand.

running board an early twentieth-century term for a narrow ledge, step, or footboard extending from the side of the door panels of a car or horse-drawn carriage to aid passengers in entering or exiting and also to provide a place to sit or to rest parcels when the vehicle is stationary. Before assisting Mary to her room in Richard Wright's *Native Son*, Bigger Thomas, the protagonist, reaches to the running board to retrieve her hat.

run out on a rail *See* ride on a rail.

rupee (*roo'* pee or roo . *pee'*) the currency of India, Sri Lanka, Mauritius, Nepal, the Seychelle Islands, Bhutan, and Pakistan. In India, Pakistan, and Nepal, the rupee equals 100 pice, paisa, or paise; other nations refer to the coins as cents. Derived from the Sanskrit for *silver cut-out*, the term is kin to the Indonesian *rupiah* and the Russian *ruble*. In Ruth Prawer Jhabvala's *Heat and Dust*, the speaker donates 5 rupees to the watchman, who turns on a light for her to examine a shrine of Hanuman, the lustful monkey hero of the *Ramayana*. *See also* pice.

rush a pithy, upright marsh plant of the sedge family that includes sweet grass, bulrush, cattail, or reeds; the plant grows in clumps on stream banks or in bogs. Rushes dry into hollow straws that can be woven into baskets, shades, partitions, chair seats, tatami mats, or trays or can be spread as a cheap, fragrant, renewable floor covering for a barn, walkway, tavern, or cottage. An Anglo-Saxon term possibly derived from the Lithuanian for *knit*, the word entered English before the twelfth century. As merrymakers approach the Capulet house in William Shakespeare's *Romeo and Juliet*, they anticipate "tickling the rushes" with their feet as they dance. *See also* rush-light; tatami mats.

rush-light a cheap, but feeble, undependable light made by dipping a marsh rush or thick stalk in melted tallow or grease and setting it in a tin shade perforated with holes to allow spots of light to spatter a wall or entranceway and to keep the shredded stalk from dropping ash or setting nearby objects ablaze. After receiving a warning letter, Pip, the protagonist of Charles Dickens's *Great Expectations*, turns away from his apartment, takes a room for the night in Covent Garden, and stares at the dots of light made by a rush-light that the chamberlain sets in a metal container. *See also* sconce.

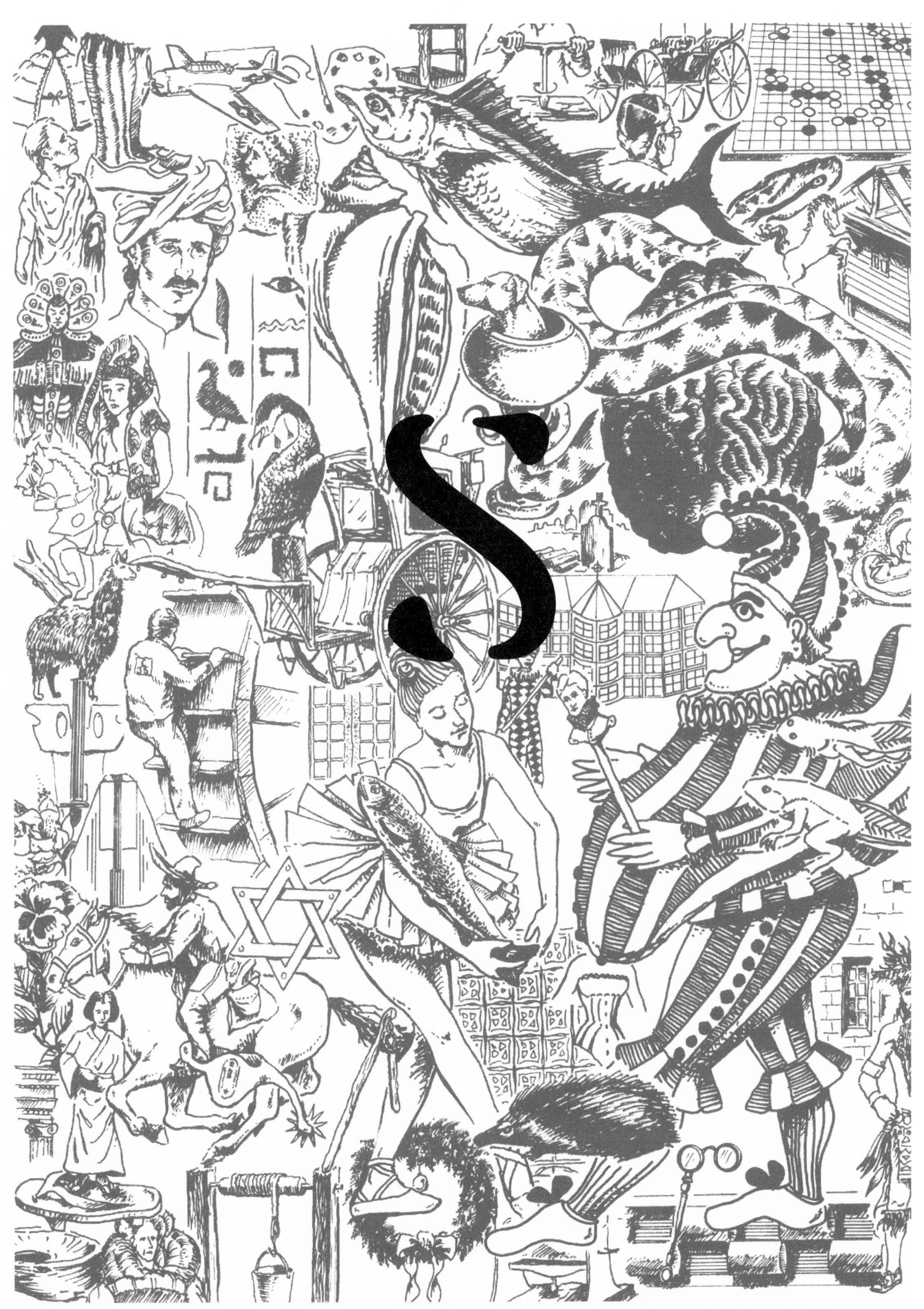
S

sabre or **saber** (*say'* b'r) a heavy, broad-bladed cavalry sword with grip, arched finger guard, sharpened cutting edge, and finely honed point capable of stabbing or slashing an adversary. A Russian term dating to the late seventeenth century, the word also refers to a more flexible curved dueling weapon or an ornamental weapon worn as officer's parade dress during inspection, presentation, and other formal occasions. When Billy Bones, an old sea dog, first appears at the Admiral Benbow tavern in Robert Louis Stevenson's *Treasure Island*, Jim Hawkins notices his rough appearance and a sabre cut, suggesting that he has lived a life of danger.

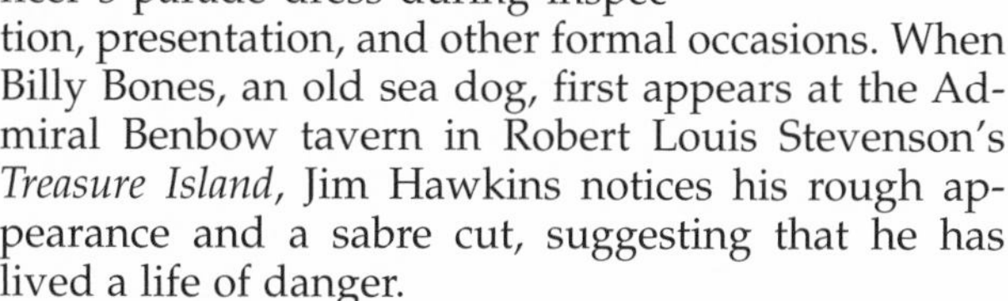

sac a fluid-filled bag, pouch, or membrane enclosing tissue or an organ of the body. Before birth, the fetus remains in a double sac, the amnion and chorion, that serves as a bumper to protect the part of the abdomen not cradled in bone. The sac ruptures before birth, releasing amniotic fluid and forcing the fetus to adapt instantly from a water animal to a land animal. During a difficult delivery in John Steinbeck's *The Red Pony*, Billy rips the mare's abdomen, bites open the sac, cuts the cord, and lifts the foal from the fluid.

sack (sak) a white wine or table-quality sherry common in England during the sixteenth and seventeenth centuries. Sack (the term derives from the French word for *dry*) was imported from the Canary Islands and parts of Spain. It was a standard drink in alehouses, inns, and ship galleys and was often carried in portable wineskins. In Daniel Defoe's *Robinson Crusoe*, the title character returns to a sunken ship to load his raft with salvaged food and five or six gallons of sack.

sackcloth and ashes as described in the Old Testament books of Genesis, Leviticus, Joshua, Samuel, Kings, Nehemiah, and Esther, a customary display of self-abasement, anguish, national calamity, or sorrow requiring the wearing of coarse cloth woven from goat or camel hair and the heaping of ashes on the head to indicate contrition, mourning, or woe. During play, Tom, the title character in Mark Twain's *The Adventures of Tom Sawyer*, explains to Huck that being a pirate is more fun than being a hermit, who must live alone and wear sackcloth and put ashes on his head. *See also* contrition, act of.

sacrarium (suh . *krehr'* ee . uhm) a part of a chapel or cathedral where worshippers approach the communion table to partake of ritual wine and wafers or bread; also, the housing or repository where viewers come to revere sacred bones, hair, images, icons, or other holy objects. After selling his wife and daughter to a sailor, Michael Henchard, the protagonist in Thomas Hardy's *The Mayor of Casterbridge*, enters the sacrarium, kneels at the communion table, and swears off strong drink on pain of a terrible punishment of deafness, blindness, and helplessness.

sacred pipe a ceremonial Native American medicine pipe or calumet composed of a stem carved of ash or sumac and a catlinite or soapstone bowl, from which smoke drifted to the four winds. Decorated with feathers, slash marks, sacred pictographs, pendants, or horsehair, the sacred pipe provided an opportunity for former enemies to smoke tobacco or kinnikinnick and make up past differences. During peacetime, the pipe and its tamper remained in a storage bag in the care of a prominent tribal leader. After offering the sacred pipe to the Six Powers, the title character in John Neihardt's *Black Elk Speaks* purifies himself with a sweat bath. *See also* pipestone; Sun Dance.

sacristy a storage room for vestments, chalices, candlesticks, trays, cups for the Eucharist, monstrances, incense, cruets, palls, altar cloths, and other necessary equipment for rituals; also, the dressing room for priests and persons serving the mass or assisting at weddings, funerals, or other religious occasions. In Isabel Allende's *The House of the Spirits*, women of the altar guild remove purple robes from the sacristy to shroud statues of saints on Maundy Thursday, the day commemorating Christ's agony in the Garden of Gethsemane. *See also* monstrance; pall; sexton.

safe a locked keeping room, closet, pantry, or ventilated storage chest or cabinet such as a pie safe that held baked goods, roasted meats, casseroles, preserves, cheese, and other cooked or processed foods to protect them from insects or theft. In the autobiographical *Narrative of the Life of Frederick Douglass*, the speaker recalls that slaves often went hungry while food lay at hand in the plantation's smokehouses and safes.

sagamore (*sa'* guh . mohr) an Abnaki term for the high rank of tribal leader or Algonquin for adviser or war leader. The term, along with *chief* and *sachem*, is not equivalent to the United States concept of commander-in-chief, but applies only to any wise spiritual leader. In James Fenimore Cooper's *The Last of the Mohicans*, Chingachgook, a Mohican and friend of Hawkeye, introduces himself as a chief and sagamore.

sagebrush artemisia; a scraggly grayish evergreen common to the rocky slopes of the American West and Mexico. Sagebrush contains a bitter, pungent oil used in soap, liqueur, pesticide, religious ceremonies, cooking, and healing. When steeped as a tea, the leaves produce a soothing beverage or wash for bathing feverish patients. In the sagebrush that grows on the hills beyond the ranch in John Steinbeck's *The Red Pony*, Jody hears the sounds of birds and grows anxious.

sahib or **saheb** (sahb or sah . *heeb'*) *fem.* **sahibah** or **memsahib** a sign of respect or courtesy title similar to *sir*, which was used in colonial India by Indians referring to prestigious or honored European male guests and government officials. Derived from the Hindi for *master*, the term entered English in the mid-seventeenth century. When the Nawab calls on Mrs. Olivia Rivers at her home in Ruth Prawer Jhabvala's *Heat and Dust*, she greets him formally as "Nawab Sahib." *See also* memsahib.

sail loft a large sewing room or storage warehouse where sail makers cut, stitch, and sell new sails for seagoing or river vessels. Also, a factory where seamers patch and repair used sailcloth for resale or recycle the fabric for whalers' breeches and coats. Along Hancock's Wharf, the setting of Esther Forbes's *Johnny Tremain*, stand counting houses, storage sheds, and sail lofts, all of which offer opportunities for artisans, apprentices, and skilled laborers.

Saint Anthony or **Saint Antony** known as a wonder-worker and powerful preacher, Saint Anthony of Padua (1195–1231) left the Augustinians and joined the Franciscans at Assisi, where he taught theology. His followers revere him as the patron of lost property, travelers, sailors, childless couples, pregnant women, and the poor. Before Frederick Henry departs for active duty in Plava in Ernest Hemingway's *A Farewell to Arms*, Catherine Barkley hands him her Saint Anthony's medal to protect him from harm.

Saint Sebastian an officer of the Roman emperor Diocletian's Praetorian Guard around A.D. 300 and patron of soldiers, athletes, and victims of plague. Upon learning that Sebastian was a Christian, his tormentors tied him to a tree for an archery target. He recovered and was drowned in a sewer. In George Orwell's *1984*, Winston Smith has a passing vision of violent sexual abuse of an unnamed young woman on the sidewalk near him, whom he envisions beating with a rubber truncheon and shooting full of arrows like the martyred Saint Sebastian to relieve pent-up sexual and emotional tensions.

sais or **syce** (sys) a manservant, groom, or horse handler who cleans and repairs harnesses, curries horses, attends to stabling and feeding, and provides transportation for a household; also, an Indian mounted guard, attendant, or chauffeur in the employ of a colonial officer or dignitary. In Rudyard Kipling's romantic story "Miss Youghal's Sais," a British soldier named Strickland poses as her sais, treats her royally by blacking the horses' hooves, and insults the general courting Miss Youghal, who sees through the disguise and helps Strickland convince the girl's father to allow them to marry.

sake or **saki** (*sah'* kee) a Japanese rice wine distilled from fermented rice gruel and served heated in tiny cups with elaborate gestures of goodwill and courtesy to guests and dignitaries. Sake is used for rituals, for toasting guests, and as a liqueur at the end of a meal. While inventorying household goods in Amy Tan's *The Joy Luck Club*, Ted's wife examines a broken domed clock, teapots, and sake sets before determining to keep her house and fight for herself against the man who had always dominated her.

salaam (suh . *lahm'*) an obeisance or gesture of fealty or ceremonial submission. Consisting of a low bow and symbolic touch to the forehead with the right palm, the salaam, derived from the Arabic for *peace*, is a common Islamic gesture of welcome, respect, or greeting in Asia and the eastern Pacific Rim. When pondering the worth of returning to India in James Hilton's *Lost Horizon*, protagonist Hugh Conway envisions introducing himself to colonial officers and accepting the salaams of servants.

salamander a red scaleless, tailed amphibian; a newt, eft, or lizard with moist, smooth skin. The salamander lives in water or trees, in burrows, or on land and eats insects, worms, and snails. In mythology, the salamander is credited with protective powers that allow it to survive in flames. In Ray Bradbury's *Fahrenheit 451*, Clarisse seems hypnotized by the salamander insignia on Guy Montag's firefighter's uniform, which symbolizes the upside-down logic of a fire company that sets fires to rid the world of books.

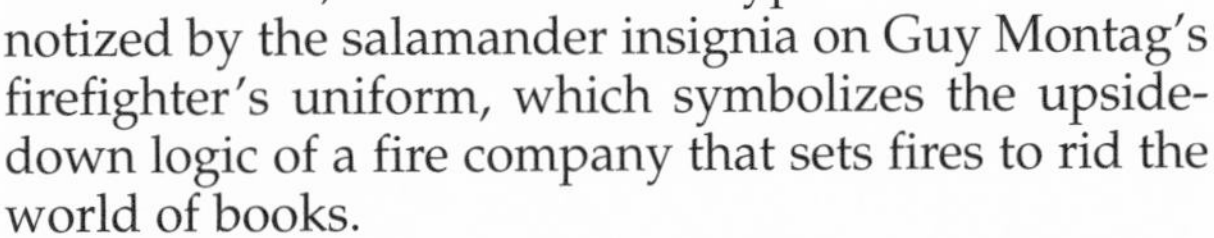

sallet (*sal'* liht) an obsolete Middle English or Appalachian dialect term for a vegetable salad consisting of the tender shoots of young green plants, including spinach, turnips, beet greens, pokeweed, cress, amaranth, or quinoa, which are eaten raw and dressed with a vinaigrette. Cooked sallet is lightly blanched or boiled with fat and served with chopped chives, cucumber, or wild onion tops or mixed with minced boiled egg, meat, or fish. In William Shakespeare's *Hamlet*, the title character, who ponders how to avenge his father's murder, speaks metaphorically of sallets or tasty tidbits, which are lacking from the harsh words he feels he must deliver.

saloon (suh . *loon'*) a central dining room; social hall for card-playing and light entertainment; reception or exhibition hall; or restaurant lounge in a steamboat, dirigible, or other passenger vehicle; also, a parlor car on a train or a public house, music hall, or tavern. In some public conveyances, the saloon offers privileges limited to first-class passengers. In Mark Twain's *Life on the Mississippi,* a gilded saloon with oil paintings, glass chandeliers, elegant upholstered furniture, and genteel occupants is the height of luxury river travel.

salsify (*sahl'* suh . fee or *sahl'* suh . fy) a wild biennial related to endive, chicory, lettuce, tarragon, and artichoke. The salsify plant produces purple flowers, strappy leaves valued as herbs or salad greens, and fleshy white tapered taproots that are steamed or cooked like potatoes or turnips; the oyster plant or vegetable oyster. As food grows scarce and exorbitantly priced, the residents of the annexe in Anne Frank's *The Diary of a Young Girl* are often limited to a single food, such as potatoes, turnips, peas, or salsify. *See also* annexe.

saltcellar or **salt-cellar** a small crystal dish and matching spoon or a glass or ceramic bottle with a perforated top for dispensing servings of salt; an obsolete term for salt shaker. Because of its use in preserving foods or bathing puncture wounds to remove infection, salt has carried so magical a value that accidental spilling is considered ill luck, which the victim wards off by sprinkling the loose grains over the left shoulder, the direction from which evil approaches. The title character in Mark Twain's *The Adventures of Huckleberry Finn* dreads bad luck after he turns over a saltcellar at breakfast.

saltpeter or **saltpetre** the common name for potassium nitrate, a salty-tasting meat preservative used in fertilizer and glass manufacture. Saltpeter is mixed with charcoal and sulfur as an essential ingredient in gunpowder, matches, and fireworks; also, a common name for sodium nitrate, a curing agent for ham. Derived from the Latin for *salt rock*, the term is a synonym for *niter*. In H. G. Wells's *The Time Machine*, the Time Traveler searches the minerals display in an abandoned museum for saltpeter or nitrates from which to make gunpowder. In Upton Sinclair's *The Jungle*, an elderly worker in a meat processing factory dies after he develops a cough and skin problems from the saltpeter that soaks through his boots.

salts *See* smelling salts.

Salvarsan (*sal'* vahr . *san*) a trade name for arsphenamine, a potentially hazardous arsenic compound used in the treatment of syphilis. In strong doses, it produces irreversible madness. Marketed by German bacteriologist Paul Ehrlich in 1909, the drug was a valuable part of pharmacopeia until the discovery of penicillin in 1928. In Ernest Hemingway's *A Farewell to Arms,* Rinaldi claims to be crazy from the gradual spread of syphilis, an occupational hazard for a soldier that is treated with mercury or Salvarsan.

samisen or **shamisen** (*sa'* muh . *sehn*) a traditional fretless Japanese lute or banjo featuring a boxy, skin-covered sounding board, horizontal tuning pegs at the end of its long neck, and three strings that are plucked or strummed with a talon-shaped pick or plectrum for lyrical solo or orchestral performance or as accompaniment to the narrative during kabuki drama. Derived from the Chinese term for *three strings*, the term for this sixteenth-century instrument entered the English language 300 years later, when Japan's trade with the West was flourishing. In Jeanne Wakatsuki Houston and James D. Houston's *Farewell to Manzanar*, the youngest Wakatsuki children misunderstand Ko's tears when he plays the samisen and weeps while singing the Japanese national anthem. *See also* kabuki.

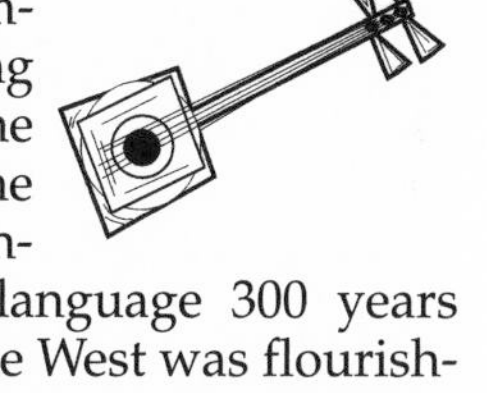

samovar (*sa'* muh . vahr) a heavy, ornate metal urn common to Russia and China for the preparation of spiced tea. The samovar is filled with water and heated by plunging a cylinder of hot coals through a hole in the top vertically into the center of the urn's contents. Hot tea pours from the spout at the bottom. Derived from the Russian for *self-boiling*, the term entered English in the early nineteenth century, when brass or silver-plated versions were displayed as conversation pieces in European tearooms and salons. On his way to visit Razumihin in Fyodor Dostoevsky's *Crime and Punishment,* Raskolnikov observes the servers clattering plates, dishes, and samovar.

sampan (*sam'* pan) a traditional Oriental dinghy, trading skiff, or light fishing boat of the eastern Pacific Rim covered with an awning and providing simple living quarters when used as a houseboat. The sampan is fitted with a junk sail in coastal waters and a short, stern-based scull or pair of sculls on rivers. Derived from the Chinese for *thin board,* the term entered English in the early seventeenth century. According to John Hersey's *Hiroshima,* a fisherman in a sampan on the Inland Sea 20 miles from the atom bomb heard the explosion and observed the flash.

samurai (*sam'* oo . *ry*) a bold chivalric warrior who earned prestige and high honor for military skills and horsemanship in feudal Japan during the seventeenth century. After the collapse of the economic system in the eighteenth century, wandering swordsmen found no employment and turned to crime as *ronin,* or brigands, who preyed on peasants and travelers. As described in Maxine Hong Kingston's *The Woman Warrior,* the samurai ranks slightly below the class of royalty and nobles.

sand-box a container or shaker of fine sand, which a writer sprinkles on freshly written copy as a means of blotting excess ink. After the sand absorbs the ink, the copyist blows the soiled sand into a waste receptacle. In Charles Dickens's *A Tale of Two Cities,* an officer sands an official document and hands it to Defarge, a revolutionary who arrests Charles Darnay and delivers him to a gloomy prison.

sanddab a general term for a family of Pacific flounder; a mottled, orangy-brown flat fish prized for its smooth white meat and ease of filleting; also, another name for plaice. When Waverly Jong accompanies her mother on shopping ventures to the fish market in Amy Tan's *The Joy Luck Club,* the sight of sanddabs with two eyes on the left side of their flat faces reminds her of a child who was hit by a car and flattened.

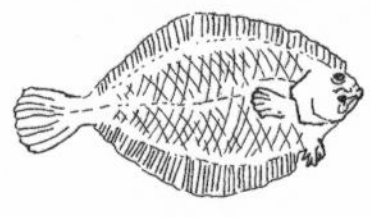

sansei (*san'* say) *pl.* **sansei** or **sanseis** the grandchildren of issei or the offspring of nisei. Derived from the Japanese for *third generation,* the term took on special meaning to Japanese-Americans who were interned or imprisoned, supposedly to prevent espionage, during World War II. In Jeanne Wakatsuki Houston and James D. Houston's *Farewell to Manzanar,* the Houston children, all sansei, learn about their family's hardships during the war by visiting the remains of Camp Manzanar, a wartime concentration camp on the edge of California's Mojave Desert. *See also* issei; nisei.

sarcophagus (sahr . *kah'* fuh . *guhs*) *pl.* **sarcophagi** a limestone, marble, alabaster, wood, terra-cotta, or lead coffin with a hinged lid or sliding fitted slab on top. Etched or carved along the top and sides, often with an effigy of the deceased on top, the most ornate sarcophagi have often been reserved for royalty or dignitaries and are placed on a raised slab or in a place of honor within a temple rather than sealed in a pyramid or family vault. Derived from the Greek for *flesh eater,* the term entered English in the early seventeenth century and refers to Egyptian tombs carved as early as 3000 B.C. and Minoan vaults from 2000 B.C. After Sam Parkhill shoots Spender in Ray Bradbury's *The Martian Chronicles,* the captain and crew arrange Spender's corpse in a Martian sarcophagus and shut the marble doors. *See also* effigy.

Sargasso (sahr . *gas'* soh) **weed** or **sargassum** a drifting mass of brown algae, or gulfweed, that is a spawning ground for eels and flying fish and is used to make fertilizer, soup, and soy sauce. The weed, buoyed by the berry-shaped gas-filled bladders attached to the bracts, remains afloat in the warmest parts of the Atlantic and western Pacific oceans. Derived from the Portuguese for *seaweed,* the term entered English in the late nineteenth century. Far from shore, Santiago, the protagonist in Ernest Hemingway's *The Old Man and the Sea,* observes natural indicators in birds, plankton, Sargasso weed, and the shapes of clouds overhead. *See also* plankton.

sarod or **sarode** (suh . *rohd'*) a Persian or north Indian lute with multiple strings, four of which are bowed or picked with a plectrum. Similar to the Japanese samisen and the Indian sitar, the sarod is a long-necked, unfretted instrument with skin-covered sound box, several strings that vibrate in harmony with the four played strings, and a four-pegged tuning anchor at the far end. It is played to accompany classical dancing or strummed as a solo performance or paired with drums. The name derives from the Persian for melody. In Ruth Prawer Jhabvala's *Heat and Dust,* Karim and Kitty maintain the ethnic atmosphere of India by playing taped sarod music in their London apartment.

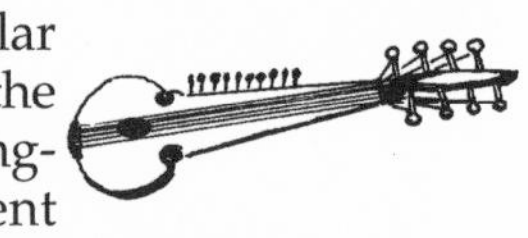

sarsaparilla (*sas* . puh . *rihl'* luh) a sweet carbonated beverage similar to root beer and made from the dried root of the tropical smilax, a prickly vine used as an herbal remedy for dermatitis, syphilis, and arthritis. Derived from the Spanish for *bramble vine*, the term entered English in the mid-sixteenth century. After Jurgis and Ona's wedding feast of sausages and sarsaparilla in Upton Sinclair's *The Jungle*, the whole family must rise early the next day and go to work to save their places in the factories.

sassafras (*sas'* suh . fras) a tall deciduous laurel tree yielding bark, shoots, aromatic oil, and roots that are boiled into a pungent flavoring for beverages, candy, tobacco, tonic, appetite suppressant, and a cure for sore throat, stomach ache, and syphilis. After Europeans learned of the healing powers of sassafras, they popularized it briefly in Europe as a cure-all. In Conrad Richter's *The Light in the Forest*, True Son stands in the shadow of sassafras trees and makes an owl call that Half Arrow recognizes.

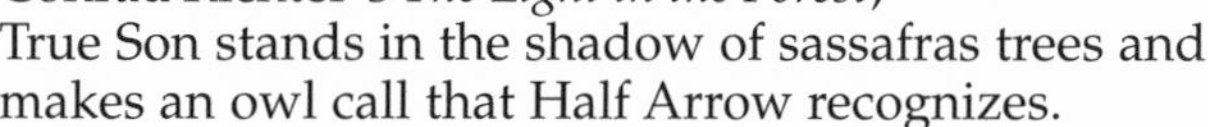

satsuma (sat . *soo'* muh) a tangy, virtually seedless Japanese tangerine or mandarin orange, one of the hardiest in the citrus family with a netted, leathery skin; juicy segmented meat; and fragrant oils. Named for a province in Kyushu, the term entered English in the late nineteenth century. In Truman Capote's "A Christmas Memory," holiday gifts include a sack of satsumas, a handmade kite, and a subscription to a religious magazine for children.

satyr (*say'* tuhr) a lustful, rowdy half-goat, half-man usually depicted as hairy-bodied and bearing goat ears, tail, and horns or horn buds. Satyrs walked on hind hooves, played flutes, and took part in orgiastic celebrations of the god Dionysius or Bacchus. Derived from the Greek for *woods deity*, the term applies to much classic and neoclassic art, sculpture, drama, and song, especially woodland idylls. In Edith Hamilton's *Mythology*, the satyrs are frisky, quarrelsome goat-men of the wilds who accompany the god Pan and the older, less troublesome sileni. *See also* Dionysiac; faun.

saveloy (*sa* . vuh . *loi'*) a cheap ready-to-eat pork sausage composed primarily of fat, dried or smoked meat scraps and skins, and pungent spices to conceal the lack of lean meat. A mid-nineteenth-century term, the word derives from Old Italian for *pig's brain*. After retrieving Kemmerich's books in Erich Maria Remarque's *All Quiet on the Western Front*, Paul Baumer rejoices at being alive and runs through the revitalizing evening air to Müller, who offers him a savory bite of saveloy.

saw grass a hardy saline or freshwater marsh sedge related to rushes and composed of clumps of long-bladed greenery edged with serrated notching and wide-ranging runners and roots. Some varieties produce rhizomes or roots that are dried and steeped in tea as purgatives. Others are cut for hay, straw, or packing material or are made into cheap paper or woven into sunshades, mats, or baskets. While Jody and his father trail Old Slewfoot the bear in Marjorie Kinnan Rawlings's *The Yearling*, the trail leads off toward thick saw grass ponds. *See also* rush.

Saxon (*saks'* uhn) a tribe member from Schleswig, a north German realm on the Baltic coast that established the early English race; a typically tall, sturdy, light-skinned people characterized by blue eyes and blond hair. The Saxons overran England in the fifth century A.D., driving the Celts west to Wales and Ireland and north into the distant parts of Scotland. The Anglo-Saxon language gave English its grammatical forms. In Herman Melville's *Billy Budd*, the speaker describes the grace, comeliness, and regular Saxon features of the 21-year-old title character. *See also* Nordic.

sayonara (*sy* . oh . *nah'* ruh) literally "May it be so," the formal Japanese term for farewell or good-bye, which is accompanied by a slow, graceful bow from the waist. In her autobiographical *So Far from the Bamboo Grove*, Yoko Kawashima Watkins speaks respectfully to the school janitor, who controls his stutter well enough to bow and say, "sayonara."

scab an American slang term for a worker who refuses to join a trade union or a union member who accepts work in a facility where union members are striking; also a temporary replacement for a striking worker, often recruited from distant factories and transported to a factory where local staff refuses to work until management meets certain demands. From the Dutch for *shrew*, the term entered English in the thirteenth century. After applying to boss Mike Scully for a job on the meat packing line in Upton Sinclair's *The Jungle*, Jurgis, desperate for money to support his family, considers working as a scab and ponders changing his political affiliation from Republican to Democrat.

scabbard (*skab'* buhrd) the thirteenth-century Middle English term for a protective sheath or carrying case for a sword, bayonet, hunting knife, or dagger. Often made of rawhide or leather worked with tooling or metal edging, a scabbard could be threaded onto a belt or bandolero. While ridiculing the overweight Montfleury in front of an audience in Edmond Rostand's *Cyrano de Bergerac*, the title character issues a veiled threat that further harassment will scare Cyrano's sword from its scabbard.

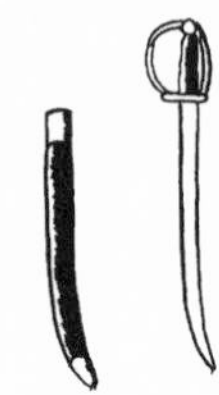

scaffold (*skaf'* fuhld) a raised staging area or platform where observers and officials watch a public beheading, hanging, mutilation, pillorying, or flogging; a place of shame or execution. A Middle English term, the word derives from the Latin for *portable tower*. In Nathaniel Hawthorne's *The Scarlet Letter*, a meteor appears to shape a scarlet A in the sky on the night that the Reverend Arthur Dimmesdale stands on the village scaffold with his daughter, Pearl, and her mother, Hester Prynne. *See also* pillory.

scaffolding temporary platforms on a raised framework erected from sturdy wood or metal uprights and moveable planking around an area where painters, window-washers, miners, welders, plasterers, masons, bricklayers, or artists are working. During the investigation of a murder in Sir Arthur Conan Doyle's "The Adventure of the Speckled Band," scaffolding indicates that the crumbling hall that Sherlock Holmes visits is under repair.

scalawag or **scallywag** (*ska'* luh . *wag*) political slang used by southern Democrats during the Reconstruction Era to vilify northern Federalists, meddlers, conniving rascals, and financial speculators and opportunists. Derived from the name of a Shetland Island pony, the term implies contempt for an undersized weakling or impostor. During a political argument between Democrats and Republicans in Ernest Gaines's *The Autobiography of Miss Jane Pittman*, a Democrat accuses a Republican scalawag of taking advantage of the postwar situation in the South by occupying a large plantation.

scalpel (*skal'* p'l) a small, maneuverable surgical, dissection, or autopsy knife featuring a thin, straight blade. Derived from the Latin for *carve*, the term entered English in the mid-eighteenth century. While trying to befriend Mike, the only human being living in the Arctic setting of *Never Cry Wolf*, Farley Mowat displays scalpels and brain spoons and a text featuring an autopsy, which terrifies Mike.

scapular (*skap'* yoo . luhr) a set of religious badges worn on the chest and back and anchored to the body with strings, tapes, or cloth bands. Worn under clothing, the badge symbolizes devotion or allegiance to a religious order or fraternity. Also, a cloak formed of two straight pieces loosely joined at the shoulder to hang in front and back of the body. A fifteenth-century term, the word derives from the Latin for *shoulder blade*. While transporting a corpse to town from the shore in Gabriel García Márquez's "The Handsomest Drowned Man in the World," villagers apply trinkets, protective charms, and a scapular.

scarification (*ska* . rih . fih . *kay'* shuhn) a form of religious marking, cutting, scratching, slitting, or laceration of the skin as an adornment or as a sign of initiation or readiness for marriage, duty, bravery in battle, nobility, or submission to tribal authority. The skin may be pricked with thorns or shards of bone or glass and the wounds marked with dye or charcoal to form a permanent plain or colored scar. Derived in the fourteenth century, the term comes from the Norse for *cut*. In a letter to Celie in Alice Walker's *The Color Purple*, Nettie observes that children of Tashi's generation resist the scarification ritual as backward and uncivilized.

scat improvised, meaningless vocal syllables of a lilting, melodic jazz song; singing that imitates the rhythmic sounds of musical instruments. Dating to the late 1920s, the origin of the term is obscure. Illustrating his Harlem days to writer Alex Haley in *The Autobiography of Malcolm X*, the Black Muslim leader stops talking and pretends to lindy-hop and scat-sing. Also, fecal droppings or excrement of an animal. From the Greek for *dung*, the second usage entered English in the same period as the first but is unrelated. In Farley Mowat's study of wolf scat in *Never Cry Wolf*, he protects himself from air-borne parasites by wearing a surgical mask.

scepter (*sehp'* tuhr) a ceremonial baton, rod, or staff held in a ritual pose by an official or dignitary; a sovereign's crest or symbol of power. From the Greek for *prop* or *shaft*, the term entered English in the fourteenth century. At a formal council of state in Homer's *Odyssey*, the hero's son, Telemachus, holds the scepter, a symbol of authority, and addresses elders concerning the internal disorder that threatens to topple Odysseus's rule.

schizophrenia (skiht . zoh . *free'* nyuh) a common psychotic disorder causing the mind to separate thoughts from emotions. The disease may manifest itself in withdrawal, fantasy, self-absorption, disorientation, delusion, hallucination, unexplained gestures, or incoherence. An early twentieth-century term derived from the Greek for *split mind*, the word applies to a complex family of psychoses. In Najib Mahfouz's "The Happy Man," the speaker laughs on his way to an appointment with a doctor who studies depression, anxiety, hysteria, and schizophrenia. *See also* psychosis.

schooner (*skoo'* nuhr) a small, top-heavy, two-masted sea vessel bearing topsails over the mainsails to give added speed. First launched from Gloucester, Massachusetts, in 1713, the schooner suited coastal traders and fishers of the eastern shore of North America because the ships were easily maneuvered by small crews, thus saving the owner money. Derived from the Scottish term for *launch*, the word may reflect the smooth action of a stone skipped on the water's surface. After saboteurs sink every tanker in Sint Nicolaas in Theodore Taylor's *The Cay*, ferry boats and native schooners remain in port.

schottische or **schottish** (*shah'* tihsh or shah . *teesh'*) a folk dance performed in a circle by couples who place hands on hips and follow intricate patterns based on a set figure of three steps and a hop or high kick. Derived from the German for *Scottish*, the word applies to lively dancing similar to a Highland fling. In Willa Cather's *My Antonia*, Jim prefers dancing with Tony, who teaches him the brisk, rapid steps of the schottische.

scimitar or **scimiter** (*sihm'* ih . tahr) a sword with a curved blade, sharpened on the bottom or convex edge, that often widens near the point. Popular in Persia, Turkey, and Arabia, the scimitar (the term derives from the Persian for *sword*) was a useful hacking or slicing weapon or ceremonial symbol of authority for entrance guards, mounted soldiers, or infantry. In the cataclysmic battle that concludes J. R. R. Tolkien's *The Hobbit*, huge goblins armed with steel scimitars rush into the valley and menace the assembled army.

sconce (skahns or skahnts) an ornate metal wall receptacle or bracket on an inside wall holding one or more candles. Projecting candles could be shielded with perforated tin or covered with a lamp glass. Sconces were often backed with shiny plate metal or mirrors to augment the light and create a brighter atmosphere for parties. Derived from the Latin for *hide*, the term entered English in the fifteenth century. The gloomy scene in which Pip gets his first view of Miss Havisham in Charles Dickens's *Great Expectations* reveals the jilted bride's romantic melancholia through the dull light of candles set in high wall sconces.

scorpion (*skor'* pyun) a predatory crawling spider native to deserts or warm, moist tropical settings. Unlike ordinary arachnids, the scorpion bears two front pincers, eight legs, and a curving, jointed tail equipped with a deadly stinger that the scorpion can arch over its back. Derived from the Greek for *stinging*, the term entered English in the twelfth century. The painful scorpion bite on Coyotito's shoulder in John Steinbeck's *The Pearl* causes the baby's parents to seek medical aid from the elitist doctor in town.

scourge (skurj) a flail or whip composed of a handle and one- to three-foot lengths of leather or hemp that is used as a flogging weapon to discipline, administer summary punishment, or inflict a masochistic gesture of self-flagellation to purify the soul of sin. A scourge may be tipped with nails or metal studs to increase damage to the flesh. The term, which entered English in the thirteenth century, derives from the Latin for *whip*. In his closet, the Reverend Arthur Dimmesdale, the unnamed father of Pearl in Nathaniel Hawthorne's *The Scarlet Letter*, lashes himself with a bloody scourge in atonement for fathering an illegitimate child.

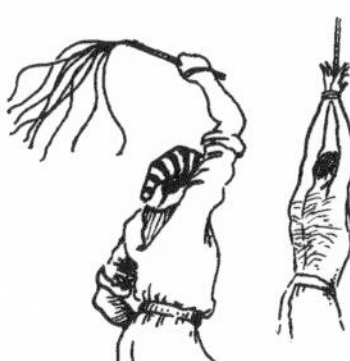

scow a slow, flat-bottomed river barge, ferry, or lighter carrying heavy loads or passengers; also, a flat-keeled racing boat. The wide-bodied, square-ended scow may be towed by a crew following a path along a watercourse, pulled by a tugboat, or propelled by oars. An obscure late seventeenth-century term, the word may derive from the German for *punt pole*. In Conrad Richter's *The Light in the Forest*, the scow moving slowly toward True Son carries a young boy who reminds him of his white brother. *See also* lighter.

scrag a pejorative or unflattering synonym for neck, particularly the neck of a thin, rawboned person or a neck or shank of mutton. Derived perhaps from the Swedish term for *crooked*, the term entered English in the Middle English period. To preserve the memory of the title character in Charlotte Brontë's *Jane Eyre*, Edward Rochester wears her pearl necklace attached to his scrag under his cravat. *See also* cravat.

screw a rotating propeller made up of a central hub surrounded by two to six symmetrical blades that force a steamship through the water. As a replacement for paddle wheels and stern-wheelers in the 1830s, the screw-driven steamer made better use of power by maintaining the propulsion mechanism underwater. In an intense search for transportation to complete his race, Phileas Fogg, protagonist in Jules Verne's *Around the World in Eighty Days*, locates the *Henrietta*, an iron-hulled vessel fitted with screw and funnel.

scrim (skrihm) a loose, gauzy fabric woven of cotton, linen, hemp, thin canvas, cambric, or synthetic fibers used in lining, upholstery, sheer curtains, or theater drapes. On the stage, scrim provides a simple, lightweight, transparent backdrop that can be painted or dyed and hung before special lights to alter the mood or create an effect of scenery. In a flashback in Arthur Miller's *Death of a Salesman*, Willy Loman's mistress dresses behind a layer of scrim.

scrimshaw *See* skrimshandering.

scrip stamps a form of welfare that supplies the needy with nonnegotiable government currency that can be exchanged only for food at a county office, particular store, distribution depot, or supply house. In Harper Lee's *To Kill a Mockingbird*, Scout explains to the teacher that the Cunninghams are poor but proud and accept no food baskets or scrip stamps. *See also* food stamps; relief.

scrivener (*skrih'* vih . nuhr) a copy clerk or stenographer, who, in addition to making additional copies of documents or letters might file, research, summarize, draft, or deliver work to other offices; an amanuensis, notary, or scribe. A fourteenth-century term, the word derives from the Latin for *write.* Today, the tiring, repetitive job of Herman Melville's "Bartleby the Scrivener" would be done by a photocopier, database, scanner, and fax machine.

scrofula (*skruhf'* yuh . luh) or **the king's evil** a tubercular condition of the neck characterized by abscesses and enlarged lymph nodes or glands. Derived from the Latin for *little sows*, the term entered English in the late eighteenth century. In William Shakespeare's *Macbeth*, the beneficent acts of King Edward the Confessor include the royal touch on sufferers of scrofula, a miraculous gesture of compassion that contrasts with the evil, self-aggrandizing acts of Macbeth, a regicide.

scullery (*skuhl'* uh . ree) a back kitchen, reserved for food preparation, dishwashing, and heavy scrubbing by the scullion, or potboy, a low-level servant. Because it was a mundane workroom where servants peeled potatoes, emptied pots, and scoured kettles, the scullery was the most menial and least pleasant of household assignments. Reassignment to the scullery was a punishment for misbehavior or inadequate performance of duties. The term, which derives from the Latin word for *drinking bowl*, entered English in the fifteenth century. In George Bernard Shaw's *Pygmalion*, Eliza Doolittle is so dirty and unpresentable that she expects to be washed in the scullery.

sculpin (*skuhl'* pihn) a small, bony, scaleless rockfish containing too large a head and skeleton and too little meat to make it a commercial food source. The sculpin is often caught for sport on the Pacific Coast. The name may derive from a mispronunciation of *scorpion.* Farley Mowat, author of *Never Cry Wolf*, observes the fishing style of wolves that reach over a stream to grab fish or, less often, grapple under rocks for sculpin.

scupper (*skuhp'* puhr) a port, vent, valve, or drain hole in a ship's bulwarks that empties water that accumulates on deck. Covered by flaps or hinged doors, scuppers open automatically from the pressure of escaping water when a ship rolls from side to side. A Middle English term, it derives from the French for *spit.* As Jim Hawkins hangs to the rigging of the *Hispaniola* in Robert Louis Stevenson's *Treasure Island*, the ship roll empties scuppers and bangs its rudder against the rocks.

scuppernong (*skuhp'* puhr . nahng) a tan, thick-skinned wild grape kin to the James grape or muscadine. Named for a river in North Carolina, scuppernongs are prized as a source of sweet fruit pulp for wine. In Harper Lee's *To Kill a Mockingbird*, Jem and Scout are not too scrupulous to eat someone's scuppernongs or swallow a squirt of milk from a neighbor's cow, but they are unsure of the rights to the Indian-head pennies that Boo Radley leaves in a hollow tree.

scurf scum, scales, flakes, crust, or debris scoured from a pot or laboratory beaker. While pigs are scrubbed, dehaired, and boiled in water during butchering, scurf rises to the top and is removed by a skimmer, slotted spoon, or seine. Entering English before the twelfth century, this word derives from the Anglo-Saxon term for *scab.* While Rob's father butchers and prepares the meat from Pinky, Rob's pet in Robert Newton Peck's *A Day No Pigs Would Die*, scurf accumulates at the surface of the scalding water.

scurvy (*skuhr'* vee) a weakening of connective tissue caused by the lack of vitamin C, or ascorbic acid, in the diet. Scurvy can cause an unhealthy pallor, bleeding gums, painful joints, bruises, spongy tissue, and physical collapse. The name is derived from *scurf.* When the mariner in Nathaniel Hawthorne's *The Scarlet Letter* attempts to allay the protagonist's concerns about contracting scurvy on the sea voyage by announcing that a doctor is accompanying the passengers, he unknowingly divulges the fact that Roger Chillingworth has learned Hester's plan of escape.

scythe (syth) an agricultural tool made up of a curved blade set at the end of a long handle with two knobs or projections for the user's hands to grasp. Use of a mowing or reaping scythe requires long, low sweeps just above root level of wheat, oats, timothy, or other grain crops or grasses. A term that entered English before the twelfth century, the word derives from the Anglo-Saxon for *saw.* Harvesters in Thomas Hardy's *Tess of the D'Urbervilles, Far from the Madding Crowd,* and *The Mayor of Casterbridge* swing scythes as they cut grain. *See also* timothy.

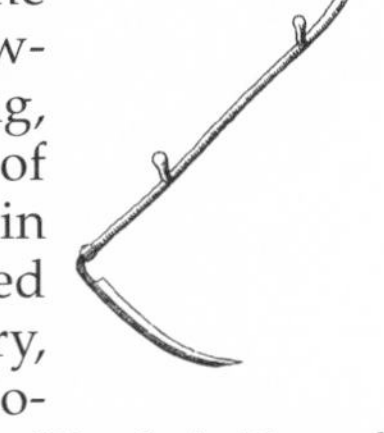

sea grape a shrub that grows along sandy seashores from the North American tropics to as far south as the southern coast of South America. The sea grape produces round, glossy leaves and clusters of purple or white grapelike berries that can be made into jam. Phillip, the survivor of marooning in Theodore Taylor's *The Cay,* signals passing ships by lighting a fire of sea grape, which produces an oily smoke.

seal a metal, wood, ivory, jade, or stone stamp carved or impressed with an insignia, crest, character, initial, design, or message; a signet ring. A seal can take the place of an artist's signature on artwork or an authorized signature on a letter or legal document as proof that the signer had permission from the owner of the seal and therefore serves as a bona fide agent or stand-in, for example, for an invalid or a soldier overseas. Well-to-do businessmen in the final vision of Charles Dickens's *A Christmas Carol* display their wealth in the form of gold seals hanging from pocket chains as they discuss the recent demise of Ebenezer Scrooge. In Pearl S. Buck's *The Good Earth,* four stones set at the corners of a piece of property bear the seal character of the House of Hwang.

sealing wax a malleable substance sold in columns or slabs to be cut into small cubes, melted, and dropped on the closed edges of a letter or at the end of a document. To prove the authenticity of the message, the sealer applies a seal stamp or signet ring, which sets the shape of an identifiable crest or initial in the cooling wax and demonstrates that the message has not been altered since it was sealed. The manager in Joseph Conrad's *The Heart of Darkness* ignores insolent servants and toys nervously with sealing wax as he explains to Marlowe the urgency of reaching Mr. Kurtz, whose fate is ironically sealed by his own greed and mistreatment of black Africans.

Secesh Army (suh . *sehsh'*) a Civil War–era slang term for secessionists. As Jane travels toward Ohio in Ernest Gaines's *The Autobiography of Miss Jane Pittman,* she observes the ragged condition of veterans of the Secesh Army, who straggle home after General Lee surrenders to General Grant and the Union Army at Appomattox, Virginia. *See also* secession.

secession (suh . *sesh'* shuhn) a political belief or separatist movement encouraging states to withdraw from the United States. In 1861, as a result of what they considered untenable federal laws, secessionists created the Confederacy, a block of southern states seeking to negate ties with the Federal Union and to preserve states' rights and an economic system based on slavery. Derived from the verb *secede,* the term names a legal position calling for a shift in allegiance with an opposing or intolerable religious or political stance. In Irene Hunt's *Across Five Aprils,* Jethro Creighton is confused by adult talk of secession and discontent over slavery.

Seconal (*see'* kuh . nahl) the trade name for a sodium salt that is compressed into quinalbarbitone, a white, odorless secobarbiturate medication used as a sedative and hypnotic for controlling psychotic patients. The sedative was introduced in 1951. The drug's name is derived from *secondary allyl.* In Ken Kesey's One Flew *over the Cuckoo's Nest,* cynical hospital staff make double use of a dose of Seconal by administering electroshock treatment while the patient is sedated. *See also* psychosis.

sect a potentially pejorative classification for a school, congregation, religious or philosophical society, political faction, or commune dedicated to a single purpose or leadership and holding a unified set of goals or aims, such as vegetarianism, pacifism, or rejection of religious ritual, for example, among Buddhists, Quakers, and Unitarians. Also, a cohesive splinter group composed of dissenters who defy or denounce the leadership of a parent group, form a schism or break with former ties, and withdraw allegiance to practice a distinct variation of general beliefs. In Arthur Miller's introduction to *The Crucible,* Europeans tolerate the fanatic sect that populates the American colonies because entrepreneurs profit from their trade goods.

sedan chair a public conveyance for one occupant consisting of a closed boxy compartment carried by two men shouldering or holding a pair of horizontal poles fastened to each side of the coach. To enter the chair, the traveler opened a door in the front and pushed up a hinged roof to accommodate large hats or ornate hairstyles. Derived from the Latin for *sit,* the term names a transportation method practiced in ancient China and Rome as well as eighteenth-century England, where the sedan chair kept the passenger from muddy streets, prying eyes, disagreeable odors, and disease and displayed wealth and privilege. On his first view of Kamala in her sedan chair in Hermann Hesse's *Siddhartha,* the title character abandons his ascetic ways to woo a mistress.

sedge *See* saw grass.

seed-drill a planting machine that sows seeds evenly along a row. The seed, which is poured into a hopper at the top of the device, falls down a slot or funnel into a small chamber alongside a rotating wheel. Holes in the wheel are cut to fit the individual seeds and allow one seed at a time to penetrate the row in a hole punctured by an automatic dibble or drill. A drag covers the hole with soil. Donald Farfrae, a key character in Thomas Hardy's *The Mayor of Casterbridge,* demonstrates a seed-drill in the marketplace, drawing both Elizabeth-Jane and his future wife, Lucetta, to view the agricultural innovation.

seer (*see'* uhr or see'r) a clairvoyant, diviner, shaman, spiritualist, soothsayer, or mystic possessing extrasensory perception (ESP), or the ability to see and interpret the future. Among the personae, or cast, of Sophocles' *Antigone* is Teiresias, a blind seer who spent part of his life as a woman and returned to manhood blessed with the wisdom of both sexes. Likewise, in William Shakespeare's *Julius Caesar,* a seer cryptically warns the title character to "beware the ides of March." *See also* medicine man; shaman.

selah (*see'* luh or *sehl'* uh) a puzzling untranslated term that ends verses or segments of the Psalms and Habakkuk and implies a musical rest or stop for soloists or instrumentalists or a halt to congregational reply to the liturgist, scripture reader, or chanter in a responsive reading. Derived from the Hebrew for *pause,* the term entered English in the early sixteenth century. In Willa Cather's *My Antonia,* Jim's pious grandfather ends a breakfast reading from a passage from the Psalms with a sonorous "selah."

selvage or **selvedge** (*sehl'* vihj) a natural edge, rim, or barrier; a tightly woven or fringed edge, composed of darker or heavier fibers, that runs along the length of fabric, and stops fraying and raveling; also, a decorative border, edge, or margin. A fifteenth-century term, the word derives from the Anglo-Saxon for *self edge.* On his first passage up the waterway west of British Columbia in Margaret Craven's *I Heard the Owl Call My Name,* the new minister observes straight crags, towering trees, and a dark selvage along the rocks below indicating low tide.

semaphore (*sehm'* uh . for) a form of telegraphy or long-distance communication system based on coded positioning of flags or shutters on a special lamp; used to pass messages or warnings from vessel to vessel, from ship to shore, or over a linked communication line of relay stations or lighthouses. Derived from the Greek for *bearing signals,* the term entered English in 1816 with the invention of Admiral Sir Home Pophal's signal lamp. In Alexandre Dumas's *The Count of Monte Cristo,* a dissembling message by semaphore encourages speculative buying of Spanish stocks, which leads to the ruin of one of Edmond Dantés's enemies.

seminary (*sehm'* uh . nehr . ee) in the nineteenth century, a private school or finishing school for young ladies; also a training center for ministers, priests, rabbis, and other students of religion. Derived from the Latin for *seed,* the term creates a metaphor for education, which puts the germ of wisdom in the fertile minds of students. Before departing for the army, Henry, the protagonist in Stephen Crane's *The Red Badge of Courage,* visits the nearby seminary and says good-bye to friends.

semi-syncope *See* syncope.

sennet (*sehn'* neht) a stage direction indicating a fanfare or coordinated trumpet or cornet call signaling the audience to rise to acknowledge the arrival of guests or nobility, announcing a banquet or a ceremonial entrance or exit of a distinguished entourage, or marking a segment of theatrical entertainment. Derived from the French for *signal*, the term entered English during the height of the English Renaissance. In William Shakespeare's *Macbeth*, the sennet that marks the arrival of Macbeth and his wife to the court suggests the peripheral privileges of royalty that mark the guilty king's rise to power. *See also* fanfare; flourish.

sen-sen (*sihn'* sihn) cinnamon and clove breath freshening lozenge that removed or masked the odor of onions, garlic, liquor, cigarettes, cigars, snuff, or chewing tobacco from the mouth. This romanticized trade name for the early twentieth-century over-the-counter deodorizer plays on the illusion of sin and the oriental allure of the product's spelling and repetition. In Zora Neale Hurston's *Their Eyes Were Watching God*, Hezekiah, clerk at Janie's store after Jody dies, steals an occasional jawbreaker and spices his breath with sen-sen to imply to local girls that he is disguising liquor on his breath.

sentinel (*sehn'* tih . nuhl) a guard, watch, or picket; also, a lookout supplied with a watchword or password that all entrants must speak to guarantee their allegiance. Dating to the late sixteenth century, the term is related to *sense* and derives from the Latin for *perceive*. The corporal doubts Wilson's acuity and alertness in his post of sentinel in Stephen Crane's *The Red Badge of Courage.*

serape or **sarape** (suh . *rah'* peh) a thick, knee-length woolen or cashmere shawl, cloak, or blanket worn as an overcoat draped across the shoulders by men and women in Latin American countries. Emulating Aztec designs, the serape is often woven in bold, bright-colored Native American patterns. In Mark Twain's *The Adventures of Tom Sawyer*, Tom and Huck are surprised to find Injun Joe wrapped in a serape and concealed beneath a sombrero.

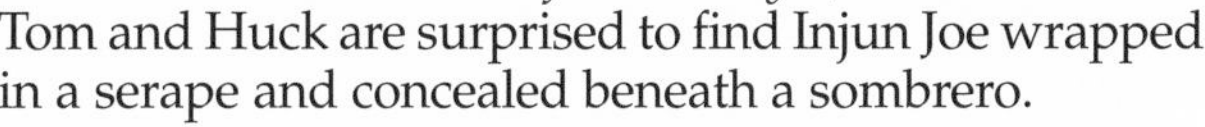

seraph (*sehr'* af) *pl.* **seraphim** a member of the highest orders of angels, or bright heavenly beings, whom the books of Isaiah, Ezekiel, and Revelation describe as God's attendants and messengers delivering divine commands or mercy. Seraphim have three sets of wings—one set covering the feet, one the head, and the third set for flying. Symbols of love, light, purity, and compassion, *seraph* and *seraphim* are Hebrew terms that derive from *burn*. The parson in Conrad Richter's *The Light in the Forest* warns Myra Butler not to expect True Son to give up Lenni Lenape ways and turn into a seraph overnight.

serf (suhrf) a feudal slave or agricultural laborer who served the master owning the piece of farmland to which the serf was bound. When the land was sold, its serfs, like farm animals and other chattel, were a negotiable part of the exchange. Derived from the Latin for *slave*, the term entered English in the early seventeenth century. In Susan B. Anthony's speech "Women's Right to Vote," delivered throughout New York in 1873, she compares the position of women in society to that of a serf during the Middle Ages, when kings and lords treated hirelings as expendable, subhuman slaves.

serviceberry or **shadberry** the purplish red fruit of a bush related to the rose, also known as the shadbush, shadblow, or juneberry, a common shrub bearing white flowers that bloom about the time that schools of shad appear in the rivers; common in the southern Appalachian Mountains. Eaten raw or dried as a flavoring for meat dishes, pemmican, or breads, the berry is rich in vitamin C. In Hal Borland's *When the Legends Die*, Tom Black Bull's parents follow Charlie Huckleberry to a mountain slope where serviceberries are ripe.

settle a high-backed solid wooden bench, stool, or settee often with arms, a drawer underneath, or a lift-up seat opening on a storage chest. The settle was placed to the side of a hearth to keep drafts from the necks and backs of persons warming themselves by the flames. Derived from the Latin for *sit*, the term dates to the mid-seventeenth century. In Charles Dickens's *Great Expectations*, customers at the Three Jolly Bargemen sit on facing settles and listen to Mr. Wopsle read aloud from the newspaper. *See also* highscreen seat.

settlement worker a social welfare worker staffing a center or settlement house sponsored by a philanthropic organization or church; a volunteer or staff member of a philanthropic body that provides a variety of services to a poor neighborhood. Workers encourage children to attend classes, women to receive help with sick infants or relief from abusive relationships, or destitute people to eat a free meal, find clothing, seek medical care, or study information about jobs, training, or locations of better lodgings. Jurgis and other characters in the tenements of Chicago in Upton Sinclair's *The Jungle* are unfamiliar with the role of settlement workers, whom they fear are religious fanatics preaching unfamiliar beliefs.

Seventh Day Adventists an evangelical Christian religious group that worships on Saturday, the day they consider the Sabbath—the day the Creator rested after making the earth. Former Millerites, the group dates to the mid-nineteenth century and centers its faith on vegetarianism, strict rules against alcohol and tobacco, daily battle against immorality, and a watchful outlook for the Second Coming when Christ will redeem the righteous. Granny, a member of the Seventh Day Adventists in Richard Wright's *Black Boy*, argues with her grandson over his need to work on Saturday to provide school clothes.

seven-up a variety of all fours, a card game played with one deck for two, three, or four players. The dealer distributes six cards face down. The seventh decides trump, the most valuable card or suit. The player to the dealer's right can accept or reject trump. More cards are distributed three at a time, two down and one facing up. The game awards points for high or low trump, the jack of trump, and the winning total of points. When the King and Duke are not operating their con games in Mark Twain's *The Adventures of Huckleberry Finn*, they gamble at games of seven-up.

sextant a navigational instrument composed of a sight, mirror, and a metal frame in the shape of a graduated 60-degree arc. The navigator or astronomer measures angles of 120 degrees or more to determine latitude and longitude by sighting the distance of heavenly bodies from the horizon. Dating to the early seventeenth century, the term derives from the Latin for *one-sixth.* As Phillip and his mother board lifeboats prior to abandoning the torpedoed *S.S. Hato* in Theodore Taylor's *The Cay*, the captain, with briefcase and sextant in hand, supervises the operations. *See also* quadrant.

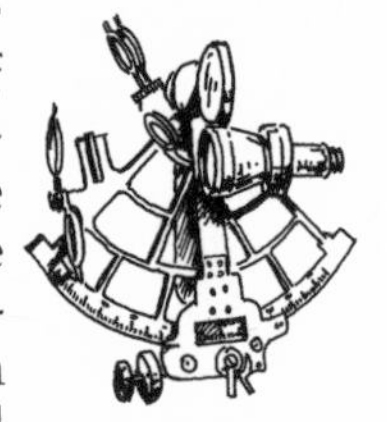

sexton (*seks'* tuhn) a lowly church employee paid to ring the church bells for services or to announce deaths in the parish, maintain security, attend to church altar equipment, wash and hang vestments and altar linen, attend the minister or priest, trim weeds in the cemetery, and dig graves. Derived from the Latin for *holy*, the term entered English in the fourteenth century. In Thomas Hardy's *Tess of the D'Urbervilles*, for a shilling and a pint of beer, the sexton buries the unbaptized swaddled infant by lamplight. *See also* sacristy.

Shabbat (shuh . *baht'*) the Jewish Sabbath, which begins at sunset on Friday and concludes at sunset on Saturday. Worshippers attending weekly Friday services wish each other "Shabbat shalom," or Sabbath peace. Following the lighting of the Sabbath candle, responsive readings from the prayer book and Torah, or scripture, the rabbi delivers a homily and the congregation sings hymns, attends to synagogue business, and enjoys fellowship. At the Shabbat table in Chaim Potok's *The Chosen*, the family enjoys tea and a reflective silence after prayers. *See also* Torah.

shadow box an early twentieth-century term for practicing jabs, breath control, and footwork against a reflection in a mirror or a shadow on the wall. Also, to spar, study combinations of moves, or train with an imaginary adversary. After conquering a bully in *Black Boy*, autobiographer Richard Wright shadow boxes and enjoys a reprieve from potential violence and humiliation.

shako (*shay'* koh) *pl.* **shakos** or **shakoes** a stiff, flat-topped, drum-shaped felt hat covered in fur and rising to a peak. Decorated with a crest or metal plate and topped with a pompon or plume, the hat features braided edges and a shiny visor and braided chin strap. Entering English in the early nineteenth century, the term derives from the Hungarian for *hat*. Enjolras tells his revolutionaries that they can mingle with the enemy by dressing themselves in shakos and cross-belts captured from army regulars in Victor Hugo's *Les Misérables. See also* cross belt.

shale (shayl) finely pigmented gray sedimentary rock related to sandstone and limestone. Stratified shale, which is collected in deposits of mud, silt, and clay, splits easily into layers. It is a source of fossils and dark crude oil that derive from living matter trapped in the strata. Entering English in the mid-eighteenth century, the term derives from Middle English for *shell*. Professor Willard in Thornton Wilder's *Our Town* describes the local geology as granite bedrock topped with basalt dotted with traces of shale and sandstone.

shaman (*shah'* muhn) *pl.* **shamans** in animistic religion; a healer, diviner, or sage possessing supernatural powers, contact with the spirit world, or the gift of prophecy. Also, a prestigious, influential member of a tribe whom members may consult on their fortunes, dream interpretation, illness, spirit visitations, or advice on personal, family, or agricultural matters. In John Neihardt's *Black Elk Speaks*, the boy develops into a shaman after many dream meetings in the spirit world. In Farley Mowat's *Never Cry Wolf*, both Ootek and Farley view each other as a variety of shaman—one from the Inuit world and one from white society. *See also* divining rod; seer.

shamisen *See* samisen.

shanty a temporary camp, ramshackle lean-to, wooden shelter, shabby hut, abandoned dwelling, rustic cabin, or poorly constructed cottage, usually in questionable condition. The shanty may be grouped with similar dwellings in a shantytown, a pejorative term for a substandard section of residences in a ghetto or the poor section of town. Derived perhaps from the Greek for *pack mule* or the Latin for *trellis*, the term entered English from Irish slang in the early nineteenth century. In Mark Twain's *The Adventures of Huckleberry Finn*, Pap Finn locks Huck in a shanty and leaves him during long bouts of drinking in town.

sharecropper a landless agricultural worker who leases land for one or more years and pays the owner a predetermined share of the crop. A poor replacement for slavery, this system of earning a living often contains a written agreement from the owner to provide seeds, tools, draft animals, and a residence for family members, who usually assist in planting, cultivating, and harvesting. After reaching manhood, Richard Wright, author of *Black Boy*, locates his father, who still lives in the South and works as a sharecropper.

Sharps rifle a breech-loading rifle firing a .52-caliber linen- or paper-wrapped cartridge from the breechblock, which offered a flash hole and slot to house the percussion cap. By sliding the block shut, the user automatically clipped the cartridge bottom and exposed the charge to a lighter inserted through the flash hole. The "American Sharps" was invented in 1850 by gunsmith Christian Sharps and found favor with soldiers during the Civil War for its accuracy and simplicity of loading. As the characters set out after villain Tom Cheney in Charles Portis's *True Grit*, Mattie Ross approves the choice of weapons—Rooster Cogburn with his Winchester and Texas Ranger LeBoeuf armed with a Sharps rifle.

shay *See* chaise.

sheet a line, rope, or chain attached to a boom or the lower corner of a sail to secure its position or alter the angle of the sail in the wind. Derived from the Anglo-Saxon for *lower corner of a sail*, the term entered English in the early Middle Ages. With Calypso's help, Odysseus, hero of Homer's *Odyssey*, fashions sails and attaches halyards and sheets before setting out once more for Ithaca.

sheik or **sheikh** or **shaikh** (sheek or shayk) a sovereign of a Middle Eastern country; a minor governor, prince, clan leader, or authority. Also, a title of respect for an Arab chieftain or influential male. In the 1920s, swashbuckling roles in movies led to the application of the term to dashing young men or alluring romantic heroes of film or stage. Derived from the Arabic for *elder*, the term entered English in the late sixteenth century. While driving in Central Park in F. Scott Fitzgerald's *The Great Gatsby*, Nick and Jordan hear the opening lines of "The Sheik of Araby," a popular song during the 1920s.

shilling a 5-penny piece or one-twentieth of a pound in Great Britain and some nations of the British Commonwealth; also, a 12-penny coin in Great Britain prior to 1971 (abbreviated s.) or a 15-cent coin in colonial America. Derived from the Anglo-Saxon for *cut piece*, the term entered English before the twelfth century. As described by Charles Dickens in *David Copperfield*, a day laborer earned 5 or 6 shillings per week for warehouse work; a farm worker might receive 10 shillings per week. In Avi's *The True Confessions of Charlotte Doyle*, the porter demands 2 shillings to pay him to carry a trunk from the dock aboard the *Seahawk*. *See also* guinea; pound.

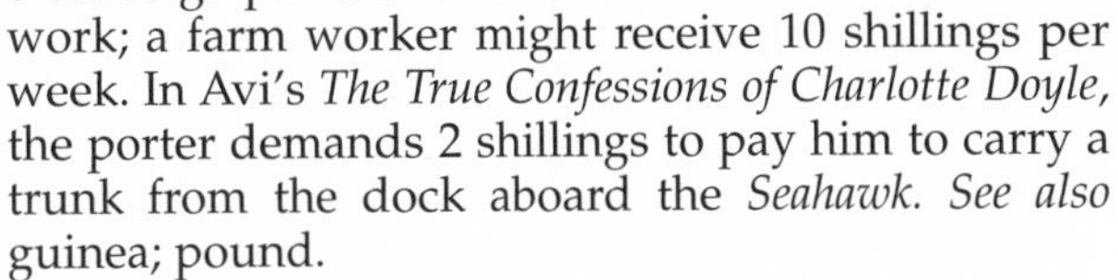

shim a mid-nineteenth century term for a whittled or tapering piece of wood or stone or a sliver of iron used as a wedge to align parts of a wooden joint or to fit between stones in masonry or between the haft and handle of a farm tool. Any small solid used to fill in a gap or cause something to stand level or fit together smoothly. In Robert Newton Peck's *A Day No Pigs Would Die*, Rob learns the importance of small chores, such as smoking the orchard to kill worms and cutting a shim to reposition an ill-fitting door.

shiner *See* guinea.

shingle a pebbly beach or seaside covered with coarse water-worn gravel. Derived from the Norse for *gravel*, the term entered English in the fifteenth century. In *Alice's Adventures in Wonderland*, Lewis Carroll sets the Lobster-Quadrille at a shingle, where the porpoise and other dancers await Alice. In a less sanguine setting, Guy Montag, protagonist of Ray Bradbury's *Fahrenheit 451*, recites "Dover Beach," which describes a shingle on which a despairing speaker proclaims the need for loyalty.

Shinto (*shihn'* toh) the fluid, undogmatic, polytheistic religion of Japan. Shintoism combines ritual prayers, processions, festivals, worship of divine heroes, and affirmation of the forces of nature with reverence for ancestors, clan leaders, and the emperor. Literally *the gods' way* in Japanese, the term, which entered English in the early eighteenth century, referred to Japan's state religion until 1945, when the emperor no longer claimed the status of a divinity. Near a Shinto shrine in John Hersey's *Hiroshima,* Mr. Tanimoto encounters his wife and child and learns how they survived the atomic bomb blast.

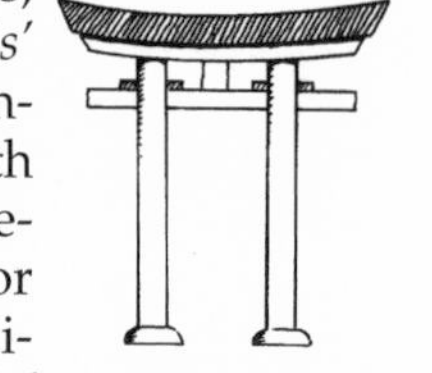

ship-chandler a dealer in nautical supplies for freshwater craft, whalers, traders, and ocean-going passenger vessels. Derived from the Latin for *candle,* the term has broadened to include a variety of goods, including hardware, tools, oil, soap, paint, varnish, cook pots, blankets, cord, rope, and chains. Among the shops of Derby Street, the speaker in "The Custom House" in Nathaniel Hawthorne's *The Scarlet Letter* reports grocers, block makers, used clothing dealers, and ship-chandlers, who draw clusters of retired seamen.

shirt front from the late nineteenth to the early twentieth century, a separate dicky, removable cellulose front with matching button-on collar and cuffs, or stitched-on panel meticulously pleated and starched to contrast with the dark cravat required of men's formal business wear or evening dress. The accountant in Joseph Conrad's *The Heart of Darkness* creates a vast sartorial chasm between himself and ill-clad Africans by keeping himself immaculate in the jungle by wearing a starched shirt front, even though the heat makes such dress unsuitable and uncomfortable.

shoal (shohl) a tricky section of a watercourse in which rocks, sandbars, coral reefs, or debris block the channel or puncture the bottom or where shallows threaten to founder or ground the keel of a vessel. Derived from the German for *shallow,* the term entered English in the early nineteenth century. The multifaceted environment of jungle, riverbanks, African observers, and treacherous shoals in Joseph Conrad's *The Heart of Darkness* causes Marlowe to struggle to keep his steamer afloat in a channel deep enough to allow safe passage.

shore-boat *See* yawl.

shovelboard or **shoveboard** an obsolete name for shuffleboard, an indoor game of skill and control invented in the early nineteenth century in which players push discs with a long-handled shovel or cue with an arched wooden endpiece. The purpose of the game is to move the discs across a smooth playing surface and have them stop on a matrix, or diagram, marked with straight lines into various shaped polygons identified with numbers. In contrast to the religious fanatics of Salem in Arthur Miller's *The Crucible,* a body of shirkers hang around Bridget's Tavern to play shovelboard.

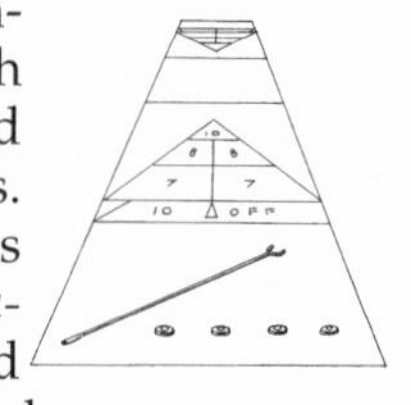

shrapnel (*shrap'* n'l) odd pieces of ricocheting metal, splintered bullet casings, and erupting antipersonnel cartridges, canisters, bombs, or mines that are designed to fling shards into soft tissue. Surgical treatment involves a tedious probing for metal bits that endanger major organs or threaten the body with infection or metal poisoning. Derived from the name of artillery officer General Henry Shrapnel, the term applies to one of the most serious hazards of armed conflict. In Walter Dean Myers's *Fallen Angels,* shrapnel sidelines the hero, Richie Perry, with light wounds that require expert treatment.

shrift an ecclesiastical term from the early Middle Ages; derived from the verb *shrive,* which comes from the Latin for *write* and means forgiveness. In the Roman Catholic Church, shrift requires a formal visit to a private confessional to recite and atone for sins and to seek spiritual advice on how to achieve redemption and forgiveness or absolution through penance and how to avoid further sins. Juliet uses shrift as an excuse to visit Friar Laurence's cell to be with Romeo in William Shakespeare's *Romeo and Juliet. See also* absolution; contrition, act of.

shrine one of a variety of places of worship, including altars, temples, reliquaries, tombs of saints, roadside icons or statues, monuments, and sacred sites of momentous religious importance, such as the birthplace of Mohammed or Jesus, the location of a sighting of the Virgin Mary, or the spot in the Mamartine Prison where martyrs were chained and tortured. Entering English before the twelfth century, the term derives from the Middle English for *chest.* In *Gilgamesh,* the speaker urges the reader to go to the temple, unlock the chest, and read accounts of the demigod who restored ancient shrines from neglect.

shroud (shrowd) a lateral four-stranded rope, cable, or wire connected from the topgallant of a mast to the side of a ship, where it attaches to a deadeye or turnbuckle that tightens the hold on chain plates welded or bolted to the ship's side for maximum stability. Woven into the shrouds are the crosspieces that form the ratlines or climbing ropes. Entering English in the Middle Ages, the term derives from the Norse for *tackle*. The title character in Herman Melville's *Billy Budd* follows an unidentified informant to the forechains where shrouds, lanyards, and backstays obscure the scene. *See also* backstay; ratline.

Shrove Tuesday See Mardi Gras.

shul (shool) the Yiddish term for school, temple, or synagogue, which also designates a congregational center where Jews go for worship, religious study, or fellowship. Derived from the Latin for *school*, the term entered English in the late nineteenth century. In Chaim Potok's *The Chosen*, Danny encourages Reuben to attend shul to meet Danny's father, who wants to learn more about his son's friend.

shuttlecock a lightweight game piece or birdie central to badminton, a sport requiring two players to earn points by volleying the shuttlecock over a net with rackets, or battledoors, in a game similar to tennis. The shuttlecock is composed of a truncated globe of cork covered with rubber to cause the object to bounce; on the flat end, a ring of feathers—either genuine or plastic—sticking vertically out of the cork provides loft. Finny, a central character in John Knowles's *A Separate Peace*, glares in disapproval at his friend Gene holding racket and shuttlecock, symbols of an effete game that Finny considers inappropriate and unmasculine. *See also* battledoor.

sibyl (*sih'* b'l) a female seer, diviner, prophet, or oracle from the classical mythology of Babylon, Egypt, Greece, and Rome. Derived from the Greek for *prophetess*, the term entered English in the Middle Ages. According to Virgil's *Aeneid*, Aeneas, the epic hero, consults the Cumaean sibyl concerning his planned visit to the Underworld to gain advice from Anchises, his deceased father, and finds her writing chaotic notes on dried leaves that swirl about her cave. *See also* seer.

sick headache a migraine headache; a debilitating pain that causes illusions of light or aura, visual or hearing impairment, stiff neck, fainting, nausea, vomiting, and prostration. Brought on by a constriction of blood vessels leading to the cranium, the condition may stem from food allergy, sinus problems, or psychogenic causes. After Johnny gives Janie a kiss during an unsupervised afternoon when her grandmother suffers from a sick headache in Zora Neale Hurston's *Their Eyes Were Watching God*, Janie's childhood comes to an abrupt end.

sideboard a long, compartmentalized dining room cupboard or banquette consisting of a flat surface for displaying flower arrangements or valuables and for serving food and beverages. The lower section is composed of drawers and cabinets for storing dishes, silverware, table linen, candles, and other essentials to fine dining. In response to his son Gregor's transformation into a cockroach in Franz Kafka's "The Metamorphosis," Mr. Samsa goes to the sideboard, fills his pocket with apples, and begins throwing them at the insect.

sight draft a sight check, bill payable, or money order that can be redeemed at a bank when presented by the person to whom it is consigned. The arrangement resembles the cashing of a traveler's check or cashier's check, both of which are guaranteed by the bank or firm that issues them. Catherine Barkley, a key character in Ernest Hemingway's *A Farewell to Arms*, mildly admonishes Frederick Henry for spending sight drafts from his family without maintaining a respectful correspondence.

signory or **signeury** or **signiory** (*see'* nyuh . ree) dominion, rights, or lordship over a manorial estate or domain; also, the feudal lord or authority who bears title to an Italian republic. A term appropriate to the division of property rights in the mid-sixteenth century, the word derives from the Latin for *elder*. In William Shakespeare's *The Tempest*, Prospero, the protagonist, laments to his daughter Miranda that he trusted his signory to his brother Antonio, who replaced him as Duke of Milan and, with help from the King of Naples, exiled Prospero and Miranda.

silage (*sy'* lihj) or **ensilage** green stems, heads, roots, and leaves of chopped plant fodder stored in a silo, haystacks or shocks, or underground pits, where natural plant acids produce anaerobic fermentation and preserve the mass for use as winter feed. While Napoleon makes few practical changes in the running of the farm in George Orwell's *Animal Farm*, Snowball helps the spread of manure by having animals drop their dung at a different spot each day.

silhouette (*sihl* . oo . *eht'*) a portrait, likeness, or outline of a head, profile, torso, or full figure preserved in chiaroscuro, as with black crayon, charcoal, or ink filling in the outline on a white background; also, a shape cut from paper with scissors or craft knife and mounted on paper of a contrasting color, usually black on white. The term was derived in the late eighteenth century from

the surname of Etienne de Silhouette, a tight-fisted French treasury officer. In Ernest Hemingway's *A Farewell to Arms*, an old man charges customers for silhouettes snipped from paper but insists on making a silhouette of Frederick Henry for his girlfriend without charge.

silk cotton tree the bombax tree, a tropical relative to the baobab and balsa. The flowering silk cotton tree yields light wood for boxes, veneer, and furniture as well as kapok or Java cotton from its seeds, a light, buoyant filler for life vests and other flotation devices, cushions, pillows, and mattresses. While spectators await the beginning of a wrestling match in Chinua Achebe's *Things Fall Apart*, drummers sit before the revered village silk cotton tree, said to contain the souls of unborn children and to bless with conception barren women who sit under its shade.

sillabub or **syllabub** (*sihl'* uh . *bub*) a frothy whip composed of wine, liquor, or cider beaten with milk, curdled or fresh cream, spices, and sugar. Other recipes call for gelatin and fruit juice added to the basic ingredients. The mid-sixteenth-century word derived from a slang expression meaning *silly stomach.* After the court finds in Johnny's favor in the suit brought by Mr. Lyte in Esther Forbes's *Johnny Tremain*, Mr. Quincy, Johnny, and his other supporters dine at a tavern, where Isannah overindulges in sillabub. *See also* flip.

simian (*sihm'* ee . yun) apelike; having the traits, behaviors, character, appetites, or attitudes of an ape. Derived from the Greek for *flat-nosed*, the word entered English in the early sixteenth century. In Aldous Huxley's *Brave New World*, the simian features and moronic behavior of an elevator operator express the dystopian concept of an epsilon-minus, a label denoting a retardate deliberately bred in the state hatchery and indoctrinated with a love of the most menial form of work.

simonize (*sy'* muh . *nyz*) to clean, wax, polish, and buff the enamel surface of a vehicle to a smooth shine; to apply a protective car wax that produces a sheen. Derived from a trade name for Simoniz car wax, this American verb entered the language in the mid-1930s. During one of his mental rambles in Arthur Miller's *Death of a Salesman*, Willy Loman recalls his red Chevy that his son Biff used to simonize.

sinew (*sihn'* yoo) the tough, fibrous tendon in a large animal—deer, elk, horse, buffalo, or moose—that is extracted from the carcass and dried and oiled for use as a waterproof bowstring, bindings for leggings or snowshoes, lanyards, sewing thread, cordage, or rope. Entering English before the twelfth century, the word derives from the Sanskrit for *bind.* When Karana builds a defensive fence around her cave in Scott O'Dell's *The Island of the Blue Dolphins*, she prefers interweaving sinew to hold the whale ribs upright like pickets.

single-tree a horizontal cross bar, whiffletree, or whippletree pivoting in the center, the single-tree swings behind a horse, ox, or mule and attaches to traces, which are harnessed to a wagon, sledge, plow, drag harrow, or other agricultural vehicle or implement. Derived from the Middle English for *swing*, the term evolved from *swingletree* to its current form to complement *doubletree.* As Bejance studies True Son weeding with a hoe like a colonial farmer in Conrad Richter's *The Light in the Forest*, he comments that the boy looks like a draft animal hitched with a harness to a single-tree.

sink hole or **swallow hole** a shallow saucer- or funnel-shaped depression in soil rich in limestone. Formed in fissures as surface water dissolves the soft bedrock, the sink hole may develop into a lake if clay or debris recede. A deeper form of sink hole results from the collapse of a limestone cave, which may be inundated by an underground stream. Because of the scarcity of potable surface or well water in Marjorie Kinnan Rawlings's *The Yearling*, Billy's family depends on a sink hole at the edge of their farm as the major source of water.

siren a fascinating mythological temptress, mermaid, or bird-woman who sings seductive songs to lure unsuspecting sailors to their deaths on a craggy coast. Modern interpretations of this phenomenon place Homer's sirens along the treacherous passage between Sicily and Italy, where the sound of wind on rocks resembles a human voice. Will Tweedy, protagonist in Olive Ann Burns's *Cold Sassy Tree*, recalls the enticement of sirens from Greek literature as he walks the trestle to reach a fishing hole.

Sister Superior or **mother superior** the ecclesiastical honorific, title, or rank of the head nun or female authority in a convent or religious order or retreat; also, the female principal of a Roman Catholic parochial school. In Sandra Cisneros's *The House on Mango Street*, Esperanza forges a note from her mother to the Sister Superior asking permission for her daughter to eat lunch in the school canteen.

sitz bath a therapeutic soak or wash of the lower body in a tub, basin, or pan filled with medicated liquid, mineral water, or plain water as a treatment, such as a reduction of inflammation in hemorrhoids or a soothing bath after giving birth. Derived from the German for *seated bath*, the term entered English in the mid-nineteenth century. To treat Tom's melancholia in Mark Twain's *The Adventures of Tom Sawyer*, Aunt Polly applies a blister plaster, sitz baths, showers, plungers, and painkiller.

sixpence (*sihks'* p'nts or *siks'* pehnts) an obsolete silver coin in Great Britain dating to the fourteenth century and worth six pennies or half a shilling. In a shouting match between Godfrey and Dunstan Cass in George Eliot's *Silas Marner*, Dunstan claims to be Godfrey's "crooked sixpence," a bent coin serving as a good luck piece or charm. *See also* shilling; sou.

six-shooter or **six-gun** a handgun featuring a rotating circular magazine holding six shots in separate chambers. The six-shooter can be fired six times without reloading. Begun with a variation on the Colt pepper box, the six-shooter or automatic pistol, created by Smith and Wesson, appeared in 1870. In John Neihardt's *Black Elk Speaks*, the title character recalls Fire Thunder's description of a hoax to draw soldiers into a trap and Fire Thunder's use of a six-shooter to kill as many as possible. *See also* Colt's revolver; pepper box.

skate a flat, diamond-shaped, cartilaginous fish kin to the manta ray, characterized by a protruding bill, prominent eyes and breathing holes, dorsal projection, and tail that, in some species, has muscles capable of giving an electrical shock. Entering English in the fourteenth century, the animal's name derives from Old Norse. While learning to adjust to blindness while marooned on an uncharted island with Timothy in Theodore Taylor's *The Cay*, Phillip steps on a skate and slips.

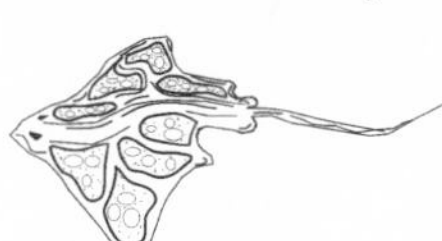

skein or **skean** or **skeane** (skayn) a coil, reel, tangled mass, or loop of sewing thread, embroidery floss, or knitting or crochet yarn. A Middle English term, the derivation appears to be French. Sitting before her embroidery frame at the convent in late afternoon in Edmond Rostand's *Cyrano de Bergerac*, Roxane takes out her skeins to begin work while she waits for her old friend to deliver his weekly collection of court gossip, which resembles tangled masses of yarn.

skeleton key the early nineteenth-century term for a pass key or master key with much of its bit removed, hollowed, or filed down so that it will fit a number of different locks. During the concealment of Jews in an Amsterdam warehouse in Anne Frank's *The Diary of a Young Girl*, a prowler, apparently carrying a skeleton key, sneaks in and inadvertently terrifies the occupants, who are hiding from the Nazis and fear that their location has been spotted.

skewer (*skyoo'* wuhr) a wooden, bamboo, or metal sliver, spit, or pin either sharpened at both ends or hooked at one end and honed at the other for holding or suspending meat, vegetables, fish, or kabobs over a grill or open flame. Also, a cook's pin used to secure a stuffed opening or fasten parts of a fowl or rolled roast during preparation. Entering English in the Middle Ages, the term is derived from the Old Norse for *slice.* While Ko sharpens a stick into a skewer to hold a roasting fish over the fire in Yoko Kawashima Watkins's *So Far from the Bamboo Grove*, her 12-year-old sister slips away to rinse the new teapot and offer her sister a prohibitively expensive New Year's gift of green tea.

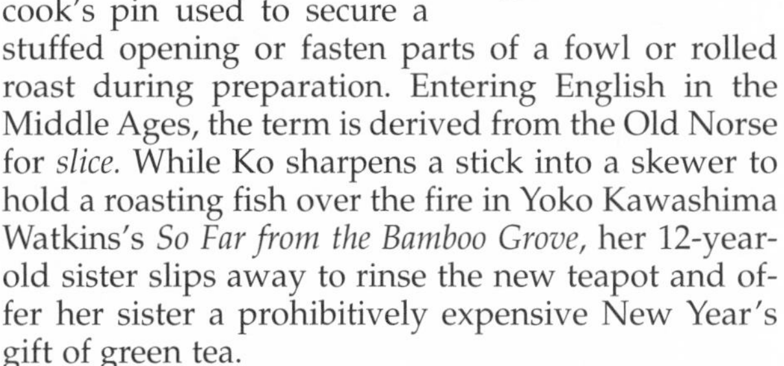

skids a wooden platform, loading pallet, open metal framework, or set of planks, logs, or sawhorses on which lumber, boxes, supplies, or stored items are stacked. Skids also assist in the moving of heavy objects or act as a support for elevation of materials above moist warehouse flooring or a ship's keel. A Middle English term, it derives from the Old Norse for *billet of wood.* On his return to the bakery in Daniel Keyes's *Flowers for Algernon*, Charlie Gordon, the retarded protagonist, places his bundle on skids and wishes that he had his spinner to play with.

skiff a small, low-sided, flat-bottomed boat, punt, or lightweight rowboat with a pointed prow and square stern and either one or two sets of oars. Also, a tender used by crew when a ship is in harbor or riding at anchor. Entering English in the fifteenth century, the term derives from the Anglo-Saxon for *ship.* To conceal the loathsome mate for his monster in Mary Shelley's *Frankenstein*, the title character rows a skiff out to sea, waits for a cloud to darken the moon, and slips the basket containing the botched corpse over the side.

skimmity-ride or **skimmington-ride** a public humiliation of a seducer, scoundrel, shrewish wife, or corrupt official by creating a procession of mummers or maskers or displaying an effigy tied to the back of a galloping horse or seated in a carriage. Derived from the Old French for *scum* or *skimmer*, the term entered

English in the early seventeenth century. As portrayed in Thomas Hardy's pivotal scene in *The Mayor of Casterbridge,* Lucetta collapses, gives birth to a stillborn fetus, and dies after the shock of seeing paired effigies of herself with Michael Henchard displayed on village streets. *See also* effigy.

skittle alley a form of nine pins, a game in which the players bowl wooden discs or balls down a grassy lawn toward wooden pins set up in a pattern or row. The person with the lowest score from the least number of tries at knocking down the skittles wins the game. Entering English in the mid-seventeenth century, the term derives from the Old Norse for *shuttle.* Sitting under a chestnut tree by the skittle alley in Erich Maria Remarque's *All Quiet on the Western Front,* Paul Baumer is too tense and depressed to drink his beer or relax.

skrimshandering or **scrimshaw** the art of carving intricate colored designs or scenes on ivory whale teeth, walrus tusks, fish jawbone, or shells with tiny dental tools, picks, jackknives, and awls. A nineteenth-century whaler's pastime or craft, the term may derive from the French for *flourish a sword* or from an unidentified Admiral Scrimshaw, an expert carver, or skrimshanderer. In *Moby-Dick,* Herman Melville comments that most skrimshanderers use a jackknife to turn out fancy carvings. *See also* awl.

skullcap a close-fitting cap lacking both brim and peak; a yarmulke or ceremonial head covering made of soft, unlined leather, velvet, linen, felt, or silk, decorated with braid, embroidery, or a feather, and worn indoors or at court gatherings. Also, an ornate netted head covering fashionably knotted and decked with beads or jewels and favored by women as an anchor for a veil or train during the Renaissance. The term, which entered English in the late seventeenth century, derived from the juncture of the Scandinavian *skull* and *cap.* Gazing down on Hester Prynne and her infant, John Wilson, a scholar wearing a skullcap in Nathaniel Hawthorne's *The Scarlet Letter,* instructs Hester to heed the questions of young Arthur Dimmesdale, her spiritual leader. *See also* netting.

slack lime a mispronunciation of slaked lime, or calcium hydroxide, a form of lime used in plaster or mortar. Slaking lime requires hydrating dry lime by soaking or mixing it with water. A fourteenth-century term, *slake* derives from the Anglo-Saxon for *slack,* a reference to the crumbly, chalky texture of calcium hydroxide. During pregnancy, Rosasharn, a character in John Steinbeck's *The Grapes of Wrath,* develops a yearning for slack lime.

slalom a downhill ski or snowmobile run in which racers follow an erratic, wavy course marked by gates, posts, flags, or other obstacles; a zigzag ski slope. Derived from the Norwegian term for *sloped course,* the term entered English in the early 1920s. During the first winter carnival at the school in John Knowles's *A Separate Peace,* participants look forward to ice carving and slalom races.

sledge (slehj) or **sled** or **sleigh** a covered, open-fronted, two-seated vehicle on skids or runners pulled by dogs, a horse, or team of horses; a toboggan. Also, a flat winter conveyance guided by a standing driver and pulled by work horses or oxen for moving heavy loads such as crates or lumber over snow, ice, mud, or uneven marshy ground. In Nikolai Gogol's "The Overcoat," Akaky leaves the part of town where drivers guided raw wooden sledges decorated with brass nailheads and entered an elite neighborhood where coachmen drive lacquered sleighs heaped with bearskin rugs.

sloe (sloh) the sweet, almond-shaped drupe, or fruit, of the blackthorn, a shrub characterized by toothed green leaves, mounds of tiny white blossoms, and rosy fruit that ripens to a bluish-black. The sloe is mixed with grain alcohol to make sloe gin, a pinkish liqueur. As a remedy for slow uterine contractions during labor, midwives may prescribe a decoction of the bark. A mid-nineteenth-century term, it derives from the Russian for *plum.* Maya Angelou recalls sloe gin, the faddish mixed drink popular during the pre–World War II era in *I Know Why the Caged Bird Sings.*

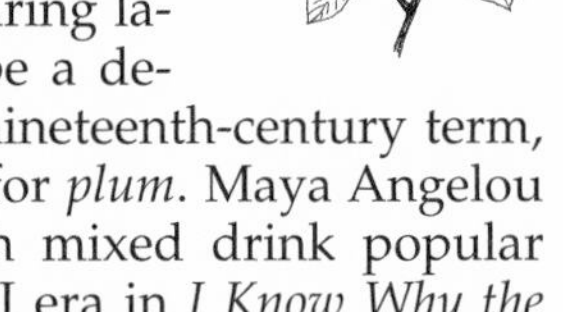

sloop a single-masted, single-jibbed sailing ship, longboat, or cutter with either a shortened bowsprit or none at all. Because of its simplicity and ease of handling, the sloop is suitable for fishing, coastal trading, or transportation of passengers or goods to market. Derived from the Dutch for *glide,* the term entered English in the early seventeenth century. In *Narrative of the Life of Frederick Douglass,* the autobiographer

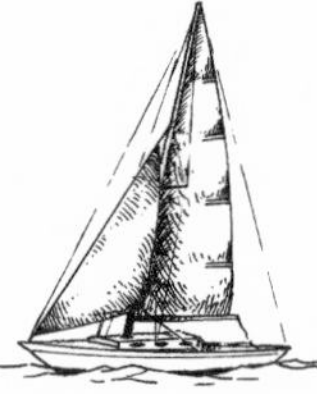

reports that his master profits by keeping a sloop to transport plantation produce to Baltimore.

slop-basin an obsolete term for a household container for dregs, leftover tea, water used for handwashing, and other domestic liquids that had to be carried outside and emptied into a ditch, drain, or gutter. Currently, a small waste bowl or receptacle that matches the other vessels in a silver tea service. On his first visit to Pip in his London apartment in Charles Dickens's *Great Expectations*, Joe Gargery grows so self-conscious about his hat that he accidentally drops it into the slop-basin.

slop jar a lidded potty or portable indoor toilet container that is either freestanding or set into an ornate covered cabinet or commode. The slop jar is used at night, during bad weather, or for people too sick or aged to walk to an outhouse or latrine; also, a similar toilet facility in a Pullman sleeping compartment or a ship's berth. Mister, the tyrannical husband in Alice Walker's *The Color Purple*, condemns Celie as a worthless handmaiden fit only to cook for Shug Avery or empty her slop jar. *See also* Pullman.

slop-seller a dealer in rags, used clothing, and cheap or poor-quality ready-made goods; an owner of a slop-shop that supplies clothing, shoes, and blankets to sailors. In "The Custom House," the introduction to Nathaniel Hawthorne's *The Scarlet Letter*, the speaker names sail lofts and slop-sellers as part of the hustle of a busy off-shore mercantile center. In Charles Dickens's *A Christmas Carol*, a more somber scene depicts the slop-seller as dickering over the value of drapes that cloaked the bed of Ebenezer Scrooge, whom a cleaning woman discovered dead that morning.

slough (sloo or slaw) a slow-running, often foul-smelling ditch, drain, or rivulet emptying a fen, swamp, or piece of marshy ground; also, a stretch of mire, bayou, bog, tidal creek, inlet, or backwater. Dating before the twelfth century, the term derives from the Anglo-Saxon for *ditch*. In Mark Twain's *The Adventures of Huckleberry Finn*, the title character drags a bag of meal to a slough and drops Pap Finn's whetstone to simulate a murder and implicate his father.

sluice (sloos) a natural or artificial channel or flow of water controlled by a series of dams, valves, or floodgates; also, a wooden framework that guides logs down a flume and into a larger body of water for loading on barges or floating to market or a collection point downstream. A fifteenth-century term, it is related to *close* and *closet* and derives from the Latin for *exclude*. During the gold rush in *The Call of the Wild*, Jack London refers to a sluice box, an artificial flow through a wooden trough used to direct water from a gold-rich stream.

smelling salts an obsolete remedy for unconsciousness; a small vial of ammonium kept handy on a chain around the neck or in a pocket, purse, or reticule for first aid to revive people—usually women—who fainted or became dizzy or disoriented, often because of tightly laced stays or corsets. Kate Chopin emphasizes Madame Ratignolle's fan and "salts" in *The Awakening*, a novel that contrasts the conventional frail wife with a daring new woman not given to fainting spells. *See also* corset; reticule; syncope.

smock frock a farm worker's wide-sleeved, square-yoked gathered shift; a traditional covering equivalent to a woman's pinafore and hanging to the knees to keep the undergarments clean while the worker performs dirty chores. Made of coarse homespun, cotton, or linen, the smock frock was a badge denoting the lowly social status of an agricultural worker or herder. Derived from the Scandinavian for *shift*, the term entered English before the twelfth century. In *Silas Marner*, author George Eliot describes working-class men as dressing in fustian jackets and smock frocks and casting their eyes down as they drink among people of greater prestige or financial worth.

smoker an early twentieth-century railroad club car, an informal meeting place designed to appeal to male passengers. The traditional smoker was fitted with a bar and chairs and tables for card-playing, reading, smoking, relaxing, or business negotiations. In a defining moment, Willy Loman, protagonist in Arthur Miller's *Death of a Salesman*, describes the demise and lavish funeral of 84-year-old Dave Singleman, a successful drummer who died the "death of a salesman," wearing green velvet slippers in the smoker of the New York, New Haven, and Hartford Railroad on its way into Boston.

smoking bishop a piquant purple punch made from pouring steaming red wine over bitter oranges, spice, and sugar, the Victorian English equivalent of the French *punch au rhum*, a blend of sugar, spice, thinly sliced lemon, and light rum, which is set aflame to maximize holiday appeal. A redeemed Ebenezer Scrooge invites his employee, Bob Cratchit, to share a bowl of smoking bishop at the conclusion of Charles Dickens's *A Christmas Carol*.

smoking papers rolling papers; a packet of thin white paper squares into which a smoker pours loose tobacco, then licks the glued edges, slides them together, and twists the ends of the cylinder to keep bits of tobacco from falling out. While an uneasy Paul D fiddles with his tobacco pouch in the absence of smoking papers in Toni Morrison's *Beloved*, Sethe divulges that she has a tree on her back, her metaphor for the lash marks that formed thick, trunklike scar tissue after the overseer beat her for trying to escape slavery at Sweet Home, a Kentucky plantation.

snap-brim hat a perky, informal hat of the early twentieth century characterized by a dented crown, turned-down brim in back, and bold, flexible upturn at the front. Because of its use by thugs and riffraff in gangster movies, the hat came to be associated with disreputable or dishonest people. In Maya Angelou's autobiographical *I Know Why the Caged Bird Sings*, Uncle Willy stays home from church to watch Mr. Murphy, Annie Henderson's shifty former husband who arrives in Stamps, Arkansas, wearing a snap-brim hat like actor George Raft, who earned fame for tough-talking gangster roles.

snow goggles a rectangular piece of perforated wood or bone worn over the face and tied at the back of the head in snowy terrain to protect the wearer from the dazzling light reflected by snow and ice. Traditional dress for kayakers, mushers or dog-sledders, and travelers in Eskimo territory, snow goggles can be easily fashioned with a pocket knife by cutting thin openings for the eyes and small holes at each side to thread thongs or rawhide ties. Russel, the protagonist in Gary Paulsen's *Dogsong*, rubs his eyes and wishes that he had wood to fashion snow goggles with small slits for each eye to ward off glare from the snow.

snowhook a barbed wooden, bone, or metal drag or brake at the rear of a dogsled, sleigh, or sledge that rotates downward to grip the snow or ice. The snowhook's chief purpose is to keep a team from slipping away or to halt a sled from sliding down a slope or off an incline. Before signaling the dog team with Oogruk's personal lip sound in Gary Paulsen's *Dogsong*, Russel loosens the snowhook and anticipates a smooth departure.

snowknife a curved blade, tusk, horn, or long utility knife consisting of a 12-inch blade attached to a horn or bone grip long enough to accommodate both hands. As described in Farley Mowat's *Never Cry Wolf*, the snowknife quickly slices and shapes snow into blocks to be stacked into an emergency shelter or igloo when a blizzard threatens.

snow mast a typical second mast on a European merchant brig, rigged with square sails in front and back and an auxiliary triangular sail or trysail extending at an angle from the main mast toward the stern for ease of maneuvering in gale weather. A late seventeenth-century term, the snow mast, of unknown derivation, is linked to Scandinavian words of similar meaning. The title character of Avi's *The True Confessions of Charlotte Doyle* boards the *Seahawk*, a two-masted brig with a snow mast. *See also* gaff; gale.

snuff powdered tobacco that eighteenth-century users gathered into a pinch between thumb and forefinger and held to the nose for inhaling to cause a tension-relieving sneeze. Elegant boxes and bottles stored the snuff to keep it dry and loose and to preserve its pungent odor; lace handkerchiefs enhanced the studied grace, discretion, and good taste of snuff-takers. In Esther Forbes's *Johnny Tremain*, both Justice Dana and Jonathan Lyte take pinches of snuff on the morning of Johnny's trial.

snuffers a fifteenth-century term for a scissorlike instrument consisting of a cutting blade and a parallel arm ending in a box for cropping and extinguishing candle wicks. To spare the fingers from burn, the user closes the pincer over the hot, blackened ends of candle wicks, which slide over the parallel arm and fall into the receptacle. After Linton, Hareton, and Joseph drop into indolent sleep, Nelly Dean, the narrator of much of Emily Brontë's *Wuthering Heights*, snips the wicks of the candles in preparation for going to bed.

soffit (*sahf'* fuht) a structural term for the underside of a bridge pier, scaffold, cantilevered deck or balcony, cornice, vault or arch, or staircase. Derived from the Latin for *fastened underneath*, the term entered English in the late sixteenth century. While fleeing in a punt in Richard Adams's *Watership Down*, Hazel and his followers cower at the clanging sound of the boat against the soffit and ask Kehaar's suggestion for a way to swim to shore and escape up the steep bank.

solar halo a refractive phenomenon resulting from a bank of cirrus clouds shielding the observer from the sun. As the rays of the sun take on a hexagonal shape, they create the effect of an aura. In Theodore Taylor's *Timothy of the Cay*, the title character studies the heat and high barometric reading, then observes thin cirrus clouds and a solar halo, all pointing to the formation of a hurricane. *See also* cirrus.

solder (*sah'* duhr) a soft, fusible alloy or pure metal cement, such as lead or tin, that is melted and applied to a joint, fissure, or patch on a less malleable metal surface or to metal-edged pieces of glass to form a stained-glass window, ornament, or decoration. A term that entered English in the Middle Ages, it derives from the Latin for *firm.* In Esther Forbes's *Johnny Tremain,* the main character takes pride in his ability to shove a bead of solder into place and smooth or blend it into nothingness.

sole a family of close-eyed, oval flatfish common to the Atlantic Ocean and similar to flounder. The term, which entered English in the thirteenth century, derives from the Latin for *sandal.* Cooks prize sole for its tender skin and succulent white meat, which is easily filleted, poached, fried, or grilled and complements a wide variety of piquant sauces and side dishes. Prefacing a reconciliation between Marius and his grandfather, Monsieur Gillenormand, in Victor Hugo's *Les Misérables,* the old gentleman urges his grandson to stop eating sole and request meat, which will restore his strength. *See also* sanddab.

solfeggio (sahl . *fehj'* jee . oh or sahl . *fehj'* jyo) voice training and sight-singing that centers on exercises in musical thirds or fifths or melodies that repeat combinations of the first, third, and fifth notes of the eight-tone scale. Dating to music theory and practice of the late eighteenth century, the term derives from the arbitrary names for the notes of the scale—do, re, mi, fa, sol, la, ti, do. Beginning in September 1991, Zlata Filipovich, author of *Zlata's Diary,* attends English class as well as weekly music and solfeggio.

sombrero (suhm . *breh'* roh) a tall-crowned straw or felt hat rolling outward into an exaggerated deep brim or sunshade, which is often banded and edged in braid or ball fringe. Derived from the Spanish for *shade,* the sombrero remains a favorite of tourists, performers, hikers, and workers in the southwestern United States and Mexico. The hired man, Otto Fuchs, dressed in sombrero and sporting pointed mustachios in Willa Cather's *My Antonia,* greets Jim by asking if he fears the Old West.

sorghum (*sor'* guhm) or **milo** a cash crop of the annual grass family that produces a tall, long-leafed stalk topped with a thick head of grain used to make protein-rich fodder, hay, silage, broom straw, bird seed, paper, whiskey, beer, syrup, and molasses. Derived in the late sixteenth century, the term may be a mispronunciation of the Latin for *Syrian grass.* On her first view of the title character in Toni Morrison's *Beloved,* Sethe concludes that the girl is fleeing labor-intensive work in a West Virginia tobacco or sorghum field.

sou (soo) a French coin worth various amounts in its history from five centimes to ten centimes and one-twentieth of a livre. Entering English in the early nineteenth century, the term derives from the Latin for *solid.* Upon his release from the galleys, Jean Valjean, protagonist of Victor Hugo's *Les Misérables,* locates manual labor paying 30 sous—or 1.5 livres—per day, but he receives half that amount—0.75 livres—because a police officer reveals that Jean carries the yellow passport of a convict.

soubrette (soo . *breht'*) a conniving or smart-mouthed maidservant, handmaiden, flirt, conceited coquette, self-absorbed clotheshorse, or go-between who carries messages between lovers. The soubrette (the term is derived from the French for deceiving) is one of many figures in world literature who fits the mold of the trickster. A minor figure in Edmond Rostand's *Cyrano de Bergerac,* the soubrette plays character roles in light comic opera, operetta, vaudeville, and stage performances.

soul food inexpensive, uncomplicated working-class food common to cafes and homes in the southern United States and influenced by African fare. Soul food ranges from yams, pork barbecue, beans and rice, turnip greens, corn bread, grits, black-eyed peas, fried chicken, biscuits, catfish, and cabbage slaw to hot sauce, chitlins, ham hock, and hog jowls. Reflecting on his childhood, the title character in Alex Haley's *The Autobiography of Malcolm X* recalls that his father, a Georgian, liked soul food but that his mother forbade her children from eating pork or rabbit.

sounding pole a notched pole marked with measures of the water's depth and studied by surveyors and navigators. Similar to the job of the leadsman on a Mississippi paddle-wheeler, the helmsman's task of sounding the depths saves the pilot from grounding the vessel or moving into unnavigable shallows. As Marlowe's steamboat chugs upriver in Joseph Conrad's *The Heart of Darkness,* the sounding pole reveals increasingly shallow water, which threatens the bottom of his boiler and disaster for the mission to rescue Mr. Kurtz. *See also* mark twain.

sou'wester (sou . *wehs'* tuhr) a sizeable all-weather hat made of oilskin or tarpaulin, a waterproof fabric consisting of tar-soaked canvas. In gale weather, the sou'wester (a corruption of "southwester") covered the back of the neck and kept rain and high waves from splashing down the back. To add to its protection, the user sometimes wore the sou'wester over a warm knitted stocking cap. In Charles Dickens's *David Copperfield,* a sou'wester is suitable head-gear for Mr. Peggotty during the rough weather that assaults the coast where his family lives. *See also* oilcloth.

sovereign (*sah'* vrihn) a heavy British gold coin. In the time of Henry II, the sovereign was worth 22 shillings and sixpence; after the establishment of the Commonwealth in 1649, the sovereign dropped in value to 11 shillings. While helping Leggatt prepare for return to shore in Joseph Conrad's "The Secret Sharer," the unnamed captain offers him three sovereigns and keeps the remaining three to pay for fresh fruits and vegetables for the crew.

sow belly mid-nineteenth-century American slang for salt pork or bacon, a form of soul food that southern cooks use to season cooked vegetables, make red-eye or sawmill gravy, or fill a biscuit. Logan, Janie's first husband in Zora Neale Hurston's *Their Eyes Were Watching God,* insults his wife by stating that no man would want to feed a woman of her background; she retorts that he reduces everything to the value of cornbread and sow belly. *See also* soul food.

spanner an adjustable two-part wrench that connects when end pieces are fitted together. A spanner is used for loosening nuts and bolts or separating segments of pipe. Entering English in the late eighteenth century, the term derives from the German for *stretch.* Winston Smith, protagonist and victim in George Orwell's *1984,* uses a spanner to empty the trap of his neighbor's backed-up drain, a symbol of the corruption in dystopian Oceania.

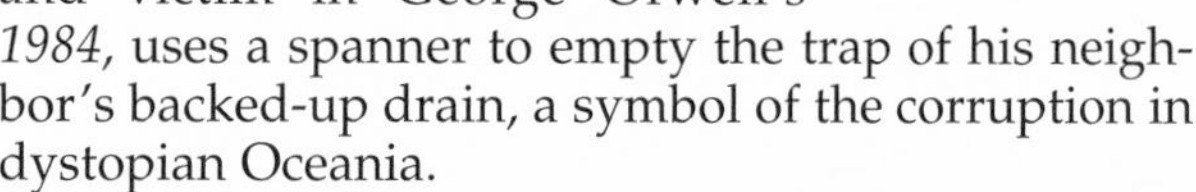

spar a general term dating to the Middle English period and designating a pole, beam, rafter, gaff, yard, boom, mast, or any wooden upright or crossbar on a ship. After the Dansker grows too old and stiff for climbing masts in Herman Melville's *Billy Budd,* he is assigned duty at the main mast, a symbolic post suggesting strength and dependability, to which "great spar" Billy goes to ask advice.

specter or **spectre** (*spehk'* tuhr) a stalking apparition, ghost, phantasm, or disembodied spirit. An apparition, such as the ghost of Hamlet's father or Banquo in *Macbeth,* haunts the mind of the observer with fear, dread, or regret. Entering English in the early seventeenth century, the word derives from the Latin for *look at.* As Henry Fleming flees his guilty conscience in Stephen Crane's *The Red Badge of Courage,* he cannot elude the specter of the tall soldier whom he watched die in a field from his battle wounds.

spencer the double-breasted, full-sleeved, waist-length jacket worn with red caps by French Revolutionaries as part of their uniform; also, a lady's tight, full-collared jacket extending to the bottom ribs and featuring capped sleeves tapering to a tight fit from elbow to wrist. These fashionable coats were made of velvet, muslin, or silk and covered bodices of gauze, voile, or muslin dresses. The rebels in Charles Dickens's *A Tale of Two Cities* wear no military uniform, but sport a variety of materials and styles in the spencers and caps that mark them as members of the revolutionary force.

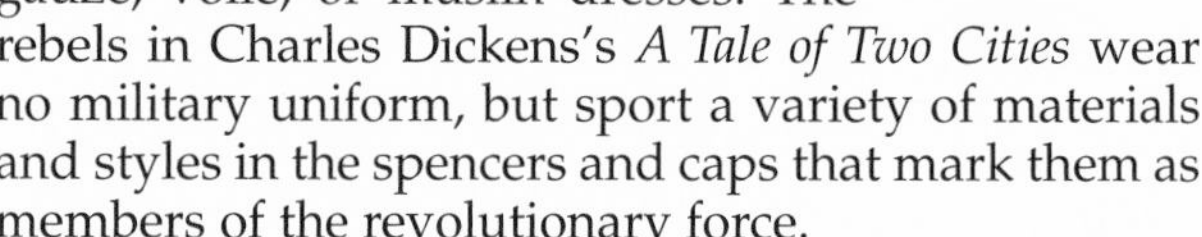

sphagnum (*sfag'* nuhm) a soft, spongy swamp moss or peat compacted with debris and decaying plant matter and used like gauze to pack wounds, as insulation around greenhouse plants to preserve moisture, or as lining for ground cloths and sled cushions and in leggings, moccasins, and gloves. Entering English in the mid-eighteenth century, the term derives from the Greek for *moss.* As described by Farley Mowat in *Never Cry Wolf,* the field biologist has difficulty protecting his food stores from the prolific colonies of mice and lemmings that thrive in burrows in the sphagnum moss that covers the Arctic tundra. *See also* lemming; peat.

sphinx (sfingks) a mythological monster consisting of the head of a hawk, ram, or human female; an eagle's wings; and the body, legs, and tail of a lion. In Sophocles' *Oedipus,* the sphinx threatens Thebes until a wanderer arrives with the answer to its riddle: What walks on four legs in the morning, two legs at noon, and three legs in the evening? Man—in infancy, the morning of life, man crawls on all fours; in adulthood, he walks upright on two legs; by old age, the sunset of life, he leans on a cane. In H. G. Wells's *The Time Machine,* the unnamed Time Traveller spies a weathered white marble sphinx atop a bronze base and seemingly hovering on outspread wings.

spice bush a tall deciduous shrub blooming with small clusters of yellow blossoms, then producing fragrant leaves and shiny red drupes, or berries. Valued by Native Americans and colonial healers, the dried bark is ground as an ingredient in a tonic or steeped in a tea to reduce fever and as a palliative for diarrhea, colds, and intestinal parasites. During the Civil War when blockades halted shipments of tea and spice, the spice bush provided useful substitutes. Awaking in his bed in the Butler home in Conrad Richter's *The Light in the Forest*, True Son regrets that he has no access to native healing, which depends on the evergreen hemlock, spring-blooming spice bush, and hazel in the fall.

spillway a permanent channel or passage leading from a dam or reservoir to safely evacuate overflowing water before it damages surrounding towns and farmland; a late nineteenth-century term. In a symbolic parallel to the struggle for civil rights, the title character in Ernest Gaines's *The Autobiography of Miss Jane Pittman* describes the Louisiana coast dwellers' attempts to dam the Mississippi River floods with dikes and sandbags; she also predicts that the engineers' concrete spillway will have no more success in subduing nature's torrents than did the dikes built during the great flood of 1927.

spindle a primitive tapered pin, rod, or staff on which thread is handmade by a process of twisting and winding. After the invention of the spinning wheel, the hand-held spindle evolved into an attached bobbin on which finished thread was wound. The silent, ungainly O-lan, ill-favored wife of Wang Lung in Pearl S. Buck's *The Good Earth*, proves to be a master of thrift: She makes her own thread from a wad of cotton on a bamboo spindle and mends clothing and bedding. *See also* distaff.

spinney a thicket or grove of small trees interspersed with vines and shrubs. The term, which entered English in the late sixteenth century, derives from the Latin for *thorn.* After the animals overthrow Farmer Jones in George Orwell's *Animal Farm*, they survey the fields, orchard, pool, and spinney. *See also* coppice.

spirit lamp a laboratory lamp or Bunsen burner with an adjustible wick that produces an intense blue flame from the combustion of ethyl alcohol or methylated gas. Near the end of his life, Jean Valjean, protagonist in Victor Hugo's *Les Misérables*, reveals how he revolutionized the jet industry by supplying workers with gum lac to be softened over a spirit lamp and shaped on a small anvil to make beads, jewelry, buckles, and combs.

spirit money in Chinese or Buddhist mythology, a ceremonial currency that enables the dead to bribe heaven's gatekeeper and gain a privileged position in the spirit world. In Amy Tan's *The Kitchen God's Wife,* Pearl's family is uncomfortable at a Buddhist funeral in Chinatown that coordinates a ritual of paid mourners, gifts of food, a farewell banner, and packets of spirit money.

spirochete or **spirochaete** (*spy'* . roh . keet) flexible, spiral-shaped, and highly mobile bacteria that burrow into body liquids in bundles that can cause syphilis, relapsing fever, yaws, and jaundice. The spirochete was discovered in 1887; the term is a hybrid of the Latin for *breathe* and the Greek for *ring*. While imitating Lucky and Pozzo in Samuel Beckett's *Waiting for Godot*, Vladimir orders Estragon to curse him; Estragon taunts him with cries of "Naughty" and "Gonococcus, spirochete," the last two naming the microbes that cause venereal diseases.

spleen a human organ that stores blood and assists the immune process by producing lymphocytes to devour pathogens. Metaphorically, the primitive psychology of the Middle Ages referred to the spleen as the storage point of human laughter, melancholy, and anger—the last producing a virulent physical and spiritual poison. To "vent spleen" meant to explode in an angry tirade and rid the body of suppressed poisons. In the breakdown of the triad that replaces the title character in William Shakespeare's *Julius Caesar*, Brutus quarrels with Cassius over money and instructs Cassius to control his raging spleen.

sponge a porous, absorbent contraceptive that is soaked in a spermicide, inserted into the vagina, and lodged against the cervix to halt the migration of sperm to the uterus and thus prevent conception. Introduced in 1918 by Scottish botanist and human sexuality expert Dr. Marie Stopes during a period when women were denied contraception, the sponge or cervical cap plus a coating of cold cream created a home birth control device that women could make and use without relying on a doctor. In a letter to God, Celie, protagonist of Alice Walker's *The Color Purple*, reports a conversation with Shug Avery, who no longer fears pregnancy because she uses a sponge as a contraceptive.

spoor (spuhr or spohr) the scent, trail, hoofprints, hair, or droppings of a hunted animal; any visual or olfactory sign of the direction taken by a prey. An Afrikaans term that entered English in the early nineteenth century, it relates to the Anglo-Saxon for *footprint.* In Joy Adamson's *Born Free,* Elsa the lion demonstrates her recovery from rickettsia by sniffing animal spoor, trailing hippos and elephants, wallowing on her back along the trail, and chasing dik-diks.

spring cart a simple, topless two-wheeled vehicle favored by produce sellers and other vendors, farmers, and country folk. In Thomas Hardy's *Tess of the D'Urbervilles,* Joan Durbeyfield complains that Mrs. D'Urberville is sending for Tess in a spring cart and not a coach, which would be more appropriate to the girl's status. *See also* dog-cart.

spring gun a charged and cocked pistol attached at the trigger or firing mechanism to a string or trip wire to fire on a thief, prowler, trespasser, poacher, or animal. In Charles Dickens's *Oliver Twist,* the title character, whom Fagin forces into housebreaking because Oliver is small enough to crawl through a window, suffers a broken arm after tripping a spring gun.

spring-line the mooring rope or cable that secures the side of a ship to the upright post or beam on a wharf or quay to allow it to move with the tide but inhibit it from drifting or striking another ship. Also, the spring-line enables the pilot to swing either bow or stern around by pulling against a taut spring-line. While acting out the job of a riverboat pilot in Mark Twain's *The Adventures of Tom Sawyer,* the title character calls for headline and spring-line. *See also* headline; quay.

spruce (sproos) a common pyramidal, cone-bearing evergreen producing fragrant needles, stout limbs, scaly bark, and trunks valued for pulpwood and timber used in piano soundboards, telephone poles, trimwork, and closet linings and as Christmas trees. The spruce exudes a gum that Native Americans chewed for relief of colds and sore throat. In Edith Wharton's *Ethan Frome,* tall, dark spruces obscure the title character and Mattie Silver during their private conversations as though the trees were disapproving chaperones or palpable images of hovering doom.

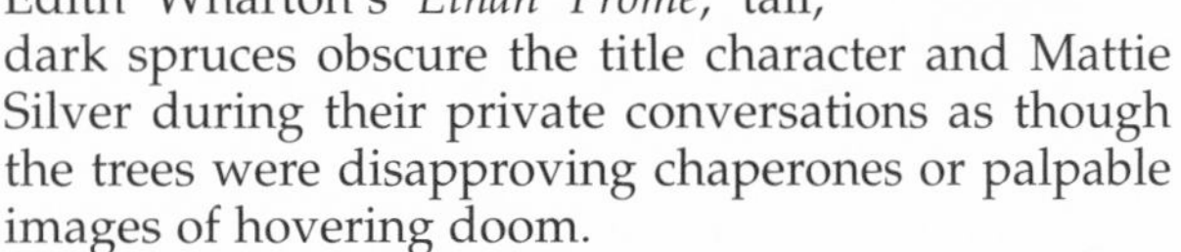

spunk-water the collected dew or rainwater that fills a decaying trunk or stump and dissolves the fungus and rotted, wormy heartwood, known as tinder or punk, into a dark, acidic solution. A term from the late sixteenth century, it derives from the Latin for *sponge.* In Mark Twain's *The Adventures of Tom Sawyer,* Huck relates a complicated rhyme and ritual using spunk-water for removing warts.

sputum a sample from the lungs of mucus, phlegm, or saliva and any accompanying blood or foreign matter; the effluvia of the respiratory tract that is coughed up, vomited, or spat from the mouth. A late seventeenth-century term, it derives from the Latin for *spit.* The rust-colored sputum of Grandpa Blakeslee in Olive Ann Burns's *Cold Sassy Tree* indicates that his lungs are leaking blood, an ominous sign.

spy-glass a small portable telescope, field glass, or opera glass. Often contained in a brass tube or a collapsing series of nested cylinders that fit into a pocket, navigator's case, or hunter's jacket, the lens magnifies objects in the distance. Black Dog, who pretends to pay a social call on Billy Bones in Robert Louis Stevenson's *Treasure Island,* notes that the old man carries a spy-glass, implying that Billy has been on the lookout for his implacable pursuer.

squadron a cavalry detail or detachment; a military unit, the army's smallest organized company. A squadron consists of four to five soldiers and is led by a staff sergeant to reconnoiter unknown terrain, disarm a guard or watch, or set up field artillery, traps, explosives, or other tactical maneuvers. Entering English in the mid-sixteenth century, the term derives from the Latin for *square.* While Hideyo conceals himself in a crate in Yoko Kawashima Watkins's *So Far from the Bamboo Grove,* a Korean squadron murders his friends and coworkers at the factory. *See also* army.

squall (skahl) a sudden wind, rain, sleet, hail, or snow storm that is brief, but violent; a passing rainstorm at sea after a lowering of barometric pressure that is followed by a steady rise. A late seventeenth-century term, it derives from the Swedish for *rush of water.* As Phillip accustoms himself to blindness and narrates to Timothy his experiences in Scharloo in Theodore Taylor's *Timothy of the Cay,* he enjoys non-visual images—the beat of rain and the sound of squall wind against the shelter. *See also* gale.

squatter a usurper, settler, or unauthorized tenant who illegally occupies a residence or cultivates land without making formal claim or acquiring a deed or title; a homesteader or nester who occupies unclaimed or reservation land under a government-supervised system of settlement. In an acceptance speech on June 16, 1858, an angry Abraham Lincoln made his famous "House Divided Speech," which typified the extension of slavery as "squatter sovereignty," a form of populist no-contest that allowed individuals to "regulate their domestic institutions in their own way."

squid (skwihd) a sea mollusk related to the octopus and cuttlefish that is capable of entrapping its prey in a blinding squirt of dark ink. Equipped with two long tentacles and five pairs of swimmers dotted with suction cups, the squid tapers to a finned triangle at the tail. Usually only a foot long, some species reach 50 feet in length and weigh over two tons. During a formal meeting about the possibility of monsters inhabiting the island in William Golding's *Lord of the Flies*, Maurice laughs nervously and comments that his father had told him stories about a squid large enough to swallow a whale.

squire (skwyr) or **esquire** the medieval designation of an aristocrat ranking between knight and gentleman; a titled owner of a considerable tract of land, buildings, country estate, or rental property. Also, an honorific for a judge, magistrate, attorney, dignitary, nobleman, or most important landowner of a district. Squire Cass, owner of the central manor in George Eliot's *Silas Marner*, is ranked as Raveloe's most prominent and prestigious citizen.

SS Adolf Hitler's Schutzstaffel or body guard; an elite commando force composed of 750,000 criminals and street toughs, who became the Third Reich's fanatical security patrol for the Nazi state. Primarily blue-eyed blonds reflecting Aryan ancestry and tattooed on the underside of their arms, they stood out from other citizens and were given special privileges, training, and advanced weaponry to help them create *judenfrei*, or Jew-free cities. In Elie Wiesel's autobiographical *Night*, the SS and its police division, the Gestapo, take charge of suppressing and exterminating Jews as well as retarded and handicapped citizens, priests, gypsies, Jehovah's Witnesses, homosexuals, dissidents, and other people declared undesirable for Hitler's master race. *See also* Aryan; Gestapo; holocaust; Nazi; Nordic.

stabilizer (*stay'* bih . *ly* . zuhr) a flap, rudder, or foil in the rear of a plane that can be raised or lowered to retard sideways swaying from turbulence and allow the plane to maintain its bearing and altitude. Brian Robeson, protagonist of Gary Paulsen's *Hatchet*, saves himself from a winter in the northern Canadian outback by diving to the sunken Cessna, entering the tail section near the stabilizer, and locating an emergency pack that contains a transmitter.

staddle (*stad'* d'l) or **steddle** a platform, pallet, framework, or stone or wood base or shelf supporting a stack of grain or rick of timbers. The term is derived from the Anglo-Saxon for *stand*. As Donald Farfrae waits for Elizabeth-Jane at the appointed time in Thomas Hardy's *The Mayor of Casterbridge*, he enters the granary doorway to shelter from the rain and leans on a staddle; turning his gaze upward, he discovers that she is hiding in the loft and staring down at him.

stagecoach or **stage** a dependable public conveyance until the mid-nineteenth century, when rail travel spread across Europe and the United States. The stagecoach delivered mail and passengers and connected with packet boats for river or sea travel. Because of diminished traffic, which could include flocks of sheep or goats or bulky hay wagons, the night coach was the most rapid overland travel. David, Steerforth, Estella, Pip, Joe, and other characters in Charles Dickens's *David Copperfield* and *Great Expectations* depend on stage schedules for hours of departure and arrival, although severe weather, breakdowns, and poor roads often delay travelers.

stair rod a horizontal rod that lies along the back of the step parallel to the riser to hold in place a loose rug, tread cover, or stair runner. Attached at each end by a cleat or screws, the stair rod, which is often made of brass and adorned at each end with a decorative finial, prevents the rug from bunching or sliding to reduce the danger of falls. At the used clothing store in Charles Dickens's *A Christmas Carol*, the rag buyer, a veteran recycler, stirs the fire with an old stair rod and studies the bundle his client has brought. *See also* riser.

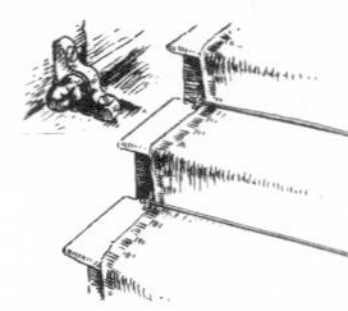

stalactite (stuh . *lak'* tyt) a conical or icicle-shaped projectile composed of calcite or aragonite and suspended from the cave roof or ceiling from which it evolved through centuries of dripping calcareous water. Below it, a stalagmite, a conical shape composed of drops of calcium carbonate or argonite from the cave roof, thrusts upward from the cave floor. The stalagmite takes centuries of steady dripping to form and soften. Ultimately, it joins with a stalactite to form a single column. Both stalactite and stalagmite, terms that entered English in the late seventeenth century, derive from the Greek word for *drip*. As Mark Twain describes the underground atmosphere in Chapter 31 of *The Adventures of Tom Sawyer,* the cave where Tom and Becky wander contains pillars formed "of great stalactites and stalagmites together."

stalagmite (stuh . *lag'* myt) *See* stalactite.

stalemate from the Middle English term for *stall,* a deadlock, standstill, tie, or draw; a impasse or one-on-one situation that prohibits either opponent in a contest from proceeding, winning, or furthering a game, political debate, or argument. During a verbal sparring match with her stubborn mother, Waverly Jong, an uncompromising character in Amy Tan's *The Joy Luck Club,* reaches a stalemate, lapses into silence, and absorbs the wisdom of her mother's point of view.

stallkeeper a traveling vendor or dispenser of a service, such as a tinker, cobbler, or barber, who sets up shop on a moveable platform, in a tent, weekly marketplace, or pavilion; at a bench, counter, or table; or out of the trunk of a car, wagon, or van. During wartime shortages of metal in George Orwell's *1984,* prole women vie noisily for an opportunity to purchase flimsy cookware from a stallkeeper.

stanchion (*stan'* chuhn) a pillar, post, support for a roof, sunshade, net, awning, or demountable stall;

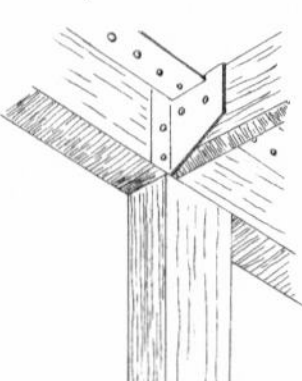

also, an upright bar, strut, stake, or beam used as a prop, as in the temporary framework of a mine shaft or the crutch that holds up the limb of a tree laden with ripening fruit or nuts. Dating to the fifteenth century, the term derives from Middle English for *stay.* As Marlowe assesses his flimsy steamboat in Joseph Conrad's *Heart of Darkness,* he observes open decks and an open cabin created from a roof and four supporting stanchions at each corner.

star-crossed astrologically unsound or unwise; lacking the confluence of favorable star patterns; cursed, ill-fated, ill-matched, or foredoomed by heaven, destiny, or supernatural powers. The prologue of William Shakespeare's *Romeo and Juliet* predicts that the love match between the star-crossed lovers Romeo and Juliet is doomed by fate because the arrangement of celestial bodies governing romance is out of balance.

stateroom a mid-seventeenth-century term for the suite, quarters, or lodging of a dignitary, ship captain, or superior officer; a private or first-class compartment or berth on a passenger train or ocean liner. Also, the apartment or ceremonial reception room in a hotel, palace, or embassy. In Joseph Conrad's "The Secret Sharer," Leggatt, the stowaway, remains in the captain's stateroom while the captain makes an appearance on deck to reassure the crew.

Stations of the Cross or **the Way of the Cross** a sacrament, meditation, devotion, or artistic or dramatic recreation of Christ's last day. This re-enactment, which evolved around the twelfth century in the Roman Catholic Church, recreates

the 14 steps of Christ on the way to crucifixion: (1) condemnation, (2) acceptance of the cross, (3) first fall on the route, (4) meeting Mary, his mother, (5) Simon of Cyrene's assistance, (6) Veronica's cool cloth on Christ's face, (7) the second stumble, (8) Christ's address to female onlookers, (9) the third fall, (10) the removal of Christ's garments, (11) the piercing of Christ's hands and feet, (12) death, (13) the removal of Christ's corpse, and (14) Christ's burial. The scenes illustrate the actions or responses of witnesses to the event; a modern addition includes the resurrection as a fifteenth station. While standing guard duty after a battle, Paul Baumer, protagonist of Erich Maria Remarque's *All Quiet on the Western Front,* imagines himself in a cathedral decorated with panels illustrating the Stations of the Cross, which symbolize his progression toward torture and death during World War I's deadly trench warfare. *See also* Calvary.

steatite (*stee'* uh . tyt) *See* sacred pipe.

steeple-crowned hat a severe, tall-topped hat for men or women worn unadorned except for a single band and buckle. In the seventeenth century, Puri-

tans divorced themselves from the frivolities of Royalists by cutting their hair short and leaving it uncurled, avoiding the frivolous styles of people they considered sacrilegious, and wearing simple, sombre-colored clothing to stress the aim of Puritanism—a desire for heaven rather than crass earthly frivolity. The throng that awaits the opening of the prison door in the opening chapter of Nathaniel Hawthorne's *The Scarlet Letter* depicts the uncharitable, sanctimonious characteristics of Puritans, symbolized by their stiff, black steeple-crowned hats.

steering oar a primitive form of vertical rudder or tiller attached to the stern by a cleat or flexible lashing. In the history of sailing before the thirteenth century, a single stout oar, usually shaped from oak, aided the helmsman in piloting a craft and keeping it on course against heavy winds or strong current. In anticipation of her lover's departure for Ithaca, Calypso lends tools to Odysseus, epic hero of Homer's *Odyssey*, who crafts keel, mast, and steering oar for his boat.

step to erect or raise a mast or main timber by simultaneously sliding and lifting the mast into the keelson, a square cradle or wood framework designed to support the heavy beam. As the mast slides into place, it must fit the step or base so that it remains steady and holds the square sail perpendicular to the keel. Stepping the mast concludes with placing sails and rigging on the beam and securing all at either side of the ship. In Avi's *The True Confession of Charlotte Doyle*, the title character notices that the crew of the *Seahawk* has stepped a new mast in preparation for their first voyage under Captain Roderick Fisk.

steppe (stehp) the Slavic term for savannah or grassland. The Soviet steppes extend from the Ukraine along the Black and Azov seas to the Altai Mountains in western Siberia. Typically too hot and dry in the short summers for gardening, the weather turns bitterly cold in winter because the flat ground offers no resistance to the freezing, drying wind. In Alexander Solzhenitsyn's *One Day in the Life of Ivan Denisovich*, the title character steps in cadence with his column and arrives on the steppe at sunrise, as the red glare strikes the icy ground.

stereopticon (*steh* . ree . *ahp'* tih . k'n) a mid-nineteenth-century projector or "magic lantern," whose name derives from the Greek for *paired vision*. The stereopticon presents two views of the same image to create the illusion of one image dissolving into the other on the screen; a hand-held stereoscope that presents two transparencies before the eyes to give the illusion of depth. To raise money for fruitcake ingredients in Truman Capote's "A Christmas Memory," Buddy and his elderly cousin put on an event featuring a freak biddy chicken and a stereopticon show.

sterling a synonym for British currency or legal money circulated in the United Kingdom. The term derives from the Old English for *little star* and the Middle English for silver penny. The ingenuous speaker in Jonathan Swift's "A Modest Proposal" predicts that an annual breeder can earn eight shillings sterling from the sale of each child. *See also* shilling.

stern the aft, tail, or rear portion of a boat, ship, or aircraft. Derived from the Old Frisian for *steering oar,* the term entered English in the fourteenth century. In Joseph Conrad's *The Heart of Darkness,* the stern wheel flops ineffectually as Marlowe's crew attempts to gain speed and leave the horror of Kurtz's landing behind. In a similarly tortuous scene, mentally replaying the scene in which Buck clings to the far side of the boat's stern in Judith Guest's *Ordinary People,* Conrad recalls the banter he shared with his brother before Buck slipped away and drowned.

stern wheel an inland steam vessel powered by a half-submerged paddle wheel fitted into the rear of the boat and favored by police, traders, passenger and mail service, and shore patrols. The boat was rapidly replaced by paddle steamers, which were propelled by two wheels amidships at either side of the boat. In Joseph Conrad's *The Heart of Darkness,* Marlowe despairs of his languid stern wheel, which flops in a struggle to push the steamship upriver against a strong current.

stetson (*steht'* s'n) the trade name for a wide-brimmed, high-crowned felt hat, often decorated with a braided or snakeskin band and pheasant feathers; a cowboy hat, often weathered and prized as a symbol of hard work or manhood. Named for John Batterson Stetson, the hat was popularized in the late nineteenth century and remains a standard feature of movies and television shows set in the Old West. To establish his status among laborers, the boss in John Steinbeck's *Of Mice and Men* sports a stetson and hooks his thumbs into his belt.

stevedore (*stee'* vuh . dohr) a manual port laborer or dock worker who loads and unloads merchant ships or other cargo vessels. A late eighteenth-century term, it derives from the Latin for *pressed together*. In Manuel Rojas's "The Glass of Milk," the sailor notices the division of labor as men carry heavy sacks down the gangplank and turn them over to stevedores, who load them through open hatches into the ship's hold.

stick bomb or **sticky bomb** an obsolete antitank explosive or grenade that was the forerunner of plastique, a self-adhering explosive used to destroy bridges, buildings, vehicles, and other large objects. Coated in adhesive so that it would adhere to the target, a stick bomb, or sticky bomb, allowed the user to place it, set the charge, and escape before the bomb exploded. In Ernest Hemingway's *A Farewell to Arms,*

Aymo points to German troops arriving armed with carbines and stick bombs, which dangle from their belts. *See also* carbine.

sticking plaster *See* poultice.

stile (styl) a narrow step, set of stairs, or ladder built into a wall, hedge, or fence in such a way as to allow passage of pedestrians but to keep animals from escaping or climbing over. Entering English before the twelfth century, the term derives from the Anglo-Saxon for *step.* On her return to Thornfield, the title character in Charlotte Brontë's *Jane Eyre* hurries toward the stile to look at the remains of the ruined hall, over which crows circle as though picking the remains of meat from a carcass.

stir a nineteenth-century American slang term, of unknown derivation, for prison, particularly solitary confinement, where inmates or prisoners of war may receive maximum security; be served limited rations through a feeding slot; remain in an unlighted cell without exercise, bedding, or personal items; hear no human voices; and rarely or never see or speak to their captors or guards, depending upon the place and country of confinement. Because of the number of letters that the protagonist sends to small-time Harlem criminals in Alex Haley's *The Autobiography of Malcolm X,* rumor suggests that "Detroit Red" has gone insane in stir.

stockade (stah . *kayd'*) a prison, enclosure, breastwork, or corral made of upright posts, often sharpened on the end or flecked with bits of metal or glass. A stockade can retain felons or other captives, or serve as a defensive wall to protect insiders from attack. In Robert Louis Stevenson's *Treasure Island,* Doctor Trelawny describes his first view of the stockade as a stout log building loopholed for muskets on all sides and surrounded by a high paling fence. *See also* musket; paling.

stocks a form of public humiliation and punishment in which the body of a petty criminal was held in an awkward position with arms, legs, and head straight forward. Derived before the twelfth century from the Old High German for *trunk,* the term is associated with the detailed laws and regulations of Puritan communities. Placed in a public square or before a courthouse, the wooden framework, whether empty or in use, served as a reminder of stiff punishment for such misdemeanors as public drunkenness, abuse of the Sabbath, or cursing. As Elizabeth-Jane and her mother approach town in Thomas Hardy's *The Mayor of Casterbridge,* Mrs. Newsom fears that her former husband may be in the workhouse or the stocks. *See also* workhouse.

stone an official British unit of weight equal to 6.35 kilograms or about 14 pounds; also, other nonstandard weights that have varied from the Middle Ages. The term applies most frequently to weighing domestic animals or humans. At maturity, Napoleon, the tyrannical pig who rules the other animals in George Orwell's *Animal Farm,* weighs 24 stone, or 336 pounds.

stoup (stoop) a drinking chalice, tankard, flagon, beaker, schooner, or bucket; also, a cask, tun, holy urn or baptismal font, or large jar, or olla, designed to hold a particular measure of liquids. Derived from the Old English for *pail,* the term entered English in the fourteenth century. In the pivotal grave-diggers' scene in William Shakespeare's *Hamlet,* one clown bids another to fetch him a stoup of ale. *See also* flagon.

strafe (strayf) to rake, harass, bombard, or attack ground-level troops or civilians with close-range machine gun fire from low-flying aircraft. Entering English during World War I, the term derives from the German *Gott strafe England* or *God punish England.* After the detonation of the atomic bomb in John Hersey's *Hiroshima,* survivors gathered in Asano Park fear that pilots of Grumman planes flying overhead intend to strafe the crowd below. *See also* Grumman.

strait waistcoat the forerunner of the straitjacket. The restraint, made of thick canvas or ticking, is laced up the back; its tight sleeves continue beyond the fingers and end in a pouch pulled shut with drawstrings. When the patient is put to bed, the arms cross over the chest and the strings tie around the waist. Derived from the French for *narrow,* the term entered English in the Middle Ages, when hysterical patients got little treatment beyond safety from harming themselves. In Bram Stoker's *Dracula,* John Sheppard wears a strait waistcoat and is chained to the walls of a padded cell.

stratosphere (*strat'* uh . sfeer) the part of the atmosphere that occupies the space from 10 to 50 miles above the earth's surface. Of lighter density and pressure, the area was named in 1909 from the Greek for *earth layer.* The speaker in George Orwell's *1984* notes that wars are designed to waste surplus goods by blowing them up, hurling them into the stratosphere, or dumping them into the ocean.

streak-a-lean an American slang term for lean bacon that fries into crisp slabs or rashers for serving with eggs or for making into bacon biscuits, a southern breakfast tradition. Because Mary Toy and Will Tweedy are not allowed pork at home in Olive Ann Burns's *Cold Sassy Tree,* their Grandmother Blakeslee keeps sausage and streak-a-lean in the warming oven for an after-school treat. *See also* sow belly.

strings of cash *See* cash.

stroke *See* apoplexy.

strop a treated canvas or leather strip of wood covered with leather used for sharpening blades, particularly straight razors, and for disciplining children. Derived from the Anglo-Saxon for *thong,* the word entered English before the twelfth century. During his first visit with his father since leaving home in Daniel Keyes's *Flowers for Algernon,* Charlie Gordon, who keeps his identity a secret while recalling his miserable childhood, cringes at the sound of the strop and flinches, causing the barber to nick his Adam's apple. *See also* Adam's apple.

strophe (*stroh'* fee) in Greek drama, the first of a triad of speeches—strophe, antistrophe, epode—recited by the chorus as commentary on the action as they dance from the right side of the stage to the left in a strict metrical movement coordinated with the chant. Derived from the Greek for *turning,* the word has been a part of literary analysis since the Golden Age of Greece in the fifth century B.C. and entered English in the early seventeenth century. In the first strophe of the opening ode in Sophocles' *Antigone,* the chorus welcomes the sun over Argos after a fierce quarrel brought about by Polyneices's anger. *See also* antistrophe; epode.

strouding (*strow'* dihng) or **stroud blanket** a coarse woolen blanket or garment traded to Indians during the late seventeenth century. Named for Stroud, a town in Gloucestershire, or possibly for an English manufacturing district, the term indicates the importance of barter between colonists and Native American tribes. Half Arrow, friend of True Son in Conrad Richter's *The Light in the Forest,* claims that his strouding will protect him from cold as he climbs into a chasm to spend the night.

strudel (*stroo'* d'l) a Bavarian dessert made of buttered, flaky noodle pastry wrapped in thin layers around spiced dried apples, chopped almonds, and currants that is then oven-poached in milk or cream, and served hot with a sprinkling of cinnamon sugar. Derived from the German for *whirlpool,* the term entered English in the late nineteenth century. In the country at Grandma's house, Zlata Filipovich enjoys strudel in an idyllic moment before the war begins, as recorded in her autobiographical *Zlata's Diary.*

stucco (*stuhk'* koh) a plaster or cement formed of powdered marble and gypsum and used for inner walls, ceilings, molded ornamentation around chandeliers, and cornices; also, an exterior paste consisting of lime, cement, and sand as a covering of brick or wood to give the impression of stone. Entering English in the late sixteenth century, the term derives from the German for *crust.* To Pearl and Hester Prynne in Nathaniel Hawthorne's *The Scarlet Letter,* the glass-studded stucco exterior of Governor Bellingham's house looks like Aladdin's palace, a rare bit of splendor in a dour Puritan community.

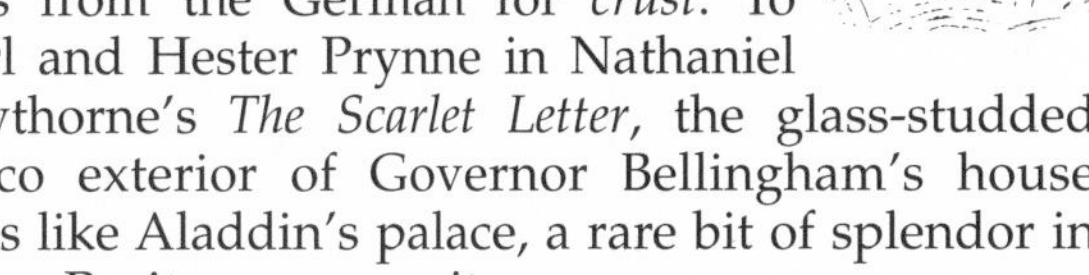

stun'sail or **stunsail** (*stuhn'* s'l) a small auxiliary sail set to catch light breezes at the far end of the yard that holds a square sail. A corruption of *studding sail,* the term derives from the German for *push* and entered English in the mid-sixteenth century. In testimony to his youth and agility, the title character and others of his rank in Herman Melville's *Billy Budd* take their ease in furled stun'sails as though swinging in hammocks.

styptic (*styp'* tihk) an astringent, hemostatic, or coagulant powder such as alum which is usually compressed into a lozenge or stick and applied to a cut or abrasion to thicken blood and halt bleeding. The term is derived from the Greek for *shrink.* While sitting in his father's barber's chair in Daniel Keyes's *Flowers for Algernon,* Charlie Gordon grows nervous and flinches, causing the razor to nick his Adam's apple, which the barber treats by applying a styptic stick, suggesting the bitter, stultifying memories of boyhood that cause Charlie's misgivings and nightmares.

subaltern (*suhb'* ahl . tuhrn) a general term for assistant or secondary officer of lower rank than the officer in charge; a subordinate, inferior, or junior officer. A sixteenth-century term, it derives from the Latin for *under* and *the other of two.* While steering the *Hispaniola* in Robert Louis Stevensons's *Treasure Island,* Jim Hawkins serves as subaltern to Israel Hands, who pilots the crewless ship.

subconscious (suhb . *kahn'* shuhs or *suhb'* kahn . shuhs) the part of the thinking process that lies below the subject's awareness and beyond the mind's powers to call in its entirety into conscious knowledge or application; the repository of suppressed or repressed thoughts, emotions, dreams, and desires. A significant part of the psychoanalytic theory of Sigmund Freud, a Viennese neurologist, the term entered English in the late nineteenth century. As Charlie Gorden keeps records of his advancing intelligence in Daniel Keyes's *Flowers for Algernon*, he comments on Dr. Strauss's explanation of the conscious mind and the subconscious, from which come dreams and suppressed thoughts. *See also* superego.

succotash (*suhk'* koh . tash) a Native American stew made by cooking a small portion of savory seafood, pork, beef, or wild bird in the broth of vegetables such as squash, corn, beans, potatoes, or pumpkin. Entering English in the mid-eighteenth century, the term derives from the Narragansett for *boiled corn kernels*. In James Fenimore Cooper's *The Last of the Mohicans*, the Delaware Indians express welcome to the Huron Magua by sharing their succotash.

succubus (*suhk'* kyoo . buhs) *pl.* **succubi** a female devil or demon who extracts semen from the penis of a human victim; an evil supernatural seducer who has sexual relations with a sleeping male. The term derives from the Latin for *recline under.* According to testimony in Arthur Miller's *The Crucible*, Reverend John Hale claims to have a book describing incubi and succubi. *See also* incubus.

sucking pig or **suckling pig** a young piglet or farrow not yet weaned; providing tender, easily carved meat, a table delicacy fit for a holiday feast. Presentation of the pig usually calls for leaves and fruit around the edge of the platter, an apple or crabapple in the pig's mouth, and a coronet of leaves. The dish is doused in brandy and set aflame to crisp the hide and make a dramatic entree. During the extravagant holiday meal featured in the visit of the second apparition in Charles Dickens's *A Christmas Carol*, roast meats include a tender sucking pig.

suffragette (*suhf* . fruh . *jeht'*) a female campaigner for women's rights to full citizenship, particularly the right to serve on juries and run for public office and to enjoy full political enfranchisement; a protestor proclaiming women's right to vote. An early twentieth-century political term, it derives from the Latin for *to allow through*. Local people ridicule the new Mrs. Blakeslee in Olive Ann Burns's *Cold Sassy Tree* because she is a Yankee free-thinker and an unapologetic suffragette.

sugar tit a forerunner of the infant's pacifier, made from a scrap of cloth filled with brown sugar and butter. The cloth was tied into the shape of a nipple and given to a baby to suck or chew. It could be tipped with laudanum or stuffed with soothing, numbing herbs to ease teething pain or colic. Stanley, an insensitive, boorish character in Tennessee Williams's *A Streetcar Named Desire*, prescribes a sugar tit for Mitch, a bachelor who admits that he will have to adjust to loneliness after his mother dies. *See also* laudanum.

suit of mail a full-body armor made of metal plates and woven wire and composed of gorget for throat protection, greaves for shinguards, breastplate over the chest, cuirasses over the thighs, helmet with visor to protect the head, flexible gauntlets to guard the hands, and a sword as a weapon. On a delivery to Governor Bellingham's home in Nathaniel Hawthorne's *The Scarlet Letter*, Hester Prynne examines the suit of mail the governor wore during the Pequod War in a significant misapplication of European tactical dress to American military exigencies. *See also* beaver; breastplate; cuirass; gauntlet; gorget.

sumac or **sumach** (*shu'* mak or *soo'* mak) a poisonous vine, native to the Americas, that produces leaves used in tanning and dyeing, in lacquer, or as an astringent. Derived from the Arabic for *red*, the term, which entered English in the fourteenth century, alludes to the vibrant color of sumac foliage in the fall. In a close encounter with Cuyloga, Lenni Lenape father of True Son, the protagonist of Conrad Richter's *The Light in the Forest*, the boy smells the man's distinctive, fragrant kinnikinnick, a pipe tobacco blended of willow and sumac.

summer house a gazebo, pavilion, glassed-in greenhouse or observatory, or belvedere; an open structure or shaded, covered picnic table in a park or garden, remote section of a manor, or gathering spot for children and governesses for summer lessons and play. Also, a weekend getaway cottage or cabin. In the Faubourg St. Germaine, a rich section of Paris in Victor Hugo's *Les Misérables*, Jean Valjean and Cosette lease the lavish, two-story summer house belonging to the president of the Paris parliament.

Sun Dance a meaningful annual summer ceremonial dance performed by Plains Indians during an annual gathering of related tribes to benefit all participants during the coming year. On a circular dance floor centered with a cottonwood pole, dancers executed complex steps, blew whistles made from bone, or slit the flesh over their pectoral muscles and inserted thongs attached to buffalo skulls as a gesture of honor to the Great Spirit. Other traditional activities included songs, fasting, incantations, prayers for the sick, and smoking of the sacred pipe. In N. Scott Momaday's *The Way to Rainy Mountain*, the speaker refers to Tai-Me as the sacred Sun Dance doll, a prized possession of the Kiowa. *See also* sacred pipe.

superego (*soo* . puhr . *ee'* goh) a symbolic construct denoting the part of the conscious mind that inhibits wrongful or shameful behavior by applying law, religious beliefs, morality, and societal safeguards. As part of psychoanalytic theory, the term came into popular language in the late nineteenth century. For a long time hampered by mental retardation, Charlie Gordon, protagonist of Daniel Keyes's *Flowers for Algernon*, learns the role of the three major parts of Dr. Sigmund Freud's paradigm of the mind—the id, ego, and superego or conscience. *See also* subconscious.

sura *See* Koran.

surcingle (*suhr'* sihn . g'l) a girth strap, band, or cincture used to anchor a saddle, packs, or saddle blanket in place on a camel, mule, burro, or horse. Derived from the Latin for *belt*, the term entered English in the fourteenth century. Tom Black Bull, protagonist in Hal Borland's *When the Legends Die*, attaches a surcingle to his pick of the herd to provide a place to hang on for a lengthy bareback ride.

surplice (*suhr'* plihs) a knee- or ankle-length white linen gown or tunic with wide, flowing sleeves worn over the cassock of a chorister or priest. Derived from the Latin for *overskin*, the term entered English in the Middle Ages. James Joyce refers to holy garments in *A Portrait of the Artist as a Young Man* during the speaker's memories of the sacristy and the stored surplices, which seemed sacred even without a priest present. *See also* sacristy.

surrey (*suhr'* rih) an inexpensive flat-topped, open-sided carriage seating four to six passengers. Later models added roll-down leather splash guards; some had isinglass windows for sightseeing. Named for a county in England, it was a popular pleasure vehicle at the end of the nineteenth century. In William Faulkner's "The Bear," the narrator and members of the hunting party travel by surrey on the annual hunt of the crippled bear, a symbol of the spirit of the North American wild who was often sighted, but never killed. *See also* isinglass; rockaway.

surtout *See* greatcoat.

suttee (suh . *tee'*) or **sati** the Indian custom of burning a widow on a funeral pyre alongside her husband's corpse in a ritual suicide or a forced public immolation or sacrifice as a form of honor and purification of the dead man and an assurance of the couple's happiness in the afterlife. A late eighteenth-century term first mentioned by Alexander the Great and derived from the Sanskrit for *devoted wife*, the term refers to a barbaric, dehumanizing custom outlawed in British India in 1830 but still practiced in some remote areas. In Jules Verne's *Around the World in Eighty Days*, rescuers race into action as local officials lead Aouda toward the statue of Kali in preparation for the suttee. *See also* fakir.

swab (swahb) or **swabby** a nautical slang pejorative referring to workers or individuals so useless that they are fit only for mopping or swabbing the sea-soaked deck, a daily job aboard ship. The term entered English in the mid-seventeenth century from the German for *mop*. In reference to Doctor Trelawny, who orders him to give up rum, Billy Bones, a crotchety character in Robert Louis Stevenson's *Treasure Island*, generalizes that all doctors are swabs or contemptible people. *See also* holystone.

swaddling a length of cotton, linen, or gauze used to wrap and restrict the motions of a newborn infant; also, clothing that easily accommodates a growing child and requires no insertion of a child's limbs into sleeves or leggings. In parts of Afghanistan, children remain safely swaddled to cradleboards out of danger and out of the way of adults until the babies reach the age to walk. Entering English in the Middle Ages, the term derives from the Anglo-Saxon for *wrap* and applies to descriptions and artistic representations of the infant Jesus, whose mother swaddled him shortly after his birth. In Kate Chopin's "Zoraïde," the title character goes insane and nurtures her delusion of motherhood by swaddling and rocking a bundle of rags.

swag a slang term for booty, stolen merchandise, or spoils of war, which could be sold outright, bartered for trade goods, or used as bounty money for paying bribes, extortion, or ransom. The term, which entered

English in the mid-seventeenth century, derives from the Old High German for *swing*. Awakened unexpectedly, Injun Joe, the villain of Mark Twain's *The Adventures of Tom Sawyer*, confers with his partner on how much swag they have left from their thievery to pay their expenses.

swagger stick a ceremonial tapered dowel, baton, riding crop, or cane with a metal ferule on one end that military officers carry as a mark of distinction. A symbol of power and discipline during England's colonial era, it derives from the Scandinavian term for *sway*. In Jeanne Wakatsuki Houston and James D. Houston's *Farewell to Manzanar*, Ko Wakatsuki returns from prison carrying a swagger stick to emphasize his authority and conceal his insecurity after the FBI arrested him and impounded his fishing boats. *See also* ferule.

swale (swayl) a shallow fen or bog; a depression or low spot where moisture collects in otherwise dry land, such as a lawn, golf course, savannah, or meadow. A late Middle English term, it derives from the Norse for *cool*. Angeline, a female wolf observed by zoologist Farley Mowat in *Never Cry Wolf*, returns across the swale on tiptoes, craning her neck toward her prey before pouncing.

swastika (*swahs'* tih . kuh) or **Hakenkreuz** an ancient four-armed hooked cross; a symmetrical rune or symbol that consists of four right angles joined at the center and pointed clockwise. The swastika became the emblem of the Nazi party and thus came to represent the deranged power-mad Third Reich and its nationalistic purge of undesirables from the Aryan race. Dressed in stylish garb and marked with a swastika, Oskar Schindler, the focal character in Thomas Keneally's *Schindler's List*, makes his appearance in Chapter 1 as he enters a chauffeured car. *See also* Aryan; holocaust; Nazi; rune; SS.

sweat lodge in Native American tradition, a domed frame or lean-to large enough for one person to sit over a fire to inhale the fragrant or hallucinogenic steam from pungent herbs or tobacco as a means of communicating with the spirit world. The narrator in John Neihardt's *Black Elk Speaks* details his communion with the spirit world through fasting and the intense moist heat of the sweat lodge. Likewise, the title character of Theodora Kroeber's *Ishi, Last of His Tribe* introduces staff from the San Francisco anthropological museum to an authentic sweat lodge. *See also* vision quest.

sweetmeat a general term indicating a delicacy with a sweet filling, whether candy, crystallized or candied fruit, pastry, cake, sugared dried fruit, coated seed or nut, honeyed conserve, or comfit. Egeus, the patriarchal father in William Shakespeare's *A Midsummer Night's Dream*, accuses Lysander of bewitching his daughter by presenting her nosegays and sweetmeats and wooing her away from Demetrius, the man to whom she is pledged. *See also* comfit.

swingel or **swingle** (*swihn'* g'l) a two-foot long beater rod or scraper with a thin edge used to shuck woody stems and coarse debris from flax or hemp; also, the sharp edge of a wooden flail. A Middle English term for a traditional agricultural tool of farmers and harvesters, the word derives from the Dutch for *lash*. On Mixen Lane, Jopp and his pals, characters in Thomas Hardy's *The Mayor of Casterbridge*, arrive, hang their swingles on pegs, and take places on settles among friend and foe to drink their ale in peace and harmony like parishioners entering a church.

switch blade a spring-loaded pocketknife, dating to the 1930s, that snaps open at the touch of a button or catch in the handle. Often associated with gang fights or death by stabbing, the term names a weapon sometimes barred from public entertainments, gatherings, and restaurants. The knife is banned by laws against concealed weapons in certain states or municipalities. In Zora Neale Hurston's *Their Eyes Were Watching God*, Tea Cake claims that his switch blade performed the job of saving Janie from a dog attack during the flood that covered the muck.

syce *See* sais.

symposium (sihm . *poh'* see . uhm) a conference or meeting bringing together scholars, professionals, or researchers who share an interest in a particular topic and who use the event to present current findings or developments. At a symposium of scientists in Daniel Keyes's *Flowers for Algernon*, facts about psychosurgery suggest that Charlie Gordon's treatment deserves a place in medical history. In a similarly intellectual setting, Pieixoto, the congenial historian in the concluding chapter of Margaret Atwood's *The Handmaid's Tale*, displays scholarly curiosity about the patriarchal society that enslaved women, as revealed on tapes made by an unidentified breeder named Offred.

synagogue (*sihn'* uh . *gahg*) the Jewish community, congregation, or assembly hall and house of worship where members come for prayer, rituals, educational lectures, and fellowship; also, the Jewish faith or Judaism itself. Derived from the Greek for *assembly*, the term entered English in the Middle Ages. In Elie Wiesel's autobiographical *Night*, the Jews of Sighet, Hungary, acquire a unity of purpose and hope by identifying with synagogue activities.

syncope (*sing'* koh . pee) loss of consciousness resulting from a lack of bloodflow to the brain, stress, trauma, hunger, or heat. Derived from the Greek for *cut short*, the term entered English in the mid-sixteenth century and serves as a medical name for fainting. Shortly before death, Jean Valjean, protagonist of Victor Hugo's *Les Misérables*, sinks into semi-syncope, then rallies briefly.

syndic (*sihn'* dihk) derived from the Latin for *representative of a corporation*, a general term dating to the early seventeenth century naming an important post, for example, a campus notable, censor, senate committee member, university dean, business agent, official, magistrate, or *chargé d'affaire*. Dr. Frankenstein, a native of Geneva, Switzerland, in Mary Shelley's *Frankenstein*, takes pride in his family's heritage of a long line of counsellors and syndics.

synovial (suh . *noh'* vee . uhl or sy . *noh'* vee . uhl) **fluid** the body's natural lubricant; a thick, colorless liquid that the joints secrete inside a synovial membrane to facilitate articulation; also, the fluid inside bursa and the sheathing of tendons. Dating to the mid-eighteenth century, the term derives from Paracelsus's term for *gout*. While examining the knee of Frederick Henry, a war casualty in Ernest Hemingway's *A Farewell to Arms*, doctors determine that the synovial fluid must re-form about the shrapnel before the fragments can be removed. *See also* shrapnel.

syrinx (*sihr'* ingks) *pl.* **syringes** *See* panpipes.

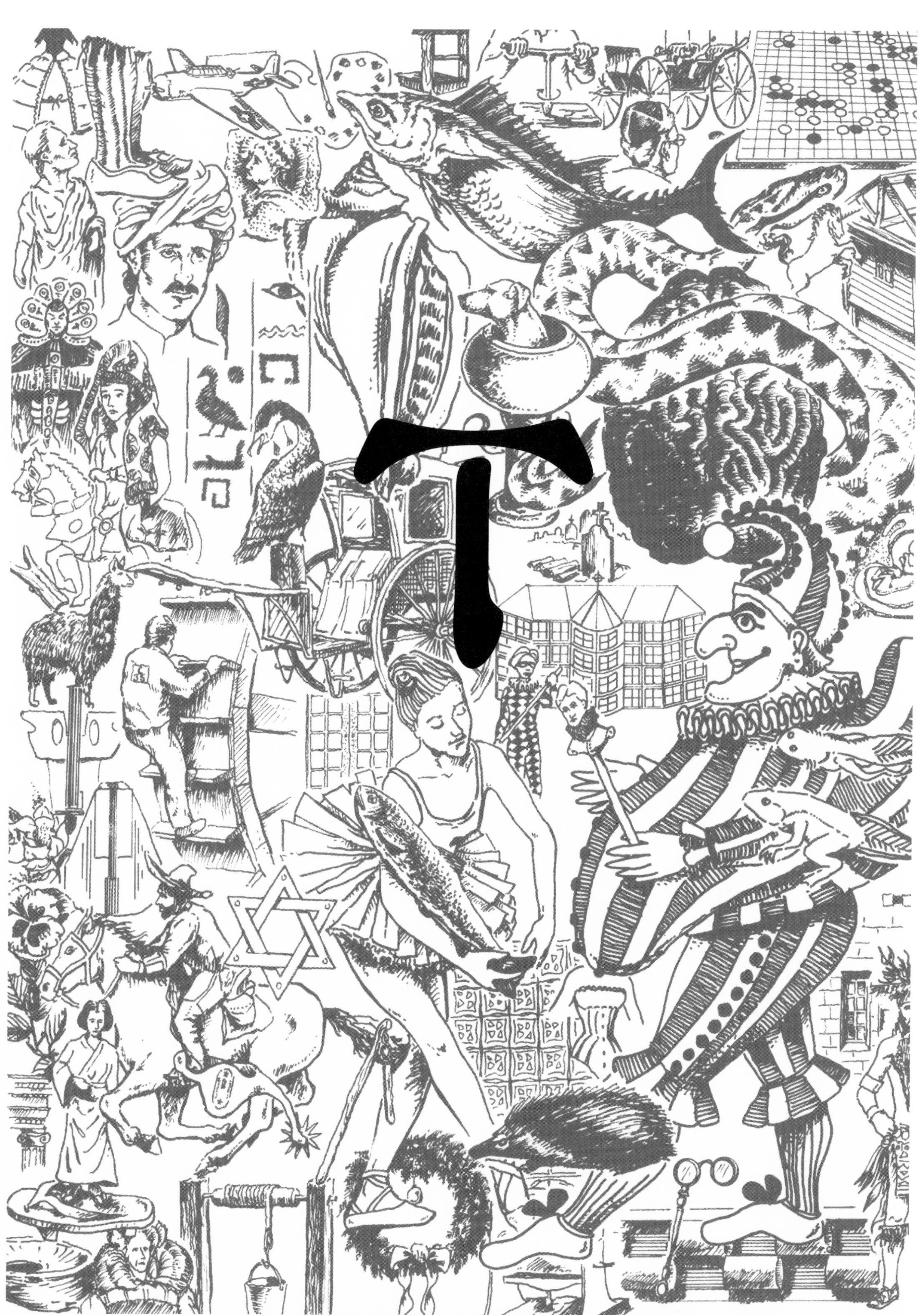
T

tabard (*tab'* uhrd) a short, loose vest dating to the Chivalric Age that was worn over a knight's armor and often bore a coat of arms, crest, initial, or official insignia. In place of side seams, the tabard tied with ribbons, thongs, or leather lacing from under the arm to the hem. The pilgrims of Geoffrey Chaucer's "Prologue to the Canterbury Tales" agree to assemble at the Tabard Inn, which, in medieval style, takes its name from a concrete noun. This tradition dates to a time when people could not read and looked for pictures on a signboard to help them find their way.

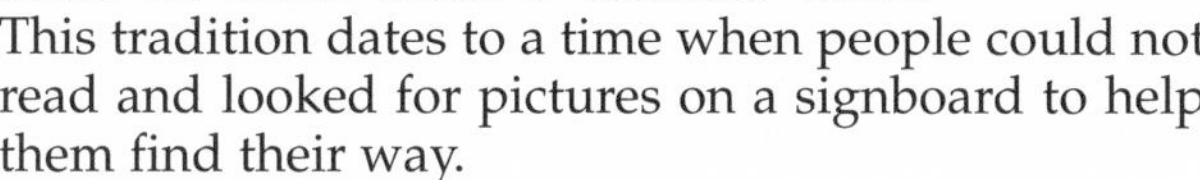

tabi (*ta'* bee) a sock designed like a mitten with a separate covering for the big toe so that it can pass alongside the thong of a geta, or wooden-soled clog. Yoko Kawashima is removing her tabi in the autobiographical *So Far from the Bamboo Grove* when Major Ryu arrives with an invitation for her and the other dancers to visit wounded veterans. *See also* geta.

tableau (*ta'* bloh) the literary term for a scene or interlude in which characters maintain a static position to illustrate a meaningful arrangement, for example, the living manger scene of Christian tradition that illustrates the visit of shepherds and magi to the Holy Family. To Mr. Tanimoto, one of the focal characters in John Hersey's *Hiroshima,* the scene in Asano Park is a vast tableau of dead, dying, and dazed people too traumatized to move or gesture.

tabloid (*tab'* loyd) an early twentieth-century term for a popularized form of news in a newspaper or broadside often half the size of a standard sheet. For ease of reading, the tabloid features short takes, generalized news, brief citations, and snippets of facts about people and events. For maximum visual effect, tabloids surround limited print with bold diagrams, photos, maps, summary headlines, captions, and cutlines. Captain Beatty characterizes the demise of the written word in Ray Bradbury's *Fahrenheit 451* by naming digests, tabloids, and condensed books and messages as examples of shortcuts to obtaining meaning from literature.

taboo or **tabu** (ta . *boo'* or tuh . *boo'*) *pl.* **taboos** a community or tribal rule, law, tradition, or ban forbidding an action or belief on religious, ethical, or moral grounds, such as the banishment of women from a patriarchal tribal festival in the men's lodge described in Herman Melville's *Typee.* The word was introduced in Europe in the late eighteenth century by Captain Cook, the explorer and cartographer of much of the Pacific Rim, who had learned the term in Melanesia. In Chinua Achebe's *Things Fall Apart,* the taboo against cutting dog meat with a knife allows the use of teeth for dismembering and preparing the meat.

tabor or **tabour** (*tay'* buhr) a small drum with a calfskin membrane suspended by a thong about the neck. Derived from Persian, the term entered English during the Middle Ages. A piper taps the tabor, coordinating beats with one hand with the playing of trumpet, panpipes, or flute with the other. Stephano, a character in William Shakespeare's *The Tempest,* is disconcerted by a melody played on the tabor by Ariel, an invisible spirit.

tack a nautical maneuver altering course or direction by bringing the bow of a sailing vessel into the wind or across it and swinging the sails athwart or at an angle from the ship's axis. A Middle English term, the word may derive from the French for *attack.* Feeling giddy with the exertion of hiding a stowaway from the steward, the unnamed captain in Joseph Conrad's "The Secret Sharer" hears a break in the shipboard silence as the mate calls for the crew to tack and pull the boat alee.

tactical police force a special detail of troops, riot squad, artillery, or peacekeeping forces deployed as an auxiliary to a military or police operation, particularly in a situation threatening to break out into riot, looting, terrorism, or anarchy. As detailed in Alex Haley's *The Autobiography of Malcolm X,* a half hour after the assassination of the title character, New York police go on alert and summon busloads of tactical police force members, who beef up security in the Harlem area.

tadpole the larval or aquatic stage of the development of a frog, toad, or other amphibian when a tail emerges and the animal breathes through gills. Derived from the Middle English for *toad head,* the term entered English in the fifteenth century. At the end of his reverse strategy to get Aunt Polly's fence whitewashed, Tom, the title character in Mark Twain's *The Adventures of Tom Sawyer,* trades work for a doorknob, a broken window sash, a few tadpoles, and assorted other goods.

taffrail (*taf'* rayl) or **tafferel** the carved and adorned finish railing around the poop deck at the top of a ship's stern. An early nineteenth-century term, it derives from the Dutch for *table.* As the longboat carries the title character in Herman Melville's *Billy Budd* away from his pals, who observe the impressment

over the taffrail, the author stresses the irony of the ship's name—*Rights-of-Man.*

tai-tai (*ty'* ty) a polite Chinese term or honorific, the equivalent of "ma'am," which an underling or subservient relative directs to the mistress, housekeeper, or lady of the house or appends to a name, as with Tai-Tai Rachel. In Amy Tan's *The Kitchen God's Wife,* young wives refer to their mothers-in-law as *tai-tai.*

talisman (*ta'* leez . m'n) *pl.* **talismans, talismen** a charm, ritual Native American medicine object, or sacred or magic item, such as a rabbit's foot, four-leafed clover, Saint Christopher's medal, or equally small object that can be carried on the person; in a pocket; or around the neck, ankle, or arm on a thong or chain. The talisman possesses occult or supernatural powers or a blessing capable of producing or assuring a miracle, good luck, health, enrichment, power over an enemy, or control over evil destiny. Derived from the Greek for *initiation into sacred mysteries,* the term entered English in the early seventeenth century. Urshanabi, the boatman in *Gilgamesh,* accuses the title character of making the crossing harder by breaking the stone talismans.

talking sheets a metaphor for the coverings of Klansmen, or nightriders, in Toni Morrison's *Beloved. See also* Ku Klux Klan.

tallith (*tah'* luhs or tah . *leht'* or *tah'* luhth) *pl.* **tallithim** a narrow prayer shawl, usually white or ivory marked with light blue stripes and ending in zizith or fringe. The tallith is worn over the shoulders or head of a Jewish male during prayers or under the outer garments of an orthodox Jewish male, especially during morning prayer. An early seventeenth-century term, it derives from the Hebrew for *cloak.* During the fundamentalist reign that terrorizes Boston in Margaret Atwood's *The Handmaid's Tale,* television reports of raids on Jews display captured Torahs, talliths, and Magen Davids.

Talmud (*tahl'* mood) a 45-volume collection of a thousand years' worth of Jewish biblical interpretation, discussion, law, and customs. A mid-sixteenth-century term, it derives from the Hebrew for *instruction* and refers to the Mishnah, a systemized text or statement of traditions, and the Gemara, or commentary. As described in Elie Wiesel's *Night,* Jewish spiritual leaders immerse themselves in the legalistic arguments of the Talmud to solve modern problems or settle disputes.

tamarisk (*ta'* muh . *rihsk*) a red- or rose-flowered Mediterranean or Asian desert shrub feathered with light-leafed bracts and exuding a sweet white gum used in dye or medicine. Derived from the Arabic for *date,* the term entered English in the fourteenth century. On the way to the beach to visit Raymond's friend in Albert Camus's *The Stranger,* Meursault observes the houses hidden behind tamarisk trees or standing naked in the sun, a symbolic representation of the killer's overt actions and covert feelings.

tanka (*tahn'* kuh) or **tan** a South Chinese houseboat or sampan suitable for sleeping a crew; also, a Cantonese neighborhood consisting of houseboat residents. To Passepartout's delight, the *Carnatic,* a steamer in Jules Verne's *Around the World in Eighty Days,* lies at anchor among a flotilla of junks, tankas, and other small craft in Hong Kong harbor at a crucial moment in Phileas Fogg's race. *See also* sampan.

tankard (*tangk'* uhrd) a tall ale-pot, schooner, or drinking mug, often made of pewter and featuring a single handle attached below the hinged lid. In alehouses where customers return regularly for a drink, personalized or initialed tankards often stood on the shelf in readiness for a night's refill. Of uncertain origin, the term entered English in the Middle Ages. A single hand grasping the tankard can hold the cylinder and extend the thumb to swing open the lid. In George Eliot's *Silas Marner,* Squire Cass's Red House displays its need for a mistress of the residence by the smell of stale dregs in tankards and the dust and general disorder of furnishings.

tanner common slang for a British sixpence. Entering English in the early nineteenth century, the term is of unknown origin. In George Bernard Shaw's *Pygmalion,* Eliza struggles to make a living from selling violets to pedestrians but runs into ill luck when she is unable to make change for a tanner.

tansu (*tahn'* soo) the Japanese term for a large cabinet, cupboard, or chest of drawers. At six o'clock on the morning of the atomic blast in John Hersey's *Hiroshima,* Mr. Tanimoto is trying to help Mr. Matsuo deliver a *tansu* filled with clothing and household items.

Tao (dow) the indescribable, elusive inner pathway to oneness with the creative life-force of the universe; a meaningful comfort to the poor, aged, handicapped, oppressed, or disenfranchised. Often represented as a paradoxical matrix, doctrine, or dogmatic structure, the Tao, an unassuming, but intriguing construct, exemplifies human experience, through which the Taoist contemplates reality. Taoism supposedly sprang from the writings of Lao Tzu, author of a book of aphorisms known as the *Tao Te Ching,* produced in the third century B.C. The power that underlies Taoism is the art of unifying earthly behavior with godliness. Thus, the seeker of the way finds beauty in simplicity, honesty, selflessness, and freedom from greed. After Waverly Jong earns a trophy for chess mastery in Amy Tan's *The Joy Luck Club,* her mother sets it beside a plastic chess set given her by a neighborhood Taoist society, a symbol suggesting that Waverly expects expertise in chess to define her being and importance.

taper (*tay'* p'r) a thin candle made from a thick wick or cord dipped lightly in wax and used to light a chandelier, pipe, hearthfire, or sconce. Derived from the Latin for *papyrus,* the term entered English in the late sixteenth century. Alone in his study, Brutus, a major character in William Shakespeare's *Julius Caesar,* calls for Lucius to bring him a taper, which burns irregularly to indicate the arrival of Julius Caesar's ghost with a warning that the phantasm will return to Brutus at Philippi. *See also* sconce.

tapestry (*ta'* pihs . trih) a handwoven textured fabric, drape, upholstery, bed curtain, or rug embroidered, woven, or painted with ornate designs or scenes from mythology, nature, the Bible, or local or national events and hung on prominent walls, particularly in an entrance hall, dining room, boudoir, or sitting or council room; often used as a tribute to a family's lineage or a scene from church or town history. Derived from the French for *carpet,* the term entered English in the late Middle Ages. In William Shakespeare's *The Taming of the Shrew,* Gremio puts on airs by claiming to own a house decorated with ivory chests, arras, fine tapestries, brass, and other treasures. *See also* arras.

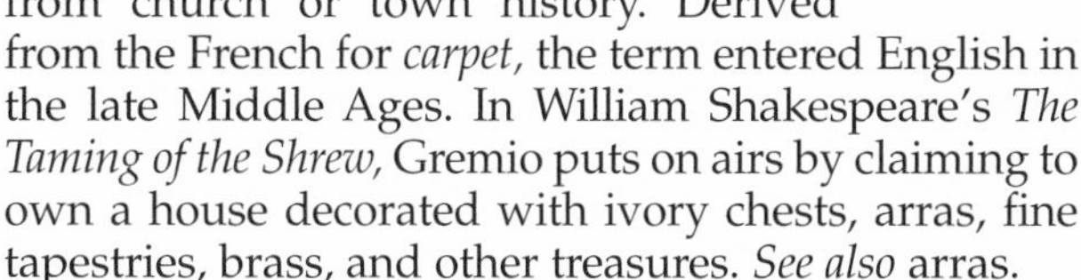

tappet (*tap'* piht) an arm, rod, or projecting lever that touches a cam shaft, valve, or other moving part in the regular operation or function of a steam or gasoline engine. An eighteenth-century term, it derives from the onomatopoetic, or imitative, sound of the rod against metal parts. Uneasy drivers—particularly Okies or midwestern migrant farm laborers—along the road to California in John Steinbeck's *The Grapes of Wrath* fear engine failure presaged by the clatter of tappets.

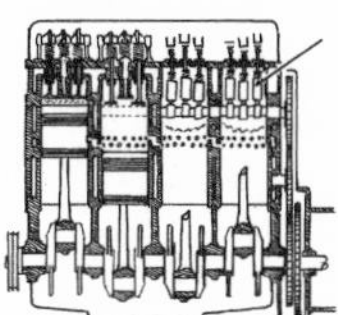

taproom a bar room, drinking counter, or public room in an alehouse where beer or ale is available on tap from a fresh keg that is tipped into a cradle or counter and "tapped," or pierced with a sharp-ended spigot for ease of serving. After his expulsion from Manor Farm, in George Orwell's *Animal Farm,* Mr. Jones complains to listeners in the taproom of his ill treatment during an uprising of his domesticated animals.

tar and feather a serious type of frontier fun practiced from Colonial times through the Reconstruction Era and consisting of coating a victim's body with hot tar, then embedding the sticky surface with feathers. Because the tar had to be removed immediately to prevent suffocation, strong solvent increased the discomfort by stripping away flesh that was pricked by feather quills. In Scott O'Dell's *Sarah Bishop,* the title character observes the victim of tarring and feathering during the unsettled times preceding the American Revolution. *See also* ride on a rail.

Tarantella (*tar* . uhn . *tehl'* luh) a melodramatic Italian folk dance based on fervid whirling, posturing, teasing, light stamps of the feet, and abrupt changes of rhythm. The dance, performed by couples or pairs of women, is accompanied by the music of mandolin, tambourine, guitar, and castanets. The dance and its ethnic costume evolved from a sixteenth-century romanticized dance cure for the bite of the poisonous tarantula or a frenzy for dancing named for Taranto, a town in southern Italy. In Henrik Ibsen's *A Doll's House,* Thorvald rehearses and browbeats his doll-like wife Nora into donning an appropriate costume and dancing the Tarantella for the guests at a party. *See also* domino.

tarmac (*tahr'* mak) or **tarmacadam** trademark name for a surfacing material for dry road beds beginning with a layer of large gravel on a raised surface covered with broken or crushed stone, or slag, and topped with a heat- and water-resistant binder created from a mix of tar, oil, and creosote mixed. Named for British chemist John London McAdam, the substance dates to 1824 and has since evolved into a formulation that recycles crushed glass into roadways, playgrounds, taxiways, and landing strips. According to Nettie's letter to Celie in Alice Walker's *The Color Purple,* the Olinka villagers anticipate that a tarmac road is being built to improve their lives rather than to disrupt and uproot them by destroying their homes and their sense of place.

taro (*tahr'* oh) *See* cocoyam.

tarp *See* tarpaulin.

tar paper or **tar-paper** a heavy paper coated or soaked in tar and used to waterproof a roof or the outside walls of a residence, outbuilding, or shed. Devised in the 1890s as a cheap form of covering plank buildings to keep out wind and weather, tar paper developed into a pejorative term for the residences of people too poor to afford shingles, siding, brick, or stone. As gale-force winds buffet Janie and Tea Cake in Zora Neale Hurston's *Their Eyes Were Watching God,* Janie seeks a cover to protect Tea Cake and grabs a piece of tar paper that flies by and threatens to carry her away. A similar building material covers internment camps such as Manzanar, the setting of Jeanne Wakatsuki Houston and James D. Houston's autobiographical *Farewell to Manzanar.*

tarpaulin (tahr . *poh'* luhn or *tahr'* poh . luhn) or **tarp** canvas or sheeting weatherproofed with tar and used to make canopies and awnings and to protect haystacks, piles of firewood, unfinished buildings, or construction materials left out in the weather. Entering English in the early seventeenth century, the term is a hybrid of *tar* and the Latin for *covering.* In "The Custom House," the introduction to Nathaniel Hawthorne's *The Scarlet Letter,* the speaker refers to the sea-going lumber traders themselves as tarpaulins, perhaps because their clothing is made of tarp cloth. *See also* sou'wester.

tarrapin *See* terrapin.

TAT or **Thematic Apperception Test** a form of subjective analysis of cognitive processes accomplished by interpreting the test-taker's projective response to a series of black-and-white pictures about common subjects, some more structured or more ambiguous than others. Devised by psychologist H. A. Murray and others in 1935 and generally administered in two one-hour sessions, the test reveals imaginative themes based on the subject's prior experiences. In Daniel Keyes's *Flowers for Algernon,* Charlie Gordon demonstrates his naiveté and simple thinking processes by making up stories about the people in the pictures that form the TAT.

tatami (tuh . *tah'* mee) **mats** *pl.* **tatami** or **tatamis** a traditional rectangular mat or area rug woven of straw or rushes that is so much a part of Japanese life that it serves as a unit of measure—1.83 by 0.91 meters or 1.66 square meters. The term entered English in the early seventeenth century. In Jeanne Wakatsuki Houston and James D. Houston's *Farewell to Manzanar,* Jeanne agrees to take odori lessons from an elderly geisha who keeps traditional Japanese quarters, with floors covered by tatami mats.

tattoo (tat . *too'*) or **tap-too** a nervous, rhythmic beat, tapping, or a military cadence used as a signal, alarm, call to arms or attention, or a pace-setter for marching or drill. Derived from the Dutch for *close the barrel tap,* it entered English in the mid-seventeenth century, a hundred years before the Polynesian *tattoo,* the practice of piercing or marking the skin with designs or symbols. As the title character exercises his horse on Boston Commons in Esther Forbes's *Johnny Tremain,* a somber tattoo precedes the execution of Pumpkin, a deserter from the Redcoat army.

taw southern slang for a large decorative marble used as a shooter in a game of marbles; a tor, alley-tor, or tolley—the British equivalent that blends *taw* with *alley,* the game enclosure where skittles were played. Of unknown origin, the term entered English in the early eighteenth century, when children placed marbles on the edge of a circle and shot at them with a taw to knock them out of the ring. The resulting game was named *ringtaw.* Tom bribes Jim into whitewashing a fence by giving him a white alley taw and showing him a sore toe, an irresistible sight in Mark Twain's *The Adventures of Tom Sawyer. See also* skittle alley.

taxi tips a term dating to the 1920s naming the money earned by a professional female dancer or escort who worked for a set fee in a nightclub, juke joint, roadhouse, dance hall, cabaret, or cafe as a paid partner or taxi dancer. After collecting tickets for each dance, the taxi dancer accepted cash or tips for herself alone or split the money in a prior arrangement with the house manager or other dancers. In Sandra Cisneros's *The House on Mango Street,* while they skip two revolving ropes simultaneously in a game of double dutch, children chant a rhyme about a waitress earning taxi tips without realizing how deeply "double dutch" compromises the lives of Hispanic women in the ghetto.

tea caddy or **tea catty** or **tea-box** a small covered box, chest, or can similar to a tobacco humidor that holds loose tea leaves in an airtight enclosure. Derived from the *kati,* a Malaysian weight equal to 600 grams or one and a third pounds, the term suggests the blocks or bricks of compressed tea that were sold by weight in the late sixteenth century. In Esther Forbes's *Johnny Tremain,* Mr. Lyte orders silver spoons and a tea caddy from Lapham's silver shop and intends to order a silver tankard if the first objects please him.

teahouse a traditional refreshment and conversation center, wayside inn, or public house in Japan or

China that sells tea and light snacks and features Asian decor and music. In Pearl S. Buck's *The Good Earth,* Wang Lung meets Lotus in a teahouse. In a description in Amy Tan's *The Joy Luck Club,* Wu Tsing's second wife had been a singer, instrumentalist, and charming escort, or paid entertainer, in a respectable teahouse. *See also* geisha.

teamster a wagoneer, hauler, or driver of a freight wagon that was often pulled by teams of mules or oxen; also, a mule skinner or muleteer, a common figure on the western frontier who took charge of harnesses, animal care, and fodder on long hauls, especially across the desert. In her ironic voice, Mattie Ross, protagonist of Charles Portis's *True Grit,* fears that the greedy landlady at the boarding house may have rented out half of Mattie's bed to a teamster or railroad detective.

tea-time a traditional afternoon refreshment, reception, or light meal in Great Britain and countries such as Bermuda, Jamaica, India, Pakistan, and New Zealand, which once made up the British Empire. Whether served in a tea room, residence, or social hall, the tea is accompanied by sugar, milk, or lemon and a selection of open-faced sandwiches, slices of cake, scones, crackers, cookies, and other pastries. In Lewis Carroll's *Alice's Adventures in Wonderland,* the Mad Hatter declares that it is always six o'clock or tea-time in Wonderland.

tefillin (tee . *fihl'* luhn) *sing. and pl.* the leathery boxes or amulets containing quotes from Hebrew scripture. Devout Jews wear tefillin on the wrist, forehead, and middle fingers as outward evidence of piety and obedience to God's law. Derived in the early seventeenth century, the term is Aramaic for attachments. Before prayers in Chaim Potok's *The Chosen,* Reuven, a devout Jew, takes prayer book and tefillin from the drawer, binds the tefillin on his head and wrist, and prays for the safety of soldiers on the beaches. *See also* phylactery.

tejano (tak . *zah'* noh or tay . *yah'* no) the Spanish term for an Hispanic settler or native of Texas. In Rudolfo Anaya's *Bless Me, Ultima,* Antonio's father loves the freedom of the open plains even after the big ranchers and *tejanos* stake claims and put up fences.

telepathy (tuh . *leh'* puh . thee) a wordless, gestureless communication of thoughts, visual images, emotions, or information by extrasensory connection of brain waves or other supernatural means that supersedes the laws of science; an unexplained system of thought transfer. Named in 1882, the word is a hybrid Greek term for *distant feeling.* To the captain's comment about a Martian's ability to speak English in Ray Bradbury's *The Martian Chronicles,* the Tyrrian woman replies that she uses telepathy to translate their conversation.

temperance revival a religious service that reviles alcohol, condemns drinkers, and maneuvers former tipplers and derelicts to "take the pledge" to abstain for life from strong drink. A melodramatic moment for the audience, especially family members, the signing of the pledge was greeted with hallelujahs, praise to God, hymn singing, and embraces from loved ones. One of the King's methods of raising money in Mark Twain's *The Adventures of Tom Sawyer,* the temperance revival is a significant part of the pseudo-religious lore from the late nineteenth and early twentieth centuries.

Temple *See* Inns of Court.

tempura (*tehm'* poo . ruh) a style of Japanese cooking that centers on dipping whitefish, prawns, shellfish, or vegetables in a light corn starch batter and frying them on a portable hibachi or grill near or at the table in view of customers or guests. Tempura servings are eaten hot, often as an appetizer or a light refreshment served at a reception or buffet. Derived from the Portuguese pidgin for *seasoning,* the term entered English from early nineteenth-century Japan, where foreign sailor's terms named local customs. In her autobiographical *I Know Why the Caged Bird Sings,* Maya Angelou recalls that the odors of raw fish and tempura from Japanese businesses give place to shops and restaurants owned by black businessmen after Japanese-Americans are interned during the early months of World War II.

tenderloin the thin strip of succulent meat or muscle tissue near the short ribs and alongside the backbone of a pig, cow, deer, or other animal served as food; a fillet steak or roast of sirloin, the choicest part of beef. After prying loose the tenderloin from a haunch of a deer in Gary Paulsen's *Dogsong,* Russel tosses the rest of the carcass to the dogs and begins cooking his meal.

tenement (*teh'* nuh . muhnt) a decrepit, overcrowded high-rise apartment house, low-rent housing, or a rickety government project, usually associated with absentee landlords who lease substandard, unsafe, or unsanitary quarters to poor ghetto dwellers, who are often the victims of public apathy, race or religious prejudice, arson, drug dealers, and gangsters. After moving from the cabin in the country, Richard Wright tells of life and vice on the streets near his family's apartment in a Memphis tenement in the autobiographical *Black Boy.*

tenon (*tehn'* uhn) *See* mortice.

tenter (*tehn'* tuhr) **hooks** derived from the Latin for *stretch,* the nails, hooks, or pegs on a drying frame or tenter over which cloth or table or bed linen is stretched to maintain its shape and prevent shrinkage or where skins or pelts are scraped and stretched during drying, curing, and glazing. In Charles Dickens's *Oliver Twist,* Mr. Bumble feels that he is "on tenter-hooks"—compromised, anxious, stressed, and tormented.

tepee or **teepee** or **tipi** a tall, conical tent or portable shelter about 15 feet in diameter, formed of lengths of hide pegged to the ground around a central lodge pole and three supporting poles that stand far enough apart to allow smoke to exit. Facing east, the entrance, a loose flap of hide secured by a lacing pin or thongs, is the main opening. In summer, the tepee walls can be rolled up to increase air flow. To hold in warmth during the winter, skins cover the ground and a dew cloth serves as an inner wall. In John Neihardt's *Black Elk Speaks,* a sacred woman commands that the people prepare a large tepee for her, where she appears to them and offers spiritual assurance.

terminus (*tuhr'* mih . nuhs) the end of the line or final depot of a train, bus, trolley, or airline; an extreme boundary or stopping place on a regular route for a transportation system or service vehicles, such as milk trucks or newspaper carriers. An early seventeenth-century term, it derives from the Latin for *boundary* or *the god of boundaries.* Dr. Sasaki takes a train to its terminus, then a streetcar to his job at the hospital, where he is inundated with victims of the atomic blast in John Hersey's *Hiroshima.*

tern (tuhrn) a family of slender migratory seabirds marked by a forked tail, long sweeping wings, webbed feet, a sharp raspy cry, and a pointed black bill with which they capture or dig into their prey, usually fish. Breeding on the Arctic tundra, the tern is a significant figure to the title character in Jean Craighead George's *Julie of the Wolves.* Contemplating the cruelty of the sea, Santiago, title figure in Ernest Hemingway's *The Old Man and the Sea,* concludes that terns and other fine, light-winged sea birds spend their lives searching the sea for food.

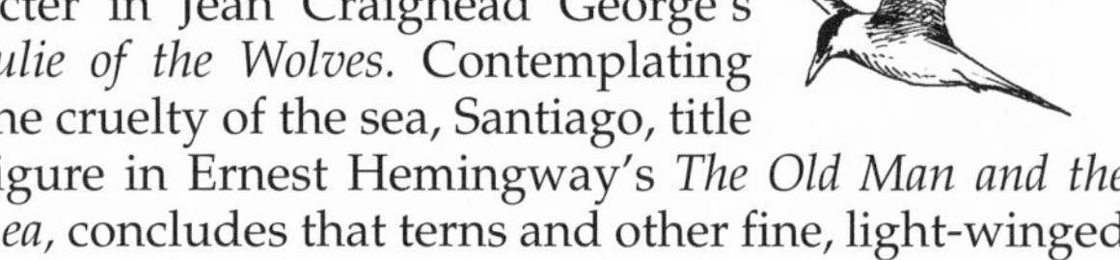

terrapin (*tehr'* ruh . p'n) or **tarrapin** a small turtle found in brackish and fresh waters along the east coast of the United States. Native Americans ate both eggs and meat and used the shell to make ritual rattles, serving dishes, and utensils. In Conrad Richter's *The Light in the Forest,* at a climactic point in True Son's illness, he relives his tribe's enjoyment of the sweet meat of rockfish and terrapin and the fragrant smoke of red willow in their pipes when he realizes that, to his Lenni Lenape family, he is dead.

tester the canopy over a four-poster bed, often crocheted or netted from yarn that ends in knotted tassels or made of thin muslin. Entering English in the fourteenth century, the term, which derives from the Latin for *shell,* may refer to a valance over an enveloping set of bed curtains. While looking up into the dimity tester, the title character in Thomas Hardy's *Tess of the D'Urbervilles* discovers a sprig of mistletoe, which Angel had carefully packed and transported. *See also* netting.

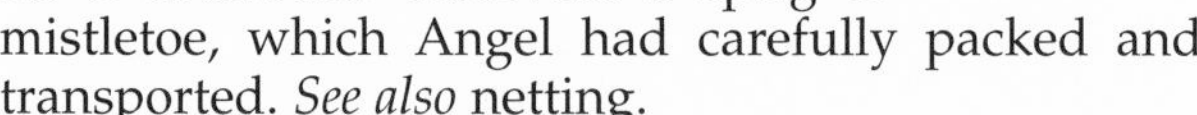

tête-à-tête (*teht'* ah . *teht*) two people sitting face-to-face in close, intimate conversation; a confidential interview or sharing of private information. From the French for *head-to-head,* the term dates to the late seventeenth century, one of many that entered English after the Royalists returned to England from exile in France during the Puritan-run Commonwealth (1649–1660). In his brusque, authoritative manner, Edward Rochester, employer of the title character in Charlotte Brontë's *Jane Eyre,* declares that he could not tolerate spending an evening *tête-à-tête* with a brat like Adèle Varens.

Teutonic (tew . *tahn'* ihk) *See* Saxon.

texas an upper deck above both the boiler deck and main deck on a steamboat; the hurricane deck. The area was restricted to pilots; hence it came to be associated with the similarly independent territory of Texas, which was a republic from 1836 until its annexation in 1845. In Mark Twain's *Life on the Mississippi,* the texas sports ornate railings as part of the upper decoration of a steamboat. *See also* gingerbread.

Texas Ranger a law enforcement officer belonging to the oldest state police in the United States. Organized and named by Stephen F. Austin in 1823 to ward off hostile Indians, the Rangers developed into a mounted frontier militia during the rowdy settlement rush following the Civil War and remained a separate entity until 1935. Rooster Cogburn degrades and ridicules LeBoeuf, a conceited Texas Ranger who carries a Sharps rifle and rides a small, sturdy range horse in Charles Portis's *True Grit.*

thane (thayn) an attendant, client, follower, freeman, or retainer of a lord; also, a feudal baron pledged to support the king. Derived from the Anglo-Saxon for *warrior,* the term entered English during the feudal era, when liegemen, who ranked below nobles, lived and worked in service to the lord of the manor, to whom they declared fealty. Hrothgar's thanes spread rumors of sightings of the title character in John Gardner's *Grendel.*

thatch a woven roof composed of rushes, plant stalks, coarse grass, reeds, straw, palm fronds, or other natural materials, common in the Middle Ages. The term derives from the Anglo-Saxon for *roof.* While searching for gold in thatch and mattresses in George Eliot's *Silas Marner,* Dunstan Cass spies a loose brick in the title character's hearth and locates a hoard of gold. *See also* rush.

theremin (*thehr'* uh . mihn) an electronic music box popular in the 1920s that was created by Russian inventor Leon Theremin from two high-frequency antennae, electrodes, or oscillators. While controlling a sound volume with one hand, the instrumentalist passes the other hand around or near a raised rod to raise or lower the pitch in an eerie tremulo, often used as the background of thriller movies. Captain Beatty, the cynical tyrant in Ray Bradbury's *Fahrenheit 451,* asks to be stung with the sound of a theremin if he is unable to respond to a play or other entertainment.

Third Reich *See* holocaust; Nazi; SS.

thistle a large family of tall, wild annual or biennial plants that serves Scotland as a national emblem; the term is of unknown derivation. Thistle produces prickly leaves and ends in a characteristic puff of red, yellow, violet, or rose spines compacted like a pin cushion. One of the most beneficial to herbalists is milk thistle, which improves lactation and drains impurities from the liver. Thistle greens are cooked as vegetables or served raw in salads. In Lewis Carroll's *Alice's Adventures in Wonderland,* during a period when the title character is very small, she ducks behind a thistle to escape a playful puppy, which is large enough to endanger her.

thole (thohl) **pin** or **thowels** a vertical wooden pin bound or pegged to a gunwale to which an oar attaches through a bracket or leather or hemp lashings; also, a double set of thole pins forming a cradle, fulcrum, or frame similar to an oarlock. The term derives from the Norse for *fir tree.* In Charles Dickens's *Great Expectations,* Pip is concerned for the noise made by the oars rotating against the thowels. In an American usage, as he sets out on his morning fishing expedition, Santiago, the title character in Ernest Hemingway's *The Old Man and the Sea,* attaches lashings to the thole pins to anchor the oars into place and begins rowing away from Cuba. *See also* oarlocks.

thong a rawhide or leather strip used by Native Americans as a cord, tie, lacing, or string to serve as a rein, lash, or cording for a quirt. Also, the thong secures headpieces, bandoleros, pouches, chaps, sandals, or leggings. Derived from the German for *tie,* the word entered English in the mid-seventeenth century. In Conrad Richter's *The Light in the Forest,* Half Arrow and True Son follow Indian tradition by floating to the trader's dock behind a log, cutting the thong that holds the trader's canoe, and continuing down river on the far side, behind the stolen canoe and out of the trader's sight.

thowel *See* thole pin.

thrall (thrahl) a servant, runner, attendant, serf, bondman, captive, or slave who is part of the spoils of war. From the late Middle Ages, the term is of German derivation. In the absence of Odysseus in Homer's *Odyssey,* Telemachus describes the stress on his father's house and realm by naming a brief catalog of suitors, their thralls, a herald, and a musician, all of whom look to Penelope and her staff for their board and lodging until the matter of a new king is decided. *See also* serf.

three gilt balls dating from the Middle Ages, when tradesmen, entertainers, barkeeps, and other professionals used concrete symbols to express the purpose of their businesses to illiterate clients, the three gilt balls on a bracket or painted on the sign of a shop or office indicated a loan office or pawn shop. After traveling on the underground, Sherlock Holmes and Dr. Watson, investigators in Sir Arthur Conan

Doyle's "The Red-Headed League," locate three gilt balls and a brown sign naming the business run by Jabez Wilson.

thrush one of 300 varieties of a stout-bodied migratory songbird with brownish speckled coat. The thrush or throstle feeds on insects and fruit and sings its loud repeated notes from woods and meadows. The term dates from before the twelfth century. A symbol of freedom and natural beauty, the thrush that lights near Julia and Winston delights them with its flutelike trill on their first outing from the tyrannical Oceania in George Orwell's *1984.*

thuggee (*tuhg'* gee) a member of a fraternal gang of Muslim or Hindu cutthroats who ravaged India from the mid-fifteenth century over a period of 300 years and took as their patron Kali, the Hindu goddess of death. The British determined to stamp out these outlaws, and during the 1830s, Sir William Sleelman succeeded in capturing more than 3,250 of the ritual brotherhood, who were either hanged, imprisoned, or transported to English colonies. The trademark of the thuggee was a quick strangulation with a ceremonial handkerchief, leaving no trace of blood. Derived from the Sanskrit for *sneak thief,* the term is the parent of the English *thug,* which applies to a less organized type of villain. In Jules Verne's *Around the World in Eighty Days,* Passepartout travels by steam train over a part of India where the thuggees once killed and robbed with abandon.

thunderbox or **thunder mug** a coarse slang expression for a private commode or indoor toilet consisting of a removable chamber pot concealed in a box and covered by an ornate lid. Ruth Prawer Jhabvala's *Heat and Dust* describes the impasse between the British colonial government and local citizens, when a girl requests a license to turn a palace into a tourist hotel so guests wouldn't be subjected to a thunderbox. *See also* slop jar.

thunderheads a mid-nineteenth-century term for a swollen upper mass of cumulonimbus clouds predicting a thunder storm. With stereotypical black hair, Captain Beatty, a main character in Ray Bradbury's *Fahrenheit 451,* rises in thunderheads of tobacco smoke, suggesting a Satanic figure wreathed in evil. *See also* cirrus.

thurible (*thoor'* ih . b'l) *See* censer.

thwart an early eighteenth-century term for a brace, bench, or rower's seat across a rowboat, punt, jolly boat, or canoe and fitted into the ribs that stabilize the sides. As True Son and Half Arrow paddle the stolen canoe toward familiar country in Conrad Richter's *The Light in the Forest,* the rifle lies across the thwart.

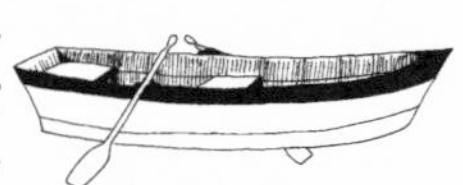

tic (tihk) an early nineteenth-century Italian term applied to an involuntary neural twitch, quiver, contraction, idiosyncratic speech pattern, or spasm of the limbs or face that appears to be involuntary and often brought on by advanced age, anxiety, or stress. While trying to comply with the Destroyer in John Gardner's *Grendel,* Ork develops a tic alongside his mouth as he frames answers to questions about the King of Gods.

tick or **ticking** or **bedtick** the strong, tightly woven linen or cotton upholstery fabric that forms a cover or casing for a pillow or mattress that holds feathers, foam rubber, shucks, straw, or other filler. Derived from the Greek for *receptacle,* the term entered English in the mid-seventeenth century. Before setting out personal items in the bunk house in John Steinbeck's *Of Mice and Men,* George lifts the tick to inspect it; Lennie mimics his actions.

tiddlywinks (*tihd'* dlee . *wihnks*) a nineteenth-century child's game involving thin colored disks of wood or plastic that players flip by pressing one against the other. The purpose of this game of skill and control is to snap or flip a maximum number of the "little winks" from a flat surface into a cup. In the mental and spiritual breakdown that consumes Winston Smith in the final scene of George Orwell's *1984,* he dreams of happy times with his sister in their childhood when they played snakes and ladders and tiddlywinks.

tie wig or **tye wig** an informal full-scalp wig for men in eighteenth-century Europe and America, used for sport, travel, and work and powdered with gray or white. For ease of movement, wearers tied the bottom half of the shoulder-length tresses with a black bow. The strands hanging at the neckline were called a cue, or cue-peruke in England and a *queue* in France. Dressed in a smart white tie wig, Merchant Jonathan Lyte, a villain in Esther Forbes's *Johnny Tremain,* sits in his red leather chair during business hours. *See also* periwig.

tiller a forerunner of the steering wheel, the horizontal wood or metal lever or helm that extends from a rudder or steering oar by which the steersman on a sailing vessel directs the ship. Derived from the Latin for *weaver's beam* or *web,* the term entered English in the Middle

Ages. In a climactic moment in Robert Louis Stevenson's *Treasure Island,* Jim Hawkins lets go of the tiller, which strikes Israel Hands and deflects him long enough for Jim to take aim at him with a pistol.

timothy or **june grass** a meadow grass with a tightly compacted seed head or cattail. Timothy is grown in damp soil for forage, grazing, open grassland, or winter feed for stock. Named for developer Timothy Hanson, who introduced the grass to the Carolinas in 1720, the plant now thrives in pastures as a staple ground cover and forage. After Ira subjects his dog Hussy to a vicious weasel in Robert Newton Peck's *A Day No Pigs Would Die,* Rob buries her remains under sweet timothy and speaks a word of farewell.

tin a container in which perishable food or juice is preserved; a metal can or pannikin. The term derives from the Norse for the metal tin. In Sir Arthur Conan Doyle's *The Hound of the Baskervilles,* Sherlock Holmes finds blankets and tins of tongue to be evidence of habitation in a deserted hut. *See also* pannikin.

tincture (*tingk'* chuhr or *tingk'* shuhr) derived from the Latin for *tint,* a preservative for spices, herbs, or other healing or invigorating tonics, such as tincture of cardamum, which was kept in a vial of brandy or grain alcohol to ward off spoilage or loss of flavor; also, a medical solution of alcohol and a healing or antibacterial substance, such as tincture of iodine. In a slick maneuver to get Rome's dictator to the Senate on the Ides of March in William Shakespeare's *Julius Caesar,* Decius interprets Calpurnia's fearful dream of Caesar's statue spouting blood from a cloyingly patriotic point of view: the blood is a symbol of the healing tincture of Caesar's spirit that serves as a tonic to all citizens.

tinderbox a metal box containing the necessities for making fire, a common household item before the invention of matches in 1827. The box protected dry tinder, such as straw, rotted heartwood, or charred linen, which was easily ignited by a spark struck from steel against flint. Smoldering linen scraps maintained the spark until other combustibles could be used to arouse a blaze. An insignificant clue in the solution of a robbery in George Eliot's *Silas Marner,* the tinderbox leads authorities no closer to recovering the money stolen from the clay pot on Silas's hearth. *See also* flint.

tinker a Middle English term for an itinerant pot and kettle seller who also mends cheap metal household utensils by applying solder, a tin alloy from which the term derives. Also, a metalsmith or jack-of-all-trades who is known for claiming an inordinate amount of expertise. While knaves tease Christopher Sly into believing that he is a gentleman in William Shakespeare's *The Taming of the Shrew,* Sly claims to be a bearherd and tinker and cites a corroborating witness to his trade. *See also* solder.

tin lantern *See* rush-light.

tintype (*tihn'* typ) a photograph taken from an exposed thin plate of tin or iron, a mid-nineteenth century method of photography derived from the daguerreotype. Also referred to as melainotype, ambrotype, stannotype, or ferrotype, the tintype was made by the wet collodion process that used a highly flammable mix of ether, alcohol, and pyroxylin as a fixative. When Jim Burden visits Antonia after her marriage in Willa Cather's *My Antonia,* he brings a bag of candy for the children and a tintype of himself with Rudolph, her son.

tipi *See* tepee.

tippet (*tihp'* piht) a streamer attached to a hood, cape, upper sleeve, or elbow of a robe, gown, minister's robe, or tunic; also, a fur or fur-lined or fur-edged shoulder cape worn around the neck and just reaching the edge of the shoulder on a woman's gown or a ranking prelate's robe. Derived from the Greek for *rug,* the term entered English in the fourteenth century. Gandalf the wizard in J. R. R. Tolkien's *The Hobbit* urges Bilbo Baggins not to mention fur, pelt, tippet, or muff in the presence of Beorn the skin-changer.

tiring house dating to the Middle Ages, an obsolete theater term for an attiring room; a dressing room for actors, musicians, mummers, or entertainers and a place where costumes, masks, and makeup are stored. While the working men practice "Pyramus and Thisbe" in William Shakespeare's *A Midsummer Night's Dream,* they use the green for a stage and a hawthorn thicket for a tiring house.

Titan (*ty'* t'n) one of the twelve children of Gaea and Uranus, gods of earth and heaven. After deposing their father, the six sons and six daughters chose Kronos, the sun god, as their leader. The myth repeats its theme of treachery and rebellion after Kronos's son Zeus replaces his father and establishes the

Olympian gods, the most familiar in Western literature. As described in Edith Hamilton's *Mythology,* the Titans were the gods of the universe during the least civilized era of Greek literature.

ti-ti (*ty'* ty or *tee'* tee) or **leatherwood** an evergreen shrub common to swamps and moist ground producing ornamental racemes covered in white blossoms, yellow drupes or fruit, and thick leaves. An early nineteenth-century term of unknown origin, it appears to derive from an Indian name. In Marjorie Kinnan Rawlings's *The Yearling,* Jody observes his mother using natural substances in her housecleaning—ti-ti for sweeping and corn husks for scrubbing.

title an honorarium or prestigious rank, often accompanied by power, an annual stipend, a residence, and land. *See also* baron; baronet; earl; thane.

T-maze a psychological puzzle requiring a laboratory animal to reach the upper end of a T and select the more pleasing of two stimuli, one on either bar of the T; also, a similar study of the subject's choice of the less painful of two stimuli in a T-maze. In Daniel Keyes's *Flowers for Algernon,* the mouse and Charlie Gordon race mazes together—with Algernon running the alleys of a T-maze and Charlie replicating the maneuver in a pencil-and-paper version.

tocsin (*tahk'* s'n) an alarm bell, omen, dread sign, or prearranged warning signal, usually auditory. Derived from the French for *stroke of the bell,* the term entered English in the late sixteenth century. As the impetus to rebellion begins to rise in Charles Dickens's *A Tale of Two Cities,* Mr. Gabelle considers the need to raise a tocsin by summoning the sacristan to unlock the church and ring the bell.

tofu (*toh'* foo) a smooth, white soy bean curd; a staple in Oriental cooking because of its availability, digestibility, high protein content, and adaptability to numerous recipes, including soups, stir fry, main dishes, and salads. Derived from the Chinese for *turning sour,* the term entered English in the late eighteenth century. After weeks of eating from hotel garbage cans, Ko and her sister relish tofu in Yoko Wakatsuki Watkins's autobiographical *So Far from the Bamboo Grove.*

toga a national garment for male citizens in Republican Rome, the toga was worn atop underwear or a tunic in cold weather and served as a designation of rank and age. Formed of a rounded piece of linen or wool between 15 and 18 feet long, the toga draped the figure in a loose, but dramatic manner and was usually unbelted and fastened at the shoulder with a brooch. Because of its great length, the free end of the toga could serve as a head covering, cloak, disguise, or shield from the sun or rain or could be left hanging over one arm. When edged in purple, the toga denoted magistrates or dignitaries, during ceremonies or patriotic duties, speeches, or attendance at public sacrifices. Because of its unusual number of folds and wrapping of the torso, the toga determined the gait and demeanor of a gentleman, who could neither run, fight, nor make other ungainly motions while swathed in its voluminous folds. In Moss Hart and George S. Kaufman's *You Can't Take It with You,* Penny paints a family guest as a discus thrower by posing him in a classic toga.

toggle point the crosspin or jutting snell on a finely honed bone, flaked stone, or iron hook, which is sometimes dabbed with poison and attached to a leister or harpoon by a length of rope or hide as a means of snaring a fish and locking the hook into place while the fisher reels in the catch. In Gary Paulsen's *Dogsong,* Oogruk insists that his lance and toggle point should be used for hunting and not placed in a museum. *See also* barb; harpoon.

toilet or **toilette** a full complement of personal care for men or women, including washing, shaving, applying makeup, dressing and arranging the hair, selecting garments and jewelry, and completing a total look before entering a dining room for meals, greeting callers, or going out in public. Jules Verne stresses in *Around the World in Eighty Days* that, out of a full day in Phileas Fogg's life, he spends only ten hours at his residence in sleeping and completing his toilet. In Tennessee Williams's *A Streetcar Named Desire,* Blanche's constant attention to a full toilette annoys Stanley, who considers her self-absorption a form of manipulating Stella and indulging herself at the family's expense.

toluache (*toh* . loo . *ah'* chay) or **toloache** a weed producing a ceremonial trance or vision during which Pacific Coast Indians contact the spirit world, initiate youths into a tribe, or divine the future by consuming boiled lavender blossoms, seeds, or roots of jimson—a narcotic of the poisonous nightshade family. Karana, the central character in Scott O'Dell's *Island of the Blue Dolphins,* uses toluache weed in a nearby spring as a means of subduing wild dogs.

tomahawk (*tah'* muh . hawk) a multipurpose ax, club, tool, or weapon made by attaching a short wood, ivory, or bone handle to a stone, metal, obsidian, or shell blade; a more complex version of the tool served a double purpose as tomahawk and peace pipe. Derived from the Algonquin *tomahack,* the term entered English in the early seventeenth century, when Europeans first came in contact with forest Indians. In Conrad Richter's *The Light in the Forest,* True Son, a defensive Lenni Lenape speaking through Del, his translator, insists that the English language uses Delaware terms, in particular, *tomahawk, wigwam,* and *Susquehanna.*

tombola (*tahm'* boh . luh) a game of chance similar to bingo in which players await the drawing of numbered tickets or stubs at random from a rotating drum and mark those that correspond to a set of numbers on the player's card. Derived from the Italian for *tumble,* the term entered English in the late nineteenth century. Before her life turns to nightmare in Zlata Filipovich's autobiographical *Zlata's Diary,* she enjoys a birthday party with a quiz, a game of tombola, and a butterfly cake.

tommy gun a slang name for the Thompson machine gun, a .45 caliber submachine gun named for John Taliaferro Thompson, World War I veteran and ordnance specialist who invented the clip-loaded weapon in the 1920s. Because of its use by law enforcement officers and criminals during the gangster era, the tommy gun has become a standard weapon in works describing the Mafia, crime, and the FBI. During the march that separates Chlomo Wiesel and his son forever from Mrs. Wiesel and her youngest daughter in Elie Wiesel's *Night,* guards holding tommy guns order men in one direction and women in the other.

tomographic scan (*toh* . moh . *graf'* ihk) a form of selective X ray that allows study of tissue on a particular plane or axis. More familiarly known as CAT, or CT, for computerized axial tomography, the procedure has become a common method of studying a cross section of the body. Derived from the Greek for *section drawing,* the term entered English in 1935. In John Hersey's *Hiroshima,* Dr. Sasaki comes close to death after voluntarily trying out the tomographic scanning equipment during a training session and awakening from anesthesia with his cancerous left lung removed.

tongue of Pentecost *See* Pentecost.

topee or **topi** (*toh'* pee) a lightweight, vented tan or white helmet sloping down from the pith or cork crown and marked with a simple band. Developed by the military in the 1830s to protect Europeans serving in India and derived from the Hindi for *sun hat,* the term delineates standard wear for British colonial officials in the tropics, where African or Asian sun and heat taxed their ability to adapt to climate and to the pressures of ruling a foreign country. Hugh Conway, protagonist of James Hilton's *Lost Horizon,* distances himself from the red-faced English colonial in a topee.

top-hat a men's hat fashionable from 1820 until well into the twentieth century, the top hat, or topper, remained in vogue through various changes, beginning with the fawn or gray color of its beaver pelt and developing to polished black silk, thin brim, and collapsible crown that was elevated by a lever releasing an internal spring. By sizing up a top-hat, Albert chain, frock coat, and vest, Sherlock Holmes, detective in Sir Arthur Conan Doyle's "The Red-Headed League," deduces much about the past of client Jabez Wilson. *See also* Albert chain; frock coat.

tops'l or **topsail** (*tahp'* s'l) a fourteenth-century term for the second sail on a mast or one of a pair of topsails on a square-sailed vessel. During a crucial moment in the stowaway's story in Joseph Conrad's "The Secret Sharer," the topsail blows away, leaving the skipper in a terrified state and incapable of comprehending or dealing sensibly with a crew member's murder.

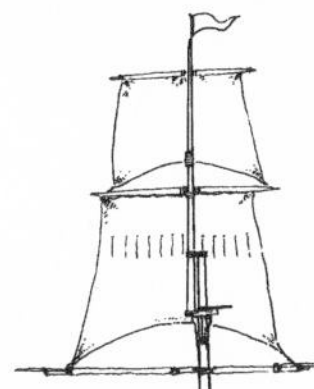

tor a jagged, rocky cliff, crag, peak, or outcropping. Derived from the Celtic for *hill,* this pre-twelfth-century term applies specifically to hills that bulge at the top or that are crested by rock piles. On the way to Baskerville Hall in Sir Arthur Conan Doyle's *The Hound of the Baskervilles,* Sherlock Holmes enters a moor marked by ominous tors and cairns.

Torah (*toh'* ruh) the Hebrew name for the Jewish scripture, handwritten on a scroll and read on the Jewish Sabbath and holy days. Preserved on ritual parchment, the text consists of the laws of Moses, prophecy, and writings detailing the history of the Hebrew people. The Torah, which is the focal point of Jewish life and study, remains stored beneath an eternal flame in a sacred niche or closet called the ark until it is removed and blessed before its presentation to worshipers. Elie Wiesel, in his autobiography *Night*, describes his youth, when he studied Torah and cabbalah and wept during his prayers. In Margaret Atwood's *The Handmaid's Tale*, set in the fundamentalist city of Gilead, Jews are murdered for openly displaying the Torah and tefillin. *See also* tefellin.

tortoiseshell *See* hawk-bill.

tosspot a sot, regular tippler, public drunk or nuisance, or noisy or quarrelsome frequenter of pubs; a derelict or ne'er-do-well. Derived from the hasty swallowing of a tankard of strong drink, the term entered English in the mid-sixteenth century. In Thomas Hardy's *The Mayor of Casterbridge*, Elizabeth-Jane contrasts the levity of local tosspots to the seriousness of purpose in Donald Farfrae, an immigrant Scot who is elected mayor.

totem (*toh'* tuhm) the Chippewa term for a marker common to animistic peoples; a tribal, clan, or family insignia, burial urn, or genealogy formed of stylized animal shapes and symbolizing a patriarch or founder and the qualities of his offspring, particularly military heroes and guardian spirits. Also, a symbol of ancestry, important events in the growth and development of a clan, or possession of tribal lands. In James Fenimore Cooper's *The Last of the Mohicans*, Uncas identifies with fellow male clan members who bear a common totem—a turtle tattoo on the chest.

touché (too . *shay'*) a sporting acknowledgement of a point scored when a fencer strikes an opponent on the area between shoulders and waist; also, a lighthearted comment from one debater to another when the opponent's logic produces sound wisdom. While sounds of card playing and flirting fill the air in the opening scene of Edmond Rostand's *Cyrano de Bergerac*, one of a pair of fencers announces a hit by calling out "Touché," an expression foreshadowing Cyrano's entrance and his deadly game of words and swords with a meddler.

tow (toh) loose fibers from flax, hemp, or jute plants that are beaten free from the stalk with a swingel and spun into yarn for burlap or tow linen, used as stuffing for mattresses and pillows, or twisted into lighters for setting the charge in a flintlock rifle; oakum. Among Pap Finn's supplies in the deserted cabin are newspapers for wadding, liquor, a sack of meal, and some tow in a scene of Mark Twain's *The Adventures of Huckleberry Finn* that details the abusive relationship that causes Huck to fake his own murder and flee. *See also* match; oakum; swingel.

Tower, the a fortress and complex of buildings and walls that has become the key national landmark in London. As the site where William the Conqueror was crowned king and where state prisoners were imprisoned and executed, the Tower remains a focal point of British legend and history. In Charles Dickens's *A Tale of Two Cities*, Dr. Manette becomes ill after Charles Darnay tells of workmen digging in the Tower and locating an unreadable manuscript under a brick marked DIG. In Mark Twain's *The Prince and the Pauper*, London's Hereditary Great Marshall is imprisoned in the Tower for treason.

towhead an early nineteenth-century colloquial term for a shoal or deposit of gravel, debris, or sand in a stream bed; an alluvial sandbar or islet amassed from particles pushed downstream by the current and partially covered in scraggly overgrowth. After Huck flees from Judith Loftus in Mark Twain's *The Adventures of Huckleberry Finn*, he and Jim take to the raft and float 16 or 17 miles from the village to a towhead.

township a settlement, hamlet, village, or segment of a parish or manor. Also, a bounded segment or division of a large urban community named as a voting district or firefighting zone. The closer True Son comes to Paxton township in Conrad Richter's *The Light in the Forest*, the less eager he feels to rejoin the Butler family, from whom he was stolen in babyhood by forest Indians.

trace one of a pair of chains, harness straps, or leather thongs on a horse collar that attaches to the singletree, a crossbar dividing draft animal from implement or wagon. Derived from the Old French for *draft*, the term entered English in the fourteenth century, when innovations in harnesses revolutionized agriculture. In Crooks's private quarters in a farm harness room in John Steinbeck's *Of Mice and Men*, the collection of broken horse collar and hames and split leather covering over a trace suggest the type of maintenance and repair work he performs. *See also* single-tree.

tracery a medieval architectural term for ornamental stonework carved into swirls, flame shapes, or curves, often billowing across the top as a decoration of a Gothic window or walls or separating glass vertically into panes or lights. At Baskerville Hall in Sir Arthur Conan Doyle's *The Hound of the Baskervilles*, fine tracery decorating the windows

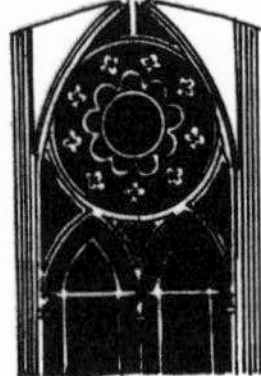

suggests a tasteful family with money to spend on expensive architectural details. *See also* mullion.

trachoma (truh . *koh'* muh) a contagious bacterial inflammation of the eyes blurring vision with a chronic accumulation of granules and thickening the conjunctiva and cornea, leading to scarring and blindness. Derived from the Greek for *rough,* the term entered English in the late seventeenth century. In William Gibson's *The Miracle Worker,* Annie Sullivan is already infected with trachoma when she arrives in Alabama to educate Helen Keller in hand spelling for the blind.

tract propaganda in the form of a pamphlet or monograph on a political or religious issue, often divisive and doctrinal in nature; also, a scholarly dissertation or treatise. Derived from the Latin for *drag,* the term entered English in the early nineteenth century. Before arriving at the witch trials in Salem, Reverend Hale, a major figure in Arthur Miller's *The Crucible,* studies the greatest minds in Europe and pores over ponderous tracts.

trademark or **trade mark** dating to 1870, an officially registered insignia, logo, label, device, symbol, word, or words written in a particular script to restrict the style of marking or advertising of a manufacturer's product, for example the scrolled letters spelling *Coca-Cola,* the alligator sewn to an Izod shirt, or the 3-M representing products of the Minnesota Mining and Manufacturing Company. To her ne'er-do-well son Biff, Linda Loman summarizes the accomplishments and downfall of her son Willy in Arthur Miller's *Death of a Salesman:* he opened new territories to an unknown trademark, then was cast off penniless in his final years as a salesman.

trades or **trade winds** the light atmospheric winds that circulate steadily over tropical waters and blow toward the northeast in the Northern Hemisphere and southeast in the Southern Hemisphere. The dependable trades result from a balance of high pressure centers in the Atlantic and Pacific oceans, the earth's rotation, and the friction of air over water. Heading for an undisclosed island that lies south-southwest in Robert Louis Stevenson's *Treasure Island,* the *Hispaniola* meets with favorable trades and makes good time.

trajectory (truh . *jehk'* trih or truh . *jehk'* toh . ree) the arc or curved path followed by a projectile as it hurtles through the atmosphere and is gradually pulled back by gravity; also, the path of a comet, or meteor. Derived from the Latin for *thrown across,* the term holds a significant place in the military, astronomy, and forensics—the study of crime that applies scientific principles to important considerations such as where a projectile originated and how far it travelled. In Erich Maria Remarque's *All Quiet on the Western Front,* soldiers listen for the whistle of shell trajectories to judge their size, speed, and destination. Captain Beatty, antagonist in Ray Bradbury's *Fahrenheit 451,* denies that the Mechanical Hound has enemies by explaining that it operates on a preset trajectory.

tram a streetcar or trolley that runs on rails and makes frequent stops for the collection and deposit of commuters in a city or urban area. Also, a motorized bus or jitney constructed like a tramcar and used to transport tourists from a large parking area to a main attraction or around the major sights of an area. Derived from the German for *beam,* the term dates to the early sixteenth century. On his return to the hospital in John Hersey's *Hiroshima,* Dr. Sasaki takes the train, then transfers to a tram that still functions despite the detonation of an atomic bomb.

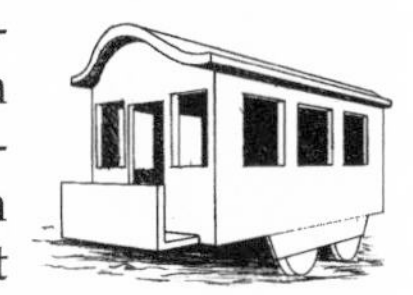

transfigure to alter the outlook, facial expression, emotional nature, or posture; to transform spiritually or emotionally, elevate or exalt, or glorify; to bring about a change of heart. Derived from the Latin for *reshape,* the term denotes an experience so electrifying that it becomes the pivotal element in a permanent change, often for the better. In John Steinbeck's *The Pearl,* Kino's neighbors recognize that good fortune has transfigured their fellow diver, changing his life forever.

transistor a small electrical unit that channels electrical current by directing it through a conductive crystal to act as a switch or to control the amount of voltage applied to the operation of an electrical device, such as a television, radio, or household appliance. Invented in 1948 at Bell Laboratories, the device enabled engineers to create smaller units or electrical housing. In a paranoid haze, the chief in Ken Kesey's *One Flew over the Cuckoo's Nest* believes that the capsules the nurses dispense are the same transistors that he recalls from military experience.

trap *See* dog-cart.

trapezius (truh . *pee'* zee . uhs) a set of large, strong triangular muscles in the top of three layers at each side of the upper back. The trapezius, which touches the cap of the shoulder and extends to the lower back of the cranium, controls the tilting and leaning motions of the head. Derived from the Greek for *a*

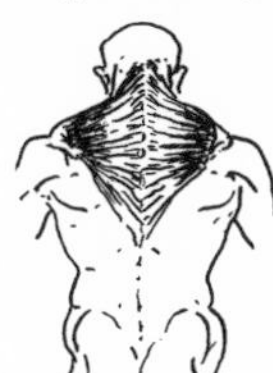

four-sided shape, the term entered English in the early eighteenth century as an important part of the study of anatomy. In minute detail, the title character in Alexandre Dumas's *The Count of Monte Cristo* declares that vengeance is not served just because a murderer has suffered death from the passage of the guillotine between his trapezius and occipital bone. *See also* occipital bone.

traps a slang term usually written in the plural and denoting portable personal goods or belongings, including weapons, baggage, clothing, wallet, watch, and other pocket items. William Portis's *True Grit* describes heroine Mattie Ross's arrival at the Fort Smith boarding house, where she collects her father's traps, which include his watch and a Colt's dragoon.

treacle (*trih'* k'l) a sweet, sticky syrup derived from raw or partially refined brown sugar; molasses. Derived from the Greek for *antidote,* the term names a medicine used to counteract poison. In a story the March Hare tells the title character in Lewis Carroll's *Alice's Adventures in Wonderland,* he makes a pun on treacle-trickle by explaining that Edith, Tillie, and Lacie live in a treacle well.

treading-yard an area in which whole stalks of grain or corn are trampled or crushed, beaten with a flail, cleaned with a swingel, or ground in a mill, then fanned or winnowed to remove the light chaff from the grain. After crawling away from the treading-yard to get out of the sun in the autobiographical *Narrative of the Life of Frederick Douglass,* the title character faces Mr. Covey, who refuses to accept an excuse of illness and beats the slave bloody. *See also* chaff; swingel; winnow.

treadle (*treh'* d'l) the foot-operated swiveling lever that is linked by belts to the crank shaft that operates moving parts. Before electrical or steam power was applied to industry, the up and down motion of the treadle powered machinery such as the needle mechanism of a sewing machine or a pump organ. An early German term for *step,* the word entered English before the twelfth century. In Kate Chopin's "The Awakening," Madame Lebrun employs a servant to pump the treadle while she sews, an arrangement that suggests the structure of a society that depends on servants for menial labor.

treadmill in nineteenth-century prisons, a revolving drum decked on the circular edge with rungs, stairsteps, or treads. As a vengeful, dehumanizing form of punishment, prisoners were forced to take turns walking up the steps, thereby turning the cylinder to no purpose except vindication of crimes or the whim of guards. In Charles Dickens's *Oliver Twist,* a prisoner is condemned to the treadmill for playing the flute.

trefoil (*tree'* foyl) a tripartite ornament, either pointed or arced, suggesting a cloverleaf or three interlocking circles or lobes; used as a decoration for windows, crests, emblems, or the tracery of windows. Derived from the Latin for *three-leafed,* the trefoil also serves in church windows, carvings, and linens as a graceful depiction of the Holy Trinity. In a flight of fantasy, Emma, the protagonist in Gustave Flaubert's *Madame Bovary,* envisions herself like a medieval lady resting on the sill of a window topped with a trefoil and watching gallant knights ride forth to pay her court. *See also* tracery.

trellis (*trehl'* lihs) a light, lacy framework or lattice of wood or metal attached to a house or building on which climbing plants, such as roses, ivy, and clematis or vegetables such as beans and cucumbers, are trained to grow upward to reach sunlight. Derived from the Latin for *bower,* the term also applies to a decorative arbor, arch, or summer house fitted with benches or seats and shaded by plants that grow over the openwork structure. The trellis in Thornton Wilder's *Our Town* serves as a stage separation between two households, yet symbolizes the ultimate union of the boy and girl who grow up in adjacent houses.

trencher a shallow wooden platter, plate, or flat board on which meat is cut or bread is sliced. A man with a hearty appetite is called a trencherman for the numbers of plates or trenchers of food he can eat. Derived from the Latin for *chop,* the term suggests the raw, unfinished inner curve of a wooden dish hewn from a piece of lumber. Caliban, Prospero's sulky servant, complains about having to fetch firewood and wash trenchers and dishes in William Shakespeare's *The Tempest.*

trench mortar a portable piece of field artillery that shoots a large explosive antipersonnel shell over a wide trajectory toward a trench or military supply dump. Because of its ease of transport, the trench mortar gains deadly accuracy by repeated adjustments to its range and aim. As Frederick Henry and his compatriots eat a meal of cheese, pasta, and wine in Ernest Hemingway's *A Farewell to Arms,* an incoming trench mortar strikes, killing and wounding by concussion or hurling fragments or shrapnel. *See also* shrapnel; trajectory.

trephine (truh . *fyn'*) to use a medical procedure that opens a path through the skull by sawing or drilling into the bone to lessen pressure, reveal a growth, remove foreign matter, or drain an abscess; also, the traditional surgical drill, derived from the Latin for *three points* and used from primitive times to bore a hole in the skull. The condition of Renfield, a raving lunatic in Bram Stoker's *Dracula,* calls for trephination to relieve intracranial swelling.

trestle (*treh'* s'l) from the Latin for *beam,* a hinged leg, sawhorse, or braced A-shaped framework that spreads to support a counter, work bench, power tools, platform, or tabletop; the bottom segment of a demountable picnic table or game board. Also, a vertical or slanting support, pylon, or brace for a bridge, railroad crossing, viaduct, high-tension wire, or masthead. In J. R. R. Tolkien's *The Hobbit,* Beorn calls for his trained dogs to set up boards and trestles and supply seating for dinner guests.

triangulate (try . *ang'* yoo . layt) to survey or measure by applying trigonometric principles based on the measurement of the legs of triangles from a calculation based on the size of each angle. By triangulating from shadows cast by objects still in position after the atomic blast in John Hersey's *Hiroshima,* analysts use the calculation methods of Pythagoras to determine that the exact center of the explosion lies under the rubble of Shima Hospital.

tribunal (try . *byoo'* n'l) a court, forum, or hall or seat of justice; a hearing, board of inquiry, or council organized to hear grievances and to address the causes of injustice. Derived from the Latin for the *magistrate's bench,* the term expands from the place to the purpose of the hearing and the judicial authority upon which rests a true, wise decision. In Susan B. Anthony's "Women's Right to Vote" speech, which she delivered numerous times in 1873 in the New York area, she calls on the logic of courts and legislative tribunals in applying constitutional rights to men as well as women.

tribute money an obligatory tax, surcharge, or tariff. Also, payment of money, privilege, or other exchange between states to assure free trade, peace, protection, or continued alliance. Derived from the Latin for *divide among tribes,* the term referred in Roman times to the safety of hostages or subject peoples captured or enslaved during war. In explaining the connection between wealth and morality in Henry David Thoreau's "Civil Disobedience," Thoreau cites the example of Christ, who asks that the citizen examine tribute money and willingly support the figure of Caesar, whose likeness was minted on the coin.

trident (*try'* d'nt) the three-pronged fishing spear; also, a general term for any three-toothed or three-tined utensil or weapon, such as the lethal fork used in gladiatorial events in a fight between gladiator and retiarius—the swordsman and the trident- and net-wielder. The term derives from the Latin for *three teeth.* In Edith Hamilton's *Mythology,* the power of Poseidon, the Greek god of the sea, or Neptune, his Roman equivalent, is symbolized by his upraised trident, which suggests the tripartite powers of Zeus, the god of heaven; Poseidon, ruler of the sea; and Hades or Dis, the god of the underworld.

trigonometry (*trih* . guh . *nah'* muh . tree) a branch of mathematics or engineering based on the ratios of the sides of triangles and the application of these ratios to measurement of angles, pieces of land, astronomical studies of celestial bodies, or other expanses of land, ocean, or space. Gene Forrester, narrator of John Knowles's *A Separate Peace,* fails a trigonometry test after spending the night with his roommate Finny on an unauthorized trip to the beach. *See also* triangulate.

trilithon (try . *lihth'* uhn or *try'* lih . thohn) or **trilith** one of three stone uprights or standing stones connected through a top groove to a crossbeam or lintel in prehistoric architecture; a post or vertical support that characterizes circular open-air temples or burial monuments built in post-and-lintel architectural style. Derived from the Greek for *three stones,* the generic term applies to many styles of ancient architecture. Awakening after a night spent at Stonehenge, the title character of Thomas Hardy's *Tess of the D'Urbervilles* surrenders to captors—waiting under trilithons—who escort her to prison for the murder of her seducer.

tripod (*try'* pahd) derived from the Greek for *three-footed,* a practical three-legged support, frame, or stand that in ancient times held a brazier, cauldron, altar, table top, wine vessel, or torch. During a state visit to Menelaus and Helen in Homer's *Odyssey,* Telemachus and his entourage present the king and queen with gold coins, a pair of tripods, and a silver basket on wheels for the queen.

trireme (*try'* reem) a Phoenician galley dating to 500 B.C. that was rowed by three vertical tiers of slaves, who extended their oars out of slots in the hull. Derived from the Latin for *three-oared,* the term, which entered English in the late sixteenth century, names a Roman transport for land soldiers. The imaginative Marlowe, a rhapsodizing storyteller in Joseph Conrad's *The Heart of Darkness,* halts his narrative to ponder the emotional impact of England on a Roman commander sent north aboard a trireme to a land of unknown customs and climate.

triumph in ancient Rome, a traditional thanksgiving and parade honoring a returning military hero with a presentation of captured vehicles, armament, siege devices, horses, women, dignitaries, royal hostages, and treasure. Derived from the Greek for *hymn to Dionysus*, the term has come to name any accomplishment, victory, or conquest. In explanation of the holiday, a Roman cobbler in William Shakespeare's *Julius Caesar* explains that the parade and festivities serve as the dictator's triumph.

troglodytic (*trah* . gluh . *dyt'* ihk) resembling a prehistoric cave dweller or primitive anthropoid race or forerunner of *Homo sapiens*. Derived from the Greek for *cave entrance,* the term entered English in the mid-sixteenth century. On first studying the shrunken form of Mr. Hyde in Robert Louis Stevenson's *The Strange Case of Dr. Jekyll and Mr. Hyde,* Mr. Utterson pities Dr. Jekyll for his connection with the perverse troglodytic figure.

troika (*troy'* kuh) derived from the Russian for *trio,* a carriage, sleigh, or sledge pulled by three horses teamed horizontally across the front with a trotter in the middle and two galloping horses on the ends. In Alexander Solzhenitsyn's *One Day in the Life of Ivan Denisovich,* Ivan ponders his wife's decision to help paint area rugs with the traditional Russian troika motif. *See also* hussar; sledge.

troller (*trohl'* luhr) a fishing boat that moves slowly over an expanse of water while fishers drag baited lines from the boat's stern and sides. The term derives from the German for *roll.* To spark enthusiasm in the apathetic men in his ward, McMurphy, the coarse, rowdy protagonist in Ken Kesey's *One Flew over the Cuckoo's Nest,* hires a troller to take them deep-sea fishing.

trot-lines cords or cables stretched over the mouth of a cove or along curved expanses of shore line and strung with vertical fishlines, an economical way to fish. The trot-line worker can pull the cable to boat level, remove fish or turtles, rebait hooks, and continue making the rounds of other trot-lines. Unlike his brother-in-law, attorney Atticus Finch in Harper Lee's *To Kill a Mockingbird,* Alexandra's unambitious husband chooses to lie in a hammock and keep tabs on his trot-lines.

trousseau (*troo'* soh) a variety of linens, jewelry, undergarments, robes, gowns, dresses, and party wear accumulated or handmade or monogrammed by an engaged woman before the wedding to serve as home accouterments or outfits suitable for receptions, dining, travel, and intimate honeymoon moments. According to gossip about Miss Love Simpson in Olive Ann Burns's *Cold Sassy Tree,* Miss Love accepted the proposal of a Texas rancher and returned to Maryland to sew her trousseau when the man jilted her for Miss Love's best friend, who was pregnant at the time of their elopement.

truckle (*truk'* ul) **bed** or **trundle bed** a low bed, cot, or pallet set on wheels or casters, which could be stored under a standard size bed when not in use and could double the amount of sleeping accommodations without taking up floor space during the day. Often, a nurse, slave, or attendant occupied the truckle bed to be near a patient or owner during the night. The term, which derives from the Latin for *pulley,* entered English in the fifteenth century. The truckle bed was a common household furnishing, particularly in inns and crowded dwellings. In Fyodor Dostoevsky's *The Brothers Karamazov,* the patient Smerdyakov lies on a truckle bed.

truffle (*truhf'* f'l) a succulent, knobby black fungus that grows underground at the base of an oak tree and is located by dogs or pigs trained to sniff out the location. Served as a delicacy in France, Perigord truffles rank above the more common white truffles of Italy, which are diced over omelets or cooked in casseroles and rice dishes. Charles ponders a night with Emma, title character in Gustave Flaubert's *Madame Bovary,* as a diner savors a meal of truffles.

truncheon (*truhn'* chuhn) derived from the Latin for *trunk,* a thick, stout club, staff, length of hose, or cudgel; also, a steel or iron baton or billy stick wrapped in hard rubber and used by riot police or guards to subdue a mob. In Elie Wiesel's autobiographical *Night,* kapos with truncheons subdue old men like Chlomo, who presumably succumbs to a head injury. *See also* kapo.

trundle bed *See* truckle bed.

trunnel (*truhn'* n'l) or **treenail** or **trenail** a wooden peg, cylinder, or shim of dry compressed lumber that is used to fasten wood parts, particularly in boats and fine, handcrafted furniture or decorated boxes. When the trunnel absorbs water, it swells to produce a tight, nail-free joint. Pa fashions a sty for Rob's pig by hammering trunnel pins into holes bored into uprights in Robert Newton Peck's autobiographical *A Day No Pigs Would Die. See also* shim.

truss a bound sheaf of grain or faggot of firewood; also, a bundle, packet, or tuft. Derived from the Latin for *twist,* the term describes how grain was bailed and transported to a barn before baling machinery was invented. As manager of Michael Henchard's grain yard, Donald Farfrae, a central character in Thomas Hardy's *The Mayor of Casterbridge,* presides over the loading of trusses of grain.

trust derived from the Anglo-Saxon for *faithful,* an object, parcel of land, amount of money, or other obligation turned over to the care and safekeeping of a reliable person, attorney, bank, or investment firm for a specified purpose over a predetermined period of time. When Cosette becomes Madame Pontmercy in Victor Hugo's *Les Misérables,* Jean Valjean tells how he came to rear her like a foster daughter and how he turns over to Marius the girl and 600 francs, which Valjean has held in trust since Cosette's childhood.

tryptych or **triptych** (*trihp'* tihk) a three-part work of art or set of panels or carvings hinged in horizontal alignment and either hung on a wall or placed freestanding on an altar, mantle, or table to depict a religious scene; an altarpiece, often with two short segments to the sides and a central scene or figure painted on the taller panel in the middle. The term derives from the Greek for *threefold.* Although not given to strong religious faith, Oskar, the title character in Thomas Keneally's *Schindler's List,* is disquieted by the theft of a tryptych, which is shipped to Nuremberg with other art objects stolen by the Nazis.

Try-Works a hybrid term from the Latin for *three* and the English *work* denoting a huge structure between the front and center masts on a whaler that shields the ten-by-eight-by-five-foot brick and mortar kiln in a watery reservoir to protect the oak deck from fire. Heated vats boil away the excess from whale blubber to enable whalers to keep the valuable portions and toss overboard the waste to lighten the load. In Herman Melville's *Moby-Dick,* the Try-Works operates two try-pots, each holding several barrels.

tub, four-clawed a raised, deep-sided bathtub attached to four decorative feet in the shape of claws or talons, which are usually depicted clutching globes and may extend upward into a carving or cast image of an eagle, hawk, or phoenix. In Sandra Cisneros's *The House on Mango Street,* the reference to the four-clawed tub suggests an intimidating home situation, where Alicia must rise early to make the lunchbox tortillas.

tuber (*tyoo'* buhr) an underground root or bulbous, thickened rhizome from which a stalk grows, as demonstrated by a dahlia bulb, yam, or sweet potato. The tuber can be stored for replanting, cut into sprouted segments, or "eyes," or eaten as a vegetable by roasting, boiling, or grating. In Chinua Achebe's *Things Fall* Apart, Okonkwo and other local males count wealth in terms of concrete objects—the number of tubers or yams raised each year.

tubercle (*too'* buhr . k'l or *tyoo'* buhr . k'l) a small round swelling, hardened mass, nodule, knob, or growth on bone or in soft tissue of the brain or lungs of a victim of tuberculosis. Derived from the Latin for *little swelling,* the term entered English in the late sixteenth century and is used primarily to describe the advancement of the symptoms of tuberculosis. In Fyodor Dostoevsky's *Crime and Punishment,* Sonia rushes from the room to aid Katerina Ivanovna, who appears to have gone insane from the growth of tubercles in her brain.

Tube station from the British colloquial term for subway, a depot or underground waiting area where subway patrons can purchase tickets, wait for a train, or greet arrivals. In his memories of his parents and the war that stretched from his childhood into the present in George Orwell's *1984,* protagonist Winston Smith recalls being led into the safety of a Tube station, where an old man reeking of gin grieved aloud that the nation should never have trusted an unspecified "them."

tucker a lace frill or fichu worn at the neck of a frock coat or a yoke or fluffy or gauzy scarf, triangle, chemisette, collar, or pleated neckpiece made of muslin or silk and used as a modesty shield to fill in the low neckline of a woman's dress or jacket. In George Eliot's *Silas Marner,* Nancy Lammeter dresses simply and elegantly for Squire Cass's New Year's party in a silver silk dress topped with a lace tucker and coral jewelry. *See also* frock coat.

tugs *See* tracery.

tumbril or **tumbrel** (*tuhm'* brihl) derived from the German for *reel,* a farm cart or tipcart that can be tilted like a dump truck. Also, a serviceable manure cart, a symbolic mode of transportation used to convey condemned prisoners to the guillotine during the French Revolution. On his ride from prison to the guillotine in Charles Dickens's *A Tale of Two Cities,* Sidney Carton, Charles Darnay's double, offers himself in exchange for the husband of Lucy, the woman Sidney secretly loves. *See also* guillotine.

tundra (*tuhn'* druh) boggy grassland of the Arctic that remains frozen much of the year. In the short summer, the treeless tundra blossoms with mosses, herbs, wildflowers, shrubs, and grasses that become a short-term habitat and breeding ground for birds, ducks, rabbits, caribou, lemmings, and bears. Tundra forms the setting of Jean Craighead George's *Julie of the Wolves,* where Miyax must correctly interpret nature's signs if she is to survive on the edge of wolf society. *See also* lemming; tern.

tunic (*tyoo'* nihk) derived from the Latin *tunica,* the most prevalent garment in human history, composed of a straight tube of material open at the neck and armholes or fitted with two smaller tubes at the shoulders to serve as sleeves. Eurycleia, the elderly nurse in Homer's *Odyssey,* takes Telemachus's tunic and hangs it on a hook as he prepares for bed, just as his father Odysseus had done when she tended him.

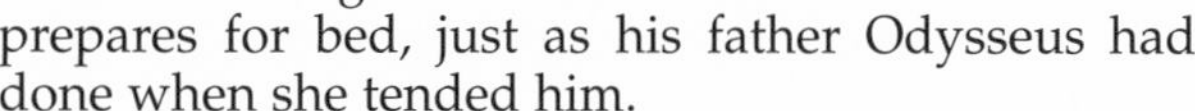

turban a wrapped headdress of Islamic origin that evolved into a high-fashion hat from medieval times to the 1920s. During this lengthy evolution, the turban received alterations and additions in the form of trains, wimples, head bands, brooches, interwoven pearls, and feather and fur trim. The term derives from the Persian for *tulip.* As ladies take their turn at the mirror in the dressing room of Squire Cass's house in George Eliot's *Silas Marner,* Miss Ladbrook holds her turban and stands politely aside so that others can use the looking glass if necessary.

Turkish bath a steam room, hot spa, or sauna where clients loll in heated herbal vapors, then are scrubbed, massaged, kneaded, oiled, and soothed with cool cloths as a means of relaxation, physical rejuvenation, and removal of body impurities through perspiration and friction from thick towels. In Arthur Miller's *Death of a Salesman,* Charley reminds Willy Loman that, in a Turkish bath, financier J. P. Morgan would look like any other nude male.

turnpike house a toll gate on a public highway, expressway, or autobahn; also, the quarters of the highway authority that oversees traffic and reports injuries and crimes to rescue squads and police. In a frantic effort to intervene in an elopement and save Lydia from ruin in Jane Austen's *Pride and Prejudice,* the Colonel looks for her at every inn and turnpike house in Hertfordshire.

turret (*tuhr'* riht) a tall lookout post or watchtower or roofline guardhouse on a fortress; later added to manor houses and compounds as decorations. The term derives from the Latin for a *portable siege tower.* In his first view of Baskerville Hall in Sir Arthur Conan Doyle's *The Hound of the Baskervilles,* Sherlock Holmes notes the central clock from which rise twin turrets marked with loopholes and crenellations like a medieval fortress.

tushes (*tuh'* shehz) a twelfth-century term naming a pair of prominent, pointed side teeth or tusks, particularly a horse's canine teeth. In George Orwell's *Animal Farm,* Major, a prize boar, reaches the age of twelve with his tushes intact, despite the fact that farmers usually remove tushes to keep them from curving back into the jaw or from piercing the hide of the pig's face.

tutu (*too'* too) a short, circular projecting frill or waist adornment or knee- or ankle-length skirt made of sheer gauze or stiffened netting and worn by a ballerina over a leotard or unitard. Derived from the infantile term for *buttocks,* the term dates to the early twentieth century. Against her father's wish to make her a traditional Japanese woman in Jeanne Wakatsuki Houston and James D. Houston's *Farewell to Manzanar,* Jeanne chooses ballet, tutus, and baton lessons over odori—the more sedate, ladylike dance of Japan.

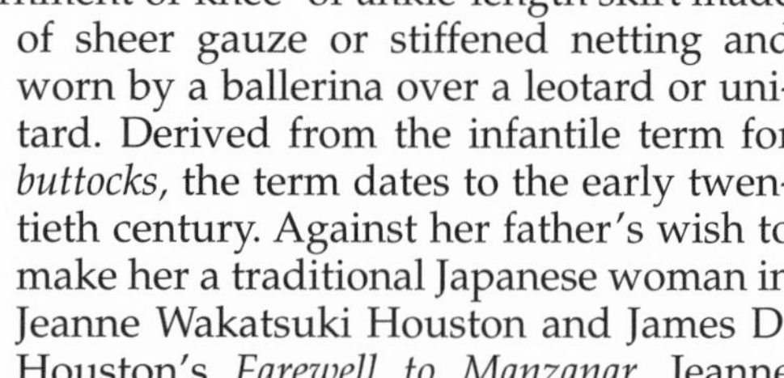

twelfth cake the European tradition of a twelfth night cake, served on January 6, or Epiphany, at the end of the Christmas season to celebrate the arrival of the Magi who visit the Christ Child. Also called Little Christmas, the custom and its many variations still exists on isolated parts of the Atlantic seaboard that were settled by the English. When the second Christmas phantasm visits Ebenezer Scrooge in Charles Dickens's *A Christmas Carol,* the room fills with fancy foodstuffs, including several decorated twelfth cakes.

two bits American slang for a quarter or twenty-five cents. Dating to the mid-eighteenth century, the term remains in use mainly as an adjective describing something that is cheap, insignificant, or rickety. In a pathetic show of bravado, Bigger Thomas, the doomed protagonist of Richard Wright's *Native Son,* bets Jack two bits that he won't assist at the planned pool hall robbery.

twopence (*tuhp'* pehns) an English silver coin; a two-penny piece. In more recent times, the term, like the American "two bits," implies worthless or insubstantial, as in "twopence worth of airport security." According to a brief, pithy aphorism from *Poor Richard's Almanack,* Ben Franklin notes: "He who pays for work before it is done has a pennyworth for twopence."

typhoid fever a long-lasting infectious form of salmonella caused by bacteria consumed in water or food or from swimming in streams contaminated by sewage. In addition to a month-long bout of fever, the disease also causes eruptions in the lymph glands, diarrhea, inflamed organs, pneumonia, and neural collapse. Typhoid fever brings Ellen and Matt Creighton together after Ellen nurses Matt back to health in Irene Hunt's *Across Five Aprils.*

typhoon derived from the Chinese for *great wind*, a tropical ocean cyclone that gathers in a low-pressure front along the Equator in the western Pacific and slowly increases from 15 up to 150 miles per hour. Destructive wind and rain can severely damage property, as can a resulting wall of water or storm surge that may accompany the typhoon when it makes landfall in a curved trajectory and quickly dissipates. The natural embankment of sand that rings the lagoon in William Golding's *Lord of the Flies* probably resulted from a typhoon. *See also* lagoon; trajectory.

typhus a disease arising from rickettsiae carried by body lice. Producing fever, chills, and headache, the flulike symptoms give way to a rash, debility, and lowered resistance. Mr. Brocklehurst, headmaster of Lowood, vacates the premises during a spring outbreak of typhus that kills Helen, friend of the title character in Charlotte Brontë's *Jane Eyre*. In Thomas Keneally's *Schindler's List* and Elie Wiesel's *Night,* incoming prisoners in Nazi concentration camps and work camps are sprayed with disinfectant to stop the spread of lice and keep down typhus.

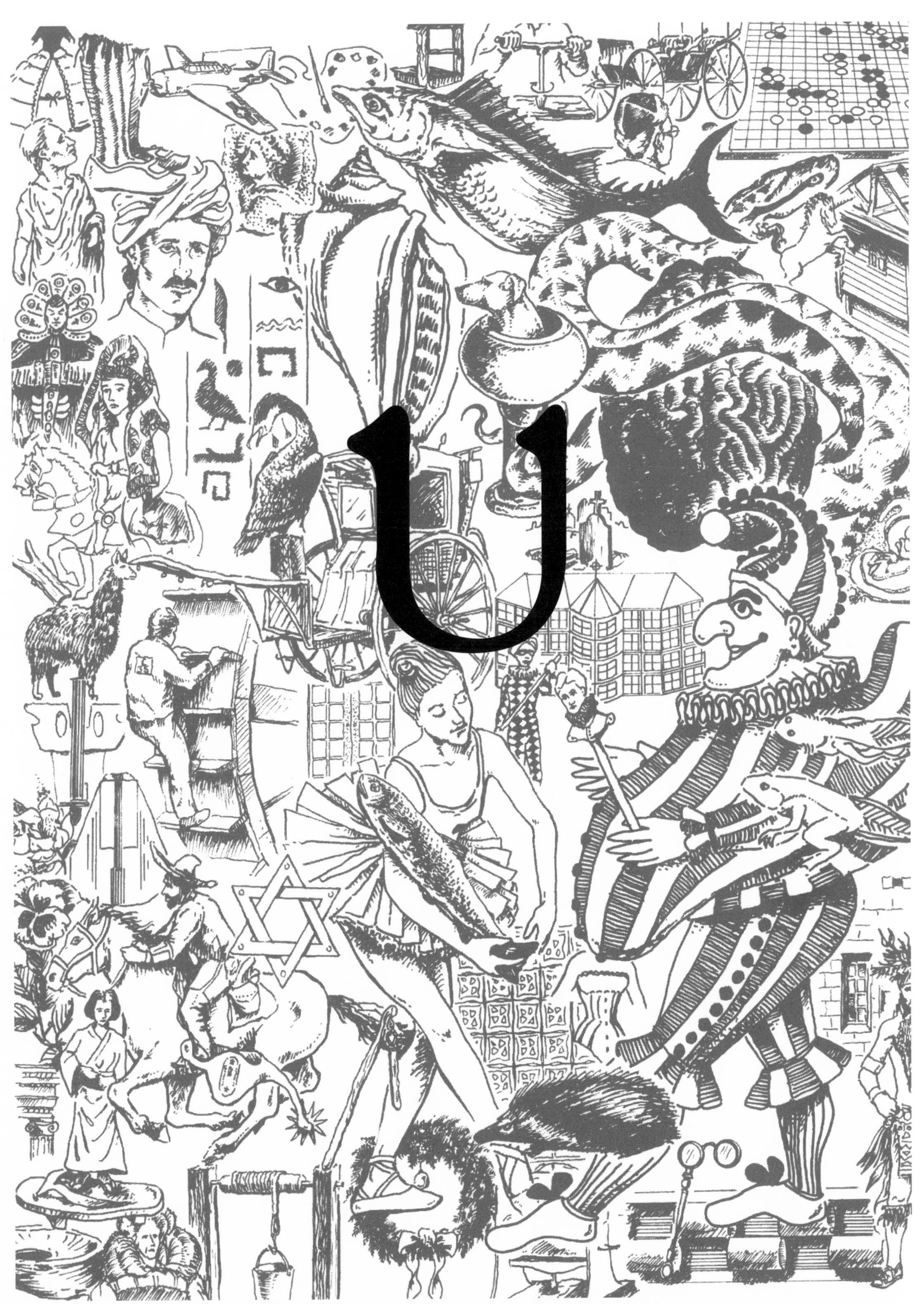

U-boat derived from the German for *under-sea boat,* the term names the general class of submarines introduced in September 1914. German tactics called for grouping six to twelve U-boats in packs for coordinated night assaults on Atlantic convoys. U-boats supported German sea power during World War I and World War II until improved radar ended their advantage in 1942. During assaults on oil tankers off Curaçao in Theodore Taylor's *The Cay* and *Timothy of the Cay,* German U-boats creep close enough to land to disrupt the production of petroleum products that aid the Allied war effort.

ulster (*uhl'* stuhr) a long, full, efficient raincoat made from coarse wool frieze or other rugged fabric and equipped with removable hood, belt, and capelet. The ulster was designed in Ulster, Ireland, in 1867 and remained popular for decades. Henry Gatz, ineffectual father of the title character of F. Scott Fitzgerald's *The Great Gatsby,* arrives at the mansion in an ulster and carrying an umbrella, a climatic commentary on the dismal day when Nick tries to locate mourners for Jay's funeral.

ulu or **oolu** (*oo'* loo) a handy knife or chopping tool that Eskimoes refer to as "the woman's knife." The ulu is shaped like a cleaver with a semicircular blade and bone or wood knob or handle; it is used for boning fish, trimming hair, scraping skins, piercing hides for sewing or lacing, or cutting cord or small twigs. In Gary Paulsen's *Dogsong,* Russel chews the barely thawed meat and hacks it free from the haunch near his lips with an ulu.

ululation (*oo* . loo . *lay'* shuhn) a high-pitched, wavering howling or wailing created by vibrating the tongue against the palate; a mournful oral lament, such as that raised by wolves. From the Latin word that imitates the sound, it entered English in the mid-seventeenth century. In Alice Walker's *The Color Purple,* Nettie writes Celie about the ululation raised by Olinka women in sorrow over their village, which was crushed by heavy machinery to allow a road to pass through.

umiak (*oo'* mee . ak) a sea-going boat propelled by four paddlers on a side and seating about two dozen Arctic whalers or fishers. Formed of bone or wood, covered in waterproof skins, and accommodating a single mast, the umiak required a single pilot to navigate. As described by Gary Paulsen's *Dogsong,* only one survivor returned with the news that Russel's grandfather had died when his umiak was destroyed during a whale hunt.

Uncle Tom a pejorative for a placating, ingratiating, ever-smiling black who maintains a positive exterior in the presence of whites to avoid giving offense. Derived from a harmless old black character in Harriet Beecher Stowe's *Uncle Tom's Cabin,* the term became an injurious taunt during the 1960s as the civil rights movement pressured whites to capitulate to black demands for equality. While interviewing his subject in preparation for the autobiography, Alex Haley, author of *The Autobiography of Malcolm X,* must accustom himself to Malcolm's use of "Uncle Tom" and "yard Negro" in denigrating less militant blacks.

underground railroad a clandestine system of assistance from Quakers, Mennonites, Covenanters, Methodists, and other Northern abolitionists to approximately 1,000 slaves per year fleeing Southern plantations because of whippings, hunger, disease, possible sale, dismemberment, loss of family, or execution. Roughly organized so that no single plan would fall into the hands of slave catchers or patrollers, the system, pressed into action after the Fugitive Slave Act of 1850, called into use barns, sheds, lean-tos, corn cribs, basements, attics, false floors, and caves as temporary stations as slaves made their way from one safe house to another. Toward the end of his commentary on race relations in *Narrative of the Life of Frederick Douglass,* the speaker questions the safety of and necessity for an underground railroad, which lures slaves from the South without solving the problem of slavery or emancipating those who are left behind. In Jessamyn West's *Except for Me and Thee,* Eliza Birdwell must act on her Quaker faith to help Lily and Burke, a runaway couple, complete a connection on the underground railroad. *See also* pateroller.

underworld the underworld of classical myth, protected by the three-headed dog Cerberus and ringed by four dark rivers. Libations had to be poured and coins placed in the mouths of the dead to pay Charon the boatman to row them across the River Styx to a judgment held in Hades' court. For heroes, an idyllic life in the Elysian Fields awaited those who had performed great deeds in their early lives. As described in Edith Hamilton's *Mythology,* the underworld forms the lowest segment of a three-part universe with Olympian gods on high, humanity on earth, and the spirits of the dead below. In Sophocles' *Antigone,* the title character pays with her life for violating King Creon's law against ritual interment for her brother, a traitor who was denied the underworld because he remained unblessed and unburied.

UNICEF the acronym for the United Nations International Children's Emergency Fund, a nonsectarian, apolitical group funded by the United Nations General Assembly in 1946 to aid children left homeless by World War II. Since that time, the agency continues to provide medical care, nutrition, and clothing to children in emergency situations, all paid through donations from member nations and from the sale of greeting cards and calendars. In the introduction to *Zlata's Diary,* by Zlata Filipovich, Janine Di Giovanni explains how UNICEF helped publish this wartime memoir in 1993.

unicorn (*yoo'* nih . kohrn) a mythic beast shaped like a horse and bearing a spiraled horn on its forehead. A worldwide symbol of whimsy and romanticism, the unicorn has for centuries graced coins, royal emblems, advertising logos, and art. The term derives from the Latin for *one horn.* Symbolic of uniqueness and of unrequited sexual urges, Laura's unicorn in Tennessee Williams's *The Glass Menagerie* ties her to a dream world beyond the gritty existence of her mother's conniving manipulation and dreams of past glory. *See also* Royal Unicorn.

Union Jack a flag representing Great Britain. Evolved with the inclusion of Ireland in the Union in 1801, the flag's upright cross (Saint Andrew's cross) is superimposed over an X-shaped cross (Saint Patrick's cross). The flag features red lines outlined in white against a blue background. On the day that royalty arrives by train to the village in Thomas Hardy's *The Mayor of Casterbridge,* Lucetta appears not to know Michael Henchard, who dresses in his seedy best and bears a Union Jack tacked to a dowel.

unit *See* squadron.

Upanishad (oo . *pan'* ih . shad) or **Vedanta** Hindu scripture composed in Sanskrit between 900 and 600 B.C. and added to the Vedas as commentaries. The literature contains a variety of pantheistic prose and verse, including didactic homilies, meditations, allegories, philosophical treatises, and aphorisms. The aim of the Upanishad is to aid the soul in locating oneness with the universal soul. To help the title character attain purity of spirit in Hermann Hesse's *Siddhartha,* Govinda recites a verse from the Upanishad recommending self-denial. *See also* Vedas.

upright piano a piano with the strings or harp in an upright position rather than horizontal, as in a grand or baby grand. Built for utilitarian purpose, the upright piano is standard in schools, churches, and music training centers where space is limited. On the morning of the atomic blast in John Hersey's *Hiroshima,* Mr. Tanimoto is weary from moving altar gear, Bibles, hymnals, and an upright piano and organ console to a donated house.

urchin (*uhr'* chihn) a ragged child or mischievous scamp of the streets; a homeless, underfed waif or foundling who survives unsupervised by stealing food, begging, or earning small amounts for running errands. Derived from the Old French for *hedgehog,* the term dates to the Middle Ages. While living with Master Hughes in *Narrative of the Life of Frederick Douglass,* the title character shares bread with white urchins who break the law by teaching him to read.

U.S. Marshal *See* marshal.

usury (*yoo'* zhur . ee) **note** a document signed by both borrower and lender explaining the terms of a personal or home loan, the interest rate, and the schedule of payments. Derived from the Latin for *interest,* the term entered English in the Middle Ages. To assure that Tony remains in his house and gets to bed on time in Willa Cather's *My Antonia,* Mr. Cutter puts her in charge of usury notes and important papers, then sneaks back during the night and finds Jim Burden sleeping in her place.

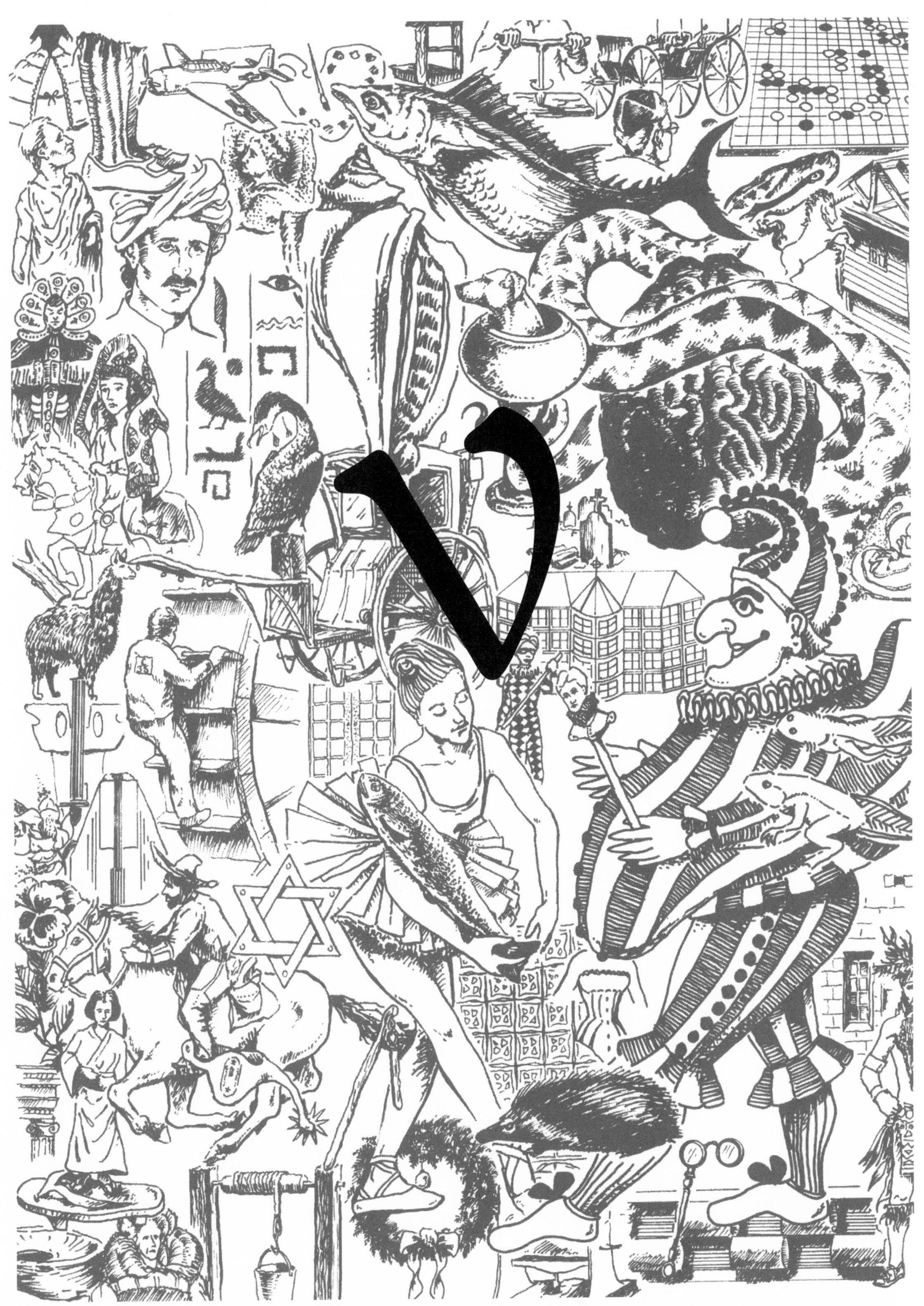
V

vail or **veil** derived from the Latin for *sail,* a scarf, kerchief, or headcloth. In ancient times, women displayed modesty and elegance as well as preparations for guests, weddings, and funerals by cloaking themselves in a ritual vail. Muslim countries were most strict about not revealing the face to strangers or visitors and required floor-length vails that covered all but the eyes. After spending the night at Boaz's feet in Ruth 3:15, Ruth obeys him and holds out her vail to receive a measure of grain and to return home without letting anyone know that she passed the night at the foot of his bed.

valance (*va'* luhntz) a draped altar cloth, table cover, bed canopy or edging, or short window cover over the upper beam that exposes most of the panes and lets in a maximum amount of sunshine. A fifteenth-century term, it derives from the city of Valance, France. In William Shakespeare's *The Taming of the Shrew,* Gremio claims to have a valance embroidered in Venetian gold.

valerian (vuh . *lihr'* ee . yuhn) a perennial herb commonly known as heliotrope, the rhizomes of which are used to treat nervous unrest and intestinal spasm. A common night-time sedative since the fourteenth century, the term derives from a Roman province named Valeria. Suffering heart palpitations, pallor, and capricious behavior, Emma, title character in Gustave Flaubert's *Madame Bovary,* receives camphor baths and valerian, which are Charles's treatments for symptoms brought on by her infatuation with a lover.

valise (vuh . *lees'*) a small suitcase, portmanteau, traveling case, makeup kit, or hand luggage. Of unknown origin, the term entered English in the early seventeenth century. Packed for her journey to the doctor, Zeena Frome, wife of the title character in Edith Wharton's *Ethan Frome,* takes along a bandbox and Ethan's old valise. *See also* bandbox.

valkyrie (*val'* kuh . ree) one of Odin's 12 female angels or supervisors of the dead who watched over battlefields to guide the spirits of slain warriors to a permanent male haven in Valhalla, the hall of heroes, where the Valkyries acted as maidservants. The term derives from the Old Norse for *chooser of the dead.* In Edith Hamilton's *Mythology,* Brynhild was a disobedient valkyrie put to sleep in a ring of fire until she was awakened by a man with a true heart. In Isak Dinesen's "The Pearls," a demure bride surprises and pleases her husband by becoming a daring valkyrie.

vampire (*vam'* pyr) a ghost, monster, or corpse with elongated canine teeth that reanimates each night at sunset, abandons its crypt, and searches for a meal of fresh blood, which it sucks from the throat of a sleeping or otherwise unsuspecting human victim. Derived from a Serbo-Croatian or Czech term, this supernatural concept entered English in the early eighteenth century. The title character in Mary Shelley's *Frankenstein* regrets releasing a vampire or spirit from the grave to prey on innocent victims.

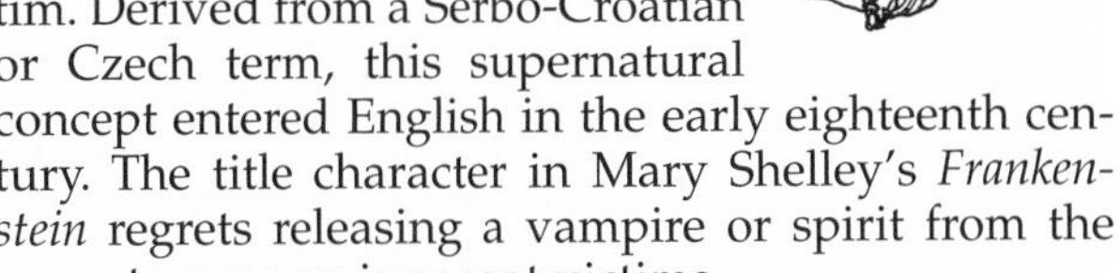

Vandyke or **Van Dyck** (van . *dyk'*) a beard trimmed close along the jowls to a deep vee on the chin in imitation of portraits of Charles I and his male courtiers. Named for painter Sir Anthony Vandyke, the style was popular in the mid-eighteenth century. Sam Westing, the protagonist in Ellen Raskin's *The Westing Game,* disappears and leaves behind an old picture of him in a Vandyke beard. *See also* goatee.

vapors a fainting spell brought on by shock, poor health, rage, indignation, hunger, pregnancy, hypochondria, depression, hysteria, or tightly laced clothing. The mock-serious colloquial term is applied only to women. In Robert Newton Peck's *A Day No Pigs Would Die,* Aunt Matty appears to collapse with the vapors because of Rob's D in English. *See also* smelling salts; syncope.

vaquero (vah . *kehr'* oh) a cowboy, mounted herder, or rodeo performer; a stockman or drover who tends cattle and drives them to market. Derived from the Latin for *cow,* the term remains in use in Hispanic communities in Texas and is related to the Americanized *buckeroo.* Antonio's father, a proud *vaquero* in Rudolfo Anaya's *Bless Me, Ultima,* dates his calling to the Spaniards who colonized New Mexico.

varicose (*va'* rih . kohs) **ulcer** an enlarged or dilated vein or blood vessel that has broken through at the surface and created a pustule or lesion. A hybrid of the Latin for *veinous* and the Greek for *wound,* the term names a condition that makes movement difficult without setting up a throbbing pain and threat of rupture and more bleeding. During Winston Smith's travail in Oceania in George Orwell's *1984,* he suffers the nagging varicose ulcer on his leg that, like the worrisome aspects of life under Big Brother, refuses to give him peace.

Varsouviana (vahr . *soo'* vyahn . uh) *See* mazurka.

V.C. or **Victoria Cross** the highest British honor for bravery, introduced in 1856 and named for Queen Victoria, who ruled from 1837 to 1901. The V.C. is composed of a red square topped by a red bar and crest and attached to the bronze cross of Saint Andrew and the words "For Valour." The general believes that Strickland deserves the V.C. in Rudyard Kipling's "Miss Youghal's Sais" because he put on the garb of a groom and pretended to be Indian.

Vedas (*vay'* duhz) the four most ancient Sanskrit canonical texts, dating from 1500 to 500 B.C., including the chants, hymns, prayers, liturgy, sacrifices, and rituals of Hinduism as well as the introduction of Vishnu and Shiva, the major Hindu deities. The term derives from the Hindi for *knowledge.* In a thirst for knowledge, the title character in Hermann Hesse's *Siddhartha* studies the Vedas and questions the Brahmans. *See also* Upanishad.

veld or **veldt** (vehlt) an open, fertile savannah or grassland; unfenced prairie country or grazing land featuring ruminant herds and few trees or bushes in South Africa, Botswana, Lesotho, and Zimbabwe. Derived from the Afrikaan for *field,* the term, which entered English in the late eighteenth century, describes rolling land primarily at elevations of 4,000 to 6,000 feet. In Doris Lessing's "No Witchcraft for Sale," the speaker comments that people who live on the veld learn of the ancient wisdom contained in nature.

veranda or **verandah** (vuh . *ran'* duh) a covered or canopied gallery, porch, lanai, piazza, portico, or patio extending from the body of a private home. Where climate allows use year round, the veranda is often a major source of entertainment, dining, and living space, particularly for women and children. Derived from the Hindi language, the term entered English in the early eighteenth century. Lying on a cool veranda in the Santa Clara Valley of California, Buck, the central character in Jack London's *The Call of the Wild,* lives a pampered pet's idyll far different from the life he chooses after being transported to the Yukon.

verdigrease a humorous mispronounciation of **verdigris** (*vuhr'* dih . grihs) copper carbonate or copper acetate, a poisonous compound used in dyes, fungicides, paint pigment, medicine, and decorative antiqueing for brass, bronze, and copper that creates a patina suggesting great age. Derived in the Middle Ages from the Old French for *green of Greece,* the term refers to the natural corrosion arising from exposure to air and saltwater that details ancient cast metal sculpture or bas-relief. Before Tom and Huck prick their fingers with a pin to sign a pact in Mark Twain's *The Adventures of Tom Sawyer,* Tom insists that they not use a brass pin because it might be tainted with poisonous "verdigrease."

Verey (*veh'* ree) **light** or **Very light** a flare gun invented in 1877 by U.S. naval ordnance specialist Edward Wilson Verey. The Verey light fired white or colored phosphorescent fireworks for use in signaling or lighting an area during night maneuvers or attacks. As the war grows more deadly in Erich Maria Remarque's *All Quiet on the Western Front,* protagonist Paul Baumer takes stock of his friends' deaths, particularly that of Müller, who was shot in the stomach with a Verey light and expired in great pain.

vermin (*vuhr'* mihn) destructive, filthy, unwholesome, loathsome, predatory, or obnoxious members of the animal kingdom that humanity considers pests because of their habits and their ability to overrun an otherwise pleasant locale. The term derives from the Latin for *overrun with maggots.* The worst examples include lice, fleas, cockroaches, bedbugs, intestinal parasites, and flies. The Morlocks, subhuman dwellers of tunnels beneath London in H. W. Wells's *The Time Machine,* obviously have adapted to a haphazard diet of vermin, such as rats, and human flesh of the Eloi, their weak alter egos on earth.

verst (vuhrst) a Russian land measure equaling 3,500 feet, two-thirds of a mile, or 1.07 kilometers. Derived from the Latin for *turn,* the term entered English in the mid-sixteenth century. Because of their lack of money, Dounia and Raskolnikov, characters in Fyodor Dostoevsky's *Crime and Punishment,* calculate the trip to St. Petersburg to be 90 versts, or 60 miles, which they can afford by traveling third class with the help of an insider on the railroad.

Vestal or **vestal** (*vehs'* t'l) **virgin** a member of an elite, extremely powerful cadre of cloistered Roman nuns or priestesses chosen at age ten for their unblemished bodies. While serving the goddess of the hearth for three decades, Vestals took a vow to abstain from even looking at any men other than brothers or fathers. At the end of a decade of training, the Vestal tended the holy fire on Rome's national hearth. After the second decade, the Vestal became a trainer for the next generation of fire-tenders. To explain the power of love-in-bloom, the flower Oberon sends for in William Shakespeare's *A Midsummer Night's Dream,* he tells Ariel that he watched Cupid accidentally hit the blossom while aiming at a Vestal, the playwright's gentle compliment to Elizabeth I, nicknamed the Virgin Queen.

vicar (*vih'* kuhr) a salaried parish priest, representative, or deputy of a bishop or ecclesiastical council or titular cleric of the Anglican faith stationed outside a parish environment in a chapel or mission to provide a variety of services. The term is derived from the Latin for *substitute.* In Margaret Craven's *I Heard the Owl Call My Name,* Mark accepts the role of vicar to a remote Kwakiutl village in British Columbia and performs jobs such as tending the motor launch, transporting the ill to hospitals, and assisting children in choosing between the white and Native American worlds.

victorine *See* tippet.

Victrola (vihk . *troh'* luh) a trademark for an early twentieth-century wind-up phonograph or gramophone, which played thick wax discs on a horizontal turntable. A jointed arm contained a needle, or stylus, that fitted its point into a groove on the record, picked up vibrations in an amplifier at the top of the arm, and transferred the sound to a large megaphone, usually ornate and quite prominent as a room decoration. To make up for disappointment and frustration, Laura Wingfield, a central character in Tennessee Williams's *The Glass Menagerie,* spends her spare time arranging glass animals and listening to her absent father's old victrola records.

viewing gauze a protective layer of opaque gauze or net placed over the face of a corpse in places and times where embalming is too expensive or not available. The purpose of the covering is to conceal or obscure from mourners harsh evidence of deterioration, disease, age, exposure to the elements, or wounds. In Boris Pasternak's *Dr. Zhivago,* the son of the deceased observes his mother through a full-length viewing gauze that envelopes the slab on which she is carried to her grave.

virginal (*vuhr'* jihn . 'l) a small, two-octave legless spinet, harpsichord, or box piano of the sixteenth and seventeenth centuries. The rectangular instrument, which contained single strands of wire plucked by a set of quills, earned its name from the Italian *virginale* because it was intended for use by young women, who held it on their laps while playing notes on the keyboard. As described in *The Diary of Samuel Pepys,* in the author's hasty departure from the London Fire of 1660, Samuel Pepys loads a lighter with household goods, including a valuable pair of virginals. *See also* lighter.

vision quest in Native American custom, a withdrawal from a tribe or community as well as from food, sex, friends, and physical comforts to pursue a glimpse of the future. Seated in a sweat lodge or alone in the wild, the male quester drank a strong purgative such as ilex or inhaled the smoke or steam from such purifying herbs as sweetgrass, wacanga, or tobacco to cleanse the body and spirit and to prepare for manhood or for a divine experience, meeting with ancestral spirits, or a dream. A significant part of John Neihardt's *Black Elk Speaks,* the vision quest accounts for the title character's development as a seer and mystic and for his belief in prophecy. *See also* sweat lodge.

voodoo *See curandera;* hamatsa; shaman.

V-2 rocket the sophisticated Vengeance Weapon 2 designed by German engineer Werner von Braun at Peenemünde, Germany, at the beginning of World War II to reach enemy territory beyond the range of artillery fire. The rocket required a liquid oxygen tank, igniter, gyroscopes, and radio homing signal to guide it to its target. The rockets had little effect on the war because of faulty direction and trigger mechanisms, but the initial effort guided post-war rocketry as a model. In Ray Bradbury's *Fahrenheit 451,* Granger explains to protagonist Guy Montag that Granger's grandfather taught him pacifism by showing him films of the V-2 rocket.

W

Wa-Alaikum-Salaam *See* Allah; As-Salaam-Alaikum; Islam.

wainscot (*wayns'* koht) or **wainscoting** fine oak paneling, planking, or finish covering, particularly the protective coating on the lower half of a wall that is divided from an ornate wallpaper, stucco, mural, fresco, or other treatment on the upper half. Entering English in the late sixteenth century, the term derives from the Dutch for *wagon crossbar*, suggesting the rail or molding that separates a two-level wall treatment or the overlapping boards that panel a fine carriage. After the cat leaps toward the wainscot in pursuit of a mouse and breaks a pickle dish in Edith Wharton's *Ethan Frome,* the falling action quickly halts the title character's plans for a romantic evening and plunges him into more desperate action: a mutual suicide with Mattie Silver.

waistcoat (*wayst'* koht) a sleeveless, tight-fitting vest, weskit, or chest covering extending from neck to waist, often lined and made of the same material as the pants and jacket of a three-piece suit for men or women. Contrasting or innovative waistcoats often sport lively colors and patterns, embroidery, a line of small metal buttons, and a double-breasted or off-center style. Fabrics vary from simple flannel or wool to brocade, silk, and moleskin. In Upton Sinclair's *The Jungle,* the speaker notes that immigrants often cling to a waistcoat, kerchief, or bauble that bears the cultural stamp of the old country; in contrast, the first generation Americans born to these immigrants prefer to be totally American and distance themselves from their parents' past.

wake a commemoration of the dead in an informal reception, feast, memorial gathering, or celebration that follows a death or funeral. A wake may include anything from music, photo albums, tears, casket vigil, and testimonials to dancing, singing, drinking, and carousing, in which the gathered mourners attempt to act out their grief and their shared evaluation of the deceased. One of Antonio's lasting memories of the *llanero's* life in Rudolfo Anaya's *Bless Me, Ultima* is the blend of laughter and tears at family weddings, funerals, births, and wakes.

walk the plank a melodramatic form of execution featured in pirate lore that requires a blindfolded, manacled brigand, captive, or menacing villain to accept a summary judgment and voluntarily step off the end of a board extending over the ocean below to drown, fall on rocks, or be eaten by sharks as recompense for a serious crime, particularly mutiny. A skilled teller of tales in Robert Louis Stevenson's *Treasure Island,* Billy Bones relates scary details of wild deeds, danger, and walking the plank, a pirate's idea of just punishment. *See also* round robin.

wall-eyed displaying an unusual amount of the cornea, or whites, of the eye by widening the lids, gazing fearfully to left and right, or staring ahead without blinking; also, dazed or unfocused, as from a shock, trauma, or sudden wakening from sleep, especially under fearful or threatening conditions. Richard Wright, author of *Black Boy,* observes the skill with which an insurance salesman terrifies his clients, who are left wall-eyed and eager to sign up for policies.

wampum (*wahm'* puhm) a beaded string, belt, baldric, or sash formed of white, lavender, or purple shell beads carved from the valve or shiny inner surface of the conch, periwinkle, whelk, or freshwater clam and threaded on sinew into tight, patterned rows. As described in James Fenimore Cooper's *The Last of the Mohicans,* Native Americans created this detailed handwork as messages, ceremonial bandoliers or insignia, or records of treaties and covenants. The term, derived from the Algonquin for *white strings*, became synonymous with money after colonists began substituting wampum for currency. *See also* baldric.

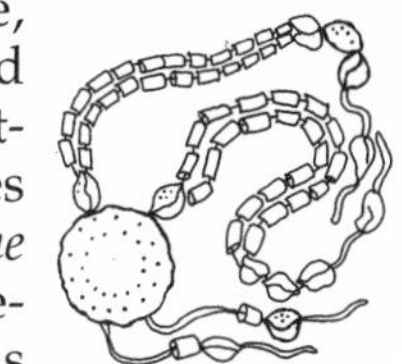

warlords perpetually quarreling Chinese feudal powermongers, despots, usurpers, or autocrats seeking absolute power over a people or territory for the purpose of self-aggrandizement, prestige, or enrichment. In the early twentieth century, Dr. Sun Yat-sen ousted the warlords and replaced them with an efficient nationalistic system. In Amy Tan's *The Kitchen God's Wife,* the extinction of warlords parallels the collapse of all-powerful husbands and feudal marriage, which relegated women to slave conditions.

warp the foundation of vertical or longitudinal threads or yarn through which a weaver intersperses varied colors, blends, and thicknesses of woof or weft threads, which pass back and forth in a shuttle as the weaver adds layers, pressing each into place with a horizontal bar to assure a tight fabric. To save the finished piece from unraveling, the weaver adds a selvedge, or selvage, a firmly interwoven edge along the warp. In a contest with Athena, the Olympian weaver in Edith Hamilton's *Mythology,* Arachne sets up warp threads on a loom and outperforms the goddess; for her arrogance, Arachne is transformed into a spider, forever weaving her web. *See also* selvage.

warrant officer a mid-level naval officer, similar to sergeant in the army, who has risen to an authorized position between commissioned officers or top brass and a noncommissioned officer. Ranking below an ensign or second lieutenant, the warrant officer usually maintains a significant role in a specialty such as helicopter repair, communications, or fire control. In Herman Melville's *Billy Budd,* the speaker skips over Captain Vere's staff of warrant officers to focus on Claggart, a troublemaking master-at-arms, who holds a minor bit of authority that he carries to the extreme by harassing the enlisted sailors beneath him.

wash bowl and pitcher an indoor lavabo or dry sink, which sometimes fit into slots or holes in a bedroom cabinet that was equipped with mirror, towel rod, and matching soap dish for limited bathing, shaving, and makeup application. Once used, it was drained into a slop pail to be carried outside for emptying. In Willa Cather's *My Antonia,* Mrs. Cutter finds an outlet for her painting skills by decorating china, such as finger bowls and wash bowl and pitcher sets, the height of the genteel toilette in an era when many people hauled their water from a pump, used an outhouse for a toilet, and bathed infrequently in a tin tub filled by hand with water heated on a woodstove. *See also* toilet.

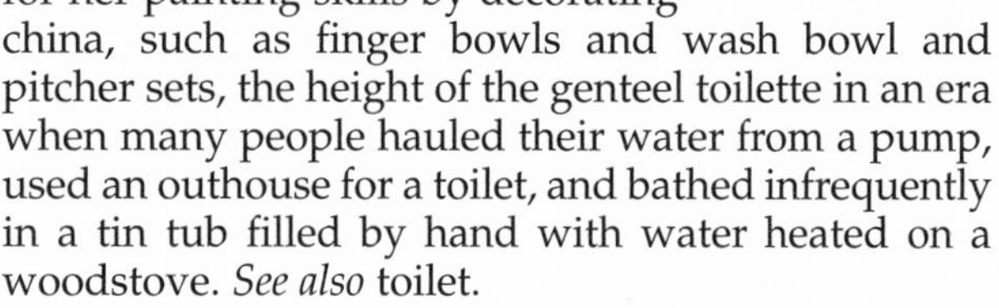

washing-pan a shallow metal pan by which miners swish effluent from a stream or sluice box to separate rocks, debris, and fool's gold from real gold. A major part of the job of panning for gold, using the washing-pan was a tedious segment of a labor-intensive task and sometimes yielded only small fragments, which, in a boom town economy pitting inflated prices against a depressed or glutted market, barely kept the worker in pocket money. At a miner's camp in spring in Jack London's *The Call of the Wild,* Jack Thornton makes a good living from the gold nuggets that glitter like metallic butter on the bottom of a washing-pan. *See also* sluice.

wassail (*was'* s'l) a hot intoxicating punch consisting of nutmeg, cinnamon, cloves, sugar, and roasted apples in hot wine or ale; a hearty drink shared by feasters and carousers who frequently lift tankards to toast their host or to pledge loyalty to a new administration or court. The Anglo-Saxon term means "be well," a contrast to the internal unrest of the title character in William Shakespeare's *Hamlet.* Prince Hamlet and his friend Horatio debate the extravagance and luxury of the usurper Claudius, who hides the murder of his brother and his hasty marriage to the queen beneath jolly banquets and calls for wassail. Obviously, the wassail is an illusion of wellness that contrasts with the corruption in Denmark's royal family.

watered silk a fine silk or a taffeta imitation woven in a solid color and damask pattern to create an undulating, lustrous glow, especially in motion by candlelight. The fabric of dance dresses, capes, underskirts, reticules, and hats as well as draperies, valances, table coverings, lamp shades and other household upholstery, watered silk became fashionable in the nineteenth century despite its tendency to spot, stain, and fade. Giving himself more airs during the growth of tyranny in George Orwell's *Animal Farm,* Napoleon strolls with his sow, each in finery—Napoleon sporting Farmer Jones's best clothes and the female pig dressed in Mrs. Jones's watered silk, emblematic of the illusion of equality that Napoleon has perpetrated on the animals. *See also* damask.

waterspout a rapidly whirling, gyrating funnel, column, or tube of mist, vapor, spray or water that extends from a cumulus or cumulonimbus cloud to a body of water; a tornado centered over water causing a reciprocating suction and expulsion of water from above and below. The term entered English in the fourteenth century. During the aftermath of an atomic bomb blast in John Hersey's *Hiroshima,* air currents produce a whirlwind over Asano Park that hovers over the river and expends its energy in a waterspout. *See also* cirrus.

wattle-and-daub (*wat'* t'l-and-*dawb'*) one of the earliest forms of building material, involving the weaving or interlacing of laths, osier, reeds, poles, or slender limbs into a rectangle and the plastering of the finished framework with mud, clay, stucco, or other materials blended with ash, dung, or plant residue. The covering, a construction material devised before the twelfth century, hardens into a firm bond to form a part of interior or exterior wall construction. Repair calls for a simple redaubing of cracks, chinks, or crevices, a simple job that even children can accomplish. In Theodore Taylor's *Timothy of the Cay,* slaves of the Alborg Estate in the Virgin Islands live in shackly wattle-and-daub huts. *See also* coppice.

wattles of osier *See* coppice; osier.

way station or **waystation** a refuge, hideaway, or safe house where runaway slaves could rest; receive messages from relatives; or request food, clothing, and directions. During the era following the Civil War, newly emancipated slaves lacked the skills to read a road map or sign posts or to trace family members who had been sold to distant plantations or slave markets. A time of danger, Reconstruction brought white backlash, violence, and retribution for financial loss; thus, the former slave could not trust white strangers to give adequate directions. For decades, wanderers depended on way stations to direct the search for missing relatives or to supply jobs, medicine, clothing, education, and housing. In Cincinnati's segment of the underground railroad in Toni Morrison's *Beloved*, Baby Suggs operates a way station that remains open to all black travelers who need assistance. *See also* underground railroad.

weir (weer) an intentional V- or Y-shaped baffle or obstruction to a creek or stream, such as a stone dam or fence woven of reed uprights, that traps or channels fish, turtles, or eels into a seine. The idyllic purling waters of the weir in Thomas Hardy's *Tess of the D'Urbervilles* offers a pleasant departure from farm labor and menace to Tess, who also enjoys nonthreatening companionship from Angel Clare, yet fails to foresee fate's weir-like trap that will pull her down to destruction.

welkin (*wehl'* kihn) a blue sky, a curved or vaulted firmament; also, heaven or the home of deities. Derived in the early Middle Ages from the German for *cloud*, the term applies to a celestial or supernatural atmosphere above the air and horizon seen by human eyes. In Herman Melville's *Billy Budd*, the main character is "welkin-eyed"—he has sky-blue eyes, a connection with otherworldliness and purity that connotes naiveté and vulnerability.

welt a ridge, lump, or swelling on the body or limbs; a lash mark produced by a blow of a whip or rod. To conceal his role in killing Professor Douglass in Ernest Gaines's *The Autobiography of Miss Jane Pittman*, Albert Cluveau claims to suffer welts from insect bites he received while gigging frogs on Grosse Tete Bayou. *See also* bayou.

wetback a pejorative or racial slur against Hispanic migrant workers and illegal aliens who dodge border control and immigrate into Texas and other border states by swimming or wading across the Rio Grande, the natural border between the United States and Mexico. Dating to the late 1920s, this offensive term captures the contempt of citizens for people who seek the benefits of American life without going through legal immigration channels. Marin, a dreamy girl ripe for disaster in Sandra Cisneros's *The House on Mango Street*, falls in love with Geraldo, a *brazer*, or wetback, who disappears because he must stay on the move to avoid discovery and deportation.

wheeler the rider or position on the left horse nearest the wheels of a carriage or coach; also, the draft animal who occupies the position nearest the driver. In mushing, the wheeler is the sled dog closest to the left front of the sled, from which position it influences lateral movement and turns. Dave, an experienced wheeler in Jack London's *The Call of the Wild*, nips Buck when he fails his post or violates sledding protocol. *See also* gee-pole; postilion.

wherry (*hwehr'* ree) *See* lighter.

whey (hway) a thin effluent that gathers at the top of a mass of curdled milk or cheese; also a nutritious beverage similar to skim milk, which is often mixed with fodder to feed pigs or other domestic animals. The term derives from the early medieval German for *milk water*. While reconnoitering the dangerous cave of Polyphemus, a cannibalistic cyclops in Homer's *Odyssey*, Odysseus takes stock of cheeses, milk, and pails running over with whey, the sign of a skilled and dedicated herder, but no assurance of safety or welcome, as the mariners soon learn.

whipping-post a post or upright where prisoners or recalcitrant slaves were manacled or tied before receiving a public caning or lashing. The number of lashes was determined by the degree of the offense, the worst being an attack on a white person. Whipping varied from a few humiliating lashes to a severe laceration of the upper body, which caused permanent scarring and even the loss of an eye or ear. Because of his egotism and pride in his reputation as a top-ranking overseer in the autobiographical *Narrative of the Life of Frederick Douglass*, Mr. Covey chooses not to punish Frederick at the whipping-post for attacking him.

whist (hwihst) a card game devised in the mid-seventeenth century resembling rook or bridge. The object is for partners to use strategy to trump or overtake cards of lower value and to accumulate the most points. The term is derived from Old Norse for *wisp* or *whisk*. Oblivious to the close calls and near misses that beset his race in Jules Verne's *Around the World in Eighty Days*, protagonist Phileas Fogg absorbs himself in friendly games of whist.

whitecaps a roiling, windswept surface or breakers on a lake, river, or sea that produces a froth, crest, or foam at the top of high, curling waves, which indicates the strength of the wind against the water. In the last night watch during a storm that produces whitecaps in the Mississippi for over a half mile around the raft in Mark Twain's *The Adventures of Huckleberry Finn,* Jim laughs at a sudden wave that sweeps Huck overboard. *See also* gale.

white-out a sudden blizzard or downpour of thick snow that obscures the landscape and snow-covered horizon and endangers pedestrians, campers, hikers, or drivers who can no longer locate landmarks except by touch or sound. The term dates to the early 1940s. While camping on the Alaskan tundra on her way to San Francisco in Jean Craighead George's *Julie of the Wolves,* Miyax recognizes the danger of a white-out, which disorients her and threatens loss of her camp and supplies that disappear in the swirl of snow.

whitewash (*hwyt'* wahsh) a thin mixture of lime, white pigment, sizing or thickener, and water used as paint; also, an insubstantial paint, gloss, or plaster covering an interior wall or the exterior of a dwelling or fence that lacks the adhesion and weather resistance of enamel or latex paint. In one of the most famous scenes from American literature, the protagonist in Mark Twain's *The Adventures of Tom Sawyer* faces a Saturday of whitewashing the fence for Aunt Polly but succeeds in finding a replacement by applying reverse psychology and pretending to glory in the job.

Whitsun (*hwiht'* s'n) or **Whitsuntide** or **White Sunday** *See* Good Friday.

wicker flexible willow or osier twigs or branches peeled of their bark, soaked, then woven into screens, baskets, cradles, chairs, mats, or sunshades. Derived from the Scandinavian for *weak,* the term *wicker* entered English in the fourteenth century. Wicker is often the style of furnishing for a sunporch, conservatory, greenhouse, lanai, porch, boathouse, or gazebo. At an afternoon tea at at the headmaster's home in John Knowles's *A Separate Peace,* Mr. Patch-Withers presides over the polite service as students perch on wicker furniture and attempt to act attentive. *See also* osier.

wicket a small gate, side door, or servants' entrance in a fence, wall, or exterior of a building; also, a bank teller's window. A wicket, either composed of grillwork, fencing, or woven wattles or made of stout planking, may adjoin a large gate or ornate iron carriage entrance for easy pedestrian passage when the gate is closed or locked for the night. Derived from the Old Norse for *turn,* this Medieval term applies to the goal in a game of cricket. In the romantic garden scene in Charlotte Brontë's *Jane Eyre,* the title character slips through the wicket and hides from her employer, but she fails to elude him or his proposal of marriage. *See also* postern; wattle-and-daub.

wigwam (*wihg'* wahm) a version of the tepee created by securing saplings from a circle of trees into a conical or domed dwelling and covering the outside with layers of woven reed mats, bark shingles, or patchwork skins. The convergence of branches at the top of the wigwam allows for ventilation and the escape of smoke. To preserve heat and keep out cold, the builder seals the wall on both sides with a layer of dirt and floors the wigwam with more skins or platform lounges. In Conrad Richter's *The Light in the Forest,* True Son boasts that the Delaware word for *wigwam* has permeated the English language. *See also* tepee.

will-o'-the-wisp *See ignis fatuus.*

wimble (*wihm'* b'l) a tool that bores holes in the ground; also an apparatus that enables a harvester to intertwine pieces of straw to form a binding rope for holding sheaves and haystacks together. Derived from the German for *auger* or *borer,* the term entered English in the thirteenth century. On his way to the fair in Thomas Hardy's *The Mayor of Casterbridge,* Michael Henchard carries the tools of his trade—a hay knife and wimble—on his back, concrete proof of a worker's skill; at the end of his life, he shoulders the same burden and returns to the dress of a simple laborer.

wimple (*wihm'* p'l) a draped head covering or veil worn in early Medieval times by nuns, novices, and nurses. The wimple crosses the forehead and hangs on either side of the head to the shoulders; a bottom portion covers the chin and throat as a deterrent to wind or an added concealment of femininity. Described as fastidious and tender-hearted in Geoffrey Chaucer's "Prologue to the Canterbury Tales," the prioress, an intriguing blend of humility and pride, wears a wimple that sets off her comely features.

Winchester carbine a late-nineteenth-century lever-action rifle, designed by the Winchester Repeating Arms Company, that could be reloaded in five seconds or less, held 15 rounds, and had a range of 200 yards. One of the items, alongside a church wedding and clothing for his child, that Kino wants for his family in John Steinbeck's *The Pearl,* the Winchester carbine demonstrates the violence, greed, and envy that muddy the simple life of the pearl diver after he makes his big discovery.

windfall a fruit that is knocked or blown from a limb before it ripens; a natural self-pruning that removes fruit from over-laden boughs so that the remaining fruit can grow to maximum size. The term may also refer to an unexpected prize or reward that is unearned and undeserved. As food grows scarce in George Orwell's *Animal Farm,* the pigs assert their importance by demanding the milk, apples, and windfalls for themselves—an ominous precedent to their eventual move into Farmer Jones's clothing, house, and easy lifestyle.

winding-sheet a length of cloth, strapping, or shroud used to wind around, encase, or mummy a corpse for burial, particularly during an epidemic when burial customs are suspended so that the dead can be interred quickly with a minimum of exposure to contagion for family, pallbearers, and funeral managers. A form of swaddling, the winding-sheet dates to the earliest tomb burials, especially for the poor, who lacked the money to embalm and deck a body in splendor. Before the visit of the first holiday phantasm in Charles Dickens's *A Christmas Carol,* Ebenezer Scrooge sees his deceased partner, Jacob Marley, still wearing a winding-sheet, his jaw tied with a rag, and his limbs hindered by chains linked to the ledger and cash box from his years of dedication to money.

windlass (*wihnd'* luhs) or **wanlace** the hand crank, handle, or lever of a winch consisting of a rotating drum between vertical uprights. It is turned by hand or belt to hoist or drop a rope, bucket, drilling shaft, or ore from a mine. Entering English in the fifteenth century, the term derives from the German for *winding pole.* A focus of Charles Dickens's *Hard Times,* the implements used by workers, such as windlasses and pumps, attest to the waning importance of human and animal muscle in an age being overtaken by steam power.

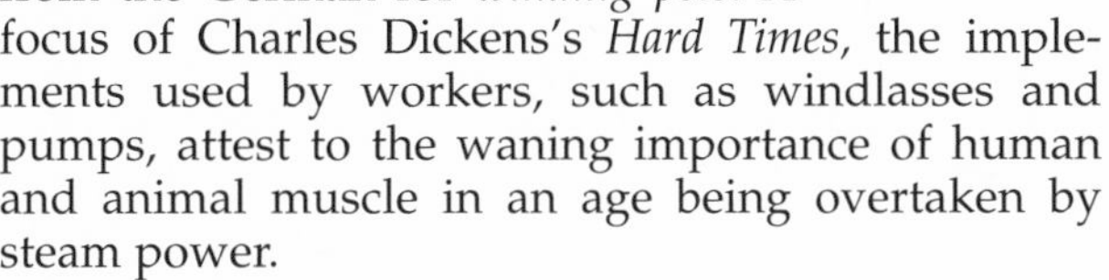

windrow (*wihnd'* roh) or **winrow** a thin row or long mound of drying wheat, corn, or other grain that is left in the field for baling or gathering into sheaves after the sun has removed excess moisture. Proper drying is crucial to hay because dampness can mold the stalks or can cause spontaneous combustion and set fire to ricks or barns. In honest, unadorned agricultural style, Pa admires Farmer Tanner for his straight windrows in Robert Newton Peck's *A Day No Pigs Would Die.*

Windsor chair (*wihnd'* suhr) a sturdy spindle-back wood chair named for the current ruling house of Great Britain. The Windsor chair features rounded railing, saddle seat, and legs canted outward to steady the user. In the rough days before rebellion freed Manor Farm in George Orwell's *Animal Farm,* Mr. Jones lolled in his Windsor chair and read the paper while tossing crusts to Moses the crow, a symbol of the hovering evil from the animal kingdom that Jones fails to suspect of conspiring to mutiny.

winnow (*wihn'* noh) to fan, toss, or expose to air currents unhusked grains to separate the heavy kernels from chaff, the nutritionless husks that are discarded or collected for bedding, mulch, fuel, or an additive to fodder. Derived from the German for *fan,* the term entered English before the twelfth century when most agricultural jobs were done by hand or with simple tools. One of O-lan's many outside jobs is to winnow wheat by fanning chaff from rice grains in Pearl S. Buck's *The Good Earth.*

wolverine (*wool'* vuh . reen) a wily, thick-pelted, compact member of the weasel family. The wolverine, a carnivore that weighs up to 70 pounds, challenges bears and cougars. In the absence of a kill, the wolverine subsists on the wintry tundra with makeshift meals of rancid bait from traps, carrion, or food stolen from nearby villages. Unable to recognize the howl of a wolverine in Jack London's *White Fang,* the title character still raises his hackles at the intruder and prepares for a fight. *See also* hackles; tundra.

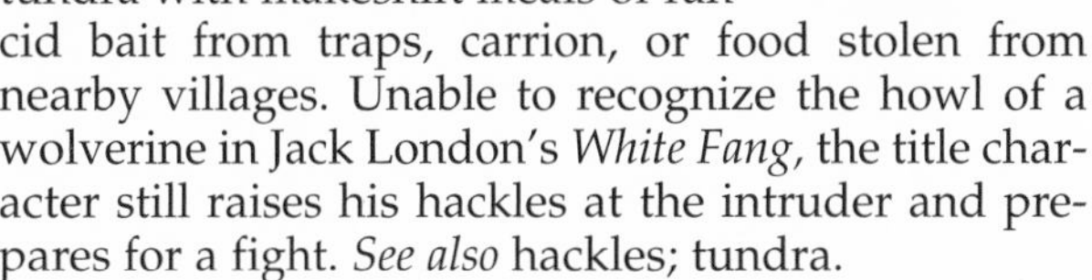

wonton (*wahn'* tahn) noodle dough that is formed into pockets and filled with a savory minced meat mixture and boiled as a dumpling in broth or fried. A Chinese culinary term, it entered English in the 1930s. In Amy Tan's *The Joy Luck Club,* Asian-American daughters doubt that the ability to make a succulent wonton proves the expertise of a good cook, the aim of Asian women in the previous generation.

woof *See* warp.

workhouse a parish refuge or shelter where destitute people—including the aged, infirm, and children—worked in exchange for minimum necessities of clothing, medical care, bedding, and food. After the passage of the Poor Laws of 1834, some parishes combined efforts by forming a union workhouse, an impersonal warehouse for society's wretched who were exploited by greedy entrepreneurs. A common setting in Charles Dickens's works, the workhouse, which is the shame-laden birthplace of the title character of *Oliver Twist,* is obliquely referred to as "the house."

wormwood a silvery-green perennial that mounds into a bush and produces feathery foliage and compact yellow flower heads. The leaves of wormwood or artemisia (called *chernobyl* in Russian) yield a bitter, poisonous juice used by healers in minute doses to induce menstruation, spark a dwindling appetite, and kill intestinal parasites. The unnamed nurse in William Shakespeare's *Romeo and Juliet* smears wormwood on her nipples to force a nursing child to give up breastfeeding.

W.P.A. the Works Progress Administration, which was created as a core contribution of President Franklin Roosevelt's New Deal and was established as a congressional relief effort in April 1935. It created jobs benefiting the public by improving roads, parks, airports, courthouses, bridges, and forests until the program's termination in 1943. In addition to the 2 million adults who performed jobs for the W.P.A., 1 million young workers assisted the national recovery from the Depression by working for the National Youth Administration, a similar program for the poor and jobless. During the childhood of the title character in Alex Haley's *The Autobiography of Malcolm X,* successful blacks shined shoes or performed manual labor; the rest lived on welfare or the W.P.A.

wreath a festive garland, spray, centerpiece, or circlet of greenery, flowers, herbs, seed pods, and fruit adorning a doorway, hearth, window, gate, shop window, or wall. The term is derived from the pre-twelfth century Anglo-Saxon word for *twist.* In ancient times, the interweaving of myrtle or laurel symbolized a victory or the love and admiration of local people for an athletic hero or triumphant general. In despair at the collapse of Brutus and Cassius's fight against Mark Antony in William Shakespeare's *Julius Caesar,* Titanius rejects a laurel wreath and falls upon his sword, an action often referred to as "the Roman way of death." *See also* triumph.

yawl a small launch, two-masted fishing boat, or jolly boat rowed to shore. The yawl transports small groups, parcels, mail, and luggage from a ship to land in a narrow harbor where boats are anchored at a distance in the roadbed or where there is not enough space at the quay or in the docks for moorage. The term is derived from the Dutch for *jolly.* Mark Twain's *Life on the Mississippi* describes the job of a visiting pilot who travels by yawl to buoy the channel or assist pilots. *See also* lighter.

yellow star the symbolic black palm-sized patch or badge containing the yellow shape of the Star of David and centered with the word *Jew.* Worn on the left breast by East European Jews, the yellow star helped Hitler's SS troops identify the oppressed group and enforce harsh laws governing daily function, education, shopping, and travel. Like Corrie ten Boom, author of *The Hiding Place* and rescuer of a stream of yellow star–marked Jews, the speaker of Margaret Atwood's *The Handmaid's Tale* identifies with a color-coded system of victimization. *See also* holocaust; Nazi; SS.

yew (yoo) a tall, thin evergreen that is considered a magical plant in English folklore. The yew, a relative of hemlock, is often associated with death and decay and is the traditional hedge of cemeteries. Its branches are used in dowsing; the plant is a sturdy ornamental that adapts to a variety of soils and climates and remains free of insect infestations. The tree is prized for pliant, fine-grained wood for bows, boat paddles, chair legs, spindles, and carvings. In literature, the yew is linked to sorrow and to immortality, possibly because of its place in Palm Sunday decorations and rituals. The yew provides slips for the pot of the three weird sisters in William Shakespeare's *Macbeth. See also* divining rod; hebona; hemlock.

yin/yang the contrast of female elements of Taoist and Confucian cosmology, for example, cold, nonaggressive, acquiescent, moist, and dark, with male elements, which are typically hot, aggressive, combative, dry, and illuminated. In Maxine Hong Kingston's *The Woman Warrior,* nursing students learn ancient beliefs about healing derived from the controlling principle of yin/yang, which symbolizes the body's fight to maintain normal temperature while fighting infection. *See also* Tao.

Yom Kippur (*yom* . kih . *poor'*) a high holy day following the Jewish New Year commemorating Moses' presentation of a second set of the ten commandments and God's offer to forgive the Hebrews' sacrilege in worshipping a golden calf. Yom Kippur requires celebrants to fast, pray, beg forgiveness, and atone for their sins by making amends to those they have wronged. In Elie Wiesel's autobiographical *Night,* concentration camp inmates are so weak from starvation and overwork that they debate the wisdom of Yom Kippur's daylong prayers and fasting. *See also* Rosh Hashanah.

yuan (*yoo'* uhn) the basic unit of Chinese currency, which breaks down into 10 jiao and 100 fen. In Amy Tan's *The Kitchen God's Wife,* when Jiang Weili is betrothed in 1937, the yuan equals 50 cents. Thus, Winnie's dowry of 4,000 yuan equalled $2,000, a sizable amount that allowed her some leverage against a spiteful, abusive husband. *See also* fen.

yuca *See* cassava.

yucca (*yuh'* kuh) a tough, versatile desert agave prized in the southwestern United States for its roots, which were made into ritual soap and a tea or rinse to treat scalp disease, rheumatism, diabetes, and digestive problems. The fibrous leaves were woven into sandals, netting, pouches, and rope or were shaped into brushes, toys, and mats. The oblong pods were roasted and eaten like yams or melons. In Rudolfo Anaya's *Bless Me, Ultima,* the *curandera* thrives on a landscape rich in healing herbs, yucca, juniper, and mesquite.

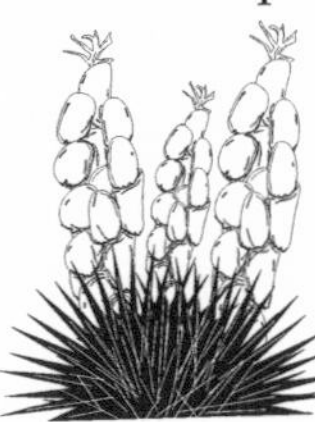

Zen (zehn) a mystical form of Buddhism derived from Lao Tzu's *Tao Te Ching* or *The Way of Life,* a brief sixth-century B.C. religious and ethical manual recommending virtue as the goal of a well-balanced life. An early eighteenth-century term, it derives from the Sanskrit for *meditation,* the clearing of the thought centers of all impediments to attain oneness with the universe. In Amy Tan's *The Kitchen God's Wife,* Pearl describes her confusion at a Zen center where no priest officiated. *See also* Tao.

Zion (*zy'* 'n) the rocky ridge that forms the nucleus of David's Jerusalem, the capital city that united a squabbling, nomadic nation for the first time in history. The scene of important moments in the lives of David, Solomon, and Moses, Zion figures as a metaphor or image in much literature and song that celebrates the Judaeo-Christian tradition. In Jerome Lawrence and Robert E. Lee's *Inherit the Wind,* the fundamentalist observers at the biology teacher's trial sing gospel hymns extolling Zion.

zoot suit a flashy fad in men's clothing of the pre–World War II era featuring sleazy fabrics, extended shoulder padding, thigh-length jackets, thin belts, and flashy, overly long watch chains. The pants to the suit tapered to a drastically narrow cuff. Before going to prison for burglary in Alex Haley's *The Autobiography of Malcolm X,* the title character conks his hair, dresses in zoot suits, and follows the pattern of young turks, gangsters, and street toughs who fill the streets of Harlem. *See also* conked head.

Bibliography

Achebe, Chinua. *Things Fall Apart*. New York: Fawcett Crest, 1959.

Adams, Richard. *Watership Down*. New York: Avon Books, 1972.

Adamson, Joy. *Born Free*. New York: Vintage Books, 1960.

Allende, Isabel. *The House of the Spirits*. New York: Bantam Books, 1986.

Anaya, Rudolfo A. *Bless Me, Ultima*. Berkeley, Calif.: Tonatiuhn-Quinto Sol International, 1972.

Anderson, Douglas. *The Annotated Hobbit*. Boston: Houghton Mifflin, 1988.

Angelou, Maya. *I Know Why the Caged Bird Sings*. New York: Bantam, 1970.

Anthony, Susan B. "Women's Right to Vote," in *The American Reader,* Diane Ravitch, ed. New York: HarperCollins, 1990.

Aristophanes. *The Birds*, Benjamin Bickley Rogers, trans. Garden City, N.Y.: Doubleday, 1955.

Atwood, Margaret. *The Handmaid's Tale*. New York: Quality Paperback Book Club, 1972.

Austen, Jane. *Pride and Prejudice*. New York: New American Library, 1980.

Avi. *The True Confessions of Charlotte Doyle*. New York: Avon, 1990.

Bambara, Toni Cade. "Blues Ain't No Mockin' Bird," in *Arrangement in Literature*. Glenview, Ill.: Scott, Foresman and Co., 1982.

Barrett, William. *Lilies of the Field*. New York: Doubleday, 1962.

Beckett, Samuel. *Waiting for Godot*. New York: Grove Press, 1982.

Beowulf. New York: Penguin, 1963.

Böll, Heinrich. "My Melancholy Face," Sandra Smith and Rainer Schulte, trans., in *World Masterpieces*. Englewood Cliffs, N.J.: Prentice-Hall, 1991.

Borges, Jorge Luis. "The Garden of Forking Paths," Donald A. Yates, trans., in *World Masterpieces*. Englewood Cliffs, N.J.: Prentice-Hall, 1991.

Borland, Hal. *When the Legends Die*. New York: Bantam Books, 1964.

Bradbury, Ray. *Fahrenheit 451*. New York: Ballantine Books, 1953.

———. *The Martian Chronicles*. New York: Bantam, 1954.

Brontë, Charlotte. *Jane Eyre*. New York: Bantam Books, 1981.

Brontë, Emily. *Wuthering Heights*. New York: New American Library, 1959.

Buck, Pearl S. *The Good Earth*. New York: Pocket Books, 1939.

Burns, Olive Ann. *Cold Sassy Tree*. New York: Dell Books, 1984.

Camus, Albert. *The Stranger*. Matthew Ward, trans. New York: Vintage International, 1989.

Capek, Karel. *R. U. R.* in *Chief Contemporary Dramatists: Twenty Plays from the Recent Drama of England, Ireland, America, Germany, France, Belgium, Norway, Sweden, and Russia.* Boston: Houghton Mifflin,1943.

Capote, Truman. "A Christmas Memory," in *America*. Boston: Houghton Mifflin, 1978.

Carroll, Lewis. *The Annotated Alice*. New York: Bramhall House, 1960.

Cather, Willa. *My Antonia*. Boston: Houghton Mifflin, 1977.

Chaucer, Geoffrey, "Prologue to the Canterbury Tales," in *British and Western Literature*. New York: McGraw-Hill, 1979.

Chekhov, Anton. "The Bet," Thomas Seltzer, trans., in *British and Western Literature*. New York: McGraw-Hill, 1979.

Chopin, Kate. *The Awakening and Selected Stories.* New York: Penguin Books, 1984.

Cisneros, Sandra. *The House on Mango Street.* New York: Vintage Contemporaries, 1989.

Confucius. *The Analects,* Arthur Waley, trans., in *World Masterpieces.* Englewood Cliffs, N.J.: Prentice-Hall, 1991.

Conrad, Joseph. *The Heart of Darkness* and *The Secret Sharer.* New York: New American Library, 1978.

———. *Lord Jim.* New York: Alfred Knopf, 1992.

Cooper, James Fenimore. *The Last of the Mohicans.* New York: Bantam Books, 1984.

Crane, Stephen. *The Red Badge of Courage.* New York: Airmont, 1962.

Craven, Margaret. *I Heard the Owl Call My Name.* New York: Dell, 1973.

Defoe, Daniel. *Robinson Crusoe.* New York: Airmont, 1963.

Dickens, Charles. *A Christmas Carol.* New York: Airmont, 1963.

———. *David Copperfield.* New York: Clarkson N. Potter, 1986.

———. *Great Expectations.* New York: Clarkson N. Potter, 1986.

———. *Hard Times.* New York: Clarkson N. Potter, 1986.

———. *Oliver Twist.* New York: Clarkson N. Potter, 1986.

———. *A Tale of Two Cities.* New York: Clarkson N. Potter, 1986.

Dinesen, Isak. "The Pearls," in *World Masterpieces.* Englewood Cliffs, N.J.: Prentice-Hall, 1991.

Dostoevsky, Fyodor. *The Brothers Karamazov,* Constance Garnett, trans. New York: Dell Publishing, 1956.

———. *Crime and Punishment,* Constance Garnett, trans. New York: Amsco, 1970.

Douglass, Frederick. *Narrative of the Life of Frederick Douglass.* New York: New American Library, 1968.

Doyle, Sir Arthur Conan. *The Adventures of Sherlock Holmes.* New York: Berkley Books, 1963.

———. *The Hound of the Baskervilles,* in *Arrangement in Literature.* Glenview, Ill.: Scott, Foresman and Co., 1982.

Dumas, Alexandre. *The Count of Monte Cristo.* Lowell Bair, trans. New York: Bantam Books, 1982.

du Maurier, Daphne. *Rebecca.* New York: Avon Books, 1938.

Eliot, George. *Silas Marner.* New York: New American Library, 1960.

Esquivel, Laura. *Like Water for Chocolate,* Carol Christensen and Thomas Christensen, trans. New York: Anchor Books, 1992.

Faulkner, William. "The Bear" in *The Portable Faulkner.* New York: Penguin Books, 1946.

Filipovic, Zlata. *Zlata's Diary.* New York: Penguin Books, 1994.

Fitzgerald, F. Scott. *The Great Gatsby.* New York: Collier Books, 1992.

Flaubert, Gustav. *Madame Bovary,* Mildred Marmur, trans. New York: Signet Classic, 1964.

Forbes, Esther. *Johnny Tremain.* New York: Dell, 1943.

Fox, Paula. *Slave Dancer.* New York: Laurel-Leaf, 1973.

Frank, Anne. *Diary of a Young Girl,* B. M. Mooyart, trans. New York: Pocket Books, 1952.

Franklin, Benjamin. *Poor Richard's Almanack* in *The American Reader.* Diane Ravitch, ed. New York: HarperCollins, 1990.

Gaines, Ernest J. *The Autobiography of Miss Jane Pittman.* New York: Bantam Books, 1971.

Gardner, John. *Grendel.* New York: Ballantine Books, 1971.

Gardner, Martin. *The Annotated Alice.* New York: Bramhall House, 1960.

George, Jean Craighead. *Julie of the Wolves.* New York: Harper & Row, 1972.

Gibson, William. *The Miracle Worker.* London: Tamarack Productions, 1960.

Gilgamesh. David Ferry, trans. New York: Farrar, Straus and Giroux, 1992.

Gogol, Nikolai. "The Overcoat," Andrew R. MacAndrew, trans., in *World Masterpieces.* Englewood Cliffs, N.J.: Prentice-Hall, 1991.

Golding, William. *Lord of the Flies.* New York: Wideview/Perigee, 1954.

Guest, Judith. *Ordinary People.* New York: Ballantine Books, 1976.

Haley, Alex. *The Autobiography of Malcolm X.* New York: Ballantine Books, 1965.

Hamilton, Edith. *Mythology*. Boston: Little, Brown & Co., 1942.

Hansberry, Lorraine. *A Raisin in the Sun*. New York: Signet Books, 1988.

Hardy, Thomas. *Far from the Madding Crowd*. New York: Airmont, 1967.

———. *The Mayor of Casterbridge*. New York: New American Library, 1962.

———. *The Return of the Native*. New York: New American Library, 1959.

———. *Tess of the D'Urbervilles*. New York: New American Library, 1980.

Hart, Moss, and George S. Kaufman. *You Can't Take It with You*, in *Three Comedies of American Family Life*. New York: Washington Square Press, 1961.

Hautzig, Esther. *The Endless Steppe*. New York: Harper & Row Junior Books, 1968.

Hawthorne, Nathaniel. *The House of the Seven Gables*, in *The Complete Novels*. New York: Modern Library, 1937.

———. *The Scarlet Letter*. New York: New American Library, 1959.

Hemingway, Ernest. *A Farewell to Arms*. New York: Charles Scribner's Sons, 1969.

———. *For Whom the Bell Tolls*. New York: Macmillan, 1940.

———. *The Old Man and the Sea*. New York: Charles Scribner's Sons, 1952.

Herriot, James. *All Creatures Great and Small*. New York: Bantam, 1985.

———. *All Things Bright and Beautiful*. New York: St. Martin's, 1975.

Hersey, John. *Hiroshima*. New York: Bantam Books, 1946.

Hesse, Hermann. *Siddhartha*. New York: New Directions Books, 1951.

Heyerdahl, Thor. *Kon Tiki*. New York: Simon & Schuster, 1990.

Hilton, James. *Lost Horizon*. New York: Pocket Books, 1960.

Homer. *Iliad*. Richmond Lattimore, trans. Chicago: University of Chicago Press, 1965.

———. *Odyssey*. Richmond Lattimore, trans. New York: Harper Colophon, 1967.

Houston, Jeanne Wakatsuki, and James D. Houston. *Farewell to Manzanar*. New York: Bantam Books, 1973.

Hsun, Lu. "My Old Home" in *Prentice-Hall Literature*. Englewood Cliffs, N.J.: Prentice-Hall, 1991.

Hugo, Victor. *Les Misérables*. Charles E. Wilbour, trans. New York: Fawcett Crest, 1961.

Hunt, Irene. *Across Five Aprils*. New York: Tempo Books, 1965.

Hurst, James. "The Scarlet Ibis," in *Arrangement in Literature*. Glenview, Ill.: Scott, Foresman and Co., 1982.

Hurston, Zora Neale. *Their Eyes Were Watching God*. New York: Harper & Row, 1990.

Huxley, Aldous. *Brave New World*. New York: Bantam Books, 1939.

Ibsen, Henrik. *A Doll's House*, in *Four Great Plays by Ibsen*. R. Farquharson Sharp, trans. New York: Bantam Books, 1958.

Jhabvala, Ruth Prawer. *Heat and Dust*. New York: Touchstone Books, 1991.

Joyce, James. *The Portrait of the Artist as a Young Man*. New York: Penguin Books, 1964.

Kafka, Franz, "The Metamorphosis," in *British and Western Literature*. New York: McGraw-Hill, 1979.

Keneally, Thomas. *Schindler's List*. New York: Touchstone Books, 1982.

Kesey, Ken. *One Flew over the Cuckoo's Nest*. New York: New American Library 1962.

Key, Francis Scott, "The Star-Spangled Banner," in *The American Reader*. Diane Ravitch, ed. New York: HarperCollins, 1990.

Keyes, Daniel. *Flowers for Algernon*. New York: Bantam Books, 1967.

King, Martin Luther. "Letter from a Birmingham Jail," in *The Negro Almanac*. Harry A. Ploski and James Williams, eds. Detroit: Gale Research, 1989.

Kingston, Maxine Hong. *The Woman Warrior*. New York: Vintage Books, 1975.

Kipling, Rudyard. *Just So Stories*. New York: New American Library, 1912.

———. "Miss Youghal's Sais," in *Plain Tales from the Hills*. New York: Oxford University Press, 1987.

Knowles, John. *A Separate Peace*. New York: Bantam Books, 1960.

Kroeber, Theodora. *Ishi, Last of His Tribe*. New York: Bantam, 1964.

Lawrence, Jerome, and Robert E. Lee. *Inherit the Wind*. New York: Bantam Books, 1955.

Lederer, William J., and Eugene Burdick. *The Ugly American*. New York: Fawcett Crest, 1958.

Lee, Harper. *To Kill a Mockingbird*. New York: Warner Books, 1960.

Lessing, Doris. "No Witchcraft for Sale," in *World Masterpieces*. Englewood Cliffs, N.J.: Prentice-Hall, 1991.

Lincoln, Abraham. "The House Divided Speech," in *The American Reader*. Diane Ravitch, ed. New York: HarperCollins, 1990.

London, Jack. *The Call of the Wild*. New York: Airmont, 1964.

———. *White Fang*. Mahwah, N.J.: Watermill Classics, 1980.

Mahfouz, Najib. "The Happy Man," Saad El-Gabalawy, trans., in *World Masterpieces*. Englewood Cliffs, N.J.: Prentice-Hall, 1991.

Mansfield, Katherine. "The Garden Party," in *The Short Stories of Katherine Mansfield*. New York: Alfred A. Knopf, 1937.

Márquez, Gabriel García. "The Handsomest Drowned Man in the World," Gregory Rabassa, trans., in *World Masterpieces*. Englewood Cliffs, N.J.: Prentice-Hall, 1991.

de Maupassant, Guy. "The Necklace," in *Approach to Literature*. New York: L. W. Singer Co., 1969.

Melville, Herman. "Bartleby the Scrivener," in *Billy Budd and Other Stories*. New York: Penguin Books, 1986.

———. *Benito Cereno* in *Four Short Novels*. New York: Bantam Books, 1959

———. *Billy Budd*. Chicago: University of Chicago Press, 1962.

———. *Moby-Dick*. New York: New American Library, 1961.

———. *Typee*. New York: New American Library, 1964.

Michener, James. *Hawaii*. New York: Random House, 1959.

Miller, Arthur. *The Crucible*. New York: Bantam Books, 1950.

———. *Death of a Salesman*. New York: Penguin Books, 1949.

Milton, John. *Paradise Lost* in *Complete Poems of John Milton*. New York: Odyssey Press, 1957.

Momaday, N. Scott. *The Way to Rainy Mountain*. Santa Fe: University of New Mexico Press, 1969.

Morrison, Toni. *Beloved*. New York: Penguin, 1988.

Mowat, Farley. *Never Cry Wolf*. New York: Bantam Books, 1963.

Myers, Walter Dean. *Fallen Angels*. New York: Scholastic, 1988.

Narayan, R. K. "An Astrologer's Day," in *World Masterpieces*. Englewood Cliffs, N.J.: Prentice-Hall, 1991.

Neihardt, John G. *Black Elk Speaks*. Lincoln: University of Nebraska Press, 1961.

O'Dell, Scott. *Island of the Blue Dolphins*. New York: Dell, 1960.

———. *Sarah Bishop*. New York: Scholastic, 1980.

———. *Sing Down the Moon*. New York: Dell, 1970.

———. *Streams to the River, River to the Sea*. New York: Ballantine Books, 1986.

Orwell, George. *Animal Farm*. New York: New American Library, 1946.

———. *1984*. New York: New American Library, 1949.

Paton, Alan. *Cry, the Beloved Country*. New York: Scribner's Sons, 1948.

Paulsen, Gary. *Dogsong*. New York: Puffin Books, 1987.

———. *Hatchet*. New York: Puffin Books, 1987.

———. *Nightjohn*. New York: Delacorte Press, 1993.

———. *Winterdance*. New York: Harcourt Brace, 1993.

———. *Woodsong*. New York: Puffin Books, 1990.

Peck, Robert Newton. *A Day No Pigs Would Die*. New York: Dell, 1972.

Pepys, Samuel. *The Diary of Samuel Pepys*. New York: Harcourt, Brace, and Co., 1926.

Pirandello, Luigi. "A Breath of Air," Lily Duplaix, trans., in *World Masterpieces*. Englewood Cliffs, N.J.: Prentice-Hall, 1991.

Portis, Charles. *True Grit*. New York: New American Library, 1968.

Potok, Chaim. *The Chosen*. New York: Fawcett Crest, 1967.

Rand, Ayn. *Anthem*. New York: New American Library, 1946.

Raskin, Ellen. *The Westing Game*. New York: Avon, 1978.

Rawlings, Marjorie Kinnan. *The Yearling*. New York: Charles Scribner's Sons, 1966.

Rawls, Wilson. *Where the Red Fern Grows*. New York: Bantam, 1974.

Remarque, Erich Maria. *All Quiet on the Western Front*. New York: Fawcett Crest, 1956.

Renault, Mary. *The Persian Boy*. New York: Random House, 1988.

Richter, Conrad. *The Light in the Forest*. New York: Bantam, 1954.

Rojas, Manuel. "The Glass of Milk," William E. Colford, trans., in *World Masterpieces*. Englewood Cliffs, N.J.: Prentice-Hall, 1991.

Rostand, Edmond. *Cyrano de Bergerac*. Lowell Bair, trans. New York: Signet Classics, 1972.

Ruth in *Holy Bible* (King James version). Cleveland, Ohio: World Publishing Co., n.d.

Salinger, J. D. *The Catcher in the Rye*. New York: Bantam Books, 1964.

Schaefer, Jack. *Shane*. New York: Bantam Books, 1949.

Scott, Walter Sir. *Ivanhoe*. New York: New American Library, 1962.

Shakespeare, William. *Hamlet*. Complete Study Edition. Lincoln, Nebr.: Cliffs Notes, 1967.

———. *Julius Caesar*. Complete Study Edition. Lincoln, Nebr.: Cliffs Notes, 1967.

———. *Macbeth*. Complete Study Edition. Lincoln, Nebr.: Cliffs Notes, 1966.

———. *A Midsummer Night's Dream*. New York: Washington Square Press, 1958.

———. *Romeo and Juliet*. Complete Study Edition. Lincoln, Nebr.: Cliffs Notes, 1968.

———. *The Taming of the Shrew*. New York: Washington Square Press, 1963.

———. *The Tempest* in *World Masterpieces*. Englewood Cliffs, N.J.: Prentice-Hall, 1991.

Shaw, George Bernard. *Pygmalion*, in *Adventures in English Literature*. New York: Harcourt, Brace & World, 1958.

Shelley, Mary. *Frankenstein*. New York: New American Library, 1965.

Sinclair, Upton. *The Jungle*. New York: New American Library, 1960.

Solzhenitsyn, Alexander. *One Day in the Life of Ivan Denisovich*. New York: Bantam Books, 1963.

Sophocles. *Antigone*. H. D. F. Kitto, trans., in *British and Western Literature*. New York: McGraw-Hill, 1979.

———. *Oedipus*, David Grene, trans., in *World Masterpieces*. Englewood Cliffs, N.J.: Prentice-Hall, 1991.

Speare, Elizabeth George. *The Witch of Blackbird Pond*. New York: Dell, 1958.

Steinbeck, John. *The Grapes of Wrath*. New York: Bantam, 1946.

———. *Of Mice and Men*. New York: Bantam, 1955.

———. *The Pearl*. New York: Bantam, 1945.

———. *The Red Pony*. New York: Bantam Books, 1938.

Stevenson, Robert Louis. *Dr. Jekyll and Mr. Hyde*. New York: Bantam Books, 1981.

———. *Treasure Island*. New York: Airmont Books, 1962.

Stoker, Bram. *Dracula*. New York: Bantam, 1981.

Swift, Jonathan. *Gulliver's Travels*. New York: Airmont, 1964.

———. "A Modest Proposal," in *British and Western Literature*. New York: McGraw-Hill, 1979.

Tagore, Rabindranath. "The Artist," Tarum Gupta, Mary Logo, and Amiya Chakravarty, trans., in *World Masterpieces*. Englewood Cliffs, N.J.: Prentice-Hall, 1991.

Tan, Amy. *The Joy Luck Club*. New York: Ivy Books, 1989.

———. *The Kitchen God's Wife*. New York: Ivy Books, 1991.

Taylor, Theodore. *The Cay*. New York: Avon Books, 1969.

———. *Timothy of the Cay*. New York: Avon, 1993.

ten Boom, Carrie. *The Hiding Place*. New York: Bantam Books, 1971.

Thoreau, Henry David. *Walden* and *Civil Disobedience*. New York: Airmont, 1965.

Tolkien, J. R. R. *The Hobbit*. New York: Ballantine Books, 1966.

Twain, Mark. *The Adventures of Huckleberry Finn*. New York: Airmont, 1962.

———. *The Adventures of Tom Sawyer*. New York: Airmont, 1962.

———. *Life on the Mississippi*. New York: Oxford University Press, 1990.

———. *The Prince and the Pauper*. New York: New American Library, 1984.

Verne, Jules. *Around the World in Eighty Days*. New York: Laurel-Leaf, 1964.

Virgil. *Aeneid*. New York: Mentor, 1961.

Walker, Alice. *The Color Purple*. New York: Pocket Books, 1982.

Watkins, Yoko Kawashima. *So Far from the Bamboo Grove*. New York: Puffin Books, 1987.

Wells, H. G. *The Time Machine*. New York: Airmont, 1964.

West, Jessamyn. *Except for Me and Thee*. New York: Avon Books, 1949.

Wharton, Edith. *Ethan Frome*. New York: Charles Scribner's Sons, 1970.

Wiesel, Elie. *Night*. New York: Bantam, 1982.

Wilder, Thornton. *The Bridge of San Luis Rey*. New York: Harper & Row, 1955.

———. *Our Town*. New York: Harper & Row, 1957.

Williams, Tennessee. *The Glass Menagerie*. New York: New Classics, 1945.

———. *A Streetcar Named Desire*. New York: Signet Books, 1947.

Wright, Richard. *Black Boy*. New York: Harper Perennial, 1966.

———. *Native Son*. New York: Harper Perennial, 1993.

Yasunari, Kawabata, "The Jay," Edward Seidensticker, trans., in *World Masterpieces*. Englewood Cliffs, N.J.: Prentice-Hall, 1991.

Yep, Laurence. *Dragonwings*. New York: HarperCollins, 1975.

Zindel, Paul. *The Effect of Gamma Rays on Man-in-the-Moon Marigolds*. New York: Bantam Books, 1972.

References

Academic American Encyclopedia. Danbury, Conn.: Grolier, 1983.

Adams, Brian, et al. *Encyclopedia of Great Civilizations.* New York: Shooting Star Press, 1994.

Alexander, David, ed. *Eerdmans' Handbook to the Bible.* San Diego, Calif.: Lion Publishing, 1973.

The American Heritage Dictionary. New York: Dell Publishing, 1983.

Anderson, Bernhard W. *Understanding the Old Testament.* Englewood Cliffs, N.J.: Prentice-Hall, 1966.

Asante, Molefi K., and Mark T. Mattson. *Historical and Cultural Atlas of African Americans.* New York: Macmillan, 1992.

Atlas of the Human Body. New York: Harper Perennial/HarperCollins, 1994.

Ayto, John. *Dictionary of Word Origins.* New York: Little, Brown and Co., 1990.

Bair, Frank E. *The Weather Almanac.* Detroit: Gale Research, 1992.

Barber, Elizabeth Wayland. *Women's Work: The First 20,000 Years.* New York: W. W. Norton, 1994.

Barrett, David G. *World Christian Encyclopedia.* New York: Oxford University Press, 1982.

Bell, Robert. *Women of Classical Mythology.* Santa Barbara, Calif.: ABC-CLIO, 1991.

Biederman, Hans. *Dictionary of Symbolism.* New York: Facts on File, 1992.

Blackburn, Simon. *The Oxford Dictionary of Philosophy.* New York: Oxford University Press, 1994.

Bowder, Diana, ed. *Who Was Who in the Greek World.* New York: Washington Square Press, 1982

———. *Who Was Who in the Roman World.* New York: Washington Square Press, 1980.

Boyce, Charles. *Shakespeare A to Z.* New York: Facts on File, 1990.

Bradfield, Nancy. *Historical Costumes of England: From the Eleventh to the Twentieth Century.* New York: Barnes & Noble, 1971.

Brockett, Oscar G. *History of the Theatre.* Boston: Allyn & Bacon, 1968.

Brown, Leslie. *The New Shorter Oxford English Dictionary.* New York: Oxford University Press, 1993.

Buckman, Peter. *Let's Dance.* Gordon Press, 1986.

Castillo, Carlos, and Otto F. Bond. *The University of Chicago Spanish-English, English-Spanish Dictionary.* New York: Washington Square Press, 1965.

Cavendish, Marshall, ed. *Man, Myth and Magic.* London: Marshall Cavendish, 1970.

Chapman, Robert. *American Slang.* New York: Harper & Row, 1987

Cirlot, J. E. *A Dictionary of Symbols.* New York: Dorset Press, 1971.

Crystal, David. *The Cambridge Encyclopedia of Language.* New York: Cambridge University Press, 1987.

Daise, Ronald. *Reminiscences of Sea Island Heritage.* Orangeburg, S.C.: Sandlapper Publishing, 1986.

Davidson, Cathy N., and Linda Wagner-Martin, eds. *The Oxford Companion to Women's Writing in the United States.* New York: Oxford University Press, 1995.

Douglas, George William. *The American Book of Days.* New York: H. W. Wilson, 1948.

Ehrlich, Eugene, ed. *The Harper Dictionary of Foreign Terms.* New York: Harper & Row, 1987.

Encyclopaedia Britannica. Chicago: Encyclopaedia Britannica, 1981.

Encyclopedia Americana. Danbury, Conn.: Grolier, 1987.

Famighetti, Robert, ed. *The World Almanac and Book of Facts.* Mahwah, N.J.: Funk and Wagnalls, 1994.

Foner, Eric, and John A. Garraty, eds. *The Reader's Companion to American History.* Boston: Houghton Mifflin, 1991.

Funk and Wagnalls New Encyclopedia. Mahwah, N.J.: Funk & Wagnalls Corp., 1993.

Gassner, John, and Edward Quinn, eds. *The Reader's Encyclopedia of World Drama.* New York: Thomas Y. Crowell, 1969.

Gentz, William H., gen. ed. *The Dictionary of Bible and Religion.* Nashville, Tenn.: Abingdon Press, 1986.

Glinert, Lewis. *The Joys of Hebrew.* New York: Oxford University Press, 1992.

Goring, Rosemary, ed. *Larousse Dictionary of Literary Characters.* New York: Larousse Kingfisher Chambers, 1994.

———. *Larousse Dictionary of Writers.* New York: Larousse Kingfisher Chambers, 1994.

Gray, Henry. *Anatomy, Descriptive and Surgical.* Philadelphia: Running Press, 1974.

Grimal, Pierre. *Dictionary of Classical Mythology.* New York: Penguin, 1990.

Growing Up with Science: The Illustrated Encyclopedia of Invention. Westport, Conn.: H. S. Stuttman, Inc., 1987.

Grunfeld, Frederic V., ed. *Games of the World.* New York: Holt, Rinehart, & Winston, 1975.

Gutek, Gerald, and Patricia Gutek. *Experiencing America's Past: A Travel Guide to Museum Villages.* 2d ed. Columbia, S.C.: University of South Carolina Press, 1994.

Hammond, N. G. L., and H. H. Scullard. *The Oxford Classical Dictionary.* Oxford: Oxford University Press, 1970.

Hammond Atlas of World History. Rev. ed. Maplewood, N.J.: Hammond, 1993.

Hammond Student's Atlas of the World. Maplewood, N.J.: Hammond, 1995.

Hart, James D. *The Oxford Companion to American Literature.* New York: Oxford University Press, 1983.

Haythornthwaite, Philip J. *The World War One Source Book.* London: Arms and Armour Press, 1992.

Heywood, V. H., ed. *Flowering Plants of the World.* New York: Oxford University Press, 1993.

Hilgard, Ernest R., et al. *Introduction to Psychology.* New York: Harcourt Brace Jovanovich, 1971.

Holman, C. Hugh, and William Harmon. *A Handbook to Literature.* New York: Macmillan, 1992.

Howatson, M. C., ed. *The Oxford Companion to Classical Literature.* New York: Oxford University Press, 1991.

The Hutchinson Dictionary of Ideas. Santa Barbara, Calif.: ABC-CLIO, 1994.

Irwin, Keith Gordon. *The Romance of Writing: From Egyptian Hieroglyphics to Modern Letters, Numbers, and Signs.* New York: Viking Press, 1956.

Israel, Fred L. *The FBI.* New York: Chelsea House, 1986.

Jacobs, Dick, and Harriet Jacobs. *Who Wrote That Song?* Cincinnati, Ohio: Writer's Digest Books, 1994.

Johnson, Kevin Orlin. *Expression of the Catholic Faith: A Guide to the Teachings and Practices of the Catholic Church.* New York: Ballantine Books, 1994.

Johnson, Otto, ed. *1995 Information Please Almanac.* Boston: Houghton Mifflin, 1995.

Kalman, Bobbie. *Early Travel.* Toronto: Crabtree Publishing, 1981.

Karenga, Maulana. *The African-American Holiday of Kwanzaa: A Celebration of Family, Country, and Culture.* Los Angeles: University of Sankore Press, 1988.

Kemp, Peter. *The Oxford Companion to Ships and the Sea.* New York: Oxford University Press, 1988.

Kincaid, Zoë. *Kabuki: The Popular Stage of Japan.* Benjamin Blom, 1965.

Krause, Chester L. *Standard Catalog of World Coins.* Iola, Wisc.: Krause Publications, 1995.

Landman, Isaac, ed. *The Universal Jewish Encyclopedia.* New York: Universal Jewish Encyclopedia Co., 1948.

Legat, Michael. *The Illustrated Dictionary of Western Literature.* New York: Continuum, 1987.

Low, W. Augustus, and Virgil A. Clift. *Encyclopedia of Black America.* New York: Da Capo, 1981.

Macaulay, David. *Castle.* Boston: Houghton Mifflin, 1977.

———. *Cathedral.* Boston: Houghton Mifflin, 1973.

McKechnie, Jean, ed. *Webster's New Universal Unabridged Dictionary.* New York: Simon & Schuster, 1983.

Maggio, Rosalie. *The Dictionary of Bias-Free Usage.* Phoenix, Ariz.: Oryx, 1991.

Merriam-Webster's Collegiate Dictionary. 10th ed. Springfield, Mass.: Merriam-Webster, 1993.

Michell, George. *In the Image of Man: The Indian Perception of the Universe Through 2000 Years of Painting and Sculpture.* New York: Alpine Fine Arts Collection, Ltd., 1982.

New Catholic Encyclopedia. Washington, D.C.: Catholic University of America, 1967.

New Grove Dictionary of Music and Musicians. New York: Macmillan, 1980.

Parrish, Thomas, ed. *The Simon and Schuster Encyclopedia of World War II.* New York: Simon & Schuster, 1978.

Partridge, Eric, ed. *The Dictionary of Slang and Unconventional English.* New York: Macmillan, 1951.

Pennick, Nigel. *The Pagan Book of Days.* Rochester, Vt.: Destiny Books, 1992.

Perkins, George, et al., eds. *Benét's Reader's Encyclopedia of American Literature.* New York: HarperCollins, 1962.

Peterson, Harold L. *The Treasury of the Gun.* New York: Golden Press, 1962.

Philip, Alex J., and W. Laurence Gadd. *A Dickens Dictionary.* London: Simpkin Marshall, 1928.

Pierce, James Smith. *From Abacus to Zeus: A Handbook of Art History.* Englewood Cliffs, N.J.: Prentice-Hall, 1991.

Ploski, Harry A., and James Williams, eds. *The Negro Almanac.* Detroit: Gale Research, 1989.

The Readers's Companion to World Literature. New York: Mentor, 1973.

Roget's International Thesaurus. New York: Harper & Row, 1977.

Rummel, R. J. *Democide: Nazi Genocide and Mass Murder.* New Brunswick, N.J.: Transaction Publishers, 1992.

Rutland, Jonathan. *An Ancient Greek Town.* London: Kingfisher Books, 1986.

———. *A Galleon.* London: Kingfisher Books, 1986.

Sattler, Helen Roney. *The Book of Eagles.* New York: Lothrop, Lee, & Shepard Books, 1989.

Schaefer, Vincent J. *A Field Guide to the Atmosphere.* Boston: Houghton Mifflin, 1981.

Shapiro, William E., ed. *The Kingfisher Young People's Encyclopedia of the United States.* New York: Larousse Kingfisher Chambers, 1994.

Shields, Mary. *Sled Dog Trails.* Fairbanks, Alaska: Pyrola Publishing, 1984.

Shumaker, David, ed. *Seven Language Dictionary.* New York: Avenel, 1978.

Smith, Henrietta M., ed. *The Coretta Scott King Awards Book: From Vision to Reality.* Chicago: American Library Association, 1994.

Snodgrass, Mary Ellen. *Black History Month Resource Book.* Detroit: Gale Research, 1993.

———. *The Great American English Handbook.* Jacksonville, Ill.: Perma-Bound, 1987.

———. *Indian Terms.* Englewood, Colo.: Libraries Unlimited, 1994.

———. *Voyages in Classical Mythology.* Santa Barbara, Calif.: ABC-CLIO, 1995.

Stern, Chaim, ed. *Gates of Prayer.* New York: Central Conference of American Rabbis, 1989.

Sullivan, George. *Slave Ship: The Story of the* Henrietta Marie. New York: Cobblehill Books, 1994.

Sykes, J. B. *The Concise Oxford Dictionary of Current English,* New York: Oxford University Press, 1982.

Unstead, R. J., ed. *See Inside a Castle.* London: Grisewood and Dempsey, 1986.

———. *See Inside a Galleon.* London: Grisewood and Dempsey, 1986.

Walton, John, Jeremiah A. Barondess, and Stephen Lock, eds. *The Oxford Medical Companion.* New York: Oxford University Press, 1994.

Watts, Karen, comp. *21st Century Dictionary of Slang.* New York: Laurel Books, 1994.

Weapons: An International Encyclopedia from 5000 B.C. to 2000 A.D. New York: St. Martin's Press, 1990.

Webster's New Geographical Dictionary. Springfield, Mass.: Merriam-Webster, 1988.

Wilson, Charles Reagan, and William Ferris. *Encyclopedia of Southern Culture.* Chapel Hill: University of North Carolina Press, 1989.

Wyman, Donald. *Wyman's Gardening Encyclopedia.* New York: Macmillan, 1971.

Yarwood, Doreen. *The Encyclopedia of World Costume.* New York: Bonanza Books, 1986.

Yeoman, R. S. *A Guidebook of United States Coins.* 46th ed. Racine, Wisc.: Western Publishing Co., 1992.

Index
by Author and Title

Achebe, Chinua
Things Fall Apart alligator pepper, bullroarer, camwood, cassava, clan, cocoyam, compound, cowrie, foo foo, harmattan, kola nut, leprosy, machete, obi, raffia, silk cotton tree, taboo, tuber
Adams, Richard
Watership Down bivouac, burrow, punt, pylon, soffit
Adamson, Joy
Born Free boma, draught, hessian bag, hookworm, hyrax, kudu, Land Rover, spoor
Allende, Isabel
The House of the Spirits novice, *patrón*, peso, sacristy
Anaya, Rudolfo
Bless Me, Ultima *abrazo*, adobe, bosque, *bruja*, carp, confirmation, conquistador, *curandera*, drunk tank, farol, Good Friday, gunny sack, half nelson, juniper, limbo, *llanero*, manzanilla, mesquite, posole, purgatory, rosary, *tejano, vaquero*, wake, yucca
Angelou, Maya
I Know Why the Caged Bird Sings abacus, arabesque, *au jus*, Bluebeard, cathead, cat's face, C.C.C., chinaberry, chow-chow, C.M.E. Church, cotton boll, crabs, *double entendre,* elder, French seams, hermaphrodite, jacks, jew's harp, juju, Ku Klux Klan, mourners' bench, mumbledypeg, numbers runner, open sesame, paisano, pedal pushers, Pharisee, Rippers, sloe, snap-brim hat, tempura
Anthony, Susan B.
"Women's Right to Vote" plebeian, serf, tribunal
Aristophanes
The Birds dupe
Atwood, Margaret
The Handmaid's Tale crèche, crowning, fanlight, flocked, matrix, *papier poudre*, primipara, Romanesque, symposium, tallith, Torah, yellow star
Austen, Jane
Pride and Prejudice backgammon, calico, cassino, chaise, coppice, curricle, earl, paling, phaeton, rectory, turnpike house
Avi
The True Confessions of Charlotte Doyle atoll, bowsprit, brigantine, dirk, foretop, frock coat, holystone, ratline, reticule, round robin, shilling, snow mast, step
Bambara, Toni Cade
"Blues Ain't No Mockin' Bird" food stamps
Barrett, William
Lilies of the Field adobe
Beckett, Samuel
Waiting for Godot the clap, cretin, dudeen, foetal posture, gonococcus, spirochete
Beowulf firedrake, meadhall, runes
Böll, Heinrich
"My Melancholy Face" quai
Borges, Jorge Luis
"The Garden of Forking Paths" crown
Borland, Hal
When the Legends Die breechclout, camas, chaps, clout Indian, falsetto, hobble, latigo, pommel, quirt, rowel, serviceberry, surcingle
Bradbury, Ray
Fahrenheit 451 adder, arc-lamp, atom-bomb mushroom, caesarian section, convolutions of the brain, flue, grille, magazine, microfilm, moonstone, praetorian guard, proboscis, salamander, shingle, tabloid, theremin, thunderheads, V-2 rocket
The Martian Chronicles psychosis, rococo, sarcophagus, telepathy
Brontë, Charlotte
Jane Eyre *bonne*, chilblain, collect, conservatory, diablerie, dressing case, false front, foundry, gingham, grange, harlequin, heather, *ignis fatuus*, negus, nonnette, portfolio, ringlet, rookery, rubric, scrag, stile, *tête-à-tête*, typhus, wicket
Brontë, Emily
Wuthering Heights battledoor, bitter herbs, cambric, coxcomb, curate, elf-bolt, gentry, gruel, gypsy, heath, kirkyard, lapwing, Michaelmas, mull, pewter, snuffers

Buck, Pearl S.
The Good Earth bound feet, Buddha, cash, chaff, concubine, court, cress, eddy, flail, fox pieces, geomancer, giblets, hasp, lacquer, lotus, lute, middleman, moon cake, opium den, pock-marked, rickshaw, seal, spindle, teahouse, winnow
Burdick, Eugene *See* William J. Lederer
Burns, Olive Ann
Cold Sassy Tree bobwhite, buckeye, Franklin car, gristmill, hello-girl, hoarhound, lockjaw, mill house, puncheon, siren, sputum, streak-a-lean, suffragette, trousseau
Camus, Albert
The Stranger assizes (court of), cassock, guillotine, indictment, tamarisk
Capek, Karel
R. U. R automaton
Capote, Truman
"A Christmas Memory" biddy chicken, rime, satsuma, stereopticon
Carroll, Lewis
Alice's Adventures in Wonderland caucus, chrysalis, comfit, courtier, cucumber frame, do-do, dormouse, fender, griffon, hookah, quadrille, shingle, thistle, treacle
Through the Looking Glass chimney-piece
Cather, Willa
My Antonia arnica, bandy legs, bile, court-plaster, finger bowl, firebreak, haymow, hieroglyphics, kolach, lariat pin, schottische, selah, sombrero, tintype, usury note, wash bowl and pitcher
Chaucer, Geoffrey
"Prologue to the Canterbury Tales" blanc mange, curteisye, palmer, Ram, tabard
Chekhov, Anton
"The Bet" panpipes
Chopin, Kate
The Awakening bath-house, Empire gown, mosquito bar, rockaway, smelling salts, treadle
"Zoraïde" swaddling
Cisneros, Sandra
The House on Mango Street anemic, ball and chain, braille, canteen, double-dutch rope, evil eye, lottery, merengue, naphtha, papaya, Sister Superior, taxi tips, tub (four-clawed), wetback
Confucius
The Analects polestar
Conrad, Joseph
The Heart of Darkness alpaca, assegai, brown holland, buccaneer, carbine, dominoes, dugout, ensign, estuary, festoon, franc, fusillade, gauntlet, half-a-crown, jetty, mangrove, Martini-Henry, ratchet-drill, rivet, sealing wax, shirt front, shoal, sounding pole, stanchion, stern wheel
"The Secret Sharer" alee, archipelago, binnacle, bulkhead, bunting, cruet stand, cuddy, fore-braces, gimbal, helmsman, pagoda, poop deck, riding light, sovereign, stateroom, tack, tops'l
Cooper, James Fenimore
The Last of the Mohicans sagamore, succotash, totem, wampum
Crane, Stephen
The Red Badge of Courage battery, breastwork, brigadier, brindle, cartridge, color sergeant, division, haversack, knapsack, orderly, paean, philippic, provost, ramrod, regiment, seminary, sentinel, specter
Craven, Margaret
I Heard the Owl Call My Name abalone, dorsal fin, fingerling, gunwale, hamatsa, ordinand, potlatch, Royal Canadian Mounted Police
Defoe, Daniel
Robinson Crusoe sack
Dickens, Charles
A Christmas Carol bedlam, biffin, blood horse, coal scuttle, gig, grog, hob, link, mince pie, penthouse, pound, seal, slop-seller, smoking bishop, stair rod, sucking pig, twelfth cake, winding-sheet
David Copperfield escritoire, excise, excommunicate, exordium, fly, guinea, sou'wester, stagecoach
Great Expectations apron, ballast, caparisoned coursers, cast, chalk scores, coal-whipper, custom house, dumb-waiter, épergne, fetters, flip, girdle, hackney chariot, hammer-cloth, hawser, hulks, indentures, Inns of Court, jack-towel, knave, limekiln, liver wing, lozenge, nosegay, ostler, pea-coat, pottle, roasting jack, rush-light, sconce, settle, slop-basin, stagecoach
Hard Times mangle, windlass
Oliver Twist nightcap, spring gun, tenter hooks, treadmill, workhouse
A Tale of Two Cities anise, balustrade, blunderbuss, cockade, dervish, equipage, escutcheon, flambeau, footpad, guillotine, jackal, jackboots, jalousie-blinds, linstock, loadstone, packet, postilion, posting-house, relief, rouleau, sand-box, spencer, tocsin, the Tower, tumbril
Dinesen, Isak
"The Pearls" alpenstock, cariole, crinoline, valkyrie
Dostoevsky, Fyodor
The Brothers Karamazov truckle bed
Crime and Punishment farthing, filigree, hypochondria, icon, parasol, pomatum, samovar, tubercle, verst

Douglass, Frederick
Narrative of the Life of Frederick Douglass apprentice, barouche, caulking, confinement, copy-book, curry, dose of salts, felon, flagellation, fodder, handspike, indictment, larboard, love-feast, man-o'-war, molasses, safe, sloop, treading-yard, underground railroad, urchin, whipping-post
Doyle, Arthur Conan
"Adventure of the Speckled Band" adder, bell-pull, dog-cart, gaiters, scaffolding
The Hound of the Baskervilles baronet, bittern, bourgeois type, cavalier, chronicle, coppice, dolichocephalic, eave, foolscap, hansom cab, jessamine, monolith, moor, mullion, *nouveau riche*, parietal fissure, quagmire, tor, tracery, turret
"The Red-Headed League" Albert chain, arc-and-compass, Freemasonry, greatcoat, three gilt balls, top-hat
Dumas, Alexandre
The Count of Monte Cristo abbé, bond, breviary, brucine, doubloon, ingot, lateen sail, occipital bone, semaphore, trapezius
du Maurier, Daphne
Rebecca entailment
Eliot, George
Silas Marner apoplexy, bandbox, beaver hat, coal-hole, dame school, farrier, finger post, flock bed, furze, gout, highscreen seat, hornpipe, I.H.S., jack, laudanum, phial, sixpence, smock frock, squire, tankard, thatch, tinderbox, tucker, turban
Esquival, Laura
Like Water for Chocolate placenta
Faulkner, William,
"The Bear" apotheosis, bayou, breech-loader, deadfall, demijohn, epitome, surrey
Ferber, Edna
Giant riata
Filipovich, Zlata
Zlata's Diary beret, Deutsche mark, flak jacket, hernia, jerrycan, solfeggio, strudel, tombola, UNICEF
Fitzgerald, F. Scott
The Great Gatsby addenda, airedale, Aryan, bond, coupé, crêpe-de-chine, Cunard, Follies, fox-trot, hawthorn, hydroplane, legend, Montenegro, Nordic, omnibus, roadhouse, roadster, sheik, ulster
Flaubert, Gustave
Madame Bovary clubfoot, emetic, fez, lorgnette, *prie-dieu*, trefoil, truffle, valerian
Forbes, Esther
Johnny Tremain alewife, annealing furnace, broadside, cress, crimping iron, crucible, derrick, flagon, flintlock, gadroon, hippogriff, hoist, holloware, inkhorn, journeyman, musket, quintal, repoussé, sail loft, sillabub, snuff, solder, tattoo, tea caddy, tie wig
Fox, Paula
Slave Dancer barracoon, bight, boll weevil, carronade, cat's cradle, hornpipe
Frank, Anne
The Diary of a Young Girl ack-ack fire, annexe, anti-Semitism, blackout, cabaret, concertina bed, eiderdown, florin, greengrocer, guilder, inkpot, kohlrabi, opklap bed, salsify, skeleton key
Franklin, Benjamin
Poor Richard's Almanack almanac, twopence
Gaines, Ernest
The Autobiography of Miss Jane Pittman Cajun, cat-o'-nine-tails, colic, Creole, flint, Freedom Beero, hoo-doo, poor white trash, praline, proclamation, scalawag, Secesh Army, spillway
Gardner, John
Grendel fontanel, hex, meadhall, nonce-rules, thane, tic
George, Jean Craighead
Julie of the Wolves jaeger, permafrost, quonset, tern, tundra, white-out
Gibson, William
The Miracle Worker trachoma
Gilgamesh acolyte, demon, gazelle, lapis lazuli, league, nether world, shrine, talisman
Gogol, Nikolai
"The Overcoat" halberd, kopek, poultice, ruble, sledge
Golding, William
Lord of the Flies after-image, apex, barb, bastion, conch, cruiser, defile, derby, diaphragm, fulcrum, garter, hambone frill, hilt, lagoon, matins, pax, precentor, runnel, squid, typhoon
Guest, Judith
Ordinary People *a cappella*, baroque, grout, recorder
Haley, Alex
The Autobiography of Malcolm X ablution, Allah, Allahu-Akbar, anti-Semitism, As-Salaikum-Salaam, cocaine, conked head, goatee, Haganah, Hajj, heroin, high yellow, hipster, homeboy, Islam, Ivy League, jump the broom, muscadine, *parrain*, pateroller, Pullman, scat, soul food, stir, tactical police force, Uncle Tom, W.P.A., zoot suit
Hamilton, Edith
Mythology acropolis, Amazon, ambrosia, bas-relief,

brand, breastplate, centaur, chimera, constellation, dolphin, faun, gad-fly, goblet, gorgon, griffon, Harpy, lyre, Maenad, mead, millet, myrtle, satyr, Titan, trident, underworld, warp

Hansberry, Lorraine

A Raisin in the Sun assegai, buckskin shoes, epitaph, ofay, peckerwood

Hardy, Thomas

Far from the Madding Crowd cock, cucumber frame, grenadier, rick, scythe

Lord Jim derby

The Mayor of Casterbridge amber, ballad sheet, bootjack, burgess, carrefour, chine, clog, felloe, fibula, flyman, furmity, fustian, glazier, granary, hair-guard, hawker, kerseymere, malt, muff, netting, round hand, Royal Unicorn, sacrarium, scythe, seed-drill, skimmity-ride, staddle, swingel, tosspot, truss, Union Jack, wimble

The Return of the Native heath

Tess of the D'Urbervilles abbot, antinomian, bailiff, barton, Candlemas, cornice, cotterel, dimity, equinox, factotum, hospice, Lady Day, lath, patten, riding crop, scythe, sexton, spring cart, tester, trilithon, weir

Hart, Moss, and George S. Kaufman

You Can't Take It with You doily, Five-Year Plan, floorwalker, G-man, mazurka, palette, peseta, toga

Hautzig, Esther

The Endless Steppe anti-Semitism

Hawthorne, Nathaniel

The House of the Seven Gables gable

The Scarlet Letter bayonet, beadle, besom, catarrh, chirography, cuirass, fiend, gauntlet, gleeman, gorget, greave, joint-stool, lattice, partridgeberry, penance, Pentecost, primer, ruff, scourge, scurvy, ship-chandler, slop-seller, steeple-crowned hat, stucco, suit of mail, tarpaulin

Hemingway, Ernest

A Farewell to Arms amphitheatre, armoire, campanile, carabinieri, cholera, concierge, feather the oars, flank, forceps, fresco, gonococcus, jaundice, liaison, luge, mufti, musette, pari-mutuel, petcock, rucksack, Saint Anthony, Salvarsan, sight draft, silhouette, stick bomb, synovial fluid, trench mortar

For Whom the Bell Tolls guerilla

The Old Man and the Sea albacore, barracuda, bitt, block and tackle, bodega, bonito, carapace, cock, condensed milk, cumulus, filaments, flying fish, guano, Gulf Stream, hawk-bill, *jota*, leader, marlin, Our Father, phosphorescence, plankton, Portuguese man-of-war, roadstead, Sargasso weed, tern, thole pin

Herriot, James

All Creatures Great and Small airedale

All Things Bright and Beautiful bots

Hersey, John

Hiroshima acupuncturist, biopsy, B-29, carcinoma, cenotaph, chromosome aberration, corrugated iron, cyclotron, electrocardiogram, Grumman, Molotov flower basket, parish, phoenix, sampan, Shinto, strafe, tableau, *tansu*, terminus, tomographic scan, tram, triangulate, upright piano, waterspout

Hesse, Hermann

Siddhartha banyan, begging bowl, bo tree, coppice, cowl, loincloth, Nirvana, sedan chair, Upanishad, Vedas

Heyerdahl, Thor

Kon Tiki balsa

Hilton, James

Lost Horizon bazaar, cadenza, chinoiserie, chupatty, col, couloir, don, D.S.O., gavotte, harpsichord, lamasery, maharajah, mango, massif, pomelo, pukka, salaam, topee

Homer

Iliad nymph, oracle

Odyssey amphora, auger, battalion, brace and bit, brazier, coffer, corded bedstead, cresset, cyclops, discus, distaff, halyard, hecatomb, moly, scepter, sheet, steering oar, thrall, tripod, tunic, whey

Houston, Jeanne Wakatsuki, and James D. Houston

Farewell to Manzanar alluvial fan, bobbysoxer, catechism, chignon, chum, geisha, goh, grunion, hana, issei, kabuki, kendo, mess kit, nisei, odori, repatriation, samisen, sansei, swagger stick, tatami mats, tutu

Hsun, Lu

"My Old Home" elements, intercalcary month

Hugo, Victor

Les Misérables antechamber, anvil, baron, barricade, capstone, censer, church warden, conduit, cross belt, damask, dormer window, dragoon, epaulet, esplanade, fiacre, firebrand, flax, grisette, gum lac, hurdy-gurdy, jet, louis d'or, *mairie*, martingale, mountebank, pantaloons, Potter's Field, prefect, prioress, *quartier*, shako, sou, spirit lamp, summer house, syncope, trust

Hunt, Irene

Across Five Aprils ironclad, secession, typhoid fever

Hurst, James

"The Scarlet Ibis" caul, Paris green

Hurston, Zora Neale
Their Eyes Were Watching God flivver, head rag, hoe cake, jack, joist, mulatto, oilcloth, palma christi, percale, quarters, quick lime, root doctor, sen-sen, sick headache, sow belly, switch blade, tar paper
Huxley, Aldous
Brave New World chypre, civet, coccyx, éclair, embryo, fire drill, fitchew, gramme, kiva, mesa, mescal, obsidian, peritoneum, pueblo, queue, simian
Ibsen, Henrik
A Doll's House consumption, domino, macaroon, Tarantella
Jhabvala, Ruth Prawer
Heat and Dust burka, dhoti, lotus pose, meccano set, memsahib, nawab, punkah, rupee, sahib, sarod, thunderbox
Joyce, James
A Portrait of the Artist as a Young Man catafalque, monstrance, novena, surplice
Kafka, Franz
"The Metamorphosis" dressing gown, livery, sideboard
Kaufman, George S. *See* Moss Hart
Keneally, Thomas
Schindler's List anti-Semitism, czardas, genocide, Gestapo, holocaust, homburg, pogrom, Reich, reichsmark, swastika, tryptych, typhus
Kesey, Ken
One Flew Over the Cuckoo's Nest birdshot, bluetick hound, catheter, chum, croupier, Dilantin, Distinguished Service Cross, electroencephalograph, EST, graphite, hydrocephalus, hydrotherapy, lobotomy, psychopath, Seconal, transistor, troller
Key, Francis Scott
"The Star-Spangled Banner" rampart
Keyes, Daniel
Flowers for Algernon brain fissure, cul-de-sac, enzyme, fugue, gestalt, hallucination, hypothesis, id, libido, mazel tov, phenylketonuria, plateau, platonic, psychosurgery, rhesus monkey, Rorschach, skids, strop, styptic, subconscious, superego, TAT, T-maze
King, Martin Luther
"Letter from a Birmingham Jail" Calvary, hemlock
Kingston, Maxine Hong
The Woman Warrior agoraphobia, bund, granny glasses, ideograph, origami, samurai, yin/yang
Kipling, Rudyard
Just So Stories djinn
"Miss Youghal's Sais" jampani, sais, V.C.
Knowles, John
A Separate Peace anarchy, apse, Blitzkrieg, Hitler Youth, knickers, puttee, shuttlecock, slalom, trigonometry
Kroeber, Theodora
Ishi, Last of His Tribe sweat lodge
Lawrence, Jerome, and Robert E. Lee
Inherit the Wind frond fan, galluses
Lederer, William J., and Eugene Burdick
The Ugly American ephemeris, ghee, ipecac, OSS, protocol
Lee, Harper
To Kill a Mockingbird ambrosia, asafoetida, blind man's bluff, capital felony, chifferobe, cootie, corset, cracklin' bread, croker sack, dunce cap, entailment, foot-washers, Franklin stove, Indian-head, jubilee, linotype, liver spot, Mrunas, rotogravure, scrip stamps, scuppernong, trot-lines
Lee, Robert E. *See* Jerome Lawrence
Lessing, Doris
"No Witchcraft for Sale" kaffir, kraal, veld
Lincoln, Abraham
"The House Divided Speech" mortice, squatter
London, Jack
The Call of the Wild aurora borealis, Colt's revolver, gee-pole, ptarmigan, sluice, veranda, washing-pan, wheeler
White Fang cribbage, faro dealer, keystone, lynx, moose-bird, pall, porte cochère, wolverine
Luke decree
Mahfouz, Najib
"The Happy Man" free association, neurosis, schizophrenia
Mansfield, Katherine
"The Garden Party" chesterfield, marquee
Márquez, Gabriel García
"The Handsomest Drowned Man in the World" astrolabe, gaff, scapular
de Maupassant, Guy
"The Necklace" garret
Melville, Herman
"Bartleby the Scrivener" cannel coal, car man, chancery, dun, folio, rockaway, scrivener
Benito Cereno Black Friars, contrition (act of), doubloon, hawse-hole, noddy, oakum
Billy Budd backstay, bluejacket, boom, bulwark, deadeye, dogwatch, drumhead court, forecastle, forechains, foretop, foreyard, frigate, impress, jewelblock, marlinspike, master-at-arms, mizzen-top, purser, quarter deck, rattan, Saxon,

shroud, spar, stun'sail, taffrail, warrant officer, welkin

Moby-Dick breach, dogvane, Fata Morgana, ferule, flukes, maelstrom, Parsee, quadrant, Ramadan, skrimshandering, Try-Works

Typee calabash, ditty bag, taboo

Michener, James

Hawaii grog, reef

Miller, Arthur

The Crucible anti-Christ, arch-fiend, clapboard, conjure, cosmology, crucible, Dionysiac, Gospel, high road, incubus, poppet, sect, shovelboard, succubus, tract

Death of a Salesman chamois, dead march, drummer, grace period, open sesame, Regents, requiem, scrim, simonize, smoker, trademark, Turkish bath

Milton, John

Paradise Lost cosmology

Momaday, N. Scott

The Way to Rainy Mountain antelope drive, antelope medicine, arroyo, peyote, Sun Dance

Morrison, Toni

Beloved bit, chain gang, chamomile, clabber, coffle, cold house, the dragon, faggot, fixing ceremony, four o'clocks, glazier, haint, head cheese, indigo, keeping room, normal school, phrenology, press, smoking papers, sorghum, talking sheets, way station

Mowat, Farley

Never Cry Wolf brain spoon, *Canis lupus*, caribou, esker, Formalin, lemming, musket, periscope, potassium cyanide, scalpel, sculpin, snowknife, sphagnum, swale

Myers, Walter Dean

Fallen Angels claymore, court-martial, Huey, Molotov cocktail, M-16, purple heart, shrapnel

Narayan, R. K.

"An Astrologer's Day" cowrie, jutka

Neihardt, John G.

Black Elk Speaks coup, heyoka, medicine man, pony drag, sacred pipe, shaman, six-shooter, sweat lodge, tepee, vision quest

O'Dell, Scott

Island of the Blue Dolphins candlefish, cormorant, devilfish, kelp, parley, sinew, toluache

Sarah Bishop tar and feather

Sing Down the Moon hogan

Streams to the River, River to the Sea bullboat, leech, pemmican, portage

Orwell, George

Animal Farm Berkshire boar, blinkers, cud, dregs, dynamo, five-pound note, governess-cart, harrow, knacker, lithograph, mangel-wurzel, manor, maxim, paddock, rheumy, silage, spinney, stone, taproom, tushes, watered silk, windfall, Windsor chair

1984 alcove, aquiline face, belfry, catapult, dace, effigy, gateleg table, hazel, kaleidoscope, pannikin, pneumatic tube, pub, Saint Sebastian, spanner, stallkeeper, stratosphere, thrush, tiddlywinks, Tube station, varicose ulcer

Pasternak, Boris

Dr. Zhivago viewing gauze

Paton, Alan

Cry, the Beloved Country absolution, clerical collar, esquire, post office book

Paulsen, Gary

Dogsong aurora borealis, bushpilot, cache, coma, gangline, gee, harpoon, Iditarod, kayak, lamp bowl, mammoth, muktuk, snow goggles, snowhook, tenderloin, toggle point, ulu, umiak

Hatchet chokecherry, Cro-Magnon, headset, stabilizer

Nightjohn cracker, rawhide

Winterdance angiogram, gee, Iditarod

Woodsong parka

Peck, Robert Newton

A Day No Pigs Would Die capstan, corn crib, cotter, crawdad, flutter mill, gilt, goiter, riser, scurf, shim, timothy, trunnel, vapors, windrow

Pepys, Samuel

The Diary of Samuel Pepys lighter, patch, virginal

Pirandello, Luigi

"A Breath of Air" dropsy, pampas

Portis, Charles

True Grit corn dodger, fee sheet, gelding, grange, Henry rifle, marshal, Mason's apron, mustang, nester, pepper box, probate, rope bed, Sharps rifle, teamster, Texas Ranger, traps

Potok, Chaim,

The Chosen apikorsim, Ark of the Covenant, bar mitzvah, caftan, chalah, cossack, earlocks, French doors, gematriya, Goy, Hasidic Jews, momzer, panzer, Passover, Shabbat, shul, tefillin

Rand, Ayn

Anthem moat

Raskin, Ellen

The Westing Game Vandyke

Rawlings, Marjorie Kinnan

The Yearling brogan, camphor, castor oil, feist, flutter mill, homespun, jerk, palmetto, paregoric, poke, pone, quire, saw grass, sink hole, ti-ti

Rawls, Wilson
Where the Red Fern Grows Adam's apple, bobcat, dutch oven, jugular, mackinaw, roasting ear
Remarque, Erich Maria
All Quiet on the Western Front anti-aircraft, billet, black-pudding, carbolic acid, clink, coal box, daisy cutter, dixie, driving-band, duck-weed, dysentery, flamethrower, garrison, hoarding, Iron Cross, latrine poles, mantilla, mustard gas, non-com, perambulator, pocket-torch, quartermaster, saveloy, skittle alley, Stations of the Cross, trajectory, Verey light
Renault, Mary
The Persian Boy eunuch
Richter, Conrad
The Light in the Forest cooperage, council house, cradler, crockery basin, gallipot, Great Spirit, hunting frock, leggings, Lenni Lenape, May apple, miasma, mow, nib, paroquet, patch box, quill, sassafras, scow, seraph, single-tree, spice bush, strouding, sumac, terrapin, thong, thwart, tomahawk, township, wigwam
Rojas, Manuel
"The Glass of Milk" stevedore, victrola
Rostand, Edmond
Cyrano de Bergerac brioche, cadet, Capuchin, chevron, colonnade, company, dice cup, duenna, fanfare, gazette, hemistitch, junta, lentil, marshal, petit four, punchinello, scaffold, skein, soubrette, touché
Ruth ephah, vail
Salinger, J. D.
The Catcher in the Rye canasta, chiffonier, daiquiri, foil, Gladstone, half gainer, highball, psychoanalyst
Schaefer, Jack
Shane buckboard, chuck wagon, corral, cowpuncher, cultivator
Scott, Sir Walter
Ivanhoe baldric, buttress
Shakespeare, William
Hamlet arras, beadle, bilboes, bodkin, canker, canon, chalice, chameleon, chopine, fardel, fennel, hebona, hobby-horse, periwig, poniard, rosemary, rue, sallet, stoup, wassail
Julius Caesar alarum, augury, awl, colossus, coronet, drachma, flourish, ides, Lupercal, mantle, pole star, praetor, spleen, taper, tincture, triumph, wreath
Macbeth adder, alarum, beldam, brindle, chamberlain, dudgeon, farrow, French hose, frieze, kite, posset, post with post, scrofula, sennet, yew
A Midsummer Night's Dream bones, buskin, chough, cloister, dewlap, harelip, masque, nine men's morris, pump, sweetmeat, tiring house, Vestal
Romeo and Juliet apothecary, *aqua vitae*, bawd, bier, bill, bite one's thumb, butt-shaft, Cynthia, doublet, dram, ducat, ell, hoodwinked, hurdle, maidenhead, marchpane, masker, partisan, passado, rosemary, rush, shrift, star-crossed, wormwood
The Taming of the Shrew argosy, bolster, ewer, farthingale, fret, metaphysics, porringer, tapestry, tinker, valance
The Tempest boatswain, elements, fathom, signory, tabor, trencher
Shaw, George Bernard
Pygmalion blackguard, brougham, dustman, laryngoscope, plinth, scullery, tanner
Shelley, Mary
Frankenstein alchemist, cabriolet, chivalry, draught, gale, portmanteau, skiff, syndic, vampire
Sinclair, Upton
The Jungle albumen, Bessemer furnace, blacklisted, crusade, dramshop, drover, evangelist, heeler, injunction, isinglass, kosher, Marseillaise, morphine, naturalization papers, sarsaparilla, scab, settlement worker, waistcoat
Solzhenitsyn, Alexander
One Day in the Life of Ivan Denisovich convoy, groats, hussar, kasha, kolkhoz, kulak, malingerer, peat, plumb line, reveille, steppe, troika
Sophocles
Antigone antistrophe, augury, Bacchic rite, decree, epode, funeral rites, libation, panoply, ploughshare, seer, strophe
Oedipus Rex expiation, garland, herald, laurel
Speare, Elizabeth
The Witch of Blackbird Pond familiar
Steinbeck, John
Grapes of Wrath ammeter, apoplexy, babbitt, carborundum, cat, clutch plates, corn dodger, hames, hob-nail, Mother Hubbard, placard, Rose of Sharon, slack lime, tappet
Of Mice and Men barley, bindle, cesspool, dugs, ejector, kewpie doll, Luger, manger, stetson, tick, trace
The Pearl ammonia, amulet, bit and bit-roller, chocolate pot, cicada, consecrated candle, fiesta, fool's gold, herring clouds, lymph, pulque, scorpion, transfigure, Winchester carbine
The Red Pony cayuse, chambray, forelock, hackamore, half-hitch, headstall, hops, morocco, rapier, riata, sac, sagebrush

Stevenson, Robert Louis
The Strange Case of Dr. Jekyll and Mr. Hyde cheval-glass, farrago, holograph, troglodytic
Treasure Island AB master mariner, after-deck, ague, blockhouse, clove hitch, coracle, coxswain, deadlights, doldrums, jib, keel-hauling, loop-hole, lugger, noggin, oilcloth, palisade, powder horn, quid, Revelation, roundhouse, rudder-head, sabre, scupper, spy-glass, stockade, sub-altern, swab, tiller, trades, walk the plank
Stoker, Bram
Dracula calèche, keep, kukri, lancet, strait waistcoat, trephine
Stowe, Harriet Beecher
Uncle Tom's Cabin abolitionist, laudanum, Uncle Tom
Swift, Jonathan
Gulliver's Travels jerkin, musket
"A Modest Proposal" fricassee, gibbet, ragout, sterling
Tagore, Rabindranath
"The Artist" pice
Tan, Amy
The Joy Luck Club aneurysm, balm, DNA, endgame, façade, grotto, karma, kowtow, macramé, mah jong, pomegranate, red egg ceremony, sake, sanddab, Tao, wonton
The Kitchen God's Wife art deco, bittermelon, characters, Chinese New Year, concubine, dim sum, fen, ginseng, herbal medicine, loss of face, Mandarin Chinese, moxa, multiple sclerosis, night soil collectors, pedicab, spirit money, *tai-tai*, warlords, yuan, Zen
Taylor, Theodore
The Cay ballast, bung, calypso, cay, crude oil, divi-divi, jumbi, langosta, petrel, pontoon bridge, refinery, schooner, sea grape, sextant, skate, U-boat
Timothy of the Cay callaloo, cay, kroner, øre, refinery, solar halo, squall, U-boat, wattle-and-daub
ten Boom, Carrie,
The Hiding Place anti-Semitism, quisling, yellow star
Thoreau, Henry David
"Civil Disobedience" lyceum, militia, tribute money
Walden freshet, penny post, purslane, ridge pole
Tolkien, J. R. R.
The Hobbit bannock, eyrie, hauberk, lentil, necromancer, portcullis, quoits, scimitar, tippet, trestle
Twain, Mark
The Adventures of Huckleberry Finn abolitionist, barlow knife, bilge, bluff bank, bottoms, bulrushes, clasp knife, corn dodger, cottonwood, dandy, *dauphin*, decanter, delirium tremens, divining rod, dog irons, doxology, frame house, hair ball, harelip, harem, heptarchy, jack-o'-lantern, melodeum, mesmerism, quarry, quicksilver, ride on a rail, saltcellar, seven-up, shanty, slough, tow, towhead, whitecaps
The Adventures of Tom Sawyer agate, belle, bowie knife, chink, cravat, cutlass, doodlebug, dupe, flying jib, gauge cock, headline, hogshead, hoopstick, hurricane deck, Mosaic Law, percussion-cap, roundabout, sackcloth and ashes, serape, sitz bath, spring-line, spunk-water, stalactite, stalagmite, tadpole, taw, temperance revival, verdigrease, whitewash
A Connecticut Yankee in King Arthur's Court hello-girl
Life on the Mississippi carpetbag, cat's-paw, daguerreotype, eagle, gangplank, gingerbread, juba, levee, mark twain, minstrel, paddle box, pow-wow, saloon, texas, yawl
The Prince and the Pauper the Tower
Verne, Jules
Around the World in Eighty Days brigantine, chronometer, fakir, grenadier, howdah, junk, mackintosh, opium den, palanquin, peristyle, porphyry, rajah, screw, suttee, tanka, thuggee, whist
Virgil
Aeneid sibyl
Walker, Alice
The Color Purple amen corner, appliqué, boater, dust devil, Epsom salts, moochie, quilt frame, scarification, slop jar, sponge, tarmac, ululation
Watkins, Yoko Kawashima
So Far from the Bamboo Grove asylum, flatcar, fusuma, futon, geta, kimch'i, koto, miso, sayonara, skewer, squadron, tabi, tofu
Wells, H. G.
The Time Machine brontosaurus, saltpeter, sphinx, vermin
West, Jessamyn
Except for Me and Thee underground railroad
Wharton, Edith
Ethan Frome almshouse, counterpane, cupola, cutter, fascinator, flagged path, harmonium, huckaback, lumbago, match safe, merino, potpourri, reel, spruce, valise, wainscot

Wiesel, Elie
Night anti-Semitism, cabbala, ghetto, kaddish, kapo, Messiah, monocle, musulman, phylactery, Rosh Hashanah, SS, synagogue, Talmud, tommy gun, Torah, truncheon, typhus, Yom Kippur
Wilder, Thornton
The Bridge of San Luis Rey osier
Our Town highboy, phosphate, shale, trellis
Williams, Tennessee
The Glass Menagerie cakewalk, Daughters of the American Revolution, Jolly Roger, Merchant Seamen, pleurosis, tub (claw-footed), unicorn
A Streetcar Named Desire atomizer, bouclé, bromo, chop suey, fox pieces, gallery, Grim Reaper, Huguenots, loving cup, Mardi Gras, neurasthenic, one-eyed jack, paddy wagon, quinine, toilet
Wright, Richard
Black Boy Armageddon, bootlegging, brickbat, crap game, flask, graft, hydrant, Jim Crow laws, pop-the-whip, Seventh Day Adventists, shadow box, sharecropper, tenement, wall-eyed
Native Son Black Belt, inquest, relief, running board, two bits
Yasunari, Kawabata
"The Jay" cataract, kimono, obi
Zindel, Paul
The Effect of Gamma Rays on Man-in-the-Moon Marigolds cloud chamber, convulsion, psoriasis

Subject Index

agriculture cat, chaff, coppice, corn crib, corral, cucumber frame, cultivator, farrow, fodder, granary, grange, hames, harrow, haymow, hobble, kolkhoz, latigo, manger, mow, nester, paddock, Paris green, ploughshare, quirt, rowel, scythe, seed-drill, silage, spinney, squatter, treading-yard, trellis, wimble, windfall, windrow, winnow. *See also* equipment, tools.

airplane ack-ack-fire, anti-aircraft, B-29, coal box, driving-band, Grumman, headset, Huey, Molotov flower basket, stabilizer, strafe, trajectory, trench mortar

animals adder, airedale, albumen, Berkshire boar, biddy chicken, blood horse, bluetick hound, bobcat, breach, brontosaurus, *Canis lupus*, caribou, cayuse, chameleon, chine, civet, cud, dewlap, do-do, dormouse, dorsal fin, dugs, embryo, eyrie, feist, filaments, fitchew, flukes, flying fish, forelock, gazelle, gelding, gilt, hyrax, jackal, kraal, kudu, leech, lemming, lynx, mammoth, mustang, rhesus monkey, rookery, sac, salamander, scat, simian, sucking pig, terrapin, trilithon, tushes, wolverine. *See also* body, human

animals, flying bittern, bobwhite, chough, chrysalis, cicada, cock, cootie, cormorant, doodlebug, gadfly, jaeger, kite, lapwing, moose-bird, noddy, paroquet, petrel, ptarmigan, scorpion, tern, thrush, vermin

animals, water abalone, albacore, alewife, barracuda, bonita, candlefish, carp, chum, conch, crawdad, dace, devilfish, dolphin, fingerling, hawk-bills, langosta, marlin, Portuguese man-of-war, sanddab, sculpin, skate, squid, tadpole

architecture apse, balustrade, baroque, belfry, buttress, campanile, capstone, carrefour, colonnade, dormer window, eave, esplanade, façade, fresco, gable, gallery, gingerbread, grotto, keystone, mortice, mullion, peristyle, plinth, porte cochère, rococo, Romanesque, sacristy, tracery, turret

art art deco, bas-relief, cast, colossus, effigy, frieze, gadroon, lithograph, origami, palette, punchinello, relief, silhouette, skrimshandering, tintype, tracery, trefoil. *See also* architecture.

athletics alpenstock, battledoor, discus, foil, half gainer, half nelson, Iditarod, kendo, laurel, luge, nine men's morris, pop-the-whip, quoits, seven-up, shovelboard, shuttlecock, skittle alley, touché

awards Distinguished Service Cross, D.S.O., escutcheon, garland, Iron Cross, laurel, loving cup, purple heart, V.C.

behavior anarchy, apikorsim, bawd, bedlam, belle, bite one's thumb, blackguard, bobbysoxer, breach, clout Indian, coxcomb, cracker, dervish, dupe, EST, foetal posture, footpad, free association, gee, hipster, homeboy, hoodwinked, kowtow, lotus pose, malingerer, mesmerism, momzer, musulman, opium den, *parrain*, pax, peckerwood, Pharisee, platonic, poor white trash, protocol, psychosurgery, queue, reveille, Rorschach test, round robin, sackcloth and ashes, sayonara, scalawag, sheik, skimmity-ride, strait waistcoast, taboo, tar and feather, TAT, T-maze, tocsin, tosspot, transfigure, ululation, Uncle Tom, urchin, wall-eyed

beliefs abolitionist, anti-Semitism, chivalry, cosmology, Daughters of the American Revolution, Freemasonry, gestalt, Huguenot, hypothesis, id, Jim Crow laws, Jolly Roger, Nirvana, subconscious, suffragette, superego, Tao, yin/yang, Zen. *See also* supernatural.

body, human Adam's apple, bandy legs, bile, brain fissure, caul, coccyx, confinement, convolutions of the brain, Cro-Magnon, crowning, diaphragm, dolichocephalic, enzyme, fontanel, hermaphrodite, jugular, libido, liver spot, lymph, maidenhead, occipital bone, parietal fissure, peritoneum, placenta, primipara, proboscis, sac, scrag, sinew, spleen, sputum, synovial fluid, trapezius. *See also* disease

buildings barracoon, bastion, bath-house, blockhouse, bodega, canteen, cold house, compound, conservatory, cooperage, custom house, dramshop, foundry, frame house, ghetto, gristmill, hospice, Inns of Court, jetty, kraal, meadhall, mill house, obi, palisade, penthouse, posting-house, pub, pueblo, quarters, quonset, rampart, refinery, roadhouse, roundhouse, rookery, sail loft, scullery, shanty, Shinto shrine, summer house, taproom, teahouse, tenement, tepee, the Tower, turnpike house, way station, wigwam

cloth alpaca, amber, bouclé, brown holland, calico, cambric, chambray, crêpe-de-chine, damask, dimity, festoon, fustian, gingham, hammer-cloth, homespun, huckaback, kerseymere, merino, netting, oilcloth, percale, scrim, strouding, tarpaulin, warp, watered silk, woof

clothing appliqué, breechclout, burka, caftan, cassock, chaps, clerical collar, cockade, corset, cravat, crinoline, cross belt, dandy, dhoti, domino, doublet, dressing gown, Empire gown, epaulet, farthingale, fascinator, fox pieces, French seams, frock coat, gaiters, galluses, garter, girdle, greatcoat, hambone frill, harlequin, hunting frock, jerkin, kimono, knickers, leggings, livery, loincloth, lorgnette, mackinaw, mackintosh, mantle, Mother Hubbard, muff, mufti, obi, pantaloons, parasol, parka, pea-coat, pedal pushers, reticule, ruff, serape, shirt front, smock frock, snow goggles, sou'wester, spencer, surplice, swaddling, swagger stick, tabard, thong, tippet, toga, trousseau, tucker, tunic, tutu, ulster, waistcoat, zoot suit. *See also* hats and head coverings, shoes and footwear.

communication *See* language.

construction alcove, annexe, antechamber, apse, balustrade, barton, belfry, boma, bund, burrow, cesspool, chimney-piece, chine, clapboard, coalhole, cornice, court, cul-de-sac, cupola, eave, fanlight, flagged path, flue, French doors, fusuma, gallery, garret, grille, grout, hoarding, joist, keep, keeping room, marquee, monolith, paling, penthouse, pontoon bridge, portcullis, pylon, riser, saloon, scaffold, scaffolding, shim, sluice, soffit, stanchion, stile, veranda, wainscot, wattle-and-daub, weir, whitewash, wicket. *See also* architecture.

containers amphora, coal scuttle, coffer, conduit, crockery basin, croker sack, demijohn, fardel, flagon, flask, gallipot, hogshead, hookah, inkhorn, inkpot, jerrycan, noggin, phial, poke, portfolio, pottle, powder horn, stoup

cooking dixie, fricassee, hob, mull, posset, roasting-jack, tempura. *See also* food.

cosmetics atomizer, chypre, *papier poudre*, patch, pomatum, toilet

crime anarchy, assizes (court of), blackguard, Bluebeard, bootlegging, buccaneer, capital felony, court-martial, the dragon, drumhead court, G-man, graft, indictment, kapo, Ku Klux Klan, numbers runner, pateroller, praetorian guard, probate, quisling, Rippers, round robin, Royal Canadian Mounted Police, SS, tactical police force, talking sheets, Texas Ranger, thuggee, tribunal, underground railroad. *See also* punishment

dance arabesque, cakewalk, czardas, dervish, Follies, fox-trot, gavotte, hornpipe, juba, mazurka, merengue, moochie, odori, quadrille, reel, schottische, Tarantella, taxi tips

disease agoraphobia, ague, anemic, aneurysm, apoplexy, bots, canker, carcinoma, cataract, catarrh, chilblain, cholera, chromosome aberration, the clap, clubfoot, colic, coma, consumption, convulsion, crabs, cretin, delirium tremens, dropsy, dysentery, fugue, goiter, gonococcus, gout, hallucination, harelip, hernia, hookworm, hydrocephalus, hypochondria, jaundice, leprosy, lockjaw, lumbago, multiple sclerosis, neurasthenic, neurosis, phenylketonuria, pleurosis, pock-marked, psoriasis, psychopath, psychosis, rheumy, schizophrenia, scrofula, scurvy, sick headache, spirochete, syncope, tic, trachoma, tubercle, typhoid fever, typhus, vapors, varicose ulcer

education dame school, dunce cap, inkhorn, inkpot, Ivy League, nib, normal school, plateau, primer, quill, Regents, seminary

equipment alpenstock, ammeter, annealing furnace, anvil, arc-lamp, babbitt, ballast, bitt, bodkin, bung, capstan, chamois, chaps, chronometer, clutch plates, coal scuttle, conduit, cotter, cotterel, crimping iron, crucible, distaff, dudeen, dumb-waiter, equipage, felloe, ferule, flint, forceps, gallipot, gauge cock, gimbal, hasp, headset, hob, holystone, hookah, hydrant, inkhorn, jack, lancet, latrine poles, leader, limekiln, linstock, lozenge, match safe, microfilm, periscope, petcock, pocket-torch, quadrant, quilt frame, roasting jack, skeleton key, skids, smoking papers, stabilizer, staddle, stair rod, stereopticon, strop, tappet, tarpaulin, tenter hooks, thole pin, thong, tinderbox, traps, treadle, trot-lines, trunnel, truss, washing-pan

direction-finders astrolabe, chronometer, dogvane, gimbal, quadrant, sextant

ships astrolabe, dogvane, forebraces, half-hitch,

halyard, quadrant, sheet, spy-glass, steering oar, Try-Works. *See also* tools, utensils.

fishing barb, chum, harpoon, toggle point, trident, troller

food black-pudding, blanc mange, chop suey, chow-chow, chupatty, clabber, dim sum, dixie, dregs, foo foo, fricassee, ghee, hoarhound, kimch'i, kolach, mince pie, molasses, muktuk, pemmican, ragout, sarsaparilla, saveloy, scurf, snuff, soul food, succotash, tempura, tofu, treacle, truffle, wonton

beverage *aqua vitae,* condensed milk, daiquiri, flip, grog, highball, mull, negus, phosphate, posset, pulque, sack, sake, sillabub, smoking bishop, wassail, whey

bread and cereal bannock, barley, brioche, cathead, chalah, corn dodger, cracklin' bread, furmity, groats, gruel, hoecake, hops, kasha, malt, miso, pone, posole

dessert ambrosia, biffin, comfit, éclair, macaroon, marchpane, moon cake, petit four, praline, strudel, sweetmeat, twelfth cake

fruit bittermelon, cassava, chokecherry, mango, muscadine, papaya, partridgeberry, pomegranate, pomelo, satsuma, scuppernong, serviceberry

meat *au jus*, giblets, head cheese, jerk, liver wing, sow belly, streak-a-lean, tenderloin

vegetable alligator pepper, callaloo, camas, cocoyam, cress, fennel, kelp, kola nut, lentil, mangelwurzel, millet, roasting ear, rosemary, rue, sallet, salsify

fuel, heat annealing furnace, arc-lamp, brand, brazier, candlefish, cresset, crude oil, deadlights, faggot, farol, flambeau, flint, Franklin stove, gimbal, limekiln, link, match safe, pocket-torch, riding light, rush-light, sconce, spirit lamp, taper, tinderbox, tow, tripod

furnishings armoire, arras, bell-pull, bolster, brazier, chesterfield, cheval-glass, chifferobe, chiffonier, chinoiserie, dog irons, doily, épergne, escritoire, fender, gateleg table, highboy, highscreen seat, holloware, jack-towel, jalousie-blinds, joint-stool, lamp bowl, macramé, mangle, press, *prie-dieu*, punkah, safe, samovar, sconce, settle, sideboard, slop jar, slop-basin, *tansu,* tapestry, tatami, thunderbox, trestle, tripod, tub (four-clawed), valance, victrola, wash bowl and pitcher, Windsor chair

beds and bedding concertina bed, corded bedstead, counterpane, eiderdown, flock bed, futon, mosquito bar, opklap bed, rope bed, tester, tick, truckle bed

games and athletics agate, alpenstock, backgammon, battledoor, blind man's bluff, bones, canasta, cassino, cat's cradle, crap game, cribbage, dice cup, discus, dominoes, double-dutch rope, draught, endgame, flutter mill, foil, half gainer, half nelson, hana, hoopstick, Iditarod, jacks, kendo, kewpie doll, knave, laurel, lottery, luge, mah jong, meccano set, mumbledypeg, nine men's morris, one-eyed jack, pax, poppet, pop-the-whip, quoits, seven-up, shadow box, shovelboard, shuttlecock, skittle alley, stereopticon, taw, tiddlywinks, tombola, touché, whist

government assizes (court of), asylum, bluejacket, bullroarer, burgess, carabinieri, caucus, chancery, clan, council house, court-martial, *dauphin*, decree, entailment, Five-Year Plan, Freedom Beero, genocide, Haganah, heeler, heptarchy, holocaust, injunction, junta, league, maharajah, *mairie*, marshal, naturalization papers, nonce-rules, OSS, parish, parley, pateroller, praetorian guard, prefect, proclamation, *quartier*, rajah, Reich, relief, repatriation, Royal Canadian Mounted Police, sagamore, scepter, Secesh Army, secession, signory, syndic, tactical police force, Texas Ranger, township, tribute money, W.P.A., warlords

hair and beard chignon, conked head, false front, goatee, periwig, ringlet, tie wig, Vandyke

harness and horses bit and bit-roller, gangline, headstall, lariat pin, martingale, riata, riding crop, single-tree, stallkeeper, surcingle, trace

hats and head coverings beaver hat, beret, boater, derby, fez, head rag, homburg, mantilla, shako, snap-brim hat, sombrero, steeple-crowned hat, stetson, top-hat, topee, turban, vail

herbs arnica, asafoetida, bitter herbs, fennel, ginseng root, hawthorn, hazel, heather, hebona, hemlock, herbal medicine, ipecac, juniper, kelp, moxa, quinine, rosemary, rue, valerian, wormwood

holidays Candlemas, Chinese New Year, fiesta, Good Friday, Lady Day, Lupercal, Mardi Gras, Michaelmas, Passover, Pentecost, Rosh Hashanah, Yom Kippur

hunting *See* weapons and hunting.

hygiene sitz bath, slop jar, slop-basin, thunderbox, tub (four-clawed), wash bowl and pitcher

insects cootie, chrysalis, cicada, doodlebug, gadfly, scorpion, vermin

institutions almshouse, cloister, dame school, Ivy League, lamasery, normal school, pagoda, penny post, rectory, seminary, shul, symposium, synagogue, UNICEF, workhouse

insults ball and chain, bawd, bite one's thumb, blackguard, clout Indian, coxcomb, cracker, dandy, dupe, eunuch, firebrand, Goy, grisette, knacker, malingerer, momzer, mountebank, nester, *nouveau riche*, ofay, peckerwood, Pharisee, plebeian, poor white trash, scab, scalawag, slop-seller, squatter, swab, tosspot, Uncle Tom, urchin, wetback

jewelry Albert chain, arc-and-compass, coronet, fibula, filigree, granny glasses, hair-guard, lapis lazuli, monocle, moonstone, seal

language addenda, bourgeois type, braille, ephemeris, epitaph, farrago, fee sheet, folio, hieroglyphics, holograph, legend, Mandarin Chinese, open sesame, parley, philippic, phylactery, placard, primer, rotogravure, rubric, rune, semaphore

lighting arc-lamp, brand, brazier, candlefish, cresset, deadlights, faggot, farol, flambeau, flint, gimbal, link, match safe, pocket torch, riding light, rushlight, sconce, spirit lamp, taper, tinderbox, tow, tripod

literature addenda, almanac, antistrophe, ballad sheet, breviary, bourgeois type, braille, broadside, characters, chirography, chronicle, copy-book, *double entendre*, ephemeris, epitaph, epode, folio, gazette, Gospel, hemistitch, hieroglyphics, holograph, ideograph, legend, Mandarin Chinese, maxim, open sesame, phylactery, primer, Revelation, rotogravure, rubric, rune, selah, strophe, tabloid, Talmud, Torah, tract, Upanishad, Vedas. *See also* theater.

luggage bandbox, bindle, carpetbag, dressing case, Gladstone, haversack, hessian bag, knapsack, musette, portmanteau, reticule, rucksack, valise

machinery abacus, ammeter, annealing furnace, automaton, babbitt, Bessemer furnace, chronometer, cloud chamber, clutch plates, cyclotron, daguerreotype, derrick, dumb-waiter, dynamo, gauge cock, gimbal, hoist, hydrant, kaleidoscope, limekiln, linotype, periscope, petcock, pneumatic tube, refinery, stabilizer, tappet, transistor, treadle, windlass

materials adobe, balsa, brickbat, carborundum, caulking, chamois, corrugated iron, flocked, graphite, grout, guano, gum lac, harmattan, hobnail, isinglass, jet, lacquer, lath, lattice, macramé, morocco, oakum, obsidian, oilcloth, peat, pewter, puncheon, raffia, rawhide, rush, saltpeter, sealing wax, skein, slack lime, smoking papers, solder, stucco, tar paper, tarmac, thatch, thong. *See also* cloth

measures *See* weights and measures

medicine ammonia, arnica, asafoetida, bromo, brucine, camphor, castor oil, cocaine, Dilantin, dose of salts, Epsom salts, fennel, Formalin, ginseng root, hebona, herbal medicine, heroin, ipecac, laudanum, moxa, paregoric, quinine, rosemary, rue, Salvarsan, Seconal, sen-sen, smelling salts, styptic, valerian, wormwood. *See also* herbs.

military alarum, army, assegai, baldric, barricade, bastion, billet, birdshot, bivouac, blackout, Blitzkrieg, breastwork, catapult, clink, coup, cross belt, flank, garrison, Iron Cross, liaison, loophole, mess kit, mufti, palisade, poniard, rampart, roundhouse, stockade, swastika, tattoo, Verey light

military clothing breastplate, cuirass, epaulet, flak jacket, gauntlet, gorget, greave, shako, suit of mail, swagger stick

military organization army, battalion, battery, company, corps, division, militia, regiment, squadron

military personnel Amazon, brigadier, color sergeant, conquistador, cossack, dragoon, grenadier, guerilla, Hitler youth, hussar, master-at-arms, noncom, orderly, provost, purser, quartermaster, samurai, sentinel, SS, warrant officer

money bond, cash, chalk scores, cowrie, crown, Deutsche mark, doubloon, drachma, ducat, eagle, farthing, fen, five-pound note, florin, food stamps, franc, grace period, guilder, guinea, Indian-head, ingot, kopek, kroner, øre, peseta, peso, pice, post office book, pound, quid, reichsmark, rouleau, ruble, rupee, scrip stamps, shilling, sight draft, sixpence, sou, sovereign, sterling, tanner, trust, two bits, twopence, usury note, wampum, louis d'or, yuan

music and musical instruments *a cappella*, cabaret, cadenza, dead march, doxology, falsetto, fanfare, flourish, fret, harmonium, harpsichord, hornpipe, hurdy-gurdy, jew's-harp, koto, lute, lyre, Marseillaise, melodeum, minstrel, paean, panpipes, potpourri, recorder, samisen, sarod, scat, sennet, solfeggio, soubrette, tabor, tattoo, theremin, upright piano, virginal. *See also* dance

optics granny glasses, lorgnette, monocle, periscope, snow goggles, spy-glass, stereopticon

plants alligator pepper, anise, banyan, barley, bitter

herbs, bittermelon, bosque, bo tree, buckeye, bulrushes, callaloo, camas, camwood, cassava, chamomile, chinaberry, chokecherry, cocoyam, cotton boll, cottonwood, cress, divi-divi, duck-weed, fennel, flax, four o'clocks, furze, hawthorn, hazel, heath, heather, hemlock, hops, indigo, jessamine, juniper, kelp, kohlrabi, kola nut, laurel, lotus, malt, mango, mangrove, manzanillla, May apple, mesquite, millet, moly, myrtle, nosegay, osier, palma christi, palmetto, papaya, partridgeberry, peyote, plankton, pomegranate, pomelo, purslane, Rose of Sharon, rush, sagebrush, salsify, Sargasso weed, sassafras, satsuma, saw grass, scuppernong, sea grape, serviceberry, silk cotton tree, sloe, sorghum, sphagnum moss, spice bush, spruce, sumac, tamarisk, thistle, ti-ti, timothy, toluache, tuber, yew, yucca

punishment bilboes, blacklisted, chain gang, clink, coffle, keel-hauling, drunk tank, fetters, flagellation, genocide, gibbet, guillotine, holocaust, hulks, hurdle, impress, paddy wagon, pogrom, reveille, ride on a rail, stir, stockade, tar and feather, the Tower, treadmill, walk the plank, whipping-post, yellow star

race Aryan, clout Indian, Creole, Goy, gypsy, high yellow, issei, Mrunas, mulatto, nisei, Nordic, poor white trash, sansei, Saxon, Tejano, Uncle Tom, wetback

ranching chaps, corral, fodder, granary, grange, hames, harrow, haymow, hobble, kolkhoz, latigo, manger, mow, nester, paddock, quirt, rowel, scythe, seed-drill, silage, spinney, squatter

real estate Black Belt, entailment, kirkyard, levee, manor, moat, roadstead

religion abbé, abbot, ablution, acolyte, Allah, Allahu-Akbar, antinomian, Ark of the Covenant, Armageddon, As-Salaikum Salaam, Bacchic rite, Black Friars, Buddha, Calvary, censer, church warden, cloister, C.M.E. Church, collect, contrition, act of, curate, elder, evangelist, funeral rites, Goy, Great Spirit, Hajj, Hasidic Jews, icon, Islam, kaddish, karma, kiva, lamasery, libation, limbo, medicine man, Messiah, Mosaic Law, novice, ordinand, Parsee, phylactery, precentor, prioress, purgatory, Revelation, rosary, sacrarium, sacred pipe, sect, Saint Anthony, seraph, Seventh Day Adventists, Sister Superior, Stations of the Cross, surplice, Talmud, temperance revival, Torah, Upanishads, Vedas, Zen. *See also* architecture, clothing, music.

ritual absolution, amen corner, bar mitzvah, bound feet, canon, catechism, chalice, confirmation, consecrated candle, crèche, Dionysiac, earlocks, fiesta, foot-washers, hecatomb, I.H.S., jubilee, jump the broom, kosher, love-feast, Mason's apron, matins, *mazel tov*, monstrance, mourners' bench, novena, Our Father, palmer, penance, peyote, potlatch, red egg ceremony, scapular, scarification, Shabbat, shrift, shrine, Sun Dance, sweat lodge, tallith, tefillin, totem, triumph, vision quest, wreath

death bier, catafalque, cenotaph, fixing ceremony, Grim Reaper, pall, Potter's Field, requiem, sarcophagus, viewing gauze, wake, winding-sheet

science after-image, aurora borealis, cannel coal, carbolic acid, constellation, daguerreotype, DNA, elements, equinox, Fata Morgana, *ignis fatuus*, jack-o'-lantern, loadstone, matrix, metaphysics, naphtha, phosphorescence, phrenology, porphyry, potassium cyanide, pow-wow, quick lime, quicksilver, saltpeter, solar halo, spillway, spunk-water, telepathy, tincture, transistor, triangulate, trigonometry, verdigrease

machinery abacus, automaton, Bessemer furnace, block and tackle, cloud chamber, cyclotron, derrick, dynamo, hoist, kaleidoscope, linotype, periscope, pneumatic tube, refinery, windlass. *See also* equipment.

shoes and footwear brogan, buckskin shoes, buskin, chopine, clog, French hose, geta, jack-boots, nightcap, patten, pump, puttee, tabi

style or prestige apotheosis, aquiline face, ball and chain, baroque, beldam, blackguard, brindle, Cajun, calypso, chinoiserie, claw-foot, concubine, Creole, effigy, epitome, eunuch, firebrand, gadroon, Goy, issei, loss of face, lozenge, mountebank, nester, nisei, nonnette, *nouveau riche*, ofay, pukka, repoussée, rococo, round hand, Royal Unicorn, sansei, scab, squatter, swastika, *tejano*, tête-à-tête, thrall, troglodytic, Union Jack, welkin, wetback

supernatural Amazon, amulet, anti-Christ, archfiend, augury, *bruja*, cabbala, conjure, diablerie, divining rod, ephemeris, evil eye, fakir, gematriya, geomancer, haint, hair ball, hamatsa, hex, heyoka, hoodoo, i'noGo tied, juju, metaphysics, moly, necromancer, nether world, open sesame, oracle, seer, shaman, sibyl, spirit money, star-crossed, suttee, talisman, Titan, underworld

animals and monsters centaur, chimera, Cyclops, demon, djinn, familiar, faun, fiend, firedrake, gorgon, griffon, Harpy, hippogriff, incubus, jumbi, Maenad, nymph, phoenix, Ram, satyr, siren, specter, sphinx, succubus, unicorn, valkyrie, vampire

theater antistrophe, domino, epode, flourish, harlequin, hobbyhorse, kabuki, patch, punchinello, scrim, sennet, soubrette, strophe, tableau

title baron, baronet, cavalier, church warden, courtier, maharajah, don, earl, elder, esquire, gentry, kaffir, Lenni Lenape, memsahib, Messiah, nawab, ordinand, *paisano*, Parsee, *patrón*, plebeian, praetor, prefect, prioress, sahib, Saint Sebastian, serf, Sister Superior, squire, *tai-tai*, thane, Uncle Tom, Vestal. *See also* religion.

tools anvil, auger, awl, besom, block and tackle, brace and bit, brain spoon, cradler, distaff, fire drill, flail, fulcrum, gaff, handspike, machete, plumb line, ratchet-drill, rivet, scalpel, snowhook, snowknife, snuffers, sounding pole, spindle, swingel, wimble

topography acropolis, alluvial fan, apex, archipelago, arroyo, atoll, bayou, bight, bluff bank, bottoms, burrow, cat's-paw, cay, col, couloir, defile, eddy, esker, estuary, firebreak , fool's gold, freshet, Gulf Stream, heath, lagoon, maelstrom, mesa, miasma, Montenegro, moor, pampas, permafrost, quagmire, quai, reef, runnel, Sargasso weed, shale, shingle, shoal, sink hole, slough, stalactite, stalagmite, steppe, stratosphere, swale, tor, towhead, tundra, veld

transportation, land apron, barouche, brougham, buckboard, cabriolet, calèche, caparisoned coursers, chaise, chuck wagon, coupé, curricle, dog-cart, felloe, fiacre, finger post, flatcar, flivver, fly, Franklin car, gee, gee-pole, gig, governess-cart, hackney chariot, hansom cab, high road, howdah, jutka, Land Rover, omnibus, palanquin, panzer, pedicab, perambulator, phaeton, pony drag, portage, post with post, postilion, Pullman, rickshaw, roadster, rockaway, running board, sedan chair, slalom, sledge, smoker, stagecoach, surrey, terminus, tram, troika, Tube station, tumbril, wheeler

transportation, water argosy, balsa, bilge, brigantine, bullboat, cat's-paw, clove hitch, convoy, coracle, cruiser, Cunard, cutter, dogwatch, dugout, feather the oars, frigate, hydroplane, ironclad, junk, kayak, larboard, lighter, lugger, maelstrom, man-o'-war, mark twain, marlinspike, packet, pole star, quadrant, quai, sampan, schooner, scow, skiff, sloop, stateroom, step, tack, tanka, trireme, troller, U-boat, umiak, whitecaps, yawl

parts of a ship or riverboat after-deck, alee, backstay, boom, bowsprit, bulwark, cuddy, deadeye, flying jib, forecastle, forechains, foretop, foreyard, gangplank, gunwale, halyard, hawse-hole, hawser, headline, hurricane deck, jewelblock, jib, lateen sail, mizzen-top, paddle box, poop deck, punt, quarter deck, ratline, rudderhead, screw, scupper, sheet, shroud, snow mast, spar, spring-line, steering oar, stern wheel, stun'sail, taffrail, texas, thwart, tiller, tops'l, Try-Works

treatment, medical amphitheatre, angiogram, balm, biopsy, caesarian section, court-plaster, *curandera*, electrocardiogram, electroencephalograph, emetic, Epsom salts, EST, forceps, free association, hoarhound, hydrotherapy, lancet, laryngoscope, leech, lobotomy, morphine, poultice, psychosurgery, Rorschach test, sitz bath, sponge, strait waistcoast, T-maze, TAT, tincture, tomographic scan, trephine, Turkish bath

practitioner acupuncturist, apothecary, psychoanalyst, root doctor

psychology and mental disorders agoraphobia, delirium tremens, EST, free association, hallucination, hydrotherapy, hypochondria, lobotomy, mesmerism, neurasthenic, neurosis, psychopath, psychosis, psychosurgery, Rorschach test, T-maze, TAT, waistcoast

utensil begging bowl, chocolate pot, cruet stand, decanter, dixie, dutch oven, finger bowl, flagon, flask, goblet, holloware, jack, noggin, pannikin, porringer, roasting jack, saltcellar, skewer, stoup, tankard, tea caddy, trencher. *See also* containers

weapons and hunting ack-ack fire, antelope medicine, anti-aircraft, assegai, atom-bomb mushroom, barb, barlow knife, bayonet, bill, birdshot, blunderbuss, bowie knife, breech-loader, butt-shaft, cache, carbine, carronade, cartridge, cat-o'-nine-tails, clasp knife, claymore, coal box, Colt's revolver, cutlass, daisy cutter, deadfall, dirk, driving-band, dudgeon, ejector, elf-bolt, flamethrower, flintlock, fusillade, halberd, harpoon, hauberk, hawker, Henry rifle, hilt, kukri, Luger, machete, magazine, Martini-Henry, Molotov cocktail, Molotov flower basket, M-16, musket, mustard gas, panoply, partisan, passado, patch box, pepper box, percussion-cap, powder horn, ramrod, rapier, rattan, sabre, scimitar, scourge, Sharps rifle, shrapnel, six-shooter, spoor, spring gun, stick bomb, switch blade, toggle point, tomahawk, tommy gun, trajectory, trench mortar, trident, truncheon, ulu, V-2 rocket, Winchester carbine

weather cumulus, doldrums, dust devil, gale, herring clouds, rime, squall, thunderhead, trades, typhoon, waterspout, white-out

weights and measures chronometer, dram, ell, ephah, fathom, fee sheet, gramme, hecatomb, ides, intercalary month, quadrant, quintal, quire, sextant, stone, verst

work and workers alchemist, apothecary, apprentice, beadle, *bonne*, cat's face, coal-whipper, concierge, curate, drummer, duenna, dun, dustman, elder, evangelist, factotum, floorwalker, glazier, greengrocer, hello-girl, herald, indentures, journeyman, middleman, ostler, *patrón*, praetor, scab, scrivener, sexton, simonize, slop-seller, three gilt balls, tinker, trademark

agriculture and livestock *abrazo*, bailiff, cowpuncher, curry, drover, farrier, knacker, kulak, night-soil collectors, sais, sharecropper, teamster

entertainment bawd, croupier, faro dealer, geisha, gleeman, grisette, taxi tips

religion or charity abbé, abbot, acolyte, Black Friars, church warden, curate, elder, evangelist, medicine man, novice, ordinand, precenter, prioress, settlement worker, sexton, shaman, Sister Superior

transportation, air or land bushpilot, car man, flyman, jampani, *llanero*, *vaquero*

transportation, water AB master mariner, boatswain, coxswain, helmsman, Merchant Seamen, quartermaster, ship-chandler, stevedore, subaltern, swab

workplaces apse, bazaar, bodega, canteen, C.C.C., cooperage, dramshop, pari-mutuel, pub, quarry, scullery, taproom

writing addenda, characters, chirography, foolscap, hieroglyphics, holograph, ideograph, inkpot, *jota*, legend, Mandarin Chinese, nib, phylactery, placard, quill, round hand, rubric, rune, sand-box